Advertising Theory

WITHDRAWN

Advertising Theory provides detailed and current explorations of key theories in the advertising discipline. The volume gives a working knowledge of the primary theoretical approaches of advertising, offering a comprehensive synthesis of the vast literature in the area. Editors Shelly Rodgers and Esther Thorson have developed this volume as a forum in which to compare, contrast, and evaluate advertising theories in a comprehensive and structured presentation. Chapters provide concrete examples, case studies, and readings written by leading advertising scholars and educators.

Utilizing McGuire's persuasion matrix as the structural model for each chapter, the text offers a wider lens through which to view the phenomenon of advertising as it operates within various environments. Within each area of advertising theory—and across advertising contexts—both traditional and non-traditional approaches are addressed, including electronic word-of-mouth advertising, user-generated advertising, and social media advertising contexts.

As a benchmark for the current state of advertising theory, this text will facilitate a deeper understanding for advertising students, and will be required reading for advertising theory coursework.

Shelly Rodgers is Associate Professor of Strategic Communication at the Missouri School of Journalism. Her research focuses on advertising, health communication, and new technology. She is Past President of the American Academy of Advertising.

Esther Thorson is Associate Dean for Graduate Studies and Research and Director of Research for the Donald W. Reynolds Journalism Institute. She has more than 100 publications on advertising, media economics, and health communication. She is a Fellow of the American Academy of Advertising.

LIVEI

D1141848

3 1

Routledge Communication Series

Selected Advertising titles include:

The Media Handbook, Fourth Edition
Katz

Advertising and Public Relations Law, Second Edition
Moore/Maye/Collins

Sex in Advertising
Reichert/Lambiase

Advertising Theory

Edited by Shelly Rodgers and Esther Thorson

Routledge
Taylor & Francis Group

NEW YORK AND LONDON

First published 2012
by Routledge
711 Third Avenue, New York, NY 10017

Simultaneously published in the UK
by Routledge
2 Park Square, Milton Park, Abingdon, Oxon OX14 4RN

Routledge is an imprint of the Taylor & Francis Group, an informa business

Library of Congress Cataloging in Publication Data
A catalog record for this book has been requested

ISBN: 978-0-415-88661-1 (hbk)
ISBN: 978-0-415-88662-8 (pbk)
ISBN: 978-0-203-14954-6 (ebk)

Typeset in Perpetua
by Wearset Ltd, Boldon, Tyne and Wear

SFI Certified Sourcing
www.sfiprogram.org
SFI-00453

Printed and bound in the United States of America
by Edwards Brothers, Inc.

In memory of Ivan Preston for his unwavering commitment to all things advertising. He will be missed.

Contents

Contributors   xii
Foreword   xx
Preface   xxii
Acknowledgments   xxx

PART I
Perspectives on Advertising and Advertising
Theory   1

1 **What Does "Theories of Advertising" Mean?**   3
   ESTHER THORSON AND SHELLY RODGERS

2 **Coloring Outside the Lines: Suggestions for Making**
   Advertising Theory More Meaningful   18
   RONALD J. FABER, BRITTANY R. L. DUFF, AND XIAOLI NAN

3 **Agency Practitioners' Theories about Advertising**   33
   GERGELY NYILASY AND LEONARD N. REID

PART II
Psychological Processes in Response to
Advertisements   49

4 **The Elaboration Likelihood Model: A 30-Year**
   Review   51
   DAVID W. SCHUMANN, MICHAEL R. KOTOWSKI, HO-YOUNG
   (ANTHONY) AHN, AND CURTIS P. HAUGTVEDT

 5 The Role of Emotion in Processing Advertising   69
    LARRY PERCY

 6 Theories of Emotion and Affect in Marketing
    Communications   85
    JON D. MORRIS

 7 Embodied Motivated Cognition: A Theoretical
    Framework for Studying Dynamic Mental Processes
    Underlying Advertising Exposure   105
    PAUL D. BOLLS, KEVIN WISE, AND SAMUEL D. BRADLEY

 8 Involvement   120
    ERIC HALEY

PART III
Specific Audiences   133

 9 A Theory of Advertising to Children   135
    RUSSELL N. LACZNIAK AND LES CARLSON

10 Theory Advancement in International Advertising:
    Drawing on Theories from Strategic Management
    and International Business   149
    CHARLES R. TAYLOR, SHINTARO OKAZAKI, AND BARBARA
    MUELLER

11 How Advertising Works Within a Cultural Context:
    Theories and Frameworks Informing the Process   162
    CARRIE LA FERLE AND WEI-NA LEE

12 The Reflexive Game: How Target and Agent
    Persuasion Knowledge Influence Advertising
    Persuasion   174
    MICHELLE R. NELSON AND CHANG DAE HAM

PART IV
Different Types of Advertising Messages   189

13   Creativity and Ad Theory   191
     SHEILA L. SASSER AND SCOTT KOSLOW

14   Creativity and Risk Theories of Advertising   212
     DOUGLAS C. WEST

15   A Rhetorical Theory of the Advertisement   227
     EDWARD F. MCQUARRIE AND BARBARA J. PHILLIPS

16   Narrative Advertisements and Narrative Processing   241
     CHINGCHING CHANG

17   Working Toward an Understanding of Persuasion
     via Engaging Narrative Advertising: Refining the
     Transportation-Imagery Model   255
     LU ZHENG AND JOSEPH E. PHELPS

18   Direct-to-Consumer Advertising of Prescription
     Drugs: Consumers, Physicians, Messages, and
     Complexity   269
     KIM BARTEL SHEEHAN

19   Theory Building for Online Health Product
     Advertising   281
     JISU HUH AND WONSUN SHIN

20   Political Advertising   297
     MARJOLEIN MOORMAN AND PETER NEIJENS

PART V
Media and Media Devices   311

21   Media Analysis and Decision Making   313
     HUGH M. CANNON

22   Managing Non-Traditional Advertising: A Message
     Processing Framework   337
     RICK T. WILSON AND BRIAN D. TILL

23 Role of Technology in Online Persuasion: A MAIN
    Model Perspective   355
    S. SHYAM SUNDAR, QIAN XU, AND XUE DOU

24 Lessons Learned for Teaching Mobile Advertising:
    Critical Review and Future Directions   373
    SHINTARO OKAZAKI

25 In-Game Advertising and Advergames: A Review of
    the Past Decade's Research   388
    SEOUNMI YOUN AND MIRA LEE

26 Social Media and Advertising Theory   402
    HARSHAVARDHAN GANGADHARBATLA

PART VI
Organizations   417

27 Toward a Social Ecology of Advertising   419
    CHRISTINE WRIGHT-ISAK

28 Brand Concepts and Advertising   434
    DEAN M. KRUGMAN AND JAMESON L. HAYES

29 I Know It When I See It: The Definability and
    Consequences of Perceived Fit in Corporate Social
    Responsibility Initiatives   449
    AMANDA B. BOWER AND STACY LANDRETH GRAU

PART VII
Contexts of Advertising   461

30 Ethics and Advertising Theory   463
    MINETTE E. DRUMWRIGHT

31 Theory and Law   480
    JEF I. RICHARDS

32 Four Theories of How IMC Works   491
    SANDRA MORIARTY AND DON SCHULTZ

33 Theories about Health and Advertising   506
    JOYCE M. WOLBURG

PART VIII
The Future of Advertising Theories   **527**

34 Human Barriers to Using Theory and Research on
    Responses to Advertising Messages   529
    IVAN L. PRESTON

35 Toward Theories of Advertising: Where Do We Go
    From Here?   541
    MARLA B. ROYNE

36 Advancing Advertising Theories and Scholarship   546
    HAIRONG LI

37 Adventures in Misplaced Theories   553
    HERBERT JACK ROTFELD

38 IMC, Advertising Research, and the Advertising
    Discipline   563
    PATRICIA B. ROSE

    Glossary   567
    Index   592

Contributors

Editors

Shelly Rodgers is Associate Professor of Strategic Communication at the Missouri School of Journalism. Her research—funded by over $7 million in grants—focuses on advertising, health communication, and new technology. She is Past President of the American Academy of Advertising.

Esther Thorson is Associate Dean for Graduate Studies and Research, and Director of Research for the Donald W. Reynolds Journalism Institute. She has 100+ publications on advertising, media economics, and health communication. She is a Fellow of the American Academy of Advertising.

Contributors

Ho-Young (Anthony) Ahn is a Doctoral Candidate and Teaching Associate at the University of Tennessee. His research is in advertising including message strategies, conflicting information processing, and health communication through social media.

Paul D. Bolls is Associate Professor and Co-director of the PRIME Lab at the Missouri School of Journalism. He investigates how the human mind processes media and co-authored the book *Psychophysiological Measurement and Meaning: Cognitive and Emotional Processing of Media* (forthcoming).

Amanda B. Bower is Associate Professor of Business Administration/Marketing and Advertising at Washington and Lee University. Her research in advertising primarily concerns exploration of source effects. She is Associate Editor of the *Journal of Advertising*.

Samuel D. Bradley is Associate Professor, Advertising Department Chairperson, and Director of the Communication and Cognition Lab at Texas Tech University. He investigates cognitive processing and media. He co-authored the book *Advertising and Public Relations Research* (2010).

Hugh M. Cannon is Adcraft/Simons-Michelson Professor of Advertising and Marketing at Wayne State University. His research includes media planning theory and the role of marketing in economic development. He received the American Academy of Advertising Outstanding Contribution to Advertising Research Award.

Les Carlson holds the Gold Distinguished Professorship at the University of Nebraska-Lincoln. He is Past President of the American Academy of Advertising and former editor of *Journal of Advertising*. He received the AAA Outstanding Contribution to Research and Kim Rotzoll Awards.

Chingching Chang is University Chair Professor at National Chengchi University (Taiwan). Her research includes advertising effects and consumer behaviors. She has published in many leading advertising and communication journals and has won multiple national research awards.

Xue Dou is a Doctoral Candidate in the College of Communications at Pennsylvania State University. Her research interests include use of new media in strategic communication and understanding psychological effects of technology in people's perception of media content.

Minette E. Drumwright is Associate Professor, Department of Advertising and Public Relations, College of Communication, University of Texas at Austin. Her research is in the areas of ethics in advertising and public relations, corporate social responsibility, and communication for nonprofit organizations.

Brittany R. L. Duff is Assistant Professor of Advertising at the Charles H. Sandage Department of Advertising at the University of Illinois. Her research interests include attention and emotion, particularly how these work separately or interact to influence perceptions of advertising.

Ronald J. Faber is Professor Emeritus of Mass Communications at the University of Minnesota and Visiting Professor of Advertising at the University of Illinois. He is a Fellow of the American Academy of Advertising and former editor of *Journal of Advertising*.

Harshavardhan Gangadharbatla is Assistant Professor in the School of Journalism and Communication at University of Oregon. His research focuses on emerging media, social and economic effects of advertising, and environmental communication. Publications include over a dozen book chapters and journal articles.

Stacy Landreth Grau is Associate Professor of Professional Practice in Marketing at the Neeley School of Business at Texas Christian University. Her primary research areas include corporate social responsibility initiatives and advertising source effects.

Eric Haley is Professor of Advertising, School of Advertising and Public Relations, University of Tennessee. He has published in *Journal of Advertising* and *Journal of Advertising Research* among others. He was Senior Associate Editor of *Journal of Advertising* and is Editor of *Journal of Current Issues in Research and Advertising*.

Chang Dae Ham is Assistant Professor at the Department of Advertising at the University of Illinois at Urbana-Champaign. His research examines why and how consumers use new media to engage with brand message creation and usage.

Curtis P. Haugtvedt is Associate Professor of Marketing in the Fisher College of Business at Ohio State University. His research includes attitude change, persuasion, and attitude strength. He was Associate Editor of *Journal of Consumer Psychology* and President of the Society for Consumer Psychology.

Jameson L. Hayes is a Doctoral Student at Grady College, University of Georgia, focusing research on areas of branding, social and new media marketing, and new media business models.

Jisu Huh is Associate Professor, School of Journalism and Mass Communication, University of Minnesota. Her research areas are advertising effects and consumer behavior in a healthcare context, including direct-to-consumer (DTC) prescription drug advertising.

Scott Koslow is Professor of Marketing, Department of Marketing and Management, Macquarie University. His research examines advertising creativity, integration, strategy, and effectiveness. He won Best Article Award by *Journal of Advertising* and was a Special Issues Editor of *Journal of Advertising*.

Michael R. Kotowski is Assistant Professor in the School of Communication Studies at the University of Tennessee, Knoxville. His research is on social influence processes, especially interpersonal persuasion and compliance gaining. He also focuses on research methodology and measurement.

Dean M. Krugman is Professor Emeritus, Grady College, University of Georgia, and Past President of the American Academy of Advertising. He received the AAA outstanding research award and is a UGA Senior Teaching Fellow. Research funding includes CDC, ACS, and NAB.

Russell N. Laczniak is Professor of Marketing and John and Connie Stafford Faculty Fellow at Iowa State University. He was editor of *Journal of Advertising* and is Past President and Treasurer of the American Academy of Advertising.

Carrie la Ferle is a Professor in the Temerlin Advertising Institute at Southern Methodist University in Dallas, Texas. Her research examines how culture impacts advertising effectiveness. She has lived and worked in Canada, Japan, and Singapore.

Mira Lee is Associate Professor of Marketing in the College of Business and Economics at Chung-Ang University. Her research focuses on the use of games for advertising purposes and consumer responses to consumer-generated content.

Wei-Na Lee is Professor of Advertising at UT-Austin. Her research focuses on culture in the process of persuasive communication. A three-time recipient of the American Academy of Advertising Research Fellowship, she is currently editor of the *Journal of Advertising*.

Hairong Li is Professor of Advertising at Michigan State University and former editor of the *Journal of Interactive Advertising*. His research covers theoretical and managerial issues of advertising, media, and branding, especially interactive and mobile advertising issues.

Edward F. McQuarrie is Professor of Marketing at Santa Clara University. His research focuses on qualitative research and persuasion via narrative and rhetoric. He has authored three books and numerous journal articles appearing in the *Journal of Consumer Research* and elsewhere.

Marjolein Moorman is Associate Professor in Political Communication at the Communication Science Department at the University of Amsterdam. Her research examines the relationship between media environments and advertising effects. Her publications include *Journal of Advertising* and *Journal of Advertising Research*.

Sandra Moriarty is retired co-founder of Colorado University's IMC Master's program, and author or co-author of 12 books on advertising, IMC, and visual communication. She has consulted with agencies, including Dentsu and BBDO, and conducted seminars in the US, Europe, and Asia.

Jon D. Morris is Professor in the Department of Advertising, University of Florida. He developed the AdSAM® measure of emotional response. His research, which examines emotional response, has appeared in major advertising, marketing, and measurement journals.

Barbara Mueller is Professor of Advertising at San Diego State University. She is author of *Dynamics of International Advertising* (2011) and *Communicating with the Multicultural Consumer* (2008), and is co-author (with Katherine Toland Frith) of *Advertising and Societies* (2010).

Xiaoli Nan is Assistant Professor in the Department of Communication at the University of Maryland. Her research is focused on persuasion processes and media effects, particularly in such domains as health communication, risk communication, and social marketing.

Peter Neijens is Dean of the Graduate School of Communication and Full Professor of Persuasive Communication, University of Amsterdam. His research examines public opinion, campaign effects, and media and advertising. He is Editor-in-Chief of the *International Journal of Public Opinion Research* and Past President of European Advertising Academy.

Michelle R. Nelson is Associate Professor in the Department of Advertising at the University of Illinois at Urbana-Champaign. Her research includes persuasion knowledge of product placement, advergames, and video news releases as well as cultural influences on consumption and persuasion.

Gergely Nyilasy is Lecturer at the University of Melbourne in Australia. His research interests are practitioner cognition and professionalism, advertising effects, and ethical issues. He was a planner at JWT and head of R&D at Hall & Partners, both in New York.

Shintaro Okazaki is Associate Professor of Marketing at Universidad Autónoma de Madrid. His research focuses on international and interactive marketing. He is Associate Editor of *Journal of Advertising* and recipient of Best Academic of the Year award from Mobile Marketing Association.

Larry Percy has worked for over 35 years in the "'real world" of advertising and marketing as well as academia. Currently a consultant in marketing and communications, he also holds appointments as Visiting Professor of Marketing at several top European business schools.

Joseph E. Phelps is Professor and Chair of the Department of Advertising and Public Relations at the University of Alabama. He served as Head of the Advertising Division of AEJMC and is Past President of the American Academy of Advertising.

Barbara J. Phillips is the Rawlco Scholar in Advertising and Professor of Marketing, University of Saskatchewan. Her research focuses on visual images in advertising. With Edward McQuarrie, she received the Dunn Award and the "Best Article" award in *Journal of Advertising*.

Ivan L. Preston, Professor Emeritus in the University of Wisconsin-Madison School of Journalism and Mass Communication, died shortly after completing this chapter. A Past President of the American Academy of Advertising, he was one of the most honored members of the organization.

Leonard N. Reid is Professor of Advertising, University of Georgia. He is recipient of the American Academy of Advertising's Outstanding Research Award, former editor of *Journal of Advertising* and recipient of *JA*'s Best Article Award. He is an AAA Fellow.

Jef I. Richards is the Chair and Professor in the Department of Advertising, Public Relations and Retailing at Michigan State University. He is Past President of the American Academy of Advertising.

Patricia B. Rose is Executive Director, American Academy of Advertising and Professor Emeriti, Florida International University, and is a Past President of the American Academy of Advertising. She served as editor of *Journal of Advertising Education* and worked 25+ years in industry.

Herbert Jack Rotfeld is Auburn University Professor of Marketing and decade-long *Journal of Consumer Affairs* editor; he received the American Academy of Advertising's Outstanding Contribution to Research Award, Kim Rotzoll Award for Advertising Ethics and Social Responsibility, and served as AAA President in 2011.

Marla B. Royne is First Tennessee Professor and Chair of Marketing, University of Memphis, and Past Editor of *Journal of Advertising*. She twice received the American Academy of Advertising fellowship, and was awarded the Palmer Professorship and Distinguished Research Award.

Sheila Sasser is Associate Professor of Marketing and Ronald Collins Outstanding Faculty Researcher at Eastern Michigan University, Visiting Professor at Michigan, and Editor of the *Journal of Advertising* Special Issue on Creativity Research, receiving many awards for her breakthrough creativity research.

Don Schultz is Professor Emeritus of Integrated Marketing Communications, Northwestern University. His BBA is from University of Oklahoma, and his MA and PhD are from Michigan State University. He is President of Agora, Inc., a global marketing, communication, and branding consulting firm.

David W. Schumann holds the William J. Taylor Professorship of Business in the Department of Marketing and Logistics at the University of Tennessee and Director, Tennessee Teaching and Learning Center. As a consumer psychologist, his research focuses on audience response to marketing communication.

Kim Bartel Sheehan is Professor of Advertising at the University of Oregon, bringing 12 years of industry experience to the program. She has written six books and over two dozen academic papers, focusing on online privacy, advertising ethics, and DTC prescription drug advertising.

Wonsun Shin is Assistant Professor at the Wee Kim Wee School of Communication and Information, Nanyang Technological University, Singapore. Areas of research include interactive advertising, consumer socialization, and youth and new media.

S. Shyam Sundar is Distinguished Professor and Founding Director of the Media Effects Research Laboratory (www.psu.edu/dept/medialab) at Penn State. He investigates social psychological effects of interactivity and other technological elements on processing and perception of media content.

Charles R. Taylor is the John A. Murphy Professor of Marketing at Villanova University. He is editor of *International Journal of Advertising* and Past President of the American Academy of Advertising. His research includes international advertising, public policy, and information processing.

Brian D. Till is Visiting Professor of Marketing at Loyola University (Chicago). His research interests are primarily in the areas of associative learning, brand associations, non-traditional media, and creativity in advertising.

Douglas C. West is Professor of Marketing at Birkbeck, University of London. He is researching creative risk decision-making. He is Executive Editor of *Journal of Advertising Research* and co-author of *Strategic Marketing: Creating Competitive Advantage* (2010).

Rick T. Wilson is Assistant Professor of Marketing and International Business at Hofstra University. His research includes non-traditional advertising, creativity in advertising, cross-cultural marketing, country branding, and Eastern Europe.

Kevin Wise is Associate Professor and Co-director of the PRIME Lab at the Missouri School of Journalism. He investigates how features of online media affect cognition and emotion. He is Associate Editor of the *Journal of Interactive Advertising*.

Joyce M. Wolburg is Professor of Advertising and Associate Dean in the Diederich College of Communication at Marquette University. Her research interests include health communication messages and ritual behavior. She is co-author of *Advertising, Society, and Consumer Culture* (2010) with Roxanne Hovland.

Christine Wright-Isak is Assistant Professor of Marketing at Florida Gulf Coast University. She worked 15 years as advertising researcher and strategic planner for BBDO New York and Young & Rubicam New York, receiving the Gold David Ogilvy award in 1998.

Qian Xu is Assistant Professor in the School of Communications at Elon University. Her research interests are on the psychological effects of online technology in human–computer interaction, computer-mediated communication, and online strategic communication.

Seounmi Youn is Associate Professor in the Department of Marketing Communication at Emerson College. Her research interests include interactive advertising effectiveness and adolescents' online socialization, specifically privacy concerns.

Lu Zheng is Assistant Professor in the Department of Advertising at the University of Florida. Her research involves construction of a persuasion model, persuasion via narrative advertising, cross-cultural advertising, media planning, and health communication on OTC and DTC advertising.

Foreword

For more than 100 years, advertising scholars have been interested in the topic of advertising theory. In 1903, Walter Dill Scott published his book *The Psychology of Advertising in Theory and Practice*, in which he applied psychology to various business practices, including advertising. Scott, who went on to serve as President of Northwestern University from 1920 until 1939, maintained that the theory of advertising is "a simple exposition of the principles of psychology in their relationship to successful advertising."

Later, in 1936, C. H. "Sandy" Sandage introduced the first edition of his long-selling textbook, *Advertising Theory and Practice*, which was used in the first advertising classes taken by many of us. Sandy wanted to focus not on the practical training of students but also to provide them with the underlying principles of advertising, thus, the theories that underlie advertising practice.

In the 1960s, S. Watson Dunn took up the mantle of advertising theory, encouraging scholarship to explore and define specific theories of advertising, apart from those borrowed from other disciplines; he continued this emphasis throughout his career at Wisconsin, Illinois, and Missouri. During his career at Houston, Illinois, Texas, and Alabama, teaching-award winner Arnold Barban, along with many others, always integrated supporting theoretical foundations in advertising courses, providing students with information about what theories underpin the practice of advertising.

Over the years and continuing today, too much of advertising is practiced with little or no understanding of advertising theory, which often results in poor advertising, wasted investments, and disappointing results. Even those practitioners who rely on theory often place their faith in simple theses such as reach, frequency, and exposure. These simple theoretical underpinnings relate to message, media, and product specifics, as well as competition and, a bit more deeply, consumer behavior. Of course, these principles are important, but they involve applying theories from other disciplines, such as the social and behavioral sciences, to the process and operation of advertising. Helpful as these analyses may be, success may often hinge on a deeper understanding of the underlying facets of advertising.

Now, after more than a century of study and contemplation, we have this book, *Advertising Theory*, which explores more deeply than ever before what theories relate to advertising, what theories lie behind advertising itself, and the applications of advertising theory to the philosophical as well as the practical aspects of advertising. By necessity, this exploration of advertising theory involves current theoretical analysis in advertising, marketing, and communications practice. Yet this book provides much more, including behavioral, legal, research, and ethical theories as they relate to advertising. For the first time, theoretical underpinnings of social media, children's advertising, health communications, mobile media, and gaming have been gathered together in one volume.

In addition, theoretical relevance from a number of cognate disciplines is presented, including behavioral, social, rhetorical, cultural, and political aspects. Also included is a review of how advertising practitioners think about and use theory in pragmatic applications.

Among the authors of these chapters are some of the leaders in philosophy, research, and teaching about advertising. This volume's editors, both highly respected leaders in advertising education, have provided a real and lasting service with this book.

Don Jugenheimer

Preface

Advertising Theory

Advertising Theory provides a comprehensive set of theories about advertising that challenge and advance current definitions, concepts, and theories of advertising. *Advertising Theory* is for advertising students, scholars, researchers, and educators. It is also created for scholars not directly in advertising but in related fields such as public relations, marketing, public health, and communication, as well as those who want to deepen their understanding of and ability to support ad functions in their organization. The book offers key theories and insights related to advertising and related areas such as branding and integrated marketing communication, to name a couple.

Our purpose in editing this volume was to provide beginning students and seasoned scholars who want greater familiarity with the various areas of advertising, a comprehensive understanding of how advertising works and how advertising relates to its environments such as regulatory, political, or international. A central rationale for putting together a volume on "Advertising Theory" is that advertising is a unique phenomenon with important theories that have been developed to help understand how advertising works. The authors represent a variety of fields and disciplines including advertising, marketing, journalism, and mass communication. Together, these authors present a diverse set of perspectives on advertising and advertising theory.

The idea for this book grew out of a series of informal discussions between the coeditors—conversations in which we complained that while there are lots of undergraduate textbooks about principles of advertising, branding, and marketing communications, there was no significant effort to bring together, compare and contrast, and evaluate advertising theories. This led to a panel on "Advertising Theory" at the annual conference of the American Academy of Advertising in Cincinnati, OH, in 2009, which expanded and grew into a 1-day pre-conference at the AAA conference in Minneapolis, MN, in 2010. Many of our authors participated in those meetings.

Advertising Theory provides a rich theoretical perspective and is unified by a common framework presented by the editors in Chapter 1, "Components of the Advertising Process Circle" model, illustrated in Figure 1.1. All of the chapters in the book—and the organization of the book—are situated within the components of advertising outlined in Figure 1.1. Even though a number of our authors disagree with this configuration of the field, all of our authors commented on where their work was located in terms of Figure 1.1. While we do not offer this volume as the final story about advertising theory, we do address some fundamental starting points toward bringing together all the work that now comprises advertising theory and the research that supports it.

We hope the book speaks to readers in ways that are not only theoretical and academic but also practical and useful. To that end, contributors have provided key terms and a glossary is provided at the end of the book. Throughout the book, our authors include websites, URLs, case studies, and examples to illustrate complex points. An eResource website is available to be used as a complement to the text—in- and outside the classroom. The eResource website contains additional examples of advertisements, commercials, advertising campaigns, etc.—materials can be accessed by instructors and students who adopt the book, to be used in the classroom and in research projects.

Our experience in working with students teaches us that many students want tips and suggestions to guide their future research and dissertations. For these students, "Additional Readings" are provided at the end of the chapters. The Additional Readings also serve the purpose of offering professors a way to link ideas in the book to ideas and discussions in the classroom. Additional Readings might be used to stimulate class discussions, to give substance to oral presentations, or serve as the basis of student papers.

Unarguably, there are theories in the field of advertising that are either missing from this volume, or may not be given sufficient attention. But it is our contention that students and scholars who read and study this volume will be well on their way to having a broad view of advertising theory.

We welcome your feedback on this collaborative text. And we want to hear your suggestions for improving and further developing the next edition of this book. You can email Shelly Rodgers at srodgers@missouri.edu or Esther Thorson at thorsone@missouri.edu.

What follows is a brief overview of the 38 chapters that comprise this volume. We have organized the chapters into eight parts, which reflect the components of Figure 1.1 of Chapter 1. We think this configuration will help the reader see linkages across areas of advertising theory that may eventually become more integrated with each other.

Part I: Perspectives on Advertising and Advertising Theory provides an overview for the whole book. The chapters in this part provide three contrasting approaches to thinking about advertising theory. Together, they provide a broad perspective and can help guide how to fit subsequent chapters into an integrated whole. Thorson and Rodgers (Chapter 1) review a number of definitions of advertising that have been offered by advertising textbooks or by advertising scholars. They also suggest that McGuire's model that combines stages of communication with stages of effect is—in combination with unique variables and contexts of advertising—a good way to understand many of the most important questions about advertising. After introducing the model in Figure 1.1 that guides this text, they conclude with a brief discussion about whether advertising is its own unique field and offer suggestions on what is needed to further establish advertising as an academic field.

Faber, Duff, and Nan (Chapter 2), argue that the McGuire approach provided in Chapter 1, while legitimate, fails to address how advertising is a different process from other communication types. They distinguish between a variable field vs. a level field and suggest four characteristics of advertising that differentiate it from other types of communication.

Nyilasy and Reid (Chapter 3) contrast what advertising scholars think about advertising theory with what advertising professionals think, and explore why there is so little communication between advertising scholars and practitioners. After depth interviews with many professionals, they conclude that the underlying theory most espoused by professionals involves three central beliefs, outlined in their chapter. They go on to compare this "professional" theory about how advertising works to some scholarly work, predominantly the Persuasion Knowledge Model, which is discussed in-depth again in Chapter 12.

We note the consistencies in Chapters 2 and 3. Both are concerned with breakthrough of advertising into awareness and the challenge of dealing with consumer skepticism. Of course, all three approaches are concerned with how "creativity" in advertising is invented and how it works. These three chapters together provide a much more inclusive approach to theorizing about advertising.

In *Part II: Psychological Processes in Response to Advertisements*, we ask about the psychological interface between advertising and its various impacts on people. Schumann et al. (Chapter 4) overview one of the most influential theories of attitude change of the past 30 years, the Elaboration Likelihood Model (ELM), and review 30 years of research in advertising. They conclude by offering suggestions for future studies that involve a number of psychological processes, attention, involvement, and cognition.

Percy (Chapter 5) focuses on the psychological process of emotion as being critically important to how well an ad persuades. Percy's analysis of emotion suggests four crucial ideas about emotion as it is related to advertising, and explores the importance of effectively embodying emotion in the behaviors and facial expressions of the actors in advertisements.

Morris (Chapter 6) reviews some of the major theories of advertising that include emotion as important variables, and elaborates on a three-component theory of emotion: valence, intensity, and dominance/submission. Morris concludes with a discussion of SAM (the Self-Assessment Manikin) and offers important insights into advertising with this measurement system.

Bolls, Wise, and Bradley (Chapter 7) introduce a new way of measuring the impact of advertising, one that focuses on the concept of Embodied Motivated Cognition. The authors relate Embodied Motivated Cognition to the ideas of receivers, channels, and messages that are central components of responses to advertising, and suggest that a particularly good way to study these components is through psychophysiology, which connects brain activity with behavioral and cognitive variables.

Finally, Haley (Chapter 8) delves into the psychology of involvement as a process that determines how successfully ads persuade people. He overviews the history of the involvement concept in advertising and then talks about involvement and learning, rational vs. emotional involvement, enduring vs. situational involvement, involvement with media channels themselves, and elaborates on how involvement plays a role in other theories of advertising.

Part III provides an overview on *Specific Audiences*. The four chapters in this part focus on two specific audiences for advertising: children and consumers from countries other than the US. In Chapter 9, Laczniak and Carlson carefully bring together all the generalizations they consider sufficiently verified by research to serve as "Laws" about children in relation to advertising—the most important is that we know advertising influences children's behavior, and that children initially do not understand the "selling purpose" of advertising but this understanding develops as they mature. The chapter closes with a preview of where children and advertising research is likely to move in the future.

Taylor, Okazaki, and Mueller (Chapter 10) introduce management-based theories about international advertising, including Global Consumer Culture Theory, Global Brand Positioning Theory, Resource Advantage Theory, and Global Marketing Strategy Theory. In the second part of their chapter they review Hofstede's theory of culture, asking what its primary implications are for understanding and managing advertising in other countries and cultures.

La Ferle and Lee (Chapter 11) also look at international advertising but approach it quite differently. Their central focus is how the encoding and decoding of advertising varies from one culture or subculture to another. They introduce Kanter's (1977) Theory of Proportional Representation and overview a number of theories that lead to specific predictions about the problems in creating advertising that does not inadvertently create a negative response in some of the different cultures that encounter it. Nelson and Ham (Chapter 12) overview how the Persuasion Knowledge Model (PKM)—developed to understand the intuitive theories that ordinary people have about how advertising works—has developed around an understanding of the "intrinsically negative audience." The authors review research that applies PKM to advertising and suggest directions that future research should take to make the theory even more useful.

Part IV provides eight chapters on *Different Types of Advertising Messages*. These eight chapters are concerned with categories of ads—ranging from what makes them "creative" to narrative ads that tell a story, to ads for health products, to ads for pharmaceuticals, to political ads. Chapter 13 reviews studies on creativity that fit within the 3Ps of Person, Place, and Process, to shed light on the many ways creativity in advertising can be explained. Chapter 14 reviews trends in advertising creative research and focuses on advertising organizations, i.e., ad agencies and creatives who are paid to create and evaluate advertising. Chapter 15 offers a rhetorical theory of advertising, conceptualized as a distinct kind of message, and provides theoretical propositions about print ads for future research and testing. Chapter 16 compares narrative and analytical process of advertising by reviewing three factors that trigger narrative processing including narrative ads, specific ad executions, and individual differences, and explains how people understand narratives and how narrative processing works. Chapter 17 presents an emerging model with much potential to explain the processing and effects of narrative advertising, namely, the Transportation-Imagery Model, and offers additional routes to persuasion beyond the two identified by ELM.

Chapter 18 looks at DTC advertising and connects DTC advertising to other relevant advertising theories. Chapter 19 discusses unique characteristics of online healthcare product advertising, proposes the trust construct as a key element in theory-building, and presents an empirical study testing the role of trust in consumers' interactions with and responses to pharmaceutical advertising websites. Chapter 20 defines and examines research on political advertising and some of the complex realities of studying effects of political advertising including different types of voters, candidates, sponsors, elections, political markets, political systems, media systems, messages, and timing and frequency of messages. The authors suggest that popular characteristics of political ads be integrated as moderators in effects models and be given more attention to the processes underlying the effects, and to model these processes as mediators.

Part V on *Media and Media Devices* considers the importance of the channels by which advertising reaches people. Chapter 21 addresses the methods by which advertising messages are actually delivered to the people for whom they were intended, i.e., receivers, and develops a general framework for understanding how interactions among the various advertising contexts affect the way consumers process information within a media channel. It draws on this framework as a basis for understanding media planning strategy, beginning with the broad concept of integrated marketing communications (IMC) and links it with conventional media planning. Chapter 22 presents the Non-traditional Advertising Message Processing (NAMP) framework, which uses the capacity theory of attention and message response involvement theory to provide a better understanding of how to maximize advertising effectiveness. Chapter 23 outlines the MAIN model, which offers a theoretical framework for understanding the role of technology in online persuasion and extends existing studies on consumers' cognitive processing and persuasive outcomes by taking into account both the technology and the psychology of its use. The chapter identifies cues in the technology of the interface that can impact users' cognitions and attitudes. Chapter 24 provides a comprehensive review on mobile advertising theories and conceptualizes the ubiquity concept, which is a core benefit of mobile devices. The chapter offers explanations on using mobile advertising theories to advance advertising research and to teach advertising courses at the university level. Chapter 25 reviews key findings of prior studies on in-game advertising and advergames while highlighting major psychological mechanisms that explain how in-game brand placements influence brand memory, attitude, or product choice will be discussed. The chapter describes how game players' characteristics and strategic features of brand placements affect players' processing of brand placements in games and provides scholars with directions for future research in these areas. Chapter 26 defines social media and identifies key characteristics that distinguish social media from other media channels and devices, and suggests new areas of study that will shape and build the future of advertising theory.

Part VI: Organizations, focuses on the organizational functions within advertising. The organizations that create ads, i.e., advertising agencies, are a significant component of the field of advertising. Wright-Isak (Chapter 27) is concerned with the sociology of advertising organizations and the ways in which advertising is a profession. In asking the latter question, Wright-Isak integrates what has been said about how to define advertising, an issue that almost all of the authors of this volume have touched upon. She also addresses again the question of creativity. A particularly important point is that advertising is an activity with highly permeable boundaries, that is, the definition of advertising fluctuates, especially with the coming of so many new digital channels and devices.

Many argue—including authors Krugman and Hayes (Chapter 28)—that the central task for most advertising is to define brands and increase their value to companies. They elaborate on how brand health is integral to successful business practices, as well as on the relations between advertising and brands. Advertising provides brands with long-lasting images and creates customer trust in and preference for brands. The authors discuss the science of determining monetary value of brands and link that valuation with advertising associated with it.

In the last chapter of this part, Bower and Grau (Chapter 29) investigate how advertiser organizations conceptualize their social responsibility to consumers. "Corporate social responsibility" is a controversial concept in that it sometimes pits stockholder profit against the value of "doing good" for causes. Bower and Grau elaborate the idea of "fit" between companies and their causes, providing examples of two guiding concepts, which are commonality between company and issue and complementarity.

Part VII is about *Contexts of Advertising*. Advertising occurs within many contexts, the features of which influence all kinds of aspects of advertising. In the four chapters in this part, we look at the roles and impact of ethical and legal environments in which advertising operates, the role of advertising in relationship to other persuasive tactics, and in terms of health concerns.

Drumwright (Chapter 30) discusses implications of advertising theory within the context of ethics. She distinguishes between "message ethics" and "business ethics," both of which are important to consider for ethics questions in advertising. The author outlines two different sets of ethics questions for individuals working in advertising, and argues that an important part of both of these sets of considerations is to identify ethical issues and to think through the alternative decisions that could be made to insure moral behavior.

Of course, one way to deal with aggregate problems is through legal regulation. This is the focus for Richards in Chapter 31, who first points out how complicated the legal environment is for advertising. Every brand carries specific and different regulatory issues—from dog food to cosmetics to banking services. Richards then turns to the issue of what "legal theory" means, a concept that has several very different meanings. Richards closes the chapter with analysis of how social science theory can bridge the gap between advertising and the application of legal theories to it.

Integrated Marketing Communications (IMC) is an approach to promotion that combines persuasion tools like advertising, public relations, promotions, and media choices. In Chapter 32, Moriarty and Schultz overview IMC and introduce four kinds of theories about it, including Interactive Communication Theory, Perceptual Integration Theory, Reciprocity Theory, and Process Theory. The authors argue that these four theories of IMC are useful because they help tame the complexity of understanding and doing IMC.

In the last chapter of this part, Wolburg (Chapter 33) reviews the environment of public health as a context in which advertising operates, when specialized forms of advertising like public service announcements and social marketing campaigns become central. Wolburg points out that sometimes these messages involve "unmarketing" as in the case of ad messages that discourage behaviors like staying out of the sun, and the importance of the concept of "risk" in these endeavors. The chapter ends with a discussion of how advertising for health products can also be thought of as part of the public health environment of advertising and is, thus, connected with Sheehan's Chapter 18 on DTC and Huh and Shin's Chapter 19 concerning online health advertising.

In our final *Part VIII: The Future of Advertising Theories*, we bring together a number of scholars and editors of academic journals to do some "big thinking" about advertising and what will come next. Preston (Chapter 34) discusses some of the human barriers to using theory and research on responses to advertising messages. Professor Preston, in his lifetime of work on the basic idea that the meaning of messages lies in people not in the messages themselves, asks how research of advertising's meaning to people could become more important within the law and for advertising professionals. Preston's concept of "puffery" for many years has served as one of the most basic of demonstrations of differences between what an ad "says" and what it means to people.

Royne (Chapter 35), as former editor of the *Journal of Advertising*, offers a different perspective on both the definition of advertising and of how important it is to develop advertising theory. Royne endorses permeability in the definition of advertising as the digital revolution progresses. She also suggests that developing advertising theory should not come at the expense of relevance to professionals.

Li (Chapter 36), as co-founder and long-time editor of *Journal of Interactive Advertising*, provides suggestions on advancing advertising theories and scholarship. Li's central advocacy is of innovation in theory that speaks directly to the new media landscape and that strays from many of the classic theories that have been elucidated in this text.

Somewhat related to Li's call for new theories in advertising, Rotfeld (Chapter 37) suggests that some theories applied to advertising have worn out their utility. As long-time editor of the *Journal of Consumer Affairs*, Rotfeld brings a "critical" perspective to advertising theories by highlighting contradictions in advertising theories and definitions, and by arguing that there is a pragmatic need to connect theory and research.

Rose, in Chapter 38, goes over the implications of IMC, advertising research, and the advertising discipline from her perspective as editor of the *Journal of Advertising Education*. She discusses the impact of IMC on research, where it has helped to switch the focus from messages to consumers, and on advertising education, where she believes there remains a need to have much more emphasis on integrating the skills and tactics that students learn.

Acknowledgments

Many perspectives are represented within the pages of this book. To acknowledge these perspectives, our first expression of thanks goes to all of our contributors. Editing your work was a privilege and, boy, did we learn a lot from you! Thanks also to our publisher, Linda Bathgate, for the amount of time and energy spent getting the book ready for publication. Thanks also to early readers and the wonderful editors of our manuscript for valuable feedback and suggestions.

Shelly wishes to thank her husband, Jon Stemmle, for his invaluable support and encouragement throughout the whole process, and for formatting the book—the best Valentine's gift ever! Shelly also thanks her two children, Brianna (8) and Brandon (5), for their hugs of support through the arduous publishing process. Thank you, also, to Shelly's family and friends who offered emotional support as our book went from rough draft to the bookstore. Shelly thanks Esther for her brilliance and sense of humor that helped keep us sane throughout the coediting process. Special thanks to my J8000 students for piloting the book.

Esther sends a big hug and thank you to her brother and sister-in-law, Joel and Carol Whiteside, who picked up a lot of the responsibilities to care for their parents while Esther was working on the book. There were so many weekends she couldn't head out to Kansas City for parent care, so Joel and Carol added weekends to their weekly caretaking! Thanks, Guys! And to Shelly, whose work ethic is like Swiss trains—always on time, meticulous in all work aspects, but with some laughs along the way!

SR
ET

Part I

Perspectives on Advertising and Advertising Theory

Chapter 1

What Does "Theories of Advertising" Mean?

Esther Thorson and Shelly Rodgers

As we designed and brought this book together our first job was to agree on what "theories" were and, of course, what "advertising" was. These activities led us to this effort to introduce and provide a rationale for organizing the field of "advertising." Although theorizing about advertising is made up of many borrowed components from other fields, it is our contention that advertising's uniqueness follows from how the components are organized and used. The scholars who contributed to this volume have each explored how their approach relates to the overview of advertising and theory as we've explicated it in this chapter. We don't offer this chapter as the final story about advertising theory, but we address some fundamental starting points toward bringing together all the work that now comprises advertising theory and the research that supports it.

Before we can consider advertising theory, we have to agree on how to define advertising. Figure 1.1 shows a chart of the components argued to be

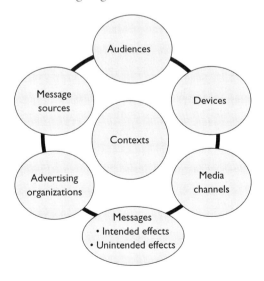

Figure 1.1 Components of the Advertising Process Circle.

required attributes of a message in order for it to be considered "advertising." The common denominator of the field is that every aspect relates, finally, to advertising messages. Table 1.1 provides a summary of textbook definitions of advertising and shows that advertising messages are commonly defined as *paid* communication from an *identified sponsor* using *mass media* to *persuade* an audience. With notable exceptions, these elements bear similarities to the definition provided by Richards and Curran (2002) who undertook the Delphi Method with a group of advertising experts, to arrive at essential elements of advertising that constitute a definition. Our model is an attempt to expand upon this definition and provide readers with a schema that helps to organize the vast literature on advertising theories, or perhaps more aptly put, *theories of advertising.*

Of course, there are many ways to promote ideas, brands, politicians, or issues but advertising involves mostly professionally designed commercials ("commercial" implies television or video) or advertisements ("advertisement" implies print or online display advertising). Mass media like television, radio, newspapers, and magazines are paid to carry those messages to their audiences. Advertisements can also occur on the Internet, and this medium can be more "individualized" than the mass media (e.g., email advertising is designed and delivered very specifically). And there is now recognized a new form of advertising created by ordinary people ("user generated" advertising) rather than professionals. But in spite of these current variations in messages that are referred to as advertising—a phenomenon caused mainly by the digital revolution—the definition above is generally accepted (for exceptions, see Richards & Curran, 2002).

Nevertheless, it is important to distinguish advertising from other promotional tools. Marketing refers to everything done to promote a brand, e.g., creating the product, pricing it, placing it where it can be bought, and promoting it, i.e., the "4 Ps," including product, price, place, promotion. Thus, advertising is a subcategory of marketing and falls under the fourth "P—promotion." Other forms of promotion, which differ from advertising, are public relations, sales promotion, and personal selling. Public relations focuses on management activities carried out between a company and its various publics to enhance long-term mutual understanding, goodwill, and support (Smith, 2002; Wilcox & Cameron, 2010). Messages are involved in public relations, for example, press releases to the media, but it does not involve paid advertising carried by the media. Sales promotions are incentives that organizations use to temporarily change the perceived value of a product or service (Schultz, Robinson, & Petrison, 1998). A coupon, contest, reward, or price discount are all sales promotions. Sales promotions may be targeted toward consumers or toward retail organizations. Personal selling is a fourth type of promotions and involves face-to-face persuasion to sell a product (Anderson, Dubinsky, & Mehta, 2007) as in the case of a car salesman or door-to-door home demonstrations that, while more targeted than traditional advertising messages, are also more costly.

In addition to these distinctions, advertising varies according to media (e.g., television commercials, newspaper advertisements) and devices (smart phones, televisions, e-Readers, laptops) that carry it. Political advertising promotes candidates for office. Issue advertising promotes ideas from the public service domain (forest fire or crime prevention), health advertising promotes behaviors that increase healthiness (promotion of vaccines, admonishments to engage in safe sex, smoking cessation), children's advertising promotes directly to the young, corporate advertising promotes the viewpoints of companies (e.g., that they are environmentally responsible, or that they are sorry for product failure or accidents).

Our organizational scheme for thinking about theories of advertising is shown in Figure 1.1. Before we look at each of the components, we ask, "What is advertising for?" that is, what are the utilities of advertising messages? In general, there are four utilities. Brand building means creating concepts and beliefs about brands in the minds of consumers. Lead generation means the advertising message has attracted people who are in the market for purchase. Driving purchase means there is a direct relationship between encountering the advertising messages and buying the advertised brand. Changing life behaviors means the advertising messages lead directly to behaviors like losing weight, reducing smoking, using safe sex methods, and brushing your teeth more often. Note that all four utilities refer to what the entity that pays for the advertising intends to have it accomplish. There are, however, many hypothesized "unintended" effects and these are also included in the "effects" circle of Figure 1.1.

Advertising, as represented in Figure 1.1, can easily be organized in terms of the classic communication components (see McGuire, 1969). We have, however, added two circles to those components. The first is "advertising organizations." Table 1.2 shows examples of the variables that make up these organizations—advertising agencies, corporations that advertise, regulatory organizations, and professional or academic associations. This circle can even contain advertising departments.

The next circle is "Messages." Advertising messages can be of a variety of types and have a variety of features. Table 1.2 shows examples like the sensory dimensions of ads, i.e., whether they are print, contain images, or video. Advertising messages can also vary by their appeal (sex, taste, emotion, rational argument, problem solution). They can vary by what is being sold: brands, behaviors, politicians, or issues. They can vary in length, by how often they are repeated, and by the media content they are embedded in (i.e., program or editorial contexts).

"Channels" refers to the common sense notion of what brings the advertising message to its audience. This is, of course, far more complex technologically

Table 1.1 Textbook definitions of advertising

Reference	Source	Message	Channel	Effect	Mediated or not	Objects
AMA (1960)	Identifiable sponsor	Paid	–	–	Non-personal message	–
Dunn (1969)	Identified business firms, nonprofit organizations and individuals	Paid	Through various media	–	Non-personal communication	–
Cohen (1972)	Identified sponsor	Paid	–	–	Non-personal presentation and promotion	Ideas, goods, or services
Kaufman (1980)	Identified sponsor	Paid	–	–	Non-personal presentation	Goods, services, or ideas
Bolen (1981)	Identified sponsor	–	–	Inform and persuade	Controlled form of non-personal presentation and promotion	Ideas, goods, or services
Dunn and Barban (1986)	Identifiable source	Paid	Through a mass-mediated channel	Persuade	Non-personal message	–
Bovée and Thill (1992)	Identified sponsors	–	Through various media	Persuasive	Non-personal communication of information	Products, services, or ideas
Arens (1996)	Identified sponsors	Paid	Through various media	Persuasive	Non-personal communication	Products (goods and services) or ideas
Bearden et al. (1998)	Identified sponsor	Paid	Through mass channels	Promote the adoption of goods, services, persons, or ideas	Non-personal	Goods, services, persons, or ideas

Source					
Belch and Belch (1998)	Identified sponsor	Paid	–	–	Non-personal communication	Organization, products, service, or ideas
Wells et al. (1998)	Identified sponsor	Paid	Using mass media	Persuade or influence an audience	Non-personal communication	–
Perreault and McCarthy (1999)	Identified sponsor	Paid	–	–	Non-personal presentation	Ideas, goods, or services
Zikmund and d'Amico (1999)	Identified sponsor	Paid	Carried by non-personal medium	Informative or persuasive message	Non-personal medium	Organization or product
Vanden Bergh and Katz (1999)	Identified sponsor	Paid	–	Influencing an audience	Non-personal communication	Products, services, or ideas
Armstrong and Kotler (2000)	Identified sponsor	Paid	–	–	Non-personal presentation and promotion	Ideas, goods, or services
Czinkota et al. (2000)	Identified sponsor	Paid	Mass communication	–	Non-personal communication	–
Lamb et al. (2000)	Marketer	Paid	One-way mass communication	–	Impersonal	Product or organization
O'Guinn et al. (2000)	–	Paid	Mass-mediated attempt	Persuade	–	–
Richards and Curran (2002)	Identifiable source	Paid	–	Persuade the receiver to take some action, now or in the future	Mediated form of communication	–
Leckenby and Li (2000) "interactive advertising"	Identified sponsor	Paid and unpaid	Through mediated means	–	Mutual action between consumers and advertisers	Products, services, and ideas

Source: chart aggregated by Joonghwa Lee (doctoral student, Missouri School of Journalism) and Chang Dae Ham (assistant professor, Advertising, University of Illinois).

Table 1.2 Examples of the components of the Advertising Process Circle

Contexts
Historical
Business
Ethical
Legal

Advertising Organizations
Advertising agencies
Corporations
Regulatory organizations
Self-regulatory organizations
Professional or Scholarly Associations (ARF, AAA)

Message sources
Corporations
Politicians
Celebrities
Spokespersons
Ordinary citizens

Messages
Content
  Features like print, video, audio, still images
  Appeals
Types
  Brand
  Product
  Corporate
  Public service announcement
  Political
  Issue
  Health

Channels
Newspapers
Magazines
Radio
Television
Internet
Social Media
Search

Devices
Smartphone
e-Reader
Netbook
Laptop
Desktop

Audiences or Message Receivers
Demographic features of consumers (age, education, race)
Segments (bird watchers, fashionistas)
Children
Various cultures or geographies (international)

Table 1.2 Continued

Intended Effects
Purchase
Intention to purchase
Attitude toward the ad
Attitude toward the brand
Memory
Attention
Involvement
Immediate vs. delayed
Unintended (e.g., materialism)
Behavior change beyond purchase

Unintended Effects
Materialism
Purchase of what is unneeded
Unhealthy behaviors
Miscomprehension

than in the past. Some of the complexity we overlook, for example, the content of your television may come from your phone line, a cable, or a satellite. But to you the viewer, it's "television," so we consider it a channel. But watching a movie on your iPhone or your iPad, or your television are different experiences because now the "devices" are different. And their features are different—you get at the movie through different activities—and may pay different prices for it. In some cases, you may be mobile outside your home while enjoying the movie. To "watch a movie on *television*" you have to be in your living room. Thus, we distinguish between channels and devices. As technology continues to develop and our ways of dealing with those technologies changes—to get content, channels, and devices—are also likely to change.

"Devices" are the noticeably different instruments that are used for mass communication. They include, for example, e-Readers, notebooks, laptops, and smart phones. Whether mobile, social, or local, digital devices are more important than ever to advertisers too. Audiences are the intended and actual receivers of advertising messages. Receivers vary in terms of who they are, demographically speaking, what groups they belong to, as in differing market "segments," what media and devices they use, and so on.

Returning to Figure 1.1, we have already talked about "Effects." The sponsor of the advertising message can intend certain effects, and they can simultaneously create unintended effects, and because the processes by which unintended effects occur, and the methodological approaches for studying them often differ, we provide a separate circle for unintended effects.

At the center of the advertising circle is "Advertising Contexts." Because the field of advertising involves anything that relates to advertising messages, contexts can include a very large variety of other areas. Advertising is studied in many contexts because it plays a role in domains as diverse as the political, economic, legal, ethical areas, and history (see Richards & Curran, 2002). To demonstrate the important role that contexts play in advertising, we offer the following discussion on ethics as an advertising context.

There are many analyses of ethical problems related to advertising. As Hovland and Wohlburg (2010) point out, "advertising is inherently controversial." Most advertising historians claim that advertising developed hand in hand with a "consumer culture." Just like any kind of mass communication message, advertising can contain falsities or it may contain only true statements but be misleading (see Preston, 1996). Advertising can promote what some consider a negative trait, "materialism." Advertising can lead to the use of dangerous products like cigarettes or dangerous behaviors like reckless driving of automobiles as they are shown in commercials. Advertising has been accused of preying on vulnerable audiences like children and/or those likely to become addicted to alcohol, gambling, overeating. Advertising is often accused of stereotyping— women, men, children, family relationships, minorities, really just about anything it depicts. From these examples, it can be seen that ethics is clearly another "context" in which advertising messages play an important role (for a discussion, see Chapter 30).

This model (in Figure 1.1) of the advertising field—as revolving around advertising messages that relate to all of the communication components, and that vary by the contexts in which they play a role—provides our rationale for suggesting that all aspects of advertising can be categorized in terms of this model. This model is not a theory of advertising, but is an attempt to organize the vast field of advertising scholarship. Although Table 1.2 comes nowhere near to identifying all the possible variables of the communication components, we suggest that all variables could be added in one of these categories. We test this model of advertising by looking at some fundamental aspects of advertising and then classifying that area by a combination of the analytic categories of Figure 1.1.

There is research on all kinds of effects that advertising is argued to have beyond persuading people, many of them, although not all, unintended. Advertising is acknowledged as the engine that drives consumer purchasing and, therefore, advertising "keeps the wheels of the economy turning." Advertising traditionally has been the support function for news. For example, until very recently newspapers relied on advertising for 80% of their revenues with consumers paying only about 20% or less of the cost of newspapers. Advertising teaches people about new ideas and products. Some researchers claim that many Americans get most of their knowledge of politics from political advertising. Thus, the society is another good example of a "context" in which advertising plays a significant role.

The model of advertising in Figure 1.1 can also be used to classify any theory of advertising. We use the family of "multiattribute theories" as an example. Multiattribute theories include the Theory of Reasoned Action, and the Theory of Planned Behavior. The concept of attitude has been a mainstay in social psychology since the 1920s. An attitude is an orientation toward an object (like a brand) that is associated with beliefs about that brand (it's inexpensive, cleans well) and affect (I like it). Ajzen and Fishbein (1972) introduced to advertising the idea that an attitude results from the summation of a series of beliefs that a brand has attribute "a," attribute "b," and so on to attribute "n." "Multiattribute theory" can be represented by the equation $A_j = \sum b_{ij} a_i$, where "A" is the attitude toward "a" brand, "b" is the belief that attribute "a" is associated with the brand, and "a" is the evaluation of that attribute. In the late 1960s and throughout the 1970s there was in advertising a dominant focus on the "cognitive algebra" of how people developed attitudes toward brands.

Fishbein and Ajzen (1975) developed the theory of reasoned action, which asserted multiattribute theory as one of its assumptions. Fishbein and Ajzen (1977) reasoned that attitudes toward behaviors would predict behaviors only when the attitude and the behavior were compatible, that is, if behaviors are performed in response to a particular target in a given context and at a particular time. For example, I might prefer all the attributes of a heavy-duty laundry detergent (removes tough stains, costs less, has a pleasant scent) but whether I buy the detergent or not is also related to social norms (my friends argue that detergents damage water sources) and motivation to comply with the social norm (maybe I don't care what my friends think). Thus, Theory of Reasoned Action says that behavior (toward a brand) is determined by multiattribute calculations (beliefs about attributes multiplied by the evaluation of those attributes), but also normative beliefs about others and the motivation to comply with those beliefs. This model has been used extensively in attempts to determine all the brand attributes that people thought about when deciding what to purchase, when different kinds of social norms were relevant and so on.

Recently, Ajzen (2005) added a third variable to the model. He suggested that intentions to behave are not the same as behaving. Behavior can be thwarted by lack of behavioral control. For example, a person may intend to marry by the age of 30, but fails to do so because finding a potential partner is not fully under his control.

Clearly, this rationality and attitude-based family of theories was borrowed from psychology, but it has often been applied in the advertising literature to the relationships between advertising messages and receivers. Many advertising applications of multiattribute theory also include source variables.

It is also the case that variables that have been commonly studied in advertising can be represented in terms of the communication components of Figure 1.1.

We look at advertising involvement as an example. Krugman (1972) was one of the first advertising researchers to talk about involvement. He defined it as interest and attention to messages. The study of involvement developed during the 1980s and it became clear that there are many types of involvement, for example, emotional vs. intellectual, the involvement of needing to buy some product (like a car or a new kind of athletic shoe). There is also involvement in product category, involvement with the brand, and involvement in the advertising message itself. Overall, there is clear evidence that the more involvement (or "engagement") there is in advertising, the greater the impact of the ad on memory, message believability, attitude toward the ad, and intention to purchase. Muehling, Laczniak and Andrews (1993) provide a relatively early but thorough review of what advertising involvement can mean, how to measure it, and its effects on persuasion.

Depending on which kind of involvement is being studied, this variable is generally defined by the relationships between messages and receivers. Depending on the nature of the question, channels and devices might also be included.

What we are positing is that everything that has to do with advertising messages can be classified in terms of combinations of the components shown in Figure 1.1. This would include the ways in which professionals go about designing advertising campaigns and the academic literature of advertising.

Is Advertising a Scientific Field?

The model proposed in Figure 1.1 interacts with an important question that has been asked recently about "advertising," i.e., is advertising a scientific field? Advertising is a relatively young field that draws on conceptual frameworks and theories of older, more established fields and disciplines (Pasadeos, Phelps, & Edison, 2008). Nan and Faber (2004), citing Paisley (1972), point out that there are "level fields" like psychology, sociology, anthropology, biology, and physics, and there are "variable fields" that borrow theories and methods from level fields. Advertising is a variable field, and variable fields are unique in that they contribute new variables to the study of advertising and advertising effects (Nan & Faber, 2004).

So fields can have borrowed theories, i.e., theories that come from other fields, and theories that are unique to a field (Pasadeos et al., 2008). The advertising field has been criticized as not having any genuine "advertising" theories (Nan & Faber, 2004). We argue that both borrowed and unique theories are necessary to establish and build a field of advertising. In this book, contributors draw upon borrowed theories from psychology (Chapter 4), social psychology (Chapter 23), biology and physiology (Chapters 5 and 7), sociology (Chapter 27), rhetoric (Chapter 15), marketing (Chapter 12), strategic management and business (Chapter 10), persuasion (Chapters 17 and 22), ethics (Chapter 30), and law (Chapter 31), to name a few. As you'll see from these chapters, borrowed theories shed light on how advertising works in two ways: (1) by taking older more established concepts, theories, and contexts and applying them to advertising, and (2) by identifying new concepts, variables, and contexts unique to advertising and applying them to borrowed theories from the social sciences and other disciplines. There are also chapters that offer theories that are, arguably, unique to advertising. For example, unique theories of advertising are presented and developed in Chapter 3 on practitioners' theories about advertising, Chapter 9 on children and advertising, and Chapter 15 on rhetoric and advertising. New and borrowed theoretical frameworks and models are offered to explain a host of advertising attributes and contexts including: the Elaboration-Likelihood model (Chapter 4), which explains the degree and type of processes individuals use in processing advertising; the Transportation-Imagery Model (Chapter 17), which explains processing and effects of narrative advertising beyond the two persuasion routes identified by ELM; the Non-traditional Advertising Message Processing (NAMP) model (Chapter 22), which explains message processing of non-traditional advertising; and the Modality-Agency-Interactivity-Navigability (MAIN) model (Chapter 23), which provides an understanding of the role of technology in online persuasion. Chapter 30 offers a unique theory of advertising ethics. Drumwright argues that advertising theory can draw profitably from other fields such as psychology and social psychology, which are predominant fields used to develop advertising theory, as well as fields not drawn as heavily upon, including organizational studies, political science, and philosophy. New and borrowed concepts are offered to explain responses to advertising in a variety of new technologies such as mobile media (Chapter 24), advergames (Chapter 25), and social media (Chapter 26), including emotional responses (Chapter 6) and responses to narrative advertising (Chapter 17). New and borrowed measures, research tools, data-gathering techniques, and statistical methods—often spawned by digital technology—are also noted in the pages of this text. In expanding current and building new theories of advertising, we cannot ignore important concepts that help to explain consumer behavior such as involvement (Chapter 8), risk (Chapters 14 and 33), complexity (Chapter 18), trust (Chapter 19), ubiquity (Chapter 24), and fit (Chapter 29). Chapter 21 on media analysis and decision-making, Chapter 28 on branding, and Chapter 32 on IMC demonstrate how both basic and applied research can be used to generate theoretical frameworks that link both areas of inquiry.

In general, then, we suggest that yes, advertising is a scientific field formed around "advertisements," and some of its unique attributes are listed in Table 1.2 that relate to advertisements in important ways. A good example is that advertisements are messages that are repeated, often many times. Therefore, "repetition" becomes an important variable in the advertising field (Chapter 2). McQuarrie and Phillips (Chapter 15) argue that an advertisement has a whole series of rhetorically defined features, e.g., ads are generally located in content that people process as their primary goal and, therefore, the advertising is secondary. Although not all the features of our advertising circle are unique, all of the variables listed in Table 1.2 have had treatment within one or more theories about advertising. As Figure 1.1 shows, it is not enough to offer a theoretical perspective on advertising—borrowed, unique, or otherwise—in isolation of its context. To that end, there are chapters on a variety of advertising contexts including international (Chapter 10), cultural (Chapter 11), health and medical (Chapters 18, 19, and 33), political (Chapter 20), ethical (Chapter 30), and legal (Chapter 31), to name a few.

The goal, then, is to focus more on key elements that make advertising unique (Nan & Faber, 2004) in order to develop robust theories on advertising within the larger societal contexts in which advertising occurs. However, as the field of advertising matures, there is a need to develop synergy between existing theories of advertising and other disciplines. The chapters in this book discuss how theories of advertising relate to or build on existing advertising theories, models, or paradigms, and how new theories of advertising can come from existing theories. As noted in Chapters 3 and 36, we need to do a better job of communicating our relevance to other academic fields and to industry. Chapter 3 notes that we, as a field, have problems disseminating theoretical knowledge to industry. The authors go on to explain that it's not enough to simply disseminate research findings but that information must be packaged in a way that industry will find it both readable and useful. Chapter 34 highlights situations in which the ad industry rejects or ignores research findings presumably due to the potential negative implications of the results, and offers suggestions on how to minimize potential backlash. As Chapter 38 argues, advertising research findings on IMC and other areas need to be translated and taken back to the classroom as well as to industry. In sum, we need to give more attention to disseminating our research, not just to advertising practitioners and educators, but also to the news media.

We should point out that the present volume does not focus on the relationship between advertising theory and professionals, but a number of the chapters provide insights about that relationship. Nyilasy and Reid (Chapter 3) explicate the "theory" of advertising in that they infer that professionals really advocate when they are interviewed about how they think advertising works. It turns out that the most important aspects of this theory are all represented in the theories in this book. Professionals focus on how important it is for the creative aspects of advertisements (Sasser and Koslow, Chapter 13) to "break through" clutter of primary messages (McQuarrie and Phillips, Chapter 15) and the intrinsic negativity of audiences (Nelson and Ham, Chapter 12). Royne (Chapter 35) also discusses the sometimes-troubled relationship between academic advertising research and the advertising profession, as does Wright-Isak (Chapter 27), Preston (Chapter 34), and Rotfeld (Chapter 36).

In short, we believe the chapters in this book comprise a solid foundation for "theories of advertising" that represent a diversity of perspectives, theories, and contexts on how advertising works. The premise of the book is that no aspect of advertising can be understood in isolation. Advertising's very nature and effectiveness is shaped by its interaction with the social, cultural, economic, legal, and psychological context in which it is delivered. In other words, advertising is a complex phenomenon that, arguably, is distinct from every other form of communication. Implicit in this approach is the fact that we can address its complexity by breaking it down into its fundamental dimensions and identifying the theoretical principles by which these dimensions interact, as noted by Cannon in Chapter 21 of this text. The chapters in this book provide lots of ideas for expanding advertising research, strengthening current "borrowed" theories, and creating "new" theories that are unique to advertising. Obviously, we feel the book further advances advertising as its own scientific field, comprised of unique theories, borrowed theories, and theories yet to come.

References

Ajzen, I. (2005). Laws of human behavior: Symmetry, compatibility, and attitude-behavior correspondence. In A. Beauducel, B. Biehl, M. Bosniak, W. Conrad, G. Schönberger, & D. Wagener (Eds.), *Multivariate research strategies* (pp. 3–19). Aachen, Germany: Shaker Verlag.

Ajzen, I., & Fishbein, M. (1977). Attitude–behavior relations: A theoretical analysis and review of empirical research. *Psychological Bulletin, 84*, 888–918.

American Marketing Association (1960). *Definitions: A Glossary of Marketing Terms*. Chicago, IL: American Marketing Association.

Anderson, R. E., Dubinsky A. J., & Mehta, R. (2007). *Personal selling: Building customer relationships and partnerships* (2nd ed.). Boston, MA: Houghton Mifflin Harcourt.

Arens, W. F. (1996). *Contemporary advertising* (6th ed.). Chicago, IL: Richard D. Irwin.

Armstrong, G., & Kotler, P. (2000). *Marketing: An introduction*. Upper Saddle River, NJ: Prentice-Hall.

Bearden, W. O., Ingram, T. N., & LaForge, R. W. (1998). *Marketing: Principles and perspectives* (2nd ed.). New York: Irwin McGraw-Hill.

Belch, G. E., & Belch, M. A. (1998). *Advertising and promotion: An integrated marketing communications perspective* (4th ed.). New York: Irwin/McGraw-Hill.

Bolen, W. H. (1981). *Advertising*. New York: John Wiley & Sons.

Bovée, C. L., & Thill, J. V. (1992). *Marketing*. New York: McGraw-Hill, Inc.

Cohen, D. (1972). *Advertising*. New York: John Wiley.

Czinkota, M. R. (2000). *Marketing: Best practices*. Orlando, FL: Dryden Press.

Dunn, S. W. (1969). *Advertising: Its role in modern marketing* (2nd ed.). New York: Holt, Rinehart and Winston.

Dunn, S. W., & Barban, A. M. (1986). *Advertising: Its role in modern marketing*. Chicago: Dryden Press.

Fishbein, M., & Ajzen, I. (1975). *Belief, attitude, intention, and behavior: An introduction to theory and research*. Reading, MA: Addison-Wesley.

Hovland, R., & Wolburg, J. (2010). *Advertising, society and consumer culture*. Armonk, NJ: M.E. Sharpe.

Kaufman, L. (1980). *Essentials of advertising*. New York: Harcourt Brace Jovanovich.

Krugman, H. E. (1972). Why three exposures may be enough. *Journal of Advertising Research*, 12 (6), 11–14.

Lamb, C. W., Hair, J. F., & McDaniel, C. (2000). *Marketing* (5th ed.). Cincinnati, OH: South-Western College Publishing.

Leckenby, J. D., & Li, H. (2000). From the editors: Why we need the Journal of Interactive Advertising. *Journal of Interactive Advertising, 1* (1), 1–3.

McGuire, W. J. (1969). An information-processing model of advertising effectiveness. In H. L. Davis & A. J. Silk (Eds.), *Behavioral and management science in marketing* (pp. 156–180). New York: Ronald Press.

Muehling, D. D., Laczniak, R. N., & Andrews, J. C. (1993). Defining operationalizing and using involvement in advertising research: A review. *Journal of Current Issues and Research in Advertising, 15* (1), 21–57.

Nan, X., & Faber, R. J. (2004). Advertising theory: Reconceptualizing the building blocks. *Marketing Theory, 4* (1/2), 7–30.

O'Guinn, T. C., Allen, C. T., & Semenik, R. J. (2000). *Advertising* (2nd ed.). Cincinnati, OH: South-Western College Publishing.

Paisley, W. (1972). *Communication research as a behavioral discipline*. Palo Alto, CA: Stanford University Institute for Communication Research.

Pasadeos, Y., Phelps, J., & Edison, A. (2008). Searching for our "own theory" in advertising: An update of research networks. *Journalism and Mass Communication Quarterly, 85* (4), 785–806.

Perreault, W. D., & McCarthy, E. J. (1999). *Basic marketing: A global-managerial approach* (13th ed.). New York: McGraw-Hill Publishing.

Preston, I. (1996). *The great American blow-up: Puffery in advertising and selling* (Rev. ed.). Madison: University of Wisconsin Press.

Richards, J. I., & Curran, C. M. (2002). Oracles on "advertising": Searching for a definition. *Journal of Advertising, 31* (2), 63–78.

Schultz, D. E., Robinson, W. A., & Petrison, L. A. (1998). *Sales promotion essentials: The 10 basic sales promotion techniques . . . and how to use them* (3rd ed.). Chicago: NTC Business Books.

Smith, R. D. (2002). *Strategic planning for public relations*. Mahwah, NJ: Lawrence Erlbaum Associates.

Vanden Bergh, B. G., & Katz, H. (1999). *Advertising principles: Choice, challenge, change.* Lincolnwood, IL: NTCI Contemporary Publishing Group.

Wells, W., Burnett, J., & Moriarty, S. (1998). *Advertising principles and practices* (4th ed.). Upper Saddle River, NJ: Prentice-Hall.

Wilcox, D. L., & Cameron, G. T. (2010). *Public relations: Strategies and tactics* (10th ed.). Boston: Allyn & Bacon.

Zikmund, W. G., & d'Amico, M. (1999). *Marketing* (6th ed.). Cincinnati, OH: South-Western College Publishing.

Chapter 2

Coloring Outside the Lines

Suggestions for Making Advertising Theory More Meaningful

Ronald J. Faber, Brittany R. L. Duff, and Xiaoli Nan

> The mere formulation of a problem is far more essential than its solution . . . To raise new questions, new possibilities, to regard old problems from a new angle requires creative imagination and marks real advances in science.
>
> (Albert Einstein (1879–1955))

Introduction

Theories are the building blocks of any discipline. Our theories direct our research and even our thinking about a topic. Yet, all too often, we don't give sufficient thought to where our theories should come from.

This volume has taken as its starting point an expanded version of McGuire's (1969, 1973) persuasion matrix (see Figure 1.1). However, it is important to remember that no one model can fully represent a field. Instead:

> Each model emphasizes certain points its creator feels are relevant in the communication process or structure. By selecting certain aspects of communication to be included in a model, the originator of a model implies judgments of relevance and a theory about the process or structure modeled.
>
> (Severin & Tankard, 1988, p. 41)

In this sense, we can view a model as the outline of a picture, and theory as the detail and nuance that color it in and give it life. As children, we were taught that we are supposed to color within the lines. However, sometimes the lines constrained our artistic senses and, indeed, better pictures emerged if we colored outside the lines (or so we believed). In this spirit, we address some potential limitations of McGuire's model for advertising theory and suggest that a more in-depth consideration of the uniqueness of advertising as a field can enhance this model and provide a richer and more varied picture of important theoretical areas for advertising.

McGuire's model combines Lasswell's (1948) model of communication process with steps in the persuasion process reflected in hierarchy of effects models (see Barry, 1987). The focus on communication and persuasion perfectly maps onto common definitions of advertising such as: "Advertising is paid, mass-mediated attempt to persuade" (O'Guinn, Allen, & Semenik, 2009, p. 9), and "Advertising is a paid, mediated form of communication from an identifiable source, designed to persuade the receiver to take some action, now or in the future" (Richards & Curran, 2002, p. 74). However, focusing exclusively on these aspects of advertising leaves several other potentially important elements of advertising either under-appreciated or ignored in theory building. The goal of this chapter is to illuminate some of these key concepts that deserve greater attention in the development of advertising theory.

Is Advertising Different from Communication?

By relying on Lasswell's components of the communication process, McGuire fails to distinguish advertising from other forms of communication. In a previous article, we have pointed out how recognizing the ways advertising differs from other forms of communication can help identify important areas for theory building in advertising (Nan & Faber, 2004).

Academic disciplines can be subdivided into two categories—level fields and variable fields (Paisley, 1972). Level fields are disciplines that develop around an interest in a specific level of analysis. Anthropology (societal or cultural level), sociology (group level), and psychology (individual level) are examples. Level fields tend to be the first divisions in science (Berelson, 1963).

Variable fields develop later when a significant number of researchers become interested in a specific phenomenon. Political science, archeology, linguistics, education, marketing, journalism, and advertising are examples of variable fields.

Because level fields develop earlier and center on specific levels of analysis, it is within these disciplines that both methodological techniques and basic theories generally develop (Paisley, 1972). The goal of these fields is to provide theoretical generalizations that are true across a wide variety of situations. This high level of generalizability or broad application makes these theories of great value in science (Reynolds, 1971).

Unlike level fields, theory building in variable fields is much narrower, stressing the particular variables thought to be most critical in the specific phenomenon being studied (Paisley, 1972). Rather than desiring theories with broad abstract generalizations, variable fields should be concerned with identifying the boundary conditions where a broader theory might no longer be true. To do this, a variable field needs to recognize what makes it unique and to identify the variables that it can contribute to testing and qualifying broad theories from level fields.

Nan and Faber (2004) suggested four such variables for advertising to consider in theory building. These were consumer skepticism, repetition, message coordination, and clutter.

Any persuasive message, by its very intent to persuade, may arouse psychological reactance (Brehm & Brehm, 1981), a motivation to reject the persuasion attempt through source and/or message derogation. Skepticism toward a persuasive message may be seen as a type of psychological reactance, leading to questioning the motives of and claims made by the persuaders (see Boush, Friestad, & Rose, 1994). Advertising messages are particularly likely to induce reactance and skepticism, not only because of their overt persuasive intent but also because the intent is often seen to be self-serving (i.e., achieving greater profits for the company). Consumer skepticism toward advertising has been well documented from the 1930s onward (Calfee & Ringold, 1994).

Skeptical consumers often dismiss the arguments made in an advertisement by ignoring them, generating counterarguments, and/or engaging in source derogation. This skeptical perspective is important to consider in developing advertising theory and when using advertising to test broader theories.

Additionally, while skepticism of advertising is somewhat universal, the degree to which people are skeptical is influenced by cultural values and the role and practice of advertising in different countries. U.S. consumers were found to be more skeptical of advertising than people in East Asian countries (La Ferle & Lee, 2003). In another study, Ukrainian consumers, who recently experienced a reintroduction to Western-style advertising after years of communism, were significantly more skeptical of advertising than either U.S. or Western European consumers (Lutchyn, Faber, Dell'Orto, & Duff, 2010). This was attributed both to exposure to advertising for questionable products (e.g., "get-rich-quick" schemes) and to disappointment from unfulfilled economic expectations.

Another important component for advertising theory suggested by Nan and Faber (2004) is repetition. Research has typically shown that repetition creates an inverted "U" shaped relationship with advertising and brand preference (for a review, see Nordhielm, 2002). Initially, repetition leads to increased preference (i.e., ad wear-in), but additional repetitions ultimately create more negative (wear-out) effects (Batra & Ray, 1986).

Repetition is also important in helping advertisers to develop associations between brands and specific attributes, benefits, or emotions in the minds of consumers. Coca-Cola, for example, has tried to associate their brand with warmth and happiness. They do this using traditional advertising, viral videos, non-traditional advertising, and even studies released to the media about the state of happiness today (see Figure 2.1). People will not just automatically associate two ideas the first time they appear together; it is only with repetition that two ideas will become associated. Associative Learning Theory might provide useful concepts to incorporate in advertising theories. Additionally, given the potential impact of repetition, it may be useful to reassess advertising theories developed on the basis of single message exposure to see how repetition might moderate these relationships.

Figure 2.1 An example of Coca-Cola associating itself with "happiness."

Advertising repetition is concerned with the presentation of the same ad message repeatedly. A related, but equally neglected, characteristic of advertising is message coordination. Message coordination is rooted in the idea of Integrated Marketing Communication (IMC) (Keller, 2001). In an IMC program, several different communication formats may be selected to achieve unified short-term and/or long-term goals.

The fact that consumers are exposed to coordinated brand messages through different communication options raises the question of how such experiences might affect brand beliefs, attitudes, and behaviors. Extant research expounds on the impact of exposure to coordinated messages on brand memory (Keller, 2001). While multiple exposures through different channels may facilitate brand learning, exposure to different brand information through various communication options may also lead to memory interference. With a few exceptions (Edell & Keller, 1989; Stammerjohan, Wood, Chang, & Thorson 2005), there has been limited research on the implications of message coordination for advertising effectiveness. However, such knowledge can be critical in testing theory and making it relevant to the actual practice of advertising.

The importance of repetition and message coordination in advertising highlights the major distinction between viewing advertising as a solitary, standalone stimulus versus seeing it as an ongoing campaign. The practice of advertising generally develops goals and assesses outcomes over a protracted time frame (generally from about 3 months to a year or longer). Academic research in advertising, however, often looks only at a single exposure to a single stimulus. To make advertising theory more relevant to advertising practice, we need to consider multiple exposures over an extended time period and from various sources. Advertising's focus on extended, coordinated campaigns rather than single messages can be one of its greatest contributions to the testing of basic social science theories.

A final feature that characterizes advertising to a much greater degree than other forms of communication is clutter. Clutter can come from the editorial content an advertisement is embedded in, advertisements from competing brands, or other advertisements in general. Clutter decreases viewer attention, memory, and recognition, as well as the number of thoughts generated while viewing the ad (Webb & Ray, 1979). Clutter may also induce negative affect (primarily irritation), which may lead to lower evaluations of the target ad.

Clutter is not a desirable characteristic, but some types of clutter are less detrimental than others. Kent (1993) distinguishes between noncompetitive clutter (i.e., ads from noncompeting brands being shown in close proximity) and competitive clutter (i.e., ads from competing brands being shown together). Compared to noncompetitive clutter, competitive clutter leads to more memory interference and less favorable brand evaluation (Keller, 1991). This is one reason why many advertisers require that their media placement contracts state that no competitive brands will be advertised within a given amount of space (pages) or time from when their ad is run. However, some of these same advertisers, in an effort to better reach their target audience, place their ads in a media context related to their product category (e.g., a food ad in a cooking magazine or food section of the newspaper; see Figure 2.2). More research on these potentially competing effects could tell us a lot about the relative strength of each.

While these four characteristics are important attributes of advertising and could contribute a great deal to theory development, our previous review found that they are rarely included in the advertising research published in the top U.S. advertising/marketing journals (Nan & Faber, 2004). Incorporating these, and other, key variables would help to enhance the development of advertising theory as well as improve its contributions to testing broader theories.

Advertising as Persuasion

Defining advertising as persuasive communication has led to an over-emphasis on attitude change theories. For instance, attitude change has been examined extensively and lists of the most frequently cited works are dominant in the advertising literature (Pasadeos, Phelps, & Kim, 1998; Pasadeos, Phelps,

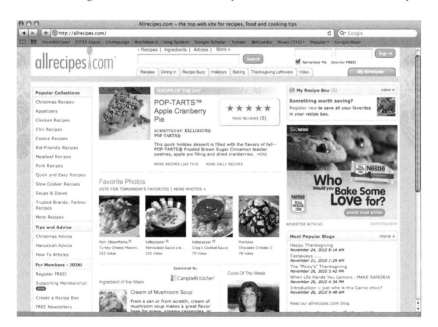

Figure 2.2 Common practice of placing ads with related editorial content.

& Edison, 2008). However, the advertising literature also points to critical limitations on the ability of advertising to change attitudes or behaviors. In a classic article, Ehrenberg (1974) claimed that advertising is generally a weak force and its role is primarily reinforcing rather than persuading. He makes an important distinction between stimulating primary versus selective demand. Primary demand refers to the total sales of all brands in a given product or service category (e.g., all car sales) while secondary or selective demand refers to the sales of a specific brand within that category (e.g., sales of Toyota cars). Except for the introduction of a new product category, very little advertising is directed at stimulating primary demand (Berkowitz, Kerin, Hartley, & Rudelius, 1992), and total advertising expenditures do little to affect total product category sales (Albion & Farris, 1981; Broadbent, 2008). A good example is the "Got Milk" campaign, which despite being incredibly popular, well remembered, extremely well liked, and the winner of numerous advertising awards, failed to reverse the declining consumption of milk (*Marketing News*, 1998; O'Guinn et al., 2009).

Instead, what Ehrenberg says advertising typically does is influence selective demand for a specific brand at the expense of competing brands. Most consumers have a couple of different brands that they will purchase over the course of an extended period of time (Ehrenberg, 1974; Jones, 1995). Research using panel data has found that the greatest impact on brand selection comes from seeing an ad for that brand relatively near to the actual time of purchase (Ephron, 1997; Jones, 1995). This isn't to say that advertising doesn't build awareness, knowledge, and interest in a brand (it certainly can and does), but rather the more common and important purpose of advertising is to serve as a short-term reminder to help reinforce brand loyalty and influence purchase behavior. To the degree this is true, it would seem that we should place a greater focus on theories of reinforcement and habit in developing advertising theory and less on attitude change.

Theories regarding habit may be particularly useful in explaining consumer behaviors since many frequent purchases occur relatively automatically (Dijksterhuis, Smith, van Baaren, & Wigboldus, 2005). Think about buying a loaf of bread when you are at the grocery store. Most likely, you can walk directly to the bread aisle and reach out and grab the brand you usually purchase. You don't need to consciously think about this purchase unless your usual brand is sold out or has been moved. Thus, habits allow us to act relatively automatically while freeing up time to let us think about other things. Recent research has suggested that habits are triggered by environmental cues and that advertising may be able to help build the association between a brand and relevant environmental cues (Lutchyn, 2010).

Other outcome variables have also tended to be under-examined in advertising research and theory. These include items such as attention, comprehension (and miscomprehension), and delayed retention. To his credit, McGuire includes all of these elements as steps along the way to attitude change. Furthermore, he indicates that each step can be influenced by communication variables in different ways. The problem in using this as a guide to developing advertising theory, however, is that we only consider these variables as steps toward achieving attitude change and ignore outcomes that don't further this goal.

For example, most advertising studies take place in laboratory settings where people are asked to attend to ads or media content while other activities are artificially limited. This allows experiments to control extraneous influences and focus just on the variables of interest. Although this can be beneficial in research, it does not allow for an understanding of what happens when these prior steps are not achieved. While research occasionally examines factors that enhance attention and comprehension, almost no consideration is given to the impact of ads that are unattended or miscomprehended. This is true despite the fact that lack of attention is likely to be the norm rather than the exception with advertising (see Figure 2.3).

Think back over the past 24 hours and try to remember all of the ads you encountered. Now think about how often you remember an ad, but aren't sure what brand it was for. These simple exercises should make us realize how often inattention and poor comprehension occur in advertising. It would seem that theory building in advertising needs to give greater consideration to what occurs when ads are not fully processed or consciously recalled.

We exist in a complex environment and our senses are constantly bombarded with sights, sounds, smells, and physical sensations, all competing for our highly limited attentional resources. As a result, consumers must

Figure 2.3 Attention to advertising is limited.

continually screen their environments, actively attending to some stimuli while ignoring many others.

The first goal of advertising is to gain attention. This often involves using attention-getting devices (e.g., animation, celebrity endorsers) or obtrusive methods (e.g., pop-up ads). However, consumers have different goals that often include actively avoiding ads. Thus, most often, we are either passively exposed to ads while browsing or multitasking, or actively trying to ignore them. Advertising research and theory need to pay much greater attention to what happens when ads in our environment are actively avoided.

One potentially important outcome variable that might be affected is memory accessibility. Memory accessibility refers to the ease and speed at which one thinks of a specific response when prompted by a cue. For example, what brands come to mind when you think of "brands of ice cream?" The first brands you think of are said to have high top-of-mind (T-O-M) awareness, which is a way to measure how well brands rank in the minds of consumers. Companies that build brand awareness tend to also rank highly in "Top of Mind Awareness" (O'Guinn et al., 2009).

In some purchasing situations, high T-O-M awareness is essential. For example, if you want to go out for ice cream, you are likely to only select from among those stores that immediately come to mind (e.g., Dairy Queen, Ben and Jerry's, Baskin Robbins). This is different from going to buy ice cream at the supermarket where you can look at all of the brands on display and not have to recall a brand from memory. However, even in the grocery store, high T-O-M awareness can be important because brand names we can recall easily are perceived to be more popular and desirable (O'Guinn et al., 2009).

The primary way advertising enhances T-O-M awareness is through repetition. One relatively unknown insurance company quickly achieved high T-O-M awareness by using a trade character (duck) that keeps repeating its name throughout the commercial (Aflac). Jingles, slogans, and alliterative sounds are also successful methods for increasing brand awareness. Greater understanding of memory and linguistics may help advertising theorists to postulate other successful strategies for enhancing awareness.

Implicit versus Explicit Memory

There are two types of memory—explicit and implicit. Most advertising theory has been concerned with just explicit memory. Explicit memory involves retrieval of previously encoded information through conscious recollection. Implicit memory, on the other hand, is a memory that is not consciously retrieved, but may still exert effects on thinking and behavior. Recall and recognition, the most common memory measures in advertising research, both assess explicit memory. Implicit memory, on the other hand, is typically measured by how accessible information is when people are given an ambiguous stimulus. For example, one common implicit memory task asks people to complete a word fragment by filling in the missing letters (Tulving, Schacter, & Stark, 1982). Several different words could complete the task and the one the participant selects is considered the one that is most accessible from memory.

Research has shown that implicit memory is affected by the advertising or brands people have either frequently or recently encountered, even though they may have no conscious memory of this exposure (Shapiro & Krishnan, 2001; Yang, Roskos-Ewoldsen, Dinu, & Arpan, 2006).

Other research has shown that well-developed associations between brands and brand meanings can be activated by brand exposure even when it occurs without conscious awareness. In one study, participants were exposed to either the Apple or IBM logo at a speed that was so rapid they could not consciously tell that these logos had appeared on the screen. Afterwards, people completed a creativity test and it was found that those who had been exposed to the Apple logo performed better than those exposed to the IBM logo (Fitzsimons, Chartrand, & Fitzsimons, 2008). Importantly, this only worked for those who already had the association of Apple being a creative brand. Additional studies showed that this effect can also be achieved with overt conscious exposure to brands but the implicit effect is particularly important since it implies that ads do not need to be recalled, recognized, or consciously processed to have an impact.

Research in consumer behavior has indicated that implicit memory for advertisements can enhance attitude toward the ad (Yoo, 2009), and implicit memory of a brand name increases the likelihood that the product will be included in a consideration set (Shapiro, 1999). In one amazing demonstration of the impact of implicit memory due to incidental exposure (www.youtube.com/watch?v=f29kF1vZ62o), Derren Brown shows that an advertising campaign developed by a professional copywriter and art director can be greatly affected by what they happen to pass on their way to the office (making these images more accessible in memory).

Hence, it may be important to learn what ad situations and elements affect implicit memory. In some cases, brief partial exposure may be sufficient to affect implicit memory, but in others it may not. Take a look at the image in Figure 2.4. Despite the fact that most of the object cannot be seen most people recognize the brand very quickly.

This is because Coke uses a distinctive logo, color, and packaging. Seeing even a tiny part of this image is enough to make the brand highly accessible in memory. Yet, for a less recognizable or distinctive brand this may not be the case. More extensive theory and research may help to determine what

Figure 2.4 Recognize this brand? Brand recognition can occur with only minimal exposure.

advertising elements influence various types of memory and how each form of memory affects brand behavior. Research on issues like these would help to build a more complete theory of advertising.

Not all brief or incidental exposure to advertising is good for a brand. When people are given the task of finding specific information from articles on a news website, they actively avoid ads on that page and are unable to recall or recognize these ads (Duff, 2009; Duff & Faber, 2011). However, unlike many implicit memory studies, the impact here of avoiding ads is detrimental to the brand. Despite having no recognition of having been exposed to the ads, when later asked to rate a number of different brands, people in these studies have more negative attitudes toward the previously ignored brands than those who were not exposed to the ads. Additionally, in subsequent exposures, they take longer to notice the previously exposed brands than people who hadn't avoided the ads. The difference here is the audience member's motivational goal during exposure (Duff, 2009). When we are actively trying to avoid seeing ads to better achieve a desired task, we associate a negative affective tag to the ad and this leads to negative effects for the brand. This phenomenon is known as "distracter devaluation." These findings help to inform theory and also have practical implications for ad placement cost models such as CPM in which each potential exposure is counted regardless of what the consumer is doing during that exposure.

Conclusion

Most current advertising theories tend to focus on the impact of source and message variables in promoting attitude change. Certainly, there is a place for developing such theories. However, as we have tried to point out, this over-emphasis ignores many of the most common and important roles of advertising. Greater focus on theories examining advertising awareness, brand associations, memory accessibility, and reinforcement would help us to more adequately address the outcomes of advertising exposure. Additionally, there is often a long delay between ad exposure and the time of actual brand choice (cf. Baker & Lutz, 2000; Keller, 1993). Therefore, advertising theories need to incorporate factors affecting information retrieval along with those influencing the encoding and processing of information. This should help to determine the most relevant literature to consider in forming advertising theories.

Future theory development should also pay particular attention to the attributes that make advertising unique, and the factors that impact how people actually use and process advertising. In doing so, we can enhance our relevance to other social science disciplines while also addressing key aspects of the phenomenon we study. We have tried to point out some of these elements, but others may be able to identify important aspects we have left out. As the practice of advertising changes, some of the important dimensions that characterize it are likely to change as well. User-generated content, social media, and narrower targeting may make it worthwhile for us to look more toward interpersonal communication theories for ideas. These new forms of advertising along with methodological changes such as multilevel models (hierarchical linear analysis) may lead to greater exploration of the inter-relationship between media advertising and the interpersonal spread of information. Advances in neuroscience are likely to incorporate brain physiology and concepts of emotional response and control into theories of consumer behavior and preference (cf. Ohme, Reykowska, Wiener, & Choromanska, 2009; Koenigs & Tranel, 2008). These are exciting times for the development of advertising theory, which provide rich opportunities for the creative integration of a wide range of different disciplines into the study of advertising.

References

Albion, M., & Farris, P. (1981). *The advertising controversy: Evidence on the economic effects of advertising*. Boston: Auburn House.

Baker, W., & Lutz, R. (2000). An empirical test of the updated relevance accessibility model of advertising effectiveness. *Journal of Advertising, 29*, 1–14.

Barry, T. (1987). The development of the hierarchy of effects: An historical perspective. *Current Issues and Research in Advertising, 10*, 251–296.

Batra, R., & Ray, M. L. (1986). Situational effects of advertising repetition: The moderating influence of motivation, ability, and opportunity to respond. *Journal of Consumer Research, 12*, 432–445.

Berelson, B. (1963). *The behavioral sciences today*. New York: Basic Books.

Berkowitz, E. N., Kerin, R. A., Hartley, S. W., & Rudelius, W. (1992). *Marketing*. Homewood, IL: Irwin.

Boush, D. M., Friestad, M., & Rose, G. M. (1994). Adolescent skepticism toward TV advertising and knowledge of advertiser tactics. *Journal of Consumer Research, 21*, 165–175.

Brehm, S. S., & Brehm, J. W. (1981). *Psychological reactance: A theory of freedom and control*. New York: Academic Press.

Broadbent, T. (2008). Does advertising grow markets? More evidence from the United Kingdom. *International Journal of Advertising, 27*, 745–770.

Calfee, J. E., & Ringold, D. (1994). The 70% majority: Enduring consumer beliefs about advertising. *Journal of Public Policy and Marketing, 13*, 228–236.

Dijksterhuis, A., Smith, P. K., van Baaren, R. B., & Wigboldus, D. H. J. (2005). The unconscious consumer: Effects of environment on consumer behavior. *Journal of Consumer Psychology, 15*, 193–202.

Duff, B. R. L. (2009). The eye of the beholder: Affective and attentional outcomes of selective attention to advertising. Unpublished dissertation manuscript, University of Minnesota.

Duff, B. R. L., & Faber, R. J. (2011). Ignored ads = liked brands? Advertising avoidance and the affective devaluation of brands. *Journal of Advertising, 40* (2), 51–62.

Edell, J. A., & Keller, K. L. (1989). The information processing coordinated media campaign. *Journal of Marketing Research, 26*, 149–163.

Ehrenberg, A. S. C. (1974). Repetitive advertising and the consumer. *Journal of Advertising Research, 14*, 25–34.

Ephron, E. (1997). Recency planning. *Journal of Advertising Research, 37*, 61–65.

Fitzsimons, G. M., Chartrand, T. L., & Fitzsimons, G. J. (2008). Automatic effects of brand exposure on motivated behavior: How Apple makes you "think different." *Journal of Consumer Research, 35*, 21–35.

Jones, J. P. (1995). *When ads work: New proof that advertising triggers sales*. New York: Lexington Books, 1995.

Keller, K. L. (1991). Memory and evaluation effects in competitive advertising environment. *Journal of Consumer Research, 17*, 463–476.

Keller, K. L. (1993). Memory retrieval and advertising effectiveness. In A.A. Mitchell (Ed.), *Advertising exposure, memory and choice* (pp. 11–48). Hillsdale, NJ: Psychology Press.

Keller, K. L. (2001). Mastering the marketing communications mix: Micro and macro perspectives on integrated marketing communication programs. *Journal of Marketing Management, 17*, 819–847.

Kent, R. J. (1993). Competitive versus noncompetitive clutter in television advertising. *Journal of Advertising Research, 33*, 40–46.

Koenigs, M., & Tranel, D. (2008). Prefrontal cortex damage abolishes brand-cued changes in cola preference. *Social Cognitive and Affective Neuroscience, 3*, 1–6.

La Ferle, C., & Lee, W. (2003). Attitudes toward advertising: A comparative study of consumers in China, Taiwan, South Korea and the United States. *Journal of International Consumer Marketing, 15*, 5–23.

Lasswell, H. D. (1948). The structure and function of communication in society. Reprinted in W. Schramm & D. Roberts (Eds.), *The process and effects of mass communication* (1974, pp. 84–99). Urbana: University of Illinois Press.

Lutchyn, Y. A. (2010). A new look at associative learning in advertising: Testing an ability of ad messages to change brand-context associations. Unpublished doctoral dissertation, University of Minnesota, Minneapolis, MN.

Lutchyn, Y. A., Faber, R. J., Dell'Orto, G., & Duff, B. R. L. (2010, June). Consumer skepticism and attitudes toward advertising: Cross-cultural analysis. Paper presented at the American Academy of Advertising European Conference, Milan, Italy.

Marketing News (1998). Got results? March 2, *1*.

McGuire, W. (1973). Persuasion, resistance, and attitude change. In I. de Sola Pool & W. Schramm (Eds.), *Handbook of communication* (pp. 216–252). Chicago: Rand McNally.

McGuire, W. J. (1969). The nature of attitudes and attitude change. In G. Lindzey and E. Aronson (Eds.), *The handbook of social psychology* (Vol. 3, pp. 136–314). Reading, MA: Addison-Wesley.

Nan, X., & Faber, R. J. (2004). Advertising theory: Reconceptualizing the building blocks. *Marketing Theory, 4*, 7–30.

Nordhielm, C. L. (2002). The influence of level of processing on advertising repetition effects. *Journal of Consumer Research, 29*, 371–382.

O'Guinn, T. C., Allen, C. T., & Semenik, R. J. (2009). *Advertising* (5th ed.). Cincinnati, OH: South Western.

Ohme, R., Reykowska, D., Wiener, D., & Choromanska, A. (2009). Analysis of neurophysiological reactions to advertising stimuli by means of EEG and galvanic skin response measures. *Journal of Neuroscience, Psychology, and Economics, 2*, 21–31.

Paisley, W. (1972). *Communication research as a behavioral discipline*. Palo Alto, CA: Stanford University Institute for Communication Research.

Pasadeos, Y., Phelps, J. & Edison, A. (2008). Searching for our "own theory" in advertising: An update of research networks. *Journalism and Mass Communication Quarterly, 85*, 785–806.

Pasadeos, Y., Phelps, J., & Kim, B. H. (1998). Disciplinary impact of advertising scholars: Temporal comparisons of influential authors, works and research networks. *Journal of Advertising, 27*, 53–70.

Reynolds, P. D. (1971). *A primer in theory construction*. Indianapolis: Bobbs-Merrill.

Richards, J. I., & Curran, C. M. (2002). Oracles on "advertising": Searching for a definition. *Journal of Advertising, 31*, 63–78.

Severin, W. J., & Tankard, J., Jr., (1988). *Communication theories: Origins, methods, uses* (2nd ed.). New York: Longman.

Shapiro, S. (1999). When an ad's influence is beyond our conscious control: Perceptual and conceptual fluency effects caused by incidental ad exposure. *Journal of Consumer Research, 26*, 16–36.

Shapiro, S., & Krishnan, H. S. (2001). Memory based measures for assessing advertising effects: A comparison of explicit and implicit memory effects. *Journal of Advertising, 30*, 1–13.

Stammerjohan, C. A., Wood, C. M., Chang, Y., & Thorson, E. (2005). An empirical investigation of the interaction between publicity, advertising, and previous brand attitudes and knowledge. *Journal of Advertising, 34*, 55–67.

Tulving, E., Schacter, D. L., & Stark, H. A. (1982). Priming effects in word-fragment completion are independent of recognition memory. *Journal of Experimental Psychology: Learning, Memory, and Cognition, 8*, 336–342.

Webb, P. H., & Ray, M. L. (1979). Effects of TV clutter. *Journal of Advertising Research, 19*, 7–12.

Yang, M., Roskos-Ewoldsen, D. R., Dinu, L., & Arpan, L. M. (2006). The effectiveness of "in-game" advertising: Comparing college students' explicit and implicit memory for brand names. *Journal of Advertising, 35*, 143–152.

Yoo, C. Y. (2009). Implicit memory measures for web advertising effectiveness. Paper presented at the annual meeting of the International Communication Association, Dresden International Congress Centre, Dresden, Germany.

Additional Readings

Duff, B. R. L., & Faber, R. J. (2011). Ignored ads = liked brands? Advertising avoidance and the affective devaluation of brands. *Journal of Advertising, 40* (2), 51–62.

Ehrenberg, A. S. C. (1974). Repetitive advertising and the consumer. *Journal of Advertising Research, 14*, 25–34.

Fitzsimons, G. M., Chartrand, T. L., & Fitzsimons, G. J. (2008). Automatic effects of brand exposure on motivated behavior: How Apple makes you "think different." *Journal of Consumer Research, 35*, 21–35.

Friestad, M., & Wright, P. (1994). The persuasion knowledge model: How people cope with persuasion attempts. *Journal of Consumer Research, 21*, 1–31.

Nan, X., & Faber, R. J. (2004). Advertising theory: Reconceptualizing the building blocks. *Marketing Theory, 4*, 7–30.

Chapter 3

Agency Practitioners' Theories about Advertising

Gergely Nyilasy and Leonard N. Reid

The relationship between academia and practice is a perennial topic in the academic advertising and marketing literatures. The common notion is that there is a wide gap between the domains of academia and practice, even though their subject matter is the same: advertising and marketing phenomena (Nyilasy & Reid, 2007). In this chapter, we discuss the relationship between theory and practice in advertising, focusing specifically on advertising practitioners' theories of advertising and offer an empirically based explanation for the academician–practitioner gap in advertising: practitioners' knowledge autonomy. We locate our discussion in the broader meta-theoretical context of theory and practice and the literature of professionalization.

In the framework of McGuire's (1969) amended persuasion/communication matrix (see Figure 1.1), our discussion lies closest to the territory of "Advertising Organizations"; however, as it has to do with academic and practitioner ideas about how advertising works, studying practitioner thinking has implications for all areas of the model in Figure 1.1.

While we will argue that the gap is wider in the field of advertising than in other, more professionalized occupations (such as medicine, law, religion), it is important to acknowledge at the outset that the gap between theory and practice is a general phenomenon and not specific to advertising. We begin by considering the broader general phenomenon before proceeding to the discussion of advertising.

Theory and Practice

Activities, social milieu, problems faced and solved are all radically different in the worlds of academia and business (Weick, 2003). Practitioners have to solve problems and act, while academicians reflect on reality and try to explain it. Weick (2003) references the work of Roethlisberger (1977), who described these two very distinct worlds of activity as "A relations" (practice) and "B relations" (theoretical explanation). "A relations," which are more primary than "B relations" in the sense that they are closer to everyday lived experience, are characterized by concreteness, subjectivity, here-and-now, mutual dependence, cyclicality, emergence, diffusion, and existentiality, while "B relations" are characterized by abstractness, objectivity, there-and-then, simple cause-and-effect, linearity, planning/design, specificity, and probability—among other things. For instance, an advertising manager has to make immediate and often subjective decisions based on imperfect information and heuristics (best guesses) about concrete factors in campaign planning. Advertising campaigns have many interdependent "moving parts" and despite planning processes in place, often emerge looking like anything but the original intentions. The academic study of advertising on the other hand aims at establishing abstract and objective cause-and-effect relationships, based on well-specified circumstances controlled by strict methodological ideas.

It is important to understand the *relationship* between the two worlds of theory and practice, not merely their inherently distinct characteristics in isolation. Weick (2003), using the management literature, categorized the metatheoretical explanations of these relationships into eight groups. Relationships between academic and practice can be understood as:

1. *Correspondent* (Lewin, 1943)—"there is nothing so practical as a good theory," the idea that theoretical knowledge can be unproblematically applied to practice.
2. *Complementary* (Roethlisberger, 1977)—while the two domains are fundamentally different bundles of activities and cognitions (as captured in the concepts of "A" and "B" relations), thorough understanding of reality and organizations requires both.
3. *Incommensurable* (Sandelands, 1990)—theory and practice are incompatible and theory cannot be translated into practice; there is nothing in explanation and theory that we do not already "understand."
4. *Coordinate* (Dutton & Starbuck, 1963)—practitioners' theories are implicit and specific to the case, while academic theories are explicit and general.
5. *Parallel* (Thomas & Tymon, 1982)—it is possible to bridge the gap between academia and practice; academia can be aligned with practitioner needs if certain criteria are met in academic research (summed up in the concept of "problem-oriented research" by Hunt (2002)).
6. *Reciprocal* (Craig, 1996)—the application of theory to practice is not linear, but cyclical and reciprocal; mutual adjustment, iterative improvement can lead to alignment.
7. *Conceptually equivalent* (Argyris, 2000)—under closer scrutiny, similar concepts are used in practice and theory, both practitioners and academicians work by paradigms.

8.   *Methodologically equivalent* (Kilduff & Mehra, 1997)—from a postmodern standpoint, academia *is* practice; inquiries in academia and practice are indistinguishable from a methodological, meta-theoretical standpoint.

What each of the positions in the above typology fails to acknowledge is, irrespective of the meta-theoretical relation between theory and practice, that there is a *sociological* force at play in most occupations where theory and practice may collide, a force that cannot be ignored. This force, explained in an influential theory of the sociology of occupations, is the theory of "professionalization." According to this theory, there are special occupations in society, ones that have much higher prestige than others. Those that do not yet have this prestige aspire to it and attempt a professionalization process (Wilensky, 1964). What differentiates professions from their humbler counterparts is, fundamentally, their claim of possessing a unique and complex "theoretical knowledge base" that informs and legitimates their operations (Abbott, 1988; MacDonald, 1995). The existence of this knowledge base and an occupation's deployment of it, place the occupation on a higher sociological "shelf"; and generate higher prestige for it than more mundane occupations could otherwise achieve. The reason: professionalizing occupations respond to their customers' need for certainty about the quality of services by referencing something traditionally unquestionable in legitimacy: scientific knowledge. An occupation that can legitimate itself by referencing a theoretical knowledge base has the "upper hand" and has the key to elevate its status in society (medicine, law, religion are "classic" professions that have achieved such status).

The implication of professionalization for the theory–practice relations debates described above is that the practitioners of any occupation are incentivized to develop and deploy theoretical knowledge bases, even if they find these different from practice. In a normally functioning, professionalizing occupation one would expect emphasis on theoretical explanation and relations between theory and practice. Using Weick's (2003) typology, both practitioners and academicians ought to be *correspondent*, *complementary*, *parallel*, *reciprocal*, or *conceptually equivalent*. This should be the case even if practitioners acknowledge the uniqueness of everyday practice; according to the predictions of professionalization, which is a universal force across all occupations, the normal response from an occupation is the resounding acknowledgment of the dominance of theoretical explanation. If an occupation, however, fundamentally questions or even denies the importance of a theoretical knowledge base, we know we are facing an *anomaly* that requires further explanation.

Theory and Practice in Advertising

Advertising, according to the vast majority of commentators, is such an anomaly. We have reviewed scholarly journal articles on the topic (Nyilasy & Reid, 2007) and found that the gap indeed is wide between advertising academia and practice. Practitioners do not acknowledge the importance and usefulness of the theoretical knowledge base; and the producers of the theoretical knowledge base, academicians, often find their own work irrelevant for practice. We have grouped what the academic literature offered as explanation for the gap between the two worlds into five categories.

1. *Problems with knowledge dissemination*: academia has failed to produce appropriate knowledge distribution systems to communicate theoretical knowledge to practitioners. This is true even if one acknowledges indirect paths (such as associations, consultancies, higher education, contact with journalists)—most of the output of advertising academia fails to percolate through these dissemination channels.
2. *Problems with knowledge content and form*: academia may not produce theoretical content that would ever be useful through application and even if it does, the form of the knowledge (and not just the distribution *channels*) is inadequate for practitioners.
3. *Academic organizational structures*: current organizational characteristics of universities (such as tenure and promotion incentives) are not aligned with what would promote a practical focus in research inquiries.
4. *Philosophy of science*: according to some commentators, advertising academia should not even be useful for practice. Subscription to this idea naturally results in lowered practical usefulness in theory and research.
5. *Practitioner characteristics*: finally, the literature points to the possibility of practitioners' unwillingness and inability to process the otherwise useful theoretical knowledge base.

In our view, these explanations specific to advertising (together with the more general theory/practice differences outlined in the first section) are all valid to a degree. We felt, however, that something else was missing. What if advertising practitioners, who are constantly exposed to professionalization pressures from their clients (who want certainty about the advertising services they receive), do have theory-like cognitive constructs (if for no other reason than to reassure their clients)? What if practitioners possess individual or interpersonally solidified mental models about the content of their work? And what if these mental models are *distinct* from the theoretical knowledge academia produces—in their content, form, and use? What if, in the case of advertising at least, we need to complement our implicit model of "knowledge dissemination" (AMA

Task Force, 1988) and acknowledge that the glass that we are trying to fill is not empty in the first place: practitioners may be reluctant to accept academic theoretical knowledge because these are "crowded out" by *their own ideas*.

We called our set of hypotheses the "Practitioner Knowledge Autonomy" model.

Practitioner ideas may differ significantly from academic ones in their *content*: practitioners may think differently about how advertising works. Practitioner theories may also differ in the *presuppositions* about knowledge and the forms it takes. It is reasonable to assume that practitioner theories are less precise, may not always be empirically testable, and may contain ideas that fall outside what social science would consider its subject matter (some may be entirely "metaphysical" or closer to humanistic theories). Finally, practitioner theories may differ from academic ones in their *social context*—they may have a much stronger and more immediate "social life" than academic theory.

The idea of practitioner knowledge autonomy is not entirely new. Viewed from Weick's (2003) typology, it falls closest to the "complementary" (Roethlisberger, 1977) and the "reciprocal" (Craig, 1996) schools and has similarities to Schon's (1983) conceptualization of the "reflective practitioner." In marketing, similar ideas were expressed by Zaltman and his colleagues, who suggested that "theories-in-use" can be back-engineered into academic theory (Zaltman, LeMasters, & Heffring, 1982). Kover (1995) has researched copywriters' implicit theories of advertising and the Contemporary Marketing Practices group has conducted empirical investigations into marketing practice (Coviello, Brodie, Danaher, & Johnston, 2002).

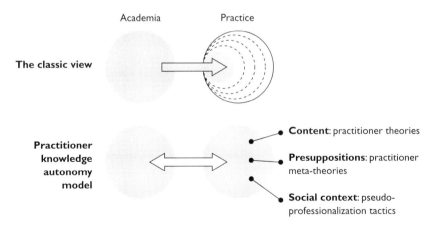

Figure 3.1 Practitioner Knowledge Autonomy Model.

Content: Practitioner Theories of Advertising

We tested our Practitioner Knowledge Autonomy model on advertising agency executives. The research involved in-depth interviews with senior practitioners in the functional roles of account management, account planning, and creative. A detailed description of the grounded theory approach used for fieldwork and data analysis is available in Nyilasy and Reid (2009b).

One of our most important findings was that practitioners indeed possess a sophisticated and complex set of native theories about how advertising works. They expressed ideas on a number of layers:

- basic building blocks of advertising effect;
- theoretical sets of statements among them ("proper" practitioner theories);
- creativity as a special theoretical area;
- boundary conditions their claims live within.

According to interviewed practitioners, the basic building blocks of advertising effects are attention, brand awareness, rational and emotional attitudes, and behavioral response. These categories are all familiar in academic advertising research as common dependent variables influenced by advertising stimulus. In this regard, there does not seem to be a great difference between academic and practitioner thinking. The difference lies in areas of emphasis. Agency practitioners invariably emphasized the importance of emotional attitude-formation effects. "Touching an emotional cord" was a predominant directive even in situations where a rational product benefit is used in the communications program (Nyilasy & Reid, 2009b).

On the second level, in more complex sets of interrelated statements (theories proper), there was also an interesting divergence between agency practitioners' theories and academic thinking. Agency practitioners reported on two core native theoretical ideas: "break through and engage" and "the mutation of effects." According to the "break through and engage" theory, advertising effects have two simple steps: getting consumer attention (the level of attention, however, does not have to be especially high) and engaging them (forming or changing, preferably emotionally based attitudes). This theory is in sharp contrast with the Hierarchy-of-Effects model, which is the most dominant theory in advertising academia (Vakratsas & Ambler, 1999). "Break through and engage" does not presuppose linearity beyond these two simple steps; neither does it presuppose that rationally based attitudes must necessarily form before positive behavioral outcomes can occur. The practitioner model suggests that advertising effects can happen in any order, based on different boundary conditions and individual cases. In this sense, the model is closest to "hierarchy-free theories" of advertising (Vakratsas & Ambler, 1999), a group of theories that is on the periphery of academic thinking.

The other core theory practitioners described is "the mutation of effects." According to this theory, one needs to take into consideration the historical context of advertising, within or outside the given product category and brand. Advertising approaches and tactics lose their effectiveness as consumer attitudes "mutate" over time and resistance develops. Advertisers therefore face not only the task of achieving point-in-time effects, by cutting through ad clutter and competitive noise, but also a broader, historically based "noise" that exists in consumers' minds. Consumers' resistance to particular approaches to persuasive argumentation forms a cognitive repository of schemas over time, schemas that intervene between any new attempts at persuasion and desired outcomes. The analogy that practitioners use is that of virology; as effective antibiotics/anti-viral drugs are developed, precisely because of their widespread use and the rules of evolutionary biology, resistance develops in the organizations targeted. The implication is that advertisers (just as virologists) constantly need to work on new approaches to finding effective "treatments." This is the reason why advertising has to be creative: to overcome the mutation of effects.

This native practitioner idea has similarities with the Persuasion Knowledge Model (Friestad & Wright, 1994), which explains resistance to marketer persuasion attempts. Practitioner thinking is different in that it focuses on the longitudinal aspect of resistance and its implications on why creativity is a necessary tool for advertising. The emphasis on historical, long-term changes in consumer cognitions make this practitioner theory incongruent with the center of the time-independent, psychology-based field of academic advertising theory.

"Mutation of effects" explains why creativity is a central concept of advertising practice. Practitioners do not only have theories about how advertising works, but also "what works best"; in other words, what characteristics of the advertising message (in academic language, what moderators or mediators) would make the communication more effective? Practitioners' answer is that *creativity* works best.

Practitioners understand creativity in two basic ways: as *artfulness* and as *innovativeness* (Nyilasy & Kreshel, forthcoming). Artfulness is a mental model that collects cognitive representations of the craft of producing creative advertising (typography, design, copywriting skill, observation of styles, trends, etc.). Innovativeness, on the other hand, is the ability to come up with "big ideas," revolutionary "creative concepts"—modes of persuasion in the context of a given campaign that are radically different from expected modes of communication.

In either sense, creativity is against the cliché, the formulaic, the uniform, which are believed to produce suboptimal effects, because of reasons discussed under the "mutation of effects" theory. Practitioners' idea that creativity is the most important cause of advertising effects also results in the prohibition of any other moderators: "The only rule in advertising is that there are no rules" (Nyilasy & Reid, 2009b). In other words, agency practitioners resist any empirical generalizations that would undermine creativity. By doing so they are in disagreement with a large portion of academic advertising research, which tries to generalize about "who says what to whom with what effect" (Hovland, Lumsdaine, & Sheffield, 1949). For example, agency practitioners do not accept research-based rules about which types of headlines to use in print ads. The only generalizations accepted about "what works best" are ideas that are in agreement with the creativity principle (for example, the suggestions that entertaining, simple, consistent, and "relevant" campaigns work better than their opposites).

Finally, agency practitioners' thinking is firmly situated within boundary conditions (circumstances under which a generalized statement would apply). To practitioners, advertising is situational and different situations may make basic theories work in different ways—in short, when it comes to regularities of advertising effectiveness, "it all depends." Conditions that would change basic theories are infinite in number. Practitioners enumerated four conditions that have the most influence on basic theoretical ideas: strategic campaign objective, product category, medium used, and history. Different campaign objectives, product categories, media, and place in advertising history make different effects more prominent. For instance, agency practitioners resist copy-testing systems that are not sensitive to specific campaign objectives (no single success metric is accepted). For a detailed summary of these contingencies, see Nyilasy and Reid (2009b).

Presuppositions: Practitioner Meta-Theories of Advertising

Agency practitioners do not only have substantive theories about how advertising works and what works best in influencing consumers. They also have meta-theories: presuppositions about the fundamental nature and possibility of knowing about these phenomena (Nyilasy & Reid, 2009a).

Overall, agency practitioners are best described as healthy skeptics. The importance of creativity has a strong influence on their meta-theoretical views. Because of the "only rule: no rules" theorem, agency practitioners are skeptical whether (a) advertising, as a creative discipline by its nature, lends itself to scientific modeling, and (b) whether methods of observation are adequate and sophisticated enough to support any solid knowledge about it. In other words, practitioners' meta-theories can be characterized by (a) ontological and (b) epistemological skepticism.

Agency practitioners' *ontological skepticism* (whether the nature of advertising itself makes it adequate for scientific theorizing and empirical research) is expressed on four levels. First, and most importantly, advertising is thought of as a discipline that is driven by innovativeness, and, as such, is unmodellable. In particular, the indeterminacy of the creative core of advertising undermines generalized directives for message content (as we saw earlier). For instance, agency practitioners would reject the idea on principle that a brand has to be mentioned a certain number of times in a TV commercial. Second, practitioners are placing the ontological status of advertising in the context of the art vs. science dichotomy, relegating it closer to art than science. In their view, advertising as an artful activity falls outside the jurisdiction of scientific legitimation. Third, agency practitioners point to their everyday work experience and emphasize that the most important determinant of advertising success is tacit skill (Polanyi, 1958), the expert performance of creating ads, a complex and personal process that eludes generalizations. Advertising from the inside is more similar to playing sports or music than to the application of generalized principles to particular cases. Fourth, while practitioners acknowledge that advertising is a composite of different ontological layers, with some layers more knowable than others (such as strategy and market research), they point to the fact that the most important layer is creativity, and we should not be deceived into thinking that just because one layer is modellable, the whole also is. Creativity's "no rules" dictate represents the essence of advertising's ontological status.

Agency practitioners also add that knowledge about advertising should be understood in *epistemological* confines. Practitioners think ability to understand the effects of advertising is limited. This epistemological skepticism is different from ontological skepticism in that it has to do with *ways of knowing* (how we can be sure what we know about advertising is true) and not the *thing-in-itself* (what the nature of advertising is). First, ad agency professionals think theories about advertising effects are severely humbled by the fact that what is most important to understand, how advertising influences purchase behavior, is hard, if not impossible, to model adequately. Second, any basic theories that professionals recognize, including their own, are perceived as "common sense." Practitioners do have basic theories of advertising, as we showed above, but they do not think these go beyond what a layman could understand after a short explanation. In contrast, what really matters in effective advertising is enwrapped in a complex tacit skill set of advertising workers and creative indeterminacy, which cannot (easily) be disentangled, and definitely not with the research tools currently available. Third, our findings corroborated earlier propositions that agency professionals have little awareness of and familiarity with academic advertising research. This does not prevent them, at the same time, from having negative views about advertising academia. Practitioners have serious validity concerns with academic research because they perceive academicians as not credible sources mainly because of their lack of practical experience. They also have validity concerns: they perceive academic advertising research as artificial and not timely. Fourth, practitioners look at commercial research with the same skepticism as they look at academic research.

In summary, agency practitioners have a distinct meta-theoretical view of advertising. They accept some basic theories as valid (such as "break through and engage" and "mutation of effects" and creativity as the most important cause of advertising effects); however, they believe these notions are common sense. They are skeptical about more detailed advertising theories, especially if they come from academia. While these ideas are proof of practitioners' "knowledge autonomy," our hypothesized model, they do not help too much with advertising's professional status.

Social Context: Pseudo-Professionalization Tactics

The gap between academia and practice in advertising is in part driven by the fact that practitioners (for "legitimate" or "illegitimate" reasons) are autonomous in their knowledge about advertising. This discrepancy is a strange anomaly in professionalization terms. In a "normally" professionalizing occupation, practitioners do find theoretical knowledge useful in legitimating their work and elevating their status. In the case of advertising, while there are professionalizing forces present, most importantly, in the form of academic advertising research, the professionalization project suffers an unexpected blow: by its own practitioners who do not believe in the project anymore.

As we have shown, practitioners' knowledge autonomy sheds light on why this is: practitioners sense a *professional paradox* (whether their perception is reality is another matter; for the professionalization project to fail, it is enough that its participants do not believe in it anymore). The professional paradox based on the analysis of practitioners' theories is this: what would be the most important form of knowledge (what works best in advertising, how creativity leads to purchase behavior) is impossible to raise to a theoretical level. Even though it is a very complex and unique knowledge-based activity to do advertising, it is encapsulated in the tacit skill and creative indeterminacy of the practitioner. Conversely, what theoretical knowledge exists, either in the form of practitioner or academic theories, is insufficient or invalid. In the case of practitioners' own theories, the perception is that whatever they can claim validly ("break through and engage," "mutation of effects") is mere common sense, too simple to meet professionalization's requirement to be unique and complex, or

meta-theories, and (3) their social use, what we called pseudo-professionalization tactics.

The "Practitioner Knowledge Autonomy" model is grounded in empirical research and as such it does not prescribe specific directives for closing the gap between academia and practice. It simply states that the unidirectional flow often assumed from academia to practical "application" is not a reality in how advertising is practiced, even if we allow for time lags and indirect flows. While it may not be possible, or even desirable to close the gap between practitioner and academic theories *entirely*, strengthening mutual understanding seems to be a goal that we all—academicians and practitioners alike—could and should agree on.

References

Abbott, A. D. (1988). *The system of professions: An essay on the division of expert labor.* Chicago: University of Chicago Press.

AMA Task Force on the Development of Marketing Thought (1988). Developing, disseminating and utilizing marketing knowledge. *Journal of Marketing, 52* (4), 1–15.

Argyris, C. (2000). The relevance of actionable knowledge for breaking the code. In M. Beer & N. Nohria (Eds.), *Breaking the code of change* (pp. 415–427). Boston: Harvard Business School Press.

Coviello, N. E., Brodie, R. J., Danaher, P. J., & Johnston, W. J. (2002). How firms relate to their markets: An empirical examination of contemporary marketing practices. *Journal of Marketing, 66* (3), 33–46.

Craig, R. T. (1996). Practical theory: A reply to Sandelands. *Journal for the Theory of Social Behavior, 26* (1), 65–79.

Dutton, J. M., & Starbuck, W. H. (1963). On managers and theories. *Management International, 6*, 1–11.

Friestad, M., & Wright, P. (1994). The Persuasion Knowledge Model: How people cope with persuasion attempts. *Journal of Consumer Research, 21* (1), 1–31.

Hovland, C. I., Lumsdaine, A. A., & Sheffield, F. D. (1949). *Experiments on mass communication.* Princeton, NJ: Princeton University Press.

Hunt, S. D. (2002). *Foundations of marketing theory: Toward a general theory of marketing.* Armonk, NY: M.E. Sharpe.

Kilduff, M., & Mehra, A. (1997). Postmodernism and organizational research. *Academy of Management Review, 22* (2), 453–481.

Kover, A. J. (1995). Copywriters' implicit theories of communication: An exploration. *Journal of Consumer Research, 21* (4), 596–611.

Lewin, K. (1943). Psychology and the process of group living. *Journal of Social Psychology, SPSSI Bulletin, 17*, 113–131.

MacDonald, K. M. (1995). *The sociology of the professions.* London: Sage.

McGuire, W. J. (1969). An information-processing model of advertising effectiveness.

In H. L. Davis & A. J. Silk (Eds.), *Behavioral and management science in marketing* (pp. 156–180). New York: Ronald Press.

Nyilasy, G., & Reid, L. N. (2007). The academician–practitioner gap in advertising. *International Journal of Advertising, 26* (4), 425–445.

Nyilasy, G., & Reid, L. N. (2009a). Agency practitioners' meta-theories of advertising. *International Journal of Advertising, 28* (4), 639–668.

Nyilasy, G., & Reid, L. N. (2009b). Agency practitioner theories of how advertising works. *Journal of Advertising, 38* (3), 81–96.

Nyilasy, G., Kreshel, P. J., & Reid, L. N. (in press). Agency practitioners, pseudo-professionalization tactics, and advertising professionalism. *Journal of Current Issues and Research in Advertising*.

Nyilasy, G., & Kreshel, P. J. (forthcoming). Ad agency professionals' mental models of advertising creativity.

Polanyi, M. (1958). *Personal knowledge: Towards a post-critical philosophy*. London: Routledge & Kegan Paul.

Roethlisberger, F. J. (1977). *The elusive phenomena*. Cambridge, MA: Harvard University Press.

Sandelands, L. E. (1990). What is so practical about theory? Lewin revisited. *Journal for the Theory of Social Behavior, 20*, 235–262.

Schon, D. A. (1983). *The reflective practitioner: How professionals think in action*. New York: Basic Books.

Thomas, K. W., & Tymon, W. G., Jr. (1982). Necessary properties of relevant research: Lessons from recent criticisms of the organizational sciences. *Academy of Management Review, 7*, 345–352.

Vakratsas, D., & Ambler, T. (1999). How advertising works: What do we really know? *Journal of Marketing, 63* (1), 26–43.

Weick, K. E. (2003). Theory and practice in the real world. In H. Tsoukas & C. Knudsen (Eds.), *The Oxford handbook of organization theory: Meta-theoretical perspectives* (pp. 453–475). Oxford, UK: Oxford University Press.

Wilensky, H. L. (1964). The professionalization of everyone. *American Journal of Sociology, 70* (2), 137–158.

Zaltman, G., LeMasters, K., & Heffring, M. (1982). *Theory construction in marketing: Some thoughts on thinking*. New York: Wiley.

Additional Readings

Abbott, A. D. (1988). *The system of professions: An essay on the division of expert labor*. Chicago: University of Chicago Press.

Kover, A. J. (1995). Copywriters' implicit theories of communication: An exploration. *Journal of Consumer Research, 21* (March), 596–611.

Nyilasy, G., & Reid, L. N. (2007). The academician–practitioner gap in advertising. *International Journal of Advertising, 26* (4), 425–445.

Nyilasy, G., & Reid, L. N. (2009a). Agency practitioners' meta-theories of advertising. *International Journal of Advertising, 28* (4), 639–668.

Nyilasy, G., & Reid, L. N. (2009b). Agency practitioner theories of how advertising works. *Journal of Advertising, 38* (3), 81–96.

Nyilasy, G., Kreshel, P. J., & Reid, L. N. (in press). Agency practitioners, pseudo-professionalization tactics, and advertising professionalism. *Journal of Current Issues and Research in Advertising*.

MacDonald, K. M. (1995). *The sociology of the professions*. London: Sage.

Schon, D. A. (1983). *The reflective practitioner: How professionals think in action*. New York: Basic Books.

Weick, K. E. (2003). Theory and practice in the real world. In H. Tsoukas & C. Knudsen (Eds.), *The Oxford handbook of organization theory: Meta-theoretical perspectives* (pp. 453–475). Oxford, UK: Oxford University Press.

Part II

Psychological Processes in Response to Advertisements

Chapter 4

The Elaboration Likelihood Model

A 30-Year Review

David W. Schumann, Michael R. Kotowski,
Ho-Young (Anthony) Ahn, and
Curtis P. Haugtvedt

Over the past three decades, the Elaboration Likelihood Model (ELM), introduced by social psychologists Richard Petty and John Cacioppo (Petty, 1977; Petty & Cacioppo, 1981; Petty & Cacioppo, 1986), has generated a great deal of attention from individuals and organizations interested in better understanding processes underlying attitude change and persuasion. Prior to the development of the ELM, reviews of the persuasion literature documented conflicting findings regarding the influence of many persuasion variables (McGuire, 1968; Wicker, 1969; Fishbein & Ajzen, 1972; Himmelfarb & Eagly, 1974; Kiesler & Munson, 1975; Norman, 1976; Greenwald & Ronis, 1978; Sternthal, Dholakia, & Leavitt, 1978; Rogers, 1983). By organizing existing theories and findings using the overarching theme of the likelihood of elaboration of message content, ELM researchers were able to explain these seemingly inconsistent findings.

ELM theorists built on the frameworks developed by their predecessors. The central route of the ELM is based on the 1960s and 1970s cognitive response model of persuasion (Greenwald, Brock, & Ostrom, 1968), which was developed in response to data that did not fit the predictions of the message learning perspective of Carl Hovland and colleagues in the 1940s and 1950s. By positing that attitudes or attitude changes that appear equal could be the result of different underlying processes, the ELM challenged the dominant views of single process models of the time (e.g., Fishbein & Ajzen, 1975). Awareness of the ELM and other dual processing frameworks (cf. the Heuristic-Systematic Model—see Chaiken, 1980) has led advertising practitioners and researchers to ask a wider range of questions about the manner in which various variables might influence persuasion outcomes.

ELM and Advertising

The ELM has been used in over 125 articles and chapters in the advertising literature since 1981 when *Advances in Consumer Research* published a paper by Petty and Cacioppo that applied the ELM to advertising. A 1983 article entitled "Central and Peripheral Routes to Advertising Effectiveness: The Moderating Role of Involvement" (Petty, Cacioppo, & Schumann, 1983) became one of the most cited articles in the advertising and consumer behavior literature (Cote, Leong & Cote, 1991).

The ELM has been noted for its usefulness in both basic and applied settings (e.g., Ajzen, 1987; O'Keefe, 1990; Pratkanis, 1989; Sears, 1988; Petty & Wegener, 1998; Choi & Salmon, 2003; Haugtvedt & Kasmer, 2008). The ELM framework has been employed in a wide range of domains, including public service announcements, political advertising, product advertising, health advertising, environmental issue advertising, and advertising via the Internet.

This chapter reviews how the ELM has influenced advertising research in the past 30 years. Suggestions are also made as to how the ELM framework can be used in future research and practice. This book follows an overarching framework within which various theoretical approaches can be attached (see Figure 1.1). As noted below, the variables studied using the ELM as a guide can be categorized as representing the dimensions of persuasion first noted by Hovland and McGuire in their pioneering work on attitudes. As the figure reflects, the content in this chapter will touch upon the dimensions of message, source, receiver, and channel.

Review of the Theory and its Tenets

The ELM offers a comprehensive theory about the degree and type of processes an individual employs in considering a persuasive message (Perloff, 2010). Petty and Cacioppo identified four key principles (Petty & Brinol, 2012) that are reflected in this framework. First, an attitude can be formed, changed, or reinforced as a result of either a high degree of thinking or a comparatively low degree of thinking. Second, the amount and type of thinking operate along a continuum, ranging from low to high elaboration. This continuum is anchored by two distinct "routes" to persuasion. The central route is characterized by extensive cognitive processing of the message, whereas the peripheral route is characterized by minimal, if any, cognitive processing. Third, the ELM posits that "central and peripheral processes determine attitudes with different probabilities at different points along the elaboration continuum" (Petty, Wegener, Fabrigar, Preister, & Cacioppo, 2006, p. 337). Attitudes formed or changed under high elaboration conditions are posited to be more persistent over time and more resistant to counterarguments than attitudes formed or changed under low elaboration conditions. Finally, the ELM explains how a variable can play multiple roles within the persuasion process. Indeed, variables can serve as cues or arguments (e.g., sheer number of arguments vs. the quality of the arguments), or they can affect the extent (amount) or direction (bias) in thinking/or the confidence in thoughts or attitudes (Petty & Brinol, in press).

Motivation and ability are variables that have received the most attention as moderators of the route to persuasion. The ELM posits that when people are highly motivated and have the ability to think about a message, the arguments for or against the issue become paramount. High levels of motivation and ability characterize the central route end of the elaboration continuum. On the other hand, those who are not motivated to carefully evaluate message arguments about the issue and/or do not have the ability to process the message (e.g., the message is in a foreign language or is too complicated), can still be influenced by other variables (serving as peripheral cues) in the communication environment. The increased influence of variables serving as peripheral cues reflects movement on the continuum toward the peripheral route end of an elaboration continuum.

Motivational variables in the advertising literature have typically included involvement with the product (e.g., Petty et al., 1983; Andrews & Shimp, 1990) and individual differences like need for cognition (NFC), "the tendency for an individual to engage and enjoy thinking" (Cacioppo & Petty, 1982; see also Cacioppo, Petty, & Kao, 1984; Haugtvedt, Petty, Cacioppo, & Steidley, 1988). Ability variables include being conversant in the language of the message, having sufficient time to think about the message, and having sufficient relevant knowledge to understand the message arguments, to name a few. For example, studies have examined the influence of situational and message factors such as distraction (e.g., Petty, Wells, & Brock, 1976), message repetition (e.g., Cacioppo & Petty, 1989; Schumann, Petty, & Clemons, 1990), time pressure (e.g., Kruglanski & Freund, 1983), and message complexity (e.g., Hafer, Reynolds, & Obertynski, 1996).

Early ELM research focused on testing hypotheses related to interaction effects predicted by the model. An important variable introduced by ELM researchers was a manipulation of the strength of arguments in order to assess the relative operation of central or peripheral route processes. One of the most common moderator variables examined in early advertising studies was a situational manipulation of personal relevance (e.g., Petty et al., 1983). Other studies employed theoretically relevant individual differences factors like NFC as moderators of the route to persuasion (Haugtvedt, Petty, & Cacioppo, 1986). Importantly, outcome variables like attitude strength (e.g., persistence, resistance, attitude confidence) have also been studied.

Variables Employed in ELM Advertising Research

We review here how a combination of variables can be used to understand the processes that take place at different points on an elaboration continuum. In particular, the influence of message, source, receiver, and channel variables are considered.

Demonstration of Processes on the Elaboration Likelihood Continuum

The purpose of Petty et al.'s 1983 article was to provide evidence for two routes to persuasion employing advertising stimuli. The study's results revealed that the attitudes of highly involved participants were more influenced by the strength of advertising message arguments while those in the low involvement conditions were more influenced by the nature of the source (celebrity as opposed to everyday citizens as endorsers). For similar manipulations of message arguments and sources, please see Andrews and Shimp (1990), Pechmann and Esteban (1991), and Yoon (1992).

In most cases, advertising programs rely on repetition to create their impact. Schumann, Petty, and Clemons (1990) examined the number of times ads were repeated and whether the repetitions of the ads were identical or varied in some way, and manipulated whether consumers were operating under high or low involvement. Low-involved participants viewing a moderate number of ads were more influenced by cosmetic variations in the ads (changes in pictures, font type), while highly involved participants were more influenced by substantive variation in the ads (changes in message arguments). This demonstrated that highly involved people who viewed the substantive variables did greater elaboration.

Persistence and Resistance

A few studies have explored the cognitive processing that underlies attitudinal persistence and/or resistance. Haugtvedt and Petty (1992) in a first study posited that the attitudes of high NFC individuals would be based on processing of message arguments while the attitudes of low NFC individuals would be based on the sheer number of message arguments. Consistent with predictions, they found that the attitudes of high NFC individuals decayed less over time than did the low NFC viewers. In a second study, Haugtvedt and Petty (1992) showed that beliefs constructed as a result of message elaboration of a first message by high NFC individuals were more resistant to a subsequent attack message than were equivalent beliefs formed on the basis of source factors by low NFC individuals. That is, the newly formed beliefs of high NFC individuals were more resistant to change than the newly formed beliefs of low NFC individuals.

The nature of repeated advertising has also been shown to influence attitude persistence and resistance. For example, Haugtvedt, Schumann, and their colleagues (1994) exposed participants to repeated ads employing either a cosmetic or substantive variation strategy under moderate levels of motivation. While repeated advertising conditions led to equal persistence over one week when a counterargument was introduced, the substantive variation condition participants were significantly more resistant. Similarly, Priester and his colleagues (1999) found that elaborative processing was important in the persistence of attitudes in a study of the sleeper effect. More recently, ELM researchers have begun to explore the influence of meta-cognitive factors like certainty and confidence in which the attitudes are held or changed. For example, respondents exposed to weak or strong arguments for an advertisement and intentionally asked to provide counterarguments or negative thoughts, were more certain of their resistance to ad messages when elaboration of message arguments was high (Tormala & Petty, 2004).

Message Variables

The beliefs and/or attitudes of highly involved participants (either manipulated, measured NFC, or created through high task involvement) have been found to be influenced more by two-sided versus one-sided arguments (Hastak & Park, 1990), by attribute quality as opposed to quantity (Booth-Butterfield & Booth-Butterfield, 1991; Booth-Butterfield & Cooke, 1994), by information-only ads as opposed to story-based testimonials (Braverman, 2008), and by the presence versus the absence of spiritual information contained in a message for breast cancer awareness (Holt, Lee, & Wright, 2008).

Studies employing the ELM framework have also considered message framing, measured message strength, and syntactic structure. Umphrey (2003) found people who were identified as processing more deeply and exposed to a loss-framed message for testicular self-examination, were more accepting (less opposed) compared to those receiving the gain-framed message. Nayakankuppam and Priester (1998) had participants provide a consideration set after ranking the strength of arguments and providing their attitude toward the brand. The results showed that participants typically did not include disliked alternatives across message strength conditions, but included liked brands only when the message arguments were stronger. Finally, Lowrey (1992) conducted a test of the complexity levels (high or low) of three psycholinguistic structures to include passive (high) versus active (low) construction, negation (high) versus affirmation (low), and left (high) versus right (low) branching sentences. Participant attitudes resulting from exposure to ads with less complex syntactic structure reflected strong versus weak arguments, while a more complex syntactic structure appeared to deter adequate message processing resulting in similar attitudes.

Sources

The use of a highly credible source typically serves as an added argument as it enhances strong arguments while potentially neutralizing weaker arguments under high elaboration conditions. Jones, Sinclaire and Courneya (2003) manipulated positive versus negative message framing for the health benefits of exercise, as well as source credibility (high and low), and found the positively framed message coupled with the credible source condition was significantly more influential in the respondent committing to future exercise. Tormala and his colleagues (2007) manipulated the timing of source credibility information and found favorability of thoughts was higher when viewing the high credibility source endorsement before the message. No differences were found, however, in thought favorability based on low or high credibility source endorsement when presented after the message. Finally, Metzler and her colleagues (2000) studied the effectiveness of HIV messages with teenagers by manipulating the quality of arguments and source factors (an HIV positive individual versus a worried mother). As expected, the teenagers exposed to the strong arguments found the message to be more persuasive and produced fewer counterarguments compared to those exposed to the message containing weak arguments. For those receiving weak arguments, however, participants exposed to the HIV positive source rated the message higher and produced fewer counterarguments.

One element of credibility is trustworthiness. In research by Priester and Petty (2003), participants were exposed to either a low or high trustworthy endorser. They found that for an endorser of suspect trustworthiness, participants more carefully processed message arguments. In a subsequent study they found that individuals exposed to the less trustworthy endorser recalled the arguments faster. For those participants exposed to high trustworthy endorsers, however, differences in argument quality were inconsequential. This finding is consistent with the possibility that some individuals default to the recommendation of a high trustworthy endorser and reduce their elaboration of message arguments (see also Meltzer et al., 2000).

Sometimes a visual stimulus may act as a peripheral source cue (e.g., a symbol), but may create a negative response rather than the expected positive response. For example, in their study manipulating the presence of a religious cross, Dotson and Hyatt (2000) found that for highly involved individuals, regardless of religious dogmatism, no effects for the cross were present and attitudes and purchase intentions were a function of the strength of the message arguments. For low-involved individuals who were highly religiously dogmatic, however, attitudes and purchase intention were lower when the cross was present than when it was not (see also Yang, Hung, Sung, & Farn 2006 for a test involving third party seals).

Receiver Variables

Several audience variables have been employed in advertising studies employing the ELM. For example, many of the studies mentioned above employed a manipulation or measurement of some form of personal involvement. It is interesting to note that Wang, Wang, and Farn (2009), employing an advertising website viewing context, added a goal-directedness manipulation (i.e., task involvement) in addition to product involvement. Those participants who were instructed to seek something specific and scored higher in product involvement, were influenced by the information appeal (substantive) as opposed to an emotional appeal (cosmetic). Participants who were told to just browse the site, and who scored low on product involvement, were influenced by the cosmetic appeal but not by a substantive variation strategy (see Schumann et al., 1990).

Sanbonmatsu and Kardes (1988) created conditions of moderate and high physiological arousal by employing exercise levels and measuring systolic blood pressure scores. Compared to moderately aroused people, highly aroused participants were more influenced by endorser status (celebrity or non-celebrity). On the other hand, moderately aroused participants were more influenced by message strength.

An individual's NFC has been the most examined of all personality traits related to elaboration likelihood. Those high in NFC, because of their desire to seek and find answers, are more likely to examine message arguments employed in advertising, while those low in NFC are more susceptible to peripheral cues. Haugtvedt, Petty, and their colleagues (1988; 1992) demonstrated that high NFC participants were more influenced by active processing of the available product message arguments, whereas individuals low in NFC were consistently influenced by the presence of a peripheral cue (see also Bailey & Strube, 1991; Peltier & Schibrowsky, 1994).

Other individual difference variables have been employed as possible moderators of elaboration. Processing and/or resultant attitudes were found to be influenced by one's self schema (Wheeler, Petty, & Bizer, 2005), identification as cognitive elaborators versus cognitive misers (Morris, ChongMoo, & Singh, 2005), variance in mood (Petty, Schumann, Richman, & Strathman, 1993), and one's confidence after exposure to an ad (Brinol, Petty, & Tormala, 2004).

Channel Variables

Using the ELM as a theoretical framework, some studies have considered the impact of time compression on message processing. Hausknecht and Moore (1986) and Moore, Hausknecht, and Thamodaran (1986), in several studies, found differences based on time compression rates. Rates exceeding 130% compression appeared to interfere directly with message processing, resulting in fewer cognitive responses related to the advertised claims (see also Lammers, Kassarjian, & Patton, 1987).

A number of studies have employed the ELM to examine ads on the Internet. A number of researchers were unable to support predictions of the ELM and thus concluded that the propositions of the ELM do not hold up in the Internet setting (e.g., Karson & Korgaonkar, 2001; SanJosé-Cabezudo, Gutiérrez-Arranz, & Gutiérrez-Cillán, 2009). To the contrary, a review of the online studies for this chapter demonstrated that when study participants are asked to do something on the Internet, their processing motivation tends to be high. Thus, manipulations of motivation (e.g., product involvement) at best create different levels of relatively higher elaboration (high and moderate). It is likely that both message quality and peripheral cues could affect persuasive outcomes within this context when task involvement is relatively high. Examples of online studies that included a message argument and examined memory, attitudes, and/or clicking behavior, used manipulations like variation in site attractiveness (Karson & Korgaonkar, 2001), source credibility (Park & Hastak, 1995), number of reviews (Park & Kim, 2008), and size of banner ads (Cho, 1999).

Issues, Misunderstandings, and Challenges

A review of how researchers in the advertising literature have conceptualized or operationalized variables to be studied with the guidance of the ELM has high-lighted several points warranting special mention. Most notable is the fact that researchers who trained under or worked closely with Richard Petty and/or John Cacioppo conceptualize and test the ELM in a particular manner with a consistent set of stimuli and a consistent method in the early stages of research. As researchers have employed new stimuli (e.g., advertising) and different methods the model has been still been shown to be supported. The fact that the model holds up well under many different testing conditions is one of the great strengths of the ELM. It is rare for a model or theory to have such consistency over its lifespan. This has been accomplished largely through programmatic research in which a basic pattern of processes is found reliably. Extensions and the identification of boundary conditions then help inform basic and applied researchers about the appropriate use of the model in a wider range of situations. We believe that the magnitude of the impact of the ELM on advertising research stems from the early programmatic research advocated and followed by the originators.

Although some researchers have accurately tested the propositions of the model, others have made erroneous assumptions about the model and have included confounds in their methods, resulting in incorrect characterizations of the model in the literature. As the literature employing the ELM moves beyond 30 years, it is imperative that those studying and using the model clearly understand the basis of the model and its limitations. Without doing so, there will likely be uncontrolled conceptual drift that decreases the usefulness of the ELM for explanatory and predictive power in applied settings. This review intentionally excluded studies that were not conceptually consistent with the ELM or were flawed methodologically.

Common Misunderstandings of the ELM in the Literature

One component of the ELM where there has been a fair amount of misunderstanding is the nature of the elaboration continuum. Occasionally an argument is presented having as its core the following: because humans are capable of cognitively processing multiple stimuli simultaneously while allocating more cognitive resources to some of these stimuli than others, the fact that the ELM posits a single elaboration continuum is flawed. This argument fails, however, because of a misunderstanding of what is meant by elaboration continuum. In the parlance of the ELM, the elaboration continuum refers to the claim that people form attitudes using more or fewer cognitive resources. Thus, confusion seems to arise because the elaboration continuum is mistakenly thought to have a cognitive corollary when, in fact, it refers to a continuum representing the likelihood of cognitive effort a person will allocate to processing a message.

Equally important, the ELM posits that one can predict the likelihood of elaboration by accounting for just two variables, motivation and ability. This chapter's literature review revealed that the relationship among these three concepts is another common area of misunderstanding. Even though people are motivated to hold subjectively correct attitudes, being cognitive misers, people by default have a low likelihood of elaboration. The ELM further posits a connection between motivation factors (e.g., mood, involvement, NFC) and elaboration likelihood. Although much of the existing literature examines the relationship between motivation and elaboration likelihood, relatively little advertising research has looked at the moderating effect of ability (and variables that affect ability like distraction and prior knowledge) on the motivation → elaboration likelihood relationship.

With the guidance of the ELM one can predict the factors primarily responsible for persuasion by knowing the level of elaboration likelihood. When the elaboration likelihood is toward the low end of the continuum, factors serving as peripheral cues are primarily responsible for persuasive outcomes; when the elaboration likelihood is toward the upper end of the continuum, message elaboration is primarily responsible for persuasive outcomes, and when the elaboration likelihood is in the middle of the continuum a combination of peripheral cues and message elaboration may be the mutual basis for persuasive outcomes. Thus, the elaboration likelihood continuum is characterized by the amount of elaboration upon factors serving as arguments and the use of factors serving as peripheral cues as basis for attitudes. The characteristics of attitudes that are outcomes of the different persuasion processes vary in attitude persistence, robustness, confidence, and accessibility. Most of the literature reviewed for this chapter focuses on the effects that occur at the extremes of the elaboration likelihood continuum. Most advertising influences, however, are perhaps likely to occur at moderate levels of the continuum.

Given the nature of the elaboration likelihood continuum and its effect on the extent to which weight is given to variables as peripheral cues, arguments, or some degree of both, it is important to point out the distinction between peripheral and central route processes and the factors themselves. According to the ELM, the peripheral and central route processes are distinct from the factors operating within the processes, but commonly conflated when discussed in the literature. Thus, it is more accurate to refer to factors serving as peripheral cues or factors serving as arguments rather than to refer to them as inherently "peripheral cues" or "arguments." This point is largely irrelevant when processing is at the extremes of the elaboration likelihood continuum because people will be giving weight mainly to factors serving a pure peripheral route process or factors serving a pure central route process. But, when processing is at the middle of the elaboration likelihood continuum this distinction matters a great deal as some relative weighting of variables will take place. Consequently, it becomes possible for factors traditionally thought of as peripheral cue prototypes like perceived source credibility to bias thoughtful processing and potentially be perceived as an argument itself. Because the majority of research in the advertising literature focuses on the two endpoints of the elaboration likelihood continuum, this aspect of the ELM is frequently overlooked and misunderstood.

What Exactly is Argument Quality?

The characteristics of weak and strong arguments have been misunderstood in many studies intending to study ELM prediction. A substantial number of studies examining the ELM reuse characteristics of weak and strong arguments as identified in earlier research. The problem with this process is that the ELM never offered a conceptual definition for argument quality that goes beyond the empirical derivation process requiring the pretesting of several different arguments until two sets of arguments are identified that are rated to be either weak or strong. Consequently, the characteristics of argument quality for any given study are dependent on the particular population, context, and topic and do not necessarily generalize.

At least two important points are worth making here. First, arguments labeled as weak or strong using the traditional ELM empirical derivation method in one study do not necessarily have the same characteristics as arguments labeled weak or strong in a different study. The lack of conceptual framework regarding argument quality makes it difficult to interpret in what ways they theoretically differ beyond the weak versus strong labels. Second, more work is needed in conceptually defining argument quality (cf. Areni, 2003). Therefore, to improve the interpretability of argument quality effects in the absence of a working theoretical framework regarding the argument quality construct it is essential for researchers and practitioners to develop and pretest weak and strong arguments for their project anytime the population, context, time, or topic deviates from earlier work.

Challenges to the ELM

Clarification of the main elements of the ELM allows attention to be turned to the main challenges that the ELM has faced. The fact that the ELM has faced challenges speaks well of the model. The value of any model (or theory) can be judged in part by the amount of debate it sparks. Models offering mundane or obviously flawed predictions generate little debate as they are dismissed from relevance quite easily. Models offering novel descriptions or counterintuitive predictions cannot be dismissed quite so easily. These models frequently break from the status quo by presenting a description of a seemingly complex set of evidence that is more elegant than the prevailing paradigm. Indeed, this was the case with the ELM in the early 1980s.

Overall, the ELM has stood up well to several challenges over the years. For example, Bitner and Obermiller (1985) critiqued the model's conceptual clarity, Stiff (1986) and Stiff and Boster (1987) argued that the ELM was not the best explanation of the variance in the persuasive effects found in the literature. Hamilton,

Hunter, and Boster (1993) attempted to translate the components of the ELM into a mathematical model but were unable to do so because they argued that the ELM is conceptually underspecified. Johnson and Eagly (1989) argued that the boomerang effect predicted by the ELM is observed with considerable variation from study to study. Each of these challenges has benefited the model because the challenge and refutation process elicited greater conceptual clarity of the ELM's components, strengthening the model in the process. The fact that the ELM has instigated and been robust to challenges over time (Petty, Cacioppo, Kasmer, & Haugtvedt, 1987; Petty et al., 1993) says a great deal about the descriptive and predictive quality of the model. The challenges have certainly helped refine what is a fairly complex model of persuasion into what advertisers today know to have high predictive, heuristic, and organizational value (cf. Petty & Brinol, 2012).

Implications for Practice and Future Research

There are many exciting avenues for future research using the ELM. In this final section, several areas are highlighted that we believe should be prioritized. Importantly, we think that ELM-based research in an advertising context has the potential to influence both theory and practice.

Message Repetition

Much more research is needed to examine the roles of message repetition and message variation in the formation and maintenance of attitudes toward products, brands, and issues. As noted above, advertising effectiveness is a function of repeated exposure. Very few studies have examined the role of repeated message exposure under conditions that allow one to understand the nature of the processes responsible for attitude change.

Attitude Strength

Both researchers and practitioners would benefit from a better understanding of the degree to which the attitudes created or changed by their efforts persist over time, resist change, or predict behavior. ELM-based research reviewed in this chapter provides some guidelines as to development of studies and measures to assess attitude strength (see also Haugtvedt & Priester, 1997) when a counterargument is introduced. Practitioners especially might realize benefits by creating normed "resistance paradigms" to which they can compare the effectiveness of various new campaigns, messages, or techniques.

Finally, persuasion researchers of the future can benefit from an understanding of the ELM framework and research methods in attempting to understand or explain the success or failure of past advertising campaigns. With knowledge of the ELM framework and tools, practitioners and scholars will be able to better understand the reasons for success or failure and thus develop effective advertising in creative new ways.

References

Ajzen, I. (1987). Attitudes, traits, and actions: Dispositional prediction of behavior in personality and social psychology. In L. Berkowitz (Ed.), *Advances in experimental social psychology* (Vol. 20, pp. 1–63). New York: Academic Press.

Andrews, J. C., & Shimp, T. A. (1990). Effects of involvement, argument strength, and source characteristics on central and peripheral processing of advertising. *Psychology and Marketing, 7*, 195–214.

Areni, C. S. (2003). The effects of structural and grammatical variables on persuasion: An elaboration likelihood model perspective. *Psychology and Marketing, 20*, 349–375.

Bailey, J. R., & Strube, M. J. (1991). Effects of need for cognition on patterns of information acquisition. In M. Lynn & J. M. Jackson (Eds.), *Proceedings of the society for consumer psychology at the 1991 annual convention of the American Psychological Association* (pp. 41–45). Madison, WI: Omnipress.

Bitner, M. J., & Obermiller, C. (1985). The elaboration likelihood model: Limitations and extensions in marketing. In E. C. Hirschman & M. B. Holbrook (Eds.), *Advances in consumer research* (Vol. 12, pp. 420–425). Provo, UT: Association for Consumer Research.

Booth-Butterfield, S., & Booth-Butterfield, M. (1991). Individual differences in communication of humorous messages. *Southern Communication Journal, 56*, 205–218.

Booth-Butterfield, S., & Cooke, P. (1994). Simultaneous versus exclusive processing of persuasive arguments and cues. *Communication Quarterly, 42*, 21–35.

Braverman, J. (2008). Testimonials versus informational persuasive messages: The moderating effect of delivery mode and personal involvement. *Communication Research, 35*, 666–694.

Brinol, P., Petty, R. E., & Tormala, Z. L. (2004). Self-validation of cognitive responses to advertisements. *Journal of Consumer Research, 30*, 559–573.

Cacioppo, J. T., & Petty, R. E. (1982). The need for cognition. *Journal of Personality and Social Psychology, 42*, 116–131.

Cacioppo, J. T., & Petty, R. E. (1989). Effects of message repetition on argument processing, recall, and persuasion. *Basic and Applied Social Psychology, 10*, 3–12.

Cacioppo, J. T., Petty, R. E., & Kao, C. F. (1984). The efficient assessment of need for cognition. *Journal of Personality Assessment, 48*, 306–307.

Chaiken, S. (1980). Heuristic versus systematic information processing and the use of source versus message cues in persuasion. *Journal of Personality and Social Psychology, 39*, 752–766.

Cho, C. (1999). How advertising works on the WWW: Modified elaboration likelihood model. *Journal of Current Issues and Research in Advertising, 21*, 33–50.

Choi, S. M., & Salmon, C. T. (2003). The elaboration likelihood model of persuasion after two decades: A review of criticisms and contributions. *Kentucky Journal of Communication, 22*, 47–77.

Cote, J. A., Leong, S., & Cote, J. (1991). Assessing the influence of Journal of Consumer Research: A citation analysis. *Journal of Consumer Research, 18*, 402–410.

Dotson, M. J., & Hyatt, E. M. (2000). Religious symbols as peripheral cues in advertising: A replication of the elaboration likelihood model. *Journal of Business Research, 48*, 63–68.

Fishbein, M., & Ajzen, I. (1972). Attitudes and opinions. *Annual Review of Psychology, 23*, 487–544.

Fishbein, M., & Ajzen, I. (1975). *Belief, attitude, intention, and behavior: An introduction to theory and research.* Reading, MA: Addison-Wesley.

Greenwald, A. G., Brock, T. C., & Ostrom, T. M. (1968). *Psychological foundations of attitudes.* New York: Academic Press.

Greenwald, A. G., & Ronis, D. L. (1978). Twenty years of cognitive dissonance: Case study of the evolution of a theory. *Psychological Review, 85*, 53–57.

Hafer, C. L., Reynolds, K. L., & Obertynski, M. A. (1996). Message comprehensibility and persuasion: Effects of complex language in counterattitudinal appeals to laypeople. *Social Cognition, 14*, 317–337.

Hamilton, M., Hunter, J., & Boster, F. (1993). The elaboration likelihood model as a theory of attitude formation: A mathematical analysis. *Communication Theory, 3*, 50–66.

Hastak, M., & Park, J. (1990). Mediators of message sidedness effects on cognitive structure for involved and uninvolved audiences. In M. E. Goldberg, G. Gorn, & R. W. Pollay (Eds.), *Advances in consumer research* (Vol. 17, pp. 329–336). Provo, UT: Association for Consumer Research.

Haugtvedt, C. P., & Kasmer, J. A. (2008). Attitude change and persuasion. In C. P. Haugtvedt, P. Herr, & F. Kardes (Eds.), *The handbook of consumer psychology* (pp. 419–436). New York: Lawrence Erlbaum Associates.

Haugtvedt, C. P., & Petty, R. E. (1992). Personality and persuasion: Need for cognition moderates the persistence and resistance of attitude changes. *Journal of Personality and Social Psychology, 63*, 308–319.

Haugtvedt, C. P., Petty, R. E., & Cacioppo, J. T. (1986, August). Creating resistant attitudes: An examination of the elaboration likelihood model. Paper presented at the Annual Meeting of the American Psychological Association, Washington, D.C.

Haugtvedt, C., Petty, R. E., Cacioppo, J. T., & Steidley, T. (1988). Personality and ad effectiveness: Exploring the utility of need for cognition. In M. J. Houston (Ed.), *Advances in consumer research* (Vol. 15, pp. 209–212). Provo, UT: Association for Consumer Research.

Haugtvedt, C. P., & Priester, J. R. (1997). Conceptual and methodological issues in advertising effectiveness: An attitude strength perspective. In W. Wells (Ed.), *Measuring advertising effectiveness* (pp. 79–94). Mahwah, NJ: Erlbaum Associates.

Haugtvedt, C. P., Schumann, D. W., Schneier, W. L., & Warren, W. L. (1994). Advertising repetition and variation strategies: Implications for understanding attitude strength. *Journal of Consumer Research, 21*, 176–189.

Hausknecht, D., & Moore, D. L. (1986). The effects of time compressed advertising of brand attitude judgments. *Advances in Consumer Research, 13*, 105–110.

Himmelfarb, S., & Eagly, A. H. (Eds.). (1974). *Readings in attitude change.* New York: Wiley.

Holt, C. L., Lee, C., & Wright, K. (2008). A spiritually based approach to breast cancer awareness: Cognitive response analysis of communication effectiveness. *Health Communication, 23*, 13–22.

Johnson, B., & Eagly, A. (1989). Effects of involvement on persuasion: A meta-analysis. *Psychological Bulletin, 106*, 290–314.

Jones, L. W., Sinclair, R. C., & Courneya, K. S. (2003). The effects of source credibility and message framing on exercise intentions, behaviors, and attitudes: An integration of the elaboration likelihood model and prospect theory. *Journal of Applied Social Psychology, 33*, 179–196.

Karson, E. J., & Korgaonkar, P. K. (2001). An experimental investigation of internet advertising and the elaboration likelihood model. *Journal of Current Issues and Research in Advertising, 23*, 53–72.

Kiesler, C. A., & Munson, P. A. (1975). Attitudes and opinions. *Annual Review of Psychology, 26* (4), 415–456.

Kruglanski, A. W., & Freund, T. (1983). The freezing and unfreezing of lay-inferences: Effects on impressional primacy, ethnic stereotyping, and numerical anchoring. *Journal of Experimental Social Psychology, 19*, 448–468.

Lammers, H. B., Kassarjian, K., & Patton, H. (1987). The effects of time compression and self-focused attention on attitude: An elaboration likelihood model perspective. In L. Alwitt (Ed.), *Proceedings of the August 1987 meetings of the American Psychological Association* (pp. 79–83). Chicago: DePaul University.

Lowrey, T. M. (1992). The relation between syntactic complexity and advertising persuasiveness. In J. F. Sherry, Jr. & B. Sternthal (Eds.), *Advances in consumer research* (Vol. 19, pp. 270–274). Provo, UT: Association for Consumer Research.

McGuire, W. J. (1968). Personality and susceptibility to social influence. In E. F. Borgatta & W. W. Lambert (Eds.), *Handbook of personality theory and research* (pp. 1130–1187). Chicago: Rand McNally.

Mazzocco, P. J., Rucker, D. D., & Brock, T. C. (2005). Assessing advertising effects: The importance of matching measurement and goals. In F. R. Kardes, P. M. Herr, & J. Nantel (Eds.), *Applying social cognition to consumer-focused strategy* (pp. 297–317). Mahwah, NJ: Lawrence Erlbaum Associates.

Metzler, A. E., Weiskotten, D., & Morgen, K. J. (2000). Adolescent HIV prevention: An application of the elaboration likelihood model. *Annual Conference of the American Psychological Association*, 3–26.

Moore, D. L., Hausknecht, D., & Thamodaran, K. (1986). Time compression, response opportunity, and persuasion. *Journal of Consumer Research, 13*, 85–99.

Morris, J. D., ChongMoo, W., & Singh, A. J. (2005). Elaboration likelihood model: A missing intrinsic emotional implication. *Journal of Targeting, Measurement and Analysis for Marketing, 14*, 79–98.

Nayakankuppam, D., & Priester, J. (1998). Consideration sets and attitudes: The role of attitude strength. *Proceedings of the SCP 1998 Winter Meeting*, 196–200.

Norman, D. A. (1976). *Memory and attention: An introduction to human information processing* (2nd ed.). New York: Wiley.

O'Keefe, D. J. (1990). *Persuasion: Theory and research*. Newbury Park, CA: Sage Publications.

Park, D., & Kim, S. (2008). The effects of consumer knowledge on message processing of electronic word-of-mouth via online consumer reviews. *Electronic Commerce Research and Applications, 7*, 399–410.

Park, J., & Hastak, M. (1995). Effects of involvement on on-line brand evaluations: A stronger test of the ELM. *Advances in Consumer Research, 22*, 435–439.

Pechmann, C., & Esteban, G. (1991). How comparative ads affect persuasion: The moderating role of prior motivation. In *Proceedings of the Society for Consumer Psychology* (p. 11). Washington, D.C.: American Psychological Association.

Peltier, J. W., & Schibrowsky, J. A. (1994). Need for cognition, advertisement viewing time and memory for advertising stimuli. In C. T. Allen & D. R. John (Eds.), *Advances in consumer research* (Vol. 21, pp. 244–250). Provo, UT: Association for Consumer Research.

Perloff, R. E. (2010). *The dynamics of persuasion: Communication and attitudes in the 21st century* (4th ed.). New York: Routledge.

Petty, R. E. (1977). The importance of cognitive responses in persuasion. *Advanced Consumer Research, 4*, 357–362.

Petty, R. E., & Briñol, P. (in press). The Elaboration Likelihood Model. In P. A. M. Van Lange, A. Kruglanski, & E. T. Higgins (Eds.), *Handbook of theories of social psychology* (Vol. 1, pp. 224–245). London, England: Sage.

Petty, R. E., & Cacioppo, J. T. (1981). Issue involvement as a moderator of the effects on attitude of advertising content and context. *Advances in Consumer Research, 8*, 20–24.

Petty, R. E., & Cacioppo, J. T. (1981). *Attitudes and persuasion: Classic and contemporary approaches*. Dubuque, IA: W.C. Brown Co. Publishers.

Petty, R. E., & Cacioppo, J. T. (1986). *Communication and persuasion: Central and peripheral routes to attitude change*. New York: Springer/Verlag.

Petty, R., Cacioppo, J., Kasmer, J., & Haugtvedt, C. (1987). A reply to Stiff and Boster. *Communication Monographs, 54*, 257–263.

Petty, R. E., Cacioppo, J. T., & Schumann, D. (1983). Central and peripheral routes to advertising effectiveness: The moderating role of involvement. *Journal of Consumer Research, 10*, 135–146.

Petty, R. E., Schumann, D. W., Richman, S. A., & Strathman, A. J. (1993). Positive mood and persuasion: Different roles for affect under high and low elaboration conditions. *Journal of Personality and Social Psychology, 64*, 5–20.

Petty, R. E., & Wegener, D. T. (1998). Attitude change: Multiple roles for persuasion variables. In S. F. D. Gilbert & G. Lindzey (Eds.), *Handbook of social psychology* (4th ed., Vol. 1, pp. 322–390). New York: McGraw-Hill.

Petty, R. E., Wegener, D. T., Fabrigar, L. R., Priester, J. R., & Cacioppo, J. T.

(2006). Conceptual and methodological issues in the elaboration likelihood model of persuasion: A reply to the Michigan state critics. *Communication Theory, 3*, 336–362.

Petty, R. E., Wells, G. L., & Brock, T. C. (1976). Distraction can enhance or reduce yielding of propaganda: Thought disruption versus effort justification. *Journal of Personality and Social Psychology, 34*, 874–884.

Pratkanis, A. P. (1989). The cognitive representation of attitudes. In A. R. Pratkanis, S. J. Breckler, & A. G. Greenwald (Eds.), *Attitude structure and function* (pp. 71–98). Hillsdale, NJ: Lawrence Erlbaum Associates.

Priester, J. R., & Petty, R. E. (2003). The influence of spokesperson trustworthiness on message elaboration, attitude strength, and advertising effectiveness. *Journal of Consumer Psychology, 13*, 408–421.

Priester, J. M., Wegener, D., Petty, R. E., & Fabrigar, L. (1999). Examining the psychological processes underlying the sleeper effect: The Elaboration Likelihood Model explanation. *Media Psychology, 1*, 27–48.

Rogers, R. W. (1983). Cognitive and physiological processes in fear appeals and attitude change: A revised theory of protection motivation. In J. R. Cacioppo & R. E. Petty (Eds.), *Social psychology: A sourcebook* (pp. 153–176). New York: Guilford Press.

Sanbonmatsu, D. M., & Kardes, F. R. (1988). The effects of physiological arousal on information processing and persuasion. *Journal of Consumer Research, 15*, 379–385.

SanJosé-Cabezudo, R., Gutiérrez-Arranz, A., & Gutiérrez-Cillán, J. (2009). The combined influence of central and peripheral routes in the online persuasion process. *CyberPsychology and Behavior, 12*, 299–308.

Schumann, D. W., Petty, R. E., & Clemons, D. S. (1990). Predicting the effectiveness of different strategies of advertising variation: A test of the repetition-variation hypotheses. *Journal of Consumer Research, 17*, 192–202.

Sears, D. O. (1988). Review of communication and persuasion: Central and peripheral routes to attitude change. *Public Opinion Quarterly, 52*, 262–265.

Sternthal, B., Dholakia, R., & Leavitt, C. (1978). The persuasive effects of source credibility: Tests of cognitive response. *Journal of Consumer Research, 4*, 252–260.

Stiff, J. B. (1986). Cognitive processing of persuasive message cues: A meta-analytic review of the effects of supporting information on attitudes. *Communication Monographs, 53*, 75–89.

Stiff, J. B., & Boster, F. J. (1987). Cognitive processing: Additional thoughts and a reply to Petty, Kasmer, Haugtvedt, and Cacioppo. *Communication Monographs, 54*, 250–256.

Tormala, Z. L., & Petty, R. E. (2004). Resistance to persuasion and attitude certainty: The moderating role of elaboration. *Personality and Social Psychology Bulletin, 30*, 1446–1457.

Tormala, Z. L., Briñol, P., & Petty, R. E. (2007). Multiple roles for source credibility under high elaboration: It's all in the timing. *Social Cognition, 25*, 536–552.

Umphrey, L. R. (2003). The effects of message framing and message processing on testicular self-examination attitudes and perceived susceptibility. *Communication Research Reports, 20*, 97–105.

Wang, K., Wang, E. T. G., & Farn, C. (2009). Influence of web advertising strategies, consumer goal-directedness, and consumer involvement on web advertising effectiveness. *International Journal of Electronic Commerce, 13*, 67–95.

Wheeler, S. C., Petty, R. E., & Bizer, G. Y. (2005). Self-schema matching and attitude change: Situational and dispositional determinants of message elaboration. *Journal of Consumer Research, 31*, 787–797.

Wicker, A. W. (1969). Attitudes vs. actions: The relationship of verbal and overt behavioral responses to attitude objects. *Journal of Social Issues, 25*, 41–78.

Yang, S., Hung, W., Sung, K., & Farn, C. (2006). Investigating initial trust toward e-tailers from the elaboration likelihood model perspective. *Psychology and Marketing, 23*, 429–445.

Yoon, D. (1992). Involvement level and the mediating role of attitude toward advertisement. *Proceedings of American Academy of Advertising Annual Conference*, 46–54.

Additional Readings

Haugtvedt, C. P., & Kasmer, J. A. (2008). Attitude change and persuasion. In C. P. Haugtvedt, P. Herr, & F. Kardes (Eds.), *The handbook of consumer psychology* (pp. 419–436). New York: Lawrence Erlbaum Associates.

Petty, R. E., & Brinol, P. (2012). The Elaboration Likelihood Model. In P. A. M. Van Lange, A. Kruglanski, & E. T. Higgins (Eds.), *Handbook of theories of social psychology* (pp. 224–245). London: Sage.

Petty, R. E., & Cacioppo, J. T. (1986). *Communication and persuasion: Central and peripheral routes to attitude change*. New York: Springer/Verlag.

Petty, R. E., Cacioppo, J. T., & Schumann, D. (1983). Central and peripheral routes to advertising effectiveness: The moderating role of involvement. *Journal of Consumer Research, 10*, 135–146.

Chapter 5

The Role of Emotion in Processing Advertising

Larry Percy

After being largely ignored for many years, there has been a renewed interest in emotion among neuroscientists in recent years. Today, emotion is conceptualized as an organizing force related to key human goals and needs. In fact, emotions are seen as essential for rational, productive behavior. But, we must be careful not to confuse "emotion" with positive affect because not all affect states qualify as emotion. Emotions are always about affect states that have objects, but something like mood is an affect feeling state without a salient object (Clore & Ortony, 2000). Nor should we treat emotion and "feelings" as synonyms. Most theorists today define emotion in terms of a number of different components, generally around what is known as the "reaction triad": physiological arousal, motor expression, and subjective feeling.

By its nature, emotion will be involved in several of the communication components outlined in the Components of the Advertising Process Circle introduced in Figure 1.1. As we shall see, the emotion shown by people in advertising (Message Sources) and the emotional responses of those exposed to it (Receivers) will inform how it is processed; and, it will be part of every appeal (Messages) and influence a number of message effects (Effects).

People experience a wide range of emotions, and many of these emotions are involuntarily expressed in things like facial expression, tone of voice, and body posture. Neuroscientists working with emotion may argue over specific emotions, but there is general agreement that there are primary emotions, along with other secondary or social emotions. Primary emotions like anger, fear, disgust, surprise, sadness, and joy are basic to all humans, and easily visible in one's demeanor. Other emotions such as guilt, pride, envy, and so forth may be experienced by everyone, but how they are interpreted within a culture can differ. For example, in Western cultures there is a strong correlation between guilt and responsibility, but in other cultures guilt is not linked to responsibility.

In this chapter we will first take a broad look at the way in which emotion is involved in how information is processed, paying particular attention to the role of the amygdala. Then we examine the close relationship between emotion and motivation. This is important because effective advertising must elicit the appropriate emotions, consistent with the motivation driving the purchase decision for the advertised product. It also bears upon the choice of creative tactics needed to optimize the likelihood of eliciting that emotion. With this as a foundation, we then explore how emotion is specifically involved in the processing of advertising, paying particular attention to the embodiment of emotion.

Emotion and Processing

In many ways, what we are really dealing with when talking about processing is *memory*. Conscious processing involves the use of declarative or "explicit" memory, and reflects what is known as "top-down" processing. Unconscious processing involves nondeclarative or "implicit" memory, and generally reflects what is called "bottom-up" processing. As we shall see, emotion is generally considered as part of nondeclarative memory.

Declarative and nondeclarative memories recruit different brain systems and use different strategies for storing memory (Heilman, 2002). Our declarative memory is for facts, assumptions, and events, the sorts of things that one can bring consciously to mind as either a verbal proposition ("that is an expensive, luxury product") or a visual image (in our mind's eye we "see" the product). Nondeclarative memories also come from experiences, but they are not expressed in terms of conscious recollections. With the exception of emotion, nondeclarative memories are generally inaccessible to the conscious mind. Such memories tend to involve knowledge that is *reflexive* rather than *reflective* in nature (Heilman, 2002). Importantly, in terms of advertising and brand learning, once something is stored in nondeclarative memory, that unconscious memory *never* becomes conscious.

The Role of the Amygdala

Recent research on emotional memory has focused specifically on pathways through the amygdala, which lies in the medial temporal lobe, in front of the hippocampus, and surrounded by the parahippocampal cortical region (Eichenbaum, 2002). The amygdala provides an important interface between visual and auditory stimuli, and in triggering emotional responses. As Winston and Dulan (2004) describe it, "the human amygdala is a crucial locus in associating stimuli with their appropriate emotional value" (p. 216). Attention to advertising, whether consciously or unconsciously, will activate emotional associations with elements within the advertisement (such as the visual images used and the brand name) that are stored in nondeclarative emotional memory.

This reflects a critical component of the nondeclarative emotional memory trace, its plasticity. This is what enables it to support emotional memories in the absence of conscious recollection. Emotional memory associations will be integrated into conscious cognitive processes that play a role in motivating considered action plans rather than just triggering rapid, reflective responses associated with other unconscious emotional memories.

When someone is exposed to an advertisement, both conscious cognitive associations in memory, as well as nondeclarative emotional memories linked to these memories, will be activated. In fact, the emotional memories will precede the cognitively based, hippocampal-dependent explicit memories into working memory for processing the message. When an advertisement activates associations in memory linked to the brand and imagery presented, the emotional memories associated with those explicit cognitive memories will immediately and unconsciously move into working memory, *ahead* of the cognitive associations, as active processing of the advertising begins. This is illustrated in Figure 5.1.

In effect, the emotional memories help frame how we process conscious memories and the words and images of an advertisement. Before we leave this concept, it is important to realize that while positive emotional associations in memory may certainly inform a positive response to an advertisement, they do not necessarily have the ability to "override" more compelling negative conscious considerations. If there is something in the message that elicits a negative cognitive response (an undesired feature, say), even though the initial emotional response to the advertising was positive because of positive emotional

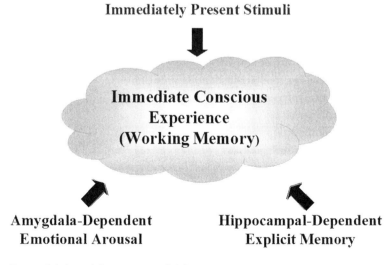

Figure 5.1 Initial Processing of Advertising.

associations with the brand or visual imagery within the execution, the new counter-attitudinal information will override the initial positive framing.

Although the amygdala is generally thought to be the key to emotional response, other areas of the brain are also believed to be involved in the perception of emotion (and other information) from facial expression, which is something we will cover later in this chapter. Neuroimaging studies have indicated medial prefrontal and orbitofrontal cortex activation by facial expression, including the anterior cingulate, insula, and regions of the occipital cortex, especially the fusiforum gyrus (Del-Ben et al., 2005).

A look at Figure 5.2 will provide a general idea of where these areas are located in the brain. While the amygdala plays the most important role, a number of other areas spread throughout the brain are involved. It is the two-way interaction between the amygdala and the cortex that permits emotion to be "felt," and for conscious thoughts to effect emotion. The specific emotion experienced depends upon which part of the cortex is activated. Different aspects of an advertising execution will have the potential of activating different parts, leading to potentially different effects.

It has also been suggested that the orbital frontal cortex plays an important role in interpreting emotion in facial expression for social reinforcement (Rolls, 1999). Additionally, accurate recognition of more complex emotions, as expressed in facial expression, may involve the somatusensory cortex, particularly the right somatusensory cortex that curls around the top of the brain like a horseshoe (Adolphs, 1999).

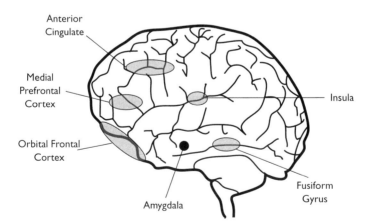

Figure 5.2 Cortical Brain Areas Believed to be Involved in the Perception of Emotion from Facial Expression.

Emotion and Motivation

Emotion and motivation are importantly linked, and this association will inform how advertising is processed. As Frijda (2004) noted, emotion *involves* motivation, accounting as it does for two distinct sets of phenomena in emotion that reflect the two traditional hallmarks of motivation: intent and the energizing of behavior. Changes in motivation and the appraisal processes that trigger them are linked to emotion. Clore and Ortony (2000) have gone so far as to suggest that emotion includes a motivational-behavioral component. A fundamental dimension of both emotion and motivation is that of approach avoidance (Lang, Bradley, & Cuthbert, 1990). Someone could be motivated by the expectation of a reward, and this would excite a feeling of happiness (approach); or fear could motivate someone to work harder to hold their job in difficult economic times (avoidance). In fact, many theorists see the link between emotion and motivation in terms of approach avoidance (Gray, Schaefer, Braver, & Most, 2005).

Rossiter and Percy (1991) long ago addressed this approach avoidance connection between emotion and motivation for advertising in terms of Hammond's reconceptualization of Mowrer's theory of emotion. For Mowrer (1960a, 1960b) emotion is a key to learning, drives that are associated with specific eliciting conditions. While they would not be considered so today, he saw fear, hope, relief, and disappointment as the fundamental emotions. External stimulus changes that might elicit emotions such as hope and relief were thought to stimulate approach behavior, while fear and disappointment were thought to stimulate avoidance behavior. If someone senses the possibility of danger, fear will be elicited. When the potential danger passes, they will experience relief. In the expectation of being safe, hope will be elicited; but if that expectation passes, disappointment will be experienced (see Figure 5.3).

Hammond's (1970) work was informed by Mowrer's notion that rewarding events lead to drive reduction and punishing events lead to drive induction. But he reworked Mowrer's original formulations, suggesting that stimuli likely to increase the occurrence of an adverse state or the occurrence of a rewarding

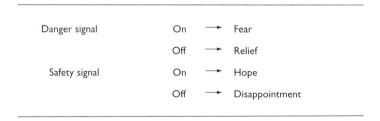

Figure 5.3 Mowrer's Theory of Emotion.

state will be *excitatory*, eliciting fear or hope. Stimuli that are likely to decrease the likelihood of either an adverse or rewarding state will be *inhibitory*, eliciting relief or disappointment (see Figure 5.4).

This fits nicely with the homeostatic concept of motivation advanced by Rossiter and Percy (1987) in which there are two fundamental motivating mechanisms, one positive and one negative. This homeostatic view follows directly from a need for advertising to facilitate the formation or reinforcement of a positive brand attitude, which is consistent with the appropriate motivation driving behavior in the category. As we shall see later on, this will inform the need for the emotional response to advertising to be not only consistent with the correct motivation, but to also reflect the correct *sequence* of emotion, as implied by Hammond's work.

Emotion and Advertising

As we have seen, emotion is an essential part of rational decision-making and behavior, which should put paid to the all-too-often erroneous distinction made between so-called "rational versus emotional" advertising. *All advertising is "emotional."* Both conscious explicit memory and nondeclarative emotional memory will be activated by an advertisement. Emotional associations are detected very fast, ahead of selective attention (e.g., work by Vuilleumier, Armary, Driver, & Dolan, 2001). One of the roles of the amygdala, noted earlier, is to link pre-perceptual or pre-attentive sensory processing with emotion. In the split second it takes to attend to something, its emotional significance is retained and evaluated, influencing how it is encoded. It is essential, if advertising is to be effectively processed, that the appropriate emotional response is elicited. This requires understanding the emotional significance of the executional elements involved by identifying those emotional associations linked to the brand, as well as key visual images to be included in an execution.

The images and text in advertising will elicit emotional associations from memory, as we have discussed. Nondeclarative emotional memories precede top-down hippocampus-dependent explicit memories into working memory in

Figure 5.4 Hammond's Reconceptualization of Mowrer's Theory of Emotion.

response to an advertisement. These emotional associations help frame how the message is processed. This means that when an advertisement elicits emotional associations with the brand and the images present in an execution, those emotional memories will immediately and unconsciously enter working memory before active, conscious processing of the advertising begins. From this processing, new associations in memory, both explicit and emotional, are possible. Any emotional learning that does occur, if linked to the brand, will then be in place to be activated when there is exposure to new advertising for the brand, when the brand is confronted at the point-of-purchase, or even when one is just "thinking" about the brand.

It should be pointed out that even if advertising is not consciously processed, processing may occur unconsciously in spite of a conscious or unconscious decision not to pay attention to the advertisement. In the time it takes to decide not to pay attention to an advertisement, the emotional response to it will still have been constructed in memory. But we must caution that we are *not* talking about implicit learning or memory here, except to the extent that one considers emotion as part of implicit memory. While there has been some suggestion over the last few years that unconscious attention and learning gives advertising a much stronger impact than is generally measured, appealing as that idea may seem, the neurology of implicit learning and memory militate against it (Bailey & Kandel, 2004). Even if some implicit learning did occur, the nature of the neural systems involved suggests that implicit memory would have no effect upon brand attitude or behavior. The only exceptions are nondeclarative emotional memories, which are generally considered as part of implicit memory (Percy, 2006).

Motivation

The important relationship between emotion and motivation bears directly upon how advertising will be processed. Depending upon the underlying motivation driving category behavior, specific creative tactics will be needed to insure optimum processing, and these will differ between positive and negative motivation. This is because when dealing with negatively motivated behavior, emotional response follows *indirectly* from an evaluation of the benefit claim. But when dealing with positively motivated behavior, the emotional response follows *directly* from the executional elements within the advertisement. The creative tactics used must reflect this (for a detailed discussion of the appropriate creative tactics needed in each case, see Rossiter & Percy, 1997).

For example, think about an advertisement for toothpaste that claims to "whiten teeth," a benefit claim reflecting a negative motivation such as problem removal. The emotional responses elicited will be indirectly associated with the benefit of whiter teeth "solving" a problem. On the other hand, consider an advertisement for ice cream. Here, we are dealing with the positive motivation of sensory gratification, and the emotional response will follow directly from how well the execution itself is able to elicit the emotion. In effect, the benefit is in the execution. It is the positive "feeling" resulting from the emotion elicited by the execution (showing, say, someone in obvious rapture while eating the ice cream). That is the benefit. It will be this "feeling" that is re-experienced when you think about the brand or it is seen at the point of purchase, and you think maybe I will feel like that too if I eat this ice cream.

While the emotional responses to stimuli are very specific, one can nonetheless look for certain types of emotion to be associated with particular motivations, very much in the spirit of Hammond's reconceptualization of Mowrer's theory. Negative motivations such as problem removal or problem avoidance are likely to follow an "annoyed" or "fearful" to "relieved" or "relaxed" sequence of emotional response. A problem occurs, thereby arousing negative emotions, followed by relief, as the problem is solved. With positive motivations, such as sensory gratification, the emotional sequence is likely to move from a dull or neutral state to one of joy or happiness.

Perhaps the most important insight here for advertising is that building or sustaining positive brand attitude through effective processing of advertising requires the eliciting of a *sequence* of emotional responses. It is inappropriate to think only in terms of a single emotion, or more precisely a single emotional state. What is likely to be involved in the optimum processing of advertising is a transfer from one emotional state to another, and this must be facilitated by the execution.

Rossiter and Percy (1987) proposed a set of specific emotional sequences that could be associated with particular negative and positive motivations for advertising executions, and some empirical support for these sequences was found by Kover and Abruzzo (1993). There is no doubt that advertising, like any stimulus, will elicit nondeclarative emotional memories, and that these will be related to motivation. But, as noted earlier, these emotional responses are *specific*, not general. Nevertheless, certain categories of emotional response sequences do seem to make sense (see Figure 5.5).

Advertising for Michelin Tires over the years provides a good example of what we are talking about. Many of their advertisements follow a "fearful to relaxed" emotional sequence, consistent with the underlying problem-avoidance motivation driving tire choice. In one commercial, a mother and small child are driving on a very dark, windy, and rainy night, evoking "fear" for their safety, reinforced by the anxious expression on the mother's face (which will be embodied by the viewer, as we shall see in the next section). This fear is resolved by reminding the viewer that with Michelin tires, you can "relax," avoiding problems with slippery roads.

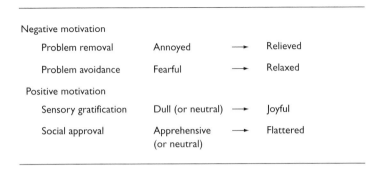

Negative motivation			
Problem removal	Annoyed	→	Relieved
Problem avoidance	Fearful	→	Relaxed
Positive motivation			
Sensory gratification	Dull (or neutral)	→	Joyful
Social approval	Apprehensive (or neutral)	→	Flattered

Figure 5.5 Emotional Sequences Associated with Motivation Appropriate for Advertising Executions (source: adapted from Rossiter and Percy, 1991).

Embodiment

Another important consideration in helping to elicit an appropriate emotional response to advertising is to insure that the people shown in an execution project the desired emotion. How a target audience perceives the emotional state of those shown in an advertisement will be used by them in interpreting and evaluating the emotional significance of what is going on in the advertisement, and will inform their own emotional response. This follows from the idea of emotional embodiment.

In effect, people will take on or imitate, i.e., "embody," the emotional behaviors they perceive in someone, from their facial expression, body language, or tone of voice. A large body of work over the last 30 years has consistently found facial, postural, and prosodic embodiment. For example, listening to someone talking in a happy versus sad voice will likely produce the same emotion in those listening (Neumann & Strack, 2000).

Other people's emotions influence our own by virtue of the information they convey (e.g., fear will convey danger or threat, happiness, safety or comfort), and this has been critical to our survival as a species. Primary emotions (such as surprise, fear, disgust, anger, happiness, or sadness) are phylogenetically ancient, informationally encapsulated reflex-like responses that are unrelated to culture. When facial expressions reflecting primary emotions are shown to people in countries all over the world, reflecting a wide range of cultural backgrounds, all agree on the emotional meaning conveyed (cf. Ekman, 2003). This is a human response, unrelated to any particular culture.

We have discussed the key role the amygdala plays in emotion. It is part of the limbic system, which is a neural system that was in place before language evolved, and which has been critical to our survival as a species. In man's earliest days, it was important to be able to interpret other people's emotions in order to know whether or not they were in a potentially dangerous situation, or whether positive social interaction would be possible. Correctly reading those situations could very well have meant the difference between life and death. While we may not need this ability today for survival, it does still operate because the limbic system does not know time. These innate responses are still in place. If, for example, fear is aroused by an advertisement, so will our defenses, looking for a solution; if happiness, we will be more open to the message, wanting to be part of it.

Niedenthal and her colleagues (Niedenthal, Barsalou, Ric, & Krauth-Gruber, 2005) have summarized evidence that people embody other people's emotional behavior, that the embodied emotion produces a corresponding emotional state in that person; imagining other people and events also produces embodied emotion and corresponding feelings; and embodied emotions mediate cognitive responses. Each of these consequences of emotion has direct bearing on the processing of advertising. The emotion expressed (if authentic, as we shall discuss later) by people shown in advertisements will be "felt" by those exposed to advertising and the feelings aroused by the embedded emotion will then inform cognitive responses to the advertising. Even if people think about the advertising later, or about the brand as informed by the advertising, the original embodied emotions will be retrieved from nondeclarative emotional memory, and help inform their thinking.

As an embodied emotional state triggers a felt emotion, it biases cognitive operations toward states consistent with that emotion. A smiling face, for example, will activate a corresponding smile in response, a tendency for approach behavior, and positive valances, leading to happiness and liking. As the smile is visually imaged, the emotion used to interpret the smile reflects the embodied state that has been activated. Perceived, authentic smiles of happiness in advertisements should lay a favorable foundation for processing the message as the receiver "feels" the positive emotional response.

There has been some suggestion that a mechanism similar to the idea of mirror neurons may apply to emotion. In a study looking at disgust, it was found that people who experienced that emotion show brain activation in areas that are similar to those activated when seeing someone else experiencing the same emotion: the left interior insular and right anterior cortex (part of the limbic system). The study concluded that this is a mirroring of the emotion involved, not a recreation of an observed goal or action (Wicker et al., 2003). Regardless of whether something like mirror neurons are being stimulated by an advertisement, advertising will stimulate an emotional response.

Facial Expression

The most prominent emotional object studied in the emotional literature is facial expression (deGelder, 2005). Among the major theoretical hypotheses in the area of emotional communication, the strongest support is for the facial feedback hypothesis (Camras, Holland, & Patterson, 1993). It suggests that there could be proprioceptive, cutaneous neural feedback, or vascular feedback, from facial expression influencing emotional experience since discrete emotions produce distinct expressions through sensory information conveyed to facial musculature. This feedback could then either create the same experience or simply influence it (Strongman, 2003).

People have a very efficient system for recognizing and processing the emotional content of facial expressions. As with all emotional responses it is the amygdala that is at the heart of processing and responding to the emotional significance of facial expression. In fMRI studies it has been shown that there is a significant increase in the activation of the left amygdala when exposed to either a happy or threatening face, when compared with a neutral face (Wright, Martis, Shin, Fischer, & Rauch, 2002).

There appears to be a direct pathway from the retina to the amygdala, involving the superior colliculus and pulvinar, but bypassing the striate area of the visual cortex. It is this subcortical pathway that seems to be involved in the processing of information about the emotional states of other people, especially as communicated through facial expressions. Figure 5.6 illustrates how the superior colliculus and pulvinar lie below the cerebral cortex, in the subcortical area of the diencephelon, just above the brain stem.

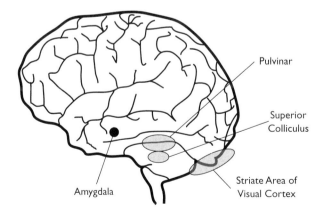

Figure 5.6 Subcortical Brain Areas Involved in a Direct Line from the Retina to the Amygdala in Processing the Emotional State of Others Bypassing the Visual Cortex.

Processing of emotional information from facial expressions seems to occur without any involvement of the visual cortex, and as some have suggested, without conscious awareness. Recent studies do appear to support the idea that there is a subcortical pathway to the amygdala, and that it is a neural substrate of unconscious emotional perception (Pasley, Mayer, & Schultz, 2004). However, it is important to remember that even when affective cues, such as facial expressions, are unconscious, they nevertheless gain their power primarily through interpretive (i.e., cognitive) processes (Clore & Colcombe, 2003).

Work by Aronoff and his colleagues (1988) found that specific geometrical properties in visual display carry critical information in determining the emotional valiance of facial expressions, and this is what provides the cues in facial expression that trigger emotional embodiment. Based upon this work, Lundqvist and Linton (as reported in Lundqvist & Öhman, 2005) created a set of schematic faces in order to study the role of eyebrows, eyes, and the mouth in conveying either happy or threatening faces.

What they found was that V-shaped eyebrows elicited a negative, threatening emotion while U-shaped eyebrows elicited a friendly, positive, emotional response. They also found that a U-shaped mouth elicited a happy feeling while a V-shaped mouth elicited an unhappy feeling. Overall, it was the V-shaped eyebrows that played the central role in communicating a negative or threatening face, and a U-shaped mouth a positive, happy face. These findings were supported by eye-tracking data that showed fixations concentrated around eyebrows when people were exposed to threatening faces and around the mouth area for happy faces. This has been further supported by image analysis of the response to the facial expressions of real people (Lundqvist & Öhman, 2005).

All of this too, of course, has important implications for advertising. Unfortunately, actors, even experienced actors, have difficulty realistically projecting emotions that are not "felt." This is especially true of smiles, owing to their evolutionary importance. Facial muscles that control smiles respond to two distinct neural systems. The evolutionary older system originates in the striatum and exerts involuntary control of facial muscles (Fridlund, 1994). The other system is evolutionarily newer, and involves voluntarily controlled muscles (Gazzaniga & Smylie, 1990).

Duchenne Smile

As a consequence of these different neural systems, intentional social smiles such as those an actor might show do not necessarily reflect a true or felt positive feeling. Voluntary smiles need only involve the mouth. Truly felt positive emotions such as happiness will also involve the muscles around the eye, and such smiles are known as "Duchenne Smiles" after the nineteenth-century anatomist who first wrote about it.

As Ekman (2003) has put it, this type of smiling is believed to occur only when someone experiences true enjoyment. It is distinguished by the combined activity of the orbicularis oculi muscle that orbits the eye, responding to the underlying emotion as well as the voluntary or intentional action of the zyomaticus major muscle that pulls up the corners of the lip. A true Duchenne Smile is an unintentional emotional signal that occurs spontaneously upon experiencing a positive feeling of happiness or joy, reflecting a true emotional state.

To be effectively embodied, emotions expressed by people smiling in advertisements must be truly felt. Only in this way can one be sure it will be seen as "real." Rossiter and Percy (1987) introduced this idea of emotional authenticity in advertising, critical for transformational advertisements (those addressing positive motivations) some time ago. We have all seen advertising where the smiles on people's faces are anything but "real." It is highly unlikely that such advertising will elicit a positive emotional response in the receiver.

Eye Gaze

Another consideration in the embodiment of emotion in facial expression is eye gaze. Following from theory of mind, for example, a person can make a well-informed guess about what someone is attending to and thinking about by perceiving that person's gaze. Haxby and his colleagues in their model of the distributed human neural system for face perception (Haxby, Hoffman, & Gobbini, 2000) do, in fact, suggest that processing the emotion content of a face and the invocation of an emotional response to it will be based on several changeable aspects of the face, including eye gaze (Haxby, Hoffman, & Gobbini, 2002). Coincidentally, the perception of a direct gaze does seem to elicit a response in the amygdala (Kawashima et al., 1999). Clearly, this is an area to be explored, and one perhaps suited to an fMRI experiment. Additionally, we know that gaze *aversion* is part of a universal gesture of embarrassment, and when observed, will elicit an attempt to help (Niedenthal, Krauth-Gruber, & Ric, 2006).

Conclusion

In this chapter, we have looked at the important role of emotion in the processing of advertising. Emotion plays a central role as an organizing force in our lives, with emotional memories associated with most aspects of our experience. These emotional memories will be a part of our responses to advertising, linked to associations with the brand and various aspects of an execution. The key to these emotional memories and responses is the amygdala, part of the limbic system and the paleomammalian mind, which has been central to our survival as a species. While responses to advertising clearly are not tied to our survival, nevertheless, the emotional responses to it are deeply rooted in primal processes.

Because of the critical role emotion plays in processing, it is essential to be able to anticipate the likely responses to an execution. In addition to our understanding of the emotional associations with a brand and specific key executional elements, it is important to use creative tactics appropriate to the underlying motivation driving category behavior. This follows from the strong connection between emotion and motivation and the approach-avoidance dimension common to both. It is because of this that a *sequence* of emotions, not a single emotion, is involved and must be accounted for in an execution. Beyond specific creative tactics, we have also seen how the receiver will embody prosody, body posture, and especially facial expression, and inform how they respond to and process advertising.

In summary, advertising will elicit emotional responses, and those responses will inform how it is processed. To be effective, advertising must utilize creative tactics that will optimize the likelihood of insuring the correct emotion— motivation association is reflected in the execution, and that the appropriate emotion will be embodied by the receiver from the facial expression of people shown in the advertising.

References

Adolphs, R. (1999). Social cognition and the human brain. *Trends in Cognitive Science, 3,* 469–479.

Aronoff, J., Barclay, A. M., & Stevenson, L. A. (1988). The recognition of threatening facial stimuli. *Journal of Personality and Social Psychology, 54,* 647–655.

Bailey, C. H., & Kendel, E. R. (2004). Synaptic growth and the persistence of long-term memory: A molecular perspective. In M. S. Gazaniga (Ed.), *The cognitive neurosciences III* (pp. 647–683). Cambridge, MA: MIT Press.

Camras, L. A., Holland, E. A., & Patterson, M. J. (1993). Facial expressions. In M. Lewis & J. M. Hoviland (Eds.), *Handbook of emotions* (pp. 199–208). New York: Guilford Press.

Clore, G. L., & Colcombe, S. (2003). The parallel worlds of affective concepts and feelings. In J. Musch & K. C. Klaver (Eds.), *The psychology of evaluative processes in cognition and emotion* (pp. 355–369). Mahwah, NJ: Erlbaum.

Clore, G. L., & Ortony, A. (2000). Cognition in emotion: Always, sometimes, or never? In R. D. Lane & L. Nadel (Eds.), *Cognitive neuroscience of emotion* (pp. 24–61). Oxford, UK: Oxford University Press.

deGelder, B. (2005). Nonconscious emotions: New findings and perspectives on nonconscious facial expression recognition and its voice and whole-body contexts. In L. Barrett, P. M. Niedenthal, & P. Winkielman (Eds.), *Emotion and consciousness* (pp. 123–149). New York: Guilford Press.

Del-Ben, C. M., Deakin, J. F. W., McKie, S., Delvai, N. A., Williams, S. R., Elliott, et al. (2005). The effect of citalopram pretreatment on neural responses to neuropsychological tasks in normal volunteers: An fMRI study. *Neuropsychopharmacology, 30*, 1724–1734.

Eichenbaum, H. (2002). *The cognitive neuroscience of memory.* Oxford, UK: Oxford University Press.

Ekman, P. (2003). *Emotions revealed: Recognizing faces and feelings to improve communication and emotional life.* New York: Times Books.

Fridlund, A. J. (1994). *Human facial expressions: An evolutionary view.* New York: Academic Press.

Frijda, N. H. (2004). Emotion and action. In A. S. R. Manstead, N. Frijda, & A. Fischer (Eds.), *Feelings and emotions: The Amsterdam symposium* (pp. 158–173). Cambridge, UK: Cambridge University Press.

Gazzaniga, M. S., & Smylie, C. S. (1990). Hemispheric mechanisms controlling voluntary and spontaneous facial expressions. *Journal of Cognitive Neuroscience, 2*, 239–245.

Gray, J. R., Schaefer, A., Braver, T. S., & Most, S. B. (2005). Affect and the resolution of cognitive control dilemma. In L. F. Barrett, P. M. Niedenthal, & P. Winkielman (Eds.), *Emotion and consciousness* (pp. 67–94). New York: Guilford Press.

Hammond, L. J. (1970). Conditional emotional states. In P. Black (Ed.), *Physiological correlation of emotion* (Ch. 12). New York: Academic Press.

Haxby, J. V., Hoffman, E. A., & Gobbini, M. I. (2000). The distributed human neural system for face perception. *Trends in Cognitive Science, 4*, 223–233.

Haxby, J. V., Hoffman, E. A., & Gobbini, M. I. (2002). Human neural system for face recognition and social communication. *Biological Psychiatry, 51*, 59–67.

Heilman, K. M. (2002). *Matter of mind.* Oxford, UK: Oxford University Press.

Kawashima, R., Sugiura, M., Kato, T., Nakamura, A., Hatano, K., Ito, K., et al. (1999). The human amygdala plays an important role in gaze monitoring: A PET study. *Brain, 122*, 779–783.

Kover, A. J., & Abruzzo, J. (1993). The Rossiter–Percy Grid and emotional response to advertising: An initial evaluation. *Journal of Advertising Research, 33* (6), 21–27.

Lang, P. J., Bradley, M. M., & Cuthbert, B. N. (1990). Emotion, attention, and the startle reflex. *Psychological Review, 97*, 377–395.

Lundqvist, D., & Öhman, A. (2005). Caught by the evil eye: Nonconscious information processing, emotion, and attention to facial stimuli. In L. F. Barnett, P. M. Niedenthal, & P. Winkielman (Eds.), *Emotion and consciousness* (pp. 97–122). New York: Guilford Press.

Mowrer, O. H. (1960a) *Learning theory and behaviour.* New York: Wiley.

Mowrer, O. H. (1960b) *Learning theory and symbolic process.* New York: Wiley.

Niedenthal, P. M., Krauth-Gruber, S., & Ric, F. (2006). *Psychology of emotion.* New York: Psychology Press.

Niedenthal, P. M., Barsalou, L. W., Ric, F., & Krauth-Gruber, S. (2005). Embodiment in acquisition and use of emotion knowledge. In L. Bartlett, P. M. Niedenthal, & P. Winkielman (Eds.), *Emotion and consciousness* (pp. 21–50). New York: Guilford Press.

Neuman, R., & Strack, F. (2000). Mood contagion: The automatic transfer of mood between persons. *Journal of Personality and Social Psychology, 79*, 211–223.

Pasley, B. N., Mayer, L. C., & Schultz, R. T. (2004). Subcortical discrimination of perceived objects during binocular rivalry. *Neuron, 42*, 163–172.

Percy, L. (2006). Unconscious processing of advertising and its effects upon attitudes and behavior. In S. Drehl & R. Terlutter (Eds.), *International advertising and communication* (pp. 110–121). Wiesbader, Germany: Deutcher Universitäter-Verlay.

Rolls, E. T. (1999). *The brain and emotion.* Oxford, UK: Oxford University Press.

Rossiter, J. R., & Percy, L. (1987). *Advertising and promotion management.* New York: McGraw-Hill.

Rossiter, J. R., & Percy, L. (1991). Emotions and motivation in advertising. In R. H. Holman & M. R. Soloman (Eds.), *Advances in consumer research* (pp. 100–110). Provo, UT: Association for Consumer Research.

Rossiter, J. R., & Percy, L. (1997). *Advertising communication and promotion management* (2nd ed.). New York: McGraw-Hill.

Strongman, K. T. (2003). *The psychology of emotion: From everyday life to theory* (5th ed.). Chichester, England: John Wity and Sons.

Vuilleumier, P., Armary, J. L., Driver, J., & Dolan, R. J. (2001). Effects of attention and emotion on face processing in the human brain: An event-related fMRI study. *Neuron, 30*, 829–841.

Wicker, B., Keysus, C., Plailly, J., Royet, J.-P., Gallese, V., & Rizzolatti, G. (2003). Both of us disgusted in my insula: The common neural bias of seeing and feeling disgust. *Neuron, 4*, 655–664.

Winston, J. S., & Dulan, R. J. (2004). Feeling states in emotion: Functional imaging evidence. In A. S. S. Manstead, N. Frijda, & A. Fischer (Eds.), *Feeling and emotion* (p. 216). Cambridge, UK: Cambridge University Press.

Wright, C. H., Martis, B., Shin, L. M., Fischer, H., & Rauch, S. L. (2002). Enhanced amygdala responses to emotional versus neutral schematic facial expressions. *Neuroreport, 13*, 785–790.

Additional Readings

Darwin, C. (1998). *The expression of emotions in man and animals* (3rd ed.). Oxford, UK: Oxford University Press.

Damasio, A. (1999). *The feeling of what happens: Body and emotion in the making of consciousness.* San Diego, CA: Harcourt, Inc.

Parkinson, B., Fischer, A. H., & Manstead, A. S. R. (2005). *Emotion in social relations.* New York: Psychology Press.

Percy, L., & Elliott, R. (2009). *Strategic advertising management* (3rd ed., Ch. 11 & 12). Oxford, UK: Oxford University Press.

Rizzolatti, G., & Sinigaglia, C. (2008). *Mirrors in the brain.* Oxford, UK: Oxford University Press

Chapter 6

Theories of Emotion and Affect in Marketing Communications

Jon D. Morris

Introduction

Emotions, unlike rational thought and behavior, are personal. They cannot be shared. There are emotional response measures for sure, but that feeling that is generated in reaction to a stimulus may be described and calculated, but unlike facts, "do you choose the item" yes or no, cannot be transmitted. Although there is this restriction, there is a complex process in the human brain that directs much of the interaction with the environment.

> On a single day, the average person can experience an extraordinary range of emotions—from happiness to sadness and from pride to guilt—and these experiences are often subtle and nuanced. It is this complexity and subtlety that makes the study of emotions so challenging. Indeed, there has been much debate about the very definition of emotion and the processes that produce it.
>
> (Stewart, Morris, & Grover, 2007)

The subject of emotion in communications is widespread (Dillard & Peck, 2000); and mass communication researchers have produced evidence of the direct and powerful influence of emotion in persuasive communications (Morris, Woo, Geason, & Kim, 2002).

Measuring emotional response in advertising seems less interesting to practitioners than other well-known and habitual marketing measures such as persuasion, intentions, and recall. Marketing communications research is all about the behavior rather than the emotional state that created it (Petty & Cacioppo, 1996; Lippmann, 1922; Lasswell, 1927).

But measures of affect as well as information should be a part of the research on persuasion. Though persuasion researchers are split into the camps supporting information processing, affect, or both, they all agree that "the most distinctive and indispensable concept in contemporary social psychology" (Allport, 1935) is that of a variable called attitude.

A change in attitude has often been linked to intended behavior and behavioral changes, but until recent years there were several studies that appeared to show that attitudes were not able to predict behaviors. And, in fact, the mid 1970s were filled with disillusionment about the attitude concept. As a result, in that period, there was a sharp decline in the study of attitudes by social psychologists. However, Fishbein and Ajzen (1975; Ajzen & Fishbein, 1977; Ajzen & Fishbein, 1980) were able to conclude, with confidence, that attitudes and behaviors were strongly linked.

What distinguished attitude from other concepts was its strongly affective nature and that "affect is the most essential part of the attitude concept" (Fishbein & Ajzen, 1975). In the mid 1980s, a direct relationship between attitudes and behavior was established, albeit cognitively (Petty & Cacioppo, 1986), but then in 2002, Morris and his colleagues showed a strong link between affective attitude and behavioral intentions.

The Role of Emotion in Persuasion

The role of emotion in response to persuasive messages and as a predictor of subsequent behavior is a relatively new field of interest for researchers. Some of the early studies that influenced communications and attitude formation research ignored or downplayed affect (Fishbein, 1963; Fishbein & Middlestadt, 1995). According to the model, attitudes can be determined by salient cognitive beliefs (i.e., Aspirin is safe) and the evaluation of those beliefs (i.e., Safety is very important).

Holbrook (1978) included affect in his model of behavior, but he gave it a secondary role. He theorized that a cognitive appraisal occurs in response to a stimulus, which then leads to an evaluation of the stimulus. The evaluation is followed by physiological changes and, finally, to subjective feelings (Holbrook & O'Shaughnessy, 1984).

The Elaboration Likelihood Model (ELM) established by Petty and Cacioppo (1981) suggested that affective reactions to persuasive messages can influence attitude under certain conditions. The model presented two routes to attitude formation: central and peripheral. The central route emphasizes information about an object and the evaluation of that information, similar to the Fishbein model. The peripheral route relies more on affective response to non-factual information like special effects or a beautiful background.

One of the earliest studies to highlight the importance of emotion was a study by Zajonc (1980). He argued that emotion may precede cognition and be entirely separate from it. He pointed to the mere exposure effect, which shows that repeated exposure increases liking of a stimulus even in the absence of recognition of the stimulus.

Shimp (1981) introduced a new component into the attitude formation literature: attitude toward the ad (A_{ad}). He distinguished between advertising that influences A_{ad} or liking of the ad and advertising that influences attitude toward the brand A_B or liking of the brand. The latter attempts to build positive perceptions of the brand by showing favorable attributes and matching these attributes to consumer needs and wants. On the other hand, advertising that focuses on A_{ad} creates a positive feeling toward the ad itself which is then transferred to the brand.

Lutz (1985) studied the determinants of A_{ad}. He stated that A_{ad} includes reactions to the advertising stimulus that are not cognitive, such as mood at the time of exposure. According to Lutz, A_{ad} mediates the impact of both emotions and cognition on brand attitude.

Edell and Burke (1987) proposed that emotions represent a dimension of A_{ad} entirely separate from thoughts about the ad. Using a feelings scale that contained a list of 169 different feelings, subjects rated their experience of each feeling on a scale from one to five for each ad. They performed the experiment using both existing and fictional brands. They found that emotions account for unexplained variance in A_{ad} and A_B, and positive and negative feelings can occur simultaneously during ad exposure and have separate effects on summary responses. They also discovered that emotion was just as important for informational ads as it was for transformational ads designed to generate feelings. Edell and Burke (1987) recommended adding a feelings scale to existing models of attitude measures, which improves the A_{ad} construct.

Holbrook and Batra (1987) also looked at emotional response as a mediator of ad content on A_{ad} and A_B. Using ads as units of observation instead of people, they assumed that ads have "emotional profiles" and that people respond homogeneously to these profiles. They content analyzed ads into six groups (emotional, threatening, mundane, sexy, cerebral, and personal) and they measured three dimensions of emotion (pleasure, arousal, and dominance) based on previous studies (Mehrabian & Russell, 1977). They found a link between content factors, emotional dimensions, A_{ad}, and A_B. Their results indicated that the three dimensions of emotions are clear mediators of ad content on A_{ad}, and they also recognized a possible link between emotion and A_B.

Stayman and Aaker (1988) proposed that A_{ad} does not account for all of the emotions generated during ad exposure. They found that A_{ad} does not completely mediate the effect of emotional responses on brand attitude. Burke and Edell (1989) also found that effects of some of the feelings generated by ads could not be accounted for by A_{ad} and therefore influence A_B directly. Thus, measuring A_{ad} without measuring emotional response ignores an important element in creating positive brand perceptions.

Because studies have shown that emotional response influences attitudes, intentions, and behavior, further studies have measured emotional response to determine important information about ads. Morris (1994) found that emotional responses to storyboards and animatics are reliable representations of emotional responses to finished commercials, showing that preproduction tests of ads are good indicators of the success of the final ads. Other research used emotional response measurements to find differences between groups. Morris, Roberts, and Baker (1993) tested African Americans' emotional responses to political ads and discovered differences between older and younger generations. Another study (Morris, Bradley, & Wei, 1994) detected cultural differences in emotional response to advertising between Americans and Taiwanese-Chinese. Significant differences were found in ads that were rated the most highly emotional by American standards. However, in another study, little difference was found between males and females in emotional response to television ads and PSAs (Morris, 1994).

Measuring Emotions

As the importance of measuring emotional reactions in marketing communications becomes apparent, researchers are seeking an effective useful scale. Some studies have attempted to devise lists of the emotions that consumers experience when they encounter ads (Aaker, Stayman, & Vezina, 1988; Zeitlin & Westwood, 1986). However, it is difficult, if not impossible, to create an exhaustive list of the full spectrum of emotions that ads generate, which makes such studies problematic. Furthermore, the large number of emotions or emotion clusters on these lists makes them unwieldy for research purposes although some researchers continue to support this approach (Nabi, 2010). Rather than looking at specific emotional categories, other researchers have attempted to find the underlying dimensions of emotion (Bolls, 2010).

A three-dimensional concept of emotion has received acceptance because a one-dimensional construct is not robust enough to incorporate all aspects of emotional response (Osgood, Suci, & Tannenbaum, 1957; Mehrabian & Russell, 1977). Havlena and Holbrook (1986) compared categorical models to dimensional models of emotions and found that the three dimensional models were more valid, more reliable, and contained more pertinent information about emotion than the categorical models. Osgood et al. (1957) pioneered the dimensional model of emotional response. They asked participants to rate verbal stimuli on 50 bipolar scales containing opposites such as hot–cold and fast–slow. A factor analysis of the results showed that most of the variance in the responses stemmed from three factors, which they labeled evaluation, activity, and potency. They also found that the same three-dimensional model worked for nonverbal information.

Based on the Osgood et al. findings, Mehabrian and Russell (1977) formulated one of the most widely accepted models of emotional response that uses pleasure, arousal, and dominance (PAD) as the three necessary and sufficient dimensions of emotion. The pleasure dimension can range from an extreme positive feeling to an extreme negative feeling. The arousal dimension can range from a state of sluggishness or disinterest to a state of excitation. The dominance dimension can range from submissive and weak to powerful and in control. Although most research recognizes the importance of the pleasure and arousal dimensions, the dominance dimension has not proved widely useful. Mehrabian and Russell (1977) provided evidence for the dominance dimension as the distinguishing factor between such similar emotions as anger (high dominance) and anxiety (low dominance) and relaxed (high dominance) and protected (low dominance).

These three dimensions of emotion are not restricted by culture and are global in nature. Using a semantic differential technique to study 22 culturally and linguistically different groups, Osgood, May, and Miron (1975) reported that the three factors, evaluation, activity, and potency, were panculturally identified. Herrman and Raybeck (1981) collected data from Spain, Vietnam, Hong Kong (Cantonese Chinese), Haiti, Greece, and the United States and used multidimensional scaling to judge the similarity of 15 emotion terms. The results yielded the two dimensions, pleasure and arousal. Through interviewing the native speakers of each language, the two dimensions: pleasure–displeasure and arousal–sleep were found in Gujarati, Croatian, Japanese, Cantonese Chinese, and English (Russell, 1983). Additionally Russell and his associates' (1989) subsequent research, which studied the facial expressions of Greek-, Chinese-, and English-speaking subjects, yielded the same two dimensions. Corraliza (1987) found all three factors, pleasure, arousal, and dominance, when analyzing Spanish emotion-related terms.

In addition, the three-dimensional approach has received support from a 2008 functional magnetic resonance imaging (fMRI) study conducted at the University of Florida (Morris et al., 2009). This study identified the processing centers of two of these dimensions in the brain. Pleasure and arousal have distinct locations in the brain for detecting changes in these dimensions. The third, dominance or control, is the subject of future research.

Nonverbal Measures of Emotional Response

Measuring emotional response using the PAD dimensions can be accomplished with two different techniques: a verbal checklist posed up to 16 bipolar adjectives in a questionnaire for respondents to express their feelings about any stimulus, or a nonverbal manikin the same stimulus. The verbal process accumulates scores from the checklist, and then collapses them into the three dimensions. For example, the following are examples of pairs used and then collapsed into the pleasure dimension: Happy–Sad, Good–Bad, Pleasant–Unpleasant, Like–Dislike, and Positive–Negative. The nonverbal, visual, manikin-based approach (Lang, 1980) is better than the verbal checklist for measuring a respondent's emotional responses, because this method reduces cognitive processing (Lang, 1985; Morris & Waine, 1993). In addition, verbal emotional response measurement can be cumbersome and take more time.

The SAM (self-assessment manikin) scale was found to be more effective and less time consuming than common verbal measures of emotional response because it does not require the respondent to translate complex emotions into words. When adjective checklists or semantic differential scales are used to assess emotional response, the precise meaning of the emotional words may vary from person to person. For example, joy or anger may mean one emotion to one person, but something slightly different to someone else. Also problematic are the use of open-ended questions that request respondents to describe their emotional responses to communication messages (Stout & Rust, 1986; Stout & Leckenby, 1986). Both approaches require a significant amount of cognitive processing. Because the self-assessment manikin does not rely on specific definitions of words, it is useful for cross-cultural studies. In addition, a problem inherent in verbal measures of emotional response is the lack of universally accepted adjectives. It is difficult to design an instrument that contains words that share the same meaning when translated from language to language. The nonverbal measurement system was developed to eliminate the language biases.

SAM was shown to be a reliable method for measuring the three dimensions of affect: pleasure, arousal, and dominance, by rating the same catalog of situations which were categorized by Mehrabian and Russell (1974). The correlations between SAM and Mehrabian and Russell's (1974) PAD results were: pleasure (+0.937); arousal (+0.938); dominance (+0.660). The finding indicated that SAM generated similar values for these situations as was obtained for the semantic differential (Lang, 1980; Lang, 1985; Morris & Waine, 1993; Morris, 1995). SAM was able to measure how respondents feel emotionally rather than what respondents think.

SAM was tested and proven to be both reliable and valid. It was used to rate responses to emotional imagery (Miller et al., 1987), sounds (Bradley, 1994), advertisements (Morris, 1995; Morris et al., 2002), and pictures (Greenwald, Cook, & Lang, 1989; Lang, Greenwald, Bradley, & Hamm, 1993). A study by Greenbaum, Turner, Cook, and Melamed (1990) used the nonverbal measure to determine the emotional response of children to the behavior of dentists. SAM was also used to generate the International Affective Picture System (IAPS), a collection of over 700 color photographs that have been rated on pleasure, arousal, and dominance dimensions by a large normative sample (Lang, Öhman, & Vaitl, 1988).

AdSAM® (the attitude self-assessment manikin) based on SAM was developed to measure emotional response to marketing communications stimuli (Morris et al., 1994) (see Figure 6.1). AdSAM® has been used to assess responses to television advertising (Morris, 1994), pre-production vs. post-production advertising (Morris, 1993), and political messages (Morris, 1995) and brand loyalty (Kim, Morris, & Swait, 2008). AdSAM® has also been used to compare global advertising between the United States and Taiwan where it proved effective in measuring responses to marketing communications across cultures (Morris, 1994).

AdSAM®, like its predecessor SAM, visually assesses each PAD dimension with a graphic character arrayed along a continuous nine-point scale. The first row of figures is the pleasure scale, which ranges from a smiling, happy face to a frowning, unhappy face. The second row is the arousal scale which ranges from extremely calm with eyes closed to extremely excited with eyes open and elevated eyebrows. The third row, the dominance dimension, represents changes in control with changes in the size of AdSAM®: from a large figure indicating maximum control in the situation to a tiny figure, which indicates being under control.

Emotional Response Modeling in Marketing Communications

A study conducted by Morris et al. (2002) found a link between emotion, cognition, and behavioral intention in an advertising context using the AdSAM® measurement. AdSAM® scores from advertising copytests were compared to other scores related to recall and belief. Purchase intention and brand interest comprised the output or dependent measure.

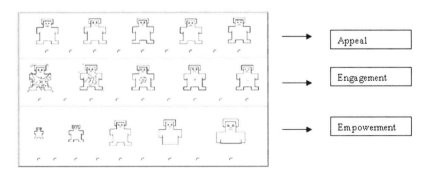

Figure 6.1 AdSAM®.

In this robust study of over 23,000 responses to 240 advertising messages, the authors examined the relationship between emotion and consumer intent and found that affect (emotion), dominated over cognition for predicting intended behavior. A structural equation model was used to examine the relationships between cognitive, affective, and conative attitude (see Figure 6.2).

Results indicate that both cognitive and affective attitudes are correlated with conative attitude or persuasion, but affective attitude as measured by emotional response is a stronger predictor of purchase intention in 12 of 13 product categories and in all types of media except radio. Emotional response accounted for more (almost twice) of the variance in predicting interest in the brand and intended behavior than cognitive (rational) response.

The study also found that liking of an advertisement may not be an accurate measure of positive feelings toward an ad. Liking was found to be as much about that product as the advertisement and therefore not good at measuring the contribution of the ad.

Although the AdSAM® model was formulated in an advertising context for consumer goods, it has also been used in measuring the value of public service announcements, health campaigns, and for determining brand loyalty and product trial (Kim et al., 2008). The Morris et al. (2002) study showed that emotional response is a powerful predictor of behavioral intention, and given its diagnostic capabilities, it can be a valuable tool for strategic planning and message formulation.

Emotion is more than just a peripheral occurrence in the process of persuasion as suggested in the Elaboration Likelihood Model. In fact, the results of one study contradict this notion. According to the ELM respondents who focus on the style of a commercial, "*cognitive misers*" would have stronger emotional responses (but lower purchase intent) than "*cognitive elaborators*." "*Cognitive*

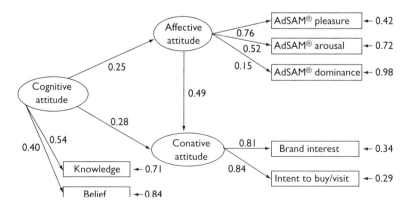

Figure 6.2 Structural Model of Affect Cognition and Conative Response.

misers" who focused on the commercial style rather than product attributes did have lower purchase intent scores, but also lower emotional response scores upon seeing commercials. It was "*cognitive elaborators*" who had higher emotional responses as well as higher purchase intent scores.

The results of the data analysis give further insight (Morris, Woo, & Singh, 2005) into the role of emotions in the process of persuasion. Cognitive processing does have an emotional core. The more cognitive group, "*cognitive elaborators*," showed significantly higher pleasure responses than the less cognitive group, "*cognitive misers.*" Higher purchase intent accompanies this increase in pleasure. This demonstrates that even though information is being processed cognitively, the procedure is not being conducted in an emotional vacuum. Cognition and emotion are inseparable (Duncan & Barrett, 2007).

The Neurology of Emotion

Affective neuroscience, at the turn of this millennium, has firmly entrenched itself in brain scan research. Drawing from the findings of forerunners such as Damasio (1994) and LeDoux (1989), researchers have established the fact that the brain circuitry of emotion and cognition is interactive, but is now shown to be separate. Data has shown that there are parts of the brain that are dedicated exclusively to affect (Morris et al., 2009). Emotion evolved to facilitate an organism's adaptation to complex challenges it faced during its past, and that emotional response is hard-wired in the brain. It has been conclusively shown that the architecture of the brain does not honor the age-old concept of segregation of cognition and affect. Most compellingly, cognition has been shown to be rudderless without emotion and studies in cognitive neuroscience and behavioral science cannot be conducted without taking emotion into account (Morris et al., 2009; Morris et al., 2002).

Case Studies

Case I

Advertisers and marketers have traditionally used beautiful women to attract attention to their products because they believe the beautiful are credible, desirable, and aspirational (Frith & Mueller, 2003; Joseph, 1982). Numerous studies have shown that the more beautiful people are, the more positive responses toward them (Dion, Berscheid, & Walster, 1972). Researchers have found that beautiful people are seen more positively upon initial introduction (Miller, 1970), have greater social acceptance (Kleck, Richardson, & Ronald, 1974), have greater social influence (Debevec, Madden, & Kernan, 1986), are better liked (Eagly, Ashmore, Makhijami, & Longo, 1991), and are attributed with more positive characteristics such as kindness, strength, warmth, friendliness, independence, and sociability (Berscheid & Walster, 1974; Chaiken, 1986; Patzer, 1985; Perlini, Bertolissi, & Lind, 1999). Moreover, abundant evidence suggests using beautiful people in ads produces positive effects for the ad and the product's evaluations (Belch, Belch, & Villareal, 1987; Joseph, 1982).

Therefore, there is a pervasive use of beautiful models as persuasion tools in advertisements. Yet how do advertisers define "beauty" besides someone who is esthetically pleasing? Research shows that both society's and the media's current characteristics of beauty include: being thin, big eyes, full lips, flawless skin, and high cheekbones (Freedman, 1986; Cunningham, Roberts, Barbee, Druen, & Wu, 1995). All these newborn-like attributes are hallmarks of youth, and all except for thinness are considered cross-cultural qualities of beauty (Sarwer, Magee, & Clark, 2004).

Even so, advertising models do not look identical. They vary in the prominence of newborn-like attributes, physical features such as hair and eye color, and their personified qualities such as elegance or sexiness (Goodman, Morris, & Sutherland, 2008). Although studies had determined that beauty can persuade women to buy products and that certain beauty types work better with certain product types, these studies had not explored women's *emotional* responses to different beauty types in advertising.

This study measured women's emotional responses to varying types of female models. The six categories of beauty combined into two basic types of beauty—*Sexual/Sensual* (formerly Sexual/Exotic and Sex Kitten) and *Classic Beauty* (formerly Cute, Classic Beauty, Girl-Next-Door). This finding is significant because it shows a clear difference in opinions from industry creatives who choose the models for fashion magazines and the female audience that views them. Thus when a company chooses a model to represent its product, the company may get better results if it uses the viewers' categorizations rather than those of fashion editors or creative directors (Goodman et al., 2008).

The first type, personified by Goldie Hawn and Calista Flockhart, has infantile qualities that make her "look like [an] adorable needy waif" (Freedman, 1986). The other type features a more mature, sexual look personified by Raquel Welch and Nicollette Sheridan. These women have an hourglass figure with full busts and round hips that "signal both eroticism and maternal security" (Freedman, 1986). In general, multidimensional beauty may be beneficial to companies because it will help them to create advertisements that feature precisely the image they wish to portray.

Most importantly, emotional reactions by young females to the two beauty types, high Classic Beauty models had significantly greater pleasure and arousal than high Sexy Sensual models. Greater degrees of sexiness and sensuality tended to produce ambivalence or a slightly negative reaction. Although the respond-ents felt a model resided strongly in the Sexy Sensual category, women had very little to no pleasure or arousal when viewing her. This finding implies two things. First, women are programmed to label certain types of beauty as "sexy" even though this type of beauty bores them. Second, there is a clear difference between how respondents view attractiveness and sexiness with the former being a posit-ive attribute and the latter being more negative. A possible explanation for these differences is that the definition of sexy has altered over time. Today's women may see sexiness as hypersexual and associate hypersexuality with negative characteristics such as incompetence, immorality, and stupidity, making Sexy Sensual images unappealing (Latteier, 1998). Furthermore, this finding may suggest that women are tired of being objectified and sexualized in advertise-ments, indicating a potential backlash effect when using Sexy Sensual images for products targeted to women, particularly if the product has no obvious tie or need to use sexual imagery (Goodman et al., 2008).

Case 2

Recent studies have shown an increase in patient involvement in physicians' healthcare recommendations including the prescribing of medications (Kravitz et al., 2005). And although this new interaction is associated with an increase in physician stress, the clinicians are strongly considering patient input in a way that encourages shared decision-making (Dubé, 2003).

Some of this focus on new influencers may be attributed to the increase in DTC (direct to consumer advertising) by pharmaceutical companies (Manning, 2002). This effort focuses prescription advertising on the consumer rather than the physi-cian and suggests the idea of shared knowledge in selecting treatment options. These consumers then use this newly acquired knowledge about the prescription products to determine emotional benefits and brand attitudes (Ruth, 2001).

This new direction in patient involvement has helped reveal the inner work-ings of the healthcare process and the findings that the system is subject to influ-ences both within the healthcare system and external to it (Mulzet, 2003). A better understanding about how low-income parents think and feel about healthcare for their children, for example, has led to the creation of messages based on relevant emotions and personal values (Bassett, 2002). In addition, evidence that a strong relationship exists between emotion and product posi-tioning (Mahajan & Wind, 2002) has led to interest in exploring the role of the various influencers and the potential for segmenting these influencers by the emotional impact.

Nowhere was this attitudinal classification more clearly demonstrated than in the 2003 NFO Healthcare Influencer study. Across 12 therapeutic categories,

1800 patients were surveyed about the impact of influencers (non-healthcare professionals such as relatives, friends, co-workers) on healthcare decision-making (e.g., prescription drug requests, lifestyle changes). In addition to demographic, attitudinal, and behavioral questions, AdSAM® questions included: how the person normally felt, how they felt about their health in general, and how they felt about having their condition. In addition the patients were asked about their feelings regarding talking to their physician, taking their medication, and about talking to the person most involved in their healthcare. Other questions focused on healthcare communications.

Understanding the emotions surrounding the condition, the patients' emotions toward the physicians, as well as other influencers, could influence a marketer's ability to communicate effectively with patients. Migraine and obesity sufferers have very negative feelings and arousing feelings about their conditions. Erectile dysfunction and obesity sufferers have more negative feelings about talking to their physicians about their condition. Obesity sufferers in particular are more relaxed about talking with an "influencer" than with their physician in making healthcare decisions. Feelings about all these conditions are generally negative, especially obesity, insomnia, and migraine. As shown in

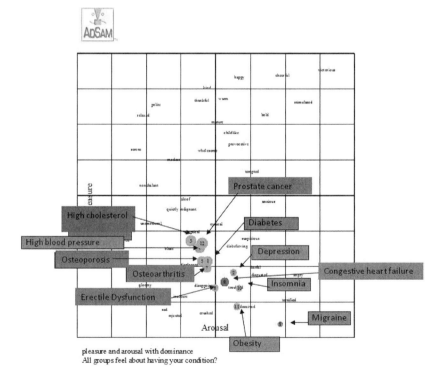

Figure 6.3 AdSAM®, Perceptional Map.

Figure 6.3, displeasure is seen in the lower two quadrants. More arousing or engaging is to the right. The size of the dot indicates control or dominance. The smaller the dot, the less control.

Emotions surrounding talking to a physician differ somewhat by condition. Obesity and erectile dysfunction sufferers have more negative feelings while prostate cancer sufferers are more comfortable talking to their doctors about their conditions (see Figure 6.4).

People suffering from any of these conditions are more relaxed about talking with an influencer or someone involved in their care, most often a woman, than with their physician. Interestingly, those who suffer from obesity and erectile dysfunction feel much more positive (comfortable) discussing the problem with an influencer or caregiver than a physician (see Figure 6.5).

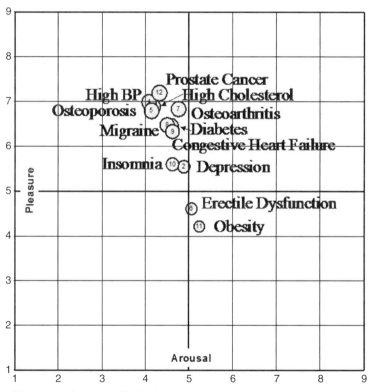

Pleasure and arousal with dominance

Figure 6.4 Locations of Diseases in AdSAM®.

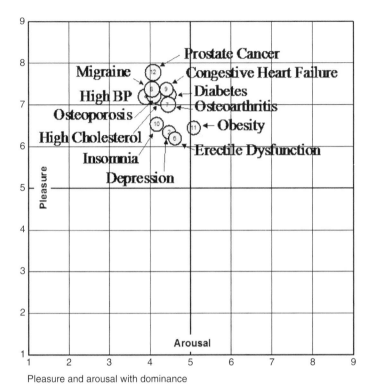

Pleasure and arousal with dominance

Figure 6.5 AdSAM® Feelings about Speaking with an Influencer.

Conclusion

Researchers have used a variety of self-report techniques in analyzing emotional responses. Some have used a discrete self-report approach that focused on specific emotions such as happiness and anger (Izard, 1977; Plutchik, 1984). Other researchers have used a more robust three-dimensional self-report approach (Osgood et al., 1957; Mehrabian & Russell, 1977; Sundar & Kalyanaraman, 2004) including physiological measures to assess the emotional response.

The discrete approach assumes that individuals can regularly distinguish their feelings using the correct words. If this were the case, then phrases like "I hate milk" or "I love orange juice" would never be heard. Emotional responses are a judgment of sensations and those are better analyzed or estimated using a dimensional rating scale.

One example of this approach is the pleasure–displeasure, arousal–calm, and dominance–submissiveness (PAD) model (Mehrabian & Russell, 1977). The three bipolar dimensions are independent of each other, and the variance of emotional responses can be identified with their positions along these three dimensions. The dimensional approach helps differentiate emotions postulated by the discrete approach by providing a numeric level of each dimension to describe the specific emotions. Specific combinations of the dimensions can identify each discrete emotion. The meaning of these specific adjectives may differ by individual, culture, or other influences; nevertheless, the method for identifying the response is universal.

Also it has been asserted here that a dimensional non-verbal approach is preferred over a verbal approach. With a verbal technique, respondents must first attempt to translate their feelings into words and then must use several pairs of words in order to produce stable dimensions. Not every pair of bipolar adjectives fits every circumstance so several different pairs are needed to create the dimensions.

With the nonverbal approach respondents react using a manikin that represents them and their feelings. This approach has not only been shown to be accurate, but gender-, culture-, and language-free. The technique can be used in any country, with any group including children. In marketing and marketing communications and advertising research, the nonverbal dimensional approach can save time and participant wear out. The average response to any stimuli is 15–20 seconds.

Regardless of the technique, measuring emotional response is an important component in gaining insights in marketing and communications. Emotional response is a leading indicator of changes in behavior. Simply measuring intentions or recall of messages does little toward determining changes in persuasion. Persuasion is a key component of changes in behavior and emotions are key to persuasion.

References

Aaker, D. A., Stayman, D. M., & Vezina, R. (1988). Identifying feelings elicited by advertising. *Psychology and Marketing, 5*, 1–16.

Ajzen, I., & Fishbein, M. (1977). Attitude–behavior relations: A theoretical analysis and review of empirical research. *Psychological Bulletin, 84*, 888–918.

Ajzen, I., & Fishbein, M. (1980). *Understanding attitudes and predicting social behavior.* Englewood Cliffs, NJ: Prentice-Hall.

Allport, G. W. (1935). Attitudes. In C. Murchison (Ed.), *Handbook of social psychology* (pp. 789–844). Worcester, MA: Clark University Press.

Bassett, B. (2002). Wirthlin Worldwide wins ARF's Ogilvy Award Grand Prize; Robert Wood Johnson Foundation's "Covering Kids" campaign recognized for effective use of research. *PR Newswire.*

Belch, G. E., Belch, M. A., & Villareal, A. (1987). Effects of advertising communications: Review of research. In *Research in marketing* (pp. 59–117). Greenwich, CT: JAI Press Inc.

Berscheid, E., & Walster, E. (1974). Physical attractiveness. In L. Berkowitz (Ed.), *Advances in experimental social psychology* (pp. 157–215). New York: Academic Press.

Bolls, P. D. (2010). Understanding emotion from a superordinate dimensional perspective: A productive way forward for communication processes and effects studies. *Communication Monographs, 77* (2), 146–152.

Bradley, M. M. (1994). Emotional memory: A dimensional analysis. In S. Van Goozen, N. E. Van de Poll, & J. A. Sergeant (Eds.), *The emotions: Essays on emotion theory* (pp. 97–134). Hillsdale, NJ: Lawrence Erlbaum.

Burke, M. C., & Edell, J. A. (1989). The impact of feelings on ad-based affect and cognition. *Journal of Marketing Research, 26*, 69–83.

Chaiken, S. (1986). Physical appearance and social influence. In C. P. Herman, M. P. Zanna, & E. T. Higgins (Eds.), *Physical appearance, stigma, and social behavior: The Ontario symposium* (pp. 143–177). Hillsdale, NJ: Lawrence Erlbaum.

Corraliza, J. A. (1987). *La experiencia del ambiente* [The experience of the environment]. Madrid, Spain: Tecnos.

Cunningham, M. R., Roberts, A. R., Barbee, A. P., Druen, P. B., & Wu, C.-H. (1995). Their ideas of beauty are, on the whole, the same as ours: Consistency and variability in the cross-cultural perception of female physical attractiveness. *Journal of Personality and Social Psychology, 68* (2), 261–279.

Damasio, A. (1994). *Descarte's error.* New York: Grosset/Putnam.

Debevec, K. K., Madden, T. J., & Kernan, J. B. (1986). Physical attractiveness, message evaluation and compliance: A structural examination. *Psychological Reports, 58*, 503–508.

Dillard, J. P., & Peck, E. (2000). Affect and persuasion: Emotional responses to public service announcements. *Communication Research, 27*, 461–495.

Dion, K., Berscheid, E., & Walster, E. (1972). What is beautiful is good. *Journal of Personality and Social Psychology, 24* (March), 285–290.

Duncan, S., & Barrett, L. F. (2007). Affect is a form of cognition: A neurobiological analysis. *Cognition and Emotion, 21* (6), 1184–1211.

Dubé, L. (2003). What's missing from patient-centered care? *Marketing Health Services, 23*, 30–35.

Eagly, A. H., Ashmore, R. D., Makhijami, M. G., & Longo, L. C. (1991). What is beautiful is good, but . . .: A meta-analytic review of research on the physical attractiveness stereotype. *Psychological Bulletin, 110*, 109–128.

Edell, J. A., & Burke, M. C. (1987). The power of feelings in understanding advertising effects. *Journal of Consumer Research, 14*, 421–433.

Fishbein, M. (1963). An investigation of relationships between beliefs about an object and the attitude toward that object. *Human Relations, 16*, 233–240.

Fishbein, M., & Ajzen, I. (1975). *Belief, attitude, intention, and behavior: An introduction to theory and research.* Reading, MA: Addison-Wesley.

Fishbein, M., & Middlestadt, S. E. (1995). Noncognitive effects on attitude formation and change: Fact or artifact? *Journal of Consumer Psychology, 4*, 107–115.

Freedman, R. J. (1986). *Beauty bound.* Lexington, MA: Lexington Books.

Frith, K.T., & Mueller, B. (2003). *Advertising and societies: Global issues*. New York: Peter Lang.

Goodman, J. R., Morris, J. D., & Sutherland, J. C. (2008). Is beauty a joy forever? Young women's emotional responses to varying types of beautiful advertising models. *Journalism and Mass Communications Quarterly, 85* (1), 147–168.

Greenbaum, P. E., Turner, C., Cook, E. W., & Melamed, B. G. (1990). Dentists' voice control: Effects on children's disruptive and affective behavior. *Health Psychology, 9*, 546–558.

Greenwald, M. K., Cook, E. W., & Lang, P. J. (1989). Affective judgment and psychophysiological response: Dimensional covariation in the evaluation of pictorial stimuli. *Journal of Psychophysiology, 3*, 51–64.

Havlena, W. J., & Holbrook, M. B. (1986). The varieties of consumption experience: Comparing two typologies of emotion in consumer behavior. *Journal of Consumer Research, 13*, 394–404.

Herrman, D. J., & Raybeck, D. (1981). Similarities and differences in meaning in six cultures. *Journal of Cross-Cultural Psychology, 12*, 194–206.

Holbrook, M. B. (1978). Beyond attitude structure: Toward the informational determinants of attitude. *Journal of Marketing Research, 15*, 545–566.

Holbrook, M. B., & Batra, R. (1987). Assessing the role of emotions as mediators of consumer responses to advertising. *Journal of Consumer Research, 14*, 404–420.

Holbrook, M. B., & O'Shaughnessy, J. (1984). The role of emotion in advertising. *Psychology and Marketing, 1*, 45–64.

Izard, C. E. (1977). *Human emotions*. New York: Plenum Press.

Joseph, W. B. (1982). The credibility of physically attractive communicators: A review. *Journal of Advertising, 11* (3), 15–24.

Kim, J. Y., Morris, J. D., & Swait, J. (2008). Antecedents of *true* brand loyalty. *Journal of Advertising, 17* (2), 99–117.

Kleck, R. E., Richardson, S. A., & Ronald, L. (1974). Physical appearance cues and interpersonal attraction in children. *Child Development, 45* (2), 305–310.

Kravitz, R. L., Epstein, R. M., Feldman, M. D., Franz, C. E., Azari, R., Wilkes, M. S., Hinton, L., & Franks, P. (2005). Influence of patients' requests for direct-to-consumer advertised antidepressants: A randomized controlled trial. *Journal of the American Medical Association, 293*, 1995–2001.

Lang, P. J. (1980). Behavioral treatment and bio-behavioral assessment: Computer applications. In J. B. Sidowski, J. H. Johnson, & T. A. Williams (Eds.), *Technology in mental health care delivery systems* (pp. 119–137). Norwood, NJ: Ablex.

Lang, P. J. (1985). *The cognitive psychophysiology of emotions: Anxiety and the anxiety disorders*. Hillsdale, NJ: Lawrence Erlbaum.

Lang, P. J., Greenwald, M. K., Bradley, M. M., & Hamm, A. O. (1993). Looking at pictures: Affective, facial, visceral, and behavioral reactions. *Psychophysiology, 30*, 261–273.

Lang, P. J., Öhman, A., & Vaitl, D. (1988). *The international affective picture system* [Photographic slides]. Gainesville, FL: Center for Research in Psychophysiology, University of Florida.

Lasswell, H. D. (1927). The theory of political propaganda. *American Political Science Review, 21*, 627–631.

Latteier, C. (1998). *Breasts: The women's perspective on an American obsession.* New York: Haworth Press.

LeDoux, J. E. (1989). *The emotional brain: The mysterious underpinnings of emotional life.* New York: Simon & Schuster.

Lippmann, W. (1922). *Public opinion.* New York: Macmillan.

Lutz, R. J. (1985). Affective and cognitive antecedents of attitude toward the ad: A conceptual framework. In L. F. Alwitt & A. A. Mitchell (Eds.), *Psychological processes and advertising effects: Theory, research, and application* (pp. 45–64). Hillsdale, NJ: Lawrence Erlbaum.

Mahajan, V., & Wind, Y. (2002). Convergence marketing. *Journal of Interactive Marketing, 16* (2), 64–79.

Manning, J. (2002). *Digit ratio: A pointer to fertility, behavior, and health.* Piscataway, NJ: Rutgers University Press.

Miller, A. G. (1970). Role of physical attractiveness in impression formation. *Psychonomic Science, 19* (4), 241–243.

Miller, G. A., Levin, D. N., Kozak, M. J., Cook, E. W., McLean, A., & Lang, P. J. (1987). Individual differences in emotional imagery. *Cognition and Emotion, 1*, 367–390.

Mehrabian, A., & Russell, J. A. (1974). *An approach to environmental psychology.* Cambridge, MA: MIT Press.

Mehrabian, A., & Russell, J. A. (1977). Evidence for a three-factor theory of emotions. *Journal of Research in Personality, 11*, 273–294.

Morris, J. D. (1994). Differences in emotional response to television ads by creative strategy typology. Presentation made at the Southern Marketing Association Annual Conference, Atlanta, GA.

Morris, J. D. (1995). SAM: The self-assessment manikin: An efficient cross-cultural measurement of emotional response. *Journal of Advertising Research, 35* (8), 63–68.

Morris, J. D., Bradley, M. M., & Wei, L. P. (1994, August). Global advertising and affective response: SAM ratings in U.S.A and Taiwan. Presentation made at the national conference of the Association for Education in Journalism and Mass Communications, Kansas City.

Morris, J. D., Klahr, N. J., Shen, F., Villegas, J., Wright, P., He, G., & Liu, Y. (2009). Mapping a multidimensional emotion in response to television commercials. *Human Brain Mapping, 30*, 789–796.

Morris, J. D., Roberts, M. S., & Baker, G. F. (1999). Emotional responses of African American voters to ad messages. In L.L. Kaid & D.G. Bystrom (Eds.), *The electronic election: Perspectives on the 1996 campaign communication* (pp. 257–274). Mahwah, NJ: Lawrence Erlbaum Associates.

Morris, J. D., & Waine, C. A. (1993). Managing the creative effort: Pre-production and post-production measures of emotional response. In E. Thorson (Ed.), *Proceedings of the 1993 Conference of the American Academy of Advertising* (pp. 158–176). Columbia, MO: American Academy of Advertising.

Morris, J. D., Woo, C., Geason, J. A., & Kim, J. (2002). The power of affect: Predicting intention. *Journal of Advertising Research, 42*, 7–17.

Morris, J. D., Woo, C., & Singh, A. J. (2005). Elaboration Likelihood Model: A Missing Intrinsic Emotional Implication. *Journal of Targeting, Measurement and Analysis, 14* (1), 79–98.

Mulzet, B. (2003). Impact of influencers on consumer healthcare decision making. *Business Wire, Inc.* Retrieved from www.businesswire.com.

Nabi, R. L. (2010). The case for emphasizing discrete emotions in communication research. *Communication Monographs, 77* (2), 153–159.

Osgood, C. E., May, W. H., & Miron, M. S. (1975). *Cross-cultural universals of affective meaning.* Urbana: University of Illinois Press.

Osgood, C. E., Suci, G., & Tannenbaum, P. (1957). *The measurement of meaning.* Urbana: University of Illinois.

Patzer, G. L. (1985). *The physical attractiveness phenomena.* New York: Plenum.

Perlini, A. P., Bertolissi, S., & Lind, D. L. (1999). The effects of women's age and physical appearance on attractiveness and social desirability. *Journal of Social Psychology, 139*, 343–354.

Petty, R. E., & Cacioppo, J. T. (1981). *Attitudes and persuasion: Classic and contemporary approaches.* Dubuque, IA: William C. Brown.

Petty, R. E. & Cacioppo, J. T. (1986). The elaboration likelihood model of persuasion. *Advances in Experimental Social Psychology, 19*, 123–205.

Petty, R. E. & Cacioppo, J. T. (1996). *Attitudes and persuasion: Classic and contemporary approaches.* Boulder, CO: Westview Press.

Plutchik, R. (1984). Emotions: A general psychoevolutionary theory. In K. R. Scherer & P. Ekman (Eds.), *Approaches to emotion* (pp. 187–214). Hillsdale, NJ: Lawrence Erlbaum.

Russell, J. A. (1983). Pancultural aspects of the human conceptual organization of emotions. *Journal of Personality and Social Psychology, 45*, 1281–1288.

Russell, J. A., Suzuki, N., & Ishida, N. (1989). Canadian, Greek, and Japanese freely produced emotion labels for facial expressions. *Motivation and Emotion, 17* (4), 337–351.

Ruth, J. A. (2001). Promoting a brand's emotion benefits: The influence of emotion categorization processes on consumer evaluations. *Journal of Consumer Psychology, 11* (2), 99–113.

Sarwer, D. B., Magee, L., & Clark, V. (2004). Physical appearance and cosmetic medical treatments: Physiological and socio-cultural Influences. *Journal of Cosmetic Dermatology, 2*, 29–30.

Shimp, T. A. (1981). Attitude toward the ad as a mediator of consumer brand choice. *Journal of Advertising, 10*, 9–15.

Sundar, S. S., & Kalyanaraman, S. (2004). Arousal, memory, and impression-formation effects of animation speed in web advertising. *Journal of Advertising, 33*, 7–17.

Stayman, D. M., & Aaker, D. A. (1988). Are all effects of ad-induced feelings mediated by Aad? *Journal of Consumer Research, 15*, 368–373.

Stewart, D. W., Morris, J. D., & Grover, A. (2007). Emotions in advertising. In G. J.

Tellis & T. Ambler (Eds.), *The Sage handbook of advertising* (pp. 120–134). Thousand Oaks, CA: Sage Publications.

Stout, P. A., & Leckenby, J. D. (1986). Measuring emotional response to advertising. *Journal of Advertising, 15* (4), 35–42.

Stout, P. A., & Rust, R. T. (1986). The effect of music on emotional response to advertising. In E. Larkin (Ed.), *Proceedings of the 1986 Convention of the American Academy of Advertising* (pp. 82–84). Norman: University of Oklahoma.

Zajonc, R. B. (1980). Feeling and thinking: Preferences need no inferences. *American Psychologist, 35*, 151–175.

Zeitlin, D. M., & Westwood, R. A. (1986). Measuring emotional response. *Journal of Advertising Research, 26*, 34–44.

Chapter 7

Embodied Motivated Cognition

A Theoretical Framework for Studying Dynamic Mental Processes Underlying Advertising Exposure

Paul D. Bolls, Kevin Wise, and Samuel D. Bradley

"This is your brain on advertising!" That exclamation, adapted from a famous 1980s anti-drug message, aptly describes one objective of research conducted under the umbrella of *neuromarketing*—a branch of research focused on measuring brain activity as consumers interact with advertising (Perrachione & Perrachione, 2008). The prospect of digging inside consumers' brains to find the "magic" route to understanding advertising effects is exciting; however, without a solid theoretical framework, this method can only document the occurrence of mildly interesting physiological responses to ads. The potential for *psychophysiological research* on advertising—of which neuromarketing is the latest version—to provide theoretical insight into the brain "on advertising" warrants the application of a rigorous theoretical framework. In this chapter, we offer Embodied Motivated Cognition (EMC) as a theoretical framework capable of offering deep insight into how the human mind processes advertising.

EMC includes basic assumptions about the mind that have tremendous implications for advertising theory. These implications intersect with how the mind ought to be investigated as the target and processor of advertising, as well as how media content and platforms can be conceptualized in a way that truly advances theory. This chapter reviews EMC, describing it at a level appropriate for readers whose background is more likely in advertising rather than *neuropsychology*. We will tease out implications of this perspective for understanding the mind and discuss the application of EMC to advertising research.

This chapter is divided into two sections. The first section reviews EMC as a theoretical framework and discusses conceptual and methodological implications of this perspective. Advertising research conducted under this perspective must include psychophysiological measures because they offer the most valid way for researchers to observe the dynamic action of mental processes occurring during advertising exposure. Thus, the last section will focus on psychophysiology as a methodological paradigm for advertising research.

EMC: "Receiver," "Message," and "Channel"

EMC is a theoretical framework through which the mind can be understood in a manner that allows for more precise explication of psychological concepts (e.g., attention, attitudes) advertisements are believed to influence. From this perspective, more specific models of advertising effects could be developed that address features of brand messages and channels, as well as mental processes and other characteristics of individuals exposed to advertising. For instance, EMC could serve as a theoretical foundation from which to develop models of the impact of sexual content in viral video ads because it describes how to conceptualize and measure basic *motivational mental processes* that are likely to significantly influence the way such content is attended to, evaluated, and remembered. EMC provides a solid foundation for explication of concepts that are central to information processing-based theories of advertising by grounding conceptual definitions in a consideration of how psychological concepts emerge from underlying biologically based processes in the brain.

In terms of addressing specific elements of the general model outlined in Chapter 1 (Thorson & Rodgers), this framework provides a theoretical perspective for conceptualizing the elements of "receiver," "message," and "channel" and theorizing about the advertising process as consisting of ongoing, dynamic, interactions between the brains of individuals who are the receivers of advertising and brand messages delivered through advertising channels.

A majority of advertising theory—and for that matter practice—has not involved in-depth consideration of the nature of the interaction between advertising and underlying mental processes that produce the conscious experience of advertising exposure. As noted by Du Plessis (2008), advertising research and practice have been conducted in a manner that essentially ignores the nature of the "processor" of advertising, the human brain. The EMC perspective addresses this issue by grounding conceptual definitions of receiver, message, and channel in a consideration of how the mind, embodied in biological processes implemented in the brain, is structured.

Conceptually Defining "Receiver"

Scholars involved in the birth of media effects research investigated the phenomenon from the *behaviorism* perspective (Sparks, 2002). Behaviorism discounted any effort to investigate the inner workings of the mind and led to a very general conceptual definition of "receiver" as simply an individual to which a message is delivered (Chaffee, 1980). Fortunately, with the occurrence of the cognitive revolution in psychology, a subset of the field of media research recognized the importance of more specifically defining receiver as an individual whose mind is actively engaged in information processing of a message (Geiger & Newhagen, 1993). EMC goes even further by more specifically articulating the nature of the mind engaged in information processing of a message.

EMC has emerged from recent research in neuropsychology exploring how the brain produces the mental experiences that constitute the mind (Berntson & Cacioppo, 2008). The foundational theoretical assumption made about the nature of the mind under this framework is that the mind is an embodied phenomenon (Cacioppo, Tassinary, & Berntson, 2007). What this means is that mental experience—including advertising exposure—emerges from the ongoing physical activity of the brain. Put more directly, mental experience does not exist without the continuous physical activity of the brain—in essence, the mind is the brain, and the brain is the mind. The brain, through its connection with every part of the body via the nervous system, directs us as we negotiate our social environment. Along the way, it produces a continuous stream of mental experiences reaching varying levels of consciousness that include the mental experience of processing and responding to advertising. This leads to the conclusion that the key defining feature of a "receiver" is the fact that it is an individual consisting of an embodied mind that is engaged in real time interactions with brand messages delivered through advertising channels. The assumption that mental experience is embodied in the brain allows researchers to use psychophysiological measures of nervous system activity associated with brain processes to investigate how receivers of advertising mentally process such messages.

The second theoretical proposition made about the nature of the mind within this framework is that the embodied mind is a motivated information processor (Lang, Bradley, & Cuthbert, 1997). This means that basic motivational processes implemented in the human brain drive information processing. The motivational system embodied in the brain is believed to consist of independent motivational subsystems referred to as the appetitive and aversive systems (Lang & Bradley, 2010). The appetitive system drives approach-related responses to environmental stimuli and is generally activated by information perceived as pleasant, while the aversive system drives defensive responses and is generally activated by unpleasant information (Lang & Bradley, 2008). An important feature of motivated processing is that activation of the appetitive and aversive systems can be reciprocal, coactive, or uncoupled (Cacioppo, Gardner, & Berntson, 1999). Reciprocal activation occurs when activation of one system decreases activation of the other; coactive activity occurs when there is an increase or decrease in activation of both systems; uncoupled activation results when activity in one system does not significantly affect activation of the other.

Under the EMC perspective, motivational activation—the level of activity in the appetitive and aversive motivational systems—is a core defining feature of information processing (Norris, Golan, Berntson, & Cacioppo, 2010). The fundamental task of the embodied mind is to determine the motivational relevance of stimuli encountered in our social environment and execute adaptive responses through motivational activation (Lang & Bradley, 2010). Adaptive responses include variation in the allocation of cognitive resources to memory, affective feelings, as well as the formation of attitudes and behavioral intentions (Yegiyan & Lang, 2010). EMC yields a unique explication of "receiver" as an individual with an embodied mind that motivationally processes brand messages delivered through advertising channels, forming memory representations of the brand and message, including affective feelings, attitudes, and behavioral intentions.

Conceptually Defining "Message" and "Channel"

A majority of advertising research has conceptualized message and channel from the perspective of advertising industry conventions. This has led to conceptually defining brand message as communication designed to promote a brand and advertising channel as the media technology used to deliver brand messages. Conceptualizing "message" and "channel" is valuable for industry practices; however, if an objective of advertising research is to provide deep insight into how the mind processes advertising, then conceptual definitions of "message" and "channel" ought to emerge from the nature of the embodied mind.

By providing a framework for understanding the nature of the mind, EMC also provides a foundation for developing conceptual definitions of "message" and "channel" that are strongly connected to the nature of the embodied mind— the receiver of advertising. Recall that our definition of receiver highlighted the fact that it is an individual consisting of an embodied mind that motivationally processes incoming sensory information in a social environment. Thus, conceptual definitions of brand message and advertising channel, emerging from the EMC perspective, need to focus on psychologically meaningful properties of of messages and channels present in the sensory information the mind processes during advertising exposure. The psychologically meaningful properties of "message" and "channel" will be those characteristics that have a significant and direct impact on embodied motivated cognitive processing of a brand message. Referring back to our conceptual definition of message receiver leads to the conclusion that the psychologically meaningful properties of message and channel will be characteristics directly related to sensory and motivational features of the message content and the technology that constructs the channel.

The above discussion leads to a conceptual definition of a brand message as information about a brand communicated in a discrete stream of mediated sensory information that varies in motivational (appetitive/aversive) significance and tone. This conceptual definition of message highlights the foundational mental categories of information (sensory and motivational) that construct a "message." Doing so does not mean other, content-specific ways of describing brand messages (e.g., sex appeal, fear appeal, and humor) are not meaningful but emphasizes the fact that from the perspective of an embodied mind, these categories of advertising content are psychologically meaningful because of the unique, sensory, motivational/emotional experience they deliver.

It should come as no surprise that the same logic used to define "message" is used to define "channel"; that is, the conceptual definition needs to highlight what is psychologically meaningful about advertising channels to the embodied mind. Here again, conceptualization of advertising channel according to industry conventions—such as television and print—fails to highlight what is psychologically relevant about channels to the embodied motivated mind. The technology that goes into constructing advertising channels delivers a unique sensory experience to receivers, and it is that aspect of "channel" that ought to be emphasized. Thus, a general conceptual definition of advertising channel is that it is a technological platform delivering unique, motivated sensory experience in the process of delivering a brand message. Specific advertising channels should be conceptualized according to the form of sensory experience they deliver. The difference between conceptual definitions of channels according to industry convention and the EMC approach can be illustrated by considering the advertising channels radio and television. The EMC approach focuses on the fact that there is nothing psychologically meaningful to the embodied mind about "television" or "radio" and redefines these advertising channels as "video advertising" and "audio advertising" independent of the specific hardware used to deliver the message. Another channel that could be reconceptualized under the approach outlined here is interactive advertising. It appears that this term is used to describe a channel that brushes over a range of technologies and creative executions that likely deliver fundamentally different motivated sensory experiences.

The larger point of the above discussion is that concepts involved in studying how the mind processes advertising need to be defined in a way that highlights the features of each concept that are most relevant to how the mind—embodied in the brain—processes advertising. This approach is consistent with the kind of conceptual and operational thinking that needs to drive advertising research focused on understanding how the mind processes advertising.

Implications of EMC for Advertising Research

Methodological implications of adopting an EMC perspective for experimental research in advertising occur on both the independent and dependent variable sides of experiments. Independent variables are usually concrete features of messages or channels (e.g., celebrity spokesperson, screen size). According to the EMC the most important characteristic of message or channel features to manipulate in experiments are those directly tied to the sensory and motivational experience of mentally processing the message. For instance, in an experiment designed to investigate how individuals process ads featuring a celebrity spokesperson, primary consideration ought to be given to the potential motivational significance (valence and arousal) associated with the presence of a celebrity versus unknown actors. Likewise, in studying mental processing of online advergames, the complexity of the sensory environment and motor responses required, as well as the motivational/emotional experience of playing the game should be a primary focus of experimental manipulations.

Dependent variables in advertising experiments are typically mental processes and states that messages and channels are hypothesized to influence. The manner in which dependent variables have been conceptualized and measured in advertising research tends to treat most dependent variables, which likely represent real-time mental processes, as existing in the form of highly conscious states rather than underlying embodied mental processes engaged during advertising exposure. Researchers often end up measuring such concepts in a way that is inconsistent with the very conceptualization of a mental process as unfolding across time. This happens any time a researcher assumes that a concept representing an underlying embodied mental process is automatically accessible to conscious self-report after individuals are exposed to a message. This inconsistency between conceptual definitions and measurement is somewhat understandable given that advertising researchers study one of the most complex phenomena in existence, the mind processing advertising. However, given a solid theoretical framework, such as EMC, for understanding the nature of the entire mental experience of processing advertising, much more rigorous, and thorough measurement of dependent variables in experiments can be accomplished.

The approach to measurement of dependent variables recommended under EMC can be better understood through review of a specific model of how the mind processes media content. Lang's (2009) *limited capacity model of motivated mediated message processing* (LC4MP) identifies concepts that ought to be included as dependent variables in experiments on mental processing of advertising and offers a rigorous approach to measurement in experiments. This model includes the assumptions of EMC—that the mind is completely embodied in the human brain and the primary purpose of embodied mental processing is to determine the motivational significance of stimuli and adaptively respond. The model further describes processing of a message as involving the allocation of limited cognitive resources to the memory subprocesses of encoding, storage, and retrieval. Both bottom-up, relatively unconscious processes, and top-down, highly conscious processes drive the allocation of cognitive resources to memory. This means that processing of an advertisement engages both underlying, embodied mental processes involved in motivational activation and memory as well as an individual's stored conscious experience involving perceptions, attitudes, and behavior. Figure 7.1 provides an illustration of processes and mental states involved in the dynamic interaction between receiver, message, and advertising channel as described by the LC4MP and EMC. The mental processes and states depicted in Figure 7.1 are the dependent variables that researchers interested in how the mind processes advertising need to measure.

Research on how the mind processes advertising needs to explore the entire mental experience of processing advertising. This is a phenomenon that includes a host of specific mental processes and states reaching varying levels of consciousness both during and after message exposure. For instance, an individual may have a general conscious perception of how much mental effort was allocated to attending to a particular message but will not have conscious access to the actual degree to which their brain allocated cognitive resources to encoding a message during exposure. This has been demonstrated through research on imagery in audio advertising. Individuals consciously report that they invest a

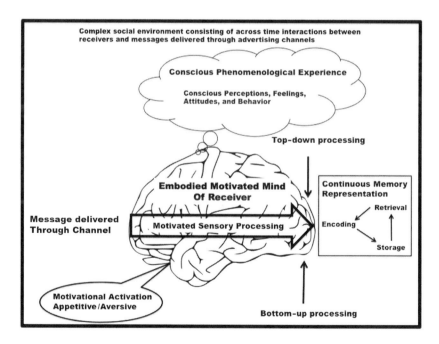

Figure 7.1 Mental Processes Engaged by Advertising Exposure as Described Under the EMC Framework and Annie Lang's LC4MP.

lot of mental effort in processing high imagery versus low imagery audio ads but data collected during real-time message exposure indicates that high imagery ads take less effort to encode than low imagery ads (Bolls & Lang, 2003). Figure 7.1 illustrates how the entire mental experience of processing advertising involves the interaction of motivated processes—associated with attention, emotion, and memory—and mental states—reflective of attitudes, conscious perceptions, and behavior—that are represented in conscious experience. The approach to measuring dependent variables in advertising experiments suggested by the EMC requires using measures that enable the observation of aspects of this entire mental experience, requiring data from a wide variety of measures.

The mental experience of processing advertising is manifested physiologically, linguistically, and behaviorally. The physiological manifestation of this mental experience is evident in the operation of embodied mental processes that evoke specific patterns of variation in nervous system activity. The linguistic aspect of the experience is reflected in verbal cognitions and words that reflect an individual's conscious access to mental constructs such as attitudes and conscious memory related to advertising exposure. The behavioral component of the experience reflects any actions an individual may be inclined to take in response to advertising exposure. This means that capturing the entire mental experience of processing advertising requires data from psychophysiological and self-report measures capable of describing embodied mental processes as well as linguistic and behavioral expression associated with advertising exposure. Each measure captures a unique aspect of the mental experience. The most valid way to measure embodied mental processes is through psychophysiological measures. Attitudes, the content of memory, as well as any potential actions an individual might take in response to a message are mental states emerging through advertising exposure that can be validly observed through self-report measures. This approach to measurement of dependent variables recommended under EMC—collecting data from a wide range of psychophysiological and self-report measures—is the most promising pathway to gaining insight into how the mind processes advertising.

Psychophysiology: A Methodological Paradigm for Advertising Research

As mentioned earlier, psychophysiological measures represent the methodological core of the EMC approach to studying advertising exposure. Research using psychophysiological measures as indicators of how the mind processes media content is becoming increasingly popular in the scholarly literature and among private advertising research firms. It is important to note, however, that psychophysiology represents more than merely a category of interesting bodily measurements a researcher can collect in advertising experiments. Psychophysiology has emerged as a unique *epistemology*—within the psychological sciences—for understanding human nature. Researchers need to fully embrace this epistemology in order for psychophysiological measures to be applied in a manner that advances advertising theory.

According to the *Handbook of Psychophysiology*, "psychophysiology can be defined as the scientific study of social, psychological, and behavioral phenomena as related to and revealed through physiological principles and events in functional organisms" (Cacioppo et al., 2007, p. 4). Psychophysiology provides a framework for interpreting specific patterns of physiological activity as indicative of specific mental processes. It is misguided to view physiological measures as indexing any form of a supposed physiological or even psychophysiological "effect" of messages on individuals. The first application of psychophysiological measures in media research occurred in the 1940s, but it was not until media researchers embraced psychophysiology as an epistemology for understanding the mind, instead of seeking psychophysiological effects of media, that these measures became more than a passing methodological fad (for an historical review see Lang, Potter, & Bolls, 2009). Researchers need to realize that the validity and reliability of psychophysiological measures comes from the unique epistemology that makes psychophysiology a distinct methodological paradigm for advertising research.

Psychophysiology includes basic assumptions researchers working under the paradigm should understand. They are discussed in great detail in other excellent sources, including a chapter in the *Handbook of Psychophysiology* (Cacioppo et al., 2007); however, here we briefly consider two primary assumptions. The most important assumption made in psychophysiology was reviewed above, namely that the mind is embodied in the human brain. This is the assumption that gives meaning to the very act of collecting physiological data in order to understand how the mind processes advertising. If you do not buy into this assumption, it is meaningless to draw inferences about, for instance, attention paid to an advertisement by interpreting variation in cardiac activity. On the other hand, if indeed the mind is completely embodied in the brain then this makes perfect sense. The researcher, diligently working under this research paradigm, can feel confident drawing conclusions about mental processing of messages from a wide range of physiological responses generated by both central and peripheral nervous system activity. Mental processes occur through the very real physical activity of the human brain, which vibrates throughout the human nervous system due to the brain's connection to every part of the body.

The second assumption we will discuss serves as a warning to researchers wishing to draw conclusions about mental processing of advertising from psychophysiological data. Researchers need to remember that the primary job of the body is to sustain life, meaning that variation in physiological activity reflective of the operation of mental processes is extremely small. This makes psychophysiological measures difficult in that the data obtained with these measures reflects multiple influences on bodily responses and researchers must work very hard to separate physiological activity dedicated to keeping an individual alive from the activity that is of interest in observing the operation of mental processes engaged by advertising exposure.

Researchers who familiarize themselves with the epistemological assumptions of psychophysiology beyond what we have discussed here are going to be at the forefront of developing rich advertising theories. The labs where psychophysiology serves as the foundation for experimental research provide an exciting environment for student and faculty researchers to work together on understanding how the mind processes advertising. Such a lab is displayed in Figures 7.2–7.4.

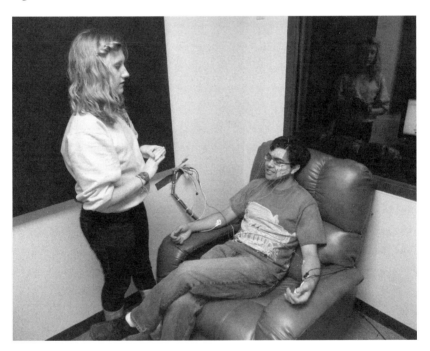

Figure 7.2 Interaction Between a Researcher and Participant in a Media Psychophysiology Lab. The collection of psychophysiological data involves the placement of recording electrodes on the surface of the skin. The participant is being prepared for the collection of heart rate, a physiological indicator of attention, skin conductance, a measure of arousal, and facial EMG, an index of emotional valence.

Figure 7.3 The Physiological Signal Collected from the Surface Electrodes is Collected Time-Locked to Exposure to Ads being shown during an Experiment using Readily Available Software Specialized for Psychophysiological Data Collection and Analysis.

The book by Potter and Bolls (2011), listed in the Additional Readings for this chapter, describes in detail many of the psychophysiological measures used in media psychophysiology labs to study how the mind processes media messages including advertising.

The most significant methodological strength of psychophysiology is that it enables the real-time observation of mental processes evoked by advertising exposure. Psychophysiological measures can index mental processes occurring on a timescale of milliseconds during advertising exposure. This not only enables researchers to draw conclusions about mental processes engaged by an entire message but also processing that occurs at very specific time points in a single message. Several researchers have already tapped into this premise. For example, EEG—the measurement of electrical activity generated by cortical areas of the brain—has been used to index changes in attention in response to very slight variation in television advertising executions such as specific gestures made by models in ads (Ohme, Reykowska, Wiener, & Choromanska, 2009). Peripheral nervous system measures, heart rate, and facial EMG, have been used to provide insight into possible defensive responses evoked at specific time points in disgust-eliciting anti-tobacco ads (Leshner, Bolls, & Wise, 2011).

Figure 7.4 The Primary Component for Psychophysiological Data Collection consists of a Configuration of Bioamplifiers and a Skin Coupler like Shown Here. The equipment shown here is used for the collection of peripheral nervous system measures (heart rate, skin conductance, and facial EMG).

Part of the promise for psychophysiology to serve as a methodological paradigm for advertising research comes from the development of new, cutting-edge measures that give researchers the ability to observe motivated cognitive processes underlying the psychological impact of brand messages by indexing low-level motivational processes and localizing brain activity during ad exposure. Functional magnetic resonance imaging—a measure that enables observation of activity in specific areas of the brain—has been used to identify specific brain networks associated with levels of pleasure and arousal evoked by television ads (Morris et al., 2009). The eye blink startle response—an indicator of aversive motivational activation—was recently used in a study of political advertising to examine the extent to which attack political ads evoke aversive motivational responses (Bradley, Angelini, & Lee, 2007). Psychophysiology is a science that continues to grow in the range of techniques and measures used to investigate embodied mental processes and advertising researchers can certainly tap into this growth and conduct research that takes our theoretical understanding of the mind processing advertising to new levels.

The promise of psychophysiology in advertising research will not be fulfilled, however, unless researchers avoid some potential pitfalls. The human brain is arguably the most complex biological entity in existence, so researchers need to be adequately trained in psychophysiology and keep up with changes.

There has been strong growth in the application of psychophysiological measures in private advertising research firms. It should be kept in mind, however, that the mission of industry research is to provide narrowly applied, practically valuable research for clients. This mission in some ways is antithetical to research solidly grounded in valid theoretical frameworks, conducted from detailed understanding of a research paradigm, such as psychophysiology. Researchers who focus too much on the measures—in this case physiological activity in the brain—as is often the case in highly applied research, may not have the proper perspective on psychophysiological measures as only one of many potential useful tools for advancing a theoretical understanding of how the mind processes advertising. Ultimately, advertising researchers must remember that the goal is to produce rich theoretical explanations of how the embodied motivated mind processes advertising, not merely index physiological activity that a researcher may have some vague inkling is possibly related to advertising effectiveness.

Conclusion

The EMC leads researchers to adopt psychophysiology as a methodological paradigm and provides the solid foundation necessary to advance theoretical explanations of dynamic mental processes underlying advertising exposure. It provides ways to conceptualize and measure psychological constructs that advertising researchers have been studying for decades. We believe this approach supplies a deep understanding of the human brain that produces a mind capable of perceiving and responding to brand messages as well as the ability to index mental processes, as embodied mental phenomena, engaged during advertising exposure. A focus on the embodied motivated mind that receives advertising and the most relevant, sensory and motivational features of messages and advertising channels can serve as an anchor for research that continues to develop relevant theoretical explanations of the important impact that advertising has on individuals across present and yet-to-be-invented forms of advertising.

References

Berntson, G. G., & Cacioppo, J. T. (2008). The functional neuroarchitecture of evaluative processes. In A. J. Elliott (Ed.), *Handbook of approach and avoidance motivation* (pp. 307–321). New York: Psychology Press.

Bolls, P. D., & Lang, A. (2003). I saw it on the radio: The allocation of attention to high imagery radio advertisements. *Media Psychology, 5* (1), 49–71.

Bradley, S. D., Angelini, J. R., & Lee, S. (2007). Psychophysiological and memory effects of negative political ads. *Journal of Advertising, 36* (4), 115–127.

Cacioppo, J. T., Gardner, W. L., & Berntson, G. G. (1999). The affect system has parallel and integrative processing components form follows function. *Journal of Personality and Social Psychology, 76* (5), 839–855.

Cacioppo, J. T., Tassinary, L. G., & Berntson, G. G. (2007). Psychophysiological science: Interdisciplinary approaches to classic questions about the mind. In J. T. Cacioppo, L. G. Tassinary, & G. G. Berntson (Eds.), *Handbook of psychophysiology* (pp. 1–18). New York: Cambridge University Press.

Chaffee, S. H. (1980). Mass media effects: New research perspectives. In G. C. Wilhoit & H. de Bock (Eds.), *Mass communication review yearbook* (Vol. 1, pp. 77–108). Beverly Hills, CA: Sage.

Du Plessis, E. (2008). *The advertised mind: Groundbreaking insights into how our brains respond to advertising*. Philadelphia, PA: Kogan Page.

Geiger, S., & Newhagen, J. (1993). Revealing the black box: Information processing and media effects. *Journal of Communication, 43* (4), 43–50.

Lang, A. (2009). The limited capacity model of motivated mediated message processing. In R. L. Nabi & M. B. Oliver (Eds.), *The Sage handbook of media processes and effects* (pp. 193–204). Thousand Oaks, CA: Sage.

Lang, P. J., & Bradley, M. M. (2008). Appetitive and defensive motivation is the substrate of emotion. In A. J. Elliot (Ed.), *Handbook of approach and avoidance motivation* (pp. 51–66). New York: Psychology Press.

Lang, P. J., & Bradley, M. M. (2010). Emotion and the motivational brain. *Biological Psychology, 84* (3), 437–450.

Lang, P. J., Bradley, M. M., & Cuthbert, B. N. (1997). Motivated attention: Affect, activation, and action. In P. J. Lang, R. F. Simons, & M. T. Balaban (Eds.), *Attention and orienting: Sensory and motivational processes* (pp. 97–135). Hillsdale, NJ: Lawrence Erlbaum.

Lang, A., Potter, R. F., & Bolls, P. (2009). Where psychophysiology meets the media: Taking the effects out of mass communication research. In J. Bryant & M.B. Oliver (Eds.), *Media effects: Advances in theory and research* (3rd ed., pp.185–206). Hillsdale, NJ: Lawrence Erlbaum.

Leshner, G., Bolls, P. D., & Wise, K. (in press). Motivated processing of fear appeal and disgust images in televised anti-tobacco ads. *Journal of Media Psychology: Theories, Methods, and Applications, 23* (2), 77–89.

Morris, J. D., Klahr, N. J., Shen, F., Villegas, J., Wright, P., He, G., & Liu, Y. (2009). Mapping a multidimensional emotion in response to television commercials. *Human Brain Mapping, 30* (3), 789–796.

Norris, C. J., Gollan, J., Berntson, G. G., & Cacioppo, J. T. (2010). The current status of research on the structure of evaluative space. *Biological Psychology, 84* (3), 422–436.

Ohme, R., Reykowska, D., Wiener, D., & Choromanska, A. (2009). Analysis of neurophysiological reactions to advertising stimuli by means of EEG and galvanic skin response measures. *Journal of Neuroscience, Psychology, and Economics, 2* (1), 21–31.

Perrachione, T. K., & Perrachione, J. R. (2008). Brains and brands: Developing mutually informative research in neuroscience and marketing. *Journal of Consumer Behaviour, 7*, 303–318.

Sparks, G. G. (2002). *Media effects research: An overview*. Belmont, CA: Wadsworth.

Yegiyan, N. S., & Lang, A. (2010). Processing central and peripheral detail: How content arousal and emotional tone influence encoding. *Media Psychology, 13* (1), 77–99.

Additional Readings

Bradley, M. M., & Lang, P. J. (2007). Emotion and motivation. In J. T. Cacioppo, L. G. Tassinary, & G. G. Berntson (Eds.), *Handbook of psychophysiology* (3rd ed., pp. 581–607). New York: Cambridge University Press.

Bradley, S. D. (2007). Dynamic, embodied, limited capacity attention and memory: Modeling cognitive processing of mediated stimuli. *Media Psychology, 9* (1), 211–239.

Potter, R. F., & Bolls, P. D. (2011). *Psychophysiological measurement and meaning: Cognitive and emotional processing of media*. New York: Routledge.

Ravaja, N. (2004). Contributions of psychophysiology to media research: Review and recommendations. *Media Psychology, 6*, 193–235.

Chapter 8

Involvement

Eric Haley

Getting attention with advertising has been a focus of industry and academic research for decades. After all, if no one sees your message, can it have an impact? People are inundated with stimuli at any given moment in their daily lives. It is believed that we cannot begin to process all we encounter, so we must actively select what we pay attention to. Theoretically, this is called selective perception, and the first step in basic perception models is selection of the particular stimuli (such as an ad) to which we will give attention at that moment.

There are many reasons you may pay attention to advertising. You may pay attention to an ad because it is novel, irritating, funny, loud, quiet, shocking, the model is attractive or familiar, you're bored, you find the ad relevant to something on your mind at that time, etc. There are various theoretical concepts that explore these motives for individuals selecting advertising as a stimulus of interest. Such concepts are often related to important advertising outcomes (e.g., what role does ad likeability play in regard to purchase intention?).

One of the earlier concepts formulated to explain why individuals may pay attention to advertising is the notion of involvement. If you venture into the office of major U.S. advertising agencies or read *Ad Age* over the years, you'll find industry people speaking of ideas such as "relevance" and "engagement." The terms change from year to year as agencies attempt to differentiate their philosophy from that of other agencies, but the basic ideas remain the same. At the core of terms like "relevance" and "engagement" is the fundamental idea of involvement.

What is Involvement?

Two germinal articles in the mid 1960s introduced the concept of "involvement" to the advertising literature, "The Impact of Television Advertising: Learning Without Involvement," and "The Measurement of Advertising

Involvement" both by Herbert Krugman (1965 and 1966, respectively). Krugman suggested that a viewer's involvement with an advertising message was evidenced by the conscious bridging associations the viewer makes between the message and his personal life. The more associations one makes the greater the involvement. In this sense, involvement is seen as a relevant connection between a message and an individual thus placing it within the "receiver" domain of the "Components of the Advertising Process Circle" model—illustrated in Figure 1.1—that guides this book.

In addition to involvement with a message, Krugman also suggested that different media created different relationships between the viewer/reader and the medium. Specifically, he said that television viewing was by nature a low-involvement activity compared to reading a magazine, for example. As a result of the media context, people learned differently from advertising.

Some argue that the main contribution of Krugman's involvement ideas was his suggestion that advertising works differently depending on the viewer's relationship to it (Maloney, 1994). It challenged the assumption that attitude formation always preceded purchase behavior. While the traditional AIDA hierarchy of effects models could be true in some situations (where awareness, interest, and desire were assumed to be antecedents to action), attitudes may be formed after action in what Krugman termed low involvement situations.

Involvement and Learning Theory

Involvement's first theoretical link was with learning theory, one of many theoretical areas within the academic discipline of psychology. Learning theory attempts to explain how people acquire, assimilate, and retrieve information. Krugman's suggestions about advertising learning opened the door for other thinkers to consider how advertising might work differently under different circumstances. These ideas were expanded beyond the ad message and media context to encompass conceptualizations of consumer behavior as being high or low involvement.

For example, Robertson (1976) used the term "commitment" to describe a person's relationship to a product or brand. Commitment was defined as the strength of the individual's belief system with regard to a product or brand. It was posited that commitment would be maximized under conditions of a high number of perceived distinguishing attributes among brands and a high level of salience (importance) attached to those attributes. This model of high-commitment consumer behavior would suggest an active audience model where consumers actively engaged in information seeking. Perhaps this describes how an average person might buy a car since a car is an expensive purchase and she may need a great deal of information about options prior to making a confident purchase decision. However, Roberts suggested that consumers may also engage in low-commitment behavior where the audience is more passive in the sense that purchase-related information seeking is rare. Buying salt or sugar at the grocery store might be an example. This suggested that most information acquisition under low commitment conditions would be based on trial of the product rather than active information seeking from other sources like advertising.

The two types of behavior suggested two definitions of advertising effectiveness. In the high-commitment scenario, advertising is effective if it moves people toward action by providing relevant product attributed-oriented information. A measure like message recall could be an important indicator of the effectiveness of an advertisement in a high-commitment scenario. However, under low-commitment conditions, mere exposure to advertising would likely equate to effectiveness. Perhaps brand name recognition might be all that's needed as an indicator for an ad in a low-commitment scenario to be considered effective.

Rational and Emotional Involvement and Learning

The FCB grid, an advertising planning tool developed by Foote Cone and Belding advertising agency, embodied an advance in the involvement concept in two key ways (Vaughn, 1983). First, it assumed that involvement (which by then was being operationalized in terms of importance of a purchase decision to an individual, the risks associated with the purchase decision, and amount of thought required for the decision) could be either "rational" or "emotional." Whereas most previous research had defined involvement or commitment (e.g., Robertson, 1976) in terms of rational attribute-oriented product evaluations, the FCB grid recognized that purchase decisions could have both rational and emotional aspects that are important to an individual. As such, a purchase decision could be highly involving on rational or "thinking" dimensions or highly involving on emotional or "feeling" dimensions. Second, the grid suggested different learning models for each involvement situation.

Each involvement context of the grid suggested a different consumer behavior model. In high involvement/thinking situations, it was posited that consumers follow the traditional informative/economic-learning model (learn–feel–do) where product attribute/benefit learning precedes attitude formation, which precedes behavior. However, in the high involvement/feeling quadrant, it was posited that consumers follow an affective/psychological model (feel–learn–do) where feeling drives learning that precedes behavior.

In both low-involvement situations, consumer action comes first, followed by learning then feeling (do–learn–feel) on the "thinking" side. The low involvement/thinking quadrant was described as habitual/responsive behavior. On the "feeling" side, action is followed by feeling then learning (do–feel–learn).

This quadrant was characterized by satisfaction/social behavior. Examples of products that could lie within each section of the grid are given in the following section regarding involvement and message strategy.

The utility of the grid has been recognized beyond purchase decisions. Specifically, Kassarjian (1981) claimed that the grid could also be useful in understanding a purchase or product use situation in terms of involvement. In illustrating this claim, Vaughn (1986) provided an example of how consumers viewed serving wine at a dinner party. For example, depending on the guest list, consumers may feel that their wine selection is more crucial to a party's success when "important" guests are present as opposed to "good friends." Thus, the wine purchase decision is more "involving" when the perceived stakes of the party are higher.

Involvement and Message Strategy

The understanding of situational consumer behavior offered by the FCB grid had advertising strategy implications. Each type of involvement suggested a different type of message strategy or product appeal for advertising. Consider the following products.

In a U.S.-based FCB grid study presented by Vaughn (1986), life insurance was found to be a high involvement/thinking purchase decision, perfume a high involvement/feeling purchase, liquid household cleaner a low involvement/thinking purchase, and Popsicles a low involvement/feeling purchase. Interestingly, the purchase of a family car was highly involving on both thinking and feeling dimensions with a slight edge toward feeling.

Once you understand the consumer's relationship to the purchase in terms of involvement, you can see how different messages might be better than others. For example, since consumers look at a life insurance purchase as highly involving on thinking dimensions, the learning model associated with such a purchase suggests the consumer wants "economic" product attribute-oriented information, thus a "reason why" copy approach (one that emphasizes the rational reasons why one should purchase the product) might work better in meeting the consumer's needs. The perfume message might stress important feelings associated with using the fragrance since it's an important purchase for the consumer but driven by emotional motives. In the low involvement examples, liquid household cleaner might best be positioned as the easy and reliable solution to everyday cleaning needs (low involvement/thinking), while Popsicles (low involvement/feeling) might be positioned as a simple feel-good treat for the whole family.

The advertising strategy and message implications of involvement as articulated in the FCB grid became the impetus for additional work in advertising message strategy. Using the high/low involvement and thinking/feeling dimensions, Puto and Wells (1984) suggested that advertising message strategy could be broadly categorized into two types—informational and transformational. Informational message strategy, which corresponds to the "thinking" side of the FCB grid, was defined as messages that provide consumers with factual, relevant brand data in a clear and logical manner such that they have greater confidence in their ability to assess the merits of buying the brand after seeing the advertisement. Relating to the "feeling" side of the grid, transformational strategy was defined a message that associates the experience of using the advertised brand with a unique set of psychological characteristics that would not typically be associated with the brand experience to the same degree without exposure to the advertisement.

Type of involvement was also incorporated into Taylor's (1999) six-segment message strategy wheel. Building upon the ideas presented in the FCB grid and Puto and Wells (1984), Taylor subdivided the informational and transformational message strategy typology into six subdivisions (three informational and three transformational). Each of the six segments was based on a specific type of consumer motivation based on what type of meaning a purchase, brand, or product use had for the consumer.

Involvement—Situational or Enduring?

As previously discussed, involvement is contextual. Part of that context has to do with the temporal nature of the consumer relationship to the ad, medium, product category, brand, message, issue, etc. Houston and Rothschild (1978) suggested that there could be a distinction made between what they called situational involvement and enduring involvement.

Situational involvement would refer to a specific moment in time such as a purchase decision or specific product use occasion. The purchase of a wedding dress might be a highly involving purchase decision, but involvement in that purchase decision would likely wane after the wedding (especially if things don't go so well!). Similarly, gift purchases may be temporarily highly involving.

Enduring involvement describes a general and more permanent concern. One might be highly involved in environmental issues, and thus more involved in products/services that exhibit pro-environment attributes or in communication that resonates with the individual's environmental concerns. One could have enduring involvement with a celebrity, and thus might feel involvement with ads, products, or programs that feature that celebrity.

Enduring Involvement with the Brand—The Case of Brand Communities

Within the consumer research literature, recent attention has been given to a special type of consumer/brand involvement, brand communities. Brand communities represent a type of enduring high consumer involvement with a brand, so much so that consumers feel a connection with other brand users (Muniz & O'Guinn, 2001; Schau, Muniz, & Arnould, 2009). Brand communities have grown up around such brands as Harley Davidson and Disney. For example, one Walt Disney World television spot acknowledged the strong connection some guests have with the parks by showing a Disney park guest gladly picking up a piece of litter on Main Street. He then looks around at the sparkling clean environment with a smile of satisfaction on his face as if he owned the park. While the Disney brand community arose organically, Disney is now attempting to leverage the power of this type of consumer involvement through their Disney-sponsored online fan club, D23.

High brand involvement might be expressed in many ways. Participating in social network fan pages, consumer brand advocacy (consumers becoming a volunteer sales person for the brand), being brand bloggers, attending brand-centered events such as a Harley Davidson rally or Disney fan club meeting, honking their horn at other VW Beetle owners while driving, visiting a brand museum (see Hollenbeck, Peters, & Zinkhan, 2008), or simply being a loyal brand purchaser/user are all ways consumers may show they have a special involvement relationship with a brand.

While brand loyalty is a likely expression of high brand involvement, not all brand loyalty can be attributed to involvement. Some brand loyalty might be driven by habit rather than strong commitment or strong attachment to the brand. For example, a consumer might buy Cheer laundry detergent simply because the consumer was satisfied with the way the product performed and buying Cheer every time is a quick and easy habitual decision (see Robertson, 1976).

Relationships Among Types of Involvement

Researchers have theorized about the relationship among various involvement types with regard to key advertising outcomes such as purchase intention. Since involvement has many antecedents and consequences and can vary depending on different situations, the scope of the involvement literature has been voluminous and varied (Kim, Haley, & Koo, 2009). Some have argued for an involvement hierarchy.

In their review of involvement literature, Day, Stafford, and Camacho (1995) suggested that involvement with general issues or activities leads to more specific involvement. For example, involvement with technology could lead to technology product category involvement (computers, phones, iPods, etc.), which could lead to involvement with ads for technology products. These authors suggest that general and product category involvement are likely to be enduring involvement while purchase decision and advertising involvement is likely to be situational.

Other research suggests that the relationship between involvement types might be more dynamic than a single hierarchy (Kim et al., 2009). For example, could involvement work differently in corporate advertising (ads that promote an entire corporation) as compared to product advertising? One study suggests it might. Kim et al. (2009) found that advertising involvement was even more important in corporate advertising than in product advertising in cases where consumers were previously unfamiliar with a company. Perhaps involvement can work in the reverse order. For example, it might be reasonable to assume that interest in a product category could develop from seeing a very involving ad, especially in the case of a pioneer brand of a new product category.

In fact, the relationship among types of involvement might not be all that linear. It could be that the linear nature of models describing the relationship among involvement types is an artifact of statistical modeling (e.g., forcing a stepwise, linear model) or of the fact that we tend to study one isolated moment in time. If we think about the relationship between people and brands, product categories, companies, issues, etc., advertising might have a different role over time for the same consumer with the same brand. Ads might create more positive feelings toward a brand or company, or they might lessen the intensity of feelings toward that brand or company. A consumer may grow tired of a brand or company and stop paying attention to its advertising. Or good advertising might re-energize that consumer's interest in the brand/company. As such it might be that the relationship among types of involvement are more dynamic and reflexive than our linear models have shown.

Involvement with the Medium

In the earliest work on involvement, Krugman (1965) suggested that certain media contexts were more involving than others for the consumer. As previously discussed, he felt that television viewing was less involving than reading magazines, thus, consumers might approach advertising in these media differently. But is magazine reading always more involving than watching TV? Or is TV viewing always less involving than reading a magazine? How about surfing the Web? Using a social network site? Can we assume that involvement is a consistent experience for consumers based on media type?

In media planning, some planners assign "weights" to advertising media exposure figures in order to better estimate exposure to an advertisement as compared to exposure to the medium. For example, with magazines, media planners value magazines with a higher subscriber to single-issue purchaser ratio. That is, if a person has sought out a particular magazine and pays for a subscription, it is likely that the person will have a higher involvement level with that magazine than someone who might buy one issue, or someone who picks up the magazine at a doctor's office or other waiting area. Someone who is truly involved in the magazine content would also likely be involved in the ads. For example, readers of fashion magazines, travel and tourism magazines, etc., likely find the information in ads just as involving or relevant to their interests as the information in articles. In this sense, magazines might be considered highly involving.

But is television always low involvement? The answer would likely depend on the motivation for TV use. If you are watching TV to pass the time, or are just "channel surfing," you might consider TV viewing low involvement. But what if you're really into a television series so much so that you must watch it every week? What if you can't wait to see who's eliminated on your favorite talent competition show? These situations suggest that TV involvement might be more contextual. In some contexts, TV might be a higher involvement context than magazines, and in other contexts, a lower one. Similar reasoning could be used for surfing the Web, reading a newspaper, radio listening, etc. In short, involvement with a medium is just like involvement with other things. It's highly situational and personal, with the key being the relevance of the object (issue, ad, medium, purchase) to the individual.

Is Involvement Always Positive?

It seems that most of the advertising literature sees creating involvement as a good thing, leading to positive outcomes for advertisers. While in many situations, this is true, could there be situations where a consumer's high involvement gets in the way of the advertising message?

Consider a situation where a highly involved consumer in environmental issues encounters "green marketing," or ads that tout the eco-friendliness of a product or company. While some pro-environment consumers may look favorably on such messages, others' high involvement in environmental issues might create more skepticism toward the marketer's claim.

How about a situation where someone is very involved in a political party? It might be reasonable to assume based on cognitive consistency theories, that a highly involved person of one political party might actively avoid messages from candidates of the opposing political party because of dissonance or irritation, etc. But there are people who hate (insert the political party of your choosing), but actively watch the ads from that party, getting really riled about them (and enjoying it) and using those ads as proof positive of the apparent stupidity, ignorance, lying, out-of-touchness, of the reviled party. The ads might even become social currency in political discussions among like-minded people. Certainly this exhibits a type of message involvement, but with "reverse" effects of what the message creators intended.

Another example of involvement with ads not always being positive would be the reaction of some U.S. Gulf Coast residents to BP advertising post-oil spill in 2010. In attempts to assure Gulf coast residents that BP was doing all it could to stop and clean up the Gulf of Mexico oil spill, the company ran daily full-page four-color ads in local newspapers. Some highly involved, angry residents paid close attention to those ads, but the ads only fueled (so to speak) their anger at the company for spending money on what they considered appearances rather than on efforts to mitigate the damage or prevent such a disaster in the first place. Whether such anger represents situational negative involvement or enduring negative involvement with BP can only be answered with time.

Role of Involvement in Other Theories

The examples just presented suggest that involvement can significantly affect information processing. In addition to its connection to learning theory discussed earlier, involvement has been used as a moderating variable when looking at various theories. For example, in the ELM chapter in this book, involvement can be seen as moderating the relationships between cognitive responses, beliefs, and ad and brand attitudes (Muehling, Laczniak, & Andrews 1993). Under high involvement situations versus low, strong message arguments will have a greater impact on attitudes. However, source credibility as a peripheral cue will be more persuasive in low involvement situations than in high. In short, central cues (message arguments) are seen as more important in high involvement conditions and peripheral cues are more important in low involvement conditions (Petty & Cacioppo, 1981; Petty, Cacioppo, & Schumann, 1983). These studies also demonstrate that higher involvement can lead to improved category and brand recall.

Strength of involvement can affect information processing as shown in the ELM, and other theories might be used to explain differential effects of involvement. For example, cognitive consistency theories might provide a window to explore. What impact would high versus low involvement have on information selection? If a consumer loves Disney (as previously discussed) cognitive consistency theories would suggest a person with strongly held beliefs that might correlate with high involvement in a brand like Disney, would either seek out positive information about Disney to reinforce the currently held beliefs and avoid negative information that might cause cognitive dissonance. Thus, strong involvement might impact information selection. On the other hand, if one is highly involved with a product category, but does not have strong beliefs one way or the other, that highly involved person might seek both positive and negative information about brands or the category. These scenarios suggest a theoretical relationship between involvement and belief strength. Such a relationship might have implications for attitude change as well.

Individual difference variables might also predict involvement. Are some people more likely than others to experience high involvement? Do some people develop involvement with things more easily than others? Perhaps people with a high need to belong look for opportunities to "belong" to a brand or product category (e.g., someone who might enjoy a brand community experience or the experience of sharing a passion for collecting postcards). Perhaps some people do not get excited or attached to anything, thus are less likely to experience involvement. Much research has addressed what happens in different involvement situations, but little has been attempted to explain why people experience involvement.

Conclusion

Involvement is a receiver-oriented construct that has been used to explore many advertising contexts. It can describe the relationship between an individual and various consumer behavior-related things such as issues, interests, product categories, brands, advertising, media, or purchase situations. It can be rational or emotional, high or low, situational or enduring. Across all of these contexts, the "involvement" construct essentially describes the same phenomenon. That is, at the core of involvement is relevance. Involvement describes the relevance of the issue, interest, product category, brand, ad (message or execution), medium, or purchase to the consumer. Involvement doesn't reside within an object; it resides in a consumer's interpretation of that object. While statistical path models may show general relationships among involvement types (as described in the section of this chapter dealing with "involvement hierarchies") a deeper understanding of consumer involvement calls for an understanding of consumer relevance. To understand how involvement might work for or against a marketer, we need to understand the consumer's meaning systems and how our ad, brand, product category, issue, etc., interacts with those systems.

Consumer meanings have long been a central focus of account planners. Through qualitative research and other interpretative methods, planners have worked to understand the relevance of brands, products/services, issues, etc., to various consumer targets. Planners can be masters at understanding consumer involvement. As such, the following readings are recommended for those wishing to learn how involvement works within the consumer.

References

Day, E., Stafford, M. R., & Camacho, A. (1995). Opportunities for involvement research: A scale-development approach. *Journal of Advertising, 24* (3), 69–75.

Hollenbeck, C. R., Peters C., & Zinkhan, G. M. (2008). Retail spectacles and brand meaning: Insights from a brand museum case study. *Journal of Retailing, 84* (3), 334–353.

Houston, M. J., & Rothschild, M. J. (1978). Conceptual and methodological perspectives on involvement. In S. C. Jain (Ed.), *Research frontiers in marketing: Dialogues and directions* (pp. 184–187). Chicago: American Marketing Association.

Kassarjian, H. H. (1981). Low-involvement: A second look. In K. B. Monroe (Ed.), *Advances in consumer research 8* (262–269). Ann Arbor, MI: Association for Consumer Research.

Kim, S., Haley, E., & Koo, G. (2009). Comparison of the paths from consumer involvement types to ad responses between corporate advertising and product advertising. *Journal of Advertising, 38* (3), 67–80.

Krugman, H. (1965). The impact of television advertising: Learning without involvement. *Public Opinion Quarterly, 29*, 349–356.

Krugman, H. (1966). The measurement of advertising involvement. *Public Opinion Quarterly, 30*, 583–596.

Maloney, J. C. (1994). The first 90 years of advertising research. In C. E. M. Clark, T. C. Brock, & D. W. Stewart (Eds.), *Attention, attitude and affect in response to advertising* (pp. 13–68). Mahwah, NJ: Lawrence Erlbaum.

Muehling, D. D., Laczniak, R. N., & Andrews, J. C. (1993). Defining, operationalizing, and using involvement in advertising research: A review. *Journal of Current Issues and Research in Advertising, 15* (1), 21–57.

Muniz, A. M., Jr., & O'Guinn, T. (2001). Brand community. *Journal of Consumer Research, 27* (4), 412–432.

Petty, R. E., & Cacioppo, J. T. (1981). Issue involvement as a moderator of the effects on attitude of advertising, content and context. In K. B. Monroe (Ed.), *Advances in consumer research 8* (pp. 20–24). Ann Arbor, MI: Association for Consumer Research.

Petty, R. E., Cacioppo, J. T., & Schumann, D. (1983). Central and peripheral routes to advertising effectiveness: The moderating role of involvement. *Journal of Consumer Research, 10* (September), 135–146.

Puto, C. P., & Wells, W. D. (1984). Informational and transformational advertising: The differential effects of time. In T. C. Kinnear (Ed.), *Advances in consumer research 11* (pp. 638–643). Provo, UT: Association for Consumer Research.

Robertson, T. S. (1976). Low-commitment consumer behavior. *Journal of Advertising Research, 16* (2), 19–24.

Schau, H. J., Muniz, A. M., Jr., & Arnould, E. J. (2009). How brand community practices create value. *Journal of Marketing, 73* (5), 30–51.

Taylor, R. E. (1999). A six-segment message strategy wheel. *Journal of Advertising Research, 39* (6), 7–17.

Vaughn, R. (1983). How advertising works: A planning model. *Journal of Advertising Research* (September), 22–28.

Vaughn, R. (1986). How advertising works: A planning model revisited. *Journal of Advertising Research* (February/March), 57–66.

Additional Readings

Bond, J., & Kirshenbaum, R. (1998). *Under the radar: Talking to today's cynical consumer.* New York: John Wiley & Sons.

Husserl, E. (2001). *Logical investigations, Volumes 1 and 2.* New York: Routledge.

Morrison, M. A., Haley, E., Sheehan, K. G., & Taylor, R. E. (2002). *Using qualitative research in advertising: Strategies, techniques and applications.* Thousand Oaks, CA: Sage.

Schutz, A. (1967). *Phenomenology of the social world.* G. Walsh & F. Lehnert (Trans.). Chicago: Northwestern University Press.

Steele, J. (1998). *Truth, lies and advertising: The art of account planning.* New York: John Wiley & Sons.

Part III

Specific Audiences

Chapter 9

A Theory of Advertising to Children

Russell N. Laczniak and Les Carlson

What is Theory?

The development of theory is an important step in creating scientific thought. Defined as a systematic set of related statements, including law-like generalizations (Reynolds, 1971), theory can (and according to most, should) be used to guide empirical research (Hunt, 1983). It affords researchers a framework for developing, categorizing, and extending knowledge with respect to a particular phenomenon. Thus, theory, by definition, is applied, in that it is applied to a phenomenon that is distinct and unique from other domains (Fischer, 1975).

The present effort was guided by the observations noted in Figure 1.1 of this text that advertising is a variable field, not a natural science, and has evolved as an area of study because scholars have shown an academic interest in it. Variable fields are largely applied and practical, and as a result are consistently evolving (Nan & Faber, 2004). Thus, while in this chapter we hope to propose a theory that is integrative and consistent, it is also likely that our conceptions of a theory of advertising to children will need to be altered over time. We propose in this chapter a set of components, i.e., empirical generalizations (to be explained below) that may represent what we know or think we know about advertising to children, though we do not intend that what follows is exhaustive.

Philosophers of science note that theories may take a number of different forms. According to one classification system (Reynolds, 1971), theories may be presented in one of three basic forms: axiomatic, causal process, or as a set of laws. The axiomatic form, which is often used in basic disciplines such as mathematics, includes a set of definitions, propositions, and/or axioms that create a system of relationships and beliefs. The causal process form (often found in well-developed scientific disciplines such as chemistry) includes a set of interrelated definitions and statements that with either deterministic or probabilistic certainty, describe the effect of one or more independent variables on one or more dependent variables. Finally, the set-of-laws form involves the provision of an *integrated set of well-supported empirical generalizations* (EGs) with a specific domain. EGs are statements that summarize the results of a number of several empirical studies. Reynolds (1971) suggests that the set-of-laws approach is a useful starting place for emerging disciplines to develop theory. Thus, given that theory development in advertising is in its developmental stage (e.g., Nan & Faber, 2004), in the present chapter we will use the set-of-laws approach to develop a theory of advertising to children. To this end, our chapter will present EGs about advertising and children, thus providing a good overview of theory development in this field.

The Development of a Theory of Advertising to Children

In developing a theory of advertising to children, it is important to consider the area's distinctive aspects and attempt to identify its unique elements (Nan & Faber, 2004). Hunt (1983) suggests that the first step in developing theory is to identify and define the phenomenon under investigation. In this case, this step is relatively simple as we have been asked to develop a chapter that deals with "advertising to children." So, the phenomenon that is the focus of this chapter is multidimensional in that it should deal with the concept of advertising and its relationship with children. Because our theory will clearly reside within the broader domain of advertising, it is imperative that we identify aspects within the area that are distinct to the topic at hand. As noted in Chapter 1 and as illustrated in Figure 1.1 of this text, these aspects include ad sponsors, messages, media, and receivers.

Although the lines between advertising and other forms of communication have been blurred in recent years (especially when targeted at children, cf. Moore & Rideout, 2007), we will focus our efforts on studying phenomena that are unequivocally identified within the traditional domain of advertising. While much research that is related to this topic has looked beyond this traditional domain (c.f. Muehling, Carlson, & Laczniak, 1992), we chose to keep its focus simple and traditional.

It is important to note that this chapter will contribute to theory by focusing on advertising's effects on a unique group of advertising receivers, namely, children. As noted by Thorson and Rodgers in Chapter 1, ad receivers constitute the targeted audience for a particular advertising message. To provide more precision to the audience in question, we relied on the developmental psychology literature to help us define children. Two of the most influential views of childhood as presented by Jean-Jacques Rousseau and Jean Piaget note that children are unique in that they lack certain aspects of a fully matured adult. Rousseau (1962) viewed children as pre-adults. Expanding slightly on this characterization, Piaget (Piaget & Inhelder, 1968) describes children as those individuals developing toward adulthood. Both characterizations carefully distinguish children, who have limitations in their cognitive and emotional systems, from adults with disabilities by noting that children are likely to have adult-like abilities in the future, barring some catastrophic complications. We view children in a similar way, defining them as ad receivers who, while not yet having the abilities of adults regarding advertising and its effects on them, are progressing toward adulthood and concomitantly will acquire these abilities as they age. Importantly, this definition appears to be consistent with the Federal Trade Commission's description of children as not yet having adult-like capabilities to deal with advertising (John, 1999).

By combining this information with the Thorson and Rodgers (Chapter 1) definition of advertising, we were able to more precisely specify the domain of this chapter. Specifically, we will focus on *paid forms of communication from identified sponsors using mass media with the intention of persuading an audience that primarily includes those who are progressing toward adulthood but who are not yet considered to be adults.* Given the definition, it should be apparent that all children are not the same—a view that has been borne out in prior work. For example, while some studies distinguish between children according to their Piagetian stage of development (e.g., Soldow, 1983), others simply distinguish between younger and older children (cf. Pechmann, Levine, Loughlin, & Leslie, 2005), with the former group referred to as pre-adolescents and the latter as adolescents.

To derive a set of laws that will constitute our theory of advertising to children, we developed EGs by identifying research hypotheses that have received at least moderate support in the existing literature (Reynolds, 1971). Research hypotheses (i.e., direct statements that predict an effect on a specific group) that have not received at least a moderate level of empirical support cannot be classified as EGs. To this end, we reviewed empirical papers that deal with advertising targeted at children; we focused, but not entirely limited, our search for relevant papers to articles published in the *Journal of Advertising* (*JA*), *Journal of Current Issues in Research and Advertising* (*JCIRA*), *Journal of Consumer Research* (*JCR*), and *Journal of Public Policy and Marketing* (*JPP&M*). We have also included a book, i.e., *Advertising to Children: Concepts and Controversies* (Macklin & Carlson, 1999). *JA*, *JCIRA*, and *JCR* are natural homes for theory-based research dealing with consumer issues (including advertising) and children. *JPP&M* was selected since it included at least one (and actually more, in a tangential sense) special section that dealt with advertising to children. Finally, the Macklin and Carlson book was based on a call for papers for a special issue in the *JA* on "advertising to children." Thus, while the review presented in the present chapter is not completely exhaustive, it is rather extensive and focuses on outlets that are fairly common for our domain of interest.

Empirical Generalizations—Advertising to Children

First and foremost, we focused on identifying empirical generalizations that deal with children as receivers of advertising messages. Since advertising's effects on children are likely to be moderated by other factors (such as parents' interactions), we generated empirical generalizations that deal with these effects as well.

Children as Ad Receivers

Prior to the 1970s, some argued that children were not targeted with advertising messages. Yet much of the research in subsequent years demonstrated that children were not only targets for advertising, but that they were affected by ads. In an effort to determine if children were potentially vulnerable to the effects of advertising, Resnik & Stern (1977) performed an experiment whereby children were (not) exposed to an ad for a fictitious brand of potato chips. Postexposure brand preferences were also assessed. Results supported the hypothesis that children's brand choices can be influenced by television ads.

Following up on Resnik and Stern (1977), Gorn and Goldberg (1982) investigated the influence of advertising on children's food and snack preferences. They hypothesized that exposure to candy and sugared soft drink ads would lead children to prefer and be more likely to choose these products compared to healthier alternatives (fruit and orange juice). Results were generally supportive of the hypothesis. Thus, the authors conclude that even though most children (aged 5 through 8 in their study) know what they *should* consume (that a doctor would want them to eat), fruit and drink fruit juice, exposure to television commercials for candy and sugared beverages influenced their choices for such products.

Goldberg and Gorn (1978) assessed the influence of parents relative to television advertising regarding children's product choices. The authors hypothesized that exposure to a toy commercial would pique a child's interest such that s/he would prefer to play with the toy in lieu of parental guidance to the contrary. They also hypothesized that exposure to a toy commercial would lead a child to prefer playing with the toy rather than interacting with peers. Results (from preschool children who tended to be middle and upper class) were supportive of these hypotheses, prompting the authors to contend that advertising directed to children has the potential to lead to parent–child conflict and to persuade children to spend more time playing with toys rather than playing with peers.

Neely and Schumann (2004) investigated preschool children's responses to animated characters' actions and voice types in ads. The authors, while not proposing specific hypotheses, contended that the presence of animated characters using the featured product would promote children's attention to, association with, and liking of ads (and the products featured in the ads). While results generally supported these contentions, statistical significance was achieved only for liking of the products featured in the ads.

In sum, this body of research suggests that children are not only targets for ads, but that they are influenced by them in a number of ways.

EG1: Children are influenced by advertising.

Understanding Advertising's Persuasive Intent

As noted by John (1999), research focusing on children as ad receivers surged in the 1970s and 1980s. Studies published at this time were based largely on arguments that were presented by developmental psychologists and other child advocates that advertising directed at children was unfair because young children do not have a complete understanding of the persuasive intent of advertising. Empirical research findings, for the most part, supported this contention. For example, results of studies published by Robertson and Rossiter (1974) and Macklin (1987) suggest that children under the age of 8 had a limited understanding of advertising's persuasive intent at best. Children were apt to see advertising as a means of entertainment (e.g., they noted that ads were funny). Yet, other studies suggest that such limitations may be diminishing. For example, Mallalieu, Palan, and Laczniak (2005), noted that many school-aged children recognized that advertising's main intent was to "sell" goods and services. One possible explanation of this study's results is that educational programs targeted at children regarding advertising and media literacy (many of which were based on study findings of the 1970s and 1980s) are working. To form a more definitive conclusion, Martin (1997) conducted a meta-analysis of studies published between 1972 and 1994 that investigated the relationship between a child's age and understanding of advertising's intent. While the correlations from this analysis suggested that there is a positive relation between these concepts, the correlation appears to be moderated by the type of dependent measure used in the study. That is, researchers were more likely to find that children understood advertising when studies employed non-verbal dependent measures. Collectively, this body of research suggests that while all children obviously do not have adult-like knowledge about advertising's intention, primary school-aged children appear to have some understanding of advertising's persuasive intent and that this comprehension continues to develop as they age.

Related to this issue were concerns that children did not have the ability to discern differences between ads and editorial content (Stephens & Stutts, 1982). In this vein, it was suggested that program–commercial separators could be used to aid young children (under the age of 8) in making this distinction. However, results of a study by Stutts, Vance, and Huddleson (1981) suggested that separators might not be effective. It is clear that as young children age (i.e., from ages 3–7), they become better able to make the distinction between editorial content and ads.

EG2: Children's understanding of advertising's persuasive intent increases with age.

Development of Persuasion Knowledge

Persuasion knowledge deals with consumers' personal knowledge of the tactics used in persuasion attempts (Friestad & Wright, 1994). Persuasion knowledge helps consumers identify how, when, and why marketers are attempting to influence them and provides tools to respond appropriately. Given advertising's importance as a persuasion mechanism for marketers, the development of persuasion knowledge could provide children with cognitive defenses that allow them to become discriminating in the beliefs that they form after ad exposure. Thus, the development of persuasion knowledge would appear to be manifested in children's use of cognitive defenses against advertising and the development of a "healthy" skepticism of advertising claims.

Results presented by Boush, Friestad, and Rose (1994) suggest that the development of persuasion knowledge increases children's skepticism toward advertising. Importantly, these researchers also determined that persuasion knowledge appears to increase with age. While additional research is needed before more definitive statements can be made regarding children's development of persuasion knowledge, it does appear that by later adolescence, most children have formed a "healthy amount" of skepticism toward advertising and developed knowledge of some advertising tactics (Mangleburg & Bristol, 1998). However, children's use of cognitive defenses against advertising is less well understood. One study (Brucks, Armstrong, & Goldberg, 1988) concluded that the ability of 9 and 10 year olds to use cognitive defenses against advertising may not be as strong as some might think. Results suggested that children do not appear to be able to retrieve prior knowledge about advertising at the time of exposure unless they are cued to do so.

Stutts and Hunnicutt (1987) investigated young children's abilities to understand disclaimer content in television ads. By using verbal and non-verbal response measures, these researchers concluded that age was related to younger children's ability to understand the meaning of ad disclaimers (especially for verbal responses). However, the researchers also noted that most children tended to pay little or no attention to disclaimers in television ads.

Pawlowski, Badzinski, and Mitchell (1998) attempted to determine if children were able to interpret and process metaphors in advertisements. Defined as a figure of thought, the authors hypothesized that older children would be better able to correctly interpret and recall ad metaphors than would younger children. In a study with second, fourth, and sixth graders, these hypotheses were partially supported. Sixth-grade children were better able to interpret metaphors than their younger counterparts and were more likely to recall ad copy than younger children.

> EG3: Children's use of persuasion knowledge increases with age.

Information Processing Abilities

In their seminal study, Petty, Cacioppo, and Schumann (1983) distinguish between ad receivers' use of central and peripheral processing tendencies. Specifically, peripheral processing involves receivers responding to peripheral cues in ads such as the popularity of the spokesperson and/or the likeability of background music as they form post-exposure brand attitudes. On the other hand, receivers using central processing focus and elaborate on the message content of an advertisement. These elaborations are then used as the basis for the receivers' formation and/or alteration of brand attitudes. Since it is based on greater elaboration of message (as opposed to peripheral) content, central processing is thought to represent a more objective and advanced form of ad processing. This contention is supported by studies which note that central processing requires higher levels of motivation and ability as compared to peripheral processing (e.g., Moore & Lutz, 2000).

Roedder (1981) associated a child's age with her/his abilities to use varying types of ad processing. This idea was tested by Moore and Lutz (2000) who investigated differences in children's processing abilities between what they referred to as limited and strategic processors. These researchers found both that younger and older children's ad attitudes influenced post-exposure brand attitudes. However, their results also support the notion that younger children tended to rely exclusively on ad liking to form brand attitudes and older children used both ad liking and brand cognitions to do so. This finding suggests that younger children are unlikely to possess the ability to use central processing when exposed to ads, and as a result, tend to use peripheral processing (Petty et al., 1983).

EG4: Children's ability to use central processing when responding to ads increases with age.

Moderating Elements

Socialization Factors

Research suggests that socialization effects will likely influence children's abilities to deal with ads (Moschis, 1985). Baumrind (1980) defined socialization as "an adult-initiated process by which developing children, through insight, training, and imitation, acquire the habits and values congruent with adaptation to their culture" (p. 640). While this definition encompasses the influence that parents and other caretakers may have on children and includes children's reactions to advertising, Baumrind's socialization perspective may ignore effects due to other entities collectively known as socialization agents (see Moschis & Churchill, 1978). These agents of socialization may be "any person or organization directly involved in socialization" (Moschis & Churchill, 1978, p. 600). Consequently, socialization agents may be represented by children's caretakers (as noted above) or other individuals or entities that interact with children and have influence over them (Moschis & Churchill, 1978). This chapter continues with an examination of socialization agents with particular emphasis on their influence as potential moderators of the empirical generalizations already discussed in this chapter.

Parents/Family as Moderators of the Influence of Advertising on Children

The family is, of course, a potent influencing agent in children's development though the definition of family is not applied consistently (Carlson & Harrison, 2010). However, at least one definition of family coincides with discussions above regarding socialization agents. For example, Galvin, Bylund, and Brommel (2004, p. 6) define family as

> networks of people who share their lives over long periods of time bound by ties of marriage, blood, or commitment, legal or otherwise, who consider themselves as family and who share a significant history and anticipated future of functioning in a family relationship.

These "networks of people" could and undoubtedly do include those who are in contact with and exert control over children. Thus, families, including parents, other siblings, caretakers, etc., all function as socialization agents in children's development.

Families are not homogeneous (Carlson & Harrison, 2010) and therefore their structures are likely to mediate how children deal with ads. For example, Moschis and his colleagues established the importance of the family's "communication structure" (for an overview see, Moschis, 1985) as a framework for understanding how families mediate the impact of advertising on children. These so-called family communication patterns (FCPs) were an attempt to move beyond mere frequency measures of parent–child communication about consumption issues to the "content and structure" of such communication interactions (Moschis, 1985, p. 901). Among other findings, Moschis and his colleagues established that different FCP formats can result in different outcomes in children such as tendencies toward being more or less materialistic (Moschis, 1985).

In addition, other authors (for example, Carlson, Laczniak, & Walsh, 2001) borrowing from work established in developmental psychology (Baumrind, 1991), have shown that methods parents use to interact with their children (i.e., beyond communication patterns) will also influence how children process advertising. Specifically, Carlson et al. (2001) explored the general preferences for interacting with and parenting children (e.g., encouraging—or not—children's participation in family decision-making, aiding—or not—children's exposure to the environment, expressing—or not—affection for children, restricting—or not—the development of children's autonomy) that are characteristic of different parental types or "styles" (Baumrind, 1968, 1971). Carlson et al. (2001) then related these tendencies to more targeted interactions regarding how the marketplace is perceived by parents as well as its influence on children. Thus, evidence exists that suggests that these parental styles may serve as moderators of at least some of the EGs that have been proposed previously.

Unfortunately for theory building, there have been few studies in marketing and advertising that have utilized Baumrind's (1991) parental-style framework to investigate actual outcomes in children which are a result of these differential family effects. A notable exception to this observation is Carlson et al. (2001) who found that children mimicked their parents' views on a number of aspects having to do with television viewing. For example, children of one parental style referred to as Authoritatives (i.e., parents who are restrictive but also warm in their interactions with children) noted the same pattern of differences on the degree to which their parents watched television with them as did their parents. This, we believe, is an example of how parental style may act as a moderator of children's interactions with the media (for a review of studies supporting this notion, see Carlson, Laczniak, & Wertley, 2011), which would likely include advertising targeted to children. Further, Carlson et al. (2001) determined that children of authoritative and indulgent mothers (i.e., parents who are warm and permissive in their overall interactions with their children) cited their mothers as having less favorable attitudes toward television advertising and programming.

> EG5: Parental influence will moderate the relation between children's understanding of advertising and children's age.
>
> EG6: Parental influence will moderate the relation between children's attitudes toward advertising and children's age.

Peers as Moderators of the Influence of Advertising on Children

Peers also serve as socialization agents and therefore are potential moderators of certain of the relations previously mentioned. In general, peers are a source of both positive and negative influence on children, particularly during adolescence (Mangleburg, Doney, & Bristol, 2004). For example, regarding the positive influences of peers on adolescents' interactions with the marketplace, Mangleburg & Bristol (1998) found that adolescents' susceptibility to various forms of peer influence is related to their skepticism of advertising. That is, adolescents' susceptibility to "normative peer influence" (attempts at gaining approval from peers for consumption decisions) is negatively related to advertising skepticism while adolescents' susceptibility to informational peer influence (obtaining information from peers regarding consumption decisions) is positively related to their skepticism of advertising (Mangleburg & Bristol, 1998).

Peers also appear to be a source for shopping information which then also contributes to teens' level of persuasion knowledge (Mangleburg & Bristol, 1998). Teen friends may serve as shopping or "purchase pals" (Mangleburg et al., 2004) and therefore function as a source for assistance during purchase decisions made at retail outlets. Moschis and Churchill (1978) found that adolescents' communication about consumption with their friends is positively correlated with the adolescents' social motivations for consuming (i.e., consumption for conspicuous purposes) as well as their own materialistic tendencies. In addition, Moschis and Churchill (1978) found that adolescents' communication with peers was related to social motivations for watching television programs and advertising. Thus, we expect that peers will also function in a moderation capacity.

EG7: Peer influence will moderate the relation between children's understanding of advertising and children's age.

EG8: Peer influence will moderate the relation between children's attitudes toward advertising and children's age.

Discussion

Our review and theorizing suggests that children have limitations as ad receivers, but these constraints tend to diminish as the child matures. For example, prior research has noted that as children become older, they (1) are more likely to be better able to distinguish ads from programs, (2) develop a greater understanding of advertising's persuasive intent, (3) have greater knowledge of advertising tactics, (4) have higher levels of ad skepticism, (5) possess a greater ability to understand ad disclaimer content, and (6) use and understand brand attribute information in ads. Importantly, the description of children as limited, cued, and strategic processors of information (Roedder, 1981) appears to somewhat adequately distinguish among children and their abilities to deal with advertising. Specifically, it seems that those younger than 8 years of age are quite limited in these abilities, while those over 12 have at least some of what might be viewed as adult-like capabilities.

There are, of course, exceptions to this generalized set of findings. One deals with children's use of cognitive defenses. As noted by Brucks et al. (1988), even older children (those in the 8–12 age group) need to be cued in order to use their cognitive defenses when processing ad information. In addition, it seems that even adolescents may have certain characteristics that may make them more vulnerable to certain types of advertising information compared to younger children (Pechmann et al., 2005). Specifically, it has been demonstrated that adolescents (as compared to younger children) will be more likely to seek out ad information for risky products (Fox, Krugman, Fletcher, & Fischer, 1998).

Interestingly, the advertising environment for children appears to be distinct from that which faces adults in a number of ways. It seems, for example, that the number of ads targeted at children has increased over the years and that these ads tend to be dominated by male actors and spokespersons. Moreover, the ads are complex in nature, with one estimate suggesting that between one-third and two-thirds of all ads directed at children contain disclaimers (Stern & Harmon, 1984; Muehling & Kolbe, 1998). While disclaimers are thought to improve a receiver's ability to process information, it is uncertain whether or not this is the case, especially in the case of children and how they process advertising stimuli. Moreover, studies also suggest that ads targeted at children are likely to be more image based (as compared to information based) (Reece, Rifon, & Rodriguez, 1999). Further, it seems that advertisers are using differing strategies to target children as opposed to adults. Such a notion suggests that parents' monitoring of the children's ad environment is critical if they are to aptly socialize their children in this regard.

Finally, it seems that many of the effects of advertising on children will be moderated by their interactions with socialization agents such as parents and peers. In particular, the efficacy of these moderation entities, especially those having to do with parents (and other caretakers of children within families), is open for further investigation. This is especially pertinent in terms of assessing how parents might moderate the EGs mentioned here (i.e., adding to or detracting from the strength of these relations). As noted, except for a few exceptions such as Carlson et al. (2001), there has been almost no research on the effects of family environments (as defined by parental types or "styles" as mentioned previously) on the children of these unique family environments regarding advertising-related outcomes. Consequently, we believe that family environmental conditions represent a ripe opportunity for assessing the viability and strength of the EGs developed in this chapter within and across contexts such as family considerations.

In sum, the EGs developed for this chapter represent an attempt at building a foundation for developing a theory of advertising to children. While we are not insinuating that the EGs we have produced are exhaustive, we do believe that they represent a solid base for understanding the scope of how advertising and children interact. We hope that these EGs then serve as an impetus for additional research focusing on establishing further their viability as central tenets of what we know about advertising to children.

References

Baumrind, D. (1968). Authoritarian vs. authoritative parental control. *Adolescence, 3* (Fall), 255–272.

Baumrind, D. (1971). Current patterns of parental authority. *Developmental Psychology Monographs, 4* (January), 1–103.

Baumrind, D. (1980). New directions in socialization research. *American Psychologist, 35* (July), 639–652.

Baumrind, D. (1991). Parenting styles and adolescent development. In R. Lerner, A. Peterson, & J. Brooks-Gunn (Eds.), *Encyclopedia on adolescence* (pp. 746–758). New York: Garland.

Brucks, M., Armstrong, G. A., & Goldberg, M. E. (1988). Children's use of cognitive defenses against television advertising and knowledge of advertiser tactics. *Journal of Consumer Research, 14* (4), 471–482.

Carlson, L., & Harrison, R. (2010). Family public policy in the United States. *Journal of Macromarketing, 30* (4), 320–330.

Carlson, L., Laczniak, R. N., & Walsh, A. (2001). Socializing children about television: An intergenerational perspective. *Journal of the Academy of Marketing Science, 29* (3), 276–288.

Carlson, L., Laczniak, R. N., & Wertley, C. (2011). What we know and what we think we know about parental style: Implications for advertising and an agenda for future research. *Journal of Advertising Research, 51* (2), 427–435.

Fischer, R. B. (1975). *Science, man, and society* (2nd ed.). Philadelphia: W.B. Saunders.

Fox, R., Krugman, D., Fletcher, J., & Fischer, P. (1998). Adolescents' attention to beer and cigarette print ads and associated product warnings. *Journal of Advertising, 27* (3), 57–68.

Friestad, M., & Wright, P. (1994). The persuasion knowledge model: How people cope with persuasion attempts. *Journal of Consumer Research, 21* (1), 1–31.

Galvin, K., Bylund, C., & Brommel, B. (2004). *Family communication: Cohesion and change.* New York: Allyn & Bacon.

Goldberg, M. E., & Gorn, G. J. (1978). Some unintended consequences of TV advertising to children. *Journal of Consumer Research, 5* (1), 22–29.

Gorn, G. J., & Goldberg, M. E. (1982). Behavioral evidence of the effects of televised food messages on children. *Journal of Consumer Research, 9* (3), 200–205.

Hunt, S. (1983). *Marketing theory: The philosophy of marketing science.* Homewood, IL: Richard Irwin Inc.

John, D. R. (1999). Consumer socialization of children: A retrospective look at twenty-five years of research. *Journal of Consumer Research, 26* (3), 183–213.

Macklin, M., & Carlson, L. (1999). *Advertising to children: Concepts and controversies.* Thousand Oaks, CA: Sage.

Macklin, M. C. (1987). Preschoolers' understanding of the informational function of television advertising. *Journal of Consumer Research, 14* (3), 229–239.

Mallalieu, L., Palan, K. M., & Laczniak, R. N. (2005). Examining children's cognitive abilities in an advertising context: Differences in breadth and depth across age groups. *Journal of Current Issues and Research in Advertising, 27* (Spring), 53–64.

Mangleburg, T., & Bristol, T. (1998). Socialization and adolescents' skepticism toward advertising. *Journal of Advertising, 27* (3), 11–21.

Mangleburg, T., Doney, P., & Bristol, T. (2004). Shopping with friends and teens' susceptibility to peer influence. *Journal of Retailing, 80*, 101–116.

Martin, M. C. (1997). Children's understanding of the intent of advertising: A meta analysis. *Journal of Public Policy and Marketing, 16* (2), 205–216.

Moore, E., & Rideout, V. (2007). The online marketing of food to children: Is it just fun and games? *Journal of Public Policy and Marketing, 26* (2), 202–220.

Moore, E. S., & Lutz, R. J. (2000). Advertising and product experiences: A multi-method inquiry. *Journal of Consumer Research, 27* (1), 31–48.

Moschis, G. (1985). The role of family communication in consumer socialization of children and adolescents. *Journal of Consumer Research, 11* (4), 898–913.

Moschis, G., & Churchill, G. (1978). Consumer socialization: A theoretical and empirical analysis. *Journal of Marketing Research, 15* (November), 599–609.

Muehling, D., & Kolbe, R. (1998). A comparison of children's and prime-time fine-print advertising disclosure practices. *Journal of Advertising, 27* (3), 37–48.

Muehling, D. D., Carlson, L., & Laczniak, R. N. (1992). Parental perceptions of toy-based programs: An exploratory analysis. *Journal of Public Policy and Marketing, 11* (1), 63–71.

Nan, X., & Faber, R. (2004). Advertising theory: Reconceptualizing the building blocks. *Marketing Theory, 4*, 7–30.

Neely, S., & Schumann, D. (2004). Using animated spokes-characters in advertising to young children. *Journal of Advertising, 33* (3), 7–23.

Pawlowski, D., Badzinski, D., & Mitchell, N. (1998). Effects of metaphors on children's comprehension and perception of print advertisements. *Journal of Advertising, 27* (2), 83–98.

Pechmann, C., Levine, L., Loughlin, S., & Leslie, F. (2005). Impulsive and self-conscious: Adolescents' vulnerability to advertising and promotion. *Journal of Public Policy and Marketing, 24* (2), 202–221.

Petty, R. E., Cacioppo, J. T., & Schumann, D. (1983). Central and peripheral routes to advertising effectiveness: The moderating role of involvement. *Journal of Consumer Research, 10*, 135–146.

Piaget, J., & Inhelder, B. (1968). *The psychology of the child*. New York: Basic Books.

Reece, B. B., Rifon, N. J., & Rodriguez, K. (1999). Selling food to children: Is fun part of a balanced breakfast? In M. C. Maklin & L. Carlson (Eds.), *Advertising to children: Concepts and controversies* (pp. 189–208). Thousand Oaks, CA: Sage.

Resnik, A., & Stern, B. (1977). Children's television advertising brand choice: A laboratory experiment. *Journal of Advertising, 6* (3), 11–17.

Reynolds, P. (1971). *A primer on theory development*. Indianapolis, IN: Bobbs-Merrill.

Robertson, T. S., & Rossiter, J. R. (1974). Children and commercial persuasion: An attribution theory analysis. *Journal of Consumer Research, 1* (1), 13–20.

Roedder, D. L. (1981). Age differences in children's responses to television advertising. *Journal of Consumer Research, 8* (2), 144–153.

Rousseau, J. J. (1962). *The Emile of Jean-Jacques Rousseau* (W. Boyd, ed. & trans.). New York: Columbia Teachers College. (Original publication, 1762.)

Soldow, G. (1983). The processing of information in the young consumer: The impact of cognitive developmental stage on television, radio and print advertising. *Journal of Advertising, 12* (3), 4–14.

Stephens, N., & Stutts, M. A. (1982). Preschoolers' ability to distinguish between television programming and commercials. *Journal of Advertising, 11* (2), 16–26.

Stern, B., & Harmon, R. (1984). The incidence and characteristics of disclaimers in children's television advertising. *Journal of Advertising, 13* (2), 12–16.

Stutts, M., Vance, D., & Hudleson, S. (1981). Program-commercial separators in children's television: Do they help a child tell the difference between Bugs Bunny and the Quik Rabbit? *Journal of Advertising, 10* (2), 16–25.

Stutts, M., & Hunnicutt, G. (1987). Can young children understand disclaimers in television commercials? *Journal of Advertising, 16* (1), 41–46.

Chapter 10

Theory Advancement in International Advertising

Drawing on Theories from Strategic Management and International Business

Charles R. Taylor, Shintaro Okazaki, and Barbara Mueller

Introduction

Based on prior reviews of the international advertising literature, there is widespread agreement that stronger conceptual frameworks can and should be developed (e.g., Miracle, 1984; Moriarty & Duncan, 1991; Taylor, 2005). In the context of Figure 1.1, this chapter addresses developing a stronger theoretical understanding of how marketers plan and execute advertising when they operate in multiple markets. Several aspects of Figure 1.1 are representative of important environmental variations that marketers must take into account in developing advertising, including social, cultural, political, economic, and legal differences. Thus, the development of comprehensive theories in the international advertising area must take into account these environmental factors. As is also depicted in Figure 1.1, consideration of the receiver of the message is essential to good advertising. In international markets, advertisers must take into account the degree to which the receiver is similar or different across markets and adjust messages and potentially channels as needed. Clearly, it has become more possible for advertisers to standardize broad strategies across at least some markets than was the case in the past. However, understanding any needed adaptation is essential to effective international advertising.

Too often in the past, individual cultural variables have been applied to attempt to explain cross-national differences in the effectiveness of various advertising executions, when the explanations for any similarities are likely more complex than a single dimension, or even a few, can explain. Many studies have used descriptive research techniques as well, resulting in only limited advances in theory about how international advertising works. At the same time, there have been relatively few attempts to test general communications and/or consumer behavior theories such as the theory of reasoned action or the elaboration likelihood model cross-nationally.

Clearly, more cross-national testing of existing general theories would be desirable. It is therefore important to ask whether a general theory holds cross-nationally, and what the implications of that are. However, the primary focus of this chapter is on recent theoretical developments from the international business and strategic management/marketing literatures that hold considerable promise for improving our understanding of international advertising.

Writing in 2005, Taylor pointed out that in spite of the area's more sophisticated studies of international advertising using more advanced methods and analytical techniques, there remains a strong need for broader and more managerially useful theoretical frameworks to be developed and empirically tested. These frameworks would provide potential to see unprecedented advances in theory development in the international advertising arena in the coming decades.

The remainder of the chapter will be divided into two major sections: one covers broad frameworks for understanding international advertising strategy and the second applies cultural dimensions to international advertising research. In the first section, the following theories are discussed: Global Consumer Culture Theory and related perspectives, Global Brand Positioning Theory, Resource Advantage Theory, and Global Marketing Strategy Theory. Pertaining to culture, Hofstede's framework and the new GLOBE framework are discussed in detail, while a few others are commented on briefly.

Global Consumer Culture Theory

Global Consumer Culture Theory has become very influential in international marketing studies. Several scholars have observed that the globalization of markets has led to the growth of a global consumer culture in which many consumers share consumption values. This culture makes it more possible than in the past to target global market segments, though it is a fairly complex process that has led to this state of affairs.

Consumer Culture Theory (CCT) refers to a family of conceptual perspectives that examine the relationships among consumer actions, the marketplace, and resultant cultural meanings (Arnould & Thompson, 2005). In a seminal work on CCT, Arnould and Thompson (2005) outlined four main research programs in CCT:

1. *Consumer identity* projects address how consumers interactively develop "co-constitutive and co-productive" mechanisms from interacting with marketer-generated communications in developing their sense of self.
2. The *marketplace culture* perspective projects oppose the traditional anthropological views of human beings as culture bearers and stress that consumers are culture producers.

3. *Socio-historic patterning of consumption* investigates the institutional and social structures that systematically affect consumption.

4. *Mass-mediated marketplace ideologies and consumers' interpretive strategies* research examines the messages that commercial media convey about consumption and the way consumers make sense of these messages and devise critical responses. CCT views consumption as continually shaped by ongoing interactions within a dynamic socio-cultural context, and is fundamentally concerned with factors "that shape consumer experiences and identities in the myriad messy contexts of everyday life" (p. 875).

Before examining specific advertising applications of CCT, the profound impact it has had on the international marketing literature should be acknowledged. Consumer Culture Theory as applied to global markets has been referred to as Global Consumer Culture Theory or GCCT. GCCT has even redefined what constitutes a global brand for many scholars. Özsomer and Altaras (2008) suggest that in contrast to the traditional view of a global brand (based largely on the marketing standardization literature), in the GCCT definition of a global brand, the consumer's perception of brand "globalness" is paramount.

GCCT has also affected perceptions of globalization among some scholars. Globalization has long been viewed as a multifaceted concept including economic, social, cultural, and political dimensions. Some scholars have assigned culture a central role in molding globalization. Waters (1995) suggests that while culture has never been and will not become completely globalized, it has shown a greater trend toward globalization than either the political or economic arenas. Nijman (1999, p. 148) offers an even stronger assessment of culture's role, asserting that: "economic globalization, in the form of consumption of globally available commodities, is predicated and dependent on the globalization of cultural values and identities." Consistent with GCCT, Nijman (1999, p. 148) defines cultural globalization as an: "acceleration in the exchange of cultural symbols among people around the world to an extent that leads to changes in local popular cultures and identities." Leading thinkers in this area argue that further growth of cultural globalization will be dependent on two factors: (1) cultural symbols; and (2) the exchange of these symbols among people in different parts of the world. In GCCT, brands are an important cultural symbol that arises out of the consumption culture (Nijman, 1999). Their exchange is highly dependent upon media content and the communication technologies that are available (Appadurai, 1990).

GCCT has also had a profound impact on thinking about cross-market segmentation. Scholars have been observing the emergence of segments of consumers around the world who share similar needs and wants and debating the degree to which it exists (Levitt, 1983; Boddewyn, Soehl, & Picard, 1986).

GCCT theorists would assert that globalization has given rise to global consumer segments and it is fair to say that this idea has become widely accepted as these segments appear to exhibit similarities in consumption patterns (Keillor, D'Amico, & Horton, 2001; Holt, Quelch, & Taylor, 2004).

The growth of global market segments that can be targeted has been closely linked with the emergence of global consumer cultures (GCC). Consumer culture functions globally because it becomes a key source of consumer identity and self-expression around the world. It is not just a matter of consumers consuming the same products, but rather the motives for consuming the same products (Waters, 1995; Nijman, 1999). According to GCCT, the global marketplace facilitates consumption and serves as a symbolic mediation, capable of providing the foundation for meaning, self-images, self-identities, and values (Baudrillard, 1988; Holt, 2002).

Advertising Applications of Global Consumer Culture Theory and Related Perspectives

Drawing on GCCT, Global Consumer Culture Positioning (GCCP) theory, as advanced by Alden, Steenkamp, and Batra (1999), suggests that firms can benefit from associating their brand with global consumer culture. One primary tenet of global consumer culture theory is that consumers across national boundaries have come to share many consumption related beliefs, symbols, and behaviors (Alden et al., 1999). As a result, cross-market segmentation of consumers across market segments such as elites or global teens has become feasible.

Archpru and Alden (2010, p. 38) state that GCC is characterized by shared symbols (likes brands) and behaviors that are "commonly understood but not necessarily shared by consumers and businesses around the world." GCC does not suggest complete homogenization or "globalization of markets" (e.g., Levitt, 1983), as it allows for the idea that marketing mixes might need to be adjusted under certain circumstances. Instead, it reflects the global diffusion of consumption signs and behaviors, predominantly from North American, European, and East Asian countries (e.g., state of the art mobile phones and computers as a status symbol for the young). While consumers understand GCC signs and behaviors, they simultaneously rely on their own values and cultural background for interpretation.

Because of the potential for different viewpoints on GCC signs and behaviors, there are multiple ways in which the marketer can make an association with GCC (Alden et al., 1999). Standardization of marketing and advertising across countries in which consumers' understandings are similar is one option. However, there are other options. These include foreign consumer culture positioning (FCCP), and local consumer culture positioning (LCCP). In GCCP, the brand is identified as a symbol of a given global culture by the advertiser (Alden et al., 1999). For example, advertising employing this technique may emphasize that consumers from all around the world purchase and use a given brand. Such ads may also call upon and reflect universal values (Archpru & Alden, 2010). In FCCP, the brand is intentionally positioned as being a symbol of a specific foreign consumer culture. With LCCP, the company does not make associations with a globally shared cultural meaning, but instead emphasizes cultural meanings that are shared by local culture. Local Consumer Culture (LCC) proponents have suggested that distinctive local consumption cultures are resistant to globalization (Jackson, 2004). Within these environments, consumers may prefer local brands and local advertising imagery as it enables them to more easily identify with local lifestyles, values, attitudes, and consumption behaviors. Clearly, there is evidence that some brands have built their success based on not offering the same products with the same advertising messages across the globe (for example, McDonald's). While this may be harder to do in the current decade, LCC advocates would argue that it can still occur.

One additional "hybrid" perspective that has been advanced should be mentioned. Advocates of "glocal" consumer cultures (GLCC) believe that some consumers value both the global and local and often "draw from all available global and local, new and old sources as they use products to position themselves in the local age, gender, social class, religion and ethnic hierarchies" (Ger & Belk, 1996). Glocalization is a mixture of both homogeneity and heterogeneity (Hermans & Kempen, 1998).

Merz, He, and Alden (2008) integrate Rosch's (1975) Categorization Theory into the discussion of whether consumer cultures globalize, glocalize, or localize. They suggest that arguments for GCC are most easily made at the most abstract level of categorization. However, their strength (versus glocal and local consumer culture) at the basic level of categorization, which is where the largest distinction among categories occurs (e.g., print advertising schemas—consumers everywhere expect to see a headline and logo in a print ad), and subordinate levels (which constitute the most specific level of categorization, for example, print advertising elements such as use of specific colors and celebrity endorsers), is moderated by whether meanings associated with consumption are perceived as primarily functional or symbolic.

Özsomer and Altaras (2008) clearly delineate the difference between GCCP and standardization in discussing two schools of thought pertaining to global brands. The first school is the marketing standardization school, which has the key advantages of standardization (e.g., cost savings) as its main focus. The second school, which has been widely adopted by GCCT researchers, is based on cross-national similarities in consumer perceptions. This view suggests that different appeals made in support of a product can be perceived similarly in different markets. In addition to Özsomer and Altaras' perspective, the notion that global strategies are effective for multinational firms is supported by the logic employed by Alden et al. (1999). They argue that the global reach of a brand plays a role in the level of brand equity realized. In this context, brand ubiquity raises global awareness and visibility of the product in many markets, while simultaneously building positive brand perceptions based solely on a mere exposure effect. In this way, marketers can employ global brand positioning (e.g., McDonald's "I'm Lovin' It" campaign), which can supersede individual domestic or foreign positioning tactics.

Since its initial development (Alden et al., 1999), a number of researchers have drawn upon GCCP in examining global advertising strategies. For example, Alden et al. (1999) found that ads employing GCCP are more likely to use soft sell appeals as opposed to hard sell appeals. Zhou and Belk (2004) applied the framework in their examination of globally versus locally positioned Chinese advertisements. They also found global advertisements used less literal or "softer" appeals, and portrayed the image of cosmopolitan sophistication. Employing GCCP in a case study approach, Amine, Chao, and Arnold (2005) examined Taiwan's country-image advertising campaign. Their study lent further support to Alden et al.'s (1999) finding that global ads employ soft selling over hard selling tactics, as Taiwan's ads portrayed an effective approach using images of culture and quality of life. Okazaki, Mueller, and Taylor (2010) examined consumer preferences for soft sell versus hard sell appeals across six countries. Data revealed that soft sell ads provoked more favorable attitudes, whereas hard sell ads were perceived as more irritating in most of the markets examined.

Perceived Brand Globalness

Perceived brand globalness (PBG) has become an increasingly prominent concept (e.g., Taylor, 2010). Degree of perceived brand globalness is a function of the interaction between the brand's positioning (done by the firm) as well as consumer perceptions of the brand (Holt et al., 2004). Steenkamp, Batra, and Alden (2003) defined PBG as the extent to which consumers "believe that the brand is marketed in multiple countries and is generally recognized as global in these countries." PBG is influenced by consumer exposure to the brand in general media and through marketing promotions (Archpru & Alden, 2010).

Steenkamp et al. (2003) found perceived brand globalness to be positively associated with consumer perceptions of brand quality and prestige in a study conducted in the U.S. and the Republic of Korea. The study suggested that there are some inherent advantages in a brand having global reach (i.e., marketed in many countries) and in being perceived by consumers as being a global brand with particular attributes like being high quality. Overall, there is growing evidence that PBG can be a key factor affecting the success of a brand. It would be fruitful for more research to focus on the magnitude of this effect, as well as the contexts in which it holds.

Archpru and Alden (2010) suggest integration of two of the above theoretical constructs in their application to advertising: GCCP and PBG. They argue that these constructs are based on two views that are critical for understanding the complexities of global consumer culture—specifically that of the firm (GCCP) and that of the consumer (PBG). Considered together, they provide a more comprehensive approach to understanding the relationship between international advertising and GCC than either the firm's or consumer's perspective alone. Based on their extensive review of the GCCP and PBG literature, Archpru and Alden (2010) argue that global brand advertising may benefit from a combined or hybrid approach. Such hybrid ads would feature globally desired attributes (such as quality and prestige) along with consumer preferences for global versus local signs and behaviors in the selection of language, visuals, and themes (Archpru & Alden, 2010, p. 49).

Resource Advantage Theory

Another promising framework that has only recently been applied directly to global advertising is Resource Advantage Theory. Resource Advantage Theory derives from the well-established resource-based view of the firm developed from strategic management. The resource-based view argues that competitive advantage is built based on effective deployment of the resources available to the firm (e.g., Wernerfelt, 1984). The well-known concepts of core competencies (Prahalad & Hamel, 1990) and core capabilities derive from this theory. A core competency is an internal capability that is central as opposed to peripheral to a company's strategy and competitiveness. Core capabilities refer to sets of linked business processes that are central to the firm's strategy and competitiveness (Schoemaker, 1992). Griffith and Yalcinkaya (2010) argue that the resource-based view has the potential to lead to better understanding of global advertising practices and effectiveness by emphasizing resource utilization and its relationship to the effectiveness of several aspects of advertising. These aspects of advertising are related to the firm's overall marketing performance. While this theory is relatively new to the study of advertising, its use has become more common in the study of marketing issues.

In general, it is worthwhile to look at which capabilities in the context of advertising drive competitive advantage. Key areas include media planning, creative strategy, cross-market segmentation, positioning, advertising research, and client–agency relationships. Applications that examine which processes are key in driving competitive advantage in global markets and, perhaps more importantly, how these processes are linked together have the potential to lead to knowledge development.

Global Marketing Strategy Theory

Global Marketing Strategy (GMS) theory as originated by Zou and Cavusgil (2002) is another conceptual framework that holds considerable potential to help advance knowledge of international advertising practices. In the original conceptualization of the theory, Zou and Cavusgil (2002) outline eight dimensions of global marketing strategy: product standardization, promotion standardization, distribution standardization, pricing standardization, concentration of marketing activities, coordination of marketing activities, global market participation, and integration of competitive moves.

A striking finding of the empirical portion of the original GMS study is that when fit (the degree to which a company's global marketing strategy matches the external environment and the firm's own organizational resources) is high, both financial and strategic performance are strong. In the context of promotion, this finding is suggestive of global advertising strategies being advisable when the external environment is conducive to it and the firm has strong organizational capabilities in this regard.

An issue that has been of particular interest to advertising scholars is the degree to which using a global advertising approach effectively enhances company reputation and profitability. Conducting promotional programs across markets generally involves two additional GMS dimensions beyond promotion standardization: global market participation and coordination of marketing ideas. GMS theory defines coordination of marketing activities as the degree to which a firm's marketing practices, for example promotions, are interdependent across countries and cultures. The theory posits that those firms with coordinated activities will achieve better outcomes. Further, those who engage in global market participation are predicted to have higher potential for success.

Okazaki, Taylor, and Zou (2006) applied GMS theory in a study of U.S. and Japanese subsidiaries operating in the EU. Specifically, the study looked at the impact of the use of standardized advertising strategy on the financial and strategic performance of the firm. The study found that the use of standardized advertising across the EU led to higher strategic and financial performance on the part of the subsidiaries. GMS also holds promise for better understanding of cross-market segmentation and associated targeting strategy (Ko, Kim, Taylor, Kim, & Kang, 2007). Zou and Volz (2010) provide several additional avenues related to the application of GMS to advertising, including some related to conditions making it more likely that firms engage in global advertising and others that examine advertising's impact on firm performance.

Dimensions of Culture

While the primary focus of this chapter has been on the application of strategic management and international business theories to the development of theory pertaining to international advertising, we will briefly overview some thinking about the use of cultural variables as a theory base in international advertising research (see, in this volume, Chapter 11 by La Ferle & Lee). While a comprehensive theory specific to culture's impact on advertising remains elusive, frameworks pertaining to cultural dimensions have been widely applied to the study of international advertising. Below, we briefly discuss those that have been applied most frequently and then offer a critique of how cultural variables have been used in international advertising research.

The cultural framework that has been most widely applied is Geert Hofstede's (1980) cultural dimensions (see de Mooij & Hofstede, 2010, for a full discussion). One or more of Hofstede's dimensions: individualism/collectivism, power distance, masculinity/femininity, uncertainty avoidance, and long-term vs. short-term orientation, have been applied to a wide variety of topics. These topics range from website visuals in advertising, to the use of nudity in advertising, to the evolution of localized advertising appeals in Japanese vs. U.S. advertising (Nelson & Paek, 2008; Okazaki & Mueller, 2008). While Hofstede's dimensions have been criticized on several grounds, they have nonetheless helped provide insight on some cultural factors that must be taken into account when conducting international advertising. As a result, recent studies continue to have proven to represent an important breakthrough and have been employed by many who use the framework (e.g., Li, Li, & Zhao, 2009; Bu, Kim, & Kim, 2009; Kwak, Larsen Andras, & Zinkhan, 2009) and helped to provide considerable insight.

The GLOBE study (Global Leadership and Organizational Behavior Effectiveness Research Program) conducted by House, Hanges, Javidan, Dorfman, and Gupta (2004) is a more recent study that developed a comprehensive set of cultural dimensions, specifically, nine cultural dimensions based on a survey of a large number of participants across more than 60 countries (Terlutter, Diehl, & Mueller, 2010). The nine dimensions are: performance orientation, in-group collectivism, institutional collectivism, power distance, uncertainty avoidance, future orientation, humane orientation, assertiveness and gender egalitarianism, in-group collectivism, institutional collectivism, power distance, uncertainty avoidance, future orientation. In addition to the dimensions that overlap with

Hofstede's framework, performance orientation and assertiveness have already begun to be applied to advertising issues.

GLOBE also differs from Hofstede in two aspects of cultural dimensions: societal practices and societal values are defined and measured (House et al., 2004). The GLOBE dimensions have already been applied to international advertising (e.g., Terlutter, Diehl, & Mueller, 2006) and it appears likely that this trend will continue (see House, Quigley, & Sully de Luque, 2010).

Additional key contributions to identifying cultural dimensions have been made by others. Edward T. Hall (1976) has discussed the concept of context, which refers to difference in the directness of communications across culture. Several studies have verified that low context cultures (e.g., the U.S.) tend to use more direct communication than high context cultures (e.g., Taylor, Miracle, & Wilson, 1997).

Although it is clear that the influence of culture on international advertising practices is a worthy topic, the sheer complexity of the concept of culture limits the degree to which cultural dimensions alone can be used to develop a fuller understanding of global advertising. Supplementing this perspective with broader theories such as those described above, or, testing general communications and consumer behavior theory in cross-national contexts is likely to lead to fuller theory development. Meanwhile, researchers are advised to measure individual level differences in culture (see Taylor, 2005) to avoid situations in which some members of a country do not even conform to the traditional cultural variable being hypothesized to lead to a difference in advertising practice.

Conclusion

In conclusion, we have reviewed several relatively new theories deriving from the areas of strategic management, international business, and international marketing that can be applied in an effort to help better understand global advertising. Whether applied in isolation or in conjunction with cultural dimensions, these theories hold the potential to contribute to significant contributions in the future.

References

Alden, D. L., Steenkamp, J. B., & Batra, R. (1999). Brand positioning through advertising in Asia, North America, and Europe: The role of global consumer culture. *Journal of Marketing, 63* (1), 75–87.

Amine, L., Chao, M. C. H., & Arnold, M. (2005). Exploring the practical effects of country of origin, animosity, and price-quality issues: Two case studies of Taiwan and Acer in China. *Journal of International Marketing, 13* (2), 114–150.

Appadurai, A. (1990). Disjuncture and difference in the global economy. In M. Featherstone (Ed.), *Global culture: Nationalism, globalization and modernity* (pp. 295–310). London: Sage.

Archpru, M. A., & Alden, D. L. (2010). Global brand positioning perceptions: International advertising and global consumer culture. *International Journal of Advertising, 29* (1), 37–56.

Arnould, E. J., & Thompson, C. J. (2005). Consumer culture theory (CCT): Twenty years of research. *Journal of Consumer Research, 31* (4), 868–892.

Baudrillard, J. (1998). *The consumer society: Myths and structures.* Newbury Park, CA: Sage.

Boddewyn, J. J., Soehl, R., & Picard, J. (1986). Standardization in international marketing: Is Ted Levitt in fact right? *Business Horizons, 29* (6), 69–75.

Bu, K., Kim, D., & Kim, S. (2009). Determinants of visual forms used in print advertising: A cross-cultural comparison. *International Journal of Advertising, 28* (1), 13–47.

de Mooij, M., & Hofstede, G. (2010). The Hofstede model: Applications to global branding and advertising strategy and research. *International Journal of Advertising, 29* (1), 85–110.

Ger, G., & Belk, R. (1996). I'd like to buy the world a Coke: Consumptionscapes of the "less affluent world." *Journal of Consumer Policy, 19* (3), 271–304.

Griffith, D. A., & Yalcinkaya, G. (2010). Resource-advantage theory: A foundation for insights into global advertising research. *International Journal of Advertising, 29* (1), 15–36.

Hall, E. T. (1976). *Beyond culture.* Garden City, NY: Anchor Press/Doubleday.

Hermans, H., & Kempen, H. (1998). Moving cultures: The perilous problems of cultural dichotomies in a globalizing society. *American Psychologist, 53* (10), 1111–1120.

Hofstede, G. (1980). *Culture's consequences: International differences in work-related values.* Newbury Park, CA: Sage.

Holt, D. (2002). Why do brands cause trouble? A dialectical theory of consumer culture and branding. *Journal of Consumer Research, 29* (2), 77–90.

Holt, D., Quelch, J. A., & Taylor, E. L. (2004). How global brands compete. *Harvard Business Review, 82* (9), 68–75.

House, R. J., Hanges, P. J., Javidan, M., Dorfman, P. W., & Gupta, V. (2004). *Culture, leadership, and organizations: The GLOBE study of 62 societies.* Beverly Hills, CA: Sage.

House, R. J., Quigley, N. R., Sully de Luque, M. F. (2010). Insights from Project GLOBE: Extending global advertising research through a contemporary framework. *International Journal of Advertising, 29* (1), 111–139.

Jackson, P. (2004). Local consumption cultures in a globalizing world. *Transactions of the Institute of British Geographers, 29* (2), 165–178.

Keillor, B. D., D'Amico, M., & Horton, V. (2001). Global consumer tendencies. *Psychology and Marketing, 18* (2), 1–19.

Ko, E., Kim, E., Taylor, C. R., Kim, K. H., & Kang, I. J. (2007). Cross-national market segmentation in the fashion industry: A study of European, Korean, and US consumers. *International Marketing Review, 24* (5), 629–651.

Kwak, H., Larsen Andras, T., & Zinkhan, G. M. (2009). Advertising to active viewers:

Consumer attitudes in the US and South Korea. *International Journal of Advertising, 28* (1), 49–75.

Levitt, T. (1983). The globalization of markets. *Harvard Business Review, 61* (3), 92–102.

Li, H., Li, A., & Zhao, S. (2009). Internet advertising strategy of multinationals in China: A cross-cultural analysis. *International Journal of Advertising, 28* (1), 125–146.

Merz, M., He, Y., & Alden, D. (2008). A categorization approach to analyzing the global consumer culture debate. *International Marketing Review, 25* (2), 166–182.

Miracle, G. E. (1984). An assessment of progress in research in international advertising. *Current Issues and Research in Advertising, 6* (2), 135–166.

Moriarty, S. E., & Duncan, T. R. (1991). Global advertising: Issues and practices. *Current Issues and Research in Advertising, 13* (1&2), 313–41.

Nelson, M. R., & Paek, H. (2008). Nudity of female and male models in primetime TV advertising across seven countries. *International Journal of Advertising, 27* (5), 715–744.

Nijman, J. (1999). Cultural globalization and the identity of place: The reconstruction of Amsterdam. *Ecumene, 6* (2), 146–164.

Okazaki, S., & Mueller, B. (2008). Evolution in the usage of localized appeals in Japanese and American print advertising. *International Journal of Advertising, 27* (5), 771–798.

Okazaki, S., Mueller, B., & Taylor, C. R. (2010). Global consumer culture positioning: Testing perceptions of soft-sell and hard-sell advertising appeals between U.S. and Japanese consumers. *Journal of International Marketing, 18* (2), 20–34.

Okazaki, S., Taylor, C. R., & Zou, S. (2006). Advertising standardization's positive impact on the bottom line: A model of when and how standardization improves financial and strategic performance. *Journal of Advertising, 35* (4), 17–33.

Özsomer, A., & Altaras, S. (2008). Global brand purchase likelihood: A critical synthesis and an integrated conceptual framework. *Journal of International Marketing, 16* (4), 1–28.

Prahalad, C. K., & Hamel, G. (1990). The core competence of the corporation. *Harvard Business Review, 68* (3), 79–91.

Rosch, E. (1975). Cognitive representations of semantic categories. *Journal of Experimental Psychology, 104* (3), 192–233.

Schoemaker, J. H. (1992). How to link strategic vision to core capabilities. *Sloan Management Review, 34* (3), 67–81.

Steenkamp, J., Batra, R., & Alden, D. A. (2003). How perceived brand globalness creates brand value. *Journal of International Business Studies, 34* (1), 53–65.

Taylor, C. R. (2005). Moving international advertising research forward: A new research agenda. *Journal of Advertising, 34* (1), 7–16.

Taylor, C. R. (2010). Towards stronger theory development in international advertising research. *International Journal of Advertising, 29* (1), 9–14.

Taylor, C. R., Miracle, G. E., & Wilson, R. D. (1997). The impact of information level on the effectiveness of U.S. and Korean television commercials. *Journal of Advertising, 26* (1), 1–18.

Terlutter, R., Diehl, S., & Mueller, B. (2006). The GLOBE study: Applicability of a new typology of cultural dimensions for cross-cultural marketing and advertising research. In S. Diehl & R. Terlutter (Eds.), *International advertising and communication: Current insights and empirical findings* (pp. 419–438). Wissenschaft, Wiesbaden, Germany: Galber Edition.

Terlutter, R., Diehl, S., & Mueller, B. (2010). The cultural dimension of assertiveness in cross-cultural advertising: The perception and evaluation of assertive advertising appeals. *International Journal of Advertising, 29* (4), 366–399.

Waters, M. (1995). *Globalization*. London: Routledge.

Wernerfelt, B. (1984). A resource-based view of the firm. *Strategic Management Journal, 5* (2), 171–180.

Zhou, N., & Belk, R. (2004). Chinese consumer readings of global and local advertising appeals. *Journal of Advertising, 33* (3), 63–76.

Zou, S., & Cavusgil, S. T. (2002). The GMS: A broad conceptualization of global marketing strategy and its effect on firm performance. *Journal of Marketing, 66* (4), 40–56.

Zou, S., & Volz, Y. Z. (2010). An integrated theory of global advertising: An application of the GMS theory. *International Journal of Advertising, 29* (1), 57–84.

Additional Reading

Griffith, D. A., & Lusch, R. F. (2007). Getting marketers to invest in firm-specific capital. *Journal of Marketing, 71* (1), 129–145.

Chapter 11

How Advertising Works Within a Cultural Context

Theories and Frameworks Informing the Process

Carrie La Ferle and Wei-Na Lee

> As a lens, culture determines how the world is seen.... As a blueprint, it deter-
> mines how the world will be fashioned by human effort.
>
> (Grant McCracken, 1986)

Introduction

When you think of Nestlé's Kit Kat chocolate bar, what comes to mind? If you said a Soy-Sauce Flavored Kit Kat you might be living in Japan and reflecting on the top-selling Kit Kat flavor of 2010. At last count there were 19 unique flavors being sold in this trendy island nation (Madden, 2010). How about the term "family?" In the U.S., family has often been referred to as the nuclear related group consisting of a mother, father, and child. For many other countries, family can include grand-parents as well as aunts and uncles and even cousins (de Mooij, 2010).

These anecdotal scenarios are meant to highlight the importance of culture influencing every aspect of our lives. Attitudes, thoughts, and behaviors are mediated by the cultural context in which we exist (Gudykunst, 1998; Markus & Kitayama, 1991) and this is becoming increasingly important for advertisers to understand as advertising dollars continue to expand to global markets and to culturally unique markets within nations (Laroche, 2007).

Prior to the 1950s, global ad spending was almost synonymous with U.S. advertising spending (Mueller, 2004). Today, U.S. ad expenditures account for less than half of the almost $450 billion forecast for global advertising expendi-tures in 2010 (Associated Press, 2010; Carat, 2007). However, it is not that American companies have lessened their efforts, but more that companies from other countries have entered the global marketplace. Clearly, global advertising practices and markets are here to stay and therefore knowledge about between-nation differences is critical, as is also knowledge about differences between groups within nations.

Nationally the necessity for cultural understanding is increasing with many countries becoming more ethnically and racially diverse. As an example, forecasts in the U.S. for 2050 indicate that a quarter of the population will be Hispanic. Currently, Hispanic Americans represent approximately 15% of the population closely followed by African Americans (~14%). Asian Americans account for approximately 5% of the population today but that percent is expected to grow to 8% by 2050 (Humphreys, 2009; Johnson, 2009; U.S. Census, 2001). Furthermore, it is predicted that the 2010 census will show approximately 80% of those 65 and over identifying as white non-Hispanics compared to only 54% of children under 18 years of age (Johnson, 2009). Cultural diversity is sure to be at the forefront of American life in the decades to come.

Many other countries find themselves in a similar place; growing into a patchwork of consumer groups with varied ages, ethnicities, and lifestyles (Cleveland & Laroche, 2007; Zhang, 2010). Similarly, a growing group of researchers is also arguing for the individual cultural group as the unit of analysis over nations. The push stems from globalization and the perceived similarities between individual consumer groups across nations while also couched in the perceived lessening of homogeneous consumers within nations (Cleveland & Laroche, 2007; Craig & Douglas, 2006). But before going any further, it is important to define several critical constructs informing the current chapter including advertising, culture, and values.

Advertising, Culture, and Values

Advertising has been defined in Chapter 1 by Thorson and Rodgers as a "*paid communication from an identified sponsor for using mass media to persuade an audience.*" And while some controversy exists over the application of this definition to advertising in the twenty-first century with the use of "mass" media, culturally speaking the controversy continues with the notion that the goal of advertising is to persuade. Several scholars of culture and international advertising have argued that the goal of advertising is more about building relationships and trust with consumers than it is about persuading (de Mooij, 2010; de Mooij & Hofstede, 2010). And culture plays a role in this argument.

Culture is a complex and multidimensional construct (Cleveland & Laroche, 2007). Part of the complexity is that the same term is used quite differently across disciplines such as biology and anthropology as well as art and advertising (de Mooij, 2010). However, as Gudykunst (1998) suggests, it is important to select a working definition to guide analysis and discussion. In this chapter, culture is conceptualized following Hofstede (1997) as "the collective mental programming of the mind which distinguishes the members of one group or category of people from another" (p. 5). It is a system of shared meanings (Geertz, 1973). Although Hofstede (1980) used this definition in his research examining work environments in different countries, we believe the definition is flexible enough to also include subcultures within a country.

Returning to Thorson and Rodgers' "Components of the Advertising Process Circle" framework represented in Figure 1.1, and borrowing from McGuire's (1969) communication process model, we can more clearly see the critical role of culture in communication and especially its role in creating effective advertising messages. According to de Mooij (2010), values are at the core of culture and are the standards that drive people's beliefs, attitudes, and behavior. They can also greatly influence communication style preferences. Culture influences both the context within which advertising and communication occurs, and has an impact on individual level processing. We can see the dual influence of culture by examining McGuire's (1969) model of persuasive communication in advertising.

McGuire's model involves (1) the sender as the advertiser and source of the message followed by (2) the message itself and the methods used to convey the message which are then (3) channeled through a medium such as TV or radio to be (4) received by the consumer, and all of this takes place within at least one if not two cultural environments. The largest area for miscommunication occurs between the advertiser wanting to encode a certain association and meaning with the brand in the advertising message, and the consumer who may decode the meaning differently.

De Mooij (2010) and Cateora and Graham (2007) have both suggested that the encoding and decoding process become even more troublesome and complex when the advertiser is from one culture and the target audience of the message is from another culture. As an example, "a golf ball manufacturing company packaged golf balls in packs of four for convenient purchase in Japan. Unfortunately, pronunciation of the word 'four' in Japanese sounds like the word 'death' and items packaged in fours are unpopular" (Kwintessential.com, 2010). Problems such as this stem from the sender and the receiver coming from different worldviews that are the lenses through which each interprets the world. According to Gudykunst (1998), dimensions of cultural variability are necessary to help explain differences between cultures. But as mentioned previously, culture exists at a variety of levels such as global, national, and within nation (Leung, Bhagat, Buchan, Erez, & Gibson, 2005).

Traditionally in international advertising research, culture has been viewed from a national level where countries have been grouped using a number of characteristics and the people within each country possess these traits more so than people from other countries (Gao, 2009; Han & Shavitt, 1994; La Ferle, Edwards, & Mizuno, 2002). This view has been criticized by some researchers recently for being quite rigid and perceiving culture as fixed and geographically based (Cleveland & Laroche, 2007; Craig & Douglas, 2006; Zhang, 2010).

Nonetheless, a significant amount of research has been undertaken at the global and national levels to warrant a brief discussion using cultural dimensions to group countries on a number of different characteristics. Gudykunst (1998) has further argued, national level distinctions of culture partially influence the values people hold and what they come to consider as normative at the individual level.

Some of the most common groupings of national-level cultural orientations include Hofstede's (1980) cultural dimensions, Hall's (1989) high and low context communication styles, Schwartz's (1992) value types and the GLOBE leadership study (2004). For a more detailed review of several of these cultural groupings such as Hofstede's individualism-collectivism refer to the chapter in this book on international advertising. However, regardless of the specific framework used, cultural orientation has been shown to influence both advertising execution decisions and consumer responses to advertising appeals (Zhang, 2010).

One theory used to explain the underlying process of the impact of cultural orientation on responses to advertising is Congruity Theory (Osgood & Tannenbaum, 1955). In simple terms the theory states that people are drawn to things that are consistent and congruent with their preexisting ideas and beliefs. As an example, Zhang and Gelb (1996) found that when culturally congruent appeals were used in advertisements such as individual appeals for people with individualistic cultural orientations, they resulted in more favorable consumer attitudes. Cultural orientation at a national level has been used as a guide to select everything in advertisements from information content (Chan & Chan, 2005) and celebrities (Choi, Lee, & Kim, 2005) to gender stereotypes (Milner & Higgs, 2004) and appeal types. However, in the past decade new research viewing culture as more fluid has begun to surface and has allowed for more studies examining individual differences within countries and cultures where people can present characteristics of many cultures (Craig & Douglas, 2006; Zhang, 2010).

Diverse Cultures within Nations

As we have discussed, there is a plethora of explanations of cross-cultural differences on how culture influences advertising in different countries. Similarly, culture influences the way persuasive messages are constructed, delivered, and received to different cultural groups within a nation. Unfortunately, literature to date on ethnic consumers and their responses toward advertising generally reflects a limited understanding of people from diverse populations (Lee, La Ferle, & Williams, 2004; Stanfield & Dennis, 1993; Williams, Lee, & Henderson, 2008). Nonetheless, there are important theories that explain how advertising works for ethnic cultural groups. We turn our attention to the need for understanding advertising in a multicultural society, and offer theoretical explanations of the way cultural forces influence individuals in different ethnic groups and how those people respond to persuasive messages. The United States is used to guide the discussion because (1) the origin of the U.S. is rooted in immigration and cultural diversity, and (2) many theories in use were developed in the U.S. out of the need to reconcile differences and facilitate communication among different ethnic cultural groups.

Given the major demographic shifts in the U.S. the first question to ask is whether the proportional representation of an individual's ethnic cultural group in the population has an impact on that person's response toward advertising and, if so, in what way. In addition, when advertisers make a concerted effort to "accommodate" preferences of different ethnic cultural groups, to what extent does this strategy work?

Kanter's (1977) Theory of Proportional Representation is an important starting point to help us understand how the representation of ethnic cultural groups relates to consumer response in the marketplace. He suggests that a person's immediate social context such as group representation expressed through proportions should have an impact on that person's thoughts and behaviors. Groups with varying proportions of demographic variables such as age, ethnicity, and gender will have different dynamics.

According to Kanter, there are four types of group: uniform groups (100:0; only one major social category): balanced groups (50:50); tilted groups (65:35); and skewed groups (85:15). Currently, Hispanics, blacks, and Asians represent 15%, 14%, and 5% of the U.S. population respectively. Therefore, the ratio of each ethnic group to non-Hispanic whites typifies the skewed group according to Kanter's classification. In skewed groups, majority members are the "dominants" because they are likely to control the environment, whereas minority members are usually treated as tokens of their respective ethnic cultural group category.

Tokenism influences how a person views him/herself and how others view them. Token individuals tend to be monitored closely and stereotyped. The perceived similarities among majority members and differences between majority and token minority members are likely to be exaggerated (Kanter, 1977). Since culture is a salient characteristic used in social categorization and identification, proportional representation based on ethnic cultures is likely to have significant influence on how individuals think, feel, and respond to advertising messages directed at them.

Social Categorization (Fiske & Taylor, 1991) and Identification Theory (Kelman, 1961) should further help explain how ethnic cultures influence consumer response to persuasive messages. The basic premise of social categorization is that as individuals we have the need to organize information in a way that is efficient for our day-to-day functions. In addition to objects, we organize people, according to their salient characteristics, into groups to facilitate our social interactions. We then apply our beliefs and affects associated with a group-to-group membership at large. The basis for categorization may be any important feature that differentiates one group from another. Ethnic culture is one such feature. Because advertising time and space are limited, this theory explains, to some extent, why advertisers resort to using stereotypes as a short-cut to help consumers recall their information and feelings about a specific group. In a similar vein, Identification Theory maintains that it is a natural tendency for people to make similarity judgments by assessing their level of similarity with a source during an interaction (Hovland & Weis, 1951; Kelman, 1961). Putting these two theories together, we can understand how individuals connect with spokespersons in advertising based on perceived similarities between themselves and the spokesperson (Kelman, 1961; Basow & Howe, 1980) and why members in ethnic cultural groups respond favorably to models of similar ethnicity (e.g., Spira & Whittler, 2004).

Interestingly, however, Deshpande and Stayman (1994) found that Hispanic Americans living in Austin, Texas (where they are an ethnic minority), were more likely to believe that a Hispanic spokesperson was more trustworthy than those Hispanics living in San Antonio, Texas (where they are an ethnic majority). One plausible explanation could be that social identification operates differently depending on an individual's majority versus minority status, or proportional representation, in the immediate social context.

For additional insights, let us consider Distinctiveness Theory. According to the theory, people tend to define themselves on traits that are numerically rare in their local environment (Appiah, 2004). These traits could be age, ethnicity, gender, etc. An individual's distinctive trait (e.g., females in engineering) may be more salient to him/her than the prevalent trait (e.g., males in engineering) possessed by others in the environment (McGuire, 1984; McGuire, McGuire, Child, & Fujioka, 1978). This could be particularly true for people who belong to an ethnic group that is part of a numeric or proportional minority. For instance, blacks would be highly aware of their "distinctiveness" in various interpersonal and social situations as a result of being a proportional minority in the U.S. Aaker, Brumbaugh, and Grier (2000) found that blacks had more favorable attitudes toward an ad featuring black models than whites had toward an ad featuring white models. In a similar way, Distinctiveness Theory may help explain findings from Deshpande and Stayman's (1994) study. When Hispanics perceive themselves as the minority in Austin, Texas, they are likely to respond positively to Hispanic spokespersons. In contrast, Hispanics are the majority in San Antonio, Texas. Therefore, they are less likely to respond positively regarding Hispanic spokespersons because their race is no longer distinctive in the immediate environment.

Past research has demonstrated that distinctive group members tend to pay more attention to ads targeted at them, process and interpret persuasive messages differently, and respond more favorably to targeted ads than non-distinctive consumers (Aaker et al., 2000; Deshpande & Stayman, 1994; Forehand & Deshpande, 2001; Forehand, Deshpande, & Reed, 2002; Grier & Brumbaugh, 1999; Grier & Brumbaugh, 2004; Grier & Deshpande, 2001; Wooten, 1995). Therefore, the key to understanding the impact of ethnicity-based proportional representation on consumer response must lie in whether an individual perceives him/herself to be "distinctive." This perception may be invoked by the immediate social context such as proportional representation (e.g., Deshpande & Stayman, 1984) or, in some instances, by the strength of an individual's ethnic identity (La Ferle & Morimoto, 2009).

According to Phinney (1992), ethnic identity is a person's knowledge of membership in a social group and the value and emotional significance attached to that membership. Those with strong ethnic identity tend to have heightened awareness of and preference for spokespersons with similar ethnicity (Appiah, 2004). However, the strength of ethnic identity may play a minor role in how whites, the majority group, respond to advertising, given our previous discussion of Distinctiveness Theory and Proportional Representation. In any case, when it comes to minority groups and accommodation considerations, the question may not be whether to accommodate but how (Green, 1999) because consumers in ethnic minority groups may be more critical toward persuasive messages directed at them than those in the majority group.

Polarized Appraisal Theory (Linville, 1982; Linville & Jones, 1980) gives us an idea of why caution is needed in accommodation. This theory is based on two premises. First, people generally have a more complex cognitive schema to evaluate in-group than out-group members as a result of their extensive in-group knowledge. Second, the lower level of cognitive schema complexity regarding the out-group will result in more extreme evaluations. For example, whites will view an ad featuring black actors with positive characteristics more positively than an ad featuring white actors with similar characteristics. Likewise, whites may view an ad featuring black actors with negative characteristics more negatively than an ad featuring white actors with similar characteristics. Therefore, while "accommodation" through the use of ethnic models for advertising messages is advisable, such a practice does have its nuanced ramifications and risks.

Unfortunately, when we delve further into research that will help us understand how best to tailor messages to individuals in different ethnic cultural groups, we do not go very far. While we know that the selection of ethnic media (e.g., BET) and the use of ethnic language (e.g., Spanish) would be the natural first steps (e.g., Lee, La Ferle, & Tharp, 2005), we know very little about how individuals simultaneously integrate their minority–majority status and identification with both origin and host cultures in their daily lives. This issue is further complicated by the ebb and flow of various cultural forces at work in the larger social environment.

Although an intuitive approach to understanding the influence of culture on ethnic cultural groups' response to advertising is to test a multitude of advertising theories or combinations of a select few on different ethnic groups and find out what works and what does not, Williams et al. (2008) suggested a more efficient approach. To untangle the complexity of ethnic cultural groups' behavior in the marketplace, they pointed out it may be easier to take the traditional marketing mix variables (product, price, place, promotion) and examine where differences occur. Subsequently, we can apply the different theories discussed earlier plus those from the consumer behavior literature (for an in-depth discussion see Shavitt, Lee, & Johnson, 2008) to gain meaningful understanding. This practice-to-theory-development approach can be highly productive both in terms of implications for practitioners and directions for evolving relevant theories.

Shavitt et al. (2008, p. 1103) poignantly pointed out that "Cultural distinctions have been demonstrated to have important implications for advertising content, persuasiveness of appeals, consumer motivation, consumer judgment process, and consumer response style." To understand the significant role of culture in advertising, we have discussed how advertising works across nations and across ethnic cultural groups within a nation. It is evident from our discussion that much more work is needed to fill the gap in our knowledge.

Conclusion

In this chapter we set out to examine what theories related to culture help to explain how advertising works. Toward this goal, we wanted to show the growing importance of culture in the advertising process, both between and within nations. We also wanted to locate culture within the "Components of the Advertising Process Circle" framework illustrated in Figure 1.1 of Chapter 1.

Our journey has made it clear that culture is both the environment within which advertising takes place and it exists at the individual level, influencing attitudes, cognitions, and behavior. Thorson and Rodgers' Figure 1.1 framework helped to emphasize these two levels, with culture being part of the "advertising context" or environment, but then also playing a role within McGuire's (1969) communication process. Specifically, culture influences the advertiser as the *source* in terms of its encoding specific associations between the product, society, and consumers through advertising. Simultaneously, culture influences the *receiver* in terms of how consumers decode the incoming messages. The process of advertising, therefore, is where advertisers and consumers negotiate their relationships both within and with cultural forces.

References

Aaker, J. L., Brumbaugh, A. M., & Grier, S. A. (2000). Nontarget markets and viewer distinctiveness: The impact of target marketing on advertising attitudes. *Journal of Consumer Psychology, 9* (3), 127–140.

Appiah, O. (2004). Effects of ethnic identification on web browsers' attitudes toward and navigational patterns on race-targeted sites. *Communication Research, 31* (3), 312–337.

Associated Press (2010, July 20). Global ad spending 2010 forecast at a glance. *ABC News.* Retrieved October 10, 2010, from http://abcnews.go.com/Business/wireStory?id=11209519.

Basow, S. A., & Howe, K. G. (1980). Role-model influence: Effects of sex and sex-role attitude in college students. *Psychology of Women Quarterly, 4* (4), 558–572.

Carat (2007). Global ad forecast. Retrieved October 10, 2010, from www.marketing-charts.com/?attachment_id=839.

Cateora, P., & Graham, J. (2007). *International marketing* (13th ed.). New York: McGraw-Hill.

Chan, K., & Chan, F. (2005). Information content of television advertising in China: An update. *Asian Journal of Communication, 15* (March), 1–15.

Choi, S. M., Lee, W., & Kim, H. (2005). Lessons from the rich and famous: A cross-cultural comparison of celebrity endorsement in advertising. *Journal of Advertising, 34* (Summer), 85–98.

Cleveland, M., & Laroche, M. (2007). Acculturation to the global consumer culture: Scale development and research paradigm. *Journal of Business Research, 60,* 249–259.

Craig, S. C., & Douglas, S. P. (2006). Beyond national culture: Implications of cultural dynamics for consumer research. *International Marketing Review, 23* (3), 322–342.

de Mooij, M. K. (2010). *Global marketing and advertising: Understanding cultural paradoxes* (3rd ed.). Thousand Oaks, CA: Sage.

de Mooij, M. K., & Hofstede, G. (2010). The Hofstede model: Applications to global branding and advertising research. *International Journal of Advertising, 29* (1), 85–110.

Deshpande, R., & Stayman, D. M. (1994). A tale of two cities: Distinctiveness theory and advertising effectiveness. *Journal of Marketing Research, 31* (1), 57–64.

Fiske, S. T., & Taylor, S. E. (1991). *Social cognition* (2nd ed.). New York: McGraw-Hill.

Forehand, M. R., & Deshpande, R. (2001). What we see makes us who we are: Priming ethnic self-awareness and advertising response. *Journal of Marketing Research, 38* (3), 336–348.

Forehand, M. R., Deshpande, R., & Reed, A. (2002). Identity salience and the influence of differential activation of the social self-schema on advertising response. *Journal of Applied Psychology, 87* (6), 1086–1099.

Gao, Z. (2009). Beyond culture: A proposal for agent-based content analyses of international advertisements. *Journal of Current Issues and Research in Advertising, 31* (1), 105–116.

Geertz, C. (1973). *The interpretation of culture.* New York: Basic Books.

GLOBE. (2004). *Culture, leadership, and organizations: The GLOBE study of 62 societies.* In R. J. House, P. J. Hanges, P. W. Dorfman, & V. Gupta (Eds.) Thousand Oaks, CA: Sage.

Green, C. L. (1999). Ethnic evaluations of advertising: Interaction effects of strength of ethnic identification, media placement, and degree of racial composition. *Journal of Advertising, 28* (1), 49–64.

Grier, S. A., & Brumbaugh, A. M. (1999). Noticing cultural differences: Ad meanings created by target and non-target markets. *Journal of Advertising, 28* (1), 79–93.

Grier, S. A., & Brumbaugh, A. M. (2004). Consumer distinctiveness and advertising persuasion. In J. D. Williams, W. Lee, & C. P. Haugtvedt (Eds.), *Diversity in advertising: Broadening the scope of research directions* (pp. 217–236). Hillsdale, NJ: Lawrence Erlbaum.

Grier, S. A., & Deshpande, R. (2001). Social dimensions of consumer distinctiveness: The influence of social status on group identity and advertising persuasion. *Journal of Marketing Research, 38* (2), 216–224.

Gudykunst, W. B. (1998). *Bridging differences: Effective intergroup communication* (3rd ed.). Thousand Oaks, CA: Sage.

Hall, E. T. (1989). *Beyond culture.* New York: Anchor Books.

Han, S., & Shavitt, S. (1994). Persuasion and culture: Advertising appeals in individualistic and collectivist societies. *Journal of Experimental and Social Psychology, 30,* 326–350.

Hofstede, G. (1980). *Culture's consequences: International differences in work-related values.* Beverly Hills, CA: Sage.

Hofstede, G. (1997). *Cultures and organizations: Software of the mind.* New York: McGraw-Hill.

Hovland, C., & Weis, W. (1951). The influence of source credibility on communication effectiveness. *Public Opinion Quarterly, 15* (4), 635–650.

Humphreys, J. M. (2009). The multicultural economy 2009. *Selig Center for Economic Growth,* Terry College of Business, University of Georgia, Vol. 69 (3). Retrieved November 5, 2010, from www.terry.uga.edu/selig/docs/GBEC0903q.pdf.

Johnson, B. (2009, October). The average American is dying off. *Business Insider.* Retrieved October 10, 2010 from www.businessinsider.com/the-average-american-is-a-dying-breed-2009-10.

Kanter, R. M. (1977). *Men and women of the corporation.* New York: Basic Books.

Kelman, H. C. (1961). Processes of opinion change. *Public Opinion Quarterly, 25* (1), 57–78.

Kwintessential.com (2010). Cross-cultural business blunders. Retrieved October 10, 2010 from www.kwintessential.co.uk/cultural-services/articles/crosscultural-blunders.html.

La Ferle, C., Edwards, S. M., & Mizuno, Y. (2002). Diffusion of the Internet in Japan: Cultural considerations. *Journal of Advertising Research, 42* (2), 65–79.

La Ferle, C., & Morimoto, M. (2009). The impact of life-stage on ethnic media use, ethnic identification and ad attitudes for Asian American females. *Howard Journal of Communication, 20* (2), 1–20.

Laroche, M. (2007). Introduction to the special issue on the impact of culture on marketing strategy. *Journal of Business Research*, *60* (3), 177–180.

Lee, W., La Ferle, C., & Tharp, M. C. (2005). Ethnic influences on communication patterns: Word-of-mouth, traditional and non-traditional media usage. In J. D. Williams, W. Lee, & C. Haugtvedt (Eds.), *Diversity in advertising* (pp. 177–200). Mahwah, NJ: Lawrence Erlbaum.

Lee, W., La Ferle, C., & Williams, J. D. (2004). Diversity in advertising: A summary and research agenda. In J. D. Williams, W. Lee, & C. Haugtvedt (Eds.), *Diversity in advertising* (pp. 3–20). Mahwah, NJ: Lawrence Erlbaum.

Leung, K. B., Baghat, T., Buchan, R. S., Erez, N. R. M., & Gibson, C. (2005). Culture and international business: Recent advances and their implication for future research. *Journal of International Business Studies, 36* (4), 357–378.

Linville, P. W. (1982). The complexity-extremity effect and age-based stereotyping. *Journal of Personality and Social Psychology, 42* (2), 193–211.

Linville, P. W., & Jones, E. E. (1980). Polarized appraisals of out-group members. *Journal of Personality and Social Psychology, 38* (5), 689–703.

McCracken, G. (1986). Culture and consumption: A theoretical account of the structure and movement of the cultural meaning of consumer goods. *Journal of Consumer Research, 13* (June), 71–84.

McGuire, W. J. (1969). An information-processing model of advertising effectiveness. In H. L. Davis & A. J. Silk (Eds.), *Behavioral and management science in marketing* (pp. 156–180). New York: Ronald Press.

McGuire, W. J. (1984). Search for the self: Going beyond self-esteem and the reactive self. In J. A. R. A. Zucker & A. I. Rabin (Eds.), *Personality and the prediction of behavior* (pp. 73–120). New York: Academic Press.

McGuire, W. J., McGuire, C. V., Child, P., & Fujioka, T. (1978). Salience of ethnicity in the spontaneous self-concept as a function of one's ethnic distinctiveness in the social environment. *Journal of Personality and Social Psychology, 36* (5), 511–520.

Madden, N. (2010, March 4). Soy-sauce-flavored kit kats? In Japan, they're No. 1. *Advertising Age*. Retrieved October 10, 2010 from http://adage.com/globalnews/article?article_id=142461.

Markus, H. R., & Kitayama, S. (1991). Cultures and the self: Implications for cognition, emotion, and motivation. *Psychological Review, 98* (2), 224–253.

Milner, L. M., & Higgs, B. (2004). Gender sex-role portrayals in international television advertising over time: The Australian experience. *Journal of Current Issues and Research in Advertising, 26* (Fall), 81–95.

Mueller, B. (2004). *Dynamics of international advertising*. New York: Peter Lang Publishing Co.

Osgood, C., & Tannenbaum, P. H. (1955). The principle of congruity in the prediction of attitude change. *Psychological Review, 62* (1), 42–55.

Phinney, J. S. (1992). The multigroup ethnic identity measure: A new scale for use with diverse groups. *Journal of Adolescent Research, 7* (2), 156–176.

Shavitt, S., Lee, A. Y., & Johnson, T. P. (2008). Cross-cultural consumer psychology. In C. Haugtvedt, P. Herr, & F. Kardes (Eds.), *Handbook of consumer psychology* (pp. 1103–1131). Mahwah, NJ: Lawrence Erlbaum.

Schwartz, S. H. (1992). Universals in the context and structure of values: Theoretical advances and empirical tests in 20 countries. In M. Zanna (Ed.), *Advances in experimental social psychology* (pp. 1–65). Orlando, FL: Academic Press.

Spira, J. S., & Whittler, T. E. (2004). Style or substance? Viewers' reactions to spokesperson's race in advertising. In J. D. Williams, W. Lee, & C. P. Haugtvedt (Eds.), *Diversity in advertising: Broadening the scope of research directions* (pp. 247–257). Hillsdale, NJ: Lawrence Erlbaum.

Stanfield, J. H., II, & Dennis, R. M. (1993). *Race and ethnicity in research methods*. Thousand Oaks, CA: Sage.

U.S. Census Bureau (2001). *The population profile of the United States: 2000*. Washington, D.C.: U.S. Government Publishing Office.

Williams, J. D., Lee, W., & Henderson, G. R. (2008). Diversity issues in consumer psychology. In C. Haugtvedt, P. Herr, & F. Kardes (Eds.), *Handbook of consumer psychology* (pp. 877–912). Mahwah, NJ: Lawrence Erlbaum.

Wooten, D. B. (1995). One-of-a-kind in a full house: Some consequences of ethnic and gender distinctiveness. *Journal of Consumer Psychology, 4* (3), 205.

Zhang, J. (2010). The persuasiveness of individualistic and collectivistic advertising appeals among Chinese generation-X consumers. *Journal of Advertising, 39* (3), 69–80.

Zhang, Y., & Gelb, B. (1996). Matching advertising appeals to culture: The influence of products' use conditions. *Journal of Advertising, 25* (3), 29–46.

Additional Readings

de Mooij, M. K. (2010). *Global marketing and advertising: Understanding cultural paradoxes* (3rd ed.). Thousand Oaks, CA: Sage.

Frith, K. T., & Mueller, B. (2010). *Advertising and societies: Global issues*. New York: Peter Lang.

Gudykunst, W. B. (2003). *Bridging differences: Effective intergroup communication* (4th ed.). London: Sage.

Hall, E. T. (1984). *Beyond culture*. New York: Doubleday.

Hofstede, G. (2003). *Culture's consequences: Comparing values, behaviors, and organizations across cultures* (2nd ed.). Newbury Park, CA: Sage.

Markus, H. R., & Kitayam, S. (1991). Culture and the self: Implications for cognition, emotion, and motivation. *Psychological Review, 98* (2), 224–253.

Triandis, H. C. (1989). The self and social behavior in differing cultural contexts. *Psychological Review, 96* (3), 506–520.

Chapter 12

The Reflexive Game

How Target and Agent Persuasion Knowledge Influence Advertising Persuasion

Michelle R. Nelson and Chang Dae Ham

One utility of advertising conforms to the direct relationship between a receiver viewing an advertising message and buying the brand (Thorson & Rodgers, Chapter 1). The receiver of a message is often referred to as the *target*, and the messages are designed and placed by advertising executive *agents* to "hit" the target. Such metaphorical language implies a "game" between the message sender and the target. In most persuasion "games," the direct effect of advertising on purchase behavior is demonstrated; however, there are cases when it is not. For example, if target consumers are suspicious about the persuasion tactics—e.g., "I think Company X is using a celebrity, who probably doesn't even use the product, just to get me to buy that shampoo"—they may reject the advertising and the product.

In persuasion games, like other games, one goal is to figure out what the other player knows or how s/he operates and then adjust individual game-play actions accordingly. Such reflexive knowledge is captured in the Persuasion Knowledge Model (PKM) (Friestad & Wright, 1994), a theoretical framework that describes ramifications of agent's and target's "everyday persuasion knowledge" for persuasion episodes, including advertising. Everyday persuasion knowledge for targets relates to their ideas about how advertising persuades or the specific tactics used (e.g., "they use good-looking people in an ad to make me want to imitate them"). Everyday persuasion knowledge for agents may relate to the way that they think targets will respond (e.g., "consumers like celebrities, so if we place this shampoo with this celebrity, they will like the brand, too"). It is likely that these sorts of ideas influence advertising persuasion. Yet, few advertising theories allow for the influence of "everyday market knowledge" on advertising effects. As such, our chapter contributes to advertising theory by highlighting the role that targets' knowledge about persuasion (and to a lesser extent, agents' knowledge) plays in interpreting and responding to persuasion attempts. Pertinent to the advertising model proposed in Figure 1.1, we review literature related to receivers' beliefs about and understanding of the message (in traditional and non-traditional advertising contexts). We first outline the components of the PKM, then present studies that investigate these components, and finally, we provide discussion on PKM processing and persuasion outcomes.

The Persuasion Knowledge Model: An Overview

Target consumers tweet, talk, and sometimes trash advertising. For example, when McDonald's used Twitter's "promoted tweet" service to reintroduce the McRib sandwich, the majority of tweeted comments were negative (Heine, 2010). A target wrote: "McRib is back and it's as bad as you remember." Another target comments on the nature of the advertising talk: "I like how 90% of the tweets related to the promoted 'McRib is back' are making fun of it." This is an example of everyday persuasion knowledge; people are evaluating the effectiveness of the promoted tweet persuasion message. How that discussion and knowledge relate to persuasion is the focus of the Persuasion Knowledge Model (PKM). Rather than a target consumer passively receiving messages, the target is an active receiver, interpreter, and responder to advertising messages.

However, the PKM is broader than this example illustrates. The PKM was created with "the ultimate goal of developing an integrated theory of the interplay between agents' and targets' persuasion knowledge, that is, what marketers believe and what consumers believe" (Friestad & Wright, 1994, p. 22). Thus, conceived of as a game, the PKM represents two teams, the Agents and the Targets (see Figure 12.1). The *Agent* represents "whomever a target identities as being responsible for designing and constructing a persuasion attempt"

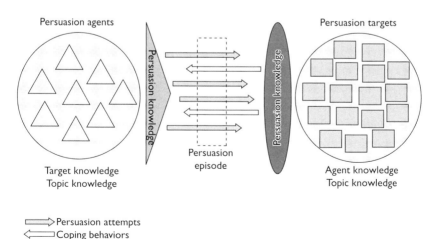

Figure 12.1 The Reflexive Game: Persuasion Knowledge Model.

(Friestad & Wright, 1994, p. 2), such as advertising agency professionals who create advertising campaigns or the companies themselves (e.g., McDonald's). On the other side of the persuasion attempt is the *Target*, defined as "those people for whom a persuasion attempt is intended" (Friestad & Wright, 1994, p. 2), such as consumers. Friestad and Wright proposed that agents and targets have their own knowledge structure about persuasion, which is made up of agent (and target) knowledge, topic knowledge, and persuasion knowledge. Each of these forms of knowledge can interact with one another to produce persuasion outcomes (e.g., acceptance or rejection of advertising messages).

Agent knowledge consists of the target's beliefs about characteristics and goals of the persuasion agent. This includes general knowledge about the advertiser (e.g., "McDonald's is a reliable, cheap fast food restaurant") as well as expertise about the agents, which has been learned by the individual target's life experiences. Individuals have accumulated agent knowledge from a variety of sources such as mass media, self-study, social interaction, or direct and indirect experience. For example, a consumer can gain knowledge about a company from the Twitter feed he reads or the friend who works at the company.

Target knowledge refers to the agent's beliefs about the persuasion target or consumer (Friestad & Wright, 1994). Target knowledge represents overall information about the persuasion target that the agent intends to persuade, which may include target audiences' profile data, their buying pattern analysis, or discussions about the agent's brands.

Topic knowledge represents beliefs about the topic of the persuasion message (Friestad & Wright, 1994), which includes the agent or the target's knowledge about product functions, the industry situation, service quality, company reputation, etc. For example, in a news article about the Twitter campaign, the McDonald's social media director (agent) presented topic knowledge about the product (e.g., "What I can tell you is that it is a quality sandwich"; Heine, 2010). To this, a target responded in a comment posted after the news article: "Um . . . It's not exactly a 'quality' sandwich, as the McDonald's rep stated. Look at the other ingredients and nutritional information—listed on the company's own website: http://mcd.to/dlAWxK." This example shows how agent and target teams interact in the marketplace as they comment on and exchange knowledge, in this case about the product.

A *persuasion attempt* is "a target's perception of an agent's strategic behavior," by which an agent intends to influence the target's beliefs, attitudes, intention, and behavior (Friestad & Wright, 1994, p. 2). This "strategic behavior" includes not only the presented message (e.g., McDonald's: "it is a quality sandwich"), but also the target's internal inference about the agent's motives, intention, and perceived consequences of the attempts (e.g., the tweets and comments regarding the agent message). Among the persuasion attempts, "a directly observable part" (p. 2) is defined as the *persuasion episode*, represented by a message in the form of an advertisement or promotional benefits delivered by a marketer. In our McDonald's case, both the "promoted tweet," "The McRib is back" and the social media director's defense of the sandwich in the news article, are examples of persuasion episodes. Subsequently, many types of persuasion episodes are included in persuasion attempts, encompassing combinations of multiple persuasion episodes such as television commercials, print ads, sales presentations, and product publicity (Friestad & Wright, 1994).

The persuasion episode or "game" is a part of the targets' *coping behavior*. When the target responds to the persuasion attempt, s/he can use agent, topic, or persuasion knowledge to "reapply" an existing brand attitude or to recalculate or adjust attitudes. In this way, the use of persuasion knowledge helps them to "cope" or control the outcome of the persuasion. Therefore, the target can fulfill the goals most salient to them (e.g., to receive accurate "health" information about this sandwich to help in the buying process). However, the coping behavior does not necessarily have to be negative. For example, if a target wants a price discount, she is likely to accept an advertiser's price discount message even though she knows the discount is a marketing tactic for increasing sales volume (i.e., matching targets' goal with agent goal). However, if the price discount is only available for buying a huge bundle, which the target does not need, s/he is likely to reject the price discount offer because the goal (i.e., buying the cheaper price for an item) does not match the agent's goal (i.e., sales increase).

Several coping mechanisms have been suggested, depending on the target's level of persuasion knowledge. Those with low PK are predicted to engage in concrete compartmentalized thinking (e.g., this ad is misleading; therefore, all TV ads must be misleading) or to ignore or reject advertising all together with reliance instead on friends' advice and interpretation (Friestad & Wright, 1994). In contrast, knowledgeable targets may offer a more nuanced approach by separating their emotional evaluation of the persuasion tactics and ad from the product information. Part of the coping process may also involve targets' beliefs about the effectiveness or the appropriateness of the tactic. Yet, not much research has investigated the forms of coping mechanisms in the persuasion process.

Application of the PKM

Persuasion Agents

Although the original PKM model included the agent and target (Friestad & Wright, 1994), most of the research in the literature has focused on targets.

Although several studies have examined the agent side of the PKM (e.g., Nyilasy & Reid, 2009; Kover, 1995), there are no known studies that have systematically measured or manipulated agents' persuasion knowledge, although there are a handful of studies that have examined advertising agents' ideas. In addition to this body of research, what is needed is to clarify the difference between the agent side of PKM and the agents' persuasion knowledge. For example, Kover (1995) conducted semi-structured interviews with 20 copywriters to discover the existence and nature of implicit communication theories. He found that for this group of Agents, a shared understanding of the target emerged as someone who is "increasingly bombarded with advertising," but someone who may or may not want to see advertising. Although not described according to the PKM, this understanding could be regarded as the "Target Knowledge" held by the Agent. As a result of this knowledge, the copywriters adjusted their actions. Many indicated that their first task was to "break through the resistance." After that, the Agents tried to create an emotional response or connection with the target. In essence, the creative brief they followed, which includes a section describing the target, is their "Target Knowledge." The process described by the copywriters (Agents) included an active role of the perceived "Target Knowledge."

Similarly, Nyilasy and Reid (2009) used semi-structured interviews among 28 advertising agency personnel in account, creative, and planning areas to discern the extent to which their knowledge about how advertising worked related to academic theories. Two key themes or "theories" emerged from the data. The first one related to that noted among Kover's (1995) creatives, that is advertising "works" when it is creative enough to break through (the clutter) and engage the target. The second theory, coined "mutation of effects," sounds like the developmental and longitudinal approach to persuasion knowledge. In essence, the agents believed that "over time, consumers develop resistance to advertising techniques and become less susceptible to overt technologies of persuasion" (Nyilasy & Reid, 2009, p. 87). Finally, the advertising executive persuasion agents believed that breaking rules by providing compelling and creative advertising that emotionally connected with consumers (targets) was the key to good advertising. In sum, these two studies offer consistency in the way that agents use their understanding of the Target to adjust their own tactics. Next, we present research related to the persuasion target.

Persuasion Targets

The PKM has been employed to examine how targets evoke their persuasion knowledge (topic, agent, or persuasion) against the agents' ulterior motivation of persuasion. To date, some studies have examined one or multiple forms of target knowledge and effects on persuasion outcomes.

Agent knowledge is usually manipulated or measured according to the level of affect, familiarity, or knowledge about the company. For example, Ahluwalia and Burnkrant (2004) examined how rhetorical questions in advertising (e.g., "Did you know that wearing Avanti shoes can reduce your risk of arthritis?") were interpreted based on the targets' agent knowledge (favorability of "agent") and dispositional persuasion knowledge (i.e., how much they know about advertising persuasion in general, either low or high). The results of their experimental studies showed that only when the persuasion knowledge was high did targets use their agent attitudes (i.e., prior attitudes/favorability toward the agent) to evaluate the persuasion tactic of the rhetorical question. In this PK condition, if the agent attitude was favorable (i.e., they believed the agent to be a socially responsible company), then the persuasion tactic of a rhetorical question was perceived to be a "more open" form of persuasion, which resulted in positive persuasion outcomes. In contrast, when prior agent attitudes were negative, respondents believed the rhetorical question format was more "pressuring," which led to negative agent attitudes. When respondents had low PK, there was no difference, presumably because they did not recognize or process the persuasion tactic.

Familiarity of the agent's brand is also a type of agent knowledge. In a series of three experiments, Wei, Fisher, and Main (2008) examined the effects of brand familiarity and activated persuasion knowledge on brand evaluations of a brand placed in a radio story. Results showed that brand familiarity moderated the influence of persuasion knowledge and perceived appropriateness of persuasion tactics on persuasion outcomes. That is, the negative effects of activated persuasion knowledge (i.e., this brand was covertly placed in the radio story, that is not appropriate) were attenuated when the brand was highly familiar.

Finally, agent knowledge was examined according to targets' evaluations of a charity (as persuasive agent) as well as their beliefs about the efficiency and effectiveness of that charity (Hibbert, Smith, Davies, & Ireland, 2007). Both forms of agent knowledge significantly and positively influenced targets' feelings of guilt when viewing a persuasive donation request message from the charity. In turn, these feelings of guilt positively influenced donation intentions. However, other aspects of persuasion knowledge (i.e., skepticism of advertising tactics in general, perceptions of manipulative intent) negatively influenced targets' feelings of guilt. Interestingly, however, there was also a *positive* direct impact of perceived manipulative intent on donor intentions. In this case, it seems that even though targets recognized that some charity tactics were manipulative, that it was deemed to be appropriate because the end goal of "helping others" was positive.

Topic Knowledge. Very few studies have examined the effect of topic knowledge on persuasion. Using a grounded theory approach, Miller and Sinclair (2009) examined how community stakeholders responded to advocacy advertising about the coal industry. Respondents in focus groups were asked their agent attitudes toward the coal industry as well as their feelings, beliefs, and knowledge about "coal" and the industry (topic knowledge) before responding to a series of advertising concepts. The authors identified several themes emerging from the texts related to targets' use of agent, topic, and persuasion knowledge. First, they found that the nature of the topic knowledge did not refer to the technical aspects of the coal process, but rather to the knowledge of the coal industry's past behavior. In addition, respondents actively evaluated the persuasive intent of the agent messages (e.g., for social good or for manipulation) as well as the perceived transparency of the organization. Such forms of knowledge impacted how these stakeholders responded to and coped with the advocacy messages (i.e., the extent to which they identified with or rejected the messages).

Persuasion Knowledge. Most PKM research has focused on how persuasion knowledge affects targets' persuasion outcomes. For example, Menon and Khan (2003) employed the PKM to explain when consumers positively perceived corporate social responsibility (CSR) activities depending on sponsorship type (i.e., advocacy ad vs. cause promotion) and congruency level between the sponsor and social issues. When people looked at cause promotions (which did not elicit persuasion knowledge), compared to the advocacy message, which evoked more elaboration, they were likely to have more positive attitudes toward the CSR activities. These relationships were moderated by sponsorship and social issue congruency. Higher congruity led to more favorable CSR evaluations for the cause message, but only when people elaborated thoughts about sponsorship activities. Rodgers (2007) examined the manipulation of skepticism of e-sponsor motives (i.e., persuasion knowledge) by asking targets about their perceptions of sponsor's ulterior motivations. Consumers' skeptical perceptions of sponsor motive moderated the influence of sponsorship congruity on targets' perceptions of credibility of e-newspapers. In all, these studies suggest the activated persuasion knowledge did not automatically lead to negative effects. Rather, the consumers seemed to implicitly or explicitly adjust the skepticism depending on the degree of prior brand attitude, familiarity, or appropriateness.

Thus, it appears that the congruity between sponsor and persuasion agent may relate to when or how persuasion knowledge is activated and related to persuasion outcomes. Now that we have reviewed literature on the major components of the model, we discuss studies related to the processing mechanisms for PKM.

PKM: Processing and Outcomes

Cognitive Capacity and Accessibility of Motives

In the inception article, Friestad and Wright (1994) propose "that consumers' persuasion knowledge, as a broad and frequently accessed knowledge structure, will 'hover' in readiness, available to them as an immediate source of help that they learn to depend on in generating valid product and agent attitudes" (p. 10). Yet, how and when persuasion knowledge (PK) gets activated is not yet fully understood. Is it a fully conscious practice or is it the case that as the everyday PK becomes so ingrained in our memory, that its influence on "how and why persuasion occurs became automatized" (Friestad & Wright, 1999, p. 180).

Some research suggests that PK cannot be evoked or activated in certain conditions. First, automatic activation of PK requires cognitive capacity, which may not always be available (Campbell & Kirmani, 2000). People first automatically draw inferences about an individual (agent) based on his/her behavior, and then correct and modify the first inference with the corresponding situational factors such as hidden motives of the individual (e.g., Gilbert, Pelham, & Krull, 1988). The first inference process is fairly automatic, which doesn't necessarily require large cognitive capacity, while the following correction inference, based on situational factors, needs more in-depth processing and much larger cognitive resources (e.g., Uleman, 1987). Therefore, when cognitive resources are constrained, PK is not likely to be activated, even though an agent's hidden motive of persuasion is salient. Without cognitive capacity, the coping mechanism is not invoked. For example, in an advergaming situation, Waiguny, Nelson and Terlutter (2011) found game players who were over-challenged by game play did not use (or could not use) PK (i.e., this advergame is an advertisement) to the same extent in their brand evaluations as those who were under-challenged by game play, presumably because the challenge of game play negatively impacted cognitive resources.

Second, Campbell and Kirmani (2000) argued that accessibility of agent motive is another significant factor influencing persuasion knowledge activation. In other words, if targets are unaware of the persuasive intent of a message, they are unable to activate PK. From social psychology literature, Higgins and King (1981) mentioned that accessibility of a construct is influenced by factors including strength of association. Thus, the degree to which the association between the agent and his/her motive is strong and highly influential is related to the accessibility of hidden motives. For example, the salesperson is highly associated with the motive to sell something whereas a blogger may not be strongly associated with the motive to sell something; in this latter case, PK may not be activated.

Similarly, for traditional advertisements, adult targets can generally understand the persuasive intent of advertising and can recognize a persuasion attempt or tactic (Friestad & Wright, 1999). For instance, U.S. adults were easily able to discuss and evaluate why ads may or may not be effective; just 20 adults generated more than 250 different psychological terms for presumed influence on how consumers attend to or respond to advertising (Friestad & Wright, 1995). In short, it appears that although most adults in the U.S. have a generally high level of PK that may be "hovering in readiness," it may or may not be activated in all persuasion settings or among younger consumers. Next, we discuss what happens when PK is activated.

Change of Meaning and Effects

The above-reviewed studies show that for traditional advertising, if targets have the cognitive capacity and understand the manipulative intent of a message, they can invoke their persuasion knowledge as a coping mechanism. For other types of persuasion tactics, including non-traditional advertising such as product placement or sponsored search advertising, the persuasive nature of the message may not be immediately obvious to the target so the persuasion knowledge is not automatically activated. For these types of messages, the PKM predicts that if the target learns that the agent's action is a persuasion tactic, a "change of meaning" will occur (Friestad & Wright, 1994, p. 13), which may impact persuasion outcomes. For example, Pechmann and Wang (2010) exposed adolescents to a television program with an "educational placement" (anti-smoking message) embedded within the storyline. When PK was activated through an epilogue (i.e., a short statement at the end of the program), which informed the audience about the planned nature of the anti-smoking placement, the smokers' realization that there was persuasive intent led them to react against the intended message. The change of meaning went from "entertaining show" to "public service persuasion device." The resultant PK led smokers to generate more favorable beliefs about smoking and intentions to smoke (opposite to the persuasion advocated).

In marketing practice, Sony came under scrutiny by game fans when the persuasive intent of a communication was revealed and the true (agent) source was identified. Sony hired a company to develop a viral video to create interest among fans for its PlayStation Portable device in November 2006 (Gupta, 2006). The video blog, "alliwantforxmasisapsp.com," was purportedly created by real-life hip-hop artists and fans, but revealed no affiliation with Sony. When the artists sang about the device with overwhelmingly positive praise, suspicious readers discovered that the website filtered out marketing-related words such as "viral," "advertisement," and "campaign." The fans wondered why a blogger would bother to filter out these words and accused the blog creators of trying to deceive them. Although Sony apologized to the community, the *change in meaning* led to negativity, backlash, and a loss of trust among game fans.

This change of meaning is predicted to influence the immediate persuasion episode as targets update their agent attitudes, but may also impact subsequent persuasion episodes—adding to overall target persuasion knowledge. In this case, such persuasion knowledge may lead to advertising skepticism (the tendency to disbelieve the informational claims of advertising; Obermiller & Spangenberg, 1998). For instance, when audiences learn about the planned nature of "educational messages" or embedded brand messages, the persuasive intent may then be applied to all similar instances. In this way, audiences may become skeptical about other pro-social themes in shows or about other brands seen in programs. For example, in a series of experiments, Darke and Ritchie (2007) found that when consumers felt they were "duped" by an advertisement for a dishwasher that they initially trusted (but then found out the ad was deceptive after reading a negative review), the negativity engendered by this experience and the suspicion it aroused led to negativity about the product and the product attitudes for unrelated products.

However, newly acquired PK will not always lead to negative outcomes. For example, knowledge of the persuasion attempt may also invoke perceptions of the effectiveness or appropriateness (perceptions of the fairness, manipulativeness, or respectfulness) of the tactic, which subsequently influence targets' agent attitudes (Friestad & Wright, 1994). For example, Yoo (2009) looked at how the difficulty of search task and perceived tactic appropriateness of search engine sponsorship influenced Internet website visitors' click-through-rate (CTR). When consumers realized that the keyword ad was sponsored by a company, they activated their PL, which in turn, negatively influenced the CTR of the keyword ad. However, the perceived tactic appropriateness of search engine sponsorship influenced targets' CTR. When the targets perceived that search engine sponsorship is appropriate, the negative effect activated by PK was attenuated. Perceived tactic appropriateness also moderated the effects of PK on brand evaluations for a familiar brand appearing in a radio news story; only those people who believed the practice to be inappropriate displayed negative brand evaluations (Wei et al., 2008).

Finally, there have been cases where increased PK did not shield the target from persuasion or lead to negative effects for the brand. For example, Mallinckrodt and Mizerski (2007) showed that for children ages 5–8 that played an advergame with Froot Loops (versus a control group), there were no *negative* effects of PK on brand preferences or intention to request the brand. In fact, more of the older children preferred the featured brand in the advergame when they actually identified the game's intent compared with the children who did not identify the intent. Also, Wood, Nelson, Atkinson, and Lane (2008) found that when respondents learned that the news story they watched for Lasik eye surgery was actually from a Video News Release (i.e., a public relations persuasion tactic), this change of meaning did not negatively impact their attitudes toward the brand, even when the credibility of the news story itself suffered.

Overall, when consumers' cognitive resources are constrained and agents' ulterior motives are not accessible, consumers are not able to infer persuasion knowledge when coping with persuasion attempts. However, as targets' gain PK about the persuasive intent of a message (e.g., "sponsored search"), they may or may not use that PK as a shield against persuasion. Future research might more carefully assess the underlying beliefs and processes for which PK leads to favorable or unfavorable outcomes.

Commentary, Critique, and Conclusion

In conclusion, the Persuasion Knowledge Model is a theoretical framework that contributes to our understanding of advertising persuasion and processes. Yet, although the research on PKM is growing, it is not yet "a dominant advertising theory, especially in a longitudinal form" (Nyilasy & Reid, 2009, Table 2, p. 92).

We believe there are several factors that hinder its development. First, studies have conceptualized, investigated, manipulated, and measured PK in too many different ways to develop an integrated literature or examination of the theory development. For example, some studies do not measure or manipulate PK directly but use it as a heuristic to explain effects (e.g., Cowley & Barron, 2008). Other studies, employing qualitative methods, add to the richness and understanding of how targets acquire, discuss, and actively use PK in their everyday lives (e.g., netnography: Nelson, Keum, & Yaros, 2004; focus groups: Miller & Sinclair, 2009), but these studies are rarely used to inform quantitative research. Even among studies that examine PKM using survey or experimental methods, there are no standard scales to measure the PK construct, especially related to advertising (see Bearden, Hardesty, & Rose, 2001, for the most commonly used scale). Part of this problem likely relates to the fact that the concepts (e.g., persuasion knowledge, topic knowledge) often present over-lapping constructs (Campbell & Kirmani, 2008) and the model itself may be too all-encompassing with so many interacting component parts to offer explanatory value. Rather, the model appears to work best when researchers use it to investigate consumers' overall PK and how that knowledge "shields" them against short-term effects of persuasion. The less-studied aspects of the model related to agents' knowledge, topic knowledge, and coping mechanisms provide ripe areas for future research. Further, what has not been investigated thoroughly is the developmental and longitudinal understanding of PK. Finally, despite the propositions and research ideas developed by Friestad and Wright (1994), few, if any, *existing frameworks* incorporate aspects of the PKM into their research. Given the development of new advertising forms into developed and developing countries, studies should investigate the development of PK among children as well as "targets" in other cultural contexts.

Future research, for instance, might examine how different age groups' PK develops over time. For example, Boush, Friestad, and Rose (1994) conducted surveys in the first and last parts of the school year for middle school children. They found that knowledge about advertising tactics and effects increased, at least for sixth and eighth graders, although levels of advertising skepticism remained stable (for a review of children's socialization as consumer, see John, 1999). Such research could be supplemented with longitudinal qualitative research that examines underlying factors and contributors to the development of PK.

In other cultural contexts, a few studies provide insight into persuasion knowledge, but do not yet tie persuasion knowledge to culture. For example, Bartholomew and O'Donohoe (2003) conducted multiple-method qualitative research with 10–12 year olds in Scotland. They found that these adolescents held very sophisticated knowledge of advertising and felt they could control advertising and limit its influence. However, results of experimental research with younger children (ages 5–8) in Australia showed that the 7 and 8 year olds who understood the commercial intent of the advergame (i.e., had high PK) actually chose the branded cereal featured in the game (Mallinckrodt & Mizerski, 2007).

References

Ahluwalia, R., & Burnkrant, R. E. (2004). Answering questions about questions: A persuasion knowledge perspective for understanding the effects of rhetorical questions. *Journal of Consumer Research, 31*, 26–42.

Bartholomew, A., & O'Donohoe, S. (2003). Everything under control: A child's eye view of advertising. *Journal of Marketing Management, 19*, 433–457.

Bearden, W. O., Hardesty, D. M., & Rose, R. L. (2001). Consumer self-confidence: Refinements in conceptualization and measurement. *Journal of Consumer Research, 28*, 121–134.

Boush, D. M., Friestad, M., & Rose, G. M. (1994). Adolescent skepticism toward TV advertising and knowledge of advertiser tactics. *Journal of Consumer Research, 31*, 529–539.

Campbell, M. C., & Kirmani, A. (2000). Consumers' use of persuasion knowledge: The effects of accessibility and cognitive capacity on perceptions of an influence of agent. *Journal of Consumer Research, 27*, 69–83.

Campbell, M. C., & Kirmani, A. (2008). "I know what you're doing and why you're doing it": The use of persuasion knowledge model in consumer research. In C. Haugtvedt, P. Herr, & F. Kardes (Eds.), *The handbook of consumer psychology* (pp. 549–573). New York: Psychology Press.

Cowley, E., & Barron, C. (2008). When product placement goes wrong: The effects of program liking and placement prominence. *Journal of Advertising, 37*, 89–98.

Darke, P. R., & Ritchie, R. J. B. (2007). The defensive consumer: Advertising deception, defensive processing, and distrust. *Journal of Marketing Research, 44*, 114–127.

Friestad, M., & Wright, P. (1994). The persuasion knowledge model: How people cope with persuasion attempts. *Journal of Consumer Research, 21*, 1–31.

Friestad, M., & Wright, P. (1995). Persuasion knowledge: Lay people's researchers' beliefs about the psychology of advertising. *Journal of Consumer Research, 22*, 62–74.

Friestad, M., & Wright, P. (1999). Everyday persuasion knowledge. *Psychology and Marketing, 16*, 185–194.

Gilbert, D. T., Pelham, B. W., & Krull, D. S. (1988). On cognitive busyness: When person perceivers meet persons perceived. *Journal of Personality and Social Psychology, 54*, 733–740.

Gupta, S. (2006, December 14). Sony confesses to creating "flog," shutters comments. *Online Media Daily*. Retrieved January 12, 2010, from www.mediapost.com/publications/?fa=Articles.showArticle&art_aid=52541.

Heine, C. (2010, November 5). "McRib is back" promotion turns into a Twitter roast. *ClickZ*. Retrieved March 10, 2011, from www.clickz.com/clickz/news/1869732/mcdonalds-mcrib-twitter-cooks-salty-comments.

Hibbert, S., Smith, A., Davies, A., & Ireland, F. (2007). Guilt appeals: Persuasion knowledge and charitable giving. *Psychology and Marketing, 24*, 723–742.

Higgins, E. T., & King, G. (1981). Accessibility of social constructs: Information-processing consequences of individual and contextual variability. In N. Cantor & J. F. Kihlstrom (Eds.), *Personality, cognition, and social interaction* (pp. 69–121). Hillsdale, NJ: Lawrence Erlbam.

John, D. R. (1999). Consumers socialization of children: A retrospective look at twenty-five years of research? *Journal of Consumer Research, 26*, 183–213.

Kover, A. J. (1995). Copywriters' implicit theories of communication: An exploration. *Journal of Consumer Research, 21*, 596–611.

Mallinckrodt, V., & Mizerski, D. (2007). The effects of playing an advergame on young children's perceptions, preferences, and requests. *Journal of Advertising, 36*, 87–100.

Menon, S., & Kahn, B. E. (2003). Corporate sponsorships of philanthropic activities: When do they impact perception of sponsor brand? *Journal of Consumer Psychology, 13*, 316–327.

Miller, B., & Sinclair, J. (2009). Community stakeholder responses to advocacy advertising: Trust, accountability, and the persuasion knowledge model (PKM). *Journal of Advertising, 38*, 37–51.

Nelson, M. R., Keum, H., & Yaros, R. A. (2004). Advertisement or adcreep game players' attitudes toward advertising and product placements in computer games. *Journal of Interactive Advertising, 5*, 3–21.

Nyilasy, G., & Reid, L. N. (2009). Agency practitioner theories of how advertising works. *Journal of Advertising, 38*, 81–96.

Obermiller, C., & Spangenberg, E. R. (1998). Development of a scale to measure consumer skepticism toward advertising. *Journal of Consumer Psychology, 7*, 159–186.

Pechmann, C., & Wang, L. (2010). Effects of indirectly and directly competing reference group messages and persuasion knowledge: Implications for educational placements. *Journal of Marketing Research, 47*, 134–145.

Rodgers, S. (2007). Effects of sponsorship congruity on e-sponsor and e-newspaper. *Journalism and Mass Communication Quarterly, 84*, 24–39.

Uleman, J. (1987). Consciousness and control: The case of spontaneous trait inferences. *Personality and Social Psychology Bulletin, 13*, 337–354.

Waiguny, M., Nelson, M. R., & Terlutter, R. (2011). Go with the flow: How persuasion knowledge and game challenge and flow state impact children's brand preference. Paper presented to the Annual Conference of the American Academy of Advertising, Mesa, AZ.

Wei, M., Fisher, E., & Main, K. J. (2008). An examination of the effects of activating persuasion knowledge on consumer response to brands engaging in covert marketing. *Journal of Public Policy and Marketing, 27*, 34–44.

Wood, M. L. M., Nelson, M. R., Atkinson, L., & Lane, J. B. (2008). Social utility theory: Guiding labeling of VNR as ethical and effective public relations. *Journal of Public Relations Research, 20*, 231–249.

Yoo, C. Y. (2009). The effect of persuasion knowledge of keyword search ads: Moderating role of search task and perceived fairness. *Journalism and Mass Communication Quarterly, 86*, 401–413.

Additional Readings

Boush, D. M., Friestad, M., & Rose, G. M. (1994). Adolescent skepticism toward TV advertising and knowledge of advertiser tactics. *Journal of Consumer Research, 21*, 165–175.

Boush, D.M., Friestad, M., & Wright, P. (2009). *Deception in the marketplace*. New York: Routledge.

Kirmami, A., & Zhu, R. (2007). Vigilant against manipulation: The effect of regulatory focus on the use of persuasion knowledge. *Journal of Marketing Research, 44*, 688–701.

McAlister, A. R., & Cornwell, B. (2009). Preschool children's persuasion knowledge: The contribution of theory of mind. *Journal of Public Policy and Marketing, 28*, 175–185.

Martin, K. D., & Smith, N. C. (2008). Commercializing social interaction: The ethics of stealth marketing. *Journal of Public Policy and Marketing, 27*, 45–56.

Wright, P. (2002). Marketplace metacognition and social intelligence. *Journal of Consumer Research, 28*, 677–682.

Part IV

Different Types of Advertising Messages

Chapter 13

Creativity and Ad Theory

Sheila L. Sasser and Scott Koslow

"We can't solve problems by using the same kind of thinking we used when we created them" according to Albert Einstein. True to this statement, creativity is ever evolving by necessity—adapting to new media, behavioral variances, cultural issues, artistic stimulation, and idiosyncratic change. Creativity requires us to think differently, to be imaginative, yet to be artistic and remain on strategy while employing novel approaches and new ideas. Creativity definitions vary widely across disciplines and are highly subjective and prone to varying interpretations, assumptions, and even organizational, environmental, sociocultural, and cross-cultural dimensions, as some scholars of the latest research streams propose. So as we look at what is creativity, to whom, and why, one of the issues with an inclusive creativity theory is that it is ever changing.

One framework that has proven useful in understanding creativity is the 3Ps of the Persons, Place, and Processes of creativity (Sasser, 2006), which enables a typology of theories to help shed light on the many ways creativity can be examined. Some researchers focus on issues involving creative people, others focus in on the creative thinking process, and still others focus on the environment surrounding the creative process. This framework was highlighted in Moriarty, Mitchell, and Wells (2009) and explored by Sasser and Koslow (2008). In this chapter, issues and theories involving each P will be examined.

The Person P: Individual-Oriented Theories of Creativity

For the person P, theoretical insights focus researchers on how creative people think about a problem, respond to a creative brief, or ideate to achieve higher levels of creativity. Historically, scholars have studied individual traits like personality, problem-solving ability, spatial skills, elaboration, experience, emotional intelligence, motivation, and passion in attempts to assess creativity. As one of the early major theorists focused on personal motivation for creativity, Amabile (1979) studied the effects of external evaluation on artistic creativity. Her book, *Creativity in Context* (1996), provided a helpful framework for many current researchers. She proposed four key factors examining why some people have more creative outputs than others: knowledge of the domain, skills in creative thinking, the social environment, and, most importantly, individual intrinsic motivation.

Creativity is a delicate thread and it is not so easily dissected and broken into component parts. Although the focus on individuals as creators has been applied to many areas, it is often the coalescence of more than one motivating factor forming complex patterns that bewilders scholars and confounds theoretical research. Like creative spaghetti, each tasty string intertwines with the total. Yet, by exploring and examining these different areas separately, as we pull them apart and then put them back together again, it is possible to better view the underlying forces that drive this messy and complex process of creativity. Co-Creation Index (CCI) is when the agency and client jointly co-create a campaign together (for additional information, refer to Sasser, 2008). Such CCI interactions may be studied to offer a clearer glimpse of creativity by looking at the person, process, and place. Like a recipe, the tables are toppings to help sort through all the creativity theories.

The Person P: Confluence Approaches

As Sternberg and Lubart (1999) point out, one model of creative production is the confluence model of individual creativity. That is, creative products are best produced when several critical factors coalesce. Such factors may include passion, expertise, support, situational, cultural, routine, priming, individual, political, process, client-based, or even motivational stimulation.

An example of a confluence model in advertising is Sasser and Koslow's (2010) PEPS framework. This considers two individual person factors: *p*assion for the work and *e*xpertise in the domain plus two situational place factors: lack of *p*olitics in the environment and organizational *s*upport for good work. Tables 13.1–13.3 display the main theories for each P category. A number of interactions are explored across the person, place, and process finding that in some cases a given factor has positive effects, while in other cases, effects are negative. Such outcomes place emphasis on individual level factors of passion and expertise. They are also consistent with the early interdisciplinary theories of Amabile, particularly the intrinsic motivation or passion component. So, the coalescence of these areas supports the confluence theory of creativity across an empirical framework.

The Person P: Intelligence, Intuitive, Innate, and Genius Theories

Large advertising agencies have been willing to pay top dollar for the most brilliant creative talent with some of these individuals achieving "rock star" celebrity fame by virtue of their work. During the golden years of advertising, some of these campaigns actually influenced pop culture and commercial art, thus achieving cult status. Similarly, some early scholars have long suspected that creative individuals have a highly innate or intuitive level of creative potential (Guilford, 1950). Guilford's work on intelligence, creativity, and their educational implications remains as one of the seminal pieces of the advertising theory puzzle for the individual "P" even now.

Likewise, genius theorist Alfred Binet, who invented the first intelligence test, believed that intelligence sparked greater creative thinking. His IQ test was widely adopted but his test of creative thinking potential was later abandoned since only the IQ test had sufficient reliability (Barron & Harrington, 1981). More recent research has connected such areas as emotional intelligence with creativity and innovation breakthroughs leading many theorists to re-examine this linkage of creativity and intelligence with intuitive thinking traits (Barczak, Lassk, & Mulki, 2010).

Practitioner groups have also looked at the specific potential to produce novel thoughts, as well. Many brainstorming and creativity think tanks including Solution People, Eureka Ranch, and Systematic Inventive Thinking (SIT), offer ideation services and training. This service offers new ideas to provide clients with breakthrough concepts as a result of their various techniques. Both agencies and their clients may attend sessions together to forge new areas and branding, so they often function as a creativity facilitator for both collaborators in the creative process, in an intermediary role.

The Person P: Cultural, Sociological, and Organizational Theories

Culture and ethnicity can also offer a saturation environment that stimulates unique creative brainstorming based on culture or ethnicity norms. Nixon and Crewe (2004) explored the notions of culture and even gender impact on creativity and debates continue on whether the place "P" impacts the person "P" or individual as a frame of interpretation. Most agree that creativity is highly subjective. Emerging researchers such as Stuhlfaut (2010) have looked at the role of culture and ethnicity in the creative process, as they qualitatively assess multicultural and ethnic agencies. Such studies are sometimes rooted in cultural anthropology and ethnographic methods and they are very helpful at the early stages of research particularly. Clients often match creative teams to clients in an assessment of the ideal creative recipe.

Everything from the role of humor to emotion in advertising campaigns has been viewed through potential cross-cultural lenses with mixed findings much like the "cosmopolitan construct" found by Cannon and Yaprak (2002), as it theorizes that people may take on an international or global citizenship. Such creative "citizenship" may be witnessed first hand at Cannes, where 10,000 advertising executives and creatives converge to bestow awards on the best campaigns globally. Taylor, Grubbs Hoy, and Haley (1996) studied how the French differ in views of advertising creativity, as they are often touted as possessing unique and original orientations. Cross-cultural international theory is dynamic and it is still constantly evolving to address advertising creativity, as Taylor (2010) has noted in several seminal works and conferences. Some researchers have considered the perceived anti-social personality characteristics of bold creative and/or innovative people (Barron & Harrington, 1981; Rogers, 2003). Ford (1996) charted his "theory of individual creative action in multiple social domains" to note some of the differing social aspects and roles. Creativity is clearly encouraged when one operates in a variety of cultural, social, or organizational circles.

Cultural, sociological, and organizational effects on creativity may be equally important and several effects may even coexist simultaneously. Intelligence and original thinking are critical capabilities that are often informed by place-based or situational variables that could be invoked by culture or environment as it shapes the creative lens. However, independent or extreme thinking is often misconstrued as non-conformist, radical, or even anti-social. Although great artists and performers have typically exhibited non-conformist characteristics, are such unique traits functioning as an enabler or a signifier of greater creativity? Or is it that we just notice what is very different, as it stands out? Kasof (1995) argued we do and that we commit a fundamental attribution bias in that we misattribute unusual behavior like creativity to individual differences rather than situational factors. Debunking conventional tendencies, habits, lifestyles, and activities as well as typical linear problem solving may be something that empowers and distinguishes creatives from more traditional roles.

The Person P: Appropriateness Construct in Creativity Theory

The individual difference issues raised above prompt the notion of differences in perceptions in what is appropriate for a creative idea. All genuinely creative ideas must be both original and appropriate to the context, but in the case of advertising, the appropriateness variable is related to creative strategy formation and involves intimate knowledge of the target segment in the individual or group brainstorming process. Thus, appropriateness of the creative campaign is a key measure, yet as Koslow, Sasser, and Riordan (2003) note in comparing creatives with account executives, they often hold vastly different views of what kind of advertising is appropriate. Kilgour and Koslow (2009) examined differences in account, creative, and student respondents in an experimental treatment for effects of various creative thinking techniques. Those three groups again have different views of what is appropriate, with some groups feeling that a mere mention of a brand name makes something appropriate, but others need much more detail presented in a campaign.

For example, Ang, Lee, and Leong (2007) and Smith, MacKenzie, Yang, Buchholz, and Darly (2007) also take different approaches to appropriateness across various contexts. There are many more possible contexts with different appropriateness measures, as cross-cultural and global creativity studies evolve. In one research article, scholars from three different countries explore the inter-relationship of creative constructs (West, Kover, & Caruana, 2008) and found that another issue is the relative balance of originality and appropriateness. Strategy may indeed be the tipping point in the see-saw balancing act waged between creatives and account people. Strategy is often privileged by account executives (Koslow et al., 2003) and it is a sticking point with clients (Sasser, Koslow, & Riordan, 2006). As strategy may be a compromise zone, it may play a central role for originality and strategy impact on the artistic approach deemed appropriate for optimal creativity.

The Process P

The Process P: Theories of Creative Idea Generation

Although there is emerging knowledge about creative individuals, the actual process of creative thinking is far more elusive. While many academics believe that individual creativity is the primary key to advertising creativity theory, others emphasize the process (Griffin, 2008) component as a learned trait. These scholars believe that creativity process can be taught to individuals as an operant or acquired skill (Kilgour, 2006, 2008). Like a recipe or formulaic invention, even those endowed with less innate creativity or expertise may become conditioned to produce award-winning campaigns. Several routine behaviors, techniques, and technologies enable increased levels of creativity to be achieved as hypothesized and found in various process-based theories and replications. In 1988, Amabile looked at the cross-disciplinary aspect of

Table 13.1 Person-based individual theories of creativity

Author	Date	Synopsis
Production-oriented/Empirical		
Reid	1977	Academics as poor judges of creative talent
Young	2000	Contrasts copywriter and art director views
Ewing & Jones	2000	Shows "strong" and "weak" theories of advertising across ad constituencies
Koslow et al.	2003	Creative, account, and media executives differences in creativity perception
El-Murad & West	2003	Creatives taking more risks win more awards
Devinney et al.	2005	Differences in clients and agency evaluation approaches, yet similarities and agreement on the identification of the best creative
Hackley & Kover	2007	How professional creatives negotiate and navigate roles and identities in ad agencies
Griffin	2008	Considers how students and creatives learn to think
West et al.	2008	Looks at the differences in what practitioners and consumers call creative advertising
Kilgour & Koslow	2009	Experimental—individuals—creative, account, and student effects of creative techniques
Production-oriented/Substantive		
Stuhlfaut	2006	Is ad creativity an individual or social process?
Nyilasy & Reid	2009	Explores how executives think advertising works
Ashley & Oliver	2010	Examines what creative leaders think leads to high creative work
Response-oriented/Empirical		
Kover et al.	1995	Consumers' emotional responses to advertising, both creative and effective are explored
Kover et al.	1997	Creatives and consumer responses to creative and effective advertising for personal enhancement to consumers, individual appeal
White & Smith	2001	Differences in practitioner, student, and general public view of creativity in advertisements
Dahlén et al.	2008	Advertising effects mediated by consumer-perceived creativity with consumers as judges
Smith et al.	2008	Considers how creativity affects the hierarchy of advertising effects
Dahlén et al.	2008	Shows creative advertising signals information to consumers like greater effort and brand ability
Goldenberg & Mazursky	2008	Demonstrates that templates-oriented advertisements have more positive and long-lasting impact on consumers
Baack et al.	2008	Examines the effects of creativity on consumer recall and recognition
Heiser et al.	2008	Shows how creative executions like cartoons influence consumers' perceptions of creativity and their responses
Poels & Dewitte	2008	Explores emotional responses to creative advertising
Van Meurs & Aristoff	2008	Looks at the creative appeal of outdoor advertisements
Heath et al.	2009	Studies how affective emotive creativity on TV is processed by individual consumers and effects

individual creativity and organizational process innovation, as the three Ps of creativity are now connected.

The Process P: Co-Creation Index and Creativity Theory

Technological advances in creative production have fueled widespread popular engagement in the creative process across various constituencies and cultures while agencies have been quick to include consumers in the creation of advertising content. YouTube, Facebook, and other social media developments have encouraged participants and members to share their creativity by posting and uploading their work for others to see. As illustrated in the co-creation index model, CCI (Sasser, Merz, & Koslow, 2008), more than one individual party typically develops, designs, interacts, and participates in the creative process. It is an interactive collaboration model between the agency creatives, clients, and even consumers as co-creators of advertising content. This approach embraces a confluence model with a process-oriented twist (Sasser, 2008).

Agencies and clients have also leveraged this by soliciting such interactions beyond merely seeking feedback with consumers. In this new era of expansive "grass roots" and "organic" co-creativity, consumers may truly "play creative director" by designing or producing a clever commercial about the brand. Many of these interactions take the form of "creative contests" or even "customization sessions" and are designed to glean consumer involvement and input in order to win some incentive prize. Fortunately, the final spot is often produced by the agency of record to insure high creative production quality.

Some clients have actually put out open creative briefs on Internet sites and discussion boards soliciting creative proposals and ideas from the World Wide Web. A key challenge is certainly managing such an open process along with all of the other considerations involved in more typical client and agency relationships. As these traditional lines have blurred between the creatives, the clients, and the consumers and as technological adeptness increases across multi-media screens, it is expected that this creative process of empowerment will continue. Forging such new areas for creative campaign exploration, beyond traditional focus groups or ad copy tests may lead to hybrid creative models and theories that are far more multifaceted in development and execution.

The Process P: Creativity Flow, Convergent, and Divergent Theories

Just as "post-modern" creativity theory privileges the individual or person humanistic aspect, systems, and process flow approaches are also alive and well

(Csikzentmihalyi, 1988). Many researchers have studied this area of the creativity phenomenon from a theoretical perspective focused on process. Early researchers such as Guilford examined a convergent thinking theoretical model (1950) while many others emphasized divergent thinking techniques. Gross (1972) developed a mathematical model of creativity suggesting that the generation of more creative ideas is optimal as a theoretical basis for this work and it unleashed a wave of other studies. For example, Reid and Rotfeld (1976) applied an associative theoretical model of creative thinking to the advertising process prompting several other studies. Vanden Bergh, Reid, and Schorin (1983) empirically test the Gross model finding that the volume of ideas is critical to the creative process while O'Connor, Willemain, and MacLachlan, (1996) replicate and extend the Gross model assuming a skewed distribution of effectiveness.

Of course, most current work is anchored on Amabile's (1996) seminal creativity motivational research across domain, task, and skill as it provides a comprehensive theoretical framework. Typically, training for creativity process proceeds in several ways (see Amabile, 1996). Even scholars who challenge Amabile such as Verbeke, Franses, Ruyten, and le Blanc (2008) do use her work as a starting point for theoretical discussion. Scholars Goldenberg, Mazursky, and Soloman's (1999) templates method of creativity theory utilizes analogies as an ideational approach. As Goldenberg and others work with Systematic Inventive Thinking (SIT) devices they often contrast and compare such things as absurd alternative exercises to illustrate an extreme opposite juxtaposition that leads to a creative idea process breakthrough. Such methods may incorporate the execution elements along with the strategy for a novel creative idea representation. Johar, Holbrook, and Stern (2001) also employ an analogy approach with copywriter and art director pairs. Kover (1995) discovers implicit communication models, used by copywriters in the creative process going beyond some of his emotional and response theory research.

The Process P: Templates and Priming Creativity Theories

Other theoretical methods enable an ordering array of ideas or an inventory of possible creative ideas and directions. Content is captured and various notions may be combined to form a new breakthrough. This process often takes the form of idea mapping in that it starts with one idea, and then radiates from that idea to several others, then another of the proposed ideas is expounded until a genuinely creative consensus or solution is reached (see Goldenberg & Mazursky, 2002). Others set parameters for generating lots of creative ideas (e.g., produce a page of ideas) or draw a phrase in one of the bubbles or light bulb areas to fill in the chart. This approach leans to the earlier Gross (1972) model of promoting and valuing the sheer volume of ideas. This technique is dubbed as "mind-scribing" discussed by Griffin (2008) as a way to imprint creativity.

Priming theories use problem-solving steps to focus and prime thinking in fertile territory that might be considered ripe for higher creative potential, if probed or prodded. Creatives are directed to a set of templates that enable thinking about certain meta-cognitive patterns in some other formats (Goldenberg et al., 1999). The emphasis on such training is not transformational, but rather it is more organizational in nature as it records, structures, and primes creative thought generation productivity. Actual change through a more radical progression of thought processes might be achieved by the random injection of diverse ideas, as divergent thinking is privileged. This "snow balling" idea generation method is noted in brainstorming sessions or in Gordon's (1961) *Synetics* training. Many trends rapidly ebb and flow in the creative realm.

The Process P: Learned Creativity, Motivation, and Passion Theories

Many creatives view such methods as a facilitation device or prop in the domain of the less skilled. Even so, ethnographies and participant observations suggest that successful creatives often do use subtle techniques that are highly complex to the point that they may not even realize it. Some of these mechanisms are beyond current creative thinking approaches. Creatives may not even be fully aware of the fact that they are employing such systems (Kilgour, 2006, 2008). As this behavior becomes second nature or automatic pilot, it complicates the exploration of creative thinking techniques and makes process research even more challenging. There are limitations and constraints on the value of such introspective or even retrospective methods for creative thinking.

There is a learning curve for creative thinking and practice is necessary due to the steep slope, which can sometimes be a slippery one. Time, energy, and trial enable creatives to explore and discover the best fit of various thinking or idea generation techniques. It is possible that years of problem solving and creative ideation leads to fundamental changes in brain mechanisms like a restructuring or reordering of individual thought patterns. While this may be true, it would require experimental or invasive MRI neurological research methods and funding to discover. Frankly, this type of study is still out of reach for most researchers and it remains controversial, as well. However, theoretically, individual intrinsic motivation or passion is still the best overall predictor of creative thinking. Such passion—i.e., intrinsic motivation—is the most central construct in the creativity literature (see Amabile, 1996) across both person and process theories. Finally, clients have a major impact on creativity as noted by

Koslow, Sasser, and Riordan (2006) as they explore factors that affect creative process.

The "big idea" of genuinely creative thought, even among professional creatives, is often taken for granted or even ignored; the process is more like a baby steps or small steps approach. Such elaboration modes or such an innovation process is the more routine approach, based on earlier work. And in most cases, a typical path-of-least-resistance problem solving suffices, and less radical or genuine creative thought is used (Moreau & Dahl, 2005). The earnest effort required to produce an idea that is both original and appropriate is often underestimated since it appears to flow so easily from top creative teams. Greater motivation may also be prone to a humanistic interaction effect since creatives work in teams or in pairs to stimulate each other's creative ideation process like priming. Many agencies attempt to inspire such collegiality within those teams.

Theoretically, the *two-step process* of creative thinking is another way to look at creativity. The first phase develops a novel idea quickly followed by a second step to integrate it internally in the process and then move on to prompt other elaborations. This second step is rarely a smooth or perfect fit, introducing a tension causing another novel departure, then an integration/elaboration, yet another tension and departure, etc., almost like a series or spiral effect.

In highly skilled creatives, this two-step cycle may take as little time as 2 or 3 seconds. Average timed observations note that such a series of creative brainstorming processes will often flow very quickly for approximately 7 minutes of heightened attention. After such a peak, there is a valley period of several minutes of "rest" characterized by reduced idea flow, and then another round of rapid idea flow. In highly skilled creatives, multiple novel ideas are produced almost simultaneously, and this two-step can go on for hours. For those with less creative skill, the amount of time spent on elaboration is relatively enormous, often comprising several minutes. In the less skilled, novel idea departures may take relatively little time. This two-step process for expert creatives is consistent with Griffin (2008) who notes how the more advanced students more easily distinguish between ideas and executions. "Expert" students downplayed and disassociated the execution of the advertisement. For more experienced creatives, this division deepens and separates across critical two steps. Griffin and Morrison (2010) explore the creative process from the inside out in their latest book based on depth interviews with creatives in agencies.

A more basic issue, however, is: why are creativity techniques needed? Although creatives usually describe what they do as problem solving, it often bears slight resemblance to how experts solve problems. Kilgour (2006) suggests that there is an inverted U-shaped relationship between expertise and creativity. Expertise is needed to aid creativity only up to a modest level. Beyond this, expertise tends to result in fixation thinking mentality that relies

Table 13.2 Process-based theories of advertising creativity

Author	Date	Synopsis
Production-oriented/Empirical		
Reid & Rotfeld	1976	Applies the associative model of creative thinking to advertising
Vanden Bergh et al.	1983	Empirically tests Gross' model premise that volume of creative idea generation is critical
Kover	1995	Copywriters' implicit communications model
Goldenberg et al.	1999	Develops the templates method of creative thinking, an analogies-based approach
Johar et al.	2001	Analogy techniques using a think-aloud task on copywriter–art director pairs
Chong	2006	Explores the advantages and disadvantages of research as perceived by creative directors
Koslow et al.	2006	Estimates the significance of the marketer client role and the impact on creativity
Borghini et al.	2010	Considers the relationship between street art and advertising
Production-oriented/Substantive		
Griffin & Morrison	2010	Examines Creative Process Inside Out
Production-oriented/Theoretical		
Gross	1972	Develops mathematical model suggesting that developing more creative ideas is optimal
Zinkhan	1993	Need more research in advertising creativity
O'Connor et al.	1996	Replicates and extends Gross' model assuming skewed distribution of effectiveness
El-Murad & West	2004	Reviews the limited literature on creativity focused on enhancing and encouraging it
Sasser	2008	Discusses appropriateness/engagement of consumers/agencies in creative process
Response-oriented/Empirical		
Stewart & Koslow	1989	Details impact of executional factors on recall, comprehension, and persuasion; argues against formulaic creativity
Ang & Low	2000	Finds that novelty (expectancy), meaningfulness (relevancy), and emotion (valence of feelings) impact response
Stone et al.	2000	Explores the relationships among advertising recall, likeability, and creativity
Pieters et al.	2002	Shows that original advertisements receive more attention, using eye-tracking method
Till & Baack	2005	Demonstrates how creative advertising facilitates unaided recall
Ang et al.	2007	Argues that consumers' view of creative advertisement is one that is novel, meaningful, and connected
Smith et al.	2007	Develops scales for consumer perceptions of creativity comparing award-winning and randomly selected advertisements
Rossiter	2008	Necessary components of creative effective ads
Response-oriented/Theoretical		
Smith & Yang	2004	Takes a general approach to creativity focusing on consumer responses

on standard solutions. Creative thinking techniques allow people to think outside this limiting set of knowledge and go beyond such limited fixation tactical approaches.

Published advertising creative thinking research deals extensively with divergent thinking, but provides little understanding of the role of convergent thinking, which Guilford (1950) argued is just as important. In agencies, convergent thinking would incorporate the critical role strategy plays in shaping advertisements and usually it shows up in the appropriateness dimension of creativity. The assumption in most creative thinking models is that increasing divergent thoughts will produce more creative advertising. If genuine creativity must be both original *and* appropriate, then it follows that increasing convergent-oriented strategic thinking may also produce more creative advertising. Runco and Charles (1993) first explored this in their article about judgments of originality and appropriateness as creativity predicators, building needed theoretical foundations for many later advertising creativity researchers. As Kilgour (2006) explains, creative thinking tasks work differently on different individuals because of their innate thinking skills. Poor divergent thinkers may benefit from traditional creative thinking tools while other tools may be useful for convergent thinkers.

The Place P

Place P: Environment Place-Based Creativity Theories

In the end, all the three Ps are needed for optimal creativity as advertising creativity theories are explored in support of this notion. Although individual scholar preferences vary by topic, agencies need talented people such as highly expert creative individuals and clients who are willing to explore. Agencies and integrated marketing communications firms especially need a process that enables the highest levels of creativity. Finally, the people involved in the creative process need a creative supportive environment or place that inspires their best work and facilitates the creative process functions in an advertising agency or integrated marketing communications setting.

Place P: Environment, Philosophy, Politics, and Risk Theories

Recently, Sasser et al. (2007) examined environment and place-based issues in an article on creative and interactive media and IMC (Integrated Marketing Communications) implementation factors. Amabile (1996) assessed work environment for creativity again from an interdisciplinary perspective in the management literature stream. From a different international angle, Li, Dou, Wang, and Zhou (2008) studied the moderating role of market conditions on agency creativity and campaign outcomes. This study took a broader view of economic factors and the impact on the place-based creativity from a succinct environmental position.

Although other frameworks are useful for flow (Csikszentmihalyi, 1988, 1996), the most important focus is developing some common threads to organize various place-based studies, as there are so many differing directions. The largest category of place-based research comprises the production-oriented empirical grouping as a tangible indicator. Many of these theories deal with risk, philosophy, information, and other specific measurable orientations (West, 1999; West & Ford, 2001). Still other theories deal with conflict (Vanden Bergh, Smith, & Wicks, 1986), roles (Hirschman, 1989), and information (Sutherland, Duke, & Abernathy, 2004). Kover and Goldberg (1995) discovered political games between account and creative executives. Other researchers have studied cross-cultural and international differences in creativity (West, 1993).

The Place P: Relationships, Attitudes, and Symbols

There are also a few early substantive and theoretical studies from the 1970s and 1980s eras, but there is such a plethora of place-based theories that some overarching meta-theoretical frameworks are truly needed to organize all the place-based theories and studies. Such environmental models in the place P focus on areas of the agency office, organization, workspace setting, or client relationships that affect people and the creative process. There are both controllable and uncontrollable factors present in the ad agency based on all these carefully cultivated creative images, structure, culture, symbols, integration, communication, styles, systems, traditions, and other factors.

Sometimes these factors are evident in the physical agency setting. Publicis agency Leo Burnett offers bowls of apples in every lobby reception area, honoring their founder. The Paris Publicis office is housed above their historic French chic drugstore on the Champs Elysée, while Saatchi New York thrives in Tribeca downtown. WPP's Ogilvy London office recreates a casual English pub atmosphere for creatives to brainstorm at work. Creativity zones or thinkubation areas have been designed in Team Detroit office space makeover. Omnicom's BBDO New York office is near the excitement of Broadway and Times Square while Organic digital agency has an auditorium theater space to host groups and clients. IPG agency offices are often in close proximity near their clients and government agencies, including some embassy and automotive locations. Doner has an impressive art collection displayed throughout its agency like a gallery space. Independent agencies like BBH are based in creative urban hub locations full of street energy. Agencies often enable creatives to work from home or use flextime. The common thread across all of these place-based theories seems to be that if people thrive and feel passionate in their environment, the intrinsic motivation to create will be optimized. It also signals clients that they invest in creativity and that it is highly important for the agency culture. All of these creative agency place-based environments along with favorite pubs or bistros flame the creative fuel that lights the fire of a big idea.

Stimulating and facilitating creativity in order to inspire creative ideas and creativity theory extends far beyond style, offering substance, psychology, and reinforcement of some intuitive notions of the place P effect on creativity. One highly creative agency takes its entire staff on an unknown mystery trip to spark their creativity and provide relief from the stress of the business. It is novel and unique and highly effective for motivation. Other agencies sponsor music, theater, arts, and cultural events to get their employees engaged in creativity. In relationship marketing, this caring theory is known as the Sternberg model of commitment, intimacy, passion, and trust and it seems very appropriate in the intense advertising creativity field. Creativity is original, unique, novel, and artistic and those who are highly creative thrive in a stimulating place-based atmosphere, as indeed they create sparks wherever they are passionately inspired!

Summary

This theoretical synopsis offers just a brief glimpse of the 3Ps framework of person, place, and process as one way to think about advertising creativity theories. Most theories and research in advertising creativity can usually be divided into these three major perspectives or themes relating to the people who create advertising, the process they follow in developing creative ideas, and their work places or environments. It can also be applied to the people who respond to advertising, the places like media, contexts, or situations involved and the thinking processes by which they interpret and perceive creative advertising. As advertising creativity theory advances, hopefully some comprehensive meta-frameworks will be forged to better focus the wide range of theories in practice. Yet, creativity is such a force as to continue to elude such capture and labeling!

Table 13.3 Place-based theories of advertising creativity

Author	Date	Synopsis
Production-oriented/Empirical		
Reid et al.	1985	Examines the creative strategies of Clio-winning advertising in a cross-national setting
Vanden Bergh et al.	1986	Investigates the conflict between creatives and account executives
Michell	1986	Compares client and agency perceptions of creativity, especially in relationship context
Hirschman	1989	Explores qualitatively roles in ad production
West	1993	Examines creative process differences among American, Canadian, and British agencies
Kover & Goldberg	1995	Documents the political games between advertising creative and account executives
Taylor et al.	1996	Four types of French creative styles: *la séduction, le spectacle, l'amour,* and *l'humour*
West & Berthon	1997	Explores client risk behavior in advertising
Reid et al.	1998	Shows that advertising has become more creative than it used to be
West	1999	Suggests agencies avoid taking creative risks and when they do, they take a portfolio approach
West & Ford	2001	Examines how agency philosophies influence the creative risks they are willing to run
Hill & Johnson	2004	Problem-solving approach clients use
Sutherland et al.	2004	Identifies the information creatives want and obtain from clients
Tippins & Kunkel	2006	Shows the mixed effects of winning creativity awards on advertiser share prices
Sasser et al.	2007	Shows relationships of interactive media, creativity, and integrated marketing communications
Verbeke et al.	2008	Tests if Amabile's KEYS framework applies to advertising and finds serious anomalies
Li et al.	2008	Explores the role of market environment on advertising creativity
Production-oriented/Substantive		
Drake	1984	Reflects on the relationship between research and creatives
Production-oriented/Theoretical		
Burke et al.	1990	Proposes normative model of ad production.
Sasser & Koslow	2008	Reviews person, process, and place theories of advertising creativity with emphasis on place
Response-oriented/Empirical		
Dahlén	2006	Creative media placement impact on consumer brand associations, attitudes, credibility.
Dahlén et al.	2009	Argues for creative media placement choices
Jayant	2010	Compares creative website design and viewer needs
Kim et al.	2010	How Korean consumers define advertising creativity

References

Amabile, T. M. (1979). Effects of external evaluation on artistic creativity. *Journal of Personality and Social Psychology, 37* (2), 221–233.

Amabile, T. M. (1988). From individual creativity to organizational innovation. In K. Gronhaug & G. Kaufmann (Eds.), *Innovation: A crossdisciplinary perspective* (pp. 139–166). Oslo: Norwegian University Press.

Amabile, T. M. (1996). *Creativity in context.* Boulder, CO: Westview Press.

Ang, S. H., & Low, S. Y. M. (2000). Exploring the dimension of ad creativity. *Psychology and Marketing, 17* (10), 835–854.

Ang, S. H., Lee, Y. H., & Leong, S. M. (2007). The ad creativity cube: Conceptualization and initial validation. *Journal of the Academy of Marketing Science, 35* (2), 220–232.

Ashley, C., & Oliver, J. D. (2010). Creative leaders. *Journal of Advertising, 39* (1), 115–130.

Baack, D. W., Wilson, R. T., & Till, B. D. (2008). Creativity and memory effects: Recall, recognition and an exploration of non-traditional media. *Journal of Advertising, 37* (4), 85–94.

Barczak, G., Lassk, F., & Mulki, J. (2010). Antecedents of team creativity: An examination of team emotional intelligence, team trust and collaborative culture. *Creativity and Innovation Management, 19* (4), 332–345.

Barron, F., & Harrington, D. M. (1981). Creativity, intelligence and personality. *Annual Review of Psychology, 32,* 429–476.

Borghini, S., Visconti, L. M., Anderson, L., & Sherry, J. F. Jr. (2010). Symbiotic postures of commercial advertising and street art. *Journal of Advertising, 39* (3), 113–126.

Burke, R. R., Rangaswamy, A., Wind, J., & Eliashberg, J. (1990). A knowledge-based system for advertising design. *Marketing Science, 9* (Summer), 212–229.

Cannon, H., & Yaprak, A. (2002). Will the real-world citizen please stand up! The many faces of cosmopolitan consumer behavior. *Journal of International Marketing, 10* (4), 30–52.

Chong, M. (2006). How do advertising creative directors perceive research? *International Journal of Advertising, 25* (3), 361–380.

Csikszentmihalyi, M. (1988). Society, culture, person: A systems view of creativity. In R. J. Sternberg (Ed.), *The nature of creativity* (pp. 325–339). New York: Columbia University Press.

Csikszentmihalyi, M. (1996). Implications of a systems perspective for the study of creativity. In R. J. Sternberg (Ed.), *Handbook of creativity* (pp. 313–335). Cambridge, UK: Cambridge University Press.

Dahlén, M. (2006). The medium as a contextual cue: Effects of creative media choice. *Journal of Advertising, 34* (Fall), 89–98.

Dahlén, M., Friberg, L., & Nilsson, E. (2009). Long live creative media choice. *Journal of Advertising, 38* (2), 121–129.

Dahlén, M., Rosengren, S., & Torn, F. (2008). Advertising creativity matters. *Journal of Advertising Research, 48* (3), 392–403.

Devinney, T., Dowling, G., & Collins, M. (2005). Client and agency mental models in evaluating advertising. *International Journal of Advertising, 24* (1), 35–50.

Drake, M. (1984). The basics of creative development research. *International Journal of Advertising, 3* (1), 43–49.

El-Murad, J., & West, D. C. (2003). Risk and creativity in advertising. *Journal of Marketing Management, 19*, 657–673.

El-Murad, J., & West, D. C (2004). The definition and measurement of creativity: What do we know? *Journal of Advertising Research, 44* (June), 188–201.

Ewing, M. T., & Jones, J. P. (2000). Agency beliefs in the power of advertising. *International Journal of Advertising, 19* (3), 335–348.

Ford, C. (1996). A theory of individual creative action in multiple social domains. *Academy of Management Review, 21* (4), 1112–1142.

Goldenberg, J., & Mazursky, D. (2002). *Creativity in product innovation*. Cambridge, UK: Cambridge University Press.

Goldenberg, J., & Mazursky, D. (2008). When deep structures surface: Design structures that can repeatedly surprise. *Journal of Advertising, 37* (Winter), 21–34.

Goldenberg, J., Mazursky, D., & Solomon S. (1999). The fundamental templates of quality ads. *Marketing Science, 18* (3), 333–351.

Gordon, W. J. J. (1961). *Synetics: The development of creative capacity*. New York: Harper & Row.

Griffin, W. G. (2008). From performance to mastery. *Journal of Advertising, 37* (4), 95–108.

Griffin, W. G., & Morrison, D. (2010). *The creative process illustrated: How advertising's big ideas are born*. Cincinnati, OH: How Books F + W Media Inc.

Gross, I. (1972). The creative aspects of advertising. *Sloan Management Review, 14* (1), 83–109.

Guilford, J. P. (1950). Creativity. *American Psychologist, 5*, 444–454.

Hackley, C., & Kover A. (2007). The trouble with creatives: Negotiating creative identity in advertising agencies. *International Journal of Advertising, 26* (1), 63–78.

Heath, R. G., Nairn, A. C., & Bottomley, P. A. (2009). How effective is creativity? *Journal of Advertising Research, 49* (4), 450–463.

Heiser, R. S., Sierra, J. J., & Torres, I. M. (2008). Creativity via cartoon spokespeople in print ads: Capitalizing on the distinctiveness effect. *Journal of Advertising, 37* (Winter), 75–84.

Hill, R., & Johnson, L. W. (2004). Understanding creative service: A qualitative study of the advertising problem delineation, communication and response (APDCR) process. *International Journal of Advertising, 23* (3), 285–307.

Hirschman, E. C. (1989). Role-based models of advertising creation and production. *Journal of Advertising, 18* (4), 42–53.

Jayant, R. K. (2010). A netnographic exploration. *Journal of Advertising Research, 50* (2), 181–196.

Johar, G. V., Holbrook, M. B., & Stern, B. B. (2001). The role of myth in creative advertising design: Theory, process and outcome. *Journal of Advertising, 30* (2), 1–25.

Kasof, J. (1995). Explaining creativity: The attributional perspective. *Creativity Research Journal, 8* (4), 311–366.

Kilgour, A. M. (2006). The creative process: The effects of domain specific knowledge and creative thinking techniques on creativity. Unpublished doctoral dissertation, University of Waikato, Hillcrest, New Zealand.

Kilgour, A. M. (2008). *Understanding creativity: The creative thinking process and how to improve it.* Staarbrucken, Germany: VDM Verlag.

Kilgour, M., & Koslow, S. (2009). Why and how do creative thinking techniques work? Trading off originality and appropriateness to make more creative advertising. *Journal of the Academy of Marketing Science, 37* (3), 298–309.

Kim, B. H., Han, S., & Yoon, S. (2010). Advertising creativity in Korea. *Journal of Advertising, 39* (2), 93–108.

Koslow, S., Sasser, S. L., & Riordan, E. A. (2003). What is creative to whom and why? Perceptions in advertising agencies. *Journal of Advertising Research, 43* (March), 96–110.

Koslow, S., Sasser, S. L., & Riordan, E. A. (2006). Do marketers get the advertising they need or the advertising they deserve? Agency views of how clients influence creativity. *Journal of Advertising, 35* (3), 85–105.

Kover, A. J. (1995). Copywriters' implicit theories of communication: An exploration. *Journal of Consumer Research, 21* (March), 596–611.

Kover, A. J., & Goldberg, S. M. (1995). The games copywriters play: Conflict, quasi-control, a new proposal. *Journal of Advertising Research, 35* (November/December), 52–61.

Kover, A. J., Goldberg, S. M., & James, W. L. (1995). Creativity vs. effectiveness? An integrative classification for advertising. *Journal of Advertising Research, 35* (November/December), 29–38.

Kover, A. J., James, W. L., & Sonner, B. S. (1997). To whom do advertising creatives write? An inferential answer. *Journal of Advertising Research, 37* (January/February), 41–53.

Li, H., Dou, W., Wang, G., & Zhou, N. (2008). The effect of agency creativity on campaign outcomes: The moderating role of market conditions. *Journal of Advertising, 37* (Winter), 109–120.

Michell, P. C. (1986). Accord and discord in agency: Client perceptions of creativity. *Journal of Advertising Research, 24* (5), 9–25.

Moreau, C. P., & Dahl, D. W. (2005). Designing the solution: The impact of constraints on consumers' creativity. *Journal of Consumer Research, 32* (June), 13–22.

Moriarty, S., Mitchell, N., & Wells, W. (2009). *Advertising Principles and Practice.* Upper Saddle River, NJ: Pearson Prentice Hall.

Nixon, S., & Crewe, B. (2004). Pleasure at work? Gender, consumption and work-based identities in the creative industries. *Consumption, Markets and Culture Journal, 7*, 129–147.

Nyilasy, G., & Reid, L. N. (2009). Agency practitioner theories of how advertising works. *Journal of Advertising, 38* (3), 81–96.

O'Connor, G. C., Willemain, T. R., & MacLachlan, J. (1996). The value of competition among agencies in developing ad campaigns: Revisiting Gross's model. *Journal of Advertising, 25* (1), 51–62.

Pieters, F. G. M., Warlop, L., & Wedel, M. (2002). Breaking through the clutter: Benefits of advertisement originality and familiarity for brand attention and memory. *Management Science, 48* (6), 765–781.

Poels, K., & Dewitte, S. (2008). Getting a line on print ads: Pleasure and arousal reactions reveal an implicit advertising mechanism. *Journal of Advertising, 37* (Winter), 63–74.

Reid, L. N. (1977). Are advertising educators good judges of creative talent? *Journal of Advertising, 6* (3), 41–43.

Reid, L. N., & Rotfeld, H. J. (1976). Toward an associative model of advertising creativity. *Journal of Advertising, 5* (4), 19 & 24–29.

Reid, L. N., King, K. W., & DeLorme, D. E. (1998). Top-level agency creatives look at advertising creativity then and now. *Journal of Advertising, 27* (2), 1–16.

Reid, L. N., Lane, W. R., Wenthe, L. S., & Smith, O. W. (1985). Creative strategies in highly creative domestic and international television advertising. *International Journal of Advertising, 4* (1), 11–18.

Rogers, E. M. (2003). *Diffusion of innovations* (5th ed.). New York: Free Press.

Rossiter, J. R. (2008). The necessary components of creative, effective ads. *Journal of Advertising, 37* (Winter), 139–144.

Runco, M. A., & Charles, R. E. (1993). Judgments of originality and appropriateness as predictors of creativity. *Personality and Individual Differences, 15* (5), 537–546.

Sasser, S. L. (2006). Creativity, innovation and integration in global advertising agency channel relationships: Creativity in the real world. ETD Collection for Wayne State University. Paper AAI3218294. http://digitalcommons.wayne.edu/dissertations/AAI3218294.

Sasser, S. L. (2008). Creating passion to engage versus enrage consumer co-creators with agency co-conspirators: Unleashing creativity. *Journal of Consumer Marketing, 25* (3), 183–186.

Sasser, S. L., & Koslow, S. (2008). Desperately seeking advertising creativity. *Journal of Advertising, 37* (4), 5–19.

Sasser, S. L., & Koslow, S. (2010). Passion, expertise, politics, and support: A dynamic framework for greater creativity. Working paper, October, 2010.

Sasser, S. L., Koslow, S., & Riordan, E. A. (2007). Creative and interactive media use by agencies: Engaging an IMC media palette for implementing advertising campaigns. *Journal of Advertising Research, 47* (September), 237–256.

Sasser, S. L., Merz, R., & Koslow, S. (2008, June 27–28). A global creativity model emerges: Evolving a theory and empirical framework for the advertising CCI. Presentation made at the ICORIA 2008 International Conference on Research in Advertising, Antwerp, Belgium.

Smith, R. E., & Yang, X. (2004). Toward a general theory of creativity in advertising: Examining the role of divergence. *Marketing Theory, 4* (12), 31–58.

Smith, R. E., Chen, J., & Yang, X. (2008). The impact of advertising creativity on the hierarchy-of-effects. *Journal of Advertising, 37* (Winter), 47–61.

Smith, R. E., MacKenzie, S. B., Yang, X., Buchholz, L. M., & Darley, W. K. (2007). Modeling the determinants and effects of creativity in advertising. *Marketing Science, 26* (6), 819–833.

Sternberg, R. J., & Lubart, T. I. (1999). The concept of creativity: Prospects and paradigms. In R. J. Sternberg (Ed.), *Handbook of creativity* (pp. 3–15). Cambridge, UK: Cambridge University Press.

Stewart, D. W., & Koslow, S. (1989). Executional factors and advertising effectiveness: A replication. *Journal of Advertising, 18* (3), 21–32.

Stone, G., Besser, D., & Lewis, L. E. (2000). Recall, liking, and creativity in TV commercials: A new approach. *Journal of Advertising Research, 40* (May/June), 7–18.

Stuhlfaut, M. W. (2006). Is advertising creativity an individual or social process? Doctoral dissertation, Michigan State University.

Stuhlfaut, M. W. (2010). How agencies differ: The influence of ethnic culture on the creative process of U.S. advertising agencies. Working paper, University of Kentucky.

Sutherland, J., Duke, L., & Abernethy, A. (2004). A model of marketing information flow. *Journal of Advertising, 33* (4), 39–52.

Taylor, C. R. (2010, June 24–26). Public opinion toward digital billboards in the United States: An analysis of recent polls. Paper presented at the International Conference on Research in Advertising, Madrid, Spain.

Taylor, R. E., Grubbs Hoy, M., & Haley, E. (1996). How French advertising professionals develop creative strategy. *Journal of Advertising, 25* (1), 1–14.

Till, B. D., & Baack, D. W. (2005). Recall and persuasion: Does creative advertising matter? *Journal of Advertising, 34* (Fall), 47–57.

Tippens, M. J., & Kunkel, R. A. (2006). Winning a Clio advertising award and its relationship to firm profitability. *Journal of Marketing Communications, 12* (1), 1–14.

Van Meurs, L., & Aristoff, M. (2009). Split-second recognition: What makes outdoor advertising work? *Journal of Advertising Research, 49* (1), 82–92.

Vanden Bergh, B. G., Reid, L., & Schorin, G. A. (1983). How many creative alternatives to generate? *Journal of Advertising, 12* (4), 46–49.

Vanden Bergh, B. G., Smith, S. J., & Wicks, J. L. (1986). Internal agency relationships: Account services and creative personnel. *Journal of Advertising, 15* (2), 55–60.

Verbeke, W., Franses, P. H., Ruyten, N., & le Blanc, A. (2008). Finding the KEYS to creativity in ad agencies: Using climate, dispersion and size to examine award performance. *Journal of Advertising, 37* (Winter), 121–130.

West, D. C. (1993). Cross-national creative personalities, processes, and agency philosophies. *Journal of Advertising Research, 37* (September/October), 53–62.

West, D. C. (1999). 360° of creative risk. *Journal of Advertising Research, 39* (January/February), 39–50.

West, D. C., Kover, A. J., & Caruana, A. (2008). Practitioner and customer views of advertising creativity: Same concept, different meaning? *Journal of Advertising, 37* (Winter), 35–45.

West, D., & Berthon, P. (1997). Antecedents of risk-taking behavior by advertisers: Empirical evidence and management implications. *Journal of Advertising Research, 37* (September/October), 27–40.

West, D., & Ford, J. (2001). Advertising agency philosophies and employee risk taking. *Journal of Advertising, 30* (1), 77–91.

White, A., & Smith, B. L. (2001). Assessing advertising creativity using the creative product semantic scale. *Journal of Advertising Research, 41* (November/December), 27–34.

Young, C. E. (2000). Creative differences between copywriters and art directors. *Journal of Advertising Research, 40* (May/June), 19–26.

Zinkhan, G. M. (1993). From the editor: Creativity in advertising. *Journal of Advertising, 22* (2), 1–3.

Additional Readings

Amabile, T. M. (1996). *Creativity in context*. Boulder, CO: Westview Press.

Goldenberg, J., Levav, A., Mazursky, D., & Solomon, D. (2009). *Cracking the ad code*. Cambridge, UK: Cambridge University Press.

Griffin, W. G., & Morrison, D. (2010). *The creative process illustrated: How advertising's big ideas are born*. Cincinnati, OH: How Books F + W Media Inc.

Kilgour, M. (2006, December). Big C versus little c: Creative findings–domain-specific knowledge combination effects on the eminence of creative contributions. In S. Karkulehto & K. Laine (Eds.), *Call for creative futures conference proceedings*, Oulu, Finland: Department of Art and Anthropology, University of Oulu. www.cream.oulu.fi/tutkimus/kuukauden.htm.

Sasser, S. L., & Koslow, S. (Eds.). (2008). Special issue on creativity research in advertising. *Journal of Advertising, 37* (4), 5–154.

Chapter 14

Creativity and Risk Theories of Advertising

Douglas C. West

Creativity is at once the least scientific aspect of business and yet often the most important (Ogilvy, 1983; Zinkhan, 1993; Pieters, Warlop, & Wedel, 2002; Heath, Nairn, & Bottomley, 2009). Creativity embraces both "originality" and "innovation"; but to be successful, advertising creativity must have impact, quality, style, and relevance (Moriarty, 1991; Im & Workman, 2004) in order to be useful as solutions to consumer and business markets. Renowned academic researchers in the field have found creativity to be among the most complex of human behaviors to describe (Till & Baack, 2005). It has even been suggested that creativity cannot be defined or measured (El-Murad & West, 2004). On the other hand, risk taking is an important part of any creative enterprise, even those in the not-for-profit sector (West & Sargeant, 2004). Managers are often hired, in part, for their ability to define and negotiate a creative risk. Risk is a characteristic of decisions to which there is uncertainty about whether potentially significant and/or disappointing outcomes will be realized. Risk is most frequently associated with outcome uncertainty. Uncertainty is generally defined in the literature in terms of the variability of outcomes, lack of knowledge of the outcomes, and the uncontrollability of the outcomes.

This chapter will review the trends in advertising creative research and address the question: what do we know about creativity and risk? Within the integrated approach to advertising theory followed in this book, based upon Figure 1.1 proposed in Chapter 1, this chapter primarily focuses upon advertising organizations. That is, the advertising agencies and advertisers that are paid to create and evaluate advertising.

Creativity

Creativity is often described in such terms as "thinking" or "ability," "problem solving," "imagination," "innovation," or "effectiveness" (Osborn, 1953; Kover, Goldberg, & James, 1995; Ang, Lee, & Leong, 2007). However, any definition of a concept that includes the concept itself is circular, and, therefore, rather unsatisfactory. Many definitions involve an aspect of problem solving, where the solution to the problem requires insight. Most involve an aspect of "originality." Originality is a required, but insufficient condition for creativity: the work must also be of value. That is, it should be "appropriate" (i.e., useful and adaptive concerning task constraints). This combination of "novelty" and "appropriateness" or "usefulness" has met with widespread acceptance in the literature (Ang & Low, 2000; Koslow, Sasser, & Riordan, 2003).

Creativity involves newness, but is not necessarily "new to the world." Fusing two or more previously existing items, materials, ideas, and thoughts is considered by many to be the essence of creativity (Reid, King, & DeLorme, 1998). It has been argued that advertising creativity is a special form of creativity, and differs from others in that originality and imagination must operate within a goal-directed and problem-solving context (Baack, Wilson, & Till, 2008). Yet, the concepts of "relevance" and "appropriateness" of mainstream creativity research imply goal attainment and problem solving, and are key features of any kind of creativity (e.g., see Sternberg & Lubart, 1999; Martindale, 1999; Amabile, 1983; Mumford & Gustafson, 1988; Unsworth, 2001). For example, architects and designers of all kinds "create" by applying their originality and imagination to solve problems and achieve goals that are set, usually, by others. An artist may paint for the purpose of self-expression, but she or he may also do it for critical recognition, fame, and fortune. In reality, advertising creatives are motivated by similar considerations, even though their ostensible primary motive is to achieve the objectives of their employers or clients (Kover, 1995). The process of creativity in business is not identical to the process of creativity in the arts and sciences, but there are many similarities (Barron, 1969; De Bono, 1971).

The Theories

Underpinning any definition of advertising creativity is some idea of a mental model (White & Smith, 2001; Devinney, Dowling, & Collins, 2005; Kilgour & Koslow, 2009; Nyilasy & Reid, 2009). The three primary theories of advertising creativity are (1) Primary Process Cognition, (2) Defocused Attention, and (3) Associative Hierarchies.

Primary Process Cognition

Primary Process Cognition suggests that creative individuals are more able to switch between primary and secondary cognitive modes, primary being the mode of dreaming, reverie, psychosis, and hypnosis (Kris, 1952). It has been argued that creative people switch between the two cognitive modes, since the primary state enables the discovery of new combinations of mental elements, whereas the secondary state involves the elaboration of creative concepts identified in the associative primary state (Martindale, 1999). Primary being the mode of dreaming, reverie, psychosis, and hypnosis—think Freud—whereas the secondary process cognition is the abstract, logical, reality-oriented waking consciousness side. This is perhaps surprising at first glance but the reality is that to develop a creative idea you need some logical thinking. In a sense, the idea of the unconscious and conscious mind brings creativity into the realms of the inexplicable.

Defocused Attention

Defocused Attention concerns the number of elements that an individual is able to keep in mind at one time (Mendelsohn, 1976). The greater this number, the more likely it is that the person can make meaningful and useful combinations and, thus, formulate creative ideas. Less creative people have a narrower-focused attention than those who are more creative.

Associated Hierarchies

However, both Primary Process Cognition and Defocused Attention support the notion that associative ability is at the core of creative ability. Mednick first proposed Analogy, or Associative Hierarchies, in the early 1960s. He stated that creativity is an associative process involving the ability to bring otherwise mutually remote ideas into contiguity to facilitate a creative solution (Mednick, 1962). This leads to a view of creativity being the process of associating previously unrelated facts to make previously unrealized relationships between them apparent (Reid & Rotfeld, 1976). In relation to the process rather than output, if a person can only give a narrow range of answers in response to divergent thinking tests, he or she is said to have a steep Associative Hierarchy. Conversely, a wide range of answers indicates a flat Associative Hierarchy. The argument is that creative individuals have flat Associative Hierarchies, so are more able to make original associations and, thus, have more creative ideas.

Risk-Taking and Creativity

There is something akin with all creative people—they work hard and do their homework (West, 1994). You are not going to paint like Picasso without first knowing how to paint classically. You are not going to develop a creative way of doing brain surgery or face transplants without any knowledge of the area. There is a chance that a layperson will come up with something creative and relevant to art or brain surgery, but it is most unlikely. The ambiguity here is that if you need to do your homework, won't such training/preparation reduce the chance of finding something new? That is, if you are more familiar with the area and all its conventions are you not less likely to think of something new and surprising? The answer is that nothing can guarantee creativity. It is to a large extent a random process (Vanden Bergh, Reid, & Schorin, 1983).

Having said this, the consideration of what is or is not creative is based on reflective thinking (Hackley & Kover, 2007). Lay people deconstruct the creative intentions of practitioners and, likewise, practitioners need to hypothesize the customer's response (Friestad & Wright, 1994); hence, congruency is needed. Why is congruency important? What would happen if the consumer or buyer did not see an advertisement as creative, however defined? Advertisements can be perfectly effective without being creative, but creativity minimizes the difficulties inherent in selective exposure (Ogilvy, 1983; Kover et al., 1995; Smith, MacKenzie, Yuang, Buchholz, & Darley, 2007; Stewart, Cheng, & Wan, 2008). If the people who create the advertisements, and consumers are not synchronized on creativity, the ad will not "grab" the audience's attention and get processed (Young, 2000). At the other end of the scale, an advertisement might be "too creative" to the extent that the audience does not "get" the point (West, Kover, & Caruana, 2009). The difficulty is that imitation may be doomed to failure unless there is some competitive advantage achieved. Much depends on the marketplace or space concerned. For example, a leading UK company selling reading glasses has successfully imitated the Axe deodorant campaign with scantily clad girls, but they are not in competition. Overall, though, creative imitation generally leads to audience apathy. That is why in any form of business creativity you normally have to take a risk at some point.

Risk Taking

Risk is paradoxical as, for example, one business may face an environment where the market constantly demands change, for example the innovative design of Nike's Air Max 360, and it would be perilous to be risk averse. Whereas another might find market resistance to any changes to its position, such as Harley Davidson has famously found with the Harley Owners Group (HOGs), which tends to reject any significant and often even minor changes to the bike's design. Creatives in the advertising business often try to convince their clients to take risks by emphasizing that "safe" advertising is a big risk in itself as it is unlikely to break through the clutter. Examples of risk include changing celebrity endorsers (for example if and when Chanel chose to replace Nicole Kidman for No. 5), developing new uses for a brand, reallocating a TV budget to direct marketing, counter-cyclical advertising in place of traditional seasonality (e.g., heavy advertising of ice cream in November), and widening the age of the target market. The point is that there is some varying degree of risk associated with decisions along the whole spectrum of business planning and execution from radically changing the offering to keeping everything the same.

Categorizing risk is not an easy issue. To use an analogy, everyone accepts that crossing a road involves some degree of risk. The main uncontrollable elements in crossing a road are location, parking, amount and speed of traffic, and the layout along with the character and intentions of the driver. On the other hand, pedestrians can manage their behavior according to what they find and how well they watch and listen as they cross. In a similar way, businesses face uncontrollable and controllable risks in the marketplace. For some, the environment is such that risks are relatively small and for others they are large, but like the pedestrian, businesses can take some control over the amount of risk taken by their actions (for a general discussion see MacCrimmon & Wehrung, 1990). Thus, the planned business risk takes account of research and any other relevant information and is based upon a sound strategy whereas the unplanned does not.

Risk Management

The best way to manage business risk is undoubtedly to establish some kind of information-gathering system that meets a company's objectives and includes some pre-testing, and additional post-testing of the decisions made (West & Shelton, 1998). However, such information gathering may be put to one side in a business that decides to simply take a risk. There are many reasons why this may happen, including a manager's experience and intuition (West, Miciak, & Sargeant, 1999). The irony, of course, is that a sophisticated risk-management system might stifle creativity.

Prospect theory (Kahneman & Tversky, 1979; Tversky & Kahneman, 1986) states that most firms are risk seeking when they are below targeted aspiration levels.[1] Figure 14.1 shows a representation of prospect theory. It can be seen in Figure 14.1 that as an organization makes gains, the utility (value) it places on those gains falls. Essentially, the more you make, the less you value incremental gains. Similarly, the more you lose, the less value you place on those losses. What this means is that when you make losses you more quickly adjust to such losses than the same amount of gains. Consider these positions on a personal level. Someone winning $20 million on the lottery who then invests the money wisely and makes another $20 million is unlikely to get the same feeling of gain from the second $20 million as the first. They certainly enjoy it, but winning the first $20 million made a much bigger difference to them than the second.

The evidence suggests people get used to losses even more quickly than when they gain, and, as losses mount, each successive loss has progressively less impact on them than the previous loss. For example, if you lose $10,000 it may feel awful, but if you make subsequent losses it does not feel as bad as the first loss. So, staying with the example, if you lose $10,000, to lose another $10,000 would not feel as bad as the original loss of $10,000. As a consequence, prospect theory suggests that to move from point A to point B in Figure 14.1, an organization or individual will be highly likely to take a chance. Once you have passed above point A the tendency will be to become risk-averse because you are beyond your "prospect point." It has certainly been found that when a target return on equity (ROE) is introduced, either at the firm or industry level, risk and return are negatively correlated for below-target firms and positively correlated for above-target firms (Fiegenbaum & Thomas, 1986). This occurs regardless of the time or the underlying environmental conditions. The lower a firm's performance relative to a target, the more likely it is to take a risk. Overall, the evidence indicates that the model is one where below-target performance drives risk-taking in the hope that if the risk pays off the organization will quickly return to its prospect point.

Take the case of the Ford Focus. The Ford Focus was launched in Europe in 1998 to replace the ageing Ford Escort. Its design ticked all the creative boxes.

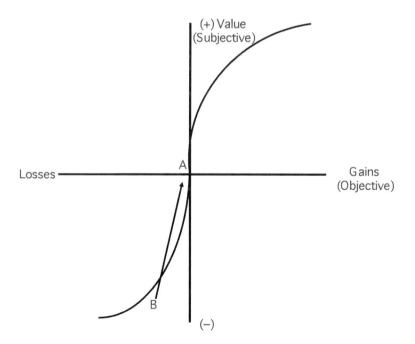

Figure 14.1 Prospect Theory.

It was fresh, original, surprising, and relevant—it was well built, handled like a much more expensive car, and had all the equipment people wanted. It jolted at first, but is now part of the landscape. The Mark II was introduced in 2004 (see Figure 14.2). The Mark II didn't surprise. It continues to be seen as a great car yet the jolt has gone. Built in collaboration with Volvo, it has the front-end of a Volvo and is wider and more "chunky" in design to meet side-impact safety. Why was the Mark I so groundbreaking and the Mark II more evolutionary? There are clearly several reasons; one is probably that Ford saw itself under great threat from Japanese and Korean competition in the 1990s. This urgency changed to greater conservatism and containment given success of the car. Put simply there was more to lose with the Mark II than the Mark I.

Advertising Risk and Culture

Risk is a managerial issue because managers set expectations and evaluate their achievements, or otherwise, and then make choices over risk (McAlister, Srinivasan, & Kim, 2007). When the business process (strategy to execution) is top-down, there will be a greater propensity to take creative risks. The reasoning is that top managers may be personally liable if things go wrong with a decision, but they have the authority and power to maintain their standing. On the other hand, executives have more to lose in the bottom-up campaign process, as their position is exposed and vulnerable. Bottom-up managers are personally accountable for the outcome. Overall, and all other factors being equal, it would be expected that the "top-down" decision process would be associated with higher levels of creative risk taking than "bottom-up." Is there a real-world example of this in advertising?

On an individual basis, research indicates that successful risk takers often feel that past successes are due to their skills rather than good fortune. According to March and Shapira (1987) history tends to interpret winners compared to losers as reflecting differences in judgment and ability. This tendency to attribute favorable outcomes to enduring features rather than good luck has been observed in organizations and individuals. To varying degrees, successful risk-taking individuals are likely to believe that they can beat the odds, that nature is good to them, and that they have special abilities.

Studies of organizational cultural risk values, risk typologies, and senior managers' risk orientations all suggest that organizations can encourage or discourage individuals to undertake risky behavior (Stoner, 1968). As noted by Coca-Cola's Marketing Director, George Bradt, if corporations penalize failure rather than reward success, people will not take risks (Nicholas, 1994).

Organizational culture is the most important factor of all (Fletcher, 1993). A "risk-seeking" culture may have the effect of providing an overall view that

Figure 14.2 Prospect Theory, Risk Aversion, and the Ford Focus Mark I and II.

virtually all performance is classified as below potential or target (West & Berthon, 1997). Similarly, a risk-seeking culture may unleash the risk-seeking potential of the "bottom-up" decision process. This is not contradictory to arguing that higher risk taking will be associated with a "top-down" campaign process. Junior managers might take more advertising risks in the bottom-up process if the culture supports taking chances and makes allowance for the inevitability that risks often fail.

Within such a culture, the key elements of risk sharing and diminished accountability come into play. Once the penalties are removed from taking risks, bottom-up managers will be more likely to take more risks. This is further enhanced by one other important factor, namely that junior managers tend to be younger and have less experience than do top managers. Research suggests that the less knowledge and experience held by a company or an individual, the more likely it is that risks may be taken (March, 1988; MacCrimmon & Wehrung, 1990; Miller & Chen, 2004).

Advertising Agencies

The advertising agency provides an interesting twist whenever consultants are involved in creative decisions. Agency personnel empathize with their clients, but will be more risk-seeking. The reason is simple—the client has the final say and controls the level of compensation. This reduces agency culpability (El-Murad & West, 2003; Koslow, Sasser, & Riordan, 2006). An advertising campaign's outcome rarely threatens an agent's livelihood, especially for senior executives, save where a major client may be lost to an agency and/or where a team has been solely allocated to one big client. As a rule, agencies diversify their client base across multiple firms and are rarely dependent upon a sole advertiser for their prosperity; thus, they can act like "agents" rather than "principals." So risk taking is linked to higher levels of creativity and creatives often feel that their managers and clients are more reluctant to take risks than they are.

Most clients do not have sufficient knowledge to understand whether agents have acted professionally or not on their behalf (Hirschman, 1989). Thus, the most effective sanction on risk-taking behavior by a consultant is peer review and comparison of work. Just because businesses have difficulty verifying the actions and activities of consultancies and consultants on their behalf, it does not mean that consultants and consultancies are uncontrollable. Consultants that take unwarranted risks will likely damage their own reputations. Consequently, they will find it increasingly difficult to find new business. For example, it has been found in advertising that the main factors in winning accounts are positive recommendations by satisfied clients and personal contacts with top management (Wills, 1992). At a micro level, unwarranted risk takers who disregard their clients' interests may also damage their personal reputation with peers and find themselves out of a job and having trouble finding a new one. Furthermore, experienced managers provide a further layer of control by imposing professional codes and norms in taking risks. Such controls on risky behavior may be more effective than any client information systems. Within this general risk "architecture," a consultant's philosophy forms the foundation of its staff belief structure of how business works and is inextricably linked to creativity and risk taking (Ewing, Napoli, & West, 2001).

In the advertising business, one underlying notion is whether there is any significant difference between the risk propensities of agents according to whether or not they have clear identities and guiding philosophies (West & Ford, 2001). Philosophies act to reduce uncertainty in the approach of agents to communications. Along with age and experience, philosophies serve to "steady the nerves" for many clients who otherwise would be at a loss as to which agency to choose. In this way, advertising agencies as a whole stakeout their positions in the marketplace and develop their own brand identities. For example, JWT is famous for its ability to brand whereas Ogilvy & Mather occupies a stronger selling position. Agency philosophies represent the packaging of the brand identity and say: "This is what we stand for—this is how we see advertising working." It is widely acknowledged that philosophies enable advertisers to reduce their risks when choosing new agencies, as they signal the values and personality of the agency brand (Channon, 1981).

Uncertainty is known to be the significant variable that influences the total amount of information gathered by any decision maker. Agents working in an agency holding a single philosophy are likely to perceive less risk when working on a campaign compared to those working in an agency using a hybrid or no philosophy. This is because the latter lacks a guiding approach and so they will treat each campaign afresh and be open to a multitude of solutions and will seek out more information. By contrast, single philosophy agencies enable their staff to frame each campaign problem according to the agency's creative beliefs. This normative approach provides a familiar framework, diminishes perceived risk, and dampens information search. The more certain you are, the more you think you know, the more likely you are to take a risk, i.e., the power of doing your homework.

An important related issue is the degree of client diversification. Agencies generally have a range of client types (given the convention that an agency may hold only one client from any competitive market) with a range of budget sizes (known in the advertising business as billings). Staff working in clear or unclear identity agencies will vary their risk-seeking according to a particular market type, e.g., car rentals or computers. However, there may be differences by perception of client size. Agents are relatively more risk-seeking with small clients than large because perceived smaller clients will not have major impacts on revenue flow within their diversified portfolios (West & Berthon, 1997; West, 1999; El-Murad & West, 2003). Furthermore, many smaller clients will have some luck with their risks and their agents may share in this good fortune. Thus, agents are more likely to take risks with smaller clients. Large clients will have a significant impact on an agency if the risk goes wrong and are, therefore, more likely to be treated with caution by the agents concerned.

Conclusion

Advertising creativity is a fusion of originality and relevance in a way that surprises an audience, and risk is an essential part of the mix because doing something new inevitably means an uncertain outcome. From the client perspective, a risk is generally something to be avoided so agencies often operate with plan A and plan B. Plan A is the risky creative they want to run whereas plan B is the safer creative that they know the client will buy. However, much depends upon a client's aspirations. Clients who feel that they are below where they expect to be are far more likely to take a creative risk than those who are happy with things as they are. The position is further complicated because some advertisers face a position where it is more risky to do something safe, such as with many fashion and youth markets, than take a chance. Furthermore, not all advertising agencies are alike. Some are fervent about new ideas and risk taking whereas others prefer safety and incremental change. In short, it's a spectrum that advertisers need to know in order to pair up with the best fit, and often that fit will not work over time as a client's aspirations change.

Note

1. "Target" is used in prospect theory, and throughout this chapter, in terms of company performance objectives.

References

Amabile, T. M. (1983). *The social psychology of creativity*. New York: Springer-Verlag.

Ang, S. H., Lee, Y. H., & Leong, S. M. (2007). The ad creativity cube: conceptualization and initial validation. *Journal of the Academy of Marketing Science, 35* (2), 220–232.

Ang, S. H., & Low, S. Y. M. (2000). Exploring the dimensions of ad creativity preview. *Psychology and Marketing, 17* (10), 835–854.

Baack, D. W., Wilson, R. T., & Till, B. D. (2008). Creativity and memory effects: recall, recognition, and an exploration of non-traditional media. *Journal of Advertising, 37* (4), 85–94.

Barron, F. (1969). *Creative person and creative process*. New York: Holt, Rinehart, & Winston.

Channon, C. (1981, March). Agency thinking and agencies as brands. *Admap*, 116–121.

De Bono, E. (1971). *Lateral thinking for management*. New York: McGraw-Hill.

Devinney, T., Dowling, G., & Collins, M. (2005). Client and agency mental models in evaluating advertising. *International Journal of Advertising, 24* (1), 35–50.

El-Murad, J., & West, D. C. (2003). Risk and creativity in advertising. *Journal of Marketing Management, 19* (5/6), 657–673.

El-Murad, J., & West, D. C. (2004). The definition and measurement of creativity: What do we know? *Journal of Advertising Research, 44*, 188–201.

Ewing, M. T., Napoli, J., & West, D. C. (2001). Creative personalities, processes, and agency philosophies: Implications for global advertisers. *Creativity Research Journal, 13* (2), 161–170.

Fiegenbaum, A., & Thomas, H. (1986). Dynamic and risk measurement perspectives on bowman's risk return paradox for strategic management: An empirical study. *Strategic Management Journal, 7*, 395–407.

Fletcher, W. (1993). *Creative people: How to manage them and maximize their creativity*. London: Hutchinson Business Books.

Friestad, M., & Wright, P. (1994). The persuasion knowledge model: How people cope with persuasion attempts. *Journal of Consumer Research, 21* (1), 1–31.

Hackley, C., & Kover, A. J. (2007). The trouble with creatives: Negotiating creative identity in advertising agencies. *International Journal of Advertising, 26* (1), 63–78.

Heath, R. G., Nairn, A. C., & Bottomley, P. A. (2009). How effective is creativity: Emotive content in TV advertising does not increase attention. *Journal of Advertising Research, 49*, 450–463.

Hirschman, E. C. (1989). Role-based models of advertising creation and production. *Journal of Advertising, 18* (4), 42–54.

Im, S., & Workman, J. P., Jr. (2004). Market orientation, creativity, and new product performance in high-technology firms. *Journal of Marketing, 68*, 114–132.

Kahneman, D., & Tversky, A. (1979). Prospect theory: An analysis of decision making under risk. *Econometrica, 2* (47), 263–288.

Kilgour, M., & Koslow, S. (2009). Why and how do creative thinking techniques work? Trading off originality and appropriateness to make more creative advertising. *Journal of the Academy of Marketing Science, 37* (3), 298–309.

Koslow, S., Sasser, S. L., & Riordan, E. A. (2003). What is creative to whom and why? Originality, strategy and artistry perceptions in advertising agencies. *Journal of Advertising Research, 43* (1), 96–110.

Koslow, S., Sasser, S. L., & Riordan, E. A. (2006). Do marketers get the advertising they need or the advertising they deserve? Agency views of how clients influence creativity. *Journal of Advertising, 35* (3), 81–101.

Kover, A. J. (1995). Copywriters' implicit theories of communication: An exploration. *Journal of Consumer Research, 21* (4), 596–611.

Kover, A. J., Goldberg, S. M., & James, W. L. (1995). Creativity vs. effectiveness? An integrative classification for advertising. *Journal of Advertising Research, 35* (November/December), 29–38.

Kris, E. (1952). *Psychoanalytic explorations in art*. New York: International Universities Press.

McAlister, L., Srinivasan, R., & Kim, M. C. (2007). Advertising, research and development, and systematic risk of the firm. *Journal of Marketing, 71* (1), 35–48.

MacCrimmon, K. R., & Wehrung, D. A. (1990). Characteristics of risk taking executives. *Management Science, 36* (4), 422–435.

March, J. G. (1988). Variable risk preferences and adaptive aspirations. *Journal of Economic Behavior and Organizations, 9*, 5–24.

March, J. G., & Shapira, Z. (1987). Managerial perspectives on risk and risk taking. *Management Science, 33* (11), 1404–1418.

Martindale, C. (1999). Biological bases of creativity. In R. J. Sternberg (Ed.), *Handbook of creativity* (pp. 137–152). Cambridge, UK: Cambridge University Press.

Mednick, S. A. (1962). The associative basis of the creative process. *Psychological Review, 69*, 220–232.

Mendelsohn, G. A. (1976). Associative and attentional processes in creative performance. *Journal of Personality, 44*, 341–369.

Miller, K. D., & Chen, W.-R. (2004). Variable organizational risk preferences: Tests of the March–Shapira model. *Academy of Management Journal, 47* (1), 105–115.

Moriarty, S. E. (1991). *Creative advertising: Theory and practice* (2nd ed.). Englewood Cliffs, NJ: Prentice-Hall.

Mumford, M. D., & Gustafson, S. B. (1988). Creativity syndrome: Integration, application, and innovation. *Psychological Bulletin, 103* (1), 27–43.

Nicholas, R. (1994, November 17). Who dares wins. *Marketing*, 24–25.

Nyilasy, G., & Reid, L. N. (2009). Agency practitioner theories of how advertising works. *Journal of Advertising, 38* (2), 81–96.

Ogilvy, D. (1983). *Ogilvy on advertising*. London: Orbis.

Osborn, A. F. (1953). *Applied imagination* (Rev. ed.). New York: Scribner's.

Pieters, R., Warlop, L., & Wedel, M. (2002). Breaking through the clutter: Benefits of advertisement originality and familiarity for brand attention and memory. *Management Science, 48* (6), 765–781.

Reid, L. N., & Rotfeld, H. J. (1976). Toward an associative model of advertising creativity. *Journal of Advertising, 5* (4), 24–29.

Reid, L. N., King, K. W., & DeLorme, D. E. (1998). Top-level agency creatives look at advertising creativity then and now. *Journal of Advertising, 27* (2), 1–16.

Smith, R. E., MacKenzie, S. B., Yang, X., Buchholz, L. M., & Darley, W. K. (2007). Modeling the determinants and effects of creativity in advertising. *Marketing Science, 26* (6), 819–833.

Sternberg, R. J., & Lubart, T. I. (1999). The concept of creativity: Prospects and paradigms. In R. J. Sternberg (Ed.), *Handbook of creativity* (pp. 3–15). Cambridge, UK: Cambridge University Press.

Stewart, D. W., Cheng, Y., & Wan, H. (2008). Creative and effective advertising: Balancing spontaneity and discipline. *Journal of Advertising, 37* (Winter), 135–139.

Stoner, J. (1968). Risk and cautious shifts in group decisions. *Journal of Experimental and Social Psychology, 4*, 442–459.

Till, B. D., & Baack, D. W. (2005). Recall and persuasion: Does creative advertising matter? *Journal of Advertising, 34* (3), 47–57.

Tversky, A., & Kahneman, D. (1986). Rational choice and the framing of decisions. *Journal of Business, 59* (4), 2.

Unsworth, K. (2001). Unpacking creativity. *Academy of Management Review, 26* (2), 289–297.

Vanden Bergh, B. G., Reid, L. N., & Schorin, G. A. (1983). How many creative alternatives to generate? *Journal of Advertising, 12* (4), 46–49.

West, D. C. (1993). Cross-national creative personalities, processes and agency philosophies. *Journal of Advertising Research, 33* (5), 53–62.

West, D. (1994). Restricted creativity: Advertising agency work practices in the US, Canada and the UK. *Journal of Creative Behavior, 27* (3), 200–213.

West, D., & Berthon, P. (1997). Antecedents of risk-taking behavior by advertisers: Empirical evidence and management implications. *Journal of Advertising Research, 37* (September/October), 27–40.

West, D., & Shelton, D. (1998). Taking advertising risks: The case of Clerical Medical. *Journal of Marketing Management, 14* (4), 251–272.

West, D. C. (1999). 360° of creative risk: An agency theory perspective. *Journal of Advertising Research, 39* (1), 39–50.

West, D. C., & Ford, J. (2001). Advertising agency philosophies and employee risk taking. *Journal of Advertising, 30* (1), 77–91.

West, D. C., Kover, A. J., & Caruana, A. (2008). Practitioner and customer views of advertising creativity: Same concept, different meaning? *Journal of Advertising, 37* (4), 35–45.

West, D. C., Miciak, A., & Sargeant, A. (1999). Advertiser risk-orientation and the opinions and practices of advertising managers. *International Journal of Advertising, 18* (1), 51–71.

West, D. C., & Sargeant, A. (2004). Taking risks with advertising: The case of the not-for-profit sector. *Journal of Marketing Management, 20* (9–10), 1027–1045.

White, A., & Smith, B. L. (2001). Assessing advertising creativity using the creative product semantic scale. *Journal of Advertising Research, 41* (6), 27–34.

Wills, J. R. (1992). Winning new business: An analysis of advertising agency activities. *Journal of Advertising Research, 32* (5), 10–16.

Young, C. E (2000). Creative differences between copywriters and art directors. *Journal of Advertising Research, 40* (3), 19–26.

Zinkhan, G. (1993). Creativity in advertising: Creativity in the Journal of Advertising. *Journal of Advertising, 22* (2), 1–3.

Additional Readings

Amabile, T. M. (1988). How to kill creativity. *Harvard Business Review, 76* (5), 76–87.

Dahlen, M., Rosengren, S., & Torn, F. (2008). Advertising creativity matters? *Journal of Advertising Research, 48* (3), 392–403.

Novremsky, N., & Kahneman, D. (2005). The boundaries of loss aversion. *Journal of Marketing Research, 42* (2), 119–128.

Sasser, S. L., & Koslow, S. (2008). Desperately seeking advertising creativity. *Journal of Advertising, 37* (4), 5–19.

West, D. C. (1999). 360° of creative risk: An agency theory perspective. *Journal of Advertising Research, 39* (1), 39–50.

Chapter 15

A Rhetorical Theory of the Advertisement

Edward F. McQuarrie and Barbara J. Phillips

> Rhetoric may be defined as the faculty of observing in any situation the available means of persuasion.
>
> (Aristotle)

In this chapter, we examine the *advertising message*, and argue that a rhetorical approach is needed to truly understand advertising messages. Many theories that address advertising messages are *communication* theories, where the focus is on the fundamental properties of all messages, of which ads are but a single example. Most of the remaining theoretical accounts of ad messages can be termed *consumer response* theories, defined as psychological accounts of how consumers process information, whether found in ads or elsewhere. Both communication and consumer response theories typically give a remarkably impoverished account of the advertisement. We will attempt something different by offering a rhetorical theory of the advertisement, conceived as a distinct kind of message. We then provide specific theoretical propositions about print advertisements for future research and testing.

What Is an Advertisement?

We limit ourselves in this chapter to theorizing about commercial advertising—paid media with a profit motive. The question now becomes: What defines a given communication attempt as an *advertisement*? Answer: the conjunction of (1) purpose, (2) form, and (3) reception environment constitute an advertisement. A message must have a particular purpose, form, and reception to be considered an advertisement (see Chapter 1). If the message under examination has some other purpose, form, or reception, it is probably some other phenomenon that requires some other theory.

As an example of ad *purpose*, consider the magazine advertisement in Figure 15.1. As with any commercial advertisement, its fundamental purpose is to

Figure 15.1 A Typical Contemporary Ad in Which the Picture Fills the Page and Few Words Appear.

predispose a consumer to buy. It may have other, more immediate purposes such as instilling a particular belief about the brand, facilitating recognition of the brand at the point of purchase, associating the brand with positive emotions, and so on, through the whole catalogue of immediate purposes proper to the domain of commercial advertising. These immediate purposes, while numerous, are a finite list. A message that is not part of an effort to predispose the recipient to buy, and does not seek one of the limited number of more immediate goals that can support that ultimate sales goal, is not a commercial advertisement.

For this reason, we deny that political advertising and commercial advertising are a single phenomenon explainable by a single theory. Both political and commercial advertising represent communication, and both are persuasion, but, theoretically, they are different. Political advertisements are always distinct in purpose, often distinct in form, and sometimes distinct in reception environment. The typical purpose of a political advertisement is to secure a vote. Voting behavior is much more restricted in range than buying behavior. Voting consists of blackening a circle, punching a card, or clicking on a screen. There is no direct economic cost to voting and no immediate economic benefit. Voting is not the same behavior as buying.

In terms of the *form* of commercial advertisements, note that the ad in Figure 15.1 is short: a single page. In general, every medium that contains ads requires a fresh specification of the forms that distinguish ad content from the remainder of the material that appears in that medium. Billboards have a form that distinguishes them from other roadside signs. Banner ads on the Web have a form that distinguishes them from other content that might appear on a Web page. Nonetheless, some formal properties are reasonably widespread across media, the most notable of which is that ads, regardless of medium, tend to be short. A theory of advertisement is likely a theory of short communications.

In terms of *reception* environment, the fundamental fact about mass media advertisements is that they are *secondary*. Some other content in the surrounding medium in which the ad is embedded is the primary focus of the consumer who encounters ads there. There are a few important exceptions where advertisements may share primary status: hobby magazines generally, and fashion magazines in particular. Even here, no individual ad is the primary object or goal of the consumer. I may open a magazine to a particular page to read the story trumpeted on the cover, but I will not pick up a magazine hunting for this month's Tide advertisement. Advertisements are encountered in passing. The consumer does not usually intend to attend to any individual ad.

A second, related aspect of advertising reception is *dismissal*. Consumers are ready to dismiss any ads that do come to their notice. To dismiss is to fail to approach; we say "fail to approach" because "avoid" is too strong and active a term. In most cases ads aren't important or consequential enough to require active avoidance; consumers simply do not give an ad any more attention than it obtains by happenstance. Thus, if one is reading an article that begins on the left side of an opened magazine and that article continues following an ad on the right side of the spread, it is difficult to get to the remainder of the article without seeing some part of that intervening ad, but that passing glance is all the consumer can be expected to give. Alternatively, if one is browsing through the magazine, turning it page by page, then an encountered ad may receive a longer glance and some portion of its words may even be read. However, the consumer will feel no obligation to complete the processing of the ad. Dismissal is the prototypical state of advertisement reception.

Exceptions to the norm of dismissal can be found. A particularly intrusive broadcast ad may trigger active avoidance, using the remote control or the radio station button. Conversely, when ads share primary focus, as in fashion magazines, the consumer does not dismiss ads per se, but nonetheless does dismiss most individual ads encountered. The baseline is always that individual ads are not chosen. Most ads are passed by, but specific ads may break through dismissal and engage the consumer.

A third aspect of the reception environment is *distance*. The purchase or intermediate action (e.g., store visit) that an advertisement is designed to affect is distant in time and space. When there is no distance, as when "operators are standing by," or when one peruses online advertising with the goal of immediate purchase, this is a distinct subcategory of advertisement ("direct response"), sufficiently distinct to demand its own theory, which we will not attempt here. We intend only a theory of typical mass media ads, which are secondary, dismissed, distant messages.

A fourth aspect of advertising reception is *cumulation*. Advertisements are one of the few kinds of human messages that are repeated, and repeated again. It would be at least a faux pas if I told my children at dinner the same story tomorrow as today; and if I told it at dinner after telling it at lunch, and did that again the next day, and the next, I would be certifiable. But individual advertisements will be repeated far more often than that, and ad components—a brand logo or a tagline—may be exposed dozens or hundreds of times within the span of a month or two, and thousands of times over a period of a year or more. Cumulation, of course, is the twin to distance; when actions will occur far in the future, messages have to be repeated over and over to make sure they are not forgotten.

A fifth aspect of the reception environment is *competition*. It is extremely unusual in day-to-day human communication to receive two (or three or four) diametrically opposed messages. But the norm in advertising is that no advertisement has the floor to itself; most advertisements are opposed by competitors.

In view of these distinguishing characteristics, the reception environment for advertisements is profoundly different from most interpersonal communication, where messages are the primary focus of a receptive audience, free of competition, delivered only once, and invite an immediate response.

Implications of the Distinctiveness of Advertisements

The point of laying out these distinguishing characteristics is to assert that each one places a boundary on causal generalization about advertising messages (McQuarrie, 1998, 2004). A rhetorical theory of advertisement, like many scientific theories, is intended to be causal: to show that one factor causes another to occur. It is the *form* of an advertisement that determines whether it can cause one of advertising's purposes, such as a change in attitudes or beliefs. In turn, the *reception environment* determines which forms can be more or less effective with respect to that given purpose. Thus, scholarly work may show that certain types of pictures can enhance memory, but not alter beliefs; or certain pictures can alter beliefs but not enhance memory; and so on. Then the reception environment determines whether ad pictures can cause these outcomes to a greater or lesser extent than can ad words. A scientific theory of advertising messages seeks to build up a network of such causal generalizations about forms of advertising within the context of the reception environments that characterize advertising. In short, a *rhetorical theory of advertisement is a set of causal sentences about a set of ad forms and outcomes, within a specified reception environment.*

A rhetorical theory of advertising messages is different from those proposed by communication or consumer theories. The latter propose theories based on contexts that do not share the same purposes, forms, or reception environments as typical mass media advertisements; they assert that such details do not matter to the overall conclusions. In contrast, a rhetorical theory of advertising messages makes no predictions about the causal impact of non-advertising forms, nor does it concern non-advertising reception environments or non-advertising purposes. A rhetorical theory of the advertisement asserts that the details matter; it questions the relevance of research done with some other purpose, form, or reception environment.

We next extend this line of reasoning to consider three examples of empirical work using non-advertising forms and non-advertising reception environments. These will serve as concrete examples that represent good scientific work, but which, we argue, cannot be generalized to advertisements.

Evaluating Arguments for a Comprehensive Exam for Graduation

As a college student subject you read a document of 1000 words (Petty & Cacioppo, 1984). Depending on condition, it argues that your (another) university should (should not) require that students pass a comprehensive exam to graduate. Depending on condition, either strong or weak arguments are used. More or fewer arguments may be supplied, and attributed to different sources. Your response consists of checking a box to indicate the extent to which you support this proposed graduation requirement, writing down the thoughts you had while reading, and indicating whether certain statements apply to you (e.g., your "need for cognition").

Given random assignment of subjects, the procedure just described allows for an internally valid scientific investigation of the causal effects of different kinds of arguments and source attributions, as influenced by specified individual differences. Such research can contribute, and has contributed, to a theoretical understanding of persuasion, broadly defined. It is good scientific work; but it is designed to be different in purpose, form, and reception environment from an advertisement. The purpose is to influence a vote; in form, there are no pictures and the communication is lengthy; in terms of reception, the message is not embedded in a media context and is thus the primary focus, the student does not have the opportunity to dismiss the message, response is immediate, and no competitive message is present. Because the experiment is so different from a commercial advertisement, the results of this research are not likely to generalize to advertising contexts and can produce little understanding about advertising.

However, the results should generalize to many political advertising contexts—for example, to material appearing in a student publication on the morning of a student government election. We are at pains to compliment this experiment as a contribution in the specific domain of political advertising to make two points: (1) there's nothing wrong with using student subjects in work on persuasion; (2) there's nothing wrong with using artificial laboratory experiments to make a contribution to scientific knowledge.

What is problematic is conducting an experiment that is distant from the purpose, form, and reception environment of advertising messages, and then claiming to be able to generalize across that profound gap. By analogy, one can't learn about the behavior of molecules if one only studies isolated atoms. Knowledge of atomic behavior is useful background because molecules are composed of atoms. But if one wants to do chemistry instead of atomic physics, sooner or later one has to work with molecules. By extension, scientists can't expect to advance a theory of advertisement if they never work with materials that correspond in purpose, form, and reception to advertisements.

Listening to Audio Messages on Headphones

Now consider another study (Anand & Sternthal, 1990). Here, you go to a language lab at your university, put on headphones, and listen to an actual radio advertisement (more or less complex radio ads, depending on condition). The ad is repeated three, five, or seven times; no other content is heard, during, before, or after these repetitions. You then answer the same sorts of questions as in the exam study.

Again given random assignment, this experiment will yield internally valid knowledge of the causal impact, under different levels of repetition, of audio messages that differ in level of complexity. The results should generalize to any reception environment where more or less complex audio messages are the primary focus of attention and there are no competing or distracting stimuli or activities. The results should also generalize to circumstances where headphones are not worn; headphone delivery is not a theoretical boundary in the way that primary vs. secondary focus of attention, and embedded vs. isolated presentation, are. But we cannot be confident that the results would generalize to a reception environment where a consumer is driving a car, listening to music on the radio, and permitting some ads to continue while switching stations in response to others. A consumer in the real world will never give the same degree of undivided attention to any radio ad as in that experiment, will never experience the same radio ad three times in a row, much less seven, will never hear radio ads in isolation from other programming, and will always be free to dismiss an ad by changing stations. We learn little about how a radio advertisement might persuade such a consumer.

It may be objected that simulating the actual radio listening environment will produce a very noisy environment making it difficult to produce the beautiful intersecting results for complexity and repetition seen in previous research (Anand & Sternthal, 1990). This argument is to imitate the drunk under the lamppost, on hands and knees, looking at the ground, who hails a passerby for help. "Did you drop something?" "Yes, I dropped my keys over there in that dark alley." "Well why are you looking for them over here?" "Because the light is so much better under the lamppost." Relative to the lamppost condition, where a fully attentive and undistracted consumer deliberately scrutinizes information about available consumption options, advertising takes place in a dark alley. But it is in that dark alley where the keys to a theory of advertisement must be found.

Strong vs. Weak Arguments

A final example of how the conjunction of purpose, form, and reception sets boundaries on generalization may be useful. Consider the stylized interaction graphed in Figure 15.2. This sort of interaction is a staple of work associated with the Elaboration Likelihood Model (ELM), itself a leading contender to be a theory of advertisement (Petty & Cacioppo, 1984). Like most social psychological theories, the ELM is positioned as a universal theory accounting for all forms of persuasion, including advertising. The graph shows that when consumer motivation, opportunity, and/or ability (MOA) are at high levels, strong arguments are more persuasive than weak; when one or more of these is insufficient, strong arguments do not outperform weak arguments. These results are interpreted as support for the underlying theory, which positions the extent of elaboration, itself contingent on MOA, as the key predictor of persuasion outcomes.

Once we accept purpose, form, and reception as boundaries on generalization, the graph in Figure 15.2 can actually be interpreted as evidence that the ELM does *not* provide a causal theory of advertisement. In the reception environment for advertising messages, ads are often secondary to other content, placed in a sea of competing messages, frequently dismissed, and relate to purchases that may be distant in the future. Thus, most ads, most of the time, for most viewers, will be viewed under conditions of insufficient motivation. The graph shows that strong arguments don't work any better than weak arguments under those conditions. Therefore, argument strength would not appear to be a key theoretical factor for most ads in a real advertising reception environment.

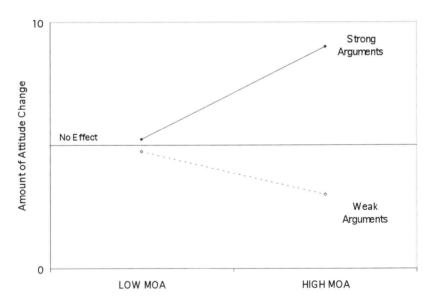

Figure 15.2 Stylized Graph of the Predicted Effect of Strong (Weak) Arguments Under the Elaboration Likelihood Model.

Note

"MOA" stands for motivation, opportunity, and ability. The prediction is that when MOA is high, strong arguments will produce more attitude change than weak arguments. Conversely, if MOA is low, arguments will not be elaborated, and there will no longer be an effect for argument strength.

Take another look at the ad in Figure 15.1. It doesn't have enough verbal text to present multiple arguments; words don't seem to play much role in the advertising message. Our point here is that strong verbal argument is a specific example of an advertising message form. This particular form is now comparatively rare in print advertising (McQuarrie & Phillips, 2008). Consequently, a theory of commercial advertisement, such as the ELM, which tries to explain all ads by using one fairly rare type of ad form, cannot succeed. However, rhetorical theories of advertisement that call out different types of forms as causal factors may lead to greater understanding of advertising outcomes. Suggestions to further such understanding are presented below.

Theoretical Propositions about Print Advertisements

A rhetorical theory of the advertisement that engages its distinct purpose, form, and reception environment leads to specific theoretical propositions that can inform and guide those studying and researching advertisements. Those developed here will focus on magazine advertisements because that is where we have the most experience; space prohibits a medium-by-medium account, but propositions fitting other media can readily be developed by interested scholars using this format.

> 1.   The available forms of advertisement are constrained by a double duality.

Under conditions of secondary focus and dismissal, an individual advertisement has to compete for consumer engagement, a competition that each ad is destined to lose most of the time with most consumers. Hence every ad, in addition to its particular purpose (e.g., change beliefs, inscribe a stronger memory trace), has the additional purpose of engaging the consumer—getting attention. This is the first duality: every ad form has to fulfill a dual purpose. It must have the capacity to achieve its particular desired outcome, but it must first get noticed, which is a universal imperative shared with virtually all ads.

Second, the form of advertisement must be such that it can accomplish its purpose at both low and high levels of engagement. This is the second duality: every ad form has to address two different kinds of audiences. As noted, most of the time ads will lose the competition for engagement; they will get only the unavoidable glance. Because this minimal engagement may constitute the majority of the audience exposure paid for, ads must be designed to accomplish whatever can be accomplished when engagement stays minimal. At the same time, the ad form must hold something in reserve for that rare consumer who does engage to a greater degree.

It follows that no experiment that forces exposure or secures engagement with an ad can give much useful insight into this fundamental challenge facing ad forms. The task of a rhetorical theory of advertisement is to find "the available means of persuasion" within the constraint of this double duality.

> **2.   The advertisement must exert its effect at a distance upon a mass.**

Within advertising research, there is a cottage industry referred to as the individual differences literature. In experimental contexts, this takes the form of administering a set of questions about personality or values (e.g., "need for cognition," "self-monitoring"), splitting the subjects into two groups using the median score on these items, and then showing that the impact of some advertising form on some purpose differs in accordance with that personality trait or value—the effect is "moderated by the individual difference," as the research lingo has it.

Well, so what? Brand advertisers never get to choose to expose their advertisements mostly to individuals high in metaphoric processing ability, or low in self-monitoring, or any other such theoretically defined disposition. Ads are exposed to a mostly unmeasured mass. At best, there is an opportunity to select media vehicles that reach larger or smaller numbers of category users, but there is no opportunity to reach preferentially individuals who are high in need for cognition. Outside the laboratory, nobody wants to think about ads, and virtually everyone is resistant to ads. Unless the targeting of print ads to a specific audience improves, such research findings fail to provide actionable findings for advertisers.

> **3.   There are a limited number of forms of advertisement. Individual advertisements in all their bewildering profusion can be understood as instantiations of a much smaller number of these basic forms. [This proposition combines with the next one to offer insight into how to best further rhetorical theories of advertising messages.]**
>
> **4.   The forms of advertisement have an internal organization; that is, the types of forms fit together in predictable and knowable ways.**

The fundamental insight about advertising forms is that there are only a limited number of gambits available to an advertiser. The set of forms available in a given medium is expected to number only in the dozens. In the past, scholars have described types and forms of advertising messages in random unordered lists. For example, when examining verbal figures of speech in ads, scholars listed rhymes (e.g., "Kitchen Aid. For the way it's made"), puns (e.g., "Why weight for success?" for a diet center), hyperbole (e.g., "Top of the heap"), antithesis ("Hot prices on cool stuff"), and dozens of other word play choices. Such a list is not helpful to understanding how the form of the verbal figure of speech influences consumer response to that form. In 1996, McQuarrie and Mick brought internal organization to verbal figures of speech, asserting that there are four main patterns in all of them: (a) repetition (such as rhyme), (b) reversal (such as antithesis), (c) substitution (such as hyperbole), and (d) destabilization (such as pun). Moreover, each step from repetition to destabilization increases the complexity of the verbal figure, which has specific implications for consumer comprehension and liking.

In summary, the older accounts were names and categories only, without links to underlying characteristics, and without any connection to cause. But today it is possible to envision a set of principles which seeks and supplies a lawful causal connection between particular advertising forms and specific advertising purposes.

5. The effectiveness of advertising forms is dynamic, and changes over time. This process can be understood to be similar to an arms race. [This proposition combines with the next to offer understanding of advertising purposes and outcomes.]

6. The greater the processing demands imposed upon the consumer, the less suitable that form is for advertisement.

An example that illustrates both these principles is the slow disappearance of lengthy verbal argument from mass media print advertisement. Dense mats of verbiage continue to appear in direct mail and other forms of direct response advertising, of course, but that is why we emphasized the importance of *distance* in formulating the boundaries of our theory of advertisement. In mass media print ads, lengthy verbal forms are now decisively less effective at achieving advertising purposes and are in the process of becoming even less effective (McQuarrie & Phillips, 2008). This is an example of the general rule that the more demanding the advertisement, the less likely it is to be effective in the advertising reception environment. This rule ties back to the fundamental imperative of double duality (#1). Demanding ads are less likely to be engaging, and less likely to be effective if only minimally engaged.

The height of demand is lengthy/verbal/argument and all three components contribute to this demand. Longer ads are more demanding than shorter ads; words are more demanding than pictures; and words that form an argument are more demanding than words that form a narrative. By "demanding" we simply mean how much effort the consumer must allocate to engage the ad and how intrinsically difficult to comprehend the ad form is. Comprehending complex pictures is much more common and automatic in the contemporary developed world than carefully reasoning one's way through multiple arguments presented in words.

Principle #6 suggests the following propositions: (a) consumers will favor pictures over words in print ads, (b) the number of words in print ads will decrease over time, and (c) non-argumentative uses of words (e.g., phatic, poetic, narrative) will be favored over time. Note that these propositions were false 100 years ago as can be seen by the ads in Figure 15.3. The left ad in Figure 15.3 is an ad from the 1920s, while the right ad is an ad from 2006; note the differences. That is what we mean by the dynamism of advertising: what worked perfectly well at one point may cease to be effective at some later point. Pictures did not unduly dominate print ads in the 1920s. Lengthy verbal arguments were not absent from 1920s ads. Print ads have changed over time.

The dynamic relationship between advertisers and consumers may be thought of as an arms race. The trajectory of dynamism in each case is the same: move provokes counter-move. Prey grows thicker skin, predator lengthens claw. Machine guns are deployed, tanks respond. Translating this model back into the language of consumption, advertisements are self-interested communication in which the advertiser seeks his or her own advantage. Consumers naturally resist this attempt by the advertiser to gain advantage. The initial advertising move was naked assertion, as in the snake oil era of the nineteenth century. Consumers soon became proof against this gambit by adopting a baseline position of skepticism. Advertisers then moved to deploy cunning arguments to link goods to cherished ideals. Consumers slowly learned not to read the ad text. In the contemporary era, advertisers more and more dispense with words and increasingly resort to rhetoricized pictures; consumers appear not yet to have well-developed defenses to these. And on it goes.

A modern example of such dynamism is the growing use of grotesque ad images in fashion magazine advertising over the last 20 years. The Jimmy Choo ad on the right-hand side of Figure 15.3 is an illustration of such a modern grotesque ad, whose imagery is strange, unusual, and even bizarre. In the picture, an Amazonian woman in a leopard bathing suit plucks a designer handbag out of a pool with a large hook; a dead man floats in the pool. Conventional wisdom suggests that fashion ads should show pretty models in luxurious settings to lead to favorable attitudes toward that brand; the weird picture in the Jimmy Choo

Figure 15.3 How the Form of Advertising has Changed Over the Past Century.

Note

On the right, a visually evocative and even grotesque modern ad in which the picture fills the page and there is no body copy; on the left, a text-heavy ad from the 1920s with its simple snapshot of happy users confined to the top portion of the page.

ad might be viewed negatively by consumers. But the use of such grotesque images in fashion ads grew over the past 20 years; grotesque ads encompass 28% of all modern fashion ads (Phillips & McQuarrie, 2011). Why?

A rhetorical theory of advertising messages, sensitive to advertising's distinctive reception environment, will understand the Jimmy Choo ad as a narrative approach to persuasion, able to break through the clutter, engage the consumer, and achieve a favorable outcome for the brand (Phillips & McQuarrie, 2010). In the case of the Jimmy Choo ad, a positive purpose for the brand is served through the visual elements of the ad which encourage consumers to complete the story in the ad for themselves.

Conclusion

In this chapter, we argued that a rhetorical theory of advertisement must address the distinct purposes, forms, and reception environment encountered by commercial mass-media advertisers in the marketplace. We took the opportunity to contrast a rhetorical theory of advertisement with other communication and consumer theories, while arguing that generalization from non-advertising forms, studied in very different reception environments, with distinct purposes, is unlikely to be successful. We then provided six theoretical propositions to guide those who wish to investigate the distinctive aspects of advertising messages. To this end, the Additional Readings section develops in more detail the variety of rhetorical forms that may be found in print advertisements, and the ways these have changed over time.

References

Anand, P., & Sternthal, B. (1990). Ease of message processing as a moderator of repetition effects in advertising. *Journal of Marketing Research, 27* (3), 345–353.

McQuarrie, E. F. (1998). Have laboratory experiments become detached from advertiser goals? A meta-analysis. *Journal of Advertising Research, 38* (6), 15–26.

McQuarrie, E. F. (2004). Integration of construct and external validity by means of proximal similarity: Implications for laboratory experiments in marketing. *Journal of Business Research, 57,* 142–153.

McQuarrie, E. F., & Mick, D. G. (1996). Figures of rhetoric in advertising language. *Journal of Consumer Research, 22* (March), 424–438.

McQuarrie, E. F., & Phillips, B. J. (2008). It's not your father's magazine ad: Magnitude and direction of recent changes in advertising style. *Journal of Advertising, 37* (3), 95–106.

Petty, R. A., & Cacioppo, J. T. (1984). The effects of involvement on responses to argument quantity and quality. *Journal of Personality and Social Psychology, 46* (1), 69–81.

Phillips, B. J., & McQuarrie, E. F. (2010). Narrative and persuasion in fashion advertising. *Journal of Consumer Research, 37* (3), 368–392.

Phillips, B. J., & McQuarrie, E. F. (2011). Contesting the social impact of marketing: A re-characterization of women's fashion advertising. *Marketing Theory, 11* (2), 99–126.

Additional Readings

McQuarrie, E. F. (2007). Differentiating the pictorial element in advertising. In M. Wiedel & R. Pieters (Eds.), *Visual marketing: From attention to action* (pp. 91–112). Hillsdale, NJ: Lawrence Erlbaum.

McQuarrie, E. F., & Phillips, B. J. (2008). *Go figure: New directions in advertising rhetoric.* Armonk, NJ: M.E. Sharpe.

Phillips, B. J., & McQuarrie, E. F. (2002). The development, change and transformation of rhetorical style in magazine advertisements 1954–1999. *Journal of Advertising, 31* (4), 1–13.

Phillips, B. J., & McQuarrie, E. F. (2004). Beyond visual metaphor: A new typology of visual rhetoric in advertising. *Marketing Theory, 4* (1/2), 113–136.

Scott, L. M., & Vargas, P. (2007). Writing with pictures: Toward a unifying theory of consumer response to images. *Journal of Consumer Research, 34* (October), 341–356.

Chapter 16

Narrative Advertisements and Narrative Processing

Chingching Chang

Introduction

Many advertisements tell stories or narratives (Chang, 2010a; Escalas, 1998), whereas others tend to offer a more analytical focus on brand features. Stories can revolve around the consumption of products (e.g., pictures of people happily cruising to Alaska) or simply recount what people desire or cherish, such as romance, relationship, achievement, or hopes (e.g., Microsoft's "Your potential, our future"). In contrast, advertisements might present product benefits or functions in an argumentative way (e.g., Listerine antiseptic commercial showing how it cleans teeth better and more deeply than toothpaste alone). (Of course there are many other names for product-attribute based ads, which tend to make factual claims about brands.) This chapter outlines some theoretical explanations for how and why these varying advertising approaches affect consumers.

The type of content in an advertisement can trigger either narrative or analytical processing (Adaval & Wyer, 1998). Through narrative processing, which is particularly likely when advertisements portray stories, consumers understand or imagine sequential events related to product consumption (Adaval & Wyer, 1998). Analytical processing of advertising instead involves close examination of product attribute information, as encouraged by advertisements that present a product's features and attributes in a list (Adaval & Wyer, 1998). These two approaches to advertising differentially affect consumers.

This chapter begins with a discussion of the distinctions between narrative and analytic modes of processing. It then reviews some comparative advantages of the narrative mode of processing, leading into a discussion of which factors might trigger this mode. Adopting an integrated advertising approach to advertising theory, and referring back to Figure 1.1 of this text, this chapter identifies three factors: *sources*, *messages*, and *receivers*. In terms of source factors, brands with established narratives encourage narrative processing. The message factors imply that advertisements in a narrative format or with specific advertising executions more readily trigger a narrative mode of processing. For receiver factors, this chapter notes individual differences in terms of processing style or accessibility of narrative prototypes, which may influence the likelihood that people engage in narrative processing.

The chapter next summarizes the functions of narrative advertisements. However, their advantages can be understood only by exploring how they are processed. The next question addressed therefore is how narrative advertisements are processed and how they persuade (their effect). The key theoretical concepts include mental simulation and being transported, both of which are typical responses to narratives. This chapter reviews the roles of both processes in enhancing persuasion. Finally, narrative processing can involve strong emotional responses, so this chapter outlines how it enhances advertising persuasion.

Narrative Versus Analytical Processing

Consumer decisions likely involve narrative and analytical processing (Adaval & Wyer, 1998). With the former, consumers imagine sequential events related to purchasing or using a product and interpret the specific implications of product features through those imagined sequential episodes. Advertisements that use narratives trigger narrative processing or elicit narrative thoughts, that is, thoughts organized in a story structure with sequential episodes connected by causal relationships (Escalas, 2004a).

When they engage in analytical processing, consumers instead undertake close examinations of product attribute information (Adaval & Wyer, 1998). An important theory describing the processing of product attributes, expectancy-value models (e.g., Fishbein & Ajzen, 1975) suggest that product attitudes are developed on the basis of assessments about product beliefs (e.g., an advertised car is likely fuel efficient) and the favorability of those beliefs for consumers (e.g., fuel efficiency is good). In other words, evaluations of product functions or performance are central to analytical processing. For example, analytic consumer processing about a restaurant would involving thinking about and elaborating on the possible restaurant's location, cuisine, and prices if they adopt an analytical processing mode.

There are several key differences between narrative and analytical processing modes. First, the narrative mode facilitates evaluations more than analytic processing. Adaval and Wyer (1998) reason that because most social experiences get stored in the form of narratives, information that triggers narrative processing is more consistent with people's knowledge representations and should be easier to process. Mattila (2000) also shows that novice consumers express more favorable attitudes when they read narratives as opposed to attribute lists in advertisements.

Second, narrative and analytical processing involve different information search patterns and evaluation strategies. For example, McGill and Anand (1989) showed that when consumers imagine owning and using studio apartments (i.e., narrative mode), they search for more information about product alternatives (i.e., various apartments) and process information in terms of those alternatives. When consumers are prompted to engage in analytical processing, they search for more information about product attributes (e.g., rent, size) and process product information in terms of those attributes.

Third, narrative and analytical processing weight the attributes of different characteristics to different degrees. Keller and McGill (1994) showed that when consumers imagine their product experiences (e.g., living in an apartment), their evaluations of the products are more affected by easily imagined product attributes (e.g., hardwood floors in the apartment) than by important attributes that they cannot imagine easily (e.g., security for the apartment). In contrast, if they receive instructions to evaluate analytically, their evaluations are more influenced by important attributes than by less important attributes that are easy to imagine.

What Triggers Narrative Processing?

Drawing upon Thorson and Rodgers' Figure 1.1, this chapter identifies three types of factors that trigger narrative processing: source factors, message factors, and receiver factors, discussed next.

Source Factors: Brand Narratives

Brand narratives refer to stories that marketers tell about their brands, which usually resonate with consumers' desires, identities, or lifestyles; when consumers choose to own a brand they possess the narrative associated with it too (Dahlen, Lange, & Smith, 2010). Marketing communication can help establish a symbolic meaning for a brand: Randazzo (2006) attributes the success of Subaru to its Outback advertising story featuring Paul Hogan, and Dahlen et al. (2010) suggest marketing campaigns have imbued Harley Davidson with the "born to be wild" association, which creates deeper self–brand relationships and sustains loyalty. Advertisements featuring a brand with a well-developed narrative, trigger narrative processing more easily than do advertisements featuring a brand without it. Thus, watching a narrative Harley Davidson commercial likely encourages consumers to imagine themselves riding on "hogs," going wild, and enjoying freedom without restrictions.

Message Factors: Advertising Narratives and Executions

Advertising Narratives

Narrative advertising accounts for 24.5% of commercials aired in prime time (Chang, 2010a). An advertisement featuring narratives is a narrative advertisement, a notion also defined by Escalas (1998) as "an ad that tells a story," such that the narrative depicts "one or more episodes consisting of actors engaged in actions to achieve goals" and involves a "sequence initiated by some events and actions result[ing] in outcome(s)" (p. 273). Two important structural features of narratives are chronology (Polkinghorne, 1991) and causality (Escalas, 1998), so narratives are organized as a series of events occurring over time, and the structure of the events clearly demonstrates their causal relationships. People progressively store more varied narratives in their minds, and exposure to advertising stories can activate existing narrative structures, trigger narrative processing, and encourage consumers to process advertising messages according to their story structures.

Narrative advertising also comes in a variety of types. Escalas' (2004a) review cites drama advertisements, specific forms of transformational advertisements, and slice-of-life advertisements. In a drama advertisement, characters talk to one another (without narration), and the audience observes product-related events unfolding through the experiences of these characters (Wells, 1989). Therefore, drama advertising is a subtype of narrative advertisements, which encompass all advertisements featuring plots acted out by advertising characters but narrators also may interpret that.

Common narrative plots include hope (e.g., Microsoft's "Your potential, our future"), romance (e.g., Google's "Parisian Love"), relationships (e.g., MasterCard's "Priceless"), and self-esteem (e.g., Dove's "True Beauty"). Advertisements in different cultures also feature different plots (Chang, 2010a): in Asia, advertisements are more likely to tell stories about relationships with others, whereas U.S. advertisements tend to focus on stories about self-image or achievement.

Being Instructed to Imagine

A common way to encourage consumers to engage in narrative processing is to invite them directly to imagine themselves in a consumption situation (Phillips, 1996). This tactic is widespread in advertising, often in the form of advertising copy that starts with an instruction phrase: "Imagine yourself...," such as "imagine yourself behind the wheel of a Lexus" or "imagine yourself cruising to

Alaska." Phillips (1996) shows that when consumers are thus instructed to imagine themselves in certain product use settings or engage in mental simulations, they generate more vivid mental imagery of product-related behaviors than when they are not so instructed. Adaval and Wyer (1998) also find that participants who are directly invited to imagine themselves in consumption situations, as opposed to those who are not, are more likely to engage in narrative processing.

Presence of Photos or Illustrations

Print advertisements commonly feature photos or illustrations that depict narrative scenarios, such as a diamond advertisement featuring a photo of an intimate couple eating in a fancy restaurant or an airline advertisement showing a family traveling in an exotic country. Adaval and Wyer (1998) argue that pictures are structurally similar to mental images of consumption and thus facilitate narrative processing. However, such enhanced effects only emerge for advertisements with narrative product information, not for those that present product information in a list. In the latter situation, analytical processing is more likely, and pictures may interfere with this mode.

Degree of Visual Detail in Pictures

Vivid pictorial information can motivate consumers to engage in narrative processing. For example, Phillips (1996) demonstrates that participants exposed to advertisements with more visual detail tend to construct self-related narratives and imagine themselves in the consumption setting. In a similar vein, Babin and Burns (1997) demonstrate that concrete pictures work better than abstract pictures for enhancing the vividness of mental imagery. Walters, Sparks, and Herington (2007) also find that more, as opposed to less, concrete pictures increase consumption vision elaboration when consumers receive instructions to engage in narrative processing.

Degree of Verbal Details in Advertising Copies

In addition to visual presentation, an implicit encouragement of narrative processing results from detailed verbal descriptions of stories. Google's "Parisian Love" is a good example, because its detailed verbal descriptions provide important bases on which consumers can construct their own mental scenarios, rendering the imagination task easier. Phillips (1996) reveals in particular that detailed verbal descriptions encourage consumers to envision themselves in similar consumption settings.

Degree of Dramatization

The degree of dramatization in a drama advertisement can determine how viewers process the advertisement (Deighton, Romer, & McQueen, 1989). Higher levels of dramatization result in fewer counterarguments and stronger emotional responses, which exemplify a narrative processing mode. These findings suggest that the degree of dramatization may encourage narrative processing. Escalas, Moore, and Britton (2004) also find that when narratives in advertising present fully developed stories, as opposed to underdeveloped ones, they can better hook consumers, a common state in response to narrative processing.

Receiver Factors: Individual Differences

Processing Styles

Advertisements may trigger different levels of narrative processing. For example, in an advertising viewing context, Chang (2010b) shows that people oriented toward visual, as opposed to rational, processing styles, and generated higher mental simulation about product consumption—an indicator of narrative processing.

Accessibility of Narrative Prototypes

Adaval and Wyer (1998) argue that when the structure of an incoming story does not match that of preexisting story representations, consumers are less likely to engage in narrative processing. Chang (2010a) compared advertising narratives in Taiwan and the United States and found that advertisements in Taiwan are more likely to tell another-related story than are U.S. advertisements, whereas as in the United States, advertisements tend to tell self-related stories, more so than advertisements in Taiwan. On the basis of the idea that cultures socialize self-concepts and alter the accessibility of narrative prototypes, Chang reasoned that people's culturally congruent narrative prototypes are more accessible, which may enable them to engage more easily in narrative processing when advertisements present culturally relevant narratives.

Functions of Narrative Advertisements

Several unique functions of narratives in advertising help explain why advertisers use them so widely. A thorough review of prior literature identifies three important functions. First, narratives present the benefits of abstract, intangible product attributes in a meaningful way (Mattila, 2000; Padgett & Allen, 1997). As Mattila (2000) notes, when promoting services, narrative advertising effectively communicates service experiences to potential consumers. Padgett and Allen (1997) further assert that narrative advertisements more effectively convey symbolic meaning (e.g., feeling secure and pampered) about service brands than do argument advertisements.

Second, narratives or stories in advertising can increase consumer involvement and entertainment (Escalas, 1998). Narrative advertisements draw in viewers and get them hooked during the viewing process (Escalas et al., 2004). To the extent that consumers are hooked by narrative advertisements, they feel more positively and express more favorable attitudes toward advertisements (Escalas et al., 2004). Among the top 10 most liked and recalled commercials aired during the live broadcast of the 2010 Super Bowl, most were narrative advertisements ("Super Bowl Top 10," 2010).

Third, narratives in advertising encourage consumers to gain product experiences through a sense of vicarious participation (Boller & Olson, 1991). According to Wells (1989), drama advertising works because it encourages viewers to infer lessons and gain experience through the characters in the stories, as well as sample emotional rewards vicariously. In addition, narratives about a product serve as "generic plots" (Escalas, 1998, p. 283) that set the scripts for future consumption; they also work as frames for interpreting future product experiences or guides that help consumers construct their product experiences.

The Process of Narrative Processing

The functions of narrative advertisements cannot be assessed without an understanding of the process of narrative processing that they trigger. When engaging in such processing, consumers experience unique cognitive processes, such as mental simulation, or enter into specific cognitive states, such as being transported. They also experience strong emotions. How people understand advertising narratives and proceed through different cognitive and affective processes therefore is the focus of this section, along with a discussion of their influences on advertising persuasion.

Understanding Narratives

When they attempt to understand a narrative advertisement, people create stories about incoming information and impose a beginning, middle, and end that enables them to infer causality (Escalas, 2004a). This process of narrative understanding relies on existing narrative knowledge structures. People store recurring narrative content or episodes with causal relations in their minds as narrative knowledge structures or event prototypes (Fiske, 1993), which facilitates their understanding of new events (Schank & Abelson, 1995; Schank & Berman, 2002). They also comprehend incoming narrative information by trying to relate it to existing structures or prototypes (Schank & Abelson, 1995; Schank & Berman, 2002).

Relatively little research explores how people understand advertising narratives, though Chang (2009b) explores the influence of repetition variation strategies on the comprehension of narrative advertisements. Narrative advertisements often revolve around a plot and involve certain characters; that is, plots and characters provide the distinguishing characteristics (Boller & Olson, 1991; Deighton et al., 1989). Chang (2009b) offers a typology of repetition variation strategies based on these two characteristics and proposes four strategies: using the same plot twice (with the same characters), using different plots with the same characters (e.g., Macy's "The Magic of Macy's" campaign), using different plots with different characters (e.g., American Express' "My Life, My Card" campaign), or using one continuous plot with the same characters (e.g., Taster's Choice). Drawing on the idea that understanding a narrative depends on relating the depicted sequential events to existing narrative knowledge structures, Chang argues that narrative advertising processing requires figuring out the plot; she also finds that repetition variation strategies that change the plot increase comprehension difficulty.

Cognitive Processes

Mental Simulation

DEFINITION

When viewing a narrative advertisement, consumers not only generate an understanding of how and why the story evolves; they also simulate similar situations for themselves, referred to as mental simulation. Mental simulation is "the cognitive construction of hypothetical scenarios or the reconstruction of real scenarios" and "the imitative mental representation of the functioning or process of some event or series of events" (Taylor & Schneider, 1989, p. 175).

In consumer research, Phillips, Olson, and Baumgartner (1995) call mental simulation that involves product consumption "consumption visions" and argue that these visions pertain to a series of visually elaborate images of the self performing a consumption activity. Consumption visions are a subtype of mental simulation, most relevant in an advertising viewing context (Chang, 2010b). Phillips and colleagues (1995) further propose that consumption visions are mostly narratives, involving "a character (the consumer's possible self), a plot (a series of events in which the character enacts behaviors and reacts to events) and a setting (an environment or context in which the action occurs)" (p. 281).

FUNCTIONS

These simulations "function as plans, prompt affect, set expectations, and lead to behavioral confirmation" (Fiske, 1993, p. 171). Thus, as Taylor and Schneider (1989) suggest, mental simulation serves two important functions: problem solving and emotional regulation. Imagining future events can help people make plans to achieve their goals or prepare contingency solutions for possible problems. Mental simulation also can regulate emotions by creating positive plausible scenarios in advance.

Mental simulation in consumption settings serves other important functions as well. First, it effectively facilitates decision making (Phillips et al., 1995). When making decisions involving product alternatives with which they have little experience, consumers who imagine themselves in alternative consumption situations can better decide among different courses of action. Second, mental simulation provides goals for potential consumers and encourages them to obtain those goals. According to Phillips and colleagues (1995), mental simulation not only depicts an ideal vision, which serves as the goal toward which consumers work, but also specifies the possible actions that should help consumers achieve these goals. Thus, a higher frequency of mental simulation leads to greater behavioral intentions. For example, Gregory, Cialdini, and Carpenter (1982) show that people involved in mental simulations of viewing cable television are more likely to express intentions to subscribe than are those who are not so involved. Third, mental simulation can enhance satisfaction. Shiv and Huber (2000) show that preference for products that can be mentally imagined easily increases after mental simulation. Therefore, mental simulation appears to increase consumers' attitudes toward products that they can imagine to a greater degree.

EFFECTS ON ADVERTISING PERSUASION

Mental simulation can enhance advertising persuasion. Escalas (2004b) demonstrates that advertising messages that encourage mental simulation lead to more favorable advertising and brand attitudes. Escalas (2004a) also shows that narrative advertisements, which presumably trigger mental simulation, generate more connections among the advertised brands and consumers' self-concepts, which further improve attitudes toward the advertisement and the brand.

Transportation

DEFINITION

Narrative processing leads consumers into a highly involved mental state, which has been referred to by many terms, including transportation (Green & Brock, 2000), being hooked (Escalas et al., 2004), and experiential immersion (Chang, 2008). Transportation is the degree to which a reader becomes immersed or absorbed in stories and undergoes a mental process that entails imagery, affect, and attentional focus (Green & Brock, 2000). Narrative advertisements can trigger transportation and the experience of being hooked (Chang, 2009a).

EFFECTS ON ADVERTISING PERSUASION

According to Green and Brock (2000, see also Escalas, 2007), transportation enhances persuasion by reducing the amount of counterarguments. Narrative processing involves imagining sequential events related to purchasing or using a product, and because this processing mode consumes cognitive capacity, it limits the extent to which people can generate cognitive resistance or counterarguments. For example, using advertising as stimuli, Escalas (2004b) demonstrated that narrative transportation leads to a decline in critical thoughts, which further improves evaluations of the advertisement and the brand.

Affective Process

When processing narratives, people also focus on emotions they are likely to experience in simulated narratives (Escalas, 1998; Kitamura, 1988; Taylor, Pham, Rivkin, & Armor, 1998; Wells, 1989). Some consumers tend to explore positive emotion in general, whereas others specify distinct emotions.

Positive Affective Responses

In general, narrative processing evokes more positive emotional responses. Escalas' (2004b) findings show that narrative transportation increases positive affect, and Deighton and colleagues (1989) show that more dramatic commercials elicit more positive feeling. When consumers receive instructions to recall consumption-related narratives that they have experienced personally, they also express more positive affect (Baumgartner, Sujan, & Bettman, 1992; Sujan, Bettman, & Baumgartner, 1993). Most important, narrative advertisements that induce positive emotion enhance persuasion (Escalas, 2004b).

Other Discrete Affective Responses

Additional studies explore discrete emotional responses. For example, Escalas and colleagues (2004) demonstrated that to the extent participants are hooked by a narrative advertising story, whether due to advertising structures or individual differences, they generate more upbeat and warm emotions. Empathy also is a common response to processing narratives (Puto & Wells, 1984), through the "involuntary and un-self-conscious merging with another's feelings" (Escalas & Stern, 2003, p. 567). Escalas and Stern (2003) established a multiple-stage model to explain the influence of drama in advertising; it suggests that drama evokes sympathy. Chang (2008) also showed that narrative public service announcements trigger greater levels of sympathy toward people whom the advertisements depict as in need of help than do argument advertisements. These discrete affective responses improve advertising persuasion (Chang, 2008; Escalas & Stern, 2003).

Discussion

This chapter summarizes extant research on narrative advertisements and narrative processing. It identifies the importance of understanding the mechanism behind narrative processing, lays out possible triggers of it, and explains their ramifications for advertising persuasion. This review thus has practical value for practitioners. First, narrative advertisements tend to be more effective than argument advertisements, especially when the product attributes are abstract and their meaning cannot be easily understood. In addition to narrative advertisements, common advertising tactics to induce narrative processing include instructing consumers to imagine themselves in the consumption scenario. Second, advertisements should feature plots that correspond to the narrative prototypes consumers store in their minds. Third, emotions portrayed in narrative advertisements enhance their effectiveness.

As long as "much of the social information we acquire in daily life is transmitted to us in the form of a narrative" (Adaval & Wyer, 1998, p. 207), narratives will remain an important form of advertising. The way people tell stories can change over time, especially with the introduction of new media, so ongoing research must continue to focus on narrative advertisements and narrative processing.

References

Adaval, R., & Wyer, R. S., Jr. (1998). The role of narratives in consumer information processing. *Journal of Consumer Psychology, 7* (3), 207–245.

Babin, L. A., & Burns, A. C. (1997). Effects of print ad pictures and copy containing instructions to imagine on mental imagery that mediates attitudes. *Journal of Advertising, 26* (3), 33–44.

Baumgartner, H., Sujan, M., & Bettman, J. R. (1992). Autobiographical memories, affect, and consumer information processing. *Journal of Consumer Psychology, 1* (1), 53–82.

Boller, G. W., & Olson, J. C. (1991). Experiencing ad meanings: Crucial aspects of narrative/drama processing. In R. H. Holman & M. R. Solomon (Eds.), *Advances in consumer research* (Vol. 18, pp. 164–171). Provo, UT: Association for Consumer Research.

Chang, C. (2008). Increasing mental health literacy via narrative advertising. *Journal of Health Communication, 13*, 1–19.

Chang, C. (2009a). Repetition variation strategies for narrative advertising. *Journal of Advertising, 38* (3), 51–65.

Chang, C. (2009b). Being hooked by editorial content: The implications for processing narrative advertising. *Journal of Advertising, 38* (1), 21–34.

Chang, C. (2010a). How people tell an ad story: Western vs. Asian styles. Working paper.

Chang, C. (2010b). The role of ad-evoked consumption visions in predicting brand attitudes: A compatibility principle model. Working paper.

Dahlen, M., Lange, F., & Smith, T. (2010). *Marketing communications: A brand narrative approach.* West Sussex, UK: John Wiley & Sons.

Deighton, J., Romer, D., & McQueen, J. (1989). Using drama to persuade. *Journal of Consumer Research, 16* (3), 335–343.

Escalas, J. E. (1998). Advertising narratives: What are they and how do they work? In B. Stern (Ed.), *Representing consumers: Voices, views, and visions* (pp. 267–289). New York: Routledge & Kegan Paul.

Escalas, J. E. (2004a). Narrative processing: Building consumer connections to brands. *Journal of Consumer Psychology, 14* (1&2), 168–180.

Escalas, J. E. (2004b). Imagine yourself in the product. *Journal of Advertising, 33* (2), 37–48.

Escalas, J. E. (2007). Self-referencing and persuasion: Narrative transportation versus analytical elaboration. *Journal of Consumer Research, 33*, 421–429.

Escalas, J. E., Moore, M. C., & Britton, J. E. (2004). Fishing for feelings? Hooking viewers helps! *Journal of Consumer Psychology, 14* (1&2), 105–114.

Escalas, J. E., & Stern, B. B. (2003). Sympathy and empathy: Emotional responses to advertising dramas. *Journal of Consumer Research, 29*, 566–578.

Fishbein, M., & Ajzen, I. (1975). *Beliefs, attitude, intention, and behavior: An introduction to theory and research.* Reading, MA: Addison-Wesley.

Fiske, S. T. (1993). Social cognition and social perception. *Annual Review of Psychology, 44*, 155–194.

Green, M. C., & Brock, T. C. (2000). The role of transportation in the persuasiveness of public narratives. *Journal of Personality and Social Psychology, 79* (5), 701–721.

Gregory, W. L., Cialdini, R. B., & Carpenter, K. M. (1982). Self-relevant scenarios as mediators of likelihood estimates and compliances: Does imagining make it so? *Journal of Personality and Social Psychology, 43* (1), 89–99.

Keller, P. A., & McGill, A. L. (1994). Differences in the relative influence of product attributes under alternative processing conditions: Attribute importance versus attribute ease of imagability. *Journal of Consumer Psychology, 3* (1), 29–49.

Kitamura, S. (1988). Unvivid imagery in vivid reproduction. *Journal of Mental Imagery, 12*, 57–62.

McGill, A. L., & Anand, P. (1989). The effect of imagery on information processing strategy in a multiattribute choice task. *Marketing Letters, 1*, 7–16.

Mattila, A. S. (2000). The role of narratives in the advertising of experiential services. *Journal of Service Research, 3* (1), 35–45.

Padgett, D., & Allen, D. (1997). Communicating experiences: A narrative approach to creating service brand image. *Journal of Advertising, 26* (4), 49–62.

Phillips, D. M. (1996). Anticipating the future: The role of consumption visions in consumer behavior. In M. Brucks & D. J. MacInnis (Eds.), *Advances in consumer research* (pp. 280–284). Provo, UT: Association for Consumer Research.

Phillips, D. M., Olson, J. C., & Baumgartner, H. (1995). Consumption visions in consumer decision making. In F. R. Kardes & M. Sujan (Eds.), *Advances in consumer research* (Vol. 22, pp. 280–284). Provo, UT: Association for Consumer Research.

Polkinghorne, D. E. (1991). Narrative and self-concept. *Journal of Narrative and Life History, 1* (2&3), 135–153.

Puto, C. P., & Wells, W. D. (1984). Informational and transformational advertising: The differential effects of time. In T. C. Kinnear (Ed.), *Advances in consumer research* (Vol. 11, pp. 572–576). Provo, UT: Association for Consumer Research.

Randazzo, S. (2006). Subaru: The emotional myths behind the brand's growth. *Journal of Advertising Research, 46* (March), 11–17.

Schank, R. C., & Abelson, R. P. (1995). Knowledge and memory: The real story. In R. S. Wyer, Jr. (Ed.), *Knowledge and memory: The real story* (pp. 1–85). Hillsdale, NJ: Lawrence Erlbaum.

Schank, R. C., & Berman, T. R. (2002). The pervasive role of stories in knowledge and action. In M. C. Green, J. J. Strange, & T. C. Brock (Eds.), *Narrative impact: Social and cognitive foundations* (pp. 287–313). Mahwah, NJ: Lawrence Erlbaum.

Shiv, B., & Huber, J. (2000). The impact of anticipating satisfaction on consumer choice. *Journal of Consumer Research, 27* (2), 202–217.

Sujan, M., Bettman, J. R., & Baumgartner, H. (1993). Influencing consumer judgments using autobiographical memories: A self-referencing perspective. *Journal of Marketing Research, 30*, 422–436.

Super Bowl Top 10 Most-Liked, Most-Recalled Ads (2010, February 9). *Advertising Age.* Retrieved August 31, 2010, from http://adage.com/article?article_id=142020.

Taylor, S. E., Pham, L. B., Rivkin, I. D., & Armor, D. A. (1998). Harnessing the imagination: Mental simulation, self-regulation, and coping. *American Psychologist, 53* (4), 429–439.

Taylor, S. E., & Schneider, S. K. (1989). Coping and the simulation of events. *Social Cognition, 7* (2), 174–194.

Walters, G., Sparks, B., & Herington, C. (2007). The effectiveness of print advertising stimuli in evoking elaborate consumption visions for potential travelers. *Journal of Travel Research, 46,* 24–34.

Wells, W. D. (1989). Lectures and dramas. In P. Cafferata & A. Tybout (Eds.), *Cognitive and affective responses to advertising* (pp. 13–21). Lexington, MA: D. C. Heath.

Additional Readings

Adaval, R., & Wyer, R. S., Jr. (1998). The role of narratives in consumer information processing. *Journal of Consumer Psychology, 7* (3), 207–245.

Dahlen, M., Lange, F., & Smith, T. (2010). *Marketing communications: A brand narrative approach.* West Sussex, UK: John Wiley & Sons Ltd.

Escalas, J. E. (1998). Advertising narratives: What are they and how do they work? In B. Stern (Ed.), *Representing consumers: Voices, views, and visions* (pp. 267–289). New York: Routledge & Kegan Paul.

Green, M. C., & Brock, T. C. (2000). The role of transportation in the persuasiveness of public narratives. *Journal of Personality and Social Psychology, 79* (5), 701–721.

Green, M. C., Strange, J. J., & Brock, T. C. (Eds.). (2002). *Narrative impact: Social and cognitive foundations* (pp. 287–313). Mahwah, NJ: Lawrence Erlbaum.

Chapter 17

Working Toward an Understanding of Persuasion via Engaging Narrative Advertising

Refining the Transportation-Imagery Model

Lu Zheng and Joseph E. Phelps

The Elaboration Likelihood Model (ELM) is discussed in detail in earlier chapters of this book. The ELM is currently the most frequently used theoretical approach to explain persuasive effects in advertising (Pasadeos, Phelps, & Edison, 2008). Despite its heavy usage by advertising researchers over many years, there is at least one major deficiency. The ELM fails to explain and predict belief changes associated with the processing of narrative advertising (Green & Brock, 2002; Chang, 2009; Appel & Richter, 2010). Narrative advertising depicts a story about product consumption (Chang, 2009) and is characterized by the content and structure of a story (Boller & Olsen, 1991).

The increasing importance of narrative advertising is perhaps best illustrated in recent studies conducted by Jupiter Research and by the Advertising Research Foundation. According to Roner (2009), this research found that advertising based on brand stories is effective and that the majority of the marketers surveyed are exploring brand "storytelling" as they see a relationship between success and the ability to tell the most engaging narratives. Given the increasing recognition of the effectiveness of narrative advertising (Chang, 2009) and of the inability of dual-process models (e.g., the ELM) to adequately address narrative processing, research dedicated to theory building in the field of narrative persuasion is highly warranted (Slater & Rouner, 2002).

The current chapter discusses an emerging model with much potential to explain the processing and effects of narrative advertising, namely, Melanie Green's (1996) Transportation-Imagery Model. The Transportation-Imagery Model, by illuminating additional routes to persuasion beyond the two identified by the ELM, holds much potential for explaining the mental processing in narrative-based belief change (Green & Brock, 2000; Appel & Richter, 2010). Furthermore, integrating the Transportation-Imagery Model and the ELM could lead to an extremely potent persuasion model that is applicable both to narrative and to rhetorical persuasion.

At this point, however, the Transportation-Imagery Model is in its infancy and much work is needed before its potential is fully realized. This developmental research will revolve around issues pertaining to advertising messages, receivers, and effects. The reader likely recognizes these elements as components of the advertising process circle presented in Figure 1.1 of this book.

Before we discuss the Transportation-Imagery Model in depth and suggest areas in which future research will refine this model, it is essential to briefly address a critical message factor, that is, the narrative versus argumentative form of an advertising message. This message factor is discussed first because the form of a message influences the information processing approach utilized by the receivers of the message. In effect, the advertising form plays a pivotal role in the theoretical accounts of advertising processing (Boller & Olson, 1991). The persuasive effects are then dependent upon the interplay of components such as the form of message, receiver characteristics, and advertising contexts.

Narrative and Argument Advertising

Wells (1989) argued that advertising consists of two basic forms: lecture and drama. Accordingly, advertising can be in the form of an argument or a narrative respectively (Boller & Olsen, 1991). Argument advertising presents product-attribute information based on arguments and evidence (Wells, 1989) and attempts to convince its audience of a claim through logical arguments and reasoning (Deighton, Romer, & McQueen, 1989). In contrast, narrative advertising often portrays a story germane to the "experiences or consequences" of the product consumption (Chang, 2009, p. 22). The content of narrative advertising consists of events, protagonists' reactions to the events, as well as their pertinent experiences. The plot, or the structure of narrative advertising, unfolds along the timeline of the characters' reactions to the events (Boller & Olsen, 1991).

Processing: Narrative versus Argument

Deighton et al. (1989) asserted that argument advertising, which substantiates its claims with appeals to objectivity, is processed in an evaluative manner, whereas narrative advertising seeks to address subjective feelings and tends to be processed in an empathic fashion. As such, advertising receivers need to "alternate between two different states of mind" in response to lecture and narrative forms of advertising (Wells, 1989, p. 14).

In argument advertising, the speaker directly addresses the audience members. In the lecture mode, ad viewers tend to process the information at arm's length (Wells, 1989). Wells (1989) contended that lectures present "argument," "evidence," as well as "exhortation" (p. 13), and are in essence "secondhand abstractions, one step removed from life" (p. 15).

Conversely, characters in drama advertising speak to one another instead of talking to audience members directly. In the narrative mode, when transported and lost into the narrative world, ad viewers become "close-in observers" of or "vicarious participants" in the narrative advertising, and they apply the lessons inferred from the advertising message to everyday circumstances they confront (Wells, 1989, p. 13). From the ad viewers' perspectives, conclusions drawn from narrative advertising are "mine" and voluntary (Wells, 1989, p. 15).

In summary, Wells (1989) maintained that lectures and dramas work in distinct fashions, and they resort to different mechanisms to persuade. The lecture mode is activated when one is exposed to argument-based stimuli, whereas the narrative mode takes effect when one consumes messages in a narrative format.

Because human beings tend to arrange information about other people and their actions in a story format (Chang, 2009), they would understand a narrative message by referring to the structure and the causal relationship of known narratives (Fiske, 1993; Schank & Abelson, 1995). In effect, such understanding also tends to facilitate mental simulation or the process of picturing oneself in the same scenario as depicted in the narrative (Taylor & Schneider, 1989).

In the next section, the evolution in the understanding of narrative processing is presented with current research culminating in the proposition of the Transportation-Imagery Model. We start with a summary of previous major research findings on narrative persuasion, and then delineate the basic components, mechanism, and consequences of narrative persuasion via transportation.

Relevant Research Prior to the Transportation-Imagery Model

Prior to the proposition of the Transportation-Imagery Model, research on narratives often viewed narrative-based belief change as the result of empathy (Booth, 1961; Martin, 1986). In narrative advertising, empathy is a "dynamic process" whereby the ad viewers vicariously participate in the product consumption experience of the advertising characters (Boller & Olsen, 1991, p. 173).

Empathy is influenced by the degree of believability. In other words, the ad viewers must find the actions and dialogues by the characters in the advertising stories believable (Todorov, 1977). Empathy with the advertising characters can be heightened by the vivid portrayal of the product consumption experience. Such empathic relationships then allow ad recipients to conceive of the advertised brand as personally relevant (Boller & Olson, 1991) and to vicariously experience the product benefits that the ad characters are enjoying in the story.

As this research evolved, a comprehensive persuasion model emerged that explains and predicts the effectiveness of the narrative-based persuasion. That model, in which the evocation of mental imagery plays a paramount role, is the Transportation-Imagery Model.

Melanie Green's Transportation-Imagery Model

It has been proposed (Green, 1996) and empirically demonstrated (Green, 1996; Green & Brock, 2000) that transportation constitutes the underlying mechanism in narrative-based belief change. According to Green and Brock (2000), transportation refers to "a feeling of being lost" (p. 701) in the story, or "an immersion into the narrative world" (p. 704). As shown in Figure 17.1, there are three antecedents in transportation, including cognitive attention, mental imagery, and emotional involvement. The synergy of these three antecedents leads to transportation, which causes belief change. The three antecedents as well as the narrative-based belief change via transportation as depicted in Figure 17.1 can be further illustrated by the following example.

When a reader of the *Lord of the Rings* trilogy is fully immersed in this highly engaging narrative, he tends to temporarily ignore the physical world around him, as all of his "mental systems and capacities" (Green & Brock, 2000, p. 701) become concentrated on the adventures unfolding in the narrative world (cognitive attention). In addition, the reader is also likely to generate a series of vivid mental imageries of magnificent sceneries, epic battles, and unworldly

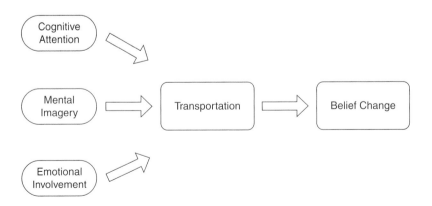

Figure 17.1 Example of Antecedents and Narrative Belief Change Process Via Transportation.

creatures in the fantasy world of Middle Earth (mental imagery). Moreover, the reader also tends to become emotionally involved with the story characters, by exhibiting positive attitude toward the Hobbits, the Elves, and Gandalf (emotional involvement). The experiences and the beliefs of these story characters exert a heightened impact on the reader. As a result, the transported reader, when mentally returning to the real world, tends to exhibit story-consonant beliefs. In our case, the reader is likely to believe in the ultimate triumph of good over evil, which is the message that the author intends to convey (belief change).

Gilbert (1991) noted that individuals are naturally inclined to believe whatever they read or hear, whereas disbelieving entails an arduous correction of such a natural tendency. As such, transportation into a narrative world dampens message recipients' motivation or ability to question any specific conclusion. In addition, the transportation experience also renders the engrossed message recipients reluctant to pause and scrutinize propositions implied by the narrative (Green & Brock, 2000).

Previous research consistently found that more transported individuals are more likely to endorse story-consistent beliefs (Escalas, 2004; Green, 2004, Green et al., 2008; Zheng, 2010). In addition, Appel and Richter (2007) empirically demonstrated that the transported individuals did not simply follow the central or the peripheral route to persuasion as identified by the ELM. Narrative persuasion does not entail cognitive elaboration but can achieve absolute sleeper effects, which are "the strongest type of long-term persuasion" (Appel & Richter, 2007, p. 118).

Advertising Research and Refining the Transportation-Imagery Model

As noted in the first chapter of this book, advertising is a variable field. Advertising scholars often borrow and adapt theories developed in more established level fields, such as psychology, in efforts to elucidate advertising processing and effects. The Transportation-Imagery Model was developed by scholars in the level field of psychology and has not been systematically investigated in an advertising context. Moreover, this model is still in its early stage of development and requires further refinement.

The remaining sections of this chapter aim to describe the current state of the transportation model and communicate suggestions for the further maturation and acclimation of the model into an advertising context. Nan and Faber (2004) contended that in order to advance advertising knowledge, when borrowing theory from other fields, advertising scholars must examine the role(s) of unique advertising variables in the theory. A number of important advertising-related variables were shown in Figure 1.1 in Chapter 1. The current discussion will focus on the essential role of message, individual receiver, and environmental or context factors in the continuing development of the Transportation-Imagery Model.

Overview of Figure 17.2

Figure 17.2 illustrates the research findings on transportation to date, notably those germane to the advertising domain. This figure represents the first attempt by advertising researchers at visually summarizing the current understanding of the transportation model. Just as importantly, Figure 17.2 illustrates critical voids within the transportation model to be addressed. Following a brief overview of Figure 17.2, a detailed discussion of the major elements within the model is presented.

In Figure 17.2, solid shapes represent Green's conceptualization of the basic structure of transportation. All other research findings and information voids are displayed in transparent shapes. Each of the three antecedents of transportation is influenced by a number of factors, some of which have been identified and examined, whereas others remain largely unexplored. We classify these factors into three categories, namely, message factors, individual/receiver factors, and environmental factors, which are represented by circles, triangles, and diamonds respectively. We use solid lines to illustrate relationships that have been proposed or confirmed by previous research and dotted lines with question marks to represent relationships that need to be identified and explored in future research.

It is best to read Figure 17.2 from left to right. The factors situated on the far left side of the figure influence the three antecedents of transportation that are represented by solid ellipses, which lead to transportation and the ensuing belief change. The reader may also note that there are also individual, message, and environmental factors located vertically above or below transportation. This arrangement illustrates that these factors have been found to influence transportation in general without being confirmed as impacting any of the three basic antecedents.

Regarding the classification of the factors, whereas the message and individual factors correspond to the message and receiver components in Chapter 1, the environmental factor is defined somewhat differently from the advertising context component. Unlike intrinsic attributes of the advertising message and receiver, environmental factors in Figure 17.2 refer to characteristics of external environment that affect transportation experience, such as the editorial context of the advertising message (Chang, 2009). In effect, our environmental factor can be viewed as a subset of the advertising context component in Figure 17.1.

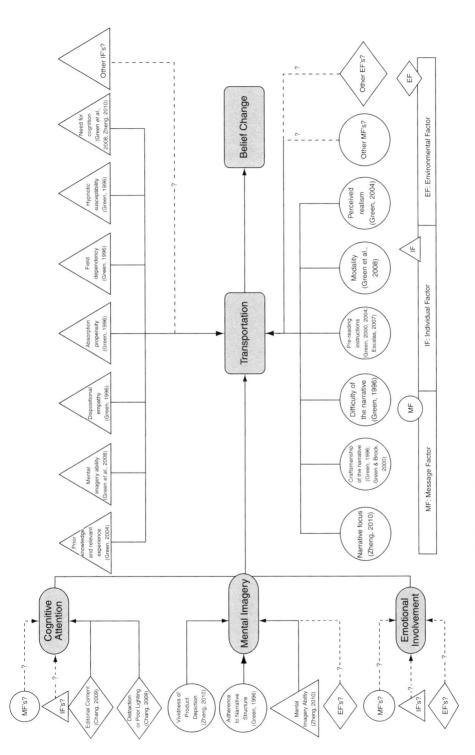

Figure 17.2 Summary of Research Findings on Transportation.

The following sections walk the reader through Figure 17.2 step by step in the following order. We start with the factors affecting each of the three antecedents of transportation, and then discuss individual, message, and environmental factors that influence transportation in general but have not been associated with the three antecedents.

Factors Influencing Cognitive Attention

Three environmental factors have been found to impact the cognitive attention antecedent of transportation, namely, editorial content of the print narrative advertising, distraction, and poor lighting. Specifically, Chang (2009) reasoned that one's cognitive capacity impinges upon the persuasiveness of narrative advertising, since adequate cognitive resources are entailed while processing narrative messages. In particular, it was found that narrative advertisements are more likely to evoke transportation when fact-based reading materials than preceded them by narrative ones (Chang, 2009). This finding could be attributed to the fact that reading narrative editorial content consumes part of one's cognitive resources and thus decreases one's cognitive capacity to process the subsequent narrative advertisement. In consequence, transportation experience is less likely to be elicited by narrative advertisement following narrative editorial content (Chang, 2009). Apart from editorial content, Chang (2009) also posited distraction and poor lighting as potential environmental factors that may influence one's cognitive capacity. As shown in Figure 17.2, the role of these two factors has yet to be empirically examined. Regarding individual receiver factors, Appel and Richter (2010) suggested that future research should examine whether need for affect, or one's dispositional tendency to approach emotions, can influence cognitive component of transportation. No other individual or message factors pertaining to cognitive attention antecedent has been proposed or explored.

Factors Influencing Mental Imagery

Two message factors and one individual factor have been found to impact mental imagery antecedent of transportation, including adherence to narrative structure (Green, 1996), vividness or sensory richness of product depiction, and mental imagery ability (Zheng, 2010).

First, the potency of mental imagery is contingent upon the narrative structure to some extent (Green & Brock, 2002). It follows that transportation is unlikely to be elicited only by the presence of provocative depictions. Instead, a transporting narrative entails an identifiable storyline, with the beginning, middle, and denouement, in which emerged questions are only answered in the later parts of the narrative (Green & Brock, 2002). In consequence, adherence to the narrative structure has been proposed as a potential message factor of mental imagery.

In an advertising context, the vividness of product depiction and one's mental imagery, or an individual's "dispositional abilities to create vivid mental images" (Marks, 1973) were found to affect the ease of mental imagery generation (Petrova & Cialdini, 2005, p. 443). Moreover, in a narrative advertising context, Zheng (2010) found that transportation, and the mental imagery antecedent in particular, was influenced by the vividness of product depiction, with vivid product depictions eliciting more transportation than their nonvivid counterparts. Therefore, vividness of product depiction is identified as a message factor that affects mental imagery. In addition, Zheng (2010) also found that one's mental imagery ability tends to influence transportation, with higher imagers being more transported into the print narrative advertisements than low imagers. As such, mental imagery ability has been identified as an individual moderator of mental imagery. No advertising research examining environmental moderators of mental imagery was found, which highlights another information void in the development of the transportation model.

Factors Influencing Emotional Involvement

One individual factor and one environmental factor have been identified as potential moderators of the emotional involvement antecedent of transportation. In the field of media psychology, Appel and Richter (2010) found that need for affect seems to influence the emotional aspect of transportation. Specifically, it was found that individuals with high need for affect, or a stronger dispositional tendency to approach emotions, were more transported to the fictional narratives than individuals with low need for affect. Note that this individual factor has yet to be empirically examined in the advertising domain. With respect to environmental factor, Chang (2009) found that editorial content of print narrative advertisements seems to influence the emotional involvement of ad receivers. No message factors or other individual and environmental factors have been proposed so far. Thus, developing a better understanding of the role played by emotional involvement and the conditions moderating and mediating that role in transportation awaits future research.

Individual Factors Influencing Transportation in General

The reader should now focus on the five triangles above the "transportation" rectangle in Figure 17.2. These triangles refer to the five potential individual moderators of transportation that have been proposed by previous research, including one's prior knowledge or pertinent personal experience, absorption propensity, private self-awareness, dispositional empathy, and need for cognition.

First, an individual's prior knowledge or personal experience germane to the narrative was found to be a significant predictor of the extent of transportedness. When readers possess knowledge pertaining to the story themes, they are more likely to be transported into the story (Green, 2004).

Second, absorption propensity was found to be moderately correlated with transportation (Green & Brock, 2000). Absorption essentially concerns one's "general tendency to become absorbed into life experiences" (Green & Brock 2000, p. 704), as measured by Tellegen's (1982) Absorption Scale.

Third, private self-awareness was also found to be moderately correlated with transportation (Green, 1996). Private self-awareness is defined as a "dispositional tendency to focus on subjective experiences" (Petrova & Cialdini, 2005) as measured by the private self-consciousness scale (Fenigstein, Scheier, & Buss, 1975).

In addition, empathy, or one's intrinsic tendency to develop empathic relationship with others, was found to be highly correlated with transportation (Green, 1996). Dispositional empathy can be measured by the Interpersonal Reactivity Index (Davis, 1983).

Furthermore, Green and her colleagues (2008, p. 518) demonstrated that need for cognition, defined as a dispositional tendency to "enjoy and engage in effortful cognitive activity" (Cacioppo & Petty, 1982) are likely to influence transportation across modality or different media types. In particular, high need for cognition individuals were more transported while reading the print narratives, whereas low need for cognition individuals were more transported while watching the cinematic version of the same narratives. Consistently, need for cognition was also found to affect one's degree of transportedness in response to print narrative advertising (Zheng, 2010).

Message Factors Influencing Transportation in General

The reader should now focus on the seven circles below the "transportation" rectangle in Figure 17.2. These circles represent seven message moderators of transportation that have been proposed by previous research, including narrative focus, writing quality of the narrative, degree of difficulty of the narrative, pre-reading instructions, sequence of the modality, pacing, and perceived realism of narrative. Note that only the first moderator, namely, narrative focus, was investigated specifically in an advertising setting, whereas the remaining six moderators were proposed to influence transportation in narrative persuasion in general.

First, Zheng (2010) found that transportation was influenced by narrative focus in narrative advertising. The focus of the narrative can be either on the process of the product usage or on the outcome (i.e., end benefits) of the product consumption (Escalas, 2004). Process-focused narrative ads were found to evoke a higher degree of transportedness than their outcome-focused counterparts (Zheng, 2010). Moreover, previous research found that more transported ad viewers were more likely to exhibit favorable brand attitude and behavioral intentions (Escalas, 2004; Zheng, 2010).

The second message factor involves the level of artistic craftsmanship or writing quality of the narrative message (Green & Brock, 2000). It has been empirically found that audience members perceived bestsellers and classic short stories to be more transporting than those experimental narratives created by the researchers (Green & Brock, 2000).

The third factor concerns the degree of difficulty of the narrative. Excessively complex narrative may inhibit the elicitation of transportation, whereas overly simple narrative may either bore the message recipients or stimulates more imagination in them (Green, 1996).

The fourth factor concerns pre-reading instructions, which have been found to influence transportation under certain conditions. For instance, when pre-reading instructions elicit a focus on surface aspects of a narrative message (e.g., grammatical errors of the text), the degree of transportation tends to be decreased relative to baseline (Green & Brock, 2000). Moreover, previous research proposed that hypnosis instructions as well as instructions capable of enhancing viewers' skepticism tend to influence transportation (Green, 2004; Escalas, 2007). Furthermore, Green (2004) posited that instructions specifically germane to one of the three antecedents of transportation could more effectively manipulate the extent of transportation. For instance, the instructions can be explicitly pertinent to the mental imagery antecedent of transportation. In particular, audience members can be instructed to form mental imageries about story protagonists and scenes depicted in the narrative. Alternatively, the instructions can directly address the emotional involvement antecedent of transportation, by asking audience members to think and feel from other people's perspectives in a given scenario (Green, 2004). Last, but not the least, if such more specific instructions can successfully affect the degree of transportation, we will be in a solid position to determine which antecedent of transportation leads to belief change (Green, 2004).

The fifth factor concerns the sequence of the modality (print, visual, or audio) of the narrative message (Green et al., 2008). Green et al. (2008) found that those who watched the same narrative twice were the least transported, whereas those who first read then watched the narrative were the most transported. As such, modality appears to be another message factor that moderates the transportation effect. Whether this finding holds true in the advertising domain remains unexplored. However, if we can pinpoint a particular pattern in terms of the presentation of the narrative advertising messages across modality, this research finding can be of practical significance in enhancing media planning efficiency. For example, if research shows that when one is exposed to the narrative ads in a magazine first, and in television and radio consecutively, the transportation effect can reach its maximum level; media planners can literally apply such findings to practice so as to produce the greatest persuasive effect.

The sixth factor concerns pacing, defined as the message receiver's ability to set the pace of processing the story elements (Green & Brock, 2002). Clearly, pacing, especially self-pacing, is closely related to modality. Specifically, some media types such as magazines and newspapers allow pacing to be maximized, because the message recipients can control the duration of their exposure and response to certain story elements. In contrast, other media types such as film render self-pacing more difficult to realize. For example, it is usually impossible for a movie viewer to pause or rewind the film in a movie theater. It is posited that self-pacing, if maximized, is likely to enhance transportation, with the experience of reading being more transporting than the experience of watching a film (Green & Brock, 2002).

The seventh factor involves perceived realism of the narrative message (Green, 2004). Green (2004) noted a positive correlation between transportation and perceived realism of the narrative information. In particular, more transported individuals tend to consider the events, settings, and characters depicted in the narrative more believable. Nevertheless, perceived realism was not a significant mediator between belief change and transportation (Green, 2004).

Conclusion

As suggested throughout this chapter, the Transportation-Imagery Model holds much potential for explaining narrative-based belief change (Green & Brock, 2000). Unleashing this potential will require research devoted to exploring message factors, receiver characteristics, environmental factors, and more.

As illustrated in Figure 17.2, although the three antecedents of transportation have been identified and the basic mechanism of belief change via transportation has been delineated, a number of information voids exist with regards to factors influencing the three antecedents and transportation in general. In addition, the bulk of the currently identified factors have yet to be empirically examined in an advertising context.

Obviously, there is much work to be done to facilitate this model's maturation. Fortunately, this work comes with the promise of great reward for scholars and for practitioners. Current models, such as the ELM, do not adequately explain narrative processing. Integrating transportation and the ELM models could lead to an extremely potent persuasion model that is applicable to both narrative and rhetorical persuasion. Furthermore, a complete and empirically supported transportation model will serve as a powerful tool for advertising practitioners to craft transporting and thus persuasive advertising messages.

References

Appel, M., & Richter, T. (2007). Persuasive effects of fictional narratives increase over time. *Media Psychology, 10*, 113–134.

Appel, M., & Richter, T. (2010). Transportation and need for affect in narrative persuasion: A mediated moderation model. *Media Psychology, 13* (2), 101–135.

Boller, G. W., & Olson, J. (1991). Experiencing ad meaning: Crucial aspects of narrative/drama processing. In R. Holman & M. R. Solomon (Eds.), *Advances in consumer research* (Vol. 18, pp. 172–175). Ann Arbor, MI: Association for Consumer.

Booth, W.C. (1961). *The rhetoric of fiction*. Chicago: University of Chicago Press.

Cacioppo, J. T., & Petty, R. E. (1982). The need for cognition. *Journal of Personality and Social Psychology, 42*, 116–131.

Chang, C. C. (2009). "Being hooked" by editorial content: The implications for processing narrative advertising. *Journal of Advertising, 38* (1), 21–33.

Davis, M. H. (1983). Measuring individual differences in empathy: Evidence for a multidimensional approach. *Journal of Personality and Social Psychology, 44*, 113–126.

Deighton, J., Romer, D., & McQueen, J. (1989). Using drama to persuade. *Journal of Consumer Research, 16* (3), 335–343.

Escalas, J. E. (2004). Imagine yourself in the product: Mental simulation, narrative transportation, and persuasion. *Journal of Advertising, 33* (2), 37–48.

Escalas, J. E. (2007). Self-referencing and persuasion: Narrative transportation versus analytical elaboration. *Journal of Consumer Research, 33* (4), 421–429.

Fenigstein, A., Scheier, M. F., & Buss, A. H. (1975). Public and private self-consciousness: Assessment and theory. *Journal of Consulting and Clinical Psychology, 43* (4), 522–27.

Fiske, S. T. (1993). Social cognition and social perception. *Annual Review of Psychology, 44*, 155–194.

Gilbert, D. T. (1991). How mental systems believe. *American Psychologist, 46*, 107–119.

Green, M. C. (1996). Mechanisms of narrative-based belief change. Unpublished master's thesis, Ohio State University, Columbus, OH.

Green, M. C. (2004). Transportation into narrative worlds: The role of prior knowledge and perceived realism. *Discourse Processes, 38*, 247–266.

Green, M. C., & Brock, T. C. (2000). The role of transportation in the persuasiveness of public narratives. *Journal of Personality and Social Psychology, 79* (5), 701–721.

Green, M.C., & Brock, T. C. (2002). In the mind's eye. In M. C. Green, J. J., Strange, & T. C. Brock (Eds.), *Narrative impact: Social and cognitive foundations* (pp. 315–341). Mahwah, NJ: Lawrence Erlbaum.

Green, M. C., Kass, S., Carrey, J., Herzig, B., Feeney, R., & Sabini, J. (2008). Transportation across media: Repeated exposure to print and film. *Media Psychology, 11*, 512–539.

Marks, D. F. (1973). Visual imagery differences in the recall of pictures. *British Journal of Psychology, 64* (1), 17–24.

Martin, W. (1986). *Recent theories of narrative.* Ithaca, NY: Cornell University Press.

Nan, X., & Faber, R. (2004). Advertising theory: Reconceptualizing the building blocks. *Marketing Theory, 4* (1/2), 7–30.

Pasadeos, Y., Phelps, J., & Edison, A. (2008). Searching for our "own theory" in advertising: An update of research networks. *Journalism and Mass Communication Quarterly, 85* (4), 785–806.

Petrova, P. K., & Cialdini, R. B. (2005). Fluency of consumption imagery and the backfire effects of imagery appeals. *Journal of Consumer Research, 32* (3), 442–452.

Roner, Lisa (2009, January 2). Narrative branding: A key to marketing success in 2009. *Eyeforpharma.* Retrieved November 16, 2010, from http://social.eyeforpharma.com/story/narrative-branding-key-marketing-success-2009.

Schank, R. C., & Abelson, R. P. (1995). Knowledge and memory: The real story. In R. S. Wyer (Ed.), *Advances in social cognition* (Vol. 8, pp. 1–85). Hillsdale, NJ: Lawrence Erlbaum.

Slater, M. D., & Rouner, D. (2002). Entertainment-education and elaboration likelihood: Understanding the processing of narrative persuasion. *Communication Theory, 12* (2), 173–191.

Taylor, S. E., & Schneider, S. (1989). Coping and the simulation of events. *Social Cognition, 7* (2), 174–194.

Tellegen, A. (1982). Brief manual for the differential personality questionnaire. Unpublished manuscript, University of Minnesota, Minneapolis.

Todorov, T. (1977). *The poetics of prose* (Trans. R. Howard). New York: Cornell University Press.

Wells, W. D. (1989). Lectures and dramas. In P. Cafferata & A. Tybout (Eds.), *Cognitive and affective responses to advertising* (pp. 13–20). Lexington, MA: Lexington Books.

Zheng, L. (2010). The impact of narrative focus, vividness of product depiction, mental imagery ability, and need for cognition on transportation in narrative advertising. Unpublished doctoral dissertation, University of Alabama, Tuscaloosa.

Chapter 18

Direct-to-Consumer Advertising of Prescription Drugs

Consumers, Physicians, Messages, and Complexity

Kim Bartel Sheehan

One of the most prevalent and controversial categories of advertising is advertising directed to consumers for prescription drugs. A prescription drug is defined as a drug that a consumer can only obtain through a prescription written by a physician or dentist and filled by a pharmacist. Prescription drugs differ from over-the-counter drugs (OTC), which are drugs that consumers can purchase without a prescription. Direct to Consumer (DTC) advertising of prescription drugs differs from virtually all other advertising messages in two important ways. First, advertisements must, by law, include both benefits and risk information about the advertised drug. The Food and Drug Administration (FDA) is responsible for developing and enforcing policies for advertising prescription drugs in the United States; these policies monitor whether DTC advertising executions meet a range of requirements.[1] Second, members of the target audience for DTC advertisements cannot, by law, purchase the advertised drug without the permission of a medical professional (e.g., a licensed physician, doctor of osteopathy, or dentist). Due to these important differences, DTC advertisements must not only persuade a consumer to want the advertised drugs—as with every other type of advertisement—but DTC ads must also persuade the consumers to have a conversation with their health professionals to request the advertised drug.

This chapter will focus primarily on two key elements identified in Thorson and Rodgers' Figure 1.1: the messages and receivers of DTC advertising. Focusing on the content of DTC messages is important because these messages include both positive and negative information about the drug, as directed by law. The focus on message receivers is important because the ultimate consumers for prescription drugs cannot make the purchase decision on their own—they require the permission of a certified medical professional—thereby making the persuasive aspect of ad messaging different from most other types of advertised products in that consumers discuss and request the medication from an authorized provider.

Industry Background

The modern pharmaceutical industry is relatively young: it began in the 1940s with the development of synthetic substances to replace naturally occurring substances (such as digitalis and opium) that had been used in healthcare (Clark, 1988). Today, the pharmaceutical industry is dominated by a small group of American, German, and Swiss companies involved not only with marketing existing drugs but also in creating, testing, and producing new drugs (Liebenau, 1990). As a result, much of the costs for a new pharmaceutical product occur long before the drug is on the market. The top five pharmaceutical companies (based on their 2009 annual reports) include Johnson & Johnson, Pfizer, Roche, GlaxoSmithKline, and Novartis. Some of the top selling drugs include Lipitor, a cholesterol drug produced by Pfizer, Advair, an asthma drug produced by GlaxoSmithKline, and Topamax, a migraine drug produced by Johnson & Johnson. In 2009, DTC advertising spending totaled almost $5 billion, one of the largest spending categories in U.S. advertising (DTC Perspectives, 2010).

Only two countries allow advertisements for prescription drugs to be directed to consumers, the United States and New Zealand, although proposed legislation in both the European Union and Canada could lift DTC advertising bans in other countries (Yan, 2008). This chapter will focus on prescription drug advertising in the United States; for information on the history and regulatory structure of the New Zealand pharmaceutical industry see Hoek, Gendall, and Calfee (2004).

In the United States, the FDA issued the first set of guidelines for pharmaceutical advertising in 1962. These guidelines required that all promotional materials that feature the name of the drug, and the medical condition the drug treats, must include a "brief summary" that consists of the drug's scientific name, the formula showing each ingredient, quantitatively, and information that discusses side effects, contraindications (such as negative interactions with other drugs), and overall effectiveness. While these early guidelines did not specifically prohibit advertising directly to consumers, the industry's tacit agreement was to focus only on physicians and other healthcare professionals and not consumers per se.

The growth of managed care organizations in the United States in the 1980s resulted in industry requests to the FDA to promote drugs directly to consumers. After significant research, the FDA approved DTC advertising utilizing the same criteria for physician advertising: inclusion of a brief summary that includes a fairly exhaustive list of a drug's risks.

Advertising directed to consumers began in 1988 with a print ad for pharmaceutical company Upjohn's hair replacement drug Rogaine. The effect of DTC advertising on drug sales was seen quickly, as Rogaine's sales increased from

$87 million in 1988 (before DTC advertising was officially allowed) to $143 million in 1992 (Nayyar, 1992).

In the early years of DTC advertising, drug companies focused primarily on print advertising, with the required brief summary information appearing as a stand-alone page near the branded DTC message. The brief summary requirement limited the use of television for DTC advertising since listing all the risks for a drug in the brief summary would take several minutes, thereby making the ad cost prohibitive in many instances.

The FDA re-evaluated the guidelines in the 1990s and the first DTC television advertisement appeared in 1997 for the allergy drug Claritin. The revised guidelines allowed broadcast messages to forego the brief summary and, instead, provide "fair balance" information that insured that advertisements presented an accurate and fair assessment of the risks as well as the benefits of the drug (FDA CDER, 1999). According to the fair balance provision, the presentation of accurate information about side effects and contraindications must be comparable in depth and detail with the claims for effectiveness or safety (FFDCA, 2004). This does not mean that a given ad must contain an equal number of benefits and risk claims. The FDA evaluates fair balance in terms of both information content and the format of the information, that is, information must be balanced in terms of prominence (the amount of time spent on risk and benefit information) and presence (the format of the risk information) in the ad (Roth, 1996).

In addition, DTC TV advertisements must include "adequate provision," that is, sources of information where consumers could find the full prescribing information about the drug. These sources include physicians, 800 numbers, and Web addresses (FDA CDER, 1999). These message requirements for DTC TV advertising are manifested in one very obvious way: the vast majority of DTC advertisements last at least 60 seconds (compared to the standard 30 second TV spot for other products) in order to provide the required risk information. This additional time allows DTC advertisers to provide a range of positive arguments that consumers can use in conversations with their physicians.

The Internet has added an additional level of complexity to DTC advertising. While the Internet has allowed consumers to learn information about all types of subjects, health information online appears to be especially salient for consumers. A 2009 study found that 61% of U.S. users used the Internet to find health information (Fox & Jones, 2009), third only to doctors (86%), and friends or family members (68%). In addition, almost half of online users have looked online for information about prescription medicine and/or OTC drugs, and most prescription drugs provide information via complex websites. Despite the popularity of the Internet for prescription drug information the FDA has not provided specific regulations on Internet communication of information for prescription drugs online.

DTC Advertising Theory

Clearly, DTC advertising is a unique type of advertising: the messages are longer than other ads, information provided is examined by a government body, and ads provide both benefit and risk information to consumers. Additionally, the ultimate goal of DTC advertising messages is not to influence the consumer to purchase the product, but, rather, for the consumer to have a conversation with his or her doctor to find out if the treatment is correct for the patient. Given these unique aspects of DTC advertising, i.e., consumers doing research online and getting information about DTC drugs from physicians and others, traditional theories may not be the best explanatory tool for DTC messaging, as illustrated in this next section.

Hierarchy of Effects Model

Lavidge and Steiner's (1961) Hierarchy of Effects (HOE) model posits that once consumers are exposed to an ad, they go through a sequential effect that moves them farther along the path to purchase. This model suggests that as consumers move through this hierarchy, they experience one of three psychological states at any given time—cognition, affect, or conation. Cognition refers to consumer understanding of factual elements about the advertised brand, affect refers to consumer development of an emotion or feeling toward the brand, and conation involves consumer choice of an action regarding the brand.

The HOE model suggests that a direct connection exists between a brand's advertising and the prospective customer's response. It also suggests that consumers generally process advertisements in similar ways, regardless of the type of product or service being advertised. As such, the model does not recognize the unique composition and complexity of DTC advertisements, particularly the fact that messages must provide both positive and negative information about the drug, which may alter consumer perceptions of such ads.

This informational requirement is likely to have a different type of effect on consumers, in that consumers may engage in a different level of processing than a typical ad. The HOE model also does not recognize any other factors that contribute to the final purchase decision (Weilbacher, 2001). For instance, consumers may be influenced by a combination of marketing factors including product quality, product availability, competitive pricing, as well as a variety of marketing communications. Thus, consumers making a decision about a prescription drug *must* access sources of information (i.e., the medical professional) other than an advertisement to make a decision. For these reasons, other theories other than HOE may better explain DTC advertising.

Social Cognitive Theory

In response to the potential limitations of HOE, noted above, Social Cognitive Theory may be better for explaining the effects of message complexity on consumer reactions and responses to DTC advertising.

Social Cognitive Theory suggests that a consumer's acquisition of knowledge is directly related to observing others within the context of social interactions, experiences, and outside media influences. One of the first published studies using Social Cognitive Theory involved "Bobo" dolls (Bandura, Ross, & Ross, 1961). In this experiment, children were exposed to an individual showing violent and aggressive behavior toward a large inflatable clown. After the exposure, children were observed in a room with a Bobo doll. Children who had watched the violent actions treated the dolls violently, while children not exposed to the violent actions did not. Subsequent versions of this experiment were conducted with videos displaying violent and aggressive behavior; watching videos induced the same imitative behavior. Social Cognitive Theory, then, suggests that we learn how to behave by observing how others behave.

Social Cognitive Theory also suggests that the learning process is more likely if there is a close identification between the observer (or the consumer) and the people being observed (such as actors in an advertisement). Further, learning is more likely to occur if the consumer has a high level of self-efficacy. Self-efficacy is the notion that an individual's perception of his or her ability to successfully perform a type of task is related to a particular context.

Applied to the current discussion, DTC advertisements may influence self-efficacy if the ads suggest that a medication regimen can positively affect one's health. Often, DTC advertisements provide language that refers to the simplicity of the regimen to achieve positive results. The erectile dysfunction drug Cialis, for example, provides this content on the home page of its website:

> Why choose Cialis for daily use? Cialis for daily use is a clinically proven, low dose tablet for erectile dysfunction that you take every day so you can be ready when the moment is right. With Cialis, men with ED can be more confident in their ability to be ready.
>
> (Cialis, 2010)

The content demonstrates the particular context of the medical problem as well as suggests the ability of the user to accomplish the proposed task. Additionally, another concept that applies here is self-efficacy, which can influence a human motivation (the decision to adopt a goal-oriented behavior), affect (emotions), and action (the actual behavior). Cialis television commercials show couples in intimate poses in restaurants, cafes, and porches, and then announces that the medication works in as little as 30 minutes. This provides both information about the efficacy of the drug as well as an indication that the drug can be as successful for the user as it apparently has been for the people in the advertisements (who are seen at the end of the ad in side-by-side bathtubs). This example connects to self-efficacy beliefs suggesting that individuals can refrain from making mistakes (e.g., not having a satisfying sexual encounter) and can perform behaviors better if they see individuals complete the behavior successfully (Bandura, 1988).

Social Cognitive Theory is often used to explain different types of health-related communications. This perspective on health communication suggests that individuals' behavior change can be facilitated by changing the way that people think and feel about the desired behaviors in order to encourage healthy behaviors (Maibach & Cotton, 1995). Again, the focus is on outcomes: if consumers believe that a favorable outcome can be obtained (and/or a negative outcome can be avoided), they are more likely to adopt a behavior (Miller, 2005). Health communications have applied social cognitive theory in health by matching the observers (consumers) to the ones performing the actions (actors in commercials) in terms of gender and ethnicity. A series of advertisements for the anti-depression drug Cymbalta features several individuals, including a young black father, a young Hispanic woman, and an older white female. The commercials display images of how "depression hurts" and shows the actors alone, looking sad and generally unkempt. The second part of the commercial shows the actors smiling, interacting with others, and opening draperies, which may symbolize a movement from darkness to light. Because depression can affect a range of people, the range of actors featured in the ads models a variety of consumers with someone to identify with, as well as suggesting actions to imitate, and shows the positive result of the action.

These advertisements are part of what Bandura (1994) characterizes as production processes and motivational processes. Production processes are those that transfer information into "guides" for behavior. In addition to helping consumers recognize the positive results for the Cymbalta ads, the guides in these ads provide sources for additional information that consumers can act on, such as an 877 number, the drug's website, an advertisement in a women's magazine, and the suggestion to talk with a doctor. Motivational processes influence the production processes. Bandura identified three different motivational processes: direct motivators, self-produced motivators, and vicarious motivators (Bandura, 1994). All three types of motivators are seen in DTC advertisements.

Direct motivators are external incentives, such as a medical or lifestyle benefit to using the advertised drug (e.g., the Cialis ad suggested a lifestyle benefit in terms of a good sex life). Self-produced motivators are self-gratifying activities that have provided previous pleasant associations, i.e., changes to responses or feelings in the past.

For instance, ads for the insomnia drug Rozerem have the tag line "your dreams miss you," suggesting that the insomniac had pleasant dreams (and therefore no insomnia) in the past. Vicarious motivators associate valued outcomes with observed behaviors (such as seen in the Cymbalta ads). Although all three motivators are seen in DTC advertisements, Young and Cline (2005) suggested that direct and vicarious motivators are key components of DTC advertising's influence on patient behavior in that DTC advertising presents rewards associated with the use (and punishments associated with nonuse) of advertised drugs.

Consumer Socialization Theory

A consumer's decision to adopt the behavior of an actor in a DTC commercial is not a sufficient action for a consumer to complete the purchase of the drug. The consumer must also obtain permission, in the form of a prescription, from his or her physician in order to purchase the drug. The physician, then, becomes both a gatekeeper and an influencer over the purchase, making the purchase not only a cognitive process, but also a social process. Consumer Socialization Theory can be used to better understand this process.

The consumer socialization framework was originally conceived as a process by which young people acquire skills, knowledge, and attitudes—in this case, to become consumers (Ward, 1974). Younger adults were an initial focus of this theoretical research because of the many changes that take place during adolescent years. These changes affect the attitudes and behaviors formed during adolescence and carry over into adulthood (Hurlock, 1980). The consumer socialization perspective is now used in "the study of consumer behavior throughout a person's life-cycle" (Moschis, 1987, p. 9), recognizing that people at any age can investigate new products and categories. This is important since many consumers find themselves adopting more prescription drugs as they age.

A key aspect of consumer socialization theory is the idea of a socialization agent, which refers to the involvement of an influencer in the persuasion process (McLeod & O'Keefe, 1972). This influencer is a person or an organization that has contact with the consumer and/or control over the rewards and punishments consumers obtain (Brim, 1966).

Two major categorizations of socialization agents are interpersonal (doctors, other healthcare workers, and peers) and mass-mediated communications (advertisements, doctor-provided information, and Web-provided information). The consumer socialization perspective suggests that interactions between a consumer and various socialization agents in specific social settings influence learning processes and, eventually, consumer behavior (Lueg & Finney, 2007).

Through these socialization agents, consumers learn how to feel about and behave toward a specific object in a given context. In a DTC advertising context, socialization agents interact with consumers to share health information, help consumers learn information from and form attitudes toward DTC advertising, and encourage discussions with doctors regarding the advertised drugs. These interactions are considered learning processes where agents use modeling to exhibit particular behaviors and intentions (Moschis & Churchill, 1978).

Consumer socialization theory expands upon Bandura's theory because it suggests that an individual's cultural background affects his/her perception of a socialization agent. For instance, in a culture or among an audience with a high level of trust in physicians, DTC advertisements may feature an actor portraying a doctor to deliver information in order to strengthen the message being communicated. Instead of relating to actors portraying characters with the illnesses in the ads, consumers relate to the information being provided by characters representing experts and other culturally relevant individuals that they trust. Consumer socialization theory also suggests that interpersonal, non-mediated communications can influence health decisions. However, there is interplay between these channels. Lee, Salmon, and Paek (2007) found that the more consumers rely on mass media and interpersonal channels for health information, the more likely they will hold positive attitudes toward DTC advertising. The researchers believe that those who learn health information through those specific socialization agents are more likely to pay attention to DTC messages and, as a result, find the advertisements from those messages most helpful in decision making.

The study also found that the more consumers rely on interpersonal channels, as opposed to mass media channels, for health information the more likely they will discuss the advertised prescription drug with their physician. Therefore, interpersonal channels have a greater influence on motivating consumers to take the action of talking with their doctors in order to make a decision. The study concluded with the idea that consumers' use of mass media channels for health information was not directly related to discussions with their healthcare professionals regarding the advertised drugs. Instead, the researchers believed that the effect of mass media channels on behavioral outcomes appears to be mediated by two factors: interpersonal channels and attitudes toward DTC advertising. This suggests that while mass media are generally effective at providing health information to consumers, interpersonal communication is an important influencer in adoption of a health-related behavior change (Backer, Rogers, & Sopory, 1992).

The Presumed Influence Model

DTC advertising may also influence the physician and, in turn, the physician serves as influencer of consumers' adoption of prescription medicine. This influence is captured in the Presumed Influence model, which suggests that presumed influence among an unintended audience (such as physicians who are not the intended audience of DTC ads) by an involved audience (physicians' patients) can significantly influence the behavior of another audience (Gunther & Story, 2003; Tsfati & Cohen, 2005).

Physicians are not the intended targets of DTC messages, though they are the gatekeepers of health information as well as a key interpersonal influence on a consumer's healthcare decision. Huh and Langteau (2007) found that physicians make assumptions about the effects of DTC messages on their patients, and these assumptions may be based on their physicians' own general attitudes toward DTC advertising.

Physicians' attitudes toward DTC advertising are mixed. Many physicians believe DTC messages encourage consumers to seek medical attention. Some physicians also believe that DTC messages have "mainstreamed" some diseases such as depression, making health-seeking behaviors among consumers more likely. The fact that consumers have information about drugs can be a challenge to the physician's authority. This is a primary concern with DTC advertising.

An FDA-sponsored survey reported that the majority of physicians (59%) felt that DTC advertisements did not help the doctor–patient relationship (Aikin, Swasy, & Braman, 2004). Nearly three-quarters of physicians who spoke with patients about DTC advertised drugs said the patient had thoughtful questions that may have resulted from DTC advertising exposure. In a more recent survey (Friedman & Gould, 2007), three-quarters of physicians agreed strongly or somewhat strongly that DTC advertising does not provide adequate information on drug risks and benefits. In this same study, more than half of the physicians surveyed (53%) believed that DTC advertisements resulted in many patients requesting unnecessary prescriptions. Almost two-thirds believed these ads create a preference for a branded drug when a lower-cost generic drug would work the same way.

Thus, the presumed influence of DTC advertising has some effects on the unintended audiences' behaviors. If a physician believes that DTC advertising as a category, in general, has a detrimental influence on patients, the doctor is less likely to prescribe a DTC drug requested by the patient based on viewing of a DTC advertisement (Huh & Langteau, 2007). If the doctor believes that DTC advertising has a positive or neutral influence, the drug is more likely to be prescribed (Huh & Langteau, 2007).

Conclusion

Direct-to-consumer advertising messages are required by law to provide a complex amount of information to consumers, and older theories of "how advertising works" are limited in their applicability to understanding the phenomenon. Consumers who need health information online are doing so for an acute reason: they (or a loved one) are suffering from an illness and need to access and comprehend a vast amount of complex information to make informed decisions. Social Cognitive Theory suggests that behavior change is the result of observing behaviors in others; behaviors provided in DTC advertisements provides a way to model appropriate health-seeking behaviors. The consumer socialization perspective provides inclusion of multiple influences (or socialization agents) in consumer decision making about drugs in DTC advertisements. Finally, the Presumed Influence model posits that physicians' beliefs about DTC advertising influences their perspectives as socialization agents.

Note

1. For more information on DTC advertising requirements, see: www.fda.gov/Drugs/ResourcesForYou/Consumers/PrescriptionDrugAdvertising/UCM076768.htm; for legal details, see: www.fda.gov/AboutFDA/CentersOffices/CDER/ucm109905.htm, both retrieved September 15, 2010.

References

Aikin, K., Swasy, J., & Braman, A. (2004). Patient and physician attitudes and behaviors associated with DTC promotion of prescription drugs: Summary of FDA survey research results. Retrieved July 12, 2010, from www.fda.gov/Drugs/ScienceResearch/ResearchAreas/DrugMarketingAdvertisingandCommunicationsResearch/ucm151498.htm.

Backer, T. E., Rogers, E., & Sopory, P. (1992) *Designing health communicaition campaigns: What works?* Newbury Park, CA: Sage.

Bandura, A. (1988). Organizational application of Social Cognitive Theory. *Australian Journal of Management, 13* (2), 275–302.

Bandura, A. (1994). Social cognitive theory of mass communication. In J. Bryant & D. Zillman (Eds.), *Media effects: Advances in theory and research* (pp. 61–90). Hillsdale, NJ: Lawrence Erlbaum.

Bandura, A., Ross, D., & Ross, S. (1961). Transmission of aggression through imitation of aggressive models. *Journal of Abnormal and Social Psychology, 63*, 575–582.

Brim, O. G. (1966). Socialization through the life cycle. In O. G. Brim, Jr. & S. Wheeler

(Eds.), *Socialization after childhood: Two essays* (pp. 1–49). New York: John Wiley & Sons.

Cialis (2010). Cialis website. Retrieved July 12, 2010, from www.cialis.com.

Clark, E. (1988). *The want makers.* New York: Viking Penguin.

DTC Perspectives (2010). A world without DTC. Retrieved February 20, 2011, from www.dtcperspectives.com/article/A-World-Without-DTC+qm+/231.html.

Federal Food, Drug, and Cosmetic Act (FFDCA) (2004). Part 202: Prescription drug advertising (21 CFR 202.1(e) (7)(viii)).

Food and Drug Administration Center for Drug Evaluation and Research (CDER) (1999, August 9). Guidance for industry: Consumer-directed broadcast advertisements. *Federal Register, 64,* 43,197–43,198 (Docket 97D-0302).

Fox, S., & Jones, S. (2009). The social life of health information. Retrieved July 10, 2010, from www.pewinternet.org/Reports/2009/8-The-Social-Life-of-Health-Information.aspx.

Friedman, M., & Gould, J. (2007). Physicians' attitudes toward direct-to-consumer prescription drug marketing. *Journal of Medical Marketing, 7,* 33–44.

Gunther, A., & Storey, J. (2003). The influence of presumed influence. *Journal of Communication, 53,* 2199–2215.

Hoek, J., Gendall, P., & Calfee, J. (2004). Direct to consumer advertising of prescription medicines in the United States and New Zealand: An analysis of regulatory approaches and consumer responses. *International Journal of Advertising, 18* (2), 93–123.

Huh, J., & Langteau, R. (2007). Presumed influence of direct-to-consumer (DTC) prescription drug advertising on patients: The physician's perspective. *Journal of Advertising, 36* (3), 151–172.

Hurlock, E. B. (1980). *Developmental psychology: A life-span approach.* New York: McGraw-Hill.

Lavidge, R. J., & Steiner, G. A. (1961). A model of predictive measurements of advertising effectiveness. *Journal of Marketing, 25* (6), 59–62.

Lee, B., Salmon, C., & Paek, H. (2007). The effects of information sources on consumer reactions on direct-to-consumer (ditch) prescription drug advertising: A consumer socialization approach. *Journal of Advertising, 36,* 107–119.

Liebenau, J. (1990). The rise of the British pharmaceutical industry. *British Medical Journal, 301,* 724–728.

Lueg, J., & Finney, R. Z. (2007). Interpersonal communication in the consumer socialization process: Scale development and validation. *Journal of Marketing Theory and Practice, 15* (1), 25–39.

McLeod, J., & O'Keefe, G., Jr. (1972). The socialization perspective and communication behavior. In G. Kline & P. Tichenor (Eds.) *Current perspectives in mass communication research* (pp. 121–168). Beverly Hills, CA: Sage.

Maibach, E., & Cotton, D. (1995). Motivating people to behavior change: A staged social cognitive approach to message design. In E. Maibach & R. Parrott (Eds.), *Designing health messages: Approaches from communication theory and public health practices.* Thousand Oaks, CA: Sage.

Miller, K. (2005). *Communication theories: Perspectives, processes, and contexts* (2nd ed.). New York: McGraw-Hill.

Moschis, G. (1987). *Consumer socialization: A life-cycle perspective*. Lexington, MA: D.C. Heath.

Moschis, G., & Churchill, G. (1978). Consumer socialization: A theoretical and empirical analysis. *Journal of Marketing Research, 15* (4), 599–609.

Nayyar, S. (1992, June 29). Green light for drug ads. *Adweek*, 9.

Roth, M. (1996). Patterns in direct-to-consumer prescription drug print advertising and their public policy implications. *Journal of Public Policy and Marketing, 15* (1), 63–75.

Tsfati, Y., & Cohen, J. (2005). The influence of presumed media influence on democratic legitimacy: The case of Gaza settlers. *Communication Research, 32* (6), 794–821.

Ward, S. (1974). Consumer socialization. *Journal of Consumer Research, 1*, 1–16.

Weilbacher, W. (2001). Point of view: Does advertising cause a "hierarchy of effects?" *Journal of Advertising Research, 41* (6), 19–26.

Yan, J. (2008). DTC advertising going global, but not without controversy. *Psychiatric News, 43* (10), 1.

Young, H., & Cline, R. (2005). Textual cues in direct-to-consumer prescription drug advertising: Motivators to communicate with physicians. *Journal of Applied Communications Research, 33* (4), 348–369.

Additional Readings

Avorn, J. (2005). *Powerful medicines: The benefits, risks and costs of prescription drugs*. New York: Alfred A. Knopf.

Bandura, A. (1976). *Social learning theory*. Upper Saddle River, NJ: Prentice Hall.

Bandura, A. (1985). *Social foundations of thought and action: A social cognitive theory*. Upper Saddle River, NJ: Prentice Hall.

Fosu, I. (2009). *Effect of risk disclosures on prescription drug advertising*. Saarbrucken, Germany: VDM Verlag.

Sheehan, K. B. (2004). *Controversies in contemporary advertising*. Thousand Oaks, CA: Sage.

Chapter 19

Theory Building for Online Health Product Advertising

Jisu Huh and Wonsun Shin

Today, the Internet is a mainstream tool for consumer information search. For many consumers, the Internet is the first place to turn to when they need information about news, products, shopping, and health. Health information search is one of the most popular online activities. According to a recent report, 76% of U.S. adults go online to search for health information (Harris Interactive, 2010).

The Internet is an optimal channel for disseminating health-related information because it provides high accessibility, privacy, immediacy, and a wide range of information in unlimited space (Bischoff & Kelley, 1999). Consumers prefer the anonymity offered by the Internet especially for seeking information about certain drugs or discussing embarrassing illnesses with others (Spain, Siegel, & Ramsey, 2001). With a growing number of consumers going online for health information, advertisers marketing healthcare products are increasing investments in online advertising including websites, banners, email advertising, and advergames (Miley & Thomaselli, 2009) (see Figures 19.1 and 19.2).

Despite the growing popularity and importance of online advertising for healthcare products, little is known about the impact and role of healthcare product advertising in consumers' healthcare decision making. To advance our knowledge of online advertising for healthcare products and to help develop a theoretical model for examining effects of such advertising, this chapter discusses unique characteristics of online healthcare product advertising, proposes the trust construct as a key element in theory-building, and presents an empirical study testing the role of trust in consumers' interactions with and responses to pharmaceutical advertising websites.

Applying the definition of online interactive advertising suggested by Leckenby and Li (2000), we define online healthcare product advertising as "paid and unpaid presentation and promotion of healthcare products by an identified sponsor through online media involving mutual action between consumers and producers." Considering the interactive nature of online advertising, it is imperative for research examining the online health-advertising phenomenon to shift

Figure 19.1 Example of Online Health Care Product Advertising Showing "Give Your Legs a Rest" Advergame to promote Mirapex (Boehringer Ingelheim Pharmaceuticals), a drug treating RLS (Restless Legs Syndrome).

from the traditional paradigm focusing on *recipients* and *message effects on them* to a new paradigm focusing on *users* and their *use of and interaction with messages* (Lievrouw & Livingstone, 2006). Thus, the primary focus of this chapter is on how consumers perceive and use healthcare product advertising as one of many types of information sources online, rather than only on influence of advertising on consumers' brand awareness, attitude, and behaviors. Among the various advertising components outlined in Figure 1.1 of Chapter 1, this chapter covers the role of advertising in the public health and policy domains with particular focus on non-traditional forms of advertising for healthcare products.

Figure 19.2 Example of Online Health Care Product Advertising Showing DTC Drug Brand Website for Clarinex.

Online Healthcare Product Advertising and Research

Online advertising for healthcare products is a relatively recent phenomenon. However, the amount of money spent and the proportion of online advertising spending out of the total advertising expenditure have shown fast growth. Pharmaceutical companies in the U.S. spent $137 million on Internet advertising in 2008, which is a 36% increase from the previous year, while at the same time total advertising spending in the pharmaceutical industry declined 4.3% (Miley & Thomaselli, 2009). Estimated total online advertising spending by U.S. pharmaceutical and healthcare industries is expected to grow to $1.52 billion in 2014 (eMarketer, 2010).

Studies about online pharmaceutical advertising and consumers' online health information seeking has multiplied with the advent of the Internet as the primary consumer information source for health-related issues and products. The majority of the existing studies about online healthcare product advertising are focused on DTC (direct-to-consumer) prescription drug websites, analyzing the content and information quality of DTC websites (e.g., Huh & Cude, 2004; Macias & Lewis, 2003; Sheehan, 2007). These studies provide important descriptive information about online healthcare product advertising practices. However, we confine our literature review to consumer research—studies investigating consumer online health information search and responses to advertising and non-advertising sources of health information online.

The literature reveals that consumers' responses to health information online are different from those in the traditional media context. Research on credibility and usefulness of the Internet as a health information source and as a healthcare product-advertising channel indicates that consumers view the Internet as a more credible source of information for prescription drugs than traditional media (Choi & Lee, 2007). However, when it comes to advertising, consumers do not view online advertising as a particularly credible or trustworthy source of health information (Huh, DeLorme, & Reid, 2005). Nevertheless, consumers frequently use both advertising and non-advertising online sources for information search (DeLorme, Huh, & Reid, 2010).

When consumers are exposed to and process online health information— including advertisements—their interactions with and responses to such information are influenced by various consumer characteristics. Previous studies have identified demographic characteristics, health status, medical conditions, and Internet use experience as significant factors influencing the way consumers search and process health information online (Choi & Lee, 2007; DeLorme et al., 2010; Goldner, 2006).

For example, consumers with medical conditions are more likely than healthy individuals to search for more diverse types of health information online (Goldner, 2006). Also, consumers with low education and high Internet skills are more likely to rate the Internet as a credible information source for prescription drugs (Choi & Lee, 2007). DeLorme et al. (2010) reported ethnic group differences—Anglo consumers perceived non-advertising health-related websites more useful than did Hispanics; for perceived usefulness of online advertising sources, the opposite was true. A recent study by the same authors found that younger consumers were more likely than older consumers to perceive both advertising and non-advertising online sources as useful in prescription drug information search (DeLorme, Huh, & Reid, 2011).

Some studies demonstrate that consumers' perceptual responses to online health advertising are linked to behavioral outcomes. Consumers who consider the Internet and online advertising as credible and trustworthy are more likely to engage in communication with doctors or other people about advertised drugs (Choi & Lee, 2007; Huh et al., 2005). Also, consumers who perceive an online health campaign message to be involving and credible were more likely to feel confident and prepared to do something to maintain and improve health in the future (Lefebvre, Tada, Hilfiker, & Baur, 2010).

Although existing studies make significant contributions to the growing body of literature on online healthcare product advertising, most of them are exploratory and descriptive rather than theoretical. For future theory-building efforts, it is critical to consider the unique characteristics of online healthcare product advertising and how this form of communication is different from advertising or non-advertising health information online. Online healthcare product advertising can contain a wealth of information, but the purpose of such communication is to promote and sell products. This makes online healthcare product advertising unique and different from non-advertising information. Due to the commercial intent and consumers' privacy concerns and skepticism toward advertising, online advertising for healthcare products is perceived and used by consumers differently from non-advertising health information (DeLorme et al., in press; Huh et al., 2005).

Compared to advertising for other products, healthcare product advertising tends to offer more information utility and is considered a legitimate source of information (DeLorme, Huh, & Reid, 2009). Healthcare products tend to be high-involvement products that require extensive information search in the purchase decision-making process (Kim & King, 2009). Therefore, consumers' reliance on and expectation of information in online ads for healthcare products are likely to be higher than in the case of other products. However, if information provided by online ads is not trusted or perceived as trustworthy, it would be unlikely that consumers would use the information presented in the online ads.

With the preceding information as a backdrop, we argue that the trust construct is a key element in developing theory about the effects and role of online healthcare product advertising in consumers' health information search.

Trust: Definitions and Sub-Dimensions

Trust has been conceptualized in many ways across different disciplines. For example, Mayer, Davis, and Schoorman (1995, p. 172) defined trust as

> the willingness of a party to be vulnerable to the actions of another party based on the expectation that the other will perform a particular action important to the trustor, irrespective of the ability to monitor or control that other party.

Nicholson, Compeau, and Sethi (2001) described trust as confidence in the other party's reliability and integrity, which is developed over the course of repeated, successful interactions. Specifically focusing on trust in the e-commerce context, Lee and Turban (2001) defined it as "the willingness of a consumer to be vulnerable to the actions of an Internet merchant based on the expectation that the Internet merchant will behave in certain agreeable ways" (p. 79).

However defined, trust is considered one of the most important factors facilitating sustainable relationships between individuals, between organizations, and between individuals and organizations. In sociology, trust is viewed as important social capital facilitating sustainable cooperation among individuals within a society (Fukuyama, 1995). In the business management literature, trust is considered a critical factor that helps maintain relationships among members of an organization (Mayer et al., 1995). Also, trust facilitates commercial transactions by reducing a buyer's perceived risks in dealing with an unfamiliar seller (Doney & Canon, 1997).

Considering the discrepancies and commonalities in the conceptualization of trust in the literature, McKnight and Chervany (2001–2002) developed the model of e-commerce customer relationships trust constructs. This interdisciplinary model proposes three distinct but interrelated constructs of trust: interpersonal, institutional, and dispositional trust. Interpersonal trust reflects beliefs in the trustworthiness of a particular entity, say, a website, brand, or advertiser. Institutional trust refers to trust in a particular situation, environment, or system such as the Internet or the e-commerce system. Finally, dispositional trust is a deep-seated personality trait of an individual that applies in a variety of settings. An individual forms this disposition through learning and experiences, and extends trust when faced with unfamiliar objects or situations (McKnight & Chervany, 2001–2002).

This model explains how different trust constructs interplay and influence online consumer behaviors. Dispositional trust and institutional trust are considered key antecedents of interpersonal trust toward a particular website. Following the logic of the Theory of Reasoned Action (Fishbein & Azjen, 1975), this model suggests that interpersonal trust in a website influences trusting intention, which results in trust-related behaviors. Trust-related behaviors include interacting with and responding to online ads, disclosing personal information to a website, and buying products (McKnight & Chervany, 2001–2002).

Antecedents and Consequences of Website Trust

A number of studies in e-commerce have examined various antecedents and consequences of website trust. Some applied the aforementioned trust model while others were more descriptive and exploratory. The antecedents identified in the previous studies can be grouped into consumer factors and website factors. Consumer factors include dispositional trust (Lee & Turban, 2001; McKnight, Choudhury, & Kacmar, 2002a, 2002b), Internet experience and usage (Bart, Shankar, Sultan, & Urban, 2005), privacy and security concerns (Metzger, 2006), and familiarity or past experience with a website (Bart et al., 2005). Website characteristics influencing consumer trust include website or company reputation (Kim, Xu, & Koh, 2004; Yoon, 2002), privacy/security, structural assurance (Bart et al., 2005; Kim et al., 2004; Schlosser, White, & Lloyd, 2006), and ease of use (Corritore, Kracher, & Wiedenbeck, 2003). Although disagreement about the conceptual definitions and operationalization of antecedents makes it difficult to directly compare results across studies, some consumer characteristics such as dispositional trust and perceived risks, seem to emerge as consistently significant predictors of website trust (McKnight et al., 2002a, 2002b; Metzger, 2006).

The e-commerce literature provides ample evidence that trust is integral to the buyer–seller relationship in the online environment. Research on the effects of website trust on consumer behavior suggests a crucial role of trust in encouraging consumers to engage in e-commerce (Lee & Turban, 2001; Pavlou, 2003) and in influencing consumer attitude and purchase intention (Bart et al., 2005; Schlosser et al., 2006). These studies demonstrate that website trust influences consumer purchase intention, especially for infrequent, high-involvement, and high-risk purchases (Bart et al., 2005; Schlosser et al., 2006).

Applicability of the Trust Construct to Online Advertising

To date, only a few existing studies have shed empirical light on the potentially important role of trust in online interactive communication (Huh & Cho, 2007; Metzger, 2006; Pavlou & Stewart, 2000). Compared to the substantial amount of scholarly research on e-commerce, studies on trust and its effects on communication behaviors in the online advertising context are scarce. Trust plays an important role in facilitating e-commerce transactions and also in influencing consumers' interactions with online ads (e.g., clicking on ads, revealing and sharing personal or personally identifiable information in online advertising sites, entering personal health information in exchange for detailed product information, free samples or coupons, and participating in online chatting or instant Q&A offered by online advertising sites), especially in the case of advertising of high-involvement and high-risk products such as pharmaceuticals. Studies on trust and online advertising in mass communication and advertising literatures—which extensively examine a related construct, i.e., credibility—are also scarce despite the potentially important role of trust in the interactive communication process. Compared to credibility, however, trust as a construct has more relational and interactive characteristics. Distinguishing ad trust from ad credibility, Soh, Reid, and King (2009) defined ad trust as "confidence that advertising is a reliable source of product/service information and willingness to act on the basis of information conveyed by advertising" (p. 86). Considering the inherent interactive nature of online advertising, the trust construct is more suitable for explaining why and to what extent consumers actively engage in the two-way interactive communication process initiated by online advertising.

Huh and Cho (2007) examined the influence of website trust on consumers' personal information disclosure to a commercial website. The results revealed a significant and direct relationship between website trust and consumers' personal information disclosure. Pavlou and Stewart (2000), taking a slightly different approach, proposed trust as one of the key measures of interactive advertising effect and effectiveness. Taken together, these studies suggest that the trust construct is applicable to research on interactive advertising as an important factor that influences consumer interactions with and responses to the ads.

An Empirical Test of the Role of Trust in Online Healthcare Product Advertising

To empirically test the role of trust in online healthcare product advertising and to contribute to theory building, we conducted a study on trust in DTC prescription drug websites and its influence on consumer responses. Specifically, our study is designed to determine antecedents of consumer trust in DTC websites and to investigate the role of website trust in consumers' attitudinal and behavioral responses.

We conducted an online survey with a nationally representative sample of U.S. adults who had searched the Internet for product/service-related information in the past 6 months. The sample was purchased from an online survey solutions provider, which offers a national random sample. From the survey panel, a sample of 325 respondents who met the selection criteria of the study was randomly drawn. Among them, 219 respondents completed the questionnaires, resulting in a completion rate of 67.4%.

The survey procedure involved the following steps: (1) filling out a Web-based questionnaire about general online product information search and health information search behaviors; (2) visiting a given DTC website and browsing for 5+ minutes or until the respondent had a good feel for the site; (3) coming back to the survey site to answer questions regarding trust, attitude, and behavioral intentions toward the visited DTC website.

The questionnaire included measurements for *dispositional trust, trust in DTC website, frequency of health information search, attitude toward DTC website, behavioral intention, perceived importance of prescription drug information, perceived health*, and demographics. *Dispositional trust* and *trust in DTC website* were both measured by nine seven-point scales from McKnight et al. (2002b). *Attitude toward DTC website* was measured by five seven-point semantic differential scales.

Behavioral intention was measured by seven-point Likert scales using the following statements: (1) I will visit this site again to get information I need for myself or someone I know; (2) I would be willing to depend on the information or advice provided by the site; (3) I will talk to my doctor about the information I found from this website; (4) I will use the information from this website as I make decisions about how to take care of myself or loved ones; and (5) I would recommend this site to a friend or family member. A seven-point scale measured items for *frequency of health information search*, *perceived importance of prescription drug information*, and *perceived health*.

Key Findings

A summated *trust in DTC website* score was computed by averaging the nine scores ($\alpha = 0.95$). The mean value of the summated website trust score was 4.40 (on a seven-point scale), which suggests that overall consumer trust in DTC websites tend to be neutral—not trusted but not distrusted either.

Dispositional Trust and Trust in DTC Websites

Correlations were conducted to test the relationship between *dispositional trust* and *trust in DTC website*. For this analysis, the summed *dispositional trust* score was created by averaging the nine measurement items ($\alpha = 0.88$). A weak but significant correlation was found ($r = 0.25$, $p = 0.00$), suggesting that consumers with higher levels of disposition to trust are more likely to trust DTC websites.

A hierarchical regression further tested the relationship between *dispositional trust* and *trust in DTC website* with demographic and health-related characteristics controlled. The predictor variables were entered in three blocks in a hierarchical manner: the first block included demographics; next, *frequency of health information search*, *perceived importance of prescription drug information*, and *perceived health* were entered; and the third block included *dispositional trust*.

As presented in Table 19.1, *dispositional trust* was found to be a significant and positive predictor of trust in DTC websites, and the relationship was significant after controlling for demographic and health-related variables, significantly increasing the predictive power of the regression equation. Of the consumer health-related and demographic characteristics examined, only *age* was found to be significantly related to *trust in DTC website*.

Relationship Between Trust and Attitude Toward DTC Website

A summed score for *attitude toward DTC website* was computed by averaging the five measurement items ($\alpha = 0.90$). A hierarchical regression analysis was

Table 19.1 Hierarchical regression for predicting trust in DTC website

Predictors	Beta
Model 1	
Age	0.19*
$df = 1$, $MS = 6.97$, $F = 6.52$, $p = 0.01$, $R^2 = 0.04$	
Model 2	
Age	0.17*
Dispositional trust	0.15*
$df = 2$, $MS = 5.58$, $F = 5.31$, $p = 0.00$, $R^2 = 0.06*$	

Notes
* $p < 0.05$.
* for R^2 indicates significance of R^2 increments.

conducted with *attitude toward DTC website* as the dependent variable. The predictor variables were entered in four blocks: the first block included demographics; next, *frequency of health information search*, *perceived importance of prescription drug information*, and *perceived health* were entered; the third block included *dispositional trust*; and the last block entered *trust in DTC website*.

As presented in Table 19.2, *trust in DTC website* emerged as a significant and positive predictor of *attitude toward DTC website*, when *dispositional trust* and demographic and health-related variables were controlled. *Dispositional trust* was not significantly associated with *attitude toward DTC website* and none of the health-related and demographic variables emerged as significant predictors.

Table 19.2 Hierarchical regression for predicting attitude toward DTC website

Predictors	Beta
Model 1	
Age	0.2 **
$df = 1$, $MS = 10.30$, $F = 7.95$, $p = 0.01$, $R^2 = 0.05$	
Model 2	
Age	0.20**
Dispositional trust	0.09
$df = 2$, $MS = 5.99$, $F = 4.63$, $p = 0.01$, $R^2 = 0.05$	
Model 3	
Age	0.12
Dispositional trust	0.01
Trust in DTC website	0.47**
$df = 3$, $MS = 19.32$, $F = 18.95$, $p = 0.00$, $R^2 = 0.26**$	

Notes
* $p < 0.05$, ** $p < 0.01$.
*, ** for R^2 indicates significance of R^2 increments.

Relationship Between Trust and Behavioral Intention

We expected that consumers with higher levels of *trust in DTC website* would be more likely to visit/revisit the site and use the information obtained there when asking questions to a doctor and making healthcare decisions. To test this relationship, a hierarchical regression analysis was conducted with a summed behavioral intention score ($\alpha = 0.91$) as the dependent variable. The predictor variables were entered in five blocks: the first block included demographics; next, *frequency of health information search*, *perceived importance of prescription drug information*, and *perceived health* were entered; the third block included *dispositional trust*; the fourth block entered *trust in DTC website*; and the last block entered *attitude toward DTC website*.

As presented in Table 19.3, when *dispositional trust*, demographic, and health-related variables were controlled, both *attitude toward DTC website* and *trust in DTC website* were significantly and positively associated with consumers' intention to revisit the DTC website and use the obtained information for their discussions with a doctor and for healthcare decision making. Based on the Beta weights of the two significant predictors and the significant amount of R^2 increase between Models 3 and 4, however, it can be inferred that *trust in DTC website* is

Table 19.3 Hierarchical regression for predicting behavioral intention

Predictors	Beta
Model 1	
Age	0.18*
$df = 1$, $MS = 11.83$, $F = 5.63$, $p = 0.02$, $R^2 = 0.03$	
Model 2	
Age	0.16*
Dispositional trust	0.15
$df = 2$, $MS = 9.54$, $F = 4.61$, $p = 0.01$, $R^2 = 0.05$	
Model 3	
Age	0.06
Dispositional trust	0.05
Trust in DTC website	0.60*
$df = 3$, $MS = 46.08$, $F = 34.21$, $p = 0.00$, $R^2 = 0.39$**	
Model 4	
Age	0.02
Dispositional trust	0.04
Trust in DTC website	0.45**
Attitude toward DTC website	0.33**
$df = 4$, $MS = 41.55$, $F = 35.16$, $p = 0.00$, $R^2 = 0.47$**	

Notes
* $p < 0.05$, ** $p < 0.01$.
*, ** for R^2 indicates significance of R^2 increments.

a stronger predictor than *attitude toward DTC website*. These results indicate that *trust in a DTC website* is a significant and direct predictor of consumers' intention to revisit the DTC website and to use the information obtained from the website for healthcare decision making.

Conclusion

Trust is a vital relationship factor that predicts and explains various human interactions including commercial transactions and interactive communication. In this chapter, we argued—and illustrated with the outlined study results— that trust construct is a key element of a theoretical framework for examining online healthcare product advertising effects. As stated earlier, and as supported by empirical evidence, trust has great potential for predicting and explaining consumer interactions with and responses to online advertising, especially when consumer involvement and perceived risks are high.

The results from our study examining consumer trust in DTC drug websites offer empirical support for the applicability of the trust construct to online healthcare product advertising. A significant relationship was found between consumers' trust in a DTC website and their intention to revisit the website and to use the information obtained when talking to a doctor and making healthcare decisions. Consumers' trust in a DTC website is also positively related to their attitude toward the DTC website.

The findings are in line with previous research showing that website trust is one of the most important predictors of consumer behavior in the context of e-commerce. However, while most existing studies address the role of trust in a commercial transaction context, our findings suggest that trust also influences consumer behavior in communicative situations such as paying attention to, processing, and responding to online advertising DTC websites.

Although our study is exploratory and has methodological limitations, it provides valuable insight into the role of trust in interactive advertising and online advertising of healthcare products in particular. The Internet has grown as one of the primary sources for consumer health information search, and many advertising websites for healthcare products require consumers to disclose personal information in exchange for useful product information, price discount, or free trial (Sheehan, 2005). When consumers encounter and interact with such websites, trust is an important factor that can prompt consumers to actively process information presented in the advertising websites and use the information for their conversations with a doctor and healthcare decision making.

Our study also provides useful practical implications for healthcare product advertisers. With an increasing number of consumers engaged in user-generated content creation and information exchanges online, advertisers have unprecedented opportunities to learn about individual consumers to a great extent and directly communicate with them with customized messages, but at the same time, face challenges stemming from heightened consumer concerns and fears about privacy and security problems and declining trust (Horrigan, 2008). Our study suggests that trust in a website should be fostered at the very early stage of consumers' exposure and experience with the site, in order to engage consumers in two-way communication and to increase the likelihood and frequency of revisits. Particularly for healthcare product advertisers, this study suggests that establishing and maintaining consumer trust is critical for their online ads to stay relevant to consumers and to fulfill the expectations set by the public and the regulatory agency, and to remain an effective communication tool.

The trust construct deserves more attention of advertising researchers and practitioners, and more research is warranted to further examine the relationship between trust and consumer responses to various forms of online health advertising. There is still much to be learned about consumers' online health information search and the role of online healthcare product advertising as a source of health information. To advance knowledge on the role and effects of online healthcare product advertising, we suggest future research investigates: (1) differences in consumers' trust and use of advertising and non-advertising health information sources on the Internet; (2) consumer characteristics influencing the level of trust in online healthcare product advertising; and (3) website features and advertising message characteristics that are likely to contribute to formation of trust in an unfamiliar advertising website. Also, in addition to the attitude and purchase intention measures of advertising effects, researchers are encouraged to examine the influence of consumer trust in online healthcare product ads on different types of interactive communication behaviors such as disclosing personal information in advertising websites, engaging in online chatting and instant Q&A offered by online advertising sites, participating in advertiser-sponsored online communities, and revealing personal health information to receive product or treatment recommendations.

References

Bart, Y., Shankar, V., Sultan, F., & Urban, G. (2005). Are the drivers and role of online trust the same for all websites and consumers? A large-scale exploratory empirical study. *Journal of Marketing, 69* (4), 133–152.

Bischoff, W. R., & Kelley, S. J. (1999). 21st century house call: The Internet and the World Wide Web. *Holistic Nursing Practice, 13* (4), 42–50.

Choi, S. M., & Lee, W. (2007). Understanding the impact of direct-to-consumer (DTC) pharmaceutical advertising on parent-physician interactions. *Journal of Advertising, 36* (3), 137–149.

Corritore, C. L., Kracher, B., & Wiedenbeck, S. (2003). On-line trust: Concepts, evolving themes, a model. *International Journal of Human–Computer Studies, 58* (6), 737–758.

DeLorme, D. E., Huh, J., & Reid, L. N. (2009). DTC advertising skepticism and the use and perceived usefulness of prescription drug information sources. *Health Marketing Quarterly, 26*, 293–314.

DeLorme, D. E., Huh, J., & Reid, L. N. (2010). Evaluation, use, and usefulness of prescription drug information sources among Anglo and Hispanic Americans. *Journal of Health Communication, 15* (1), 18–38.

DeLorme, D. E., Huh, J., & Reid, L. N. (2011). Source selection in prescription drug information seeking and influencing factors: Applying the comprehensive model of information seeking (CMIS) in an American context. *Journal of Health Communication, 16* (7), 766–787.

Doney, P. M., & Cannon, J. P. (1997). An examination of the nature of trust in buyer–seller relationships. *Journal of Marketing, 61* (2), 35–51.

eMarketer (2010). DTC pharmaceutical marketing online: A slow shift to digital. Retrieved August 27, 2010, from www.emarketer.com/Reports/All/Emarketer_2000705.aspx.

Fishbein, M., & Ajzen, I. (1975). *Belief, attitude, intention and behavior: An introduction to theory and research.* Reading, MA: Addison-Wesley.

Fukuyama, F. (1995). *Trust: The social virtues and the creation of prosperity.* New York: Free Press.

Goldner, M. (2006). How health status impacts the types of information consumers seek online. *Information, Communication, and Society, 9* (6), 693–713.

Harris Interactive (2010). "Cyberchondriacs" on the rise? *Harris Poll, 95*, 1–5.

Horrigan, J. B. (2008, February 13). *Online Shopping.* Washington, D.C.: Pew Internet and American Life Project.

Huh, J., & Cho, S. (2007, August). The role of trust in interactive communication: Antecedents and consequences of website trust. Paper presented at the 2007 AEJMC (Association for Education in Journalism and Mass Communication) Conference, Washington, D.C.

Huh, J., & Cude, B. J. (2004). Is the information "fair and balanced" in direct-to-consumer prescription drug websites? *Journal of Health Communication, 9* (6), 529–540.

Huh, J., DeLorme, D. E., & Reid, L. N. (2005). Factors affecting trust in online prescription drug information and impact of trust on behavior following exposure to DTC advertising. *Journal of Health Communication, 10* (8), 711–731.

Kim, W. J., & King, K. W. (2009). Product category effects on external search for prescription and nonprescription drugs. *Journal of Advertising, 38* (1), 5–19.

Kim, H., Xu, Y., & Koh, J. (2004). A comparison of online trust building factors between potential customers and repeat customers. *Journal of the Association for Information Systems, 5* (10), 392–420.

Leckenby, J. D., & Li, H. (2000). From the editors: Why we need the Journal of Interactive Advertising. *Journal of Interactive Advertising, 1* (1). Retrieved August 20, 2010, from http://jiad.org/article1.

Lefebvre, R. C., Tada, Y., Hilfiker, S. W., & Baur, C. (2010). The assessment of user engagement with eHealth content: The eHealth engagement scale. *Journal of Computer-Mediated Communications, 15*, 666–681.

Lee, M. K. O., & Turban, E. (2001). A trust model for consumer Internet shopping. *International Journal of Electronic Commerce, 6* (1), 75–91.

Lievrouw, L. A., & Livingstone, S. (2006). Introduction. In L. A. Lievrouw & S. Livingstone (Eds.), *The handbook of new media, updated student edition* (pp. 1–32). London: Sage.

Macias, W., & Lewis, L. S. (2003). A content analysis of direct-to-consumer (DTC) prescription drug websites. *Journal of Advertising, 32* (4), 43–56.

McKnight, D. H., & Chervany, N. L. (1998). Initial trust formation in new organizational relationships. *Academy of Management Review, 23* (3), 473–490.

McKnight, D. H., & Chervany, N. L. (2001–2002). What trust means in e-commerce customer relationships: An interdisciplinary conceptual typology. *International Journal of Electronic Commerce, 6* (2), 33–59.

McKnight, D. H., Choudhury, V., & Kacmar, C. (2002a). The impact of initial consumer trust on intentions to transact with a website: A trust building model. *Journal of Strategic Information Systems, 11* (3–4), 297–323.

McKnight, D. H., Choudhury, V., & Kacmar, C. (2002b). Developing and validating trust measures for e-commerce: An integrative typology. *Information Systems Research, 13* (3), 334–359.

Mayer, R. C., Davis, J. H., & Schoorman, F. D. (1995). An integrative model of organizational trust. *Academy of Management Review, 2*, 709–734.

Metzger, M. J. (2006). Effects of site, vendor, and consumer characteristics on website trust and disclosure. *Communication Research, 33* (3), 155–179.

Miley, M., & Thomaselli, R. (2009). Big pharma finally taking big steps to reach patients with digital media. *Advertising Age, 80* (17), 8f.

Nicholson, C., Compeau, L., & Sethi, R. (2001). The role of interpersonal liking in building trust in long term channel relationships. *Journal of the Academy of Marketing Science, 29* (1), 3–15.

Pavlou, P. A. (2003). Consumer acceptance of electronic commerce: Integrating trust and risk with the technology acceptance model. *International Journal of Electronic Commerce, 7* (3), 101–134.

Pavlou, P. A., & Stewart, D. W. (2000). Measuring the effects and effectiveness of interactive advertising: A research agenda. *Journal of Interactive Advertising, 1*. Retrieved August 20, 2010, from http://jiad.org/article6.

Schlosser, A. E., White, T. B., & Lloyd, S. M. (2006). Converting website visitors into buyers: How website investment increases consumer trusting beliefs and online purchase intentions. *Journal of Marketing, 70* (2), 133–148.

Sheehan, K. (2005). In poor health: An assessment of privacy policies at direct-to-consumer websites. *Journal of Public Policy and Marketing, 24* (2), 273–283.

Sheehan, K. (2007). Direct-to-consumer (DTC) branded drug websites. *Journal of Advertising, 36* (3), 123–135.

Soh, H., Reid, L. N., & King, K. W. (2009). Measuring trust in advertising: Development and validation of the ADTRUST scale. *Journal of Advertising, 38* (2), 83–103.

Spain, J. W., Siegel, C. F., & Ramsey, R. P. (2001). Selling drugs online: Distribution-related legal/regulatory issues. *International Marketing Review, 18* (4), 432–449.

Yoon, S. (2002). The antecedents and consequences of trust in online purchase decisions. *Journal of Interactive Marketing, 166* (2), 47–63.

Additional Readings

Bart, I. Y., Shankar, V., Sultan, F., & Urban, G. (2005). Are the drivers and role of online trust the same for all websites and consumers? A large scale exploratory empirical study. *Journal of Marketing, 69* (4), 133–152.

DeLorme, D. E., Huh, J., Reid, L. N., & An, S. (2011). Advertising in health communication: Promoting pharmaceuticals and dietary supplements to U.S. consumers. In T. L. Thompson, R. Parrott, & J. Nussbaum (Eds.), *The Routledge handbook of health communication* (2nd ed., pp. 268–290). New York: Routledge.

Huh, J., DeLorme, D. E., & Reid, L. N. (2005). Factors affecting trust in online prescription drug information and impact of trust on behavior following exposure to DTC advertising. *Journal of Health Communication, 10* (8), 711–731.

McKnight, D. H., & Chervany, N. L. (2001–2002). What trust means in e-commerce customer relationships: An interdisciplinary conceptual typology. *International Journal of Electronic Commerce, 6* (2), 33–59.

Soh, H., Reid, L. N., & King, K. W. (2009). Measuring trust in advertising: Development and validation of the ADTRUST scale. *Journal of Advertising, 38* (2), 83–103.

Chapter 20

Political Advertising

Marjolein Moorman and Peter Neijens

Introduction

Political advertising allows parties and candidates to present themselves in a direct, and unfiltered way to the electorate, without intervention from critical journalists or competing politicians (Kaid & Holtz-Bacha, 1995; Kaid, 2008). This form of political communication—represented as advertising "contexts" in Figure 1.1 of Chapter 1—has witnessed an enormous rise in interest and spending from parties and politicians during the past decade. Several societal and political factors, such as declining partisanship, weakening party ties, an increasingly volatile and fragmented electorate, weakening party ideology, single-issue politics, and populism, have contributed to this rise (Kaid & Holtz-Bacha, 2006). In recent years, political advertising has developed as one of the most dominant sources of political communication, especially in the USA. The reason that political advertising has principally rooted in the USA can be found in the U.S. Constitution. Unlike many other Western democratic countries, such as France, Germany, and the UK, the number of regulations and restrictions in the USA on political advertising is limited, since political advertising is protected as a form of free speech (Kaid, 2008). Therefore, the amount of airtime politicians, parties, and pressure groups can buy is almost boundless. Although all kinds of media are used for political advertising messages, from brochures to social media, TV is certainly the most popular media form in the USA today. The first politician to use television as a medium for political campaigning was Dwight D. Eisenhower is his 1952 presidential campaign. Eisenhower's campaign was remarkable not only because of the televised spots, but also because this campaign is generally seen as the first campaign in which methods from commercial marketing were adopted (Maarek, 2008). Kotler and Kotler (1999), however, note that political campaigning always has had a marketing orientation in the sense that candidates, to be successful, have to recognize the nature of the exchange process when they ask voters for their votes.

Political advertising research has a long-standing history (e.g., Gosnell, 1927), but with the recent growth in advertising expenditures, academic interest has revitalized. Within this stream of research, most studies have focused on television, and more specifically on negative television campaigns. In this chapter we will discuss the effects of political television advertising in general, and the effects of negative campaigns in particular. These results are mainly based on American studies, since most of the expansion in advertising expenditures has taken place in the USA, and consequently most of the research was done there. To put these results in an international perspective, first a comparison is made between various systemic variables in the USA, compared to other Western countries. Differences in the political system, the electoral system, and the media system, have caused an explosion of political television advertising in the USA, but stagnancy in other countries (Holtz-Bacha & Kaid, 2006).

Political Spots in the USA Compared to Other Countries

Holtz-Bacha and Kaid (2006, p. 4) define political advertising as "any controlled message communicated through any channel designed to promote the political interest of individuals, parties, groups, government, or other organizations." Because political advertising is controlled, instead of being produced and selected along critical journalistic criteria, it is possible to enhance the candidates' or parties' presence in the media without interference from political opponents and critical journalists. In the USA, political TV advertising has become the dominant form of communication between politicians and the public, on which half of campaign budgets is spent (Holtz-Bacha & Kaid, 2006). Franz and Ridout (2010) compared the 2004 and 2008 presidential campaigns, and showed that the air war had intensified significantly, both in volume and geographic scope. For Kerry and Bush, 461,086 ads were aired in total in 146 markets in the 2 months prior to Election Day in 2004. In the 2 months prior to Election Day in 2008, 542,199 ads were aired for Obama and McCain in 189 markets. Recently the media agency Borrell Associates Inc. (2010) has forecasted an ad spend of $4.2 billion in 2010. The lion's share of this amount will be commanded by TV broadcasters. Furthermore, Borrell Associates Inc. (2010) reveal an accelerating trend, going forward since 1996, with U.S. political ad spending doubling each 2 years.

In many other Western countries, however, political advertising, and the role of TV in particular, is much less dominant, due to regulations that restrict content, amount, and time periods during which political TV advertisements can be aired. To compensate for these limitations, nearly all countries provide free political broadcasting time on public channels.

Almost all democratic countries these days have a dual broadcasting system, with public television channels and commercial television channels. Some of these countries, such as the United Kingdom, France, Spain, Portugal, Israel, and Brazil, do not allow candidates or parties to purchase broadcasting time. Only free broadcasting time on public channels is offered to political parties, on an equal or proportional basis. The "political electoral broadcasts" (Holtz-Bacha & Kaid, 2006, p. 5) aired in this free time, are usually long (ranging from 3 to 10 minutes) during which "talking heads" provide the voters with information on policy positions of political parties (Brants, 2006). Arguments for not allowing parties and politicians to purchase air time range from "too expensive" to "too powerful." Also, protection of print media and their political advertisement revenues has been mentioned as an argument (Holtz-Bacha & Kaid, 2006).

Other countries, such as the Netherlands, Germany, Greece, Italy, Mexico, Australia, and Japan, offer free time on public channels, but also allow candidates and parties to buy broadcasting time on commercial channels. Buying political television ads has become possible in West European dual systems only since the 1990s. Although commercial political spots have entered the scene in these countries, the role of TV spots does not compare to the USA. In the Netherlands (see Brants, 2006), for example, the political culture and the financial context are not ready for political advertising on a large scale. Amateurism, low budgets, and public opinion seem to resist business and other sponsorship of political parties. Not until 1998—10 years after the introduction of commercial television—were political spots allowed in commercial time (Brants, 2006), but they still play only a minor role in campaigns.

Next to differences in media systems, legal restrictions, and prevailing political culture, the differentiations in political and electoral systems clearly leave a mark on the design of political television advertising. In those countries with a presidential system, campaigns will be much more candidate oriented instead of party oriented. In those countries where elections lead to coalitions with two or more parties instead of a single-party government, most campaigners are more careful about using negative campaigns against future or former coalition partners (Holtz-Bacha & Kaid, 2006).

We can conclude that the media system, the political culture, and the electoral system affect amount, form, and content of political advertising (Holtz-Bacha & Kaid, 2006) and account for differences between the USA and other countries.

The Effects of Political Advertising

With the rise of political television advertising as a popular campaign tool, the amount of criticism has also increased.

> In addition to complaints about the accuracy or truth of specific political ads, the most common criticisms are that political spots are too short to contain meaningful information, that television ads focus too much attention on the candidate's image at the expense of issues, and that political ads are too negative.
>
> (Kaid, 2008, p. 3665)

Most political spots are indeed quite short, with an average length of around 30 seconds (Kaid, 2008). But despite this short length, studies show political spots' ability to overcome selective exposure—the tendency of individuals to seek out media content that confirms their existing beliefs—(Atkin, Bowen, Nayman, & Sheinkopf, 1973; Surlin & Gordon, 1976). Politicians and parties are thus able to get controlled political messages across to all voters, communicating the superiority of their attributes, without intervention from their opponents (Kaid, 1991). This may contribute to a voter's broader view on politics than exposure to free media only. An experimental study by Just, Crigler, and Wallach (1990) showed that voters learned more candidate information from political advertisements than from debates.

But political commercials are not only able to come across to voters, they also have the ability to influence their political interest, knowledge, candidate evaluations, and eventually their voting behavior. Benoit, Leshner, and Chattopadhay (2009) conducted an extensive meta-analysis, and concluded that political ads have various significant effects on viewers. Their analyses revealed that political spots increased issue knowledge, influenced perceptions of the candidates' character, altered attitudes, affected candidate preference, influenced agenda setting, and altered vote likelihood (turnout). Results from various experimental (e.g., Chang, 2001; Kahn & Geer, 1994; Meirick, 2002; Pinkleton, 1997, 1998; Valentino, Hutchings, & Williams, 2004) and survey studies (Goldstein & Freedman, 2000; Franz & Ridout, 2010; Johnston, Hagen, & Jamieson, 2004; Huber & Arceneaux, 2007) showed that there is a positive impact of advertising on candidate preference in senate races as well as presidential elections (see also Benoit et al., 2009; Kaid, 2006).

Various voter-, political market-, candidate-, and message-related variables are found to moderate the effects of exposure to political spots. An experimental study by Tinkham, Weaver, Lariscy, and Johnson Avery (2009) showed that younger people show greater attitudinal vulnerability to political ads, and older voters show greater behavioral vulnerability. Maarek (2008) notes that political advertising works best with voters who are uninvolved with politics, or yet undecided, the so-called swing voters. Kaid (1997, cited in Kaid, 2006) found a gender effect, which showed that "female voters are more likely to be affected by exposure to political spots, and when they are, the spots are more likely to result in higher positive evaluations for the candidates than is true for male voters." Benoit et al. (2009) demonstrated that learning effects from exposure to political ads was larger for students than for non-students. Shaw (1999) related the number of ads to vote percentage in the years 1988, 1992, and 1996, and concluded that amount of advertising increases vote share, but the impact of advertising varied depending on the specific presidential election campaign. Franz and Ridout (2010) found that political advertising had more impact on vote share in states where there is not much competition between parties or candidates, than in battleground states. These authors also showed that political advertising had more impact on vote share in case of unknown candidates (Franz & Ridout, 2010), and that political advertising with a consistent message had more impact on vote share than political advertising with an inconsistent message coming from multiple sources (Franz & Ridout, 2010).

Another issue covered in the literature concerns the duration of advertising effects. Gerber, Gimpel, Green, and Shaw (2007) found clear evidence of important advertising effects, but these effects lasted only about a day. Hill, Lo, Vavreck, and Zaller (2007) showed in their study of various types of elections that 80–90% of advertising effects dissipate within 2 or 3 days, perhaps 10 at most. The tentative conclusion of these authors is that the findings undermine "the view that American voters are persuaded by information that accumulates during long campaigns and suggests instead the importance of tactical maneuvers by candidates to dominate the airwaves at the very end of campaigns" (Hill et al., 2007, p. 1). Their findings are in line with a memory-based model of information processing that suggests that individuals do not have fixed preferences and answer survey questions on the basis of information salient in memory (Zaller, 1992).

Various studies have examined the question of whether or not image information is dominant over issue information in political commercials (Joslyn, 1980; Patterson & McClure, 1976). This question comes of course from the widespread concern that voting decisions should be rational, based on one's evaluation of policy issues rather than a candidate's image (Kaid, 1999). To date, there seems to be no support for this concern. Results consistently show that issue content is predominant over image content in most political television commercials. However, it must also be noted that the arguments contained in political spots are often abbreviated, sometimes misleading and in any case difficult to prove (Baukus, Payne, & Reisler, 1985; Kaid, 1999).

A type of commercial that tends to be clearly more issue oriented than image oriented, is negative advertising (Kaid, 1999). Negative advertising is a common American phenomenon. More than half of American political commercials these days are negative ads (Kaid, 1999). The discussion regarding negative advertising is certainly the most dominant in research on political advertising in the past two decades. In the next section, we will discuss the effects of negative political advertising.

Negative Political Advertising

Negative advertising is advertising that degrades perceptions of the opposing candidate's character or issues they support (Merritt, 1984), or "advertising that attacks the opponent or opposing idea, rather than discussing the positive attributes of the sponsoring candidate, party, or issue" (Kaid, 2008, p. 3665). Lau, Sigelman, Heldman, and Babbitt (1999, p. 854) list different definitions for negative political advertising:

> Whereas some researchers treat as negative any ad that mentions the opponent, others distinguish among ads that mention only the sponsor (positive or advocacy ads), ads that focus exclusively or primarily on the opponent (negative or attack ads), and ads that focus on both the sponsor and the opponent (comparative or contrast ads).

(See also Klotz, 1998; Johnson-Cartee & Copeland, 1991.) Pfau and Kenski (1990) mention in addition the "response ad" for negative material answering the charges of an opponent.

A trend analysis shows that there has been a positive trend in the percent of negative spots in the USA (Johnson-Carlee & Copeland, 1991). "The use of negative information in advertising is increasing among all types of candidates and dominates a longer campaign timespan" (Jasperson & Fan, 2002, p. 4). Negative political advertising has become the dominant format for political spots in U.S. national elections (Kaid, 1999). The tone is negative in the presidential election campaigns particularly. Two factors seem to have contributed to the rise of negative spots. The first factor is the growing importance of personal and performance characteristics in campaigns due to the declining importance of ideology. The second factor is the growing role of independent groups such as interest groups, political action committees, unions, or even "billionaire tycoons." These "independent" ad expenditures have overtaken candidate ad expenditures, especially after 1996 (Marcus, 2000).

Effects of negative advertising compared to positive advertising is by far the most studied issue in political advertising research in the past two decades.

Findings are mixed. Some studies found that negative advertising is more powerful, other studies found that positive advertising generates better effects, and, finally, some studies found no difference in effects between positive and negative ads at all.

Positive effects of negative advertising are attributed to the negativity effect which indicates that greater weight is given to negative information (Fiske, 1980), and the fact that people seem to remember negative information better (Kensinger & Schacter, 2006). Lau (1982) was one of the first researchers in this branch of research who showed that negative information has more impact on creating impressions of political candidates, than positive information. A superior effect of negative advertising over positive advertising was also found by Garramone, Atkin, Pinkleton, and Cole (1990), who showed that negative commercials lead to greater candidate image discrimination, and had more effect on vote preferences than positive advertisements. Also, it was found that negative political advertising increases political interest and stimulates voter turnout (Carsey, 2000; Goldstein & Freeman, 2002; Hillygus, 2005; Jackson & Carsey, 2007; Kaid, 2006).

Negative effects of negative advertising are ascribed to the so-called backlash or boomerang effect (Roese & Sande, 1993; Garramone, 1984; Merritt, 1984). Backlash or boomerang effects are the unintended consequences of negative political ads, due to voter disapproval of negative advertising, which might result in more negative feelings toward the sponsor (Jasperson & Fan, 2002). The negative effect of political advertising on voter turnout, found by Ansolabehere and Iyengar (1995), has also been attributed to backlash. Although this is one of the most cited studies in the field of political advertising, this negative effect has not been reported ever since.

Some authors claim that the negativity effect and the backlash effect counterbalance each other, which may be the reason why some researchers have not found a difference when comparing negative and positive political spots. For example, Garramone et al. (1990) found that negative and positive commercials did not differ in their effects on involvement in the election, communication behavior regarding the election, and likelihood of turning out to vote. Also, two meta-analysis studies concluded that there was no net effect of type of advertising (positive/negative). The first meta-analysis (Lau et al., 1999) showed that in the end negative political ads appear to be no more effective than positive ads: "Most of the effect sizes fall very close to the zero point, and about as many are below as above zero" (p. 857). Furthermore, they conclude that the target of a political advertising attack "is liked less" but "this intended effect is counterbalanced by an even stronger and highly significant decrease in liking of (that is, backlash against) the sponsor, an effect that sponsors of such ads certainly do not want to achieve" (p. 857). The second meta-analysis (Allen &

Burrell, 2002) looked at the effects on attitude toward a position, attitude toward a candidate (target of the information in the ad), attitude toward the ad's sponsor, and voting. The authors found smaller effects on attitude toward position, the target, and vote intention, with a larger (backlash) effect against the ad's sponsor. This indicates no net benefit to the sponsor of negative advertising. Please note that these results do not indicate that negative advertising does not work. It simply tells us that on average negative advertising is not more successful than positive advertising.

Variables Moderating the Effects of Negative Advertising

Many variables have been studied for their possible moderating influence on the effects of negative advertising. Lau and Pomper (2001) found support for the hypothesis that partisans tend to be stimulated to vote by campaign negativism while independents are more likely to be discouraged by such campaigns. Other authors (Kahn & Geer, 1994; Kaid, 2008) found that negative political advertising is most effective when it concerns issue positions of the opposing candidate rather than personal qualities or images. Furthermore, rebuttals are found to be helpful in blunting the effects of a "negative attack" (Kaid, 1991; Garramone, 1985). "If a candidate is attacked and does not respond, the public tends to believe the attack is true" (Kaid, 2008). Also, "inoculation," by providing counterevidence or positive candidate information first, provides some protection against negative advertising (Pfau & Kenski, 1990). In order to prevent political parties and candidates from backlash effects, it is shown that it might help to bring third parties into action to sponsor political ads.

Two categories of third party ads can be distinguished: soft money advertisements, which "tend to focus on issues or candidates' positions on certain issues," and hard money, or advocacy ads, which "call for electing or defeating a particular candidate" (Shen & Wu, 2002, pp. 395–396). Contrary to candidate advertising, issue advocacy advertising enjoys First Amendment protection and is not subject to campaign finance law restrictions concerning spending limits (Dreyfuss, 1998).

Whether a third party advertising strategy is successful has been frequently studied (Garramone, 1985; Pfau, Park, Holbert, & Cho, 2001; Jasperson & Fan, 2002; Shen & Wu, 2002; Meirick, 2005; Pfau, Haigh, Sims, & Wigley, 2007). There is mixed evidence of the success of the attacks (negative advertising) of candidate versus independent sponsors. Pfau, Holbert, Szabo, and Kaminski (2002) found no main effects for type of sponsor of political ads. Shen and Wu (2002) concluded that although negative advertisements sponsored by a candidate had a negative impact on the target candidate and backfired against the sponsoring candidate, the backlash effects were minimal, however, when negative advertisements were sponsored by soft-money political organizations. Two other studies (Jasperson & Fan, 2002; Meirick, 2005) reached an opposite conclusion. They showed that third party attacks led to a boomerang effect; attacks by the candidate did not. This was true particularly for viewers with high political knowledge (Meirick, 2005). These results suggest, according to the authors, that the electorate values open and straight politicians.

Conclusions

Because of fundamental changes in the political, societal, and media landscape, political advertising has developed as one of the most dominant sources of political communication, especially in the USA. Academic interest in the topic has kept pace with the popularity of the phenomenon. The many studies on political advertising show that money spent on political advertising seems to be well spent in terms of desired impact. The studies have shown effects on variables such as political interest, political knowledge, voter turnout, candidate perceptions, candidate evaluations, and voting behavior. The studies have also identified various voter-, political market-, candidate-, and message-related variables that moderate the effects of political spots. It is easy to see how these variables relate to the source, message, receiver, and context variables included in the Components of the Advertising Process Circle framework outlined in Figure 1.1 in this text.

Political advertising operates in a complex reality with different types of voters, candidates, sponsors, elections, political markets, political systems, media systems, messages, and timing and frequency of messages. The conditions under which (field) studies of political advertising are conducted vary and therefore it is no wonder that the findings may differ as well. There is a need to integrate the particular characteristics of the various studies as moderators in effect models of political advertising. Another suggestion for future research is to pay further attention to the processes underlying the effects and to model these processes as mediators.

We should note that most studies on the effects of political advertising were conducted in the USA, have focused on television spots, and on negative campaigns. These limitations give indications for how future research into political advertising should be extended.

References

Allen, M., & Burrell, N. (2002). The negativity effect in political advertising: A meta-analysis. In J. P. Dillard & M. Pfau (Eds.), *The persuasion handbook: Developments in theory and practice* (pp. 83–96). Thousand Oaks, CA: Sage.

Ansolabehere, S., & Iyengar, S. (1995). *Going negative: How political advertisements shrink and polarize the electorate*. New York: Free Press.

Atkin, C., Bowen, L., Nayman, O. B., & Sheinkopf, K. G. (1973). Quality versus quantity in televised political ads. *Public Opinion Quarterly, 37*, 209–224.

Baukus, R. A., Payne, J. G., & Resiler, M. C. (1985). Negative polispots. In J. R. Cox, M. O. Sillars, & G. B. Walker (Eds.), *Argumentation and social practice* (pp. 236–252). Annandale, VA: Speech Communication Association.

Benoit, W. L., Leshner, G. M., & Chattopadhay, S. (2009). A meta-analysis of political advertising. *Human Communication, 10* (4), 507–522.

Borrel Associates Inc. (2010). *2010 political advertising outlook: The endless campaign*. Williamsburg, VA: Borrel Associates Inc.

Brants, K. (2006). Sure to come, but temporarily delayed. The Netherlands in search of the political ad. In L. L. Kaid & C. Holtz-Bacha (Eds.), *The Sage handbook of political advertising* (pp. 227–239). Thousand Oaks, CA: Sage.

Carsey, T. M. (2000). *Campaign dynamics: The race for governor*. Ann Arbor: University of Michigan Press.

Chang, C. (2001). The impact of emotion elicited by print political advertising on candidate evaluation. *Media Psychology, 3*, 91–118.

Dreyfuss, R. (1998). Harder than soft money. *American Prospect*, 30–37.

Fiske, S. T. (1980). Attention and weight in person perception: The impact of negative and extreme behavior. *Journal of Personality and Social Psychology, 38* (6), 899–906.

Franz, M. M., & Ridout, T. N. (2010). Political advertising and persuasion in the 2004 and 2009 presidential elections. *American Politics Research, 38* (2), 303–329.

Garramone, G. M. (1984). Voter responses to negative political ads. *Journalism Quarterly, 61*, 250–259.

Garramone, G. M. (1985). Effects of negative political advertising: The role of sponsor and rebuttal. *Journal of Broadcasting and Electronic Media, 29*, 147–159.

Garramone, G. M., Atkin, C. K., Pinkleton, B. E., & Cole, R. T. (1990). Effects of negative political advertising on the political process. *Journal of Broadcasting and Electronic Media, 34* (3), 229–311.

Gerber, A., Gimpel, J. G., Green, D. P., & Shaw, D. R. (2007). The influence of television and radio advertising on candidate evaluations: Results from a large scale randomized experiment. Presentation made at the Annual Meeting of the Midwest Political Science Association, Chicago.

Goldstein, K., & Freedman, P. (2000). New evidence for new arguments: Money and advertising in the 1996 Senate elections. *Journal of Politics, 62*, 1087–1108.

Goldstein, K., & Freedman, P. (2002). Lessons learned: Campaign advertising in the 2000 elections. *Political Communication, 19*, 5–28.

Gosnell, H. F. (1927). *Getting-out-the-vote: An experiment in the stimulation of voting*. Chicago: University of Chicago Press.

Hill, S. J., Lo, J., Vavreck, L., & Zaller, J. (2007). The duration of advertising effects in political campaigns. Presentation made at the American Political Science Association Annual Meeting, Chicago.

Hillygus, D. S. (2005). Campaign effects and the dynamics of turnout intention in election 2000. *Journal of Politics, 67*, 50–68.

Holtz-Bacha, C., & Kaid, L. L. (2006). Political advertising in international comparison. In L. L. Kaid & C. Holtz-Bacha (Eds.), *The Sage handbook of political advertising* (pp. 3–13). Thousand Oaks, CA: Sage.

Huber, G., & Arceneaux, K. (2007). Identifying the persuasive effects of presidential advertising. *American Journal of Political Science, 51*, 957–977.

Jackson, R. A., & Carsey, T. M. (2007). US Senate campaigns, negative advertising, and voter mobilization in the 1998 Midterm election. *Electoral Studies, 26*, 180–195.

Jasperson, A. E., & Fan, D. P. (2002). An aggregate examination of the backlash effect in political advertising: The case of the 1996 U.S. Senate race in Minnesota. *Journal of Advertising, 31* (1), 1–12.

Johnston, R., Hagen, M. G., & Jamieson, K. H. (2004). *The 2000 presidential election and the foundations of party politics.* Cambridge, UK: Cambridge University Press.

Johnson-Cartee, K., & Copeland, G. (1991). *Negative political advertising: Coming of age.* Hillsdale, NJ: Lawrence Erlbaum.

Joslyn, R. A. (1980). The content of political spot ads. *Journalism Quarterly, 57* (1), 92–98.

Just, M., Crigler, A., & Wallach, L. (1990). Thirty seconds or thirty minutes: What viewers learn from spot advertisements and candidate debates. *Journal of Communication, 40*, 120–133.

Kahn, K. F., & Geer, J. G. (1994). Creating impressions: An experimental investigation of political advertising on television. *Political Behavior, 16*, 93–116.

Kaid, L. L. (1991). Ethical dimensions of political advertising. In R. E. Denton (Ed.), *Ethical dimensions of political communication* (pp. 14–170). Westport, CT: Praeger.

Kaid, L. L. (1997). Effects of television spots on images of Dole and Clinton. *American Behavioral Scientist, 40*, 1085–1094.

Kaid, L. L. (1999). Political advertising. In B. I. Newman (Ed.), *Handbook of political marketing* (pp. 423–438). Thousand Oaks, CA: Sage.

Kaid, L. L. (2006). Political advertising in the United States. In L.L. Kaid & C. Holtz-Bacha (Eds.), *The Sage handbook of political advertising* (pp. 83–108). Thousand Oaks, CA: Sage.

Kaid, L. L. (2008). Political advertising. In W. Donsbach (Ed.), *The international encyclopedia of communication* (pp. 3664–3667). Oxford, UK: Wiley-Blackwell.

Kaid, L. L., & Holtz-Bacha, C. (Eds.) (1995). *Political advertising in western democracies.* Thousand Oaks, CA: Sage.

Kaid, L L., & Holtz-Bacha, C. (Eds.) (2006). *The Sage handbook of political advertising.* Thousand Oaks, CA: Sage.

Kensinger, E. A., & Schacter, D. L. (2006). Reality monitoring and memory distortion: Effects of negative, arousing content. *Memory and Cognition, 34* (2), 251–260.

Klotz, R. (1998). Virtual criticism: Negative advertising on the Internet in the 1996 Senate races. *Political Communication, 15* (3), 347–365.

Kotler, P., & Kotler, N. (1999). Political marketing: Generating effective candidates, campaigns, and causes. In B. I. Newman (Ed.), *Handbook of political marketing* (pp. 3–18). Thousand Oaks, CA: Sage.

Lau, R. R. (1982). Negativity in political perceptions. *Political Behavior, 4*, 353–377.

Lau, R. R., & Pomper, G. M. (2001). Effects of negative campaigning on turnout in U.S. Senate elections, 1988–1998. *Journal of Politics, 63*, 804–819.

Lau, R. R., Sigelman, L., Heldman, C., & Babbitt, P. (1999). The effects of negative political advertisements: A meta-analytic assessment. *American Political Science Review, 93*, 851–875.

Maarek, P. J. (2008). Political marketing. In W. Donsbach (Ed.) *The international encyclopedia of communication* (pp. 3723–3727). Oxford, UK: Wiley-Blackwell.

Marcus, R. (2000, November 6). Costliest race nears end; Bush, Gore running close; U.S. campaigns fuel $3 billion in spending. *Washington Post*, A1.

Meirick, P. C. (2002). Cognitive responses to negative and comparative political advertising. *Journal of Advertising, 31*, 49–62.

Meirick, P. C. (2005). Political knowledge and sponsorship in backlash from party- and candidate-sponsored attacks. *Communication Reports, 18* (2), 75–84.

Merritt, S. (1984). Negative political advertising: Some empirical findings. *Journal of Advertising, 13*, 27–38.

Patterson, T. E., & McClure, R. D. (1976). *The unseeing eye: Myth of television power in politics*. New York: Putnam.

Pfau, M., Haigh, M. M., Sims, J., & Wigley, S. (2007). The influence of corporate front-group stealth campaigns. *Communication Research, 34*, 73–99.

Pfau, M., Holbert, R. L., Szabo, E. A., & Kaminski, K. (2002). Issue-advocacy versus candidate advertising: Effects on candidate preferences and democratic process. *Journal of Communication, 52*, 301–315.

Pfau, M., & Kenski, H. C. (1990). *Attack politics: Strategy and defense*. New York: Praeger.

Pfau, M., Park, D., Holbert, R. L., & Cho, J. (2001). The effects of party- and PAC-sponsored issue advertising and the potential of inoculation to combat its impact on the Democratic process. *American Behavioral Scientist, 44* (12), 2379–2397.

Pinkleton, B. E. (1997). The effects of negative comparative political advertising on candidate evaluations and advertising evaluations: An exploration. *Journal of Advertising, 26*, 19–29.

Pinkleton, B. E. (1998). Effects of print comparative political advertising on political decision-making and participation. *Journal of Communication, 48*, 24–36.

Roese, N. J., & Sande, G. N. (1993). Backlash effects in attack politics. *Journal of Applied Social Psychology, 23* (8), 632–653.

Shaw, D. R. (1999). The effect of TV ads and candidate appearances on statewide Presidential votes, 1988–96. *American Political Science Review, 93*, 345–361.

Shen, F., & Wu, H. D. (2002). Effects of soft-money issue advertisements on candidate evaluation and voting preference: An exploration. *Mass Communication and Society, 5* (4), 395–410.

Surlin, S. H., & Gordon, T. E. (1976). Selective exposure and retention of political advertising. *Journal of Advertising, 5*, 32–44.

Tinkham, S. F., Weaver, L., Lariscy, R., & Johnson Avery, R. (2009). Political advertising and the older electorate. *Journal of Advertising, 38* (2), 105–119.

Valentino, N. A., Hutchings, V. L., & Williams, D. (2004). The impact of political advertising on knowledge, internet information seeking, and candidate preference. *Journal of Communication, 54*, 337–354.

Zaller, J. (1992). *The nature and origins of mass opinion*. New York: Cambridge University Press.

Additional Readings

Harris, P., & Lock, A. (Eds.). (2010). Special issue on political marketing. *European Journal of Marketing, 44* (3/4), 297–538.

Kaid, L. L., & Holtz-Bacha, C. (Eds.) (2006). *The Sage handbook of political advertising*. Thousand Oaks, CA: Sage.

Lau, R. R., Sigelman, L., Heldman, C., & Babbitt, P. (1999). The effects of negative political advertisements: A meta-analytic assessment. *American Political Science Review, 93*, 851–875.

Louden, A. (2010). Political spot advertising: Selected bibliography. Retrieved August 17, 2010, from www.wfu.edu/%7Elouden/Political%20Communication/Bibs/SPOTBIB.html.

Pfau, M., Holbert, R. L., Szabo, E. A., & Kaminski, K. (2002). Issue-advocacy versus candidate advertising: Effects on candidate preferences and democratic process. *Journal of Communication, 52*, 301–315.

Part V

Media and Media Devices

Chapter 21

Media Analysis and Decision Making

Hugh M. Cannon

The premise of this book is that no aspect of advertising can be understood in isolation. This is captured in Figure 1.1 in the introduction to this book. The nature and effectiveness of advertising is shaped by its interaction with the social, cultural, economic, legal, physical, and psychological context in which it is delivered. This is to say, advertising is an extremely complex phenomenon. Implicit in our approach is the fact that we can address its complexity by breaking it down into its constituent dimensions and identifying the theoretical principles by which these dimensions interact.

This chapter will address the advertising "channel," or the methods by which advertising messages are actually delivered to the people for whom they were intended (the "receivers" in Figure 1.1 of the introduction). Following the common parlance of advertising, we will refer to elements of the channel as advertising media. The chapter will begin by developing a general framework for understanding how interactions among the various advertising contexts affect the way consumers process information within a media channel. It will then draw on this framework as a basis for understanding media planning strategy, beginning with the broad concept of integrated marketing communications (IMC) and continuing to link it with conventional media planning. While the definition of IMC may vary in specifics from source to source, we will define it in terms of its most basic concept, that everything a company does must be considered part of its marketing communications program, and that it must all be carefully coordinated to service the company's strategic marketing objectives (see also Chapter 32 by Moriarty and Schultz).

A General Model of How Consumers Process Information within a Media Channel

In order to help you understand what the aforementioned view of media channels and IMC means in practice, let us begin by developing a broad conceptual model (Figure 21.1) of the key factors influencing the way consumers might

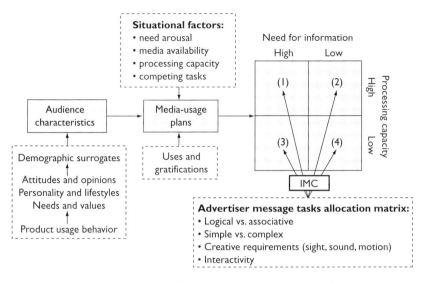

Figure 21.1 A General Model of How Consumers Process Information within a Media Channel.

process messages in a particular media context. We will look at the model from a media planning perspective, asking what media planners would need to consider when planning an IMC program.

Audience Characteristics

The first consideration is the nature of the market being targeted by the communications program. We refer to this as the *target market*. By convention, we refer to the people reached through various media as their *audience*. We use the term *target audience* to represent the practical translation of the target market membership into specific characteristics by which media audiences are measured. For instance, if we were developing a program for a new kind of energy drink, the target market might be energy-drink users, but the target audience might be men between the ages of 18 and 25.

Our example illustrates the first problem of media planning: How do we develop a target audience that closely represents our target market? This is referred to as *media-market matching* (Assael & Cannon, 1979). In Figure 21.1, the box leading to *audience characteristics* shows the process. The marketing team defined the target market in terms of product usage behavior (energy-drink users). By comparing energy-drink users with nonusers, they would be able to see the different consumer motivations growing out of consumer attitudes and opinions, personality and lifestyles, needs and values. However, because demographic groups report most media usage data, the target audience was reduced to a simple demographic surrogate: men between the ages of 18 and 25. The process is known as *indirect media-market matching* (Assael & Cannon, 1979). Clearly, this is a rather "blunt instrument" for identifying target market members, but it is probably as close as a planner could come with the demographics that are typically found for describing media audiences.

Considerable research has been conducted to find a better approach. One of the most promising is *direct media-market matching*, where modern *single-source data bases* (containing both product- and media-usage data from a single source) are used to identify media whose audiences actually contain a relatively high concentration of product users (Cannon, Smith, & Williams, 2007). While the purpose is not necessarily to reach product users, targeting them is a good way to reach the kind of people who use the product, but who might not have purchased. For instance, a campaign for a Cadillac's CTS might target recent CTS buyers. The purpose, however, would not be to reach CTS buyers, but, rather, people who share their attitudes and opinions, personality and lifestyle, needs and values, but who have not yet purchased—i.e., people who consume the same kinds of media.

Returning to the notion of how media interact with the advertising environment, the two major constraints on *media-market matching* are the availability of appropriate media and the data required to match these effectively to an advertiser's target market. Both of these depend on the innovative efforts of advertising organizations, the changing demands of modern message strategies, and the receptivity of consumers to advertising—as opposed to avoidance strategies such as *zipping* (fast-forwarding through commercials) and *zapping* (jumping between programs during commercial breaks) in television media.

Media are proliferating rapidly, including both *traditional* and *non-traditional* media. Non-traditional media include a host of new approaches to advertising, from advertising on mobile phones to highly innovative forms of in-store or outdoor signage, as noted in Chapter 22 by Wilson and Till. From an IMC perspective, the range of "media" becomes even greater, because virtually every activity of a firm is considered a form of advertising. We will refer to the resulting new forms of communication as *pseudo-media*.

In this kind of environment, we would expect enormous pressure on data providers to support the process of *media-market matching*. The growth of different kinds of media makes measurement increasingly difficult and expensive. A host of syndicated media data services such as Nielson, Arbitron, Scarborough, Simmons, and MediaMark provide data on conventional media. Furthermore, researchers are continually investigating new approaches to use them more efficiently (see Cannon et al., 2007 for a review of approaches). As data lag for non-traditional media, planners will have to substitute judgment, based on an understanding of the principles we are discussing in this chapter.

Media Usage Plans

Blindly seeking to match target markets to media-audience demographics is clearly a naïve approach to media planning. A more enlightened approach would consider a host of qualitative considerations as well. Referring again to Figure 21.1, many of these are expressed through what we refer to as *media-usage plans*. Media-usage plans refer to the specific series of intentions that govern audience members' behavior as they dedicate attention to a particular medium. Ask yourself what led you to view a particular show the last time you watched television or reviewed a supermarket flier. Each step in your involvement with the medium was governed by a sequence of mental steps—a plan—even if your decision was spontaneous and whimsical. You had to turn on the TV, select the channel, and so forth, or in the case of the supermarket flier, you had to pick it up and begin looking through the items on sale, ultimately drawing some conclusion about what to do with the information you had just acquired.

The string of behaviors governed by the plan was the result of your personal decisions to expose yourself to a particular medium. Referring again to Figure 21.1, *situational factors* (*need arousal*, *media availability*, *processing capacity*, and *competing tasks*) played a key role in motivating your plan. They are relatively self-explanatory. *Need arousal* refers to the specific emotional impetus for media exposure. For instance, the television plan might have been triggered by your remembering that it was time for one of your favorite programs which you find both relaxing and entertaining. By contrast, you might read a magazine to update your understanding of the news or some other topic. *Media availability* simply addresses the physical availability of the media when you might be receptive to using them. *Processing capacity* addresses what we now refer to as "band width" in common parlance, using the Internet metaphor to describe the intellectual and emotional resources available during media exposure. Of course, your available band width depends on *competing tasks*—the other things vying for your attention in a media-exposure situation.

Again, we see the potential role of the interactive advertising environment. Obviously, media usage plans will depend on the kinds of media created by advertising and media organizations, not to mention technological and cultural developments. Imagine the impact of DVDs, personal DVD players, MP3 players, and smart phones on the way people consume media. Increasingly, consumers plan their media usage with vehicles that do not deliver unsolicited advertising. Information services such as Google have emerged as major players on the advertising scene by providing advertising information on topics that consumers are actually investigating using their computers or smart phones.

Situational factors are often random and difficult to predict. However, in certain circumstances, they can be managed. Returning to our example of the

Cadillac CTS, Cadillac made an arrangement to feature the CTS as part of a chase scene in one of the "Matrix" movies. Anticipating that the scene would create positive need arousal for the CTS, media planners might arrange to place CTS ads during an airing of the movie on television.

Uses and gratifications refer to more general patterns of situational factors. Why do audience members *tend* to expose themselves to a particular medium? This is to say, "What kinds of need arousal characterizes the medium?" Automobile advertisers would naturally get more audience attention from media that tend to arouse automotive-related needs than those that don't—an automotive magazine, for instance, or an automotive website such as Kelly Blue Book (www.kbb.com).

The Message Task Allocation Matrix and Integrated Marketing Communications

The general idea of *media-usage plans* and their application to specific advertising situations has enormous potential for stimulating media planning creativity. However, the general principles can be used more systematically to guide the allocation of messages in an IMC program. This is portrayed in the *message task allocation matrix* on the right-hand side of Figure 21.1. To illustrate how the matrix might be used, consider a hypothetical program supporting the launch of a new voice-driven smart phone. The program includes a number of different message components, each requiring a different type of media environment.

One component seeks to create general awareness and understanding of the concept. It falls in Cell 4 of the matrix. The message is simple: this is a smart phone you can talk to instead of wrestling with a virtual keyboard. No one is looking for the message, but, once understood, it sensitizes consumers to possibilities that require much more attention, leaving them hungry for further information. This component of the campaign would be ideal for intrusive media such as television or billboards, where consumers have relatively little excess mental capacity or initial incentive to process the ad. The actual message would be associative, using evocative imagery and a high level of creativity to capture consumer attention and link the simple message to situations and needs with which they can identify.

A second component of the program would involve a much deeper explanation of what the new phone could actually do. It would fall into Cell 1 of the matrix, addressing the needs of consumers who are already interested and want more information regarding the phone. The message would be a relatively complex, logical, and informational ad, requiring a relatively high level of information processing capacity. Such a message would be well suited to magazines, the Internet (perhaps a Google ad linking to a website), or even direct mail.

Yet another component of the IMC campaign would address the sales transaction. This would involve checking out all the last-minute details, perhaps
comparing prices and features, different vendors, and so forth. In such an environment, consumers have to process a great deal of information quickly. This is
most characteristic of Cell 3. We mentioned the use of sponsored links on
Google. They provide a media environment where consumers can process a
very simple, logical message, then following a link to a much more complex,
information (Cell 1) website if more in-depth investigation appears to be
warranted.

Finally, we can envision consumers who are perfectly satisfied with their
current phones, thus making any switch to the voice-driven technology a purely
discretionary purchase. This would characterize Cell 2. Consumers would have
no need for information, but given a media environment in which they have
excess processing capacity (lots of time to dream), an associative, emotionally
arousing ad might stimulate fantasies about how fun the new phone would be to
use, leading to a desire to use the new technology. This might call for long television commercials (allowing time to emotionally process the situation portrayed in the ad), a highly evocative website, or perhaps a key product placement
in a popular movie.

The possibility of a key product placement brings us back to the philosophical driver of IMC: everything a company does should be considered as a potential form of advertising. We don't usually think of product placements as
mainstream media, but from an IMC perspective, product placements are often
the perfect media. In this case, they portray a realistic environment that captures how the phone fits into the lives of people with whom the viewing audience is already identifying.

Linking IMC with Conventional Media Planning: Media Class Decisions

The primary link between IMC and conventional media planning is through
what are traditionally referred to as *media class* decisions. Most media planning
discussions are organized around a discussion of the strengths, weaknesses, and
capabilities of the major established media classes—television, radio, magazines, newspapers, out-of-home media, and so forth. From an IMC perspective, this makes little sense. How would you classify a product placement? A
candy-bar wrapper? A cash register receipt? An employee's uniform? The
texture of a fabric on the furniture of a lawyer's office? The smells emanating
from the kitchen vents of a restaurant?

Our approach has been to focus on the basic ways consumers are likely to
process media information across different media, namely their need for

product-related information (the *need for information* dimension in Figure 21.1), their information processing capacity (the *processing capacity* dimension), and implicitly, the degree to which their need for information and processing capacity can be altered in the course of media consumption. For instance, to what extent can a Web banner ad on a cluttered Web page (a media environment characterized by moderate need for information and low processing capacity) be altered to a high need for information, high processing capacity environment by clicking on a link to the advertiser's website?

This approach relates closely to the creative strategy models growing out of the Foote, Cone, and Belding (FCB Grid) tradition (Vaughn, 1980, 1986; Ratchford, 1987; Rossiter, Percy, & Donovan, 1991; Rossiter & Percy, 1997). The FCB Grid approach looks at how consumers tend to process information for different kinds of products—by "thinking" versus "feeling," with a high versus a low level of "involvement." Rossiter and Percy (1997) look at the kind of decision process evoked by the advertising message, rather than by the product. Their approach draws on Wells' (Puto & Wells, 1984) distinction between *informational* and *transformational* advertising, arguing that informational advertising focuses on drive reduction, while transformational advertising addresses drive enhancement.

The Rossiter–Percy approach provides the better link to media strategy. Informational advertising helps consumers solve problems, while transformational advertising alerts them to possibilities. Percy and Rossiter (1992) use the example of automobile advertising to illustrate how this works in a media context. Rather than simply characterizing the kind of advertising called for by automobile decisions (as would characterize the FCB approach), they suggest that automotive print advertising is informational, while television is transformational. The print ads provide information to people who are trying to select a car from among the many available alternatives, while television stimulates them to want (a particular brand of) the car. The television ads transform the car into something that has meaning and significance for the consumers' lives. In this example, print is a high *need-for-information* environment, while television is a low *need-for-information* environment. Each plays a different, but complementary, role in the overall media/IMC program.

The question, of course, is what makes a medium create one kind of environment versus another. This question takes us back to our earlier discussion of media usage plans. We suggested that *need arousal* might reflect any number of different needs, but the two categories suggested by Rossiter and Percy (Rossiter et al., 1991; Percy & Rossiter, 1992; Rossiter & Percy, 1997) tend to stand out, namely, the need to address a particular problem (leading to a need for information) versus the need to have some kind of emotional stimulation (leading to low need for information).

The *processing capacity* dimension grows out of the simple fact that consumers are limited in the amount of information/stimuli they can process during any given interval of time. If an ad contains a lot of information and/or emotionally evocative stimuli, consumers' ability to process the ad effectively will depend on how long the exposure takes place and what else is going on during ad exposure. A 60 second television commercial accommodates higher involvement than a 30 second spot; a commercial embedded in an involving television program that you don't want to miss is likely to create more involvement than one that is running in the background while you are cleaning house.

Again, there are no absolute rules that we can apply to specific media. Television generally provides a low-information-seeking environment, but many programs (e.g., news, financial, or do-it-yourself programs) have the opposite effect; magazines generally provide a high-need-for-information environment, but some are so emotionally involving that readers are not even aware they are turning the pages. Similarly, the nature of the exposure environment depends on the audience members and what is going on in their lives (their *media-usage programs*). One person may watch a travel program with the specific idea of finding information to help them decide where to take a vacation, whereas another person might involve herself in the program as a form of vicarious experience.

Having said this, Figure 21.2 provides a general guide to how different media might fit into the message allocation matrix (Cannon, 2001), overlaying the matrix on the corresponding creative strategy dimensions the media must support. Using this as a point of departure, an understanding of the principles governing this fit can help media planners adapt these media to address the needs of a specific campaign. The process involves looking at patterns of need arousal, availability, processing capacity, and competing tasks, along with the uses and gratifications people look for from a particular medium (see Figure 21.1).

As a final point in our discussion of the *message task allocation matrix* portrayed in Figure 21.1, we need to remember that the specific communication capabilities are different for each advertising medium (or pseudo-medium, if we think of media in the broader IMC context, where every activity of the firm is a potential medium). As suggested in Figure 21.1, these include *sight*, *sound*, *motion*, and *interactivity*. But *pseudo-media* in particular can also contain tactile and olfactory characteristics. In the case of product placements, characteristics include the ability to insert a product into a realistic narrative with which consumers are identifying, unencumbered by the skepticism that often accompanies conventional advertising. Effective IMC seeks to identify media that will create customer contacts at a time, place, and in a form that will best address each of the tasks allocated to the program.

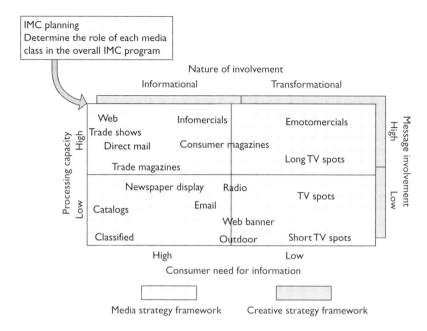

Figure 21.2 IMC Planning: Determining the Role of Each Media Class in the Overall IMC Program (source: adapted from Cannon, 2001).

Conventional Media Strategy and Planning

We have discussed how consumers process information within a media channel and how this relates to the general allocation of advertising tasks across different media classes. Now, let us turn our attention to the specific decisions media planners must make to translate their understanding into a specific media plan. To do this, we will address four stages of decision making; *media class allocations, scheduling, media vehicle decisions*, and *media schedule evaluation and refinement*.

Media Class Allocations and Scheduling

So far, we have focused on the selection of media classes to address the communications requirements of the advertiser's IMC program. However, the actual selection is more complicated. It must also consider the way the media are targeted and how much they cost. In other words, media class decisions ultimately depend on the same factors as do media vehicle decisions (summarized in Figure 21.4, below). The difference is that media class decisions tend to be based on broad qualitative considerations, whereas media vehicle decisions tend to be more quantitative and data intensive. Media class allocations and scheduling seek to be more strategic, providing general guidelines that will simplify the analytical process when selecting specific media vehicles.

None of this is to say that media class decisions do not involve quantitative decisions. Strategic guidelines can still use numbers to facilitate their implementation. The ultimate expression of a media class decision is an allocation of the media budget to the various types of media. Scheduling spreads the budget across a media calendar.

Suppose that our total budget is $60 million. In the end, we decide to allocate our budget equally across two media classes—$30 million to cable television and $30 million to the spot (local) radio. Our task is to spread this budget across 12 months, from January to December. In order to make the process manageable, we will reduce it to a mathematical exercise that can be captured on a spreadsheet. Figure 21.3 illustrates the process. While working our way through the spreadsheet is somewhat tedious, it provides an excellent way to track the logic of media class and scheduling decisions.

Avg Cost per GRP: $25,000
Overall Budget: $60,000,000

Media Class:	Cost index	Targeting Index	% alloc	Budget	Est TRPs
Cable TV	Cost index 0.400	Targeting Index 0.700	% alloc: 50%	Budget: $30,000,000	Est TRPs: 4,286
Internet	Cost index 0.450	Targeting Index 0.800	% alloc: 50%	Budget: $30,000,000	Est TRPs: 3,333

Schedule:

	Jan	Feb	Mar	Apr	May	Jun	Jul	Aug	Sep	Oct	Nov	Dec	Total	Budget
Cable TV	350	350	350	350	350	350	350	350	350	350	350	350	4,200	$29,400,000
Net Radio	250	250	250	250	250	250	250	250	250	250	250	250	3,000	$27,000,000

Total media budget: $56,400,000
Reserve for opportunistic buying: $3,600,000
Percentage held in reserve: 6.00%

Budget Summary:

	Jan-Mar	Apr-Jun	Jul-Sep	Oct-Dec	
Cable TV	$25,000 Cost per GRP	$25,000 Cost per GRP	$25,000 Cost per GRP	$25,000 Cost per GRP	
	0.40 Cost index	0.40 Cost index	0.40 Cost index	0.40 Cost index	
	1.00 Seasonal index	1.10 Seasonal index	1.00 Seasonal index	1.20 Seasonal index	
	0.70 Targeting index	0.70 Targeting index	0.70 Targeting index	0.70 Targeting index	
	1,050 GRPs or TRPs	1,050 GRPs or TRPs	1,050 GRPs or TRPs	1,050 GRPs or TRPs	
	Total cost $7,350,000	Total cost $8,085,000	Total cost $5,145,000	Total cost $8,820,000	Total: $29,400,000
Net Radio	$25,000 Cost per GRP	$25,000 Cost per GRP	$25,000 Cost per GRP	$25,000 Cost per GRP	
	0.45 Cost index	0.45 Cost index	0.45 Cost index	0.45 Cost index	
	1.00 Seasonal index	1.00 Seasonal index	1.00 Seasonal index	1.00 Seasonal index	
	0.80 Targeting index	0.80 Targeting index	0.80 Targeting index	0.80 Targeting index	
	750 GRPs or TRPs	750 GRPs or TRPs	750 GRPs or TRPs	750 GRPs or TRPs	
	Total cost $6,750,000	Total cost $6,750,000	Total cost $6,750,000	Total cost $6,750,000	Total: $27,000,000

Media Class Cost Indices:

Network TV		Magazines:		Other Media		Radio:	
30-second	1.00	4-Color	1.00	Cable	0.40	Radio (net)	0.35
60-second	1.80	B/W	0.70	Internet	0.20	Radio (spot	0.45
				Newspapers:	1.00		
Early AM	0.50	Trade	2.00	Supplements	0.30	1st Quarter	0.90
Daytime	0.30	Mass circ:	0.40	Out-of-home:	0.25	2nd Quarter	1.00
Early News	0.40	Mass/prestige	0.70	Direct Mail	20.00	3rd Quarter	1.00
Prime Time	1.00	Specialty	2.00			4th Quarter	0.90
Late Evening	0.60						
Weekend	0.70	Spot TV					
		Top 20 DMAs	1.30				
1st Quarter	1.00	Top 40 DMAs	1.30				
2nd Quarter	1.10	Top 60 DMAs	1.60				
3rd Quarter	0.70	Top 80 DMAs	1.77				
4th Quarter	1.20	Top 100 DMA	1.85				

Targeting Indices:

Cable	0.70
Direct mail	0.05
Internet	0.50
Magazine campaigns	0.70
Radio campaigns	0.80
Specialized media	0.50
Trade publications	0.10
TV campaigns	0.90

Reach and Frequency Possibilities:

Cable campaigns	0.70
Daytime TV campaign	0.50
Internet campaigns	0.75
Magazine campaigns	0.50
Outdoor campaigns	0.50
Radio campaigns	0.75

Figure 21.3 Illustration on Tracking Media-Class and Scheduling Decisions.

To begin, we need to establish a common unit of measurement for expressing the amount of advertising a company is buying. This is a *gross rating point (GRP)*. A rating point is a number of potential advertising exposures purchased by an advertiser, expressed as a percentage of the population. If a television program reached 10% of the population, an ad in that program would deliver 10 gross rating points. Gross rating points are an expression of the amount of advertising without regard to duplication. To continue the example, a media schedule containing 200 GRPs includes a number of potential advertising exposures equal to twice the population.

A related concept is a *target rating point (TRP)*. It is identical to GRP, except that it considers only advertising exposures to members of the target market. If a schedule consists of media that include high concentrations of target market members, TRPs would be higher than GRPs. For instance, if the media in a 200-GRP schedule contains twice the concentration of target market members found in the population as a whole, the schedule would deliver 400 TRPs. This is important, because a company might reduce its media costs by choosing specialized media. If a highly specialized class of media could consistently deliver 400 TRPs from a 200-GRP schedule, it would cut the effective cost of media in half, all else being equal.

With this background, consider the spreadsheet in Figure 21.3. It begins by assuming that the average cost for advertising media is $25,000 per rating point (cell C1). The actual number, of course, changes over time. You can accommodate these changes by simply changing the number in the spreadsheet. The same is true for the various indices used to help estimate the amount of advertising a company can buy with a given media budget. The spreadsheet includes a number of *cost* and *targeting indices*. *Cost indices* express the average cost of different media classes relative to the standard cost upon which the overall cost per rating point ($25,000) is based. *Targeting indices* provide an estimate of the potential savings available through targeting using the different media classes. If your product has a relatively unique user profile, planners will often use TRPs instead of GRPs for their planning, using specialized media to reduce wasted exposures. For instance, direct mail is very expensive (cost index of 20.00 from cell F36), but it is also very specialized (targeting index of 0.05 from cell C48). The indices provided in Figure 21.3 can be used to illustrate the planning process. While the numbers change over time and with the way a particular company defines the media classes they address, this can again be easily addressed by simply altering the initial value in the spreadsheet.

In our hypothetical example, we have a total media budget of $60 million (cell C2). The first step in our analysis is to estimate how much advertising this will provide in the two media classes we have selected (*cable TV* and local, or *spot radio*). Drawing on the tables of *cost* and *targeting indices* shown at the bottom of Figure 21.3, we link the cable and network radio cost indices (cells E3 and E4) with the corresponding cost indices from the table (cells F31 and H31), yielding values of 0.40 and 0.45, respectively. We link the cable and radio targeting indices (cells G3 and G4) with the targeting indices from the table (0.70 and 0.80 from cells C47 and C51). The result is to effectively reduce the estimated cost per rating point from $25,000 to ($25,000 × 0.40 × 0.70 =) $7000 and ($25,000 × 0.45 × 0.80 =) $9000, respectively.

These are crude estimates, of course. But they provide a useful starting point for the planning process. By multiplying the media class allocations (cells I3 and I4) by the total campaign budget (cell C2), we get a budget for each media class ($30,000,000 in cells K3 and K4). Dividing these budgets by the estimated costs per rating point, we get an estimated number of TRPs with which to work (4286 for cable and 3333 for spot radio, as shown in cells M3 and M4).

In the second stage of planning, we simply spread the TRPs over the schedule, with the distribution depending on how you believe the exposures will impact on the audience. For instance, if your message requires strong initial impact, with a lighter schedule to follow for reinforcement, you would place more media weight early in the schedule; if you believed your consumers would be more receptive during key buying periods (such as spring graduation and/or the Christmas season), you would place more media weight there. Cells N8 and N9 total up the TRPs actually allocated (4200 and 3000 TRPs, respectively) to help us keep track.

Below the media schedule, we have developed a more detailed summary of the actual media budget, summing the TRPs by quarter, and applying all the applicable cost indices, including seasonality. To illustrate, cells B15 through C20 summarize the budget for the first quarter's cable TV campaign. They adjust the initial cost per rating point (cell B15, linked from cell C1) by the cost index for cable TV (cell B16, linked from cell F31), the first-quarter seasonality index (cell B17, linked from B41), and the cable-TV targeting index (cell B18, linked from cell C47). We then multiply the adjusted cost per rating point by the number of TRPs (cell B19, summing the first quarter TRPs from cells B8 through D8). The resulting first-quarter budget ($7,350,000 in cell C20) is summed with the other quarters to summarize the actual cable-TV budget ($29,400,000 in cell O20). The spreadsheet links the actual media class budgets to the final cells of the media schedule (cells O8 and O9) for convenience, summing to an actual total ($56,400,000 in cell O10).

Cell O11 (cell C2 to cell O10) contains the amount ($3,600,000), and cell O12 the proportion (6.00%), of the original budget that is not specifically allocated to the media schedule. Often an advertiser will keep a reserve of 5% or so available for opportunistic media buys—opportunities created by unsold advertising slots that are steeply discounted in order to generate at least some revenue before the ad spots expire.

Once the spreadsheet has been constructed, we can proceed with the third stage where we adjust the schedule to deliver the kind of campaign we are seeking. For instance, if our initial schedule delivers too few TRPs to address the needs of our monthly schedule, we might look for less expensive media that would still be suitable for delivering the required message. In the case of cable TV, we might choose a less expensive time slot—early morning, late evening, or weekends, for instance. The spreadsheet enables us to quickly change our assumptions to better meet campaign objectives.

Media Vehicle Decisions

Media vehicle decisions involve comparisons of specific media within a given class, such as a comparison of cable programs. However, a little thought suggests that the *class vehicle* distinction is somewhat arbitrary. A comparison of two cable programs would be treated as a media vehicle decision. However, financial programs and news programs could be considered as two different media classes. Again, the same criteria apply to both media class and media vehicle decisions. The real distinction lies in the way the decisions tend to be made. As we have seen, media class decisions tend to emerge from qualitative considerations, such as the audience's *need for information* and *information processing capacity*, along with an evaluation of general cost, targeting, and message-delivery capabilities. By contrast, media vehicle decisions tend to be much more quantitative, drawing on specific estimates of the cost effectiveness of exposures. We have formalized this approach in Figure 21.4 as *cost-per-thousand effective target market exposures* (CPM_{ETM}). This is expressed in equation (1):

$$CPM_{ETM} = \frac{C}{TA \cdot E}. \tag{1}$$

where: C = cost per ad in a given media vehicle; TA = number of target market members ('000) reached by the ad; and E = probability that a given target market audience member will be effectively exposed.

Cost. The *cost* of an ad is given by media *rate cards*—what amounts to the posted retail price for advertising space. These prices vary by *media options*—the length of a television commercial, whether a magazine ad is full color or black-and-white, the placement and size of the ad, and so forth.

In practice, prices are highly negotiable for most media. They are also subject to substantial volume *discounts*. Many companies have centralized their media buying in order to capitalize on these discounts. For instance, in the early 1990s, General Motors consolidated its multi-billion dollar advertising budget into

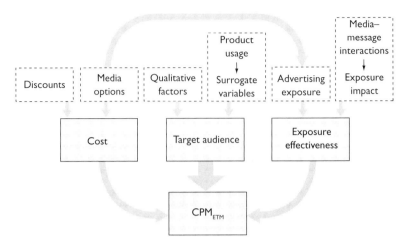

Figure 21.4 Cost-Per-Thousand Effective Target Market Exposures (CPM$_{ETM}$).

GM Mediaworks in order to get more pricing leverage and buying efficiency for its advertising media.

Target Audience. The concept of *target audience* grows out of our earlier discussion of *audience characteristics* (Figure 21.1). It is the practical translation of the target market membership into specific characteristics by which media audiences are measured. We noted that one of the best indicators of target market potential is product usage. Media vehicles with relatively high concentrations of product users in their audiences are likely to reach the kind of people who would be interested in buying a particular product.

Returning to our earlier discussion of *direct* and *indirect media-market matching*, we see the role of the *surrogate variables* referred to in Figure 21.3. These are generally demographics because most media data are broken down by demographics, thus enabling advertisers to target demographic groups. We suggested that people who consume energy drinks (*product users*) might be characterized as men between the ages of 18 and 25 (a *demographic surrogate variable*).

In practice, *product usage* can also be too broad a category to use as a target audience. People can use a product for a host of different reasons. For instance, energy-drink users could be habitual users to look for a boost in energy to support their intense lifestyle, or they could be more conservative people who often face work deadlines that periodically demand extra performance. We have referred to these differences in Figure 21.3 as *qualitative factors* because they are not readily apparent from commonly used media data. Media planners will often assign a subjective weight to one vehicle over another, based on such factors. They might also be inferred from media data, even if they are not readily apparent. For example, even if younger people were the primary users of energy drinks, a careful analysis might reveal a subcategory of energy-drink users with higher income and a somewhat older, more professional profile. Such a discovery could lead to the development of a drink aimed specifically at this segment. Segment members might be addressed with a more elaborate data-based *target audience*, including both product usage and demographic data. More likely, media planners would target them through a more refined selection of media that includes *subjective factors* as well as audience data. For instance, they might look for media whose audiences included relatively high concentrations of energy-drink users, but also had an older, more professional profile.

Exposure Effectiveness. The most obvious element of exposure effectiveness is the difference between what media planners call *opportunity to see* (*OTS*) and *actual advertising exposure*. The classic story illustrating this point is how water meters show dramatic fluctuations during commercial breaks on Monday night football. People who report watching Monday night football are counted as part of the media audience (having an OTS for commercials placed in that media vehicle). However, audience members use the breaks to visit the water closet or tend to any other necessary tasks without missing any of the football action, thus missing some of the ads. The difference between OTS and *effective exposure* is characteristic of all media. For instance, in magazines, Starch Communications publishes *AdNorms*, a report that provides analyses of actual advertising exposure, measuring what percentage of readers remember seeing a given ad, associated it with the sponsor, and read most of the copy in various magazines. The percentage of audience members exposed to ads varies by both media vehicle and by the nature of the ad placed in the vehicle.

This leads to the second element of *exposure effectiveness—exposure impact*. Drawing on magazine exposure as an example, the exposure impact of an ad that is associated with its sponsor is obviously greater than the impact of an ad that an audience member simply remembers seeing. Or to make the point even more dramatically, ask yourself whether an ad for disposable diapers would be more effective in *Soap Opera Digest* or *Parents* magazine, all else being equal? By all else being equal, we mean, "assuming that the same people are reading both magazines." The principle is rooted in our earlier discussion of *media usage plans*. People read *Parents* magazine to learn about things that are relevant to their role as parents, whereas they read *Soap Opera Digest* to learn about the fantasy world of their favorite soap operas. Clearly, disposable diapers are more relevant to the former than the latter media usage plan.

From a practical perspective, media planners might actually quantify *exposure effectiveness* (E in equation 1) using statistical sources such as Starch *AdNorms*, or they may simply take it into account as they make subjective adjustments in their media evaluations, based on cost and audience considerations.

Even if planners supply their own subjective judgments to represent *exposure effectiveness*, one can argue that converting the judgments to specific quantitative values is a useful process. It forces planners to be specific in judgments they are making, sensitizing them to the implications of different kinds of assumptions.

Cost-Per-Thousand Effective Target Market Exposures (CPM$_{ETM}$). Again, media class and media vehicle evaluation are very similar in theory. The difference is in the quantitative detail used to make the vehicle decisions, ultimately resulting in an estimate of *cost-per-thousand effective target market exposures (CPM$_{ETM}$)*. Whereas media class evaluation looks at average cost per rating point for vehicles within a particular media class, media vehicle evaluation looks at the specific cost for one vehicle versus another. For instance, suppose your campaign targeted users of a particular home-improvement product and that there were five million of these people in the market. If an ad in "This Old House" costs $100,000, reached one million target market members, and effectively exposed 75% of the people who saw the ad, the CPM_{ETM} would be ($100,000/(1000 thousand $\times$ 0.75 =) $133.33.

Compare this to the $7000 per TRP estimate used when developing the media schedule. *Cost per TRP* does not include exposure effectiveness. However, we know that the ad reaches (1,000,000/5,000,000 =) 20% of the target market. We can calculate the cost per TRP as ($100,000/20 =) $5000. This suggests that "This Old House" would likely be a good vehicle to include when implementing the media strategy. Its actual value, relative to other vehicles being considered, would depend on the CPM_{ETM} of the various vehicles.

Media Schedule Evaluation and Refinement: Frequency Value Planning

Our final task in conventional media planning is to incorporate the effects of multiple exposures into our planning process. Clearly, a second exposure to an ad will not have the same effect as a first exposure. Nor will a third, fourth, fifth, and so forth. These effects are reflected in an *advertising response curve*, where the number of advertising exposures is graphed against the probability of a desired audience member's response. Traditionally, the shape of the curve is assumed to take one of two forms, as illustrated in Figure 21.5—an S-shaped curve, where a "threshold effect" requires multiple exposures for the advertising to become effective, and a concave curve where the first advertising exposure is the most effective, followed by continually diminishing returns.

The shape of the response curve determines the media scheduling strategy. Given a fixed advertising budget, if it is S-shaped, the strategy will be to emphasize *frequency* (high levels of exposure) over *reach* (the proportion of the target population being reached by the campaign). The key will be to expose as many

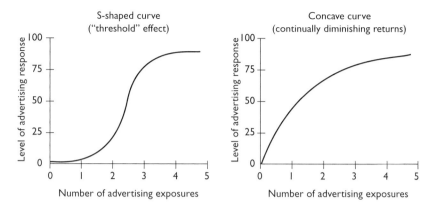

Figure 21.5 S-Shaped versus Concave Advertising Response Curves.

target market members as possible above the "threshold" level portrayed by the curve. Conversely, if the curve is concave, the strategy will be to emphasize reach over frequency, since the first exposures would be the most effective and therefore deliver a greater return for a company's advertising budget. Of course, a company can increase both reach and frequency by increasing its budget, but the budget will always become fixed at some point, implying some kind of trade-off.

Traditionally, media planners have addressed the trade-off judgmentally by selecting media to deliver reach or frequency as the situation appears to demand. In support of this, a number of advertising researchers sought to develop algorithms for estimating reach and frequency from media data (Agostini, 1961; Bower, 1963; Caffyn & Sagovsky, 1963; Kuhn, 1963; Marc, 1963; Hofmans, 1966; Claycamp & McClelland, 1968). As the research progressed, a host of different algorithms were developed to estimate *frequency distribution* rather than simple reach and average frequency (Metheringham, 1964; Greene & Stock, 1967; Liebman & Lee, 1974; Beardon, Haden, Klompmaker, & Teel, 1981; Rust & Klompmaker, 1981; Leckenby & Kishi, 1982; Rust & Leone, 1984; Leckenby & Boyd, 1984; Leckenby & Kishi, 1984; Leckenby & Rice, 1985; Danaher, 1988, 1989, 1991, 1992; Leckenby & Hong, 1998). Frequency distribution is the proportion of a target market reached at various exposure levels by a media schedule—0, 1, 2 times and so forth. There was general agreement within the advertising industry that frequency distributions provided better information than reach and average frequency. The question was how to use them. In 1979, Naples introduced the concept of *effective frequency*, arguing that a certain number of exposures are needed to be effective. The concept suggests that planners need only focus on *effective reach*, defining reach as the proportion of the target population who have received the requisite number of exposures.

If the *effective frequency* were judged to be three exposures, and if the frequency distribution indicated that 50% of the target population were exposed three or more times, *effective reach* would be 50%.

One of the problems with the *effective frequency* approach is that it places no value on any exposure below the "effective" level. In essence, it assumes a radical S-shaped advertising response curve, where the threshold is the level of effective frequency (Cannon & Riordan, 1994). While many advertisers have traditionally espoused the S-shaped curve as descriptive of how advertising works, the weight of empirical studies appears to support a concave curve (Simon & Arndt, 1980; Schultz & Block, 1986; Zielske, 1986). More recent studies suggest that an S-shaped curve might describe advertising response in some cases, but not others (Feinberg, 1992; Feinberg, 2001; Vakratsas, Feinberg, Bass, & Kalyanaran, 2004). One of the problems with response-curve research is that it involves empirically fitting a theoretically preconceived curve to actual advertising response data. It is dependent on the researcher's theory and is highly sensitive to random errors ("noise") in the data. However, the results clearly do not support a planning system such as *effective frequency* that depends on an S-shaped response curve.

Cannon, Leckenby, and Abernethy (2002) address this problem by suggesting a planning system (*frequency value planning*, or *FVP*) that easily accommodates any type of response curve. They illustrate using an S-shaped and concave curve, noting that each can be estimated from three points. For instance, suppose you were developing a "brand awareness" campaign and estimated that you would get a zero response for no advertising exposures, 45% probability of response to a single exposure, and a response probability of 88%, for five exposures. This would enable you to fit a concave response curve such as the one shown in Figure 21.5. Estimates of 0%, 2%, and 88% would have fit an S-shaped curve. Either way, the estimates are no more demanding than those required to implement *effective frequency*. The difference is that once planners have fitted the response curve, it enables them to estimate advertising response for any number of advertising exposures. To illustrate, consider a frequency distribution where 20% of the target market is unexposed, 40% exposed once, 23% exposed twice, 10% exposed three times, 5% four times, and 2% five times. Using the concave curve shown in Figure 21.5 to estimate response rates, we can construct the *FVP* analysis shown in Table 21.1.

Note that the *advertising response* column is derived from the advertising response curve, matching each level of exposure with the corresponding level of response–brand awareness, in our example. The *exposure value* column is simply the *advertising response* weighted by the proportion of the target market receiving the corresponding number of advertising exposures, as shown in the *exposure distribution* column. The *total exposure value* is the sum of the advertising

Table 21.1 An illustrative *FVP* analysis

Media exposures	Exposure distribution	Advertising response	Exposure value
0	20%	0%	0.0%
I	40%	45%	18.0%
2	23%	68%	15.6%
3	10%	80%	8.0%
4	5%	85%	4.3%
5	2%	0.88%	1.8%
		Total Exposure Value: 47.7%	

response stimulated by the exposure distribution of the media schedule—47.7%, in this case. In other words, based on the estimates given, we believe that we will achieve a total of 47.7% improvement in brand awareness as a result of the schedule.

As with the media planning spreadsheet shown in Figure 21.3, the *FVP* analysis provides an iterative tool for fine-tuning the media schedule. However, the input will be based on specific media vehicle schedules, each designed under the same budget constraint and general schedule, as described in Figure 21.3. Each media vehicle schedule will yield a unique frequency distribution, which in turn, will interact with the established advertising response curve to deliver a total exposure value. Media planners may experiment with any number of different schedules to seek an optimal value.

Beyond Frequency Value Planning

One of the problems with *frequency value planning*, along with its antecedent approaches, is its simplistic definition of frequency. Specifically, it fails to account for *prior learning effects*, *exposure interval effects*, and *cross-media effects*. While both academics and practitioners are well aware of these, the effects are much like frequency distributions prior to the advent of *effective frequency* and *frequency value planning*. We have not yet developed a practical and systematic way of incorporating them into media planning systems. Such systems will no doubt emerge in the future. Until then, media planners will be left to address the effects intuitively through their judgments regarding the way they structure their media schedules.

Prior Learning Effects. In our discussion of advertising response curves, we suggested that one of the three points from which the curve could be estimated would be zero response for zero advertising exposures. This makes sense, of course. How could audience members respond to something they are not exposed to? But it begs the issue of prior learning. Advertising rarely addresses a totally new idea. Even if the ad takes a totally new approach, people might know something about the product. If the product is new, they might know something about the product category. If the product category is new, they will still link it to other things they know and understand. All of this will affect the way they respond to the campaign. For instance, Vakratsas et al. (2004) suggest that the broad support found in the literature for a concave response curve is due to the fact that studies typically address audiences whose prior knowledge moves them past the "threshold" that would exist and drive an S-shaped curve if the product were totally unknown. Nor is prior learning necessarily limited to an S-shaped or concave curve. Research suggests that, in some circumstances (i.e., high involvement), too much repetition can actually have a negative effect on advertising response (Batra & Ray, 1986; Nordhielm, 2002). Unlike *effective frequency*, *frequency value planning* is compatible with any type of advertising response curve. However, we have yet to integrate our knowledge into clear guidelines for determining the kind of curve we should seek to use in any given situation.

Exposure Interval Effects. One of the most troubling problems with *frequency value planning* is the fact that there is no such thing as true frequency. That is, people don't process multiple exposures at the same time, and the time between exposures makes a big difference. The advent of single-source data has given rise to a host of studies demonstrating the short-term effect of advertising on sales, governed by a concave response curve (Wood, 1990; Jones, 1995; Longman, 1997; Wood, 2009). The effect gradually decays in the days and weeks following exposure. This suggests that advertising schedules should emphasize continuity (Ephron, 1995, 1997; Jones, 1995, 1997; Longman, 1997; VonGonten & Donius, 1997). Of course, the primary purpose of advertising is usually not to stimulate short-term sales, but to change attitudes, the effects of which will only be felt over the long run, through interaction with other elements of the marketing mix (Colley, 1961). Fortunately, the same research that supports short-term sales effects for advertising suggests that long-term effects are mediated by short-term advertising response (Jones, 1995; Longman, 1997; VonGonten & Donius, 1997). This, in turn, suggests that *exposure interval effects* may not present a severe problem. If the research is correct, planners need only focus on reach and continuity—schedules that are spread evenly over key buying periods—and the composite effect of the short-term response curves will be a long-term concave curve.

Cross-media effects. When several different media are involved in an advertising campaign, one of the logical questions is how they interact with each other. By this, we are not asking their relative values as media alternatives; this has already been addressed in our discussion of media vehicles, where we seek to estimate the cost-per-thousand effective target market exposures (CPM_{ETM}) of each alternative (see Figure 21.4). Any difference in the exposure impact of one medium or media option versus another would be addressed through the probability of effective exposure. However, what if one type of media increases or decreases the effectiveness of another? For instance, Pfeiffer and Zinnbauer (2010) find that traditional media are very useful early in a campaign for stimulating brand-related Internet (social networking) activity. Later in the campaign, after achieving initial awareness and a measure of brand equity, online advertising is adequate to drive social networking. The Pfeiffer and Zinnbauer study is only illustrative. Notwithstanding the fact that our approach to IMC is built on the unique roles, and presumably interactions, among media classes, we still know relatively little about cross-media effects. Once we develop a better understanding, we will still be faced with the problem of incorporating them into a practical media scheduling and evaluation tool.

Conclusions

The purpose of this chapter was to systematize and review the logic and major components of media analysis and decision making. Underlying the effort, however, there were two major themes. The first is the integrative nature of modern media planning. There was a time when advertising media were viewed primarily as a means of delivering advertising messages. Today, we broadly recognize that this view was naïve. This chapter seeks to show how media selection is linked to creative strategy. Progress not withstanding, many of the media–creative interactions are still not well understood. Nevertheless, it helps to identify them, so we know where to focus future research. This is what we have sought to do.

The second major theme is that we should seek to quantify, or at least systematize, our judgments whenever possible. The purpose is not to replace judgment with mechanistic, mathematical decision processes. Rather, it is to impose a logical discipline on our thinking. Indeed, developing decision models is not the major objective. If properly done, the modeling process forces us to be explicit about our assumptions and to articulate subtle, but important, distinctions in concepts and relationships. Too often, our intuitive mind misses these in favor of broad patterns that gloss over important details. This chapter illustrates the direction taken in the media literature, and suggests areas that need further development.

References

Agostini, J. M. (1961). How to estimate unduplicated audiences. *Journal of Advertising Research, 1* (1), 11–14.

Assael, H., & Cannon, H. (1979). Do demographics help in media selection? *Journal of Advertising Research, 19* (6), 7–11.

Batra, R., & Ray, M. L. (1986). Situational effects of advertising repetition: The moderating influence of motivation, ability, and opportunity to respond. *Journal of Consumer Research, 12* (4), 432–445.

Beardon, W. O., Haden, R. S., Klompmaker, J. E., & Teel, J. E. (1981). Attentive audience delivery of TV advertising schedules. *Journal of Marketing Research, 18* (2), 187–191.

Bower, J. (1963). Net audiences of U.S. and Canadian magazines: Seven tests of Agostini's formula. *Journal of Advertising Research, 3* (1), 13–20.

Caffyn, I. M., & Sagovsky, M. (1963). Net audiences of British newspapers: A comparison of the Agostini and Sainsbury methods. *Journal of Advertising Research, 3* (1), 21–25.

Cannon, H. M. (2001, April). Addressing new media with conventional media planning. *Journal of Interactive Advertising, 1* (2). Retrieved from http://jiad.org/article11.

Cannon, H. M., Leckenby, J. D., & Abernethy, A. (2002). Beyond effective frequency: Evaluating media schedules using frequency value planning. *Journal of Advertising Research, 42* (6), 33–47.

Cannon, H. M., & Riordan, E. A. (1994). Effective reach and frequency: Does it really make sense? *Journal of Advertising Research, 34* (2), 19–28.

Cannon, H. M., Smith, J. A., & Williams, D. A. (2007). A data-overlay approach to synthesizing single-source data. *Journal of Advertising, 36,* 7–18.

Claycamp, H. J., & McClelland, C. W. (1968). Estimating reach and the magic of K. *Journal of Advertising Research, 8* (2), 44–51.

Colley, R. H. (1961). *Defining advertising goals for measured advertising results.* New York: Association of National Advertisers.

Danaher, P. (1988). Parameter estimation for the dirichlet-multinomial distribution using supplementary beta-binomial data. *Communications in Statistics, A17* (6), 777–778.

Danaher, P. (1989). An approximate log-linear model for predicting magazine audiences. *Journal of Marketing Research, 26* (4), 473–479.

Danaher, P. (1991). A canonical expansion model for multivariate media exposure distributions: A generalization of the "duplication of viewing law." *Journal of Marketing Research, 28* (3), 361–367.

Danaher, P. (1992). A Markov-chain model for multivariate magazine-exposure distributions. *Journal of Business and Economic Statistics, 10* (4), 401–407.

Ephron, E. (1995). More weeks, less weight: The shelf-space model of advertising. *Journal of Advertising Research, 35,* 18–23.

Ephron, E. (1997). Recency planning. *Journal of Advertising Research, 37* (4), 61–65.

Feinberg, F. M. (1992). Pulsing policies for aggregate advertising models. *Marketing Science, 11,* 221–234.

Feinberg, F. M. (2001). On continuous-time optimal advertising under S-shaped response. *Management Science, 47* (11), 1476–1487.

Greene, J. D., & Stock, J. S. (1967). *Advertising reach and frequency in magazines.* New York: Marketmath Inc. and Reader's Digest Assciation.

Hofmans, P. (1966). Measuring the cumulative net coverage of any combination of media. *Journal of Marketing Research, 3* (3), 267–278.

Jones, J. P. (1995). Single-source data begins to fulfill its promise. *Journal of Advertising Research, 35* (3), 9–18.

Jones, J. P. (1997). What does effective frequency mean in 1997? *Journal of Advertising Research, 37* (4), 14–20.

Kuhn, W. (1963). Net audiences of German magazines: A new formula. *Journal of Advertising Research, 3* (1), 30–33.

Leckenby, J. D. & Boyd, M. (1984). An improved beta binomial reach/frequency model for magazines. *Current Issues and Research in Advertising, 7* (1), 1–24.

Leckenby, J. D., & Hong, J. (1998). Using reach/frequency for web media planning. *Journal of Advertising Research, 38* (2), 7–20.

Leckenby, J. D., & Kishi, S. (1982). Performance of four exposure distribution models. *Journal of Advertising Research, 22* (2), 35–44.

Leckenby, J. D., & Kishi, S. (1984). The Dirichlet multinomial distribution as a magazine exposure model. *Journal of Marketing Research, 21* (1), 100–106.

Leckenby, J. D., & Rice, M. (1985). A beta binomial network TV exposure model using limited data. *Journal of Advertising, 14* (3), 13–20.

Liebman, L. & Lee, E. (1974). Reach and frequency estimation services. *Journal of Advertising Research, 14* (4), 23–25.

Longman, K. A. (1997). If not effective frequency, then what? *Journal of Advertising Research, 37* (4), 44–40.

Marc, M. (1963). Net audiences of French business papers: Agostini's formula applied to special markets. *Journal of Advertising Research, 3* (1), 26–29.

Metheringham, R. A. (1964). Measuring the net cumulative coverage of a print campaign. *Journal of Advertising Research, 4* (4), 23–28.

Naples, M. J. (1979). *Effective frequency: The relationship between frequency and advertising effectiveness.* New York: Association of National Advertisers.

Nordhielm, C. L. (2002). The influence of level of processing on advertising repetition effects. *Journal of Consumer Research, 29* (3), 371–382.

Percy, L., & Rossiter, J. R. (1992). A model of brand awareness and brand attitude advertising strategies. *Psychology and Marketing, 9* (4), 263–274.

Pfeiffer, M., & Zinnbauer, M. (2010). Can old media enhance new media? How traditional advertising complements the online social network. *Journal of Advertising Research, 50* (1), 42–49.

Puto, C. P., & Wells, W. D. (1984). Informational and transformational advertising: The differential effects of time. *Advances in Consumer Research, 11*, 638–643.

Ratchford, B. T. (1987). New insights about the FCB Grid. *Journal of Advertising Research, 27* (4), 24–38.

Rossiter, J. R., & Percy, L. (1997). *Advertising communications and promotion management* (2nd Ed.). New York: McGraw-Hill.

Rossiter, J. R., Percy, L., & Donovan, R. J. (1991). A better advertising planning grid. *Journal of Advertising Research, 31* (5), 11–21.

Rust, R. T., & Klompmaker, J. E. (1981). Improving the estimation procedure for the beta binomial TV exposure model. *Journal of Marketing Research, 18* (4), 442–448.

Rust, R. T., & Leone, R. P. (1984). The mixed media Dirichlet-multinomial distribution: A model for evaluating television-magazine advertising schedules. *Journal of Marketing Research, 21* (1), 89–99.

Schultz, D., & Block, M. E. (1986). Empirical estimation of advertising response functions. *Journal of Media Planning, 1* (1), 17–24.

Simon, J. L., & Arndt, J. (1980). The shape of the advertising response function. *Journal of Advertising Research, 20* (4), 11–28.

Vakratsas, D., Feinberg, F. M., Bass, F. M., & Kalyanaram, G. (2004). Advertising response functions revisited: A model of dynamic probabilistic thresholds. *Marketing Science, 23* (1), 109–119.

Vaughn, R. (1980). How advertising works: A planning model. *Journal of Advertising Research, 20* (5), 27–33.

Vaughn, R. (1986). How advertising works: A planning model revisited. *Journal of Advertising Research, 26* (1), 57–66.

VonGonten, M. F., & Donius, J. (1997). Advertising exposure and advertising effects: New panel-based findings. *Journal of Advertising Research, 37* (4), 51–60.

Wood, L. (1990). Single source solutions. *Television Symposium*. Tarrytown, NY: Communications Operations.

Wood, L. (2009). Short-term effects of advertising: Some well-established empirical law-like patterns. *Journal of Advertising Research, 49* (2), 186–192.

Zielske, H. A. (1986). Using effective frequency in media planning. *Journal of Media Planning, 1* (1), 53–56.

Chapter 22

Managing Non-Traditional Advertising

A Message Processing Framework

Rick T. Wilson and Brian D. Till

Introduction

Traditional advertising is giving way to a variety of new methods to communicate and interact with consumers. This trend is driven by technology (e.g., wireless text messaging to phones, Internet search advertising, GPS-based location advertising on PDAs, self-destructing SMS messages, QR coded posters), pure opportunism (e.g., free-floating holograms, guerilla light projections, street theater, moving billboards), and sheer ingenuity (e.g., subway turnstiles, airplane tray tables, parking lot stripes, water coolers). Its rise also comes at a time of a general decline in the use and fragmentation of traditional media, a shift in the amount of time consumers spend outside the home, and the pervasiveness of technology in media—both in ad-avoidance technology (such as DVRs) and new capabilities in ad transmission (such as digital billboards and mobile/cell phone advertising) (Chafkin, 2007; Francese, 2004).

The absolute number and variety of non-traditional advertising can make its study and use appear daunting. However, despite its seemingly eclectic and varied nature, non-traditional advertising does share some theoretical commonalities that help to understand, evaluate, and implement its use. To organize these commonalities, we present the Non-traditional Advertising Message Processing (NAMP) framework, which is simple yet theoretically sound and robust. Our NAMP framework uses the capacity theory of attention and message response involvement theory to frame the relevant issues pertaining to McGuire's (1969) receiver and channel components while the resource-matching hypothesis is used to frame issues concerning the message component. The NAMP framework additionally takes into account Thorson and Rodgers' Figure 1.1 advertising "context" to better understand how to maximize advertising effectiveness.

Non-Traditional Advertising

Not surprisingly, "non-traditional advertising" covers a lot of ground and includes both relatively new media options (e.g., cell phones) as well as new uses of traditional media in a new way (e.g., augmented reality). Our goal in this section is not necessarily to present an exhaustive list of non-traditional advertising, but rather to develop a reasonable taxonomy that provides a good sense of the range of possibilities and to highlight some particularly interesting applications.

In this section we also introduce the NAMP framework, which is a useful and powerful tool to explain the effectiveness of non-traditional advertising. As shown in Figure 22.1, the framework dichotomizes the target audience and media into four quadrants based upon whether media is fixed or mobile and the target audience captive or mobile. The importance of these classifications will be explained later. To begin we start with the basic distinction that non-traditional advertising could either be fixed (e.g., airport terminal board) or mobile (e.g., bus wrap).

Fixed Advertisement

Non-traditional advertising of this nature includes bus, train, subway and taxi interiors, in-store video, grocery cart advertising, video game advertising,

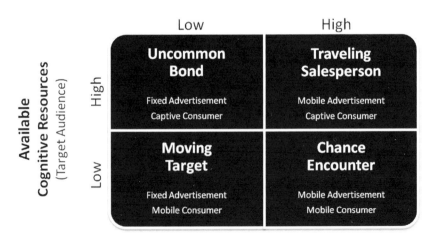

Figure 22.1 Non-Traditional Advertising Message Processing Framework.

cinema pre-show advertising, webisodes, public restroom advertising, gas pump handles, airplane trays, digital billboards, cell phones, wall murals, benches, bus shelters, street branding, ski area displays, spectaculars (extra large outdoor boards), and office/waiting room advertising. The extent of message development is influenced both by the size of the medium (airplane tray vs. waiting room poster) as well as the average length of exposure (gas pump handle vs. cinema pre-show advertising).

The use of digital in-store media will continue to grow as the technology moves away from relatively complicated PC-based systems toward solid-state technology requiring less programming sophistication. With new developments in this area, making timely changes to messaging is much easier, improving managers' ability to easily modify video. Digital screens coupled with RFID location technology on shopping carts allows the targeting of grocery customers based on location in the store.

Webisodes are short entertainment integrated with the sponsoring brand and delivered via the Web (Hulu, YouTube, etc.). BMW pioneered this medium commissioning prominent film directors to produce short stories featuring BMW automobiles. Webisodes allow a longer exposure to the brand than a more traditional 30 second TV spot, but because they are less intrusive (viewers need to proactively seek them out), it is critical that the story content be engaging and relevant to the target audience. For example, BMW's short films, about 5 minutes in length, were engaging stories in which the brand was an integral part, but the films had stand-alone entertainment value.

Augmented reality is the interaction of digital image and the real world via a smartphone or computer application. Again, BMW has used augmented reality to manipulate a 3D image of their Z4 convertible and to "drive" the car in a way that the car "paints" color tracks with its tires, consistent with the brand's print and TV campaign. Visitors to BMW's website were able to use the camera on their computer to transmit the special symbol in BMW's ad to then control a "virtual Z4" and "drive" the car on their computer screen. As the car moved around on the computer screen, its wheels left track marks in the colors of various paints, allowing the visitor to create art with the car.

Because non-traditional media can sometimes be highly idiosyncratic in nature, there can be opportunities to find the perfect match between brand meaning, medium, and target audience. Ski lift supports are wrapped with a protective pad to protect skiers. Volvo puts their tagline "Volvo for Life" on these pads—the perfect medium for their safety message and a great fit with their more upscale target audience.

We include mobile phone advertising in this category as while the audience is mobile, the medium is fixed relative to the audience. Phone geographic tracking software can make targeting advertising (text messages, BlueTooth delivered content, etc.) to be tied closely to the user's location. However, while there are over three billion cell phones worldwide, a fairly small portion are smartphones able to maximize audio/visual content.

Digital billboards are revitalizing outdoor media. Digital billboards are more engaging and allow for quicker and easier programming and customization of messages and brands by daypart as well as easy "board sharing" where different brand advertising is rotated on a timed cycle. Mini Cooper has been able to very creatively use digital boards by special programming and sensors that detect owners' key fobs (key chains) so that when a Mini Cooper driver passes by the board it displays a personalized message such as "Great Car, Dave!"

Street branding includes chalking and other forms of markings on the street and is also an opportunity for creative use. To highlight the slimness of Sony's Cyber Shot camera, the line "the ultra-slim Cyber Shot T1" was chalked on a street with a wrist strap cord disappearing into a street grate crack. No camera was actually present but the creative chalking and cord placement certainly made the point.

Mobile Advertisement

In this category, we include such examples as taxi and bus boards, bus wraps, truck exteriors, human moving boards, towed boards, sky writing, airplane banners, race car sponsorship, and promotional vehicles.

While subject to increased FAA regulation in a post 9/11 world, the use of sky writing and airplane banners is a fairly simple way to deliver a short message to a geographically concentrated audience. Local restaurants and entertainment spots will occasionally tow a large sign around such venues as baseball stadiums shortly after a game ends. Red Bull has become particularly effective with this type of non-traditional advertising. They sponsor a performance plane for air races, several race cars including in the World Rally Championship series and the highly prestigious Formula One series. Red Bull also has the Mobile Energy Team, which is a stable of cars decked in the Red Bull livery and adorned with a large Red Bull can on the roof. These cars are driven around at various sporting and festival events.

Creative use of this media, though, can break through what is often an advertising-dense and distracting urban environment. For example, taxis featuring a roof board for HBO's Soprano's series also had a fake arm sticking out of the trunk, reinforcing the mafia theme of the show. A bus board (placed at the back end of bus) for a stop smoking aid featured a man's head with the smoking tailpipe where his mouth would be and the line "Ready to Quit?"

Theoretical Foundation

The NAMP framework draws upon three theoretical domains—capacity theory of attention, message response involvement theory, and the resource-matching hypothesis. Capacity theory of attention originates from cognitive psychology and recognizes that people have limited cognitive or mental resources available for tasks such as message processing. Message response involvement theory explains why people attend to advertisements, what factors hinder and aid in message processing, and how these issues affect advertising (MacInnis & Jaworski, 1989). Finally, the resource-matching hypothesis offers strategies for enhancing advertising effectiveness for non-traditional advertising based upon a match between the cognitive resources available for message processing and the resources required for the task (Anand & Sternthal, 1989).

Capacity Theory of Attention and Message Response Involvement Theory

Exposure to non-traditional advertising is often incidental and people do not always pay full attention. Thus, some people have limited cognitive resources available for message processing and the amount of mental resources available to people for processing non-traditional advertising may be very limited. Some non-traditional advertising is more difficult to notice or process because they are peripheral to what people see or are moving (e.g., bus advertising, airplane banners). This can make some non-traditional advertising methods more cognitively demanding.

The implications for message processing can best be understood by the capacity theory of attention. According to the theory, the amount of cognitive resources available is limited (Kahneman, 1973). Although limited, these scarce resources may be allocated among concurrent tasks with the amount of cognitive resources dedicated to any one task depending on demands imposed by the task and the individual's personal motivation. Thus, if a person is driving, which is a more difficult task, fewer cognitive resources are available for the processing of roadside advertising and the effectiveness of the medium may suffer.

Effectiveness of non-traditional advertising can be measured by the extent that the message is understood, the retention of message components or brand information in memory, and the extent to which attitudes toward the ad or brand develop (MacInnis, Moorman, & Jaworski, 1991).

The attention that people are able or willing to allocate to message processing is not solely dependent upon the task such as driving. Message response involvement theory also suggests three additional factors—motivation, opportunity, and ability (Batra & Ray, 1985; MacInnis & Jaworski, 1989). People may be more *motivated* to process a particular ad due to their own individual needs or interests. Regardless of one's motivation to attend to non-traditional advertising, the two remaining factors may act to further stimulate or hinder message processing. People may have limited *opportunity* to process advertising if the message length or its appearance is brief or if many distractions are present (e.g., heavy pedestrian or road traffic, talking to a companion or on a cellular phone, billboard partially blocked by vegetation). Similarly, those with limited *ability* may have insufficient product knowledge or intelligence to fully comprehend an ad as when an ad's execution is complex or otherwise difficult to read.

As motivation, opportunity, and ability increases, the amount of attention paid to the ad increases and less attention is paid to secondary tasks leading to a greater amount of working memory allocated to processing ad and brand information. Deeper processing leads to more encoding of brand and ad information into memory and the development of stronger attitudes (MacInnis & Jaworski, 1989). Applying the capacity theory of attention and message response involvement to non-traditional advertising works well if we no longer categorize it by traditional means (e.g., out-of-home, digital, ambient) but rather categorize it by context. That is, whether the advertising (channel) is fixed or mobile and whether the audience (receiver) is captive or mobile. This distinction permits us to organize non-traditional advertising by the difficulty in message processing and offers a foundation to build a framework to understand, evaluate, and implement non-traditional advertising in a variety of advertising contexts.

Media Channel Issues: Fixed vs. Mobile Advertising

Non-traditional advertising that is fixed is stationary with respect to the audience viewing the ad and includes items such as Internet search advertising, billboards, benches, public telephones, bus shelters, cinema advertising, and bus, train, and airport terminal displays. Mobile advertisements, on the other hand, are advertisements affixed to objects that move with respect to the audience viewing it and includes such advertisements found on the outside of taxis and buses as well as aerial advertisements such as hot air balloons, blimps, or airplane banners.

As compared to fixed advertising, mobile advertising tends to be more difficult to process because it is often fleeting and people have limited exposure time. However, fixed ads are not without their own issues. The opportunity to process fixed ads may be hindered by obstruction or visual clutter. Outdoor ads can easily be blocked by overgrown vegetation, buildings and structures, people, and other advertising. Research in transit facilities shows that recognition rates for advertising are as much as 8% lower in areas where ads are routinely obstructed by passengers (Wilson & Till, 2008). Visual clutter, on the other hand, not only reduces the overall visibility of non-traditional advertising but also reduces the attention-getting prominence or novelty of an ad (Cole & Hughes, 1984). Too many billboards in a particular stretch of highway can impede message processing by diverting attention to one billboard at the expense of another (Young, 1984). Similar effects have been found in sports arenas where large amounts of advertising vie for attention (Turley & Shannon, 2000). This suggests, based on our initial framework, that although some types of ads may appear less cognitively demanding such as fixed ads, their ability to attract attention may be limited due to distractions.

Receiver Issues: Captive vs. Mobile Audiences

As with the advertising outlined earlier, we can categorize the audience for non-traditional advertising as either captive (fixed) or mobile, recognizing that people may have more difficulty processing ads if they are moving. A mobile person can be, for example, a pedestrian, driver, or passenger.

Mobile audiences generally have fewer cognitive resources than do captive audiences. Mobile people, whether walking or driving, require more time to stop or change direction because of their forward momentum and the number of interacting variables which must be processed in parallel in order to avoid other pedestrians, vehicles, or objects (Halford, Wilson, & Phillips, 1998). This task is cognitively demanding and as such people spend fewer seconds on any given object in their purview including advertising (Crundall & Underwood, 1998). Driving studies have found that as traffic increases or as the environment becomes more urban, the number and length of glances at advertising dramatically decreases (Beijer, 2002; Smiley et al., 2005). Another study found that bus advertising was noticed 52% of the time by captive people waiting for a bus, 35% of the time by walking people, and only 4% of the time by people who were driving (Prendergast & Hang, 1999). A study of roadside advertising found that 97% of the glances at advertising were within 25 degrees of a driver's forward-looking field of vision and 75% were within 10 degrees of this field of vision (Beijer, 2002). Not surprisingly, billboards placed on the right-hand side of the road are found to have recall scores as much as 7% greater than those on the left-hand side of the road (Donthu, Cherian, & Bhargava, 1993).

While seemingly ideal targets for non-traditional advertising, captive audiences have issues as well like talking, reading, or taking notice of other disruptive activities (Wilson & Till, 2008). A study of cinema advertising found that captive people who reported talking to their movie companion, talking or playing on a cellular phone, or reading recalled 50% fewer ads as compared to those who did not participate in such distracting activities (Wilson & Till, 2011). Perhaps the most distracting activity associated with a captive audience—and a mobile audience for that matter—is talking on a cellular phone. In a simulated driving experiment, individuals who did not speak on the phone had five incidents (e.g., speeding, running a stop sign, failing to yield, following too close) whereas an individual talking to a passenger in the car had 10 incidents and an individual talking on a cellular phone had 22 incidents (Hutton & Rose, 2005).

Non-traditional Advertising Messaging Processing (NAMP) Framework

The NAMP framework is a unique method of categorization and a starting point for ensuring the effectiveness of non-traditional advertising as measured by brand recall/recognition, attitude toward the ad/brand, and message persuasion (see Figure 22.1). The NAMP framework places the amount of cognitive resources available to an audience along the vertical axis (receiver) while the amount required to process a message is along the horizontal axis (channel). Two levels of cognitive resources (low, high) along each axis divide the framework into four quadrants. This division into quadrants allocates non-traditional media and its intended audience based upon the amount of cognitive resources made available by the recipient to the amount of resources needed for successful processing of the ad.

Quadrant 1 illustrates the combination of cognitive resources and the ads requiring the fewest resources to process. Quadrants 2 and 3 represent incrementally more difficult situations in terms of cognitive resources in that either few resources are available by the audience (quadrant 3) or too many are required by advertisements (quadrant 2) for successful processing. Quadrant 4 exemplifies the most difficult of situations for message processing as audiences have few cognitive resources available and advertisements here require the most resources to process.

Quadrant 1: Uncommon Bond

Within the first quadrant, audiences have greater flexibility in allocating their limited supply of cognitive resources since they are captive and advertisements take fewer resources to process because they are fixed. In this scenario, people have ample time sitting in the movie theater or traveling on a train and may welcome the diversion or distraction that non-traditional advertisements may provide. In fact, an "*Uncommon Bond*" may be formed between the audience and the advertisement in that the recipient is entertained by the advertisement and the advertisement is able to depart its message to the recipient.

Quadrant 2: Traveling Salesperson

The media and audiences in the second quadrant are analogous to a "*Traveling Salesperson*" who must quickly gain your attention before the door is slammed in his/her face. Here too mobile advertisements must break through a world filled with clutter and distractions in order to quickly gain attention. Many of these advertisements move at speeds greater than 30 mph creating an even more challenging scenario for message processing. Quadrant 2 pits captive audiences who have greater flexibility in allocating their cognitive resources against mobile advertisements which require greater levels of cognitive resources to process.

Quadrant 3: Moving Target

Advertisements found within the third quadrant are fixed but the audience is mobile and a "*Moving Target*." Examples of mobile audiences include automobile drivers and passengers, moving pedestrians, and commuters onboard trains and buses. Automobile drivers and moving pedestrians generally have limited cognitive resources available to process messages as they are more likely to be concerned about sidewalk or road traffic and other distractions than they are about advertising in the immediate area. Passengers and commuters may have more flexibility to process these advertisements because they are not operating a vehicle or walking but because they are still moving with respect to the fixed advertisement and/or talking with their driver or fellow passengers, they have limited resources available for message processing (Lee & Triggs, 1976).

Quadrant 4: Chance Encounter

With both people and advertisements moving, the likelihood of a person taking notice of a mobile advertisement as postulated in quadrant 4 of the NAMP framework is likened to a "*Chance Encounter*." Here audiences are required to expend a great amount of effort to process mobile advertisements at a time when they have the fewest amount of cognitive resources available. Thus, this quadrant is perhaps one of the most challenging to address.

Using NAMP to Maximize Advertising Effectiveness

To insure that audiences are able to process the entire message as intended by the advertiser, we draw upon the resource-matching hypothesis. In this way, advertisers can maximize effectiveness by crafting ads based upon the appropriate NAMP quadrant.

Resource-Matching Hypothesis

The resource-matching hypothesis states that when the amount of cognitive resources required to process an ad matches the amount of cognitive resources held by the target audience, advertising effectiveness is maximized (Anand & Sternthal, 1989, 1990). However, when too few cognitive resources are available, message processing is hindered and the advertisement may not be fully processed or it may be processed superficially.

Conversely, if the amount of cognitive resources available to the target audience exceeds the amount of resources necessary to process a message, the message recipient may begin excessive elaboration on the ad's message. While the increased elaboration may bring about favorable thoughts toward the ad or brand it may just as easily produce irrelevant, idiosyncratic, or negative thoughts as well (Meyers-Levy & Peracchio, 1995; Peracchio & Meyers-Levy, 1997). Therefore it is important that marketing communications be designed so that the level of cognitive resources required matches the level available. We call this process of matching resources "*cognitive congruency*."

Admittedly, it is more difficult for marketing practitioners to influence the receiver side of the equation than it is for the message side when attempting to achieve cognitive congruency (Anand & Sternthal, 1989). Consequently, the onus is placed upon practitioners to create ads that fit both the context of ad placement and the type of activity the target audience is likely to be engaged in when encountering the advertisement. This means, for example, designing a billboard at the intersection of Main and Broadway very differently from a billboard along an interstate. This type of strategic and analytical thinking toward non-traditional advertising may require marketers to expend more time and cost during a campaign's development. The resource-matching hypothesis suggests several strategies to either reduce or increase the amount of resources required for message processing. These strategies are discussed in the next section.

Achieving Cognitive Congruency through Message Design

Figure 22.2 is presented as a guide to help achieve cognitive congruency through message design. It uses each of the four quadrants as a starting point in the design process.

While each one of the quadrants categorizes advertising contexts by the cognitive limitations or opportunities created by each combination of mobile and captive audiences and mobile and fixed advertisements, we can't assume that the message recipient's cognitive state is stable within each quadrant. As

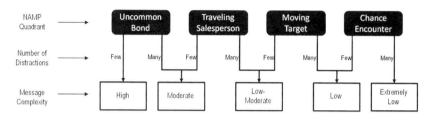

Figure 22.2 Achieving Cognitive Congruency through Message Design Framework.

discussed previously, distractions may be present that may limit an individual's opportunity or ability to process advertising. Therefore, we must understand what our target audience is likely doing in our chosen context. For example, if we target subway riders through transit advertising within the subway car (*Uncommon Bond*), we must discern whether our intended target is a commuter who takes the subway during rush hours or a casual rider who may travel in off-peak hours. The distinction helps us understand if there are few or many distractions present in this captive environment. For example, a daily commuter who travels during rush hour often contends with limited opportunity to process advertising due to the sheer number of people present or ads that may be partially blocked by standing passengers.

Consider another example—a billboard alongside a busy, urban highway (*Moving Target*). Advertising here should use a simpler design since the available cognitive resources a driver has is limited and very unlikely to be reallocated in any great quantity to message processing due to the complexity of the driving task in a congested area full of distractions. However, if the intended target passes the billboard several times during the week or month, then the message design can utilize a low-moderate complex design as the driver has increased opportunity for message processing.

Advertising researchers have identified a number of strategies to vary the level of complexity within an ad to match the message recipient's availability of cognitive resources (Anand & Sternthal, 1989). To increase the complexity of advertisements, message design might employ quantitative arguments, rich narrative ad copy, or message incongruity. Quantitative arguments, as shown in Figure 22.3, require more resources to process as message recipients evaluate and elaborate on such claims. Likewise, rich narrative copy shown in Figure 22.4 is more resource demanding as product or service assertions are embedded within in a story-like presentation (Peracchio & Meyers-Levy, 1997). Message incongruity, which presents information that contrasts prior expectations, also requires more cognitive resources to process (see Figure 22.5) (Anand & Sternthal, 1989).

Figure 22.3 Increasing Messaging Complexity Using Quantitative Arguments.

Figure 22.4 Increasing Messaging Complexity Using Narrative Copy.

Figure 22.5 Increasing Messaging Complexity Using Incongruity.

Simplifying the message, on the other hand, can be achieved by using fewer words or presenting information in a more direct, logical, and expository style (Peracchio & Meyers-Levy, 1997). For instance, listing product or service features in a straightforward factual manner as opposed to a narrative or story-like manner makes for easier and quicker message processing (see Figure 22.6). Complexity can also be reduced by using a simple layout or an easy-to-follow appeal (see Figure 22.7). Finally, qualitative arguments within the message, as shown in Figure 22.8, promote faster message processing as there are fewer concrete facts to evaluate (Anand & Sternthal, 1989).

For particular executions where it may be desirable to present complex messages in contexts where people are overwhelmed with distractions or unwilling

Figure 22.6 Decreasing Messaging Complexity Straightforward Factual Copy.

to expend the required cognitive resources for message processing, a couple of strategies are worth noting. The first is to increase an individual's motivation to process the ad by enhancing brand relevance. This may include using rhetorical questions, fear appeals, and sources that are similar to the message recipient (MacInnis et al., 1991). Another strategy is to employ novelty or creativity to draw the individual into the ad. However, for creativity to be truly effective, the ad's placement must be conspicuous otherwise the tactic may go fully unnoticed (Baack, Wilson, & Till, 2008). For example, an urban billboard affixed to the side of a building in a pedestrian neighborhood is unlikely to be processed for more than 1 or 2 seconds by an individual walking by and therefore should utilize a simple design. However, if it is able to grab an individual's limited attention through its use of a unique layout, vibrant or contrasting colors, or movement, a more complex message design may be permissible. Figure 22.9 is such an example. Here Calvin Klein Jeans uses a provocative headline and a QR code to capture attention and encourage passersby to stop and process the ad more fully. QR coding is similar to the technology behind bar codes. Utilization of this technology allows mobile phones to scan the code and have URLs, text-messaging addresses, or phone numbers appear on the screen of their phone.

Figure 22.7 Decreasing Messaging Complexity Using a Simple Appeal.

Figure 22.8 Decreasing Messaging Complexity Using Qualitative Arguments.

Figure 22.9 Attention Capture through QR Codes.

Conclusion

If scholarly research and effective practitioner use of non-traditional advertising is to move forward, a conceptual framework organizing emerging knowledge and applications is important. We present our NAMP framework as such a structure. To be certain, success in this seemingly disparate category of advertising must in fact not be seen as categories (e.g., outdoor, digital, ambient) but rather as contexts—contexts in which audiences have varying amounts of cognitive resources available for message processing. Thus, in order to ensure advertising effectiveness is maximized, message design must be made cognitively congruent such that ads are made simpler or more complex in order to match the available cognitive resources of the intended target.

References

Anand, P., & Sternthal, B. (1989). Strategies for designing persuasive messages: Deductions from the resource matching hypothesis. In P. Cafferata & A. M. Tybout (Eds.), *Cognitive and affective responses to advertising* (pp. 135–159). Lexington, MA: Lexington Books.

Anand, P., & Sternthal, B. (1990). Ease of message processing as a moderator of repetition effects in advertising. *Journal of Marketing Research, 27* (3), 345–353.

Baack, D. W., Wilson, R. T., & Till, B. D. (2008). Creativity and memory effects: Recall, recognition, and an exploration of nontraditional media. *Journal of Advertising, 37* (4), 85–94.

Batra, R., & Ray, M. L. (1985). How advertising works at contact. In L. F. Alwitt & A. A. Mitchell (Eds.), *Psychological processes and advertising effects: Theory, research, and applications* (pp. 13–44). Hillsdale, NJ: Lawrence Erlbaum.

Beijer, D. D. (2002). Driver distraction due to roadside advertising (Master's thesis). University of Toronto, Ontario, Canada.

Chafkin, M. (2007). Ads and atmospherics: Outdoor campaigns are suddenly hip. *Inc., 29* (2), 39–41.

Cole, B. L., & Hughes, P. K. (1984). A field trial of attention and search conspicuity. *Human Factors, 26* (3), 299–313.

Crundall, D. E., & Underwood, G. (1998). Effects of experience and processing demands on visual information acquisition in drivers. *Ergonomics, 41* (4), 448–458.

Donthu, N., Cherian, J., & Bhargava, M. (1993). Factors influencing the recall of outdoor advertising. *Journal of Advertising Research, 33* (3), 64–72.

Francese, P. (2004). More homeless. *American Demographics, 25* (8), 40–41.

Halford, G. S., Wilson, W. H., & Phillips, S. (1998). Processing capacity defined by relational complexity: Implications for comparative, developmental, and cognitive psychology. *Behavioral and Brain Sciences, 21* (6), 803–864.

Hutton, J., & Rose, J. M. (2005). Cellular telephones and driving performance: The effects of attentional demands on motor vehicle crash risk. *Risk Analysis, 25* (4), 855–866.

Kahneman, D. (1973). *Attention and effort*. Englewood Cliffs, NJ: Prentice-Hall.

Lee, P. N., & Triggs, T. J. (1976). The effects of driving demand and roadway environment on peripheral visual detections. *Australian Road Research Board Conference Proceedings, 8* (5), 7–11.

MacInnis, D. J., & Jaworski, B. J. (1989). Information processing from advertisements: Toward an integrative framework. *Journal of Marketing, 53* (4), 1–23.

MacInnis, D. J., Moorman, C., & Jaworski, B. J. (1991). Enhancing and measuring consumers' motivation, opportunity, and ability to process brand information from ads. *Journal of Marketing, 55* (4), 32–53.

Meyers-Levy, J., & Peracchio, L. A. (1995). Understanding the effects of color: How the correspondence between available and required resources affects attitudes. *Journal of Consumer Research, 22* (2), 121–138.

Peracchio, L. A., & Meyers-Levy, J. (1997). Evaluating persuasion-enhancing techniques from a resource-matching perspective. *Journal of Consumer Research, 24* (2), 178–191.

Prendergast, G., & Hang, C. C. (1999). The effectiveness of exterior bus advertising in Hong Kong: A preliminary investigation. *Journal of International Consumer Marketing, 11* (3), 33–50.

Smiley, A., Persaud, B., Bahar, G., Mollett, C., Lyon, C., Smahel, T., et al. (2005). Traffic safety evaluation of video advertising signs. *Journal of the Transportation Research Board: Transportation Research Record, 1937*, 105–112.

Turley, L. W., & Shannon, J. R. (2000). The impact and effectiveness of advertisements in a sports arena. *Journal of Services Marketing, 14* (4), 323–336.

Wilson, R. T., & Till, B. D. (2008). Airport advertising effectiveness: An exploratory field study. *Journal of Advertising, 37* (1), 57–70.

Wilson, R. T., & Till, B. D. (2011). Recall of pre-show cinema advertising: A message response involvement perspective. *Journal of Marketing Communications*, forthcoming.

Young, E. (1984). Visibility achieved by outdoor advertising. *Journal of Advertising Research, 24* (4), 19–21.

Additional Readings

Dou, X., & Li, H. (2008). Creative use of QR codes in consumer communication. *International Journal of Mobile Marketing, 3* (2), 61–67.

Gambetti, R. C. (2010). Ambient communication: How to engage consumers in urban touchpoints. *California Management Review, 52* (3), 34–51.

OBIE Awards, Outdoor Advertising Association of America, available at www.oaaa.org.

Outdoor Advertising Magazine, available at www.oam.net.

Samanta, S. K., Woods, J., & Ghanbari, M. (2009). MMS to improve mobile advertising acceptance and replace billboards. *International Journal of Mobile Marketing, 4* (2), 61–67.

Chapter 23

Role of Technology in Online Persuasion

A MAIN Model Perspective

S. Shyam Sundar, Qian Xu, and Xue Dou

Advertisements reach us through a variety of media, from traditional print and broadcast vehicles to newer digital devices, such as computers and mobile phones. As consumers, we tend to focus on the content and form of the ads rather than the media technology used to deliver the ad. However, advertisers know fully well that technology can make a profound difference, as they develop separate campaigns for different media. Advertising budgets are drawn out separately for each medium, with online media attracting a growing share in recent years. Scholarly work, such as that proposed by Figure 1.1 in Chapter 1 of this text, acknowledges that "channels" and "devices" can play a role in determining how advertisements are created, developed, deployed, and received.

As evident in Marshall McLuhan's famous quote, "the medium is the message," media technology is not a mere vacant channel. Rather, each medium possesses certain characteristics that shape the mediated environment and thereby affect people's perception of the information presented. According to McLuhan (1964), the psychological effects of media can be powerful enough to surpass the effects of actual message content. Studies in advertising have suggested that we process information differently from different media by demonstrating significant differences in ad recall, attitude towards ads and brands, and purchase intentions (e.g., Dahlen, 2005).

The past decade has witnessed an explosion in the development of information and communication technologies that enable easy and rapid communication between advertisers and consumers. As the Internet becomes ever more multi-faceted, with newer devices (e.g., iPad) and newer venues (e.g., social networking sites) offering unprecedented opportunities to advertisers and retailers for reaching their target consumers and promoting their products and services, there has been a growing interest in exploring the role of technology in the persuasive context. Early studies were centered on comparing the effects of online media with offline media. For example, Sundar, Narayan, Obregon, and Uppal (1998) found that individuals actually remembered more of the ad when the same advertisement was presented in the print version of a newspaper than when it was presented on a website. As the technology surrounding online ads matured, studies began comparing the effects of different types of online ads, such as banner and pop-up (Chatterjee, 2008), ads with and without pull-down menus (Brown, 2002), 2D ads and 3D ads (Li, Daugherty, & Biocca, 2002), and those with and without virtual direct experiences (Griffith & Chen, 2004). In the area of online marketing and e-commerce, the role of media technology has been examined in terms of both functionality, such as different levels of interactivity (Sundar & Kim, 2005), and metrics generated by such functionality, such as consumer reviews and product rankings (Chevalier & Mayzlin, 2006).

On the face of it, technological features of online advertisements, such as the 3D effect and interactivity, appear as visual accoutrements, designed primarily to dazzle the consumer by promoting a loose association between their presence on the interface and positive attitudes toward the product advertised. However, these features also bring with them certain additional functions that allow consumers to explore product information more deeply and make a more informed purchasing decision. Therefore, a fundamental theoretical question relates to the nature and depth of cognitive processing engendered by the technology of modern-day advertising. Dual process models in social psychology provide an excellent framework for addressing this and related questions because they conceptualize the dichotomy of shallow as well as effortful consideration of advertisements by consumers.

Dual Process Model

Given that advertisements have the ultimate goal of "persuading target consumers to adopt a particular product, service, or idea" (Meyers-Levy & Malaviya, 1999, p. 45), researchers studying the psychology of advertising and marketing have leaned heavily on persuasion theories that shed light on how individuals process commercial information. A general class of theories, called Dual Process Models, has been widely embraced in the field of advertising and marketing (e.g., Petty, Cacioppo, & Schumann, 1983). Dual-process models posit that we do not always process the central arguments of an advertising message actively and effortfully (systematic processing). Oftentimes, "peripheral cues" embedded in the context of advertising lead us to apply judgmental rules to make quick decisions or "heuristics" (Chaiken, 1980; Petty & Cacioppo, 1986). These judgmental rules are already stored in our memory based on our previous learning experiences. For example, we tend to trust product claims made by an expert (e.g., doctor in a white lab coat) more than that by a non-expert (e.g., an everyday consumer) without even scrutinizing the content of those claims. This is because we directly apply the expertise heuristic (i.e., experts' statements can be trusted) by relying on cues such as lab coat and the endorser's qualification (e.g., Dr. or MD associated with their name) presented in the context of the ad, and proceeding to buy into their claims. If individuals indeed recognize the cues, they could well process them systematically (or centrally) by using it as another piece of evidence for making a decision about the product. Heuristic processing typically occurs if message receivers are not consciously aware of the cues and/or their role in influencing a judgment based on a mental shortcut (Sundar, Oeldorf-Hirsch, & Garga, 2008a).

Studies in social psychology have attributed the occurrence of heuristic processing to the inherent human tendency for being miserly with cognitive resources. In general, we spend the bare minimum of cognitive resources that are necessary for making a judgment (Fiske & Taylor, 1984). This is particularly true for advertisements because we encounter so many of them (e.g., Lee & Sundar, 2002) in a given day, month, or year, and, barring a few exceptions (e.g., when we are in the market for a high-priced product), we lack the motivation or involvement to process them in an effortful way. Therefore, the primary way in which advertisements persuade us is through cues in the context that trigger mental shortcuts or heuristics.

MAIN Model

One source of such cues is the technology of the medium used for conveying advertising and marketing messages. Each communication technology brings with it a set of affordances that can shape consumers' perception of the content delivered by the technology, including their stance toward advertising and marketing appeals. These affordances are "action possibilities" (Norman, 1999) that determine the presentation of content as well as consumers' states of mind when using them. For instance, the presence of a spin-to-get-a-360-degree-view feature on an e-commerce product webpage would give consumers the impression that they can examine the product more vividly by mimicking the act of rotating the product from different angles in a brick-and-mortar store. The existence of a feature to mouse-over to zoom-in/out will enable consumers to get an enlarged view of details, just like walking closer to a product in offline stores. Such novel features might stimulate consumers' curiosity in the product and persuade them to explore it in greater depth.

As shown in Figure 23.1, the MAIN Model (Sundar, 2008) classifies such affordances into the following four broad categories: Modality (M), Agency (A), Interactivity (I), and Navigability (N). Modality refers to the variety of ways in which information is presented. Agency focuses on the ability of the medium to let users serve as sources of content. Interactivity pertains to the choices provided to users and the ability to go back and forth with the

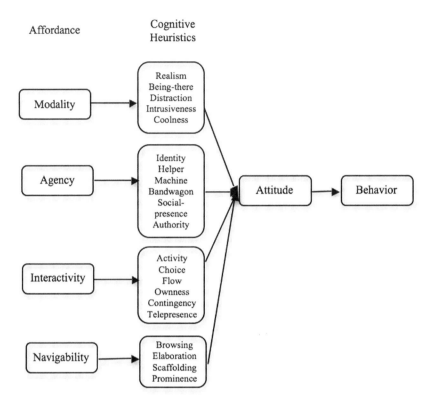

Figure 23.1 MAIN Model for Online Advertising and Marketing.

interface. Navigability refers to user movement through the mediated environment. All these affordances comprise the structure of interfaces. They can be
found in advertising/marketing media to varying degrees. Each affordance is
associated with a set of heuristics depending on how it manifests itself through
cues on the interface, with differential impact on product judgments. For
example, modality affordances may manifest themselves through cues such as
the 360-degree-view feature described above, which, by letting users experience the product in a lifelike fashion, serves to trigger the *realism heuristic*, i.e.,
the site's portrayal of the product is quite real, therefore it is genuine. The same
affordances, if presented through new tools, may cue the *novelty heuristic*,
whereby consumers would apply the positive affect created by the novelty of
the modality tool to their evaluation of the product experienced by using that
tool.

Thus, the same affordance may convey different cues leading to various
heuristics-based judgments. These judgments, and the consequent attitudes
and behaviors might be either positive or negative. If an e-commerce website

provides consumers with a variety of options to change the display of product information, it may trigger the *choice* heuristic. Consumers may enjoy the freedom to make selections. However, if it is hard for consumers to switch between options, the frustration resulting from the inability to control the technology features would lead to negative attitude towards the ad even though it provides them with more options. Here, the *control* heuristic is triggered in the negative.

In applying the MAIN model to explain the effect of technology on advertising and marketing, it is important to clarify the central concepts involved in this model. The first is *affordance*. It refers to the capacity possessed by the medium to initiate or facilitate a certain action (Norman, 1988), as long as users can visually perceive it. Therefore, users are an integral part of the conceptualization of affordances. For example, the click-to-spin feature affords the possibility to see the product from different perspectives. However, the realization of this feature depends upon whether consumers can perceive this action possibility. A *cue* is any salient aspect of the mediated presentation that might allow for quick evaluation of the underlying product information, possibly by triggering heuristics (Sundar, Oeldorf-Hirsch, & Xu, 2008b). The mere presence of a technology affordance can be a cue, such as the click-to-change-color feature or the drag-to-rotate feature. In addition to that, the aggregated data metrics generated by the medium (Sundar et al., 2008a), such as the number of customer reviews, star ratings, and number of website visitors, are also considered cues. A *heuristic* refers to the mental shortcut used as a judgment rule (often based on generalizations of knowledge and experience) for making quick evaluations (Chaiken, Liberman, & Eagly, 1989; Sundar et al., 2008b). For example, the presentation of a product on an e-commerce site with a high star rating based on user reviews will serve to cue the bandwagon heuristic, which is basically a judgment rule that goes something like this: "if a lot of others like this product, then I must, too."

Although the original formulation of MAIN model (Sundar, 2008) pertained to credibility evaluations of content delivered by media interfaces, the heuristics triggered by technological affordances can affect a variety of outcomes (Sundar et al., 2008a). In the context of advertising and marketing, they could affect consumers' attitudes as well as behavioral intentions towards the product or service.

Modality

We encounter messages everyday in various modes through various types of media. For example, we receive advertisements in the form of text (e.g., newspaper), audio (e.g., radio), and video (e.g., TV). Our perceptions of the content of the message have been found to differ based on the modality of presentation (e.g., Sundar, 2000). In addition to traditional modes of communication mentioned in the above example, modality also includes other structural aspects relating to data presentation, such as screen size, animation, pop-ups, and so on (Sundar et al., 2008a). According to the MAIN model, digital media offer a number of modality-related affordances that possess cues capable of triggering a variety of heuristics to psychologically influence users' perception of content (Sundar, 2008).

Studies in online advertising have shown the effect of modality on consumers' perceptions of commercial messages. For example, Appiah (2006) manipulated modality used for presenting product testimonials in a retailer's website, and found that audio/video yielded better attitudes towards both website and product than text/picture. The results of this study can be explained by the MAIN model framework in terms of the *realism heuristic*. The audiovisual presentation of the testimonial probably served to boost the realism (and therefore genuineness) of the endorsement, which, in turn, positively influenced participants' judgment of the website and product. Somewhat similar to this is the *being-there heuristic*. Studies in online product presentation have shown that, compared to traditional 2D images, using 3D visualization to present products can make consumers feel as if they are co-present with the product, leading to a more authentic experience, and therefore better attitudes toward the brand, brand recall, and purchase intentions (Li et al., 2002; Grigorovici & Constantin, 2004).

As mentioned earlier, modality heuristics can also be triggered by structural aspects related to presentation of content. For example, Heo and Sundar (2004) noticed higher arousal for large (compared to small) screen size only when receiving entertainment content and advertising, not when viewing news content. This content-specific effect suggests that screen size mattered only when the content is processed heuristically, and probably triggered the *being-there* or *coolness* heuristic, the latter being "a conscious acknowledgement of the 'hipness' of the digital device suggested by its newer modalities" (Sundar, 2008, p. 82). Other structural features of online advertising, such as animation and pop-ups, have been known to be quite effective in hijacking consumers' attention (Diao & Sundar, 2004) and directing them to specific parts of the screen (Constantin & Sundar, 2007). While memory for ad content is often heightened by such innovative modalities, their effect on consumers' impressions of the site and product attitudes are generally negative (Edwards, Li, & Lee, 2002), with pop-ups being perceived as more obtrusive than pop-unders (Stavrositu & Sundar, 2004). For example, Sundar and Kalyanaraman (2004) found that ads with fast animation speeds are more attention grabbing and more likely to increase advertising recall than slow animation ads, but less likely to lead to behavioral intentions (ad conation), thus suggesting the cueing of a negative heuristic, such as *intrusiveness* and *distraction*.

In sum, it appears that certain modality affordances, especially those related to enhancing viewer presence in the mediated environment, serve to trigger positive heuristics such as realism, being there, and coolness, with favorable spillover effects on the products advertised. However, newer modalities unique to online media, such as animation and pop-ups, while cognitively effective in garnering user attention and retention of ad content, serve to cue intrusiveness and/or distraction heuristics, thereby resulting in poorer attitudes toward the advertised product.

Agency

Research on traditional advertising, marketing, and consumer behavior has long indicated that source is an important factor influencing consumers' attitudes and behavioral intentions (Wilson & Sherrell, 1993). Expertise, physical attractiveness, and similarity of the source have been found to consistently affect the effectiveness of persuasion (Wilson & Sherrell, 1993). Digital media have forced a reconceptualization of the notion of source. When an ad goes viral and receivers get creative and embellish it with their own additions and redesigns, and you receive a YouTube link of a mashed-up version of the ad via email from a friend who picked it up from his Facebook feed, who or what is the source of this ad? Facebook? YouTube? The person who first posted the ad on YouTube or on Facebook? Your friend? Email client? All the people along the way who added creative tweaks to the ad? As you can tell from this example, the concept of source becomes quite murky in online, especially social media.

Sundar (2008) refers to online sourcing as the "agency" affordance of media. Modern digital interfaces offer users tremendous variety in exerting their own agency as well as experiencing the agency of others. Agency refers not only to the user himself or herself as source, but also to others as sources. In other words, the agency affordances of digital media essentially serve two functions: (1) let an individual assert his/her own control over the interface, and (2) let one be aware of and/or anticipate others' agency. The cues elicited by agency affordances are manifested through a variety of technological features such as customization, personalization, and interface agents.

For instance, Franke and Piller (2004) found in their experiment that when consumers were given the chance to customize their own watches online, which in turn were produced by the manufacturer, they were willing to pay a considerable premium for the product, even though it was of the same technical quality as the non-customized version of the watch. Therefore, the online toolkit's ability to allow customers to customize products to suit their individual preferences created value for them in this particular e-commerce transaction. In this process, the customization tool probably triggered the *identity* heuristic, which serves to communicate the consumer's idiosyncrasies to others.

Unlike the customization tools, which give consumers the full ability to express their preference, personalization features of the website cater to consumers' potential likes and dislikes in a relatively passive manner by providing recommendations. Numerous websites, ranging from Amazon.com to your hometown bank site, provide personalized recommendations, based on your previous activities or other consumers' similar behaviors. These are found to induce significantly higher commitment and higher tendency to stay with the website than those without any personalized recommendations (Fung, 2008). This personalization affordance might elicit the *helper* heuristic, such that the recommendations provided by the website are considered benevolent and convenient for facilitating further transactions on the site. Kim and Sundar (2010) found that when a search-engine site served up text ads in the form of sponsored links, consumers showed significantly more positive attitudes toward the ads and the site when those links were relevant, rather than irrelevant, to the search. So much so that they appreciated ad clutter! Clearly, the helper heuristic triggered by the site made users look favorably upon ad content, which is otherwise received with a great deal of negativity.

In a direct test of different kinds of agency, the personalized suggestion offered by the recommendation agent on a retail website was found to be more positively influential on consumers' product choices than the recommendations from other human sources, such as "human experts" and "other consumers" (Senecal & Nantel, 2004). The reason why non-human recommendation led to more effective persuasion can be explained by the *machine* heuristic cued by the personalization function. The fact that the recommendation agent isn't human makes it appear more objective and unbiased and therefore more trustworthy in guiding shopping decisions.

In addition to asserting and confirming one's needs and wants, agency affordance also enables consumers to experience the agency of other consumers. Thanks to collaborative filtering technology (Breese, Heckerman, & Kadie, 1989), consumer ratings, recommendations, and ranks can now be found on almost all e-commerce websites. These ratings compiled based on other consumers' opinions are found to significantly influence consumers' product and purchase intentions and attitudes (Sundar, Xu, & Oeldorf-Hirsch, 2009). Cues, such as star ratings, signifying the collective agency of other consumers, served to elicit the *bandwagon* heuristic (Sundar et al., 2008b). For instance, Sundar et al. (2009) found that the higher the star ratings generated by other consumers' reviews, the more favorable the consumers' attitudes toward the product, all else being equal.

When the website or the computer system is no longer treated as an impersonal system, but as a personified recommendation agent or customer-service agent in the form of an avatar, the *social presence* heuristic is likely to be activated in the minds of consumers. They will consider the retail website as a community with a social entity rather than as an inanimate object. The anthropomorphic cues and human characteristics of an avatar would encourage them to apply social rules in their interaction with the avatar. Indeed, perceptions of social presence have been shown to lead subsequently to better persuasive outcomes. Using an avatar sales agent was found to generate more satisfaction with the retailer, more positive attitude towards the product, and greater purchase intention compared to not using it (Holzwarth, Janiszewski, & Neumann, 2006).

In addition to online recommendation agents and websites, even computers can serve as agents of persuasion, as claimed by Fogg (2003), who uses the term "captology" to refer to computers as persuasive technologies. Koh and Sundar (2010) revealed that consumers exposed to specialist computers, websites, and agents focusing exclusively on wine products, showed greater trust in media technology and product descriptions than those exposed to generalist computers, websites, and agents selling a variety of products. In this particular case, the expertise conveyed by specialization served to cue the *authority* heuristic, leading to greater trust in machine agency at all source layers of human–website interaction.

In sum, agency affordances affect consumers' attitudes toward products, either by triggering the identity heuristic accruing from self-agency or bandwagon heuristic arising from peer agency. Furthermore, non-human agency attributed to the site affects consumer attitudes by triggering machine, authority, helper, and social-presence heuristics.

Interactivity

Interactivity is probably the most distinctive affordance of digital media. The concept of interactivity suggests that the medium should be responsive to users' needs and therefore take into account variations in users' input during the interaction (Sundar, 2007, 2008). Therefore, the meaning of this concept may involve providing choices, enabling users' control over media (Jensen, 1998), and the system being responsive to users' inputs (Rafaeli, 1988). Based on such attributes, the interactivity affordance in online advertising and marketing might cue a variety of cognitive heuristics.

In comparing the effectiveness of Web banner advertisements with and without pull-down menus, Brown (2002) found that consumers who were exposed to banner advertisements with pull-down menus paid more attention, perceived more novelty, showed more liking toward the advertisement, and generated more click-throughs. The action possibilities offered by the pull-down menus might have triggered the *activity* heuristic, implying that the advertisement was inviting consumers to interact with it, thereby leading to positive persuasion outcomes.

Chen, Griffith, and Shen (2005) provided consumers with more action options beyond simple click-to-get information in their study comparing three apparel websites with different levels of interactivity: a basic color palette and fabric choices for low interactivity, plus a generic body model that could try the apparels in the medium interactivity site, and a more elaborated customizable virtual model that can replicate the consumer's body features in the high interactivity version. By offering functional options to display the apparel, these websites might have activated the *choice* heuristic, such that the high interactivity website was considered better since it offered more choices for consumers to access the product. To the extent the affordance makes consumers feel that they created a unique design all by themselves, it may cue the *ownness* heuristic, leading possibly to such behaviors as saving one's profile and returning to the same site for future purchases.

By varying the hyperlinked layers of online advertisements (one layer without hyperlink for low interactivity ad, two hierarchical layers with clickable hyperlinks for medium interactivity ad, and three or more hyperlinked layers for high interactivity ad), Sundar and Kim (2005) revealed that interactivity, when attended upon, was a strong affordance aiding the persuasive function of online ads. Advertisements with more layers led to higher perceived product knowledge, product involvement, and purchase intention than those with fewer hyperlinked layers. Manipulating interactivity via hyperlinked layers served to cue consumers with the *contingency* heuristic. Study participants could feel the reciprocity between their actions and the reactions of the online advertisement. The fact that the responses from the advertisement were contingent upon user actions heightened their affinity to the website and the product advertised in the interactive marketing unit.

Another feature of interactivity lies in its potential to modify content and form in real time (Steuer, 1992), thereby cueing the *telepresence* heuristic. Consumers would feel that they are having an authentic interaction with the product/service in reality when in fact they are experiencing it virtually. For example, Griffith and Chen (2004) found in their study that online apparel ads employing virtual direct experience were more effective in persuasion than online ads alone. When the system responds in tune with user's expectations, it is likely to trigger the *flow* heuristic, realized often in the reverse when there is a break in flow. As Xu and Sundar (2011) noted, interactive affordances trigger an expectation for further action and depth among users. If the site does not match these expectations, it results in negative product attitudes.

In sum, interactivity affordances in online advertisements trigger activity, choice, control, and flow heuristics by allowing user actions. They trigger the contingency heuristic by providing output that is relevant to their actions, telepresence heuristic by providing a responsive virtual environment, and ownness heuristic by allowing them to build something unique. When cued positively, all these heuristics are likely to lead to favorable product attitudes.

Navigability

Navigability refers to the interface's ability to facilitate user navigation or movement through the device, site, or even a multi-layered advertisement. Online consumers have come to depend on navigational aids for finding desired information from media (e.g., menubar, tabs). While information has been traditionally presented in a linear narrative style, information on the Web can be presented in a nonlinear fashion through associative links (Sundar, 2008). It presents many opportunities for designers, but at the same time, can bring negative consequences, such as making users confused or irritated. Therefore, the design of navigation aids is a critical issue for ensuring successful user experience of digital products and venues.

Many studies have stressed the importance of navigability in website design, and demonstrated that consumers show different cognitive, affective, and behavioral outcomes depending on the types and number of navigability aids used in a website (Geissler, Zinkhan, & Watson, 2006). For example, Spyridakis, Mobrand, Cuddihy, and Wei (2007) manipulated navigation by way of linking structure. Study participants were exposed to a webpage with a series of links that were embedded in a text preview about linked materials, presented as a list after the text preview, or presented as a list only. Although individuals in the list-only condition explored more of the website, their comprehension of information presented in the website was lower than their counterparts in the links-embedded-in-text-preview condition. These results can be explained by *browsing* heuristic and *elaboration* heuristic in the MAIN model. The sheer presence of links in the list-only condition perhaps served as a cue for triggering the browsing heuristic, which encourages users to quickly skim the site and explore the various links. On the other hand, participants in the other condition were probably cued the elaboration heuristic because the links, when interwoven with the main content, make the user think about the relationship between a given link and the site's content. This in turn enhances users' elaborative processing and higher knowledge-structure density (Sundar, 2008). This is probably why individuals in the text-preview condition had higher comprehension.

The sheer presence of navigation aids can also enhance users' perception of the website by cueing the *scaffolding* heuristic. In their study, Spyridakis et al.

(2007) also found that simply having a navigation menu on the webpage can increase users' perceived usability of the website. This is understandable because people have established a schema that navigation aids are there for maximizing the efficiency of users' browsing experiences. Thus, when users recognize navigation aids on a website, they will be cued the scaffolding heuristic and perceive the website to be more usable even without using any of the aids themselves.

Another important heuristic related to navigability is the *prominence heuristic*, which is associated with the order in which the information is presented on websites. In advertising and marketing, search-engine optimization is regarded as a useful way to introduce consumers to a commercial website (Kharbanda, 2006). This is because we often assume that information shown higher up in a search result must be more relevant and therefore more likely to click on it (e.g., Pan et al., 2007). Heo and Sundar (2001) have documented strong position effects, with banner ads at the bottom of the page leading to better ad recognition than those at the top. Another study (Heo & Sundar, 2000) showed that visual attention was greatest for ads positioned along the sides of the page. As online advertisers try new formats and users habituate to them, the exact location of prominence is likely to be a moving target, but the overall theoretical construct of prominence is an important determinant of user navigation of online spaces.

In sum, navigability affordances in online ads and sites can facilitate user exploration by cueing the browsing heuristic and encourage cognitive engagement by cueing the elaboration heuristic. They can also trigger the scaffolding heuristic by affording easy tools for comparison shopping and the prominence heuristic by dictating the placement of commercial messages.

Conclusion

As evident in the preceding sections, the MAIN model offers a fertile theoretical framework for understanding the role of technology in online persuasion, by simply changing the outcome variable from credibility to attitudes and behaviors (Figure 23.1). As discussed in the preceding sections, technological features in online ads and e-commerce sites can be conceptualized as affordances (i.e., action possibilities) with cues that trigger cognitive heuristics, both positive and negative. These heuristics are said to affect consumers' evaluation and attitude toward the media interface and subsequently their attitudes toward the promoted product or service. Based on the elaboration likelihood model (Petty & Cacioppo, 1986), if individuals are either of lower ability or of lower motivation, they would be more likely to rely on such peripheral cues for making judgments and forming attitudes. Following the theory of planned behavior (Ajzen, 1991), attitudes would predict behavioral intentions and subsequent behaviors.

For advertising and consumer behavior researchers, this model represents a social-cognition approach to understanding the psychological mechanisms by which technology plays a role in the persuasion context. At the same time, it also extends existing studies on consumers' cognitive processing and persuasive outcomes by shedding a different kind of light on the proverbial black box of media effects. Cognitive variables such as ad memory, physiological variables such as eye-tracking, and behavioral variables such as log data have all produced rich insights into the effects of online media, but they have not explicitly conceptualized the technological triggers for user responses. The MAIN model is an attempt to provide a theoretical account that takes into account both the technology and the psychology of its use. Given that the vast majority of persuasive content is unsolicited, receivers are unlikely to process it systematically. Therefore, it is important to conceptualize them in terms of heuristic cues. Work in social psychology has already documented a variety of heuristics triggered by cues embedded in the content. The focus of the MAIN model lies in identifying cues in the technology of the interface that can impact user cognitions and attitudes, regardless of the content of the persuasive appeals. The heuristics listed in this chapter are far from exhaustive. They are merely illustrative. With the advancement and emergence of new technologies and newer forms of advertising and marketing using emergent media forms, we will see more cues that are capable of triggering already identified heuristics as well as new ones.

Practical Implications

In addition to motivating theory, the application of MAIN model to advertising and marketing has practical implications for online persuasion. With a plethora of information online, making consumers aware of your advertisement and websites, and eventually making them want to click to get more information, are certainly major challenges. In such an environment, creating a positive first impression of the site can mean the difference between success and failure. When designers approach a medium for disseminating their commercial messages, they often rely on simple heuristics such as novelty and coolness, triggered typically by new modality affordances. Our model encourages designers to look beyond modality and into other species of affordances, namely agency, interactivity, and navigability.

In addition, advertisers and designers can refer to the model for making necessary trade-offs between features that trigger positive heuristics and those that trigger negative heuristics. It not only helps them to strategically adopt technologies to their own websites, but also assists them in making decisions about the placement of online advertisements. As noted throughout, interface designs are found to influence content perceptions, including perceptions of advertisements and other commercial appeals. Therefore, it is better to gauge the design features of a website when advertisers make decisions of the design and deployment of their ads. The MAIN model can be a useful tool during such decision processes.

All these years, advertisers have been focused on persuasiveness of content and issues related to placement, reach, and frequency. The MAIN model forces them to consider the affordances of the interface through which persuasive content is presented—what do these affordances mean to users? What actions do they trigger and how do users interpret the availability of those actions? How best can we capitalize on the positive meanings conveyed by those actions and distance ourselves from negative ones, while designing content, format, and placement of online advertisements? These are the kinds of questions motivated by the MAIN model.

Acknowledgment

This research is supported by the Korea Science and Engineering Foundation under the WCU (World Class University) program at the Department of Interaction Science, Sungkyunkwan University, Seoul, South Korea (Grant No. R31–2008–000–10062–0), where the first author holds a visiting appointment.

References

Ajzen, I. (1991). The theory of planned behavior. *Organizational Behavior and Human Decision Processes, 50*, 179–211.

Appiah, O. (2006). Rich media, poor media: The impact of audio/video vs. text/picture testimonial ads on browsers' evaluations of commercial websites and online products. *Journal of Current Issues and Research in Advertising, 28* (1), 73–86.

Breese, J., Heckerman, D., & Kadie, C. (1989). Empirical analysis of predictive algorithms for collaborative filtering. *Proceedings of the Fourteenth Conference on Uncertainty in Artificial Intelligence*, 43–52.

Brown, M. (2002). The use of banner advertisements with pull-down menus: A copy testing approach. *Journal of Interactive Advertising, 2* (2). Retrieved October 6, 2010, from http://jiad.org/article24.

Chaiken, S. (1980). Heuristic versus systematic information-processing and the use of source versus message cues in persuasion. *Journal of Personality and Social Psychology, 39* (5), 752–766.

Chaiken, S., Liberman, A., & Eagly, A. H. (1989). Heuristic and systematic information processing within and beyond the persuasion context. In J. S. Uleman & J. A. Bargh (Eds.), *Unintended thought* (pp. 212–252). New York: Guilford.

Chatterjee, P. (2008). Are unclicked ads wasted? Enduring effects of banner and pop-up ad exposures on brand memory and attitudes. *Journal of Electronic Commerce Research, 9* (1), 51–61.

Chen, Q., Griffith, D. A., & Shen, F. (2005). The effects of interactivity on cross-channel communication effectiveness. *Journal of Interactive Advertising, 5* (2). Retrieved October 7, 2010, from http://jiad.org/article60.

Chevalier, J. A., & Mayzlin, D. (2006). The effect of word of mouth on sales: Online book reviews. *Journal of Marketing Research, 43* (9), 345–354.

Constantin, C., & Sundar, S. S. (2007, May). Do pop-ups enhance processing of online news? A test of attentional spotlight, cognitive load, and affect-as-information theories. Paper presented at the 57th annual conference of the International Communication Association, San Francisco, CA.

Dahlen, M. (2005). The medium as a contextual cue: Effects of creative media choice. *Journal of Advertising, 34* (3), 89–98.

Diao, F., & Sundar, S. S. (2004). Orienting responses and memory for web advertisements: Exploring effects of pop-up window and animation. *Communication Research, 31* (5), 537–567.

Edwards, S. M., Li, H. R., & Lee, J. H. (2002). Forced exposure and psychological reactance: Antecedents and consequences of the perceived intrusiveness of pop-up ads. *Journal of Advertising, 31* (3), 83–95.

Fiske, S., & Taylor, S. (1984). *Social cognition*. Reading, MA: Addison-Wesley.

Fogg, B. J. (2003). *Persuasive technology: Using computers to change what we think and do*. San Francisco, CA: Morgan Kaufmann Publishers.

Franke, N., & Piller, F. (2004). Value creation by toolkits for user innovation and design: The case of the watch market. *Journal of Product Innovation Management, 21* (6), 401–415.

Fung, T. K. F. (2008). Banking with a personalized touch: Examining the impact of website customization on commitment. *Journal of Electronic Commerce Research, 9* (4), 296–309.

Geissler, G. L., Zinkhan, G. M., & Watson, R. T. (2006). The influence of home page complexity on consumer attention, attitudes, and purchase intent. *Journal of Advertising, 35* (2), 69–80.

Griffith, D. A., & Chen, Q. (2004). The influence of virtual direct experience (VDE) on online ad message effectiveness. *Journal of Advertising, 33* (1), 55–68.

Grigorovici, D. M., & Constantin, C. D. (2004). Experiencing interactive advertising beyond rich media: Impacts of ad type and presence on brand effectiveness in 3D gaming immersive virtual environments. *Journal of Interactive Advertising, 5* (1), 22–36. Retrieved September 29, 2010, from www.jiad.org/article53.

Heo, N., & Sundar, S. S. (2000, June). Visual orientation and memory for web advertising: A study of animation and position effects. Paper presented at the 50th annual conference of the International Communication Association, Acapulco, Mexico.

Heo, N., & Sundar, S. S. (2001, May). Memory for web advertisements: Exploring effects of animation, position, and product involvement. Paper presented at the 51st annual conference of the International Communication Association, Washington, DC.

Heo, N., & Sundar, S. S. (2004, May). The role of screen size in inferring the effects of content type on attention, arousal, memory, and content evaluation: A search for content-specific effects. Paper presented at the 54th annual conference of the International Communication Association, New Orleans, LA.

Holzwarth, M., Janiszewski, C., & Neumann, M. M. (2006). The influence of avatars on online consumer shopping behavior. *Journal of Marketing, 70*, 19–36.

Jensen, J. F. (1998). Interactivity: Tracing a new concept in media and communication studies. *Nordicom Review, 19* (1), 185–204.

Kharbanda, S. (2006). Web advertising acceptability and usefulness: Attaining top positions on search engines is more cost-effective than a yellow page or directory listing. *Journal of Website Promotion, 2* (1/2), 185–193.

Kim, N. Y., & Sundar, S. S. (2010). Relevance to the rescue: Can smart ads reduce negative response to online ad clutter? *Journalism and Mass Communication Quarterly, 87* (2), 346–362.

Koh, Y. J., & Sundar, S. S. (2010). Effects of specialization in computers, web sites and web agents on e-commerce trust. *International Journal of Human-Computer Studies, 68*, 899–912.

Lee, S. Y., & Sundar, S. S. (2002, July). Psychological effects of frequency and clutter in Web advertising. Paper presented at the 52nd annual conference of the International Communication Association, Seoul, South Korea.

Li, H., Daugherty, T., & Biocca, F. (2002). Impact of 3-D advertising on product knowledge, brand attitude, and purchase intention: The mediating role of presence. *Journal of Advertising, 31* (3), 43–57.

McLuhan, M. (1964). *Understanding media: The extensions of man.* New York: McGraw-Hill.

Meyers-Levy, J., & Malaviya, P. (1999). Consumers' processing of persuasive advertisements: An integrative framework of persuasion theories. *Journal of Marketing, 63*, 45–60.

Norman, D. A. (1988). *The design of everyday things.* New York: Doubleday.

Norman, D. A. (1999). Affordances, conventions, and design. *Interactions, 6* (3), 38–43.

Pan, B., Hembrooke, H., Joachims, T., Lorigo, L., Gay, G., & Granka, L. (2007). In Google we trust: Users' decisions on rank, position, and relevance. *Journal of Computer-Mediated Communication, 12* (3). Retrieved September 30, 2010, from http://jcmc.indiana.edu/vol12/issue3/pan.html.

Petty, R. E., & Cacioppo, J. T. (1986). *Communication and persuasion: Central and peripheral routes to attitude change.* New York: Springer-Verlag.

Petty, R. E., Cacioppo, J. T., & Schumann, D. (1983). Central and peripheral routes to advertising effectiveness: The moderating role of involvement. *Journal of Consumer Research, 10* (2), 135–146.

Rafaeli, S. (1988). Interactivity: From new media to communication. In R. P. Hawkins, J. M. Wiemann, & S. Pingree (Eds.), *Advancing communication science: Merging mass and interpersonal processes* (pp. 110–134). Newbury Park, CA: Sage.

Senecal, S., & Nantel, J. (2004). The influence of online product recommendations on consumers' online choices. *Journal of Retailing, 80*, 159–169.

Spyridakis, J. H., Mobrand, K. A., Cuddihy, E., & Wei, C. Y. (2007). Using structural cues to guide readers on the internet. *Information Design Journal, 15* (3), 242–259.

Stavrositu, C., & Sundar, S. S. (2004, May). Interstitials and their relevance to Website content: Influence on Website credibility. Paper presented at the 54th annual conference of the International Communication Association, New Orleans, LA.

Steuer, J. (1992). Defining virtual reality: Dimensions determining telepresence. *Journal of Communication, 42* (4), 73–93.

Sundar, S. S. (2000). Multimedia effects on processing and perception of online news: A study of picture, audio, and video downloads. *Journalism and Mass Communication Quarterly, 77* (3), 480–499.

Sundar, S. S. (2007). Social psychology of interactivity in human-website interaction. In A. N. Joinson, K. Y. A. McKenna, T. Postmes, & U.-D. Reips (Eds.), *The Oxford handbook of internet psychology* (pp. 89–104). Oxford, UK: Oxford University Press.

Sundar, S. S. (2008). The MAIN model: A heuristic approach to understanding technology effects on credibility. In M. J. Metzger & A. J. Flanagin (Eds.), *Digital media, youth, and credibility* (pp. 73–100). Cambridge, MA: MIT Press.

Sundar, S. S., & Kalyanaraman, S. (2004). Arousal, memory, and impression-formation effects of animation speed in Web advertising. *Journal of Advertising, 33* (1), 7–17.

Sundar, S. S., & Kim, J. (2005). Interactivity and persuasion: Influencing attitudes with information and involvement. *Journal of Interactive Advertising, 5,* 6–29. Retrieved September 29, 2010, from www.jiad.org/article59.

Sundar, S. S., Narayan, S., Obregon, R., & Uppal, C. (1998). Does web advertising work? Memory for print vs. online media. *Journalism and Mass Communication Quarterly, 75* (4), 822–835.

Sundar, S. S., Oeldorf-Hirsch, A., & Garga, A. K. (2008, October). A cognitive-heuristics approach to understanding presence in virtual environments. Paper presented at the 11th Annual International Workshop on Presence, Padova, Italy.

Sundar, S. S., Oeldorf-Hirsch, A., & Xu, Q. (2008). The bandwagon effect of collaborative filtering technology. *Proceedings of the Conference on Human Factors in Computing Systems (ACM SIGCHI), 26,* 3453–3458.

Sundar, S. S., Xu, Q., & Oeldorf-Hirsch, A. (2009). Authority vs. peer: How interface cues influence users. *Proceedings of the Conference on Human Factors in Computing Systems (ACM SIGCHI), 27,* 4231–4236.

Wilson, E. J., & Sherrell, D. L. (1993). Source effects in communication and persuasion research: A meta-analysis of effect size. *Journal of the Academy of Marketing Science, 21* (2), 101–112.

Xu, Q., & Sundar, S. S. (2011, May). Lights, camera, music, interaction! Interactive persuasion in e-commerce. Paper presented at the 61st annual conference of the International Communication Association, Boston, MA.

Additional Readings

Chen, S., & Chaiken, S. (1999). The heuristic-systematic model in its broader context. In S. Chaiken & Y. Trope (Eds.), *Dual process theories in social psychology* (pp. 73–96). New York: Guilford.

Gibson, J. J. (1977). The theory of affordances. In R. Shaw & J. Bransford (Eds.), *Perceiving, acting, and knowing: Toward an ecological psychology* (pp. 67–82). Hillsdale, NJ: Lawrence Erlbaum.

Sundar, S. S. (2004). Theorizing interactivity's effects. *Information Society, 20,* 385–389.

Sundar, S. S. (2008). Self as source: Agency and customization in interactive media. In E. A. Konijn, S. Utz, M. Tanis, & S. Barnes (Eds.), *Mediated interpersonal communication* (pp. 58–74). New York: Routledge.

Sundar, S. S., & Nass, C. (2001). Conceptualizing sources in online news. *Journal of Communication, 51* (1), 52–72.

Chapter 24

Lessons Learned for Teaching Mobile Advertising

Critical Review and Future Directions

Shintaro Okazaki

Introduction

Since the first text message was sent from a computer to a mobile phone in the UK in 1992, the mobile communication medium has been growing at an astonishing pace (Michael & Salter, 2006). In 2010, the penetration of third generation (3G) mobile devices increased to almost 35% in most of the 8G countries. Japan is ranked at the top with 87%, followed by South Korea (71%), and Australia (50%) (Morgan Stanley, 2009). As a result, an increasing number of both global and local firms incorporate the mobile device as part of their marketing mix, and use a diverse range of its functionalities.

Of these, mobile advertising is the earliest and most visible marketing tool. The main objective of mobile advertising is to generate or support new customer acquisition. This includes both "push" communications initiated by the marketer, and "pull" communications initiated by the consumer, in response to either a "push" communication or a perceived consumer need. Push advertising is usually sent via Short Message Service (SMS) or Multimedia Message Service (MMS), while pull advertising places advertisements on a website, banner, display, search, or applications (Barnes, 2002). Mobile advertising spending in all formats is projected to reach $3.5 billion in 2010 and $5.55 billion in 2012, in Western Europe (SFN, 2010). In the US, the compound annual growth rate is predicted to be 37.3% between 2008 and 2013, with total spending jumping from $320 million to $1.56 billion (eMarket, 2010).

As higher-capacity 3G technologies have boosted consumer demand for more sophisticated applications, mobile advertising has received increasing attention as a teaching subject. This seems to be a natural move, given the increasing interest in online social media and new technology adoption. However, educational materials related to mobile advertising are surprisingly scarce. The objective of this chapter is to move one step forward, by providing a comprehensive state of the art on mobile advertising theories. Such a resource is indispensable for understanding theory and its application to mobile advertising and teaching mobile advertising courses at the university level, since theories play a vital role in connecting new media with our existing knowledge. In particular, there has been an explicitly stated need to conceptualize the ubiquity concept, which is a core benefit of a mobile device. Ubiquity has been conceptualized as flexibility in time and space, but a thorough theoretical exploration has not yet been conducted. However, parallel to interactivity in the more traditional "wired" Internet, ubiquity seems to hold the key to responding to an unanswered question: why does mobile advertising have a potentially greater reach, regardless of time and location?

In this light, this chapter considers "advertising contexts" as shown in Figure 1.1 of Chapter 1, although here the notion of "context" may differ considerably from other media. In mobile-based communication, "context" refers to both the physical and social environments, which can be paraphrased as "situation" (Belk, 1975). Mobile media is a personalization tool that fits a range of situational variables so that the applications needed are available at any time, and any place. Although the actual practice of mobile advertising goes far beyond the academic literature, it is our hope that scholarly work will develop meaningful theories to explain how and why this ubiquitous personalization would work.

The remainder of the chapter is structured as follows. First, a brief overview of earlier mobile advertising research is presented. Then, based on systematic article selection criteria, a critical review of the existing literature is performed, and it identifies the major theoretical frameworks used in prior research, and the gaps to be filled. In closing, we suggest future research directions.

Earlier Research

The dawn of mobile advertising research begins with two seminal works: Barnes (2002) and Barwise and Strong (2002). The former is conceptual and the latter is empirical. Barnes (2002) drew the first comprehensive map of the then unknown mobile communication technology for marketing scholars. In his paper, a farsighted conceptualization of push versus pull, simple versus rich, and stand-alone versus interactive mobile advertising ("wireless advertising" in his words) were presented, while he also hinted at the important determinants of consumer information processing, such as social norms, user motives, mode, and time and location. However, perhaps even more important is the contribution of the first-ever empirical study, conducted by Barwise and Strong (2002). The authors conducted a trial of permission-based "push" SMS message advertising in the UK. On recruitment, respondents were paid cash incentives and then received more than 100 messages in the six-week trial period. Almost all respondents were satisfied or very satisfied. The study found that 81% read all messages, 63% responded or took action, and 17% forwarded at least one message. As many as 84% of respondents were "likely to recommend" the service to their friends whereas only 7% were "likely to abandon" the service. This research not only pioneered mobile advertising, but also resulted in many replications, establishing it as a research area on "permission-based" SMS advertising.

However, it was not until 2004 that the next empirical research appeared in scholarly journals. At approximately the same time, Tsang, Ho, and Liang (2004) and Okazaki (2004) conducted similar studies in two Asian countries: Taiwan and Japan, respectively. As one of the most cited studies, Tsang et al. (2004) examined attitudes toward SMS "push" advertising among Taiwanese. Their proposed structural model consists of two parts: (1) entertainment, informativeness, irritation, and credibility as antecedents of attitudes, which in turn led to an intention–behavior chain; and (2) incentives as an antecedent of intention. In addition, the existence of permission (i.e., opt-in) was used as a moderator of attitudes. Based on the data collected from 380 student samples, their findings indicate that (1) consumers generally have negative attitudes toward mobile advertising unless they have been informed and have pre-consented (i.e., opted-in) to the ads, and (2) there seems to be a direct and positive relationship between consumers' attitudes and behavior. The authors noted further that consumers' intention to accept mobile ads is affected by incentives.

Similarly, but in a "pull" advertising framework (Barnes, 2002), Okazaki (2004) set out to identify the factors influencing consumers' motives to click text banner ads in a mobile portal platform. This platform attracted more than one million subscribers who accessed freely the promotional information delivered by various companies. The study found that three constructs—content credibility, infotainment, and irritation—affected the formation of attitudes toward wireless ads, which in turn determined the level of intention to click the ads. Interestingly, the demographic analysis revealed that the unmarried working youth segment has a higher propensity to access such pull mobile ads. Okazaki (2006) furthered the analysis by clustering consumer segments that are likely to access the mobile portal platform based on the uses and gratifications theory and demographic variables.

Although earlier researchers claimed that both push and pull types of mobile advertising would grow as consumer needs became more complex (Barnes 2002; Rodriguez-Perlado & Barwise 2004), the research trends have been heavily skewed toward push advertising (e.g., Carroll, Barnes, Scornavacca, & Fletcher, 2007; Choi, Hwang, & McMillan, 2008; Gao, Rau, & Salvendy, 2009; Okazaki, Katsukura, & Nishiyama, 2007). On the other hand, as far as publication quantity is concerned, mobile advertising seems to have been highlighted as an emerging research topic only recently. Special issues of leading marketing journals have been issued only twice, in 2008 (*Psychology and Marketing*) and 2009 (*Journal of Advertising Research*), which may lead us to conclude that publication on mobile advertising has been only sporadic. Nonetheless, a keyword search with mobile advertising in Google yields numerous publications, although some of their findings are unsubstantiated. To clarify this point, a compressive citation analysis based on objective criteria seems necessary.

Theoretical Review

Past researchers have reviewed major marketing journals in order to investigate the patterns and developments in general m-commerce research (e.g., Varnali & Toker, 2010). However, the state of the art on mobile advertising has not yet been established. Furthermore, little attention has been paid to the question of what kinds of theories are used as the conceptual base. To this end, we conducted an exhaustive literature review of the mobile advertising research published in major academic journals from 1993 to August 2010. This 20-year block is adequate as a time frame, in that the first commercial SMS was deployed in Sweden in 1992 (Michael & Salter, 2006). The selection of the articles consisted of three phases. The first phase aimed to perform an exhaustive search of the mobile marketing literature in various disciplines, including marketing, management, business, psychology, engineering, information technology, information systems, finance, and operations research. The following online databases were used to create a pool of articles that might be relevant to mobile advertising: ABI/INFORM Global, Academic Research Library, Arts & Humanities Full Text, EBSCOhost Business Source, Emerald, Elsevier SD Freedom Collection, IEEE Xplore, and Wiley InterScience. The literature search was based on such keywords as "mobile advertising," "m-advertising," "SMS advertising," and "wireless advertising." As a result, we found a total of 179 articles from 92 journals. In the second phase, each article was then manually examined to ascertain that it satisfied the following four criteria:

1. The article's main focus should be on advertising in the broad sense of marketing communications (including events and experience, sponsorship, product placement, and electronic word-of-mouth), in order to generate or support *new* customer acquisition in particular.
2. The article's main focus should not be on a loyalty program, trust building, or the customer value of *existing* customers.
3. The study's main focus should be on theoretical advancement, with empirical exploration in terms of *attitudinal and/or behavioral models*.
4. The study's empirical evidence should be well substantiated with a reasonable sample that represents the population the study intends to examine.

5. The journal in which the article appears should be indexed in Thomson Reuters Web of Knowledge multidisciplinary databases in the sciences, social sciences, or humanities.

This procedure yielded 26 articles from 12 journals.

Theories and Models in Prior Research

In this article, we do not intend to present an exhaustive list of the theories identified in our selected articles. For a pedagogic reason, we prefer to provide a more synthetic view of the theories most frequently used in the past. Although our literature review reveals no clear trend in terms of advertising theories, the following theories seem consistently salient as conceptual foundations.

Uses and Gratifications Theory

The uses and gratifications (U&G) theory was originally developed by communications researchers to understand consumers' motivations to use different media (Brackett & Carr, 2001; Dholakia, Bagozzi, & Pearo, 2004; Ducoffe, 1996; Flanagin & Metzger, 2001; Lin, 1999). The U&G theory explains why individuals often seek out media in a goal-setting fashion to fulfill a core set of motivations. This suggests that media users control their own decisions. It has proven to be an axiomatic theory (a theory logically driven from a set of propositions) because its principles are generally accepted, and it is readily applicable to a wide range of situations involving mediated communications.

U&G theory aims to explain the psychological needs that motivate people to engage in media use behaviors, and that derive gratifications to satisfy those intrinsic needs, under a particular socio-cultural environment. Lin (1999) explains the basic underlying assumptions of U&G theory as follows:

> individuals differ along several psychological dimensions, which in turn prompt them to make different choices about which media to patronize, and even individuals exposed to the same media content will respond to it in different ways, depending on their characteristics.

Furthermore, U&G theory assumes that consumers are (1) goal-directed in their behavior, (2) active media users, and (3) aware of their needs, and select media to gratify those needs (Katz, Blumler, & Gurevitch, 1974).

U&G theory has been employed on numerous occasions to identify online consumers' needs or motivations regarding the fixed Internet (Lin, 1999). Thus, it seems reasonable to assume that it can also be applied to wireless

Internet adoption. For example, Tsang et al. (2004) and Okazaki (2004) used the U&G paradigm, and proposed three motivational antecedents of mobile push and pull advertising, respectively. The former used entertainment, information, and irritation as major motives to accept SMS ads, while the latter proposed infotainment and irritation as major motives to access a mobile portal site. There seem to exist numerous derivatives of these studies in both journals and conference proceedings. In a study on mobile phone usage among 175 adolescents, Grant and O'Donohoe (2007) identified five gratifications: "Convenient entertainment," "Social stimulation," "Experiential learning," "Escapism," and "Purchase information and advice." In the context of mobile-based word-of-mouth, Okazaki (2009) expanded Dholakia et al.'s (2004) social influence model to propose group–person connectivity, intrinsic enjoyment, and purposive value as motives to spread the word—in either commercial or noncommercial messages—via mobile communication.

Attitude–Behavior Models

The theory of reasoned action (TRA) (Fishbein & Ajzen, 1975) is one of the most important social psychological theories for predicting and understanding behavior. It was designed to model how any specific behavior under volitional control is produced by beliefs, attitude, and intention to perform that behavior. In this model, the formation of a behavioral intention is the immediate antecedent of action, and it mediates the influence of other variables on behavior (Fishbein & Ajzen, 1975). More specifically, intention is caused by both the individual's attitude toward performing that behavior, and the individual's perceptions of the social pressures on him or her to perform, or not, that behavior. Fishbein and Ajzen (1975) termed the latter as a subjective norm.

Tsang et al. (2004) examined attitudes toward SMS "push" advertising among Taiwanese. Their proposed structural model is based on attitude, intention, and behavior, which are the three major constructs in the TRA. Muk (2007) combined TRA with Rogers' (1995) diffusion of innovation as a theoretical base, to examine cross-culturally the antecedents of young consumers' behavioral intention to sign up with wireless advertisers in the US and South Korea. The findings suggest that although attitudes towards SMS advertising affect their intention to opt in to SMS ads more strongly than social influences, the relationship between attitudes and intentions was stronger for young Korean consumers.

Fishbein and Ajzen's TRA appears to hold reasonably well within the constraints they define. However, researchers have become increasingly interested in the understanding and prediction of situations that do not fit "neatly" within Fishbein and Ajzen's framework. In particular, a model was needed to address specifically why people accept or reject information systems. Shedding light on this question, Davis (1989) proposed the technology acceptance model (TAM), which quickly became the most frequently used model in IT research. TAM is one of the most influential adaptations of TRA, and is specifically designed to apply only to computer usage behavior. TAM uses TRA as a theoretical basis, but it replaces many of TRA's attitude measures with two technology acceptance measures: ease of use (EOU) and perceived usefulness (PU). Perceived usefulness refers to the extent to which a prospective user believes that using a specific system will improve his or her job performance, whereas perceived ease of use refers to the extent to which a user expects the use of a specific system to be relatively effort free (Davis, 1989).

The central idea underlying TAM is that EOU and PU ultimately determine a person's behavioral intention to use a "system." Because effort is a finite resource that a person may allocate to the various activities for which he or she is responsible (Radner & Rothschild, 1975), TAM posits that, all else being equal, an application that is perceived to be easier to use than another is more likely to be accepted by users. In TAM, PU is seen as being directly impacted by EOU, with intention to use serving as a mediator of actual system use. However, it should be noted that Davis, Bagozzi, and Warshaw (1989) concluded that attitude did not appear to mediate fully the effect of perceived usefulness and perceived ease of use on behavioral intention, as originally anticipated, and they therefore removed it from the model. Thus, the original TAM should be understood as Davis et al. (1989), which was the final model proposed without attitude (Venkatesh & Davis, 1996).

The TAM has received extensive empirical support through validations, applications, and replications across a diverse range of information technology, including mobile advertising. Zhang and Mao (2008) applied TAM to SMS advertising acceptance in China. Their model posits that perceived usefulness, perceived ease of use, trust, and subjective norms predict intention, while perceived usefulness is determined by both the information and sociality utilities offered by using SMS advertising messages, and trust is influenced by users' psychological disposition to trust, and perceived ease of use. Based on 262 responses from those aged between 21 and 35 years old, the findings suggest that the four proposed factors were strong determinants of behavioral intention to use SMS advertising messages. Similar explorations with TAM variations can be found in Muk (2007), Kim, Park, and Oh (2008), and Zhang and Mao (2008), among others.

Research Gaps

Ubiquitous Context

What is missing in prior mobile advertising research is a profound conceptualization of the ubiquitous context. Although ubiquitous computing has long been an established field of research in computer science, this topic has seldom been taken into account in the advertising literature. Prior research unanimously claims that ubiquity—or the usage flexibility of time and location—represents the most important feature of the mobile Internet. Curiously, however, it seems that the comprehensive understanding of this concept has been far less optimal. When we look at prior research on m-commerce, a surprisingly small number of studies actually incorporated ubiquity into their adoption models. So far, the majority of published studies—either in marketing or information science—view ubiquity as either a combined flexibility of time and space (Okazaki, Li, & Hirose, 2009), time consciousness (Kleijnen, Ruyter, & Wetzels, 2007), or an enhanced mode of interactivity (Gao et al., 2009). Otherwise it is a practically untouched area.

The *Merriam–Webster Dictionary* defines "ubiquitous" as "existing or being everywhere at the same time." In computer science, the concept of ubiquitous computing arises from the Xerox Palo Alto Research Center (PARC), in which each user continuously interacts with new kinds of wirelessly interconnected computers. There, the computers are available but invisible to the users throughout the physical environment. Marc Weiser called this next-generation computing environment "ubiquitous computing," and it is a complex integration of human factors, computer science, engineering, and social sciences. In his vision, computer hardware and software will become an effective part of our environment, performing tasks that support our broad purposes without our continual direction, thus allowing us to be largely unaware of them. It is in effect the opposite of virtual reality: where virtual reality puts people inside a computer-generated world, ubiquitous computing forces the computer to live out here in the world with people. Thus, ubiquity means being invisible or seamless so that the computer does not intrude on users' consciousness. More recently, *The Global Information Technology Report* (Dutta & Mira, 2009) notes that

> The goal may be simple but it is ambitious: Internet ubiquity offers connectivity to people wherever they are, whenever they want to access the network, with the device of their choosing. Ubiquity features safe, reliable, and continuous high-speed connectivity. Above and beyond Internet availability, ubiquity means that the Internet follows users seamlessly, rather than users searching for it as they move about during the day from place to place, device to device.

(p. 37)

Again, despite its importance, however, the concept of ubiquity has rarely been discussed in the mobile advertising literature. In marketing, a pioneering discussion was presented by Watson, Pitt, Berthon, and Zinkhan (2002), who describe ubiquity as synonymous with omnipresence, meaning "not only that they are everywhere but also that they are, in a sense, 'nowhere,' for they become invisible as we no longer notice them" (p. 332). In the context of e-commerce, Hoffman, Novak, and Venkatesh (2004) proposed a conceptual model of Internet indispensability, in which they define ubiquity in terms of two major elements: (1) the different segments of the society using the Internet and the contexts of use, and (2) the access points for its use. They claim that

> the underlying idea is that as more segments of the population use the Internet in different contexts (work, family, school, etc.), the greater its diffusion and potential impact. Similarly, the greater the access points for the Internet the greater its use and impact.

Thus, it is the access points that directly impact the nature of Internet users' daily routines and activities. More recently, Kleijnen, de Ruyter, and Wetzels (2007) define ubiquity as "the ability it offers to engage in commerce anytime and anywhere," while Okazaki et al. (2009) envisage it as the combination of time and place flexibility.

Time–Space Perspective

The core concept of ubiquity seems to stem from the so-called "time–space perspective," whose origin can be traced to the work of Hägerstrand at the University of Lund, Sweden. He focused on the organization of activities into temporal and spatial terms, which can be employed to define the performance of human activities. This was the very first step in so-called time-geography, an attempt to stress the factors associated with the spatial and temporal spread of innovations within particular environments. According to Lenntorp (1999), time-geography constitutes a foundation for a general geographical perspective. It represents a new structure of thought under development, which attempts to consolidate the spatial and temporal perspectives of different disciplines on a more solid basis than has thus far occurred. Time-geography is not a subject area per se, or a theory in the narrow sense, but rather an attempt to construct a broad structure of thought that may form a framework capable of fulfilling two tasks. The first is to receive and bring into contact knowledge from highly distinct scientific areas, and from everyday praxis. The second is to reveal relations, the nature of which escapes researchers as soon as the object of research is separated from its given milieu, in order to study it in isolation, experimentally, or in some other distilled way (Lentorp, 1999).

Hägerstrand (1975) argues that the importance of spatial factors is demonstrated by interpersonal communications, where most influence is transferred within local social systems or the "neighborhood effect." According to him, both terrestrial and social distance barriers impede diffusion, in that human activities form environments that have a hierarchical ordering to the extent that those who have access to power in a superior domain frequently use it to restrict the set of possible actions permitted inside the subordinate domains. On this basis, Hägerstrand (1970) developed the basics of time-geographic notation, in order to have a means to keep track simultaneously of both the spatial and temporal dimensions.

In Hägerstrand's theory, there is a "time–space" entity called a "domain." A domain is defined as "a time–space entity within which things and events are under the control of a given individual or a given group" (Hägerstrand, 1970, p. 16). In a domain, activities and events are under the control and influence of specific individuals or organizations. Domains, such as a school or an office building, often serve as stations for individuals to bundle. The ability of an individual or an organization to navigate through the domain depends on the following three time–space constraints that characterize information technology (Hägerstrand, 1970): capability constraints, coupling constraints, and authority constraints.

Coupling constraints require the user's presence at a specific time and place, and therefore they are instrumental, physiological, and cognitive limitations. That is, individuals must join other individuals or organizations in order to form production, consumption, social, and other activity bundles. Capability constraints refer to the user's resources and ability to overcome spatial separation at a specific moment. They circumscribe the amount of effort needed for people to associate themselves with others and with material artifacts at specific places and times for certain durations, in order to realize production, consumption, and transactions. Finally, authority constraints become important when several activities are pretended to be packed into a limited space. Authority constraints subsume such limited space occupation in terms of rules, laws, economic barriers, and power relations, which determine who does or does not have specific access to specific domains at specific times in specific spaces.

Although Hägerstrand's theory is derived from a different discipline, the concepts of coupling, capability, and authority constraints are very relevant to our conceptualization of the ubiquity concept. Telecommunication systems allow humans to eliminate distance for some types of activities and interactions. Transportation, along with telecommunication and settlement systems, grows and declines in response to human activities in space and time. They influence economic, social, and knowledge networks, and in turn shape human activities and their locations in time and space. No coupling constraints—presence and timing—are relevant when using Twitter or MySpace, because users are allowed to form social networks via the wireless Internet connection at any time, and in any place. Similarly, capability constraints become unimportant when search engines enable users to overcome spatial distance, and to reach almost all spatial information at any moment. Finally, mobile banking and payment functions overcome authority constraints, because the right and freedom to control specific domains at specific times is drastically extended.

Personal Extensibility Theory

In terms of theory building for ubiquity, personal extensibility theory may be more specific to human mobility. The personal extensibility concept attempts to measure the ability of a person (or group) to overcome the friction of distance through transportation or communication. Fundamentally, it pertains to "the scope of sensory access and knowledge acquisition and dispersion, and to people's horizons as social actors." Janelle (1973) claims that personal extensibility is "conceptually the reciprocal of time–space convergence," and argues that the rapid advances in communication and transportation technologies and their associated institutions imply a "shrinking world," with expanding opportunities for extensibility. That is, the focal point of this theory lies in the expansion of opportunities for human interaction, rather than improved abilities for movement over greater distances. Here, of special interest to us is that personal extensibility depends on developments in communications technology, because such innovation will reduce the time required to interact with persons in distant places.

Personal extensibility can be anywhere on a continuum of high to low. In a high personal extensibility situation, one can satisfy important information needs, while moving away or toward a destination, by the use of a mobile device. For example, a stockbroker has just left home, and walking along a street toward a commuter train station. On the way, he turns on his mobile to check real-time Dow Jones prices, because he needs to make a buying decision this afternoon. In this case, his perceived extensibility is high, because he can access the information he needs, as he could not have done without his mobile. By contrast, in a low personal extensibility situation, one stays in a static place, and thus takes little advantage of the device's portability. For example, a sales manager enjoys her quiet Sunday morning at home. She may or may not use a mobile device to check a weather forecast for her afternoon picnic, or simply turn on her TV or laptop in the living room. In this case, her perceived extensibility is low, because she may not feel any desperate information needs that require her to use her mobile to catch up. Such changes in the significance of distance affect economic, political, and cultural life. For example, Adam (1995) argues that "as distant connections become easier to maintain, spatial patterns of social interaction change; work and home, resources and industries, management and labor assume varying spatial configurations" (pp. 267–268). This is precisely the result of the rapid advances in the Internet in general, and the mobile device in particular.

Conclusion

Although both scholars and marketers have paid much attention to mobile advertising research, progress has been slow. Clearly, our research does not correspond to industry practice, and, thus, theories tested in prior research may not have been of much interest to practitioners. The majority of published studies still focus on SMS-based advertising, but actual practice goes much further. Social networking, branded entertainment, and even more sophisticated modes of mobile marketing communications should therefore be explored theoretically.

Regardless of the type of mobile advertising, it is extremely important to conceptualize the concept of ubiquity, which has been considered the most important characteristic of the mobile device. For some reason, no formal theory has been proposed in the existing literature. The time–space perspectives from time-geography may provide us with a key to conceptualize ubiquity. Hitherto ubiquity has either been known either as only temporal or spatial flexibility (Okazaki et al., 2009), or it has been discussed as a conceptual derivative of interactivity (Barnes, 2002; Gao et al., 2009). No further scrutiny of ubiquity has been performed. However, without further exploration of it, our progress in mobile advertising research will be limited.

In terms of teaching, mobile advertising should be clearly distinguished from traditional online advertising, from various standpoints. Needless to say, ubiquity is the key to understanding its uniqueness as a medium, and thus active discussion through the use of real examples is encouraged to attain deeper understanding. In addition, the relevant theories associated with context awareness—the main objective of ubiquitous computing—should be explored in terms of mobile advertising effectiveness. Currently, many industry examples are to be found in MMA's annual awards, from top industry practice to best academic of the year (MMA, 2010). These examples should be used in courses, so that theoretical explanations can be easily translated into ongoing reality. In this light, much closer collaboration between industry practitioners and academics in developing teaching materials may be necessary, to foster societal understanding of mobile advertising.

Acknowledgment

The preparation of this chapter has been facilitated by a grant from the Spanish Ministry of Science and Innovation (National Plan for Research, Development and Innovation EC02008–01557).

References

Adams, P. C. (1995). A reconsideration of personal boundaries in space-time. *Annals of the Association of American Geographers, 85* (2), 267–285.

Barnes, S. J. (2002). Wireless digital advertising: Nature and implications. *International Journal of Advertising, 21* (3), 399–420.

Barwise, P., & Strong, C. (2002). Permission-based mobile advertising. *Journal of Interactive Marketing, 16* (1), 14–24.

Belk, R. W. (1975). Situational variables and consumer behavior. *Journal of Consumer Research, 2* (3), 157–164.

Brackett, L. K., & Carr, B. N. (2001). Cyberspace advertising vs. other media: Consumer vs. mature student attitudes. *Journal of Advertising Research, 41* (5), 23–33.

Carroll, A., Barnes, S., Scornavacca, E., & Fletcher, K. (2007). Consumer perceptions and attitudes towards SMS advertising: Recent evidence from New Zealand. *International Journal of Advertising, 26* (1), 79–98.

Choi, Y., Hwang, J., & McMillan, S. (2008). Gearing up for mobile advertising: A cross-cultural examination of key factors that drive mobile messages home to consumers. *Psychology and Marketing, 25* (8), 756–768.

Davis, F. D. (1989). Perceived usefulness, perceived ease of use and user acceptance of information technology. *MIS Quarterly, 13* (3), 319–340.

Davis, F. D., Bagozzi, R. P., & Warshaw, P. R. (1989). User acceptance of computer technology: A comparison of two theoretical models. *Management Science, 35* (8), 982–1003.

Dholakia, U. M., Bagozzi, R. P., & Pearo, L. K. (2004). A social influence model of consumer participation in network- and small-group-based virtual communities. *International Journal of Research in Marketing, 21*, 241–263.

Ducoffe, R. H. (1996). Advertising value and advertising on the Web. *Journal of Advertising Research, 36* (5), 21–35.

Dutta, R., & Mira, I. (2009). *The global information technology report 2008–2009 mobility in a networked world.* Geneva: World Economic Forum.

eMarket (2010, January 10). Mobile ad spending trends. *AdWeek.* Retrieved September 1, 2010, from www.adweek.com/aw/content_display/news/agency/e3if-5f773e59310e059c43c985188622dc1.

Fishbein, M., & Ajzen, I. (1975). *Beliefs, attitude, intention and behaviour: An introduction to theory and research.* Reading, MA: Addison-Wesley.

Flanagin, A. J., & Metzger, M. J. (2001). Internet use in the contemporary media environment. *Human Communication Research, 27*, 153–181.

Gao, Q., Rau, P., & Salvendy, G. (2009). Perception of interactivity: Affects of four key variables in mobile advertising. *International Journal of Human–Computer Interaction, 25* (6), 479–505.

Hägerstrand, T. (1970). What about people in regional science? *Papers of the Regional Science Association, 24*, 1–12.

Hägerstrand, T. (1975). Space, time and human conditions. In A. Karlqvist, L. Lundquist, & F. Snickars (Eds.), *Dynamic allocation of urban space* (pp. 3–14). Lexington: Saxon House Lexington Books.

Hoffman, D. L., Novak, T. P., & Venkatesh, A. (2004). Has the Internet become indispensable? *Communications of the ACM, 47* (7), 37–42.

Janelle, D. (1973). Measuring human extensibility in a shrinking world. *Journal of Geography, 72* (5), 8–15.

Janelle, D. (1969). Spatial reorganization: A model and concept. *Annals of the Association of American Geographers, 59*, 348–364.

Katz, E., Blumler, J. G., & Gurevitch, M. (1974). Utilization of mass communication by the individual. In J. G. Blumler & E. Kats (Eds.), *The uses of mass communications: Current perspectives on gratifications research* (pp. 19–32). Beverly Hills, CA: Sage.

Kim, G. S., Park, S. B., & Oh, J. (2008). An examination of factors influencing consumer adoption of short message service (SMS). *Psychology and Marketing, 25* (8), 769–786.

Kleijnen, M., Ruyter, K., & Wetzels, M. (2007). An assessment of value creation in mobile service delivery and the moderating role of time consciousness. *Journal of Retailing, 83* (1), 33–46.

Lenntorp, B. (1999). Time-geography: At the end of its beginning. *GeoJournal, 48*, 155–158.

Lin, C. A. (1999). Uses and gratifications. In G. Stone, M. Singletary, & V. P. Richmond (Eds.), *Clarifying communication theories: A hands-on approach* (pp. 199–208). Ames: Iowa State University Press.

Michael, A., & Salter, B. (2006). *Mobile marketing: Achieving competitive advantage through wireless technology*. Oxford, UK: Elsevier.

MMA (Mobile Marketing Association) (2010). Mobile advertising guidelines. Retrieved August 20, 2010, from www.mmaglobal.com/mobileadvertising.pdf.

Morgan Stanley (2009). *The mobile internet report*. New York: Morgan Stanley.

Muk, A. (2007). Consumers' intentions to opt in to SMS advertising: A cross-national study of young Americans and Koreans. *International Journal of Advertising, 26* (2), 177–198.

Okazaki, S. (2004). How do Japanese consumers perceive wireless ads? A multivariate analysis. *International Journal of Advertising, 23* (4), 429–454.

Okazaki, S. (2006). What do we know about mobile Internet adopters? A cluster analysis. *Information and Management, 43* (2), 127–141.

Okazaki, S. (2009). Social influence model and electronic word of mouth: PC versus mobile internet. *International Journal of Advertising, 28* (3), 439–472.

Okazaki, S., Katsukura, A., & Nishiyama, M. (2007). How mobile advertising works: The role of trust in improving attitudes and recall. *Journal of Advertising Research, 47* (2), 165–178.

Okazaki, S., Li, H., & Hirose, M. (2009). Consumer privacy concerns and preference for degree of regulatory control: A study of mobile advertising in Japan. *Journal of Advertising, 38* (4), 63–77.

Radner, R., & Rothschild, M. (1975). On the allocation of effort. *Journal of Economic Theory, 10* (June), 358–376.

Rodriguez-Perlado, V., & Barwise, P. (2004). Mobile advertising: A research agenda. In M. R. Stafford and R. J. Faber (Eds.), *Advertising, promotion, and new media* (pp. 261–277). New York: M.E. Sharpe.

Rogers, E. M. (1995). *The diffusion of innovations* (4th ed.). New York: Free Press.

SFN (2010, April 22). SFN report: Mobile ad spending to exceed $5 billion in Western Europe and Asia Pacific in '12. *sfnblog.com*. Retrieved September 1, 2010, from www.sfnblog.com/industry_trends/2010/03/sfn_report_global_mobile_advert-ising_to.php.

Tsang, M., Ho, S., & Liang, T. (2004). Consumer attitudes toward mobile advertising: An empirical study. *International Journal of Electronic Commerce, 8* (3), 65–78.

Varnali, K., & Toker, A. (2010). Mobile marketing research: The-state-of-the-art. *International Journal of Information Management, 30*, 144–151.

Venkatesh, V., & Davis, F. D. (1996). A model of the antecedents of perceived ease of use: Development and test. *Decision Sciences, 27* (3), 451–481.

Watson, R. T., Pitt, L. F., Berthon, P., & Zinkhan, G. M. (2002). U-commerce: Expanding the universe of marketing. *Journal of the Academy of Marketing Science, 30* (4), 333–347.

Zhang, J., & Mao, E. (2008). Understanding the acceptance of mobile SMS advertising among young Chinese consumers. *Psychology and Marketing, 25* (8), 787–805.

Additional Readings

Habuchi, I., Dobashi, S., Tsuji, I., & Iwata, K. (2005). Ordinary usage of new media: Internet usage via mobile phone in Japan. *International Journal of Japanese Sociology, 14*, 94–108.

Kavassalis, P., Spyropoulou, N., Drossos, D., Mitrokostas, E., Gikas, G., & Hatzista-matiou, A. (2003). Mobile permission marketing: Framing the market inquiry. *International Journal of Electronic Commerce, 8* (1), 55–79.

Nysveen, H., Pedersen, P. E., & Thorbjornsen, H. (2005). Explaining intention to use mobile chat services: Moderating effects of gender. *Journal of Consumer Marketing, 22* (5), 247–256.

Okazaki, S. (2012). *Fundamentals of mobile marketing: Theory and practice*. New York: Peter Lang.

Wu, J. H., & Wang, S. C. (2005). What drives mobile commerce? An empirical evaluation of the revised technology acceptance model. *Information and Management, 42* (5), 719–729.

Chapter 25

In-Game Advertising and Advergames

A Review of the Past Decade's Research

Seounmi Youn and Mira Lee

Introduction

As game play continues to grow in popularity among consumers, advertisers are increasingly relying on video, computer, or online games as a platform to deliver branded entertainment. Advertisers use games in two different ways to place brands: in-game advertising and advergames (Lee & Youn, 2008). In-game advertising refers to the placement of advertisers' brands in a commercial game to promote their products or services to the target demographic (e.g., male 18–34). With in-game advertising, multiple brands are typically displayed in the background of the game (e.g., a billboard in a car-racing game). Game players are often incidentally exposed to the brands embedded in games while playing games (Lee & Faber, 2007; Yang, Roskos-Ewoldsen, Dinu, & Arpan, 2006). Another type of in-game brand placements is the advergame, a free online game primarily developed for promoting advertisers' brands or branded products. In a typical advergame, one brand is featured (Mallinckrodt & Mizerski, 2007) and the embedded brand or product is a central part of the game. Advergames are relatively easy to play, thus attracting casual adult gamers or children. Advergames are available on brand websites and drive traffic to brand websites (Cauberghe & De Pelsmacker, 2010; Gross, 2010).

Research on in-game advertising and advergames has received extensive scholarly attention in the past decade since Nelson's (2002) seminal study on the effectiveness of product placements in a computer racing game was published in *Journal of Advertising Research*. An overview of previous research on in-game advertising and advergames is briefly presented in Table 25.1. Among various aspects identified in the integrated approach to advertising theory (see Figure 1.1 in Chapter 1), this chapter endeavors to examine in-game advertising and advergames as *an advertising channel* that conveys advertisers' messages to receivers, both adults and children.

Specifically, this chapter will review key findings of prior studies on in-game advertising and advergames while highlighting theories applied in those studies.

Table 25.1 Summary of research on in-game product placements

	In-game advertising	Advergames
Effects of exposure to in-game placements	Nelson, 2002; Yang, Roskos-Ewoldsen, Dinu, & Arpan, 2006	Mallinckrodt & Mizerski, 2007; Pempek & Calvert, 2009
Psychological mechanisms: Flow or telepresence	Grigorovici & Constantin, 2004; Schneider & Cornwell, 2005; Nelson, Yaros, & Keum, 2006	
Game player characteristics:		
Attitude toward advertising, product placement, or brand	Nelson, 2002; Nelson, Keum, & Yaros, 2004;	
Game experience	Chaney, Lin, & Chaney, 2004; Schneider & Cornwell, 2005; Lee & Faber, 2007	
Mode of exposure: Play vs. Watch	Nelson, Yaros, & Keum, 2006	
Game-playing repetition		Cauberghe & De Pelsmacker, 2010
Product placement strategies:		
Brand prominence or product placement proximity	Schneider & Cornwell, 2005; Lee & Faber, 2007	Cauberghe & De Pelsmacker, 2010
Brand-game congruity	Lee & Faber, 2007	Wise, Bolls, Kim, Venkataraman, & Meyer, 2008; Gross, 2010
Content analysis studies		Weber, Story, & Harnack, 2006; Moore & Rideout, 2007; Lee & Youn, 2008; Lee, Choi, Quilliam, & Cole, 2009; Culp, Bell, & Cassady, 2010

In doing so, major psychological mechanisms that explain how in-game brand placements influence brand memory, attitude, or product choice will be discussed. In addition, this chapter will describe how game players' characteristics and strategic features of brand placements affect players' processing of brand placements in games. A systematic understanding of previous work on in-game advertising and advergames provides scholars with directions for future research in these areas, and helps identify room for improvement to conduct theoretically and methodologically rigorous studies.

A Review of Prior Research on In-Game Brand Placements

The Psychology of Games

To understand the psychological processes underlying how in-game brand placements work, some researchers have explored how game players process brand messages in games. Processing brands embedded in a game while playing the game involves dual tasks: playing a game is considered a primary task, while processing brand identifiers (e.g., brand logo, branded product) placed in the game is a secondary task. Due in part to such unique information processing, the limited capacity model of attention has been widely adopted as a theoretical framework (Lee & Faber, 2007; Nelson, Yaros, & Keum, 2006). According to the limited capacity model of attention, an individual's total attentional capacity at any specific point in time is limited and divided between the primary task and the secondary task (Kahneman, 1973). The more an individual allocates his or her cognitive capacity to processing the primary task, the less he or she has capacity to process the secondary task. In the context of in-game brand placements, this model has been explicated under a set of conditions—for example, placement proximity, prior game experiences, or mode of exposure (play versus watch)—where the effect of in-game brand placements on brand memory is more or less pronounced (Lee & Faber, 2007; Nelson et al., 2006).

There have also been other psychological processes explaining the effects of in-game brand placements on brand memory. Compared to the passive context of watching TV or movies, the context of game play is highly interactive because players maneuver around the game (Chaney, Lin, & Chaney, 2004; Yang et al., 2006). Because of the nature of game play, researchers have examined flow (Schneider & Cornwell, 2005). Flow involves experiencing an enjoyable sense of control and total concentration in an activity, which requires an adequate level of skill and challenge (Csikszentmihalyi, 1990). Game players can experience flow because game-playing activities provide players with a sense of control over gaming environments and are intrinsically motivated for the sake of pleasure. Schneider and Cornwell (2005) expected a positive relationship between flow and brand memory under the assumption that a flow experience leads to a focusing of attention on game play, thus resulting in higher brand memory. However, the effects of flow on brand recall and recognition were not found in their study.

As another game-induced psychological reaction, telepresence is viewed as individuals' immersion or transportation ("you are there") inside the game, which is "the feeling of being in the game" (Nelson et al., 2006, pp. 95–96). Telepresence increases with interactivity, which enables players to control the game environment. It is argued that telepresence leads players to attend to and recall central stimuli of the primary experience (e.g., playing the game) while weakening recall of stimuli that are not related to the experience (e.g., embedded brands) (Nelson et al., 2006). Related to this argument, Grigorovici and Constantin (2004) found that the engagement factor of telepresence had an inhibitory effect on recall and recognition of brands in 3D gaming environments. In contrast, Nelson et al.'s (2006) study using adult game players did not show negative effects of telepresence on recall of background brands embedded in a computer racing game.

Given that game play is a pleasant activity, several researchers have applied the affect transfer mechanism to explain the persuasive impact (e.g., attitude toward the brand) of brand placements in games (Nelson et al., 2006; Wise, Bolls, Kim, Venkataraman, & Meyer, 2008). Telepresence has been regarded as one of the positive psychological responses induced by game playing and such positive feelings caused by telepresence may spill over into brands sponsored in the games through affect transfer. Along this line, Nelson et al. (2006) found that telepresence positively influenced perceived persuasion of the product placements in the game.

In conjunction with psychological mechanisms of in-game brand placements, the next section discusses specific findings of studies on in-game advertising and advergames in terms of strategic features of product placements and game players' characteristics.

Effects of Product Placement Strategies

Brand placement strategies in games may vary depending on where brand messages are located in the game. As suggested in the literature on product placement in movies (e.g., Gupta & Lord, 1998), a placement strategy in relation to the brand location in games is referred to as brand prominence (Cauberghe & De Pelsmacker, 2010; Schneider & Cornwell, 2005) or product placement proximity (Lee & Faber, 2007). Prominent (or focal) placement is defined as integrating brand identifiers in a central part of the game, while subtle (or peripheral) placement involves displaying brand identifiers on a billboard or signage in the background of the game.

The limited capacity model of attention explains the effect of the brand location in games on brand memory. Gamers pay primary attention to the action in the game rather than the background of the game. In the prominent or focal placement, the brands appear in the center of the action in the game and therefore the brands receive a great deal of attention from game players.

Conversely, gamers are more likely to have limited resources available to process brands appearing in the peripheral area because they use most of their cognitive resources playing the game. Prior research on in-game advertising has consistently found that prominent or focal placement leads to a better memory of brands embedded in games than subtle or peripheral placement (Lee & Faber, 2007; Schneider & Cornwell, 2005). These findings align with Cauberghe and De Pelsmacker's (2010) results showing that prominent brand placement in an advergame resulted in a stronger brand recall than subtle brand placement.

Another brand placement strategy used for in-game brand placements likely to affect brand memory is game–product congruity, the relevance or fit between the content of the game and the product category of the brand embedded in the game (Gross, 2010; Lee & Faber, 2007; Wise et al., 2008). In the context of in-game advertising, Lee and Faber (2007) found that college student participants recalled the highly incongruent brands better than moderately incongruent brands or the highly congruent brands, after playing an online car racing game. It has been asserted that incongruent information may receive additional mental processing at the time of encoding because it is novel and irrelevant. Further, game players may engage in more intensive cognitive activities when processing incongruent information (versus congruent information) in order to resolve the incongruity, thus facilitating retrieval of incongruent information later on (Srull & Wyer, 1989).

However, in the context of advergames, Gross (2010) found that college student participants who played the high-congruent advergames showed higher scores on both implicit brand memory, which was measured with a word-fragment completion task, and 1-week delayed explicit brand memory, which was measured with recognition, compared to the low-congruent advergames. The spreading activation theory (Anderson, 1983) was applied in her study to explain this effect. According to this theory, one's memory storage is viewed as an associated network, which consists of information nodes and links between nodes (Anderson, 1983). It has been argued that a brand embedded in a game would be easily remembered, when a link between the node representing the brand and the node representing the game content is thematically connected. This would be because high thematic connections between nodes (e.g., game content and brand) easily activate one's memory of the embedded brand in the game by associating it with the game (Carlston & Smith, 1996).

Further, Wise et al. (2008) investigated how the thematic connection between an advergame and a brand influences the relationship between attitude toward the advergame and attitude toward the brand. Two theories were applied to this study: affect transfer and spreading activation theory. Positive feelings induced by game play are likely to be transferred to gamers' attitude toward the brand. This affect transfer is more likely to be facilitated when the game content and the featured brand are thematically relevant (versus irrelevant) because the node representing the game content is speculated to easily activate the brand node. Indeed, the study revealed that advergame enjoyment had a stronger positive effect on brand attitude when participants played the thematically relevant advergames, compared to the irrelevant advergames.

Game Player Characteristics

The effects of exposure to brands in games on brand memory and brand attitudes may also vary depending on gamers' characteristics. One individual difference factor that has been found to influence the effectiveness of in-game advertising is an individual's attitude toward product placement in games. Nelson, Keum, and Yaros (2004) found that attitudes toward advertising in general had positive effects on attitudes toward product placements in computer games, which, in turn, positively affected the perceived influence of product placement in games on purchase intention.

Another individual difference factor likely to influence brand memory is an individual's prior experience in game play (Chaney et al., 2004; Lee & Faber, 2007; Schneider & Cornwell, 2005). It has been argued that individuals who have greater experience levels in playing games are armed with stronger skills to manipulate game-playing environments and are expected to easily master the game. These experienced players may, thus, have a sufficient level of spare cognitive capacity necessary to process brands placed in games. In contrast, novice players are more likely to spend intensive mental efforts in learning how to play games due to a lack of skills and, hence, do not have spare resources to attend to brands embedded in games (Chaney et al., 2004; Lee & Faber, 2007).

Indeed, in an experimental study with a computer racing game, Schneider and Cornwell (2005) observed that college student participants' level of skill in game play appeared to be positively related to the level of recall and recognition of brands placed in the game. Lee and Faber (2007) considered an individual's prior game experience as a moderator that influences the effect of product placement proximity on brand memory. They predicted that, due to their enhanced ability to handle secondary tasks (e.g., process the embedded brands in games), experienced players are able to devote their attention to the embedded brands, regardless of the placement location—focal or peripheral. In contrast, for novice players, focal brands (versus peripheral brands) are more likely to induce brand recall because they pay more attention to focal brands than peripheral brands. In fact, Lee and Faber (2007) detected greater differences in memory for focal versus peripheral brands among inexperienced players relative to experienced players.

Mode of Exposure to In-Game Advertising

Individuals often play games in a social environment, sharing their game-play experience with others. When they do so, they often watch other people play as well. Nelson et al. (2006) explored the influence of playing and watching on individuals' brand processing. Drawing insights from the limited capacity model of attention in the context of game playing, it has been contended that game players actively participate in goal-oriented central tasks of a game, while game watchers get involved in an attention task only. Thus, game players have limited resources available to process peripheral elements of the game (e.g., brands on billboards), whereas game watchers have more spare cognitive resources to attend to the brands. Reflective of this argument, Nelson et al. (2006) found that non-student adult participants who played a computer racing game recalled fewer embedded brands than those who watched the pre-recorded game. Nelson et al. (2006) suggest that practitioners develop turn-taking games, which can provide players with cognitive resources necessary for processing peripheral elements of the game.

Effects of Game-Playing Repetition

Repetitive exposure to advertising stimuli has been examined as one of the factors that influence individuals' memory of and attitudes toward ads and brands (Cox & Cox, 1988; Nan & Faber, 2004; Pechmann & Stewart, 1988). Researchers have explained the effects of advertising repetition by applying the wear-in and wear-out mechanism to memory and attitudes. The wear-in phase through repetition involves learning, which fosters familiarity with advertising stimuli and, thus, enhances brand memory and attitudes. Alternately, the wear-out phase over repetition leads to boredom, irritation, or psychological reactance toward the ad stimuli, which diminishes positive attitudinal effects while failing to augment brand memory. Cauberghe and De Pelsmacker (2010) asserted that this wear-in and wear-out effect is accelerated when individuals are repeatedly exposed to simple stimuli such as advergames. Due to faster wear-in and wear-out resulting from message simplicity of the advergame, Cauberghe and De Pelsmacker (2010) found that playing the advergame multiple times showed no effects on brand recall, but shaped brand attitudes negatively.

Children as Target Audience

Chapter 9 of this volume talks extensively about children as a specific target audience. The preceding discussions suggests that placing brand messages in a game has a potential to influence adult game players' attitudes toward brands embedded in the game. Such effect of in-game brand placements on brand attitudes through affect transfer can emerge partly because brand messages are woven into the content of the game and, thus, selling or persuasive intent of brand messages is "hidden." It has long been suggested that younger children are vulnerable to advertising because they are unable to distinguish commercial content from non-commercial content and do not recognize the selling intent of advertising messages (John, 1999). Given the fact that advergames blur the lines between entertainment and commercial content (Moore & Rideout, 2007) as well as the interactive nature of advergame play, it has been argued that children may be vulnerable to advergames and, thus, marketing to children using advergames is problematic (Lee, Choi, Quilliam, & Cole, 2009; Mallinckrodt & Mizerski, 2007; Moore & Rideout, 2007).

Recognizing the public concerns over the rising childhood obesity rate and the potential impact of advergames on children's attitudes toward brands embedded in advergames, researchers have examined the prevalence and content of food advergames that might be accessed and played by children. Researchers have consistently found that advergames were present on the majority of websites for food brands that are frequently marketed to children (Culp, Bell, & Cassady, 2010; Lee et al., 2009; Moore & Rideout, 2007; Weber, Story, & Harnack, 2006). For example, Moore and Rideout (2007) identified 546 advergames on 77 websites of food companies whose primary audience was judged as children or whose content was of interest to children. Recently, Culp et al. (2010) analyzed 19 websites of food, beverage, and restaurant brands advertised on two children's networks on TV. Among those 19 websites, 16 offered a total of 247 advergames.

Beyond counting the number of advergames available on websites of food companies, Lee et al. (2009) analyzed the content of food advergames that might be accessed and played by children and the nutritional content of the food products promoted in those advergames. Specifically, they found that about 67% of the 220 advergames analyzed integrated brand identifiers as game pieces, such as tools or equipment that children use in order to complete game missions or as objects that they collect or catch in order to earn points. This type of integration allows children to "play with" the virtual food items. More alarming is the finding that the majority of the food products promoted in those advergames (83.8%) were considered unhealthy. Taken together, these content analytic studies have demonstrated that food marketers heavily use advergames to promote their food products to children, and these advergames allow children to interact with their food products in virtual game worlds.

Researchers have also started to examine the impact of food advergame play on children's food preferences and choices. Mallinckrodt and Mizerski (2007) found that children who played the advergame for the stimulus cereal, which should be consumed in moderation by children due to the amount of sugar, preferred the stimulus cereal brand to other brands of cereal and to other types of foods (e.g., a hamburger, a sandwich, or fruit salad) more often than those who did not play the advergame. Opposite to what researchers have often argued, however, this study found that children's knowledge about the intent of the advergame or persuasion knowledge had no impact on their preference for the stimulus cereal brand and for the cereal category (see also Chapter 9).

Additionally, Pempek and Calvert (2009) had children play either an advergame for healthier foods or an advergame for less healthy foods and asked them to choose and eat foods promoted in those advergames. They found that children who played the advergame for the healthier foods chose and ate a greater number of healthier foods than did those who played the advergame for the less healthy foods. These studies show that advergames are effective in influencing children's food preferences and choices.

Conclusion

A review on studies spanning the past decade provides us with guidance for future studies in terms of theoretical and methodological issues. Since only a few researchers have conducted theory-driven studies, only a few select theories have been applied to explain the effectiveness of in-game brand placements.

In a game playing context, it is argued that processing brands displayed in games may be more challenging, compared to processing brands placed in TV programs or movies, because players are engrossed in game play. Given that game players engage in dual tasks when processing brands embedded in a game, the limited capacity model of attention has been employed as an overarching theoretical perspective to explain the effect of in-game brand placements on brand memory. Several researchers have also identified the conditions under which in-game brand placements are more or less effective in increasing brand memory, such as product placement prominence (or proximity), prior game-playing experience, and mode of exposure (play versus watch) (Chaney et al., 2004; Lee & Faber, 2007; Nelson et al., 2006). Future research should continue to apply the limited capacity model to the context of in-game advertising or advergames to demonstrate its robustness and examine conditions that interact to influence brand memory.

Game–product congruity has been explored as a product placement strategy likely to affect brand memory. Within the context of in-game advertising, it has been found that the incongruent brands placed in a game are so distinctive and irrelevant that those brands are retrieved better than the congruent brands (Lee & Faber, 2007). Conversely, game–product congruity in advergames showed contradictory findings such that the congruent advergame led to higher brand recall than the incongruent advergame (Gross, 2010). In fact, such inconsistent findings have appeared in consumer research for decades. Researchers need to further investigate inconsistent findings in in-game brand placements and examine why these inconsistent results occur.

Based on media context effects, several researchers have accounted for the effect of in-game brand placements on brand attitudes through the affect transfer mechanism (Nelson et al., 2006; Wise et al., 2008). Although previous studies found significant relationships between game-induced psychological responses, such as telepresence and game liking, and brand attitudes (Nelson et al., 2006; Wise et al., 2008), empirical evidence has not been readily available regarding the direct impact of exposure to brands in games on persuasion through affect transfer. This is another area of research that warrants increased attention in future studies.

Recognizing the immersive nature of game play, researchers have also adopted the concept of telepresence as a theoretical framework in the context of in-game advertising. The findings on the effect of telepresence on brand memory have been mixed across studies showing no impact (Nelson et al., 2006) or an inhibitive impact (Grigorovici & Constantin, 2004). However, the effect of telepresence on attitudes and persuasion has been positive (Nelson et al., 2006). More research should be conducted to assess under what conditions telepresence produces negative impact on brand memory in the context of in-game advertising and under what conditions it leads to no or negative impact.

More recently, recognizing the public concerns about a potential contribution of advergames promoting unhealthy food products to children on the increasing childhood obesity rate, researchers have started to examine the effects of food advergames on children's food preference and choice (Mallinckrodt & Mizerski, 2007; Pempek & Calvert, 2009). Children's age-based cognitive capacities and the persuasion knowledge model (Friestad & Wright, 1994; Wright, Friestad, & Boush, 2005) have been used to explain such effects (Mallinckrodt & Mizerski, 2007). Given the lack of research in this area, however, many questions still remain unanswered regarding why and how food advergames influence children's food preferences and choices. More theory-based research should be conducted in this area to contribute to our understanding of the effects of food advergames on children's dietary behaviors. Such research will also provide public policy makers with insights into how to better protect children from a potential negative effect of advergames for unhealthy food products on children's dietary behaviors.

A review of studies on in-game brand placements offers future research directions in terms of the methodology as well. Recall and recognition of brands embedded in games have been most commonly measured when examining the effectiveness of in-game brand placements. Some scholars have also assessed implicit memory of the brands by using a word fragment completion test (Gross, 2010; Yang et al., 2006). It has been argued that implicit memory would be more appropriate for investigating unconscious recollection of information that occurs when players do not fully attend to the brands promoted in games while playing games (Gross, 2010; Lee & Faber, 2007; Yang et al., 2006). Future research would benefit from measuring implicit memory and its subsequent role in product choice to gauge the effectiveness of in-game brand placements more accurately.

Although in-game advertising and advergames share some similarities, they also differ in the game's complexities and design (Cauberghe & De Pelsmacker, 2010). Due to unique characteristics of each format, advertisers may try to achieve different goals when using in-game advertising and advergames. To gauge the effectiveness of each format appropriately, therefore, different outcome variables need to be measured. Within the context of typical in-game advertising, multiple brands compete for attention from players because a single game often includes multiple billboards or signage featuring multiple brands within the game. Therefore, assessing brand memory such as brand recall or recognition as effectiveness outcomes would be more appropriate for in-game advertising.

However, advergames are usually available on brand websites and, thus, advergame players are already aware of which brand(s) is featured in the advergame even before they play the advergame. Additionally, one brand is typically given sole or primary prominence in an advergame. In the context of advergames, therefore, it would be more appropriate to measure brand attitudes or brand choice, rather than brand recall or recognition, to assess the effectiveness of advergames. The use of more suitable measures to gauge effectiveness outcomes merits future investigation on product placement in games.

Although a growing number of researchers have examined the effects of in-game advertising or advergames, little research has examined specific features or placement strategies of in-game advertising or advergames (Wise et al.,

2008). In order to enhance our understanding of in-game advertising and advergames, it is recommended that researchers examine a variety of features of in-game advertising and/or advergames (e.g., brand placement strategies) potentially influencing brand memory, brand attitudes, or product choices. The lack of research examining specific features of in-game advertising or advergames may be largely due to the difficulty and high cost of manipulating specific features. A strategic partnership with the game development industry should be considered to prevent restricting research ideas due to difficulties in stimulus development.

During the past decade, researchers have contributed to our understanding of in-game advertising and advergames to a great extent. However, as noted earlier, there is room remaining for improvement. It is hoped that an increasing number of researchers can use this review to conduct theoretically and methodologically rigorous studies in in-game advertising and advergames.

References

Anderson, J. R. (1983). A spreading activation theory of memory. *Journal of Verbal Learning and Verbal Behavior, 22* (3), 261–295.

Carlston, D. E., & Smith, E. R. (1996). Principles of mental representation. In E. T. Higgins & A. W. Kruglanski (Eds.), *Social cognition: Impact on social psychology* (pp. 184–210). New York: Academic Press.

Cauberghe, V., & De Pelsmacker, P. (2010). Advergames: The impact of brand prominence and game repetition on brand responses. *Journal of Advertising, 39* (1), 5–18.

Chaney, I. M., Lin, K., & Chaney, J. (2004). The effect of billboards within the gaming environment. *Journal of Interactive Advertising, 5* (1), 37–45.

Cox, D. S., & Cox, A. D. (1988). What does familiarity breed? Complexity as a moderator of repetition effect in ad evaluation. *Journal of Consumer Research, 15*, 111–116.

Csikszentmihalyi, M. (1990). *Flow: The psychology of optimal experience.* New York: Harper & Row.

Culp, J., Bell, R. A., & Cassady, D. (2010). Characteristics of food industry websites and "advergames" targeting children. *Journal of Nutrition Education and Behavior, 42* (3), 197–201.

Friestad, M., & Wright, P. (1994). The persuasion knowledge model: How people cope with persuasion attempts. *Journal of Consumer Research, 21* (1), 1–31.

Grigorovici, D. M., & Constantin, C. D. (2004). Experiencing interactive advertising beyond rich media: Impacts of ad type and presence on brand effectiveness in 3D gaming immersive virtual environments. *Journal of Interactive Advertising, 5* (1), 22–36.

Gross, M. L. (2010). Advergames and the effects of game-product congruity. *Computers in Human Behavior, 26*, 1259–1265.

Gupta, P. B., & Lord, K. R. (1998). Product placement in movies: The effect of prominence and mode on audience recall. *Journal of Current Issues and Research in Advertising, 20* (1), 47–59.

John, D. R. (1999). Consumer socialization of children: A retrospective look at twenty-five years of research. *Journal of Consumer Research, 26* (December), 183–213.

Kahneman, D. (1973). *Attention and effort.* Englewood Cliffs, NJ: Prentice Hall.

Lee, M., Choi, Y., Quilliam, E. T., & Cole, R. T. (2009). Playing with food: Content analysis of food advergames. *Journal of Consumer Affairs, 43* (1), 129–154.

Lee, M., & Faber, R. J. (2007). Effects of product placement in on-line games on brand memory: A perspective of the limited-capacity model of attention. *Journal of Advertising, 36* (4), 75–90.

Lee, M., & Youn, S. (2008). Leading national advertisers' uses of advergames. *Journal of Current Issues and Research in Advertising, 30* (2), 1–13.

Mallinckrodt, V., & Mizerski, D. (2007). The effects of playing an advergame on young children's perceptions, preferences, and requests. *Journal of Advertising, 36* (2), 87–100.

Moore, E. S., & Rideout, V. (2007). The online marketing of food to children: Is it just fun and games? *Journal of Public Policy and Marketing, 26* (2), 202–220.

Nan, X., & Faber, R. J. (2004). Advertising theory: Reconceptualizing the building blocks. *Marketing Theory, 4* (1/2), 7–30.

Nelson, M. R. (2002). Recall of brand placements in computer/video games. *Journal of Advertising Research, 42* (2), 80–92.

Nelson, M. R., Keum, H., & Yaros, R. A. (2004). Advertainment or adcreep game players' attitudes toward advertising and product placements in computer games. *Journal of Interactive Advertising, 5* (1), 3–21.

Nelson, M. R., Yaros, R. A., & Keum, H. (2006). Examining the influence of telepresence on spectator and player processing of real and fictitious brands in a computer game. *Journal of Advertising, 35* (4), 87–99.

Pechmann, C., & Stewart, D. W. (1988). Advertising repetition: A critical review of wearin and wearout. *Current Issues and Research in Advertising, 11* (2), 285–330.

Pempek, T. A., & Calvert, S. L. (2009). Tipping the balance: Use of advergames to promote consumption of nutritious foods and beverages by low-income African American children. *Archives of Pediatrics and Adolescent Medicine, 163* (7), 633–637.

Schneider, L., & Cornwell, T. B. (2005). Cashing in on crashes via brand placement in computer games: The effects of experience and flow on memory. *International Journal of Advertising, 24* (3), 321–343.

Srull, T. K., & Wyer, R. S. (1989). Person memory and judgment. *Psychological Review, 96* (1), 58–83.

Weber, K., Story, M., & Harnack, L. (2006). Internet food marketing strategies aimed at children and adolescents: A content analysis of food and beverage brand websites. *Journal of the American Dietetic Association, 106* (9), 1463–1466.

Wise, K., Bolls, P. D., Kim, H., Venkataraman, A., & Meyer, R. (2008). Enjoyment of advergames and brand attitudes: The impact of thematic relevance. *Journal of Interactive Advertising, 9* (1), 27–36.

Wright, P., Friestad, M., & Boush, D. M. (2005). The development of marketplace persuasion knowledge in children, adolescents, and young adults. *Journal of Public Policy and Marketing, 24* (2), 222–233.

Yang, M., Roskos-Ewoldsen, D. R., Dinu, L., & Arpan, L. M. (2006). The effectiveness of "in-game" advertising: Comparing college students' explicit and implicit memory for brand names. *Journal of Advertising, 35* (4), 143–152.

Additional Readings

An, S., & Stern, S. (2011). Mitigating the effects of advergames on children. *Journal of Advertising*, *40* (1), 43–56.

Jeong, E. J., Bohil, C. J., & Biocca, F. A. (2011). Brand logo placement in violent games: Effects of violence cues on memory and attitude through arousal and presence. *Journal of Advertising*, *40* (3), 59–72.

Marolf, G. (2007). *Advergaming and In-game advertising: An approach to the next generation of advertising*. VDM Verlag, Saarbrucken, Germany.

Chapter 26

Social Media and Advertising Theory

Harshavardhan Gangadharbatla

Introduction

Six years ago there was no Facebook. Today, Facebook has over 500 million active users (Facebook, 2010). YouTube was created in 2005 and, every minute, 24 hours of video is uploaded onto the site and people watch over two billion videos a day on YouTube (YouTube, 2010). Even younger than Facebook and YouTube is Twitter, which was created just 4 years ago. According to a study by PEW Research Center, one in 10 American adults who use the Internet are Twitter users (Gaudin, 2010) and nine in 10 Americans visit online social networks every month (comScore, 2011). Not only has social media adoption increased multifold over the last couple of years, but the time spent on these websites has also increased by 82% from 2008 with users spending an average of 6 hours or more on social networking sites per month (Nielsen, 2010a). According to some estimates, social media account for 11–16% of all time spent online in the United States (comScore, 2011; SAS Institute, 2010). Therefore, it comes as no surprise that social media websites have become the most popular activity on the Web, surpassing pornography for the first time in the history of the Internet (Qualman, 2009).

Collectively called social media, websites such as Facebook, YouTube, Twitter, Four Square, MySpace, LinkedIn, Delicious, and Yelp are also referred to as social networking sites, user-generated content, Web 2.0 technologies, social computing, social web, citizen media, participatory media, and consumer-generated media. Several definitions for social media exist in the literature but the most commonly cited definition is by Andreas and Haenlein (2010). According to them, social media "is a group of Internet-based applications that build on the ideological and technological foundations of Web 2.0, and that allow the creation and exchange of User Generated Content" (p. 61). Social media can also be defined as

> web-based services that allow individuals to (a) construct a public or semi-public profile within a bounded system, (b) articulate a list of other users with

whom they share a connection, (c) view and traverse their list of connections and those made by others within the system and (d) create and share content.

(boyd & Ellison, 2007, p. 2)

Brian Solis in his new book *Engage* defines social media as "the democratization of information, transforming people from content readers into publishers. It is the shift from a broadcast mechanism, one-to-many, to a many-to-one model, rooted in conversations between authors, people, and peers" (Solis & Kutcher, 2010, p. 37).

From an historical perspective, the roots of social media can be traced to the early days of the Internet, which itself began as a giant Bulletin Board System that allowed individuals to exchange information; but the technological advancements over the last 20 years have created a more powerful and efficient means of sharing/exchanging information (Andreas & Haenlein, 2010) now commonly referred to as "social media." While there are literally thousands of websites that fit these definitions of social media, an element of commonality running through all of these websites and services is that most of the content on these sites is created by the users of the sites. Distinguishing features of social media include participation, openness, conversation, community, and connectedness (Mayfield, 2008). Social media websites use technologies and mechanisms that facilitate a high degree of participation from users whether through comments, "like" buttons, or feedback; they also encourage openness and conversation with relatively few barriers to accessing and/or creating content on these sites; and, finally, there is a high degree of connectedness and community building on social media websites that allows users to find and network with other users (Mayfield, 2008).

Other characteristics that distinguish social media from "traditional" media relate to barriers to entry, immediacy, and shelf life. To create content on traditional media such as television, radio, or print, one needs to be a professional and be skilled at or trained in "media," i.e., writing for television, creating radio ads, etc. Furthermore, content in traditional media must go through "gatekeepers" (editors, owners, and publishers) and must gain the financial support of private or governmental entities in terms of advertising or public funding. On the other hand, these barriers to entry are fewer and, in some cases, nonexistent on social media websites. Anyone with access to the Internet can create and distribute content. It also takes longer to create content in traditional media than social media. For instance, shooting, editing, and producing a television show might take months but an individual armed with a Flip camera or an iPhone can shoot, edit, and upload videos to social media websites within a matter of hours or minutes. Finally, content on social media has a longer shelf life than traditional media. People hold on to traditional newspapers for days, magazines for weeks, and DVDs for years but content on social media is relatively permanent in that it is indexed to be searchable, copied, revised, and shared with others and remains on the Internet virtually forever.

While there are many differences between traditional media and social media, the common aspects pertain to the revenue models. Thus far, both traditional and social media rely heavily on advertising for survival and existence. Advertising has supported traditional media for almost 100 years and many social media websites are hoping it would do the same for them. Social media can generate revenue either by subscriptions or by advertising. Under the subscription model, the user pays either a one-time fee or a recurring (monthly or yearly) fee to gain access to content but access to content is free under the advertising model. According to a recent Nielsen survey of 27,000 consumers across 52 countries, almost 85% of users prefer content to remain free on the Internet (Nielsen, 2010b). With such an overwhelming number of people preferring not to pay for content online, social media will inevitably have to rely on advertising for survival. Forrester predicts that ad spending on social media will reach $3.1 billion by 2014 (Ostrow, 2009a).

Given the proliferation of social media and increased ad spending on these sites, often at the expense of traditional media, it is imperative that we examine how social media can impact and change advertising theory. Using the framework for advertising theory (McGuire, 1969; Rodgers & Thorson, Chapter 1, this volume), the current chapter delineates how social media impact the key components of the model depicted in Figure 1.1 of Chapter 1—message sources, messages, channels, receivers, and effects. The goal is to better our understanding of how social media are transforming advertising theory by examining social media's effect on each of the components in the model on how advertising works in Chapter 1. In doing so, several areas of research for advertising scholars are expected to emerge that will shape and build the future of advertising theory.

Who says What on Social Media

For decades, advertising scholars have used Lasswell's (1948) "*Who* says *What* in *Which Channel* to *Whom* with *What Effects*" as a framework to develop theories of how advertising works. In traditional models of advertising or communication, the *Who* and *What* refer to "message sources" and "messages." With the advent of social media, our understanding of "who" in the traditional models of communication/advertising is evolving in that the "who" on social media is not necessarily a professional creator of advertising (like an ad agency or ad professional) but is oftentimes an everyday consumer. In a traditional advertising context, "message sources" pertain to whoever appears to be behind the advertising message—corporations, politicians, celebrities, and spokespersons (see Chapter 1). In a social media environment, most of the content is user generated so "message sources" now include individuals who are oftentimes operating independently. User-generated content is video, audio, or written content created by end users of a website that is largely publicly available for others to consume, comment on, or further modify. Messages on social media can originate partially or entirely from sources (individuals or users) that are not connected to the advertiser. For instance, any individual can create a profile or a fan page on Facebook or a blog for a brand, and generate content that is shared and transmitted throughout the network. Similarly, everyday consumers can tweet—saying positive and/or negative things—about a brand, product, or service. Many social media users have also created commercials in the traditional 30-second format and uploaded them to YouTube for easy consumption and distribution. In all these cases, it is the end user, or consumer, who creates and disseminates the advertising message and not the "advertiser," as represented by traditional models of advertising (see Figure 1.1). With recent technological advancements, the quality of user-generated messages is sometimes on par with professional ads that even consumers fail to differentiate between the two in some cases. Frequent discussions in the form of comments on YouTube debating whether a particular commercial is authentic or not (a spoof) are an indication of the evolving nature of *Who* in Lasswell's (1948) model. For example, during the 2008 democratic primaries, several ads appeared on YouTube supporting Barack Obama. The user comments on those ads indicated some confusion as to who was behind those ads. It was later established that most of those ads were user-generated ads from supporters who were not part of the official campaign team.

When consumers create and share content about brands on their own, there is a noticeable shift in power and control. What has traditionally been an advertiser-controlled message can now potentially turn into a consumer-driven one. Some advertisers have boldly embraced this phenomenon by inviting consumers to create commercials and ads for a client or a brand. For instance, consumers have produced ads for Doritos, CareerBuilder, and Heinz that were used extensively on dedicated websites and on TV during Super Bowl (Thomaselli, 2010). Sometimes the role of consumers in message creation and propagation is complex and not quite as evident. In the advertising model in Figure 1.1, the component "messages" refers to advertisements that vary by appeal, product, length, repetition, and by media content they are embedded in (see Chapter 1). In a social media context, "messages" can take on all of the traditional formats and, additionally, some new ones. For example, consumers on social media can post their shopping and consumption behaviors on their profiles, thereby "advertising" to everyone in their network on behalf of the brand. Recently, a newsfeed item on my Facebook indicated that 52 friends of mine were fans of a local Thai restaurant, which prompted me to visit the restaurant for lunch one afternoon. In other instances, advertisers can provide mechanisms (or space on websites or forums) by which consumers can comment, write reviews, and recommend brands. Such strategies designed to encourage peer-to-peer communication by leveraging the power of online social networks are often called viral marketing strategies (Eckler & Rodgers, 2010). Similar to viral marketing, user-generated content is easier to measure and quantify, and spreads at a much faster rate than traditional word of mouth. Marketers and advertisers can influence the propagation of user-generated content by targeting key individuals in a social network and providing them with a reason to create and/or disseminate information.

Another way for individuals to create and disseminate information on social media is through location-based services. Location-based services are defined as information or entertainment services that use the geographical position of a mobile device to inform other users of an individual's whereabouts. This is achieved by means of "checking-in" to various locations (bars, restaurants, and stores), brands, or even content. By letting others in their network know of their whereabouts and consumption habits, consumers engage in the creation of "messages" on behalf of advertisers and brands. For instance, services like Gowalla, Four Square, and Facebook enable users to check-in at various businesses physically and share that information online with either a select group of friends in their social network or everyone on the Internet if their profiles are public. Several advertisers like Starbucks, GAP, and the National Hockey League (NHL) are already taking advantage of this by providing incentives to users to check-in at their stores (brick-and-mortar) and venues (e.g., Madison Square Garden) (Bowman, 2010). Users check-in for a variety of reasons: as a means to define or brand oneself, for game dynamics such as earning a badge or button, as means to share and/or discover new things, and to maintain a personal history of where one has been (Giegerich, 2011). In addition to location-based sharing, two other types of sharing are becoming increasingly popular; brand-based sharing and content-based sharing. Consumers can now check-in to various brands, TV shows, books, and movies using apps such as GetGlue, Miso, Philo, Tunerfish, LooptStar, SCVNGR, and Shopkick and broadcast the same to everyone on the Internet. Furthermore, they earn rewards and points for doing so.

These location-based, content-based, and brand-based check-ins are changing the "what" of the traditional advertising model in Figure 1.1. As mentioned earlier, the "what" in the traditional model is a clearly demarcated advertisement bounded by time (e.g., 30-second spot) or space (e.g., full- or half-page ad) but in a social media context it becomes a complex ongoing message that illustrates the consumption behavior and habits of individuals who choose to share, and thereby, implicitly recommend the brands to everyone in their network or on the Internet if their profiles are public.

Message Propagation on Social Media

In this section, we examine how social media work as "channels" to facilitate the propagation of advertising messages. In Figure 1.1 of Chapter 1, "channels" refer to the media that bring advertising messages to the audience. Several communication theories exist that explain how channels operate and how information propagates in a traditional mass media context. For instance, the two-step flow of information suggests that information travels from mass media to individuals via an intermediary group of people called the opinion leaders (Katz & Lazarsfeld, 1955). Opinion leaders are individuals who act as key links between media sources and the public at large. Also, traditional mass media come with gatekeepers who control and, ultimately, determine what content sees the light of the day and what does not (McCombs & Shaw, 1972; Shaw, 1979). For social media, there are fewer or no gatekeepers and the barriers to entry are relatively low. This has led many researchers to claim that social media are revolutionizing the way information propagates among consumers, thereby forcing brands and organizations to become more open and transparent (Gillin, 2007; Mooney & Rollins, 2009). As technology makes it easier to create and share content with others on the Internet, there should be a shift in power and control from major corporations to everyday consumers. For example, GAP recently changed its decades-old logo, which prompted consumers to complain on social media and create a barrage of tweets and pages on Facebook protesting the change that GAP immediately abandoned the idea and returned to its original logo (Fredrix, 2010).

Researchers have just started to examine how information travels on social media. The author of *Socialnomics*, Erik Qualman (2009), suggests that individuals no longer search for information; rather information finds individuals on social media. This changes our understanding of "channels" as illustrated in Figure 1.1. First, users of social media have more control over the channel than audiences in traditional advertising. Second, the interconnectedness of social media users allows for information to travel and present itself (via newsfeeds, tweets, and updates) to individuals in ways that are more relevant than in traditional contexts.

Audience and Social Media

In traditional advertising, "audiences" are primarily the group of individuals that advertisers are interested in appealing or talking to and an audience can be grouped by demographics and other segmentation strategies (see Figure 1.1). Advertisers then proceed to carefully craft messages to target these specific groups of consumers. Social media is, however, about speaking "with" people and not "at" people (Solis, 2010). This idea of speaking with your consumers stems from the fact that consumers today are more connected with others than ever before. This shared connectedness and a sense of community among users is one of the distinguishing features of social media (Mayfield, 2008). The audience in a traditional environment can be connected as well via shared commonalities such as geographical proximity, brand loyalty and usage characteristics, demographics, politics, and religion. However, traditional and social media connections differ in that social media offer unique advantages by erasing the boundaries created by time and distance, thereby making it infinitely easier for individuals to form and maintain relationships online with others in and out of their networks (Shirky, 2010). This shared connection on social media facilitates increased flow of information between consumers who in a traditional media context are not as connected. Communication between audiences in traditional media is expected to be less frequent and more difficult given the time and distance constraints. For face-to-face conversations, an individual needs to be in physical proximity with others. The limitation for conversations by phone is that it has to happen in the same time continuum. On social media, however, conversations are not limited by either time or distance. An individual can watch a commercial or video on YouTube and leave a comment for others to respond to at a later time and from an entirely different geographic area.

The lack of time and space constraints on social media has numerous implications for advertising theory. First, the very nature by which "receivers" could be connected is evolving. Prior to social media, researchers estimated the total number of meaningful connections and/or relationships an individual could have to be around 150 based on the size of the neocortex, the part of the brain involved in higher functions such as perception, reasoning, thought, and language (Dunbar, 1993). This number, called the Dunbar number, is now estimated to be around 600 given the power of social media and the high degree of connectedness that social media yield (Tapscott, 2009). Furthermore, technologies such as Four Square and GetGlue now provide for additional and easier ways to connect with others around brands, events, books, television shows, and other media content. In fact, companies such as Hot Potato have created Apps for mobile phones that let users check-in to virtual spaces and even abstract concepts. For instance, on Hot Potato, I could check-in to "thinking and writing about social media" and broadcast that message to all the users of that App, thereby creating an opportunity for others to connect and share ideas on my topic.

Social Media and Advertising Effects

The next component in Figure 1.1 that social media change significantly is "advertising effects." All changes to our understanding of message sources, messages, channels, and audiences in social media should translate to some "effect" they ultimately produce. Meaning, for instance, if message sources now include individuals not related to the brand or not acting as paid spokespersons, that message should elicit a higher level of trust or credibility depending on how close and strong the tie strength is between the source and receiver. Seeing someone you trust and respect on Twitter tweet about how much they enjoy using a product or a service should produce a different reaction from when watching a commercial for that product or service. Similarly, knowing that a friend "likes" a particular brand on Facebook might persuade one differently from when exposed to a traditional banner ad of that brand.

The traditional measures of advertising effectiveness include attitude toward the ad, attitude toward the brand, memory, attention, involvement, purchase intentions, and actual purchase behavior (Chapter 1). These measures are typically considered good substitutes for measuring or gauging the actual return on investment (ROI). Counting eyeballs or measuring hits has thus far been the norm in measuring effectiveness of advertising, but social media introduces a new metric called "engagement" (Solis, 2010; SAS Institute, 2010). While it is difficult to define or measure engagement, it roughly translates to some evidence that the individual, i.e., audience member, an advertiser is trying to reach is responding in some way to the message, e.g., by clicking the "like" button or by commenting on the advertiser's wall on Facebook or by writing a review for a brand or product or by retweeting (RT) or downloading an App (SAS Institute, 2010). Engagement explains *who*, *how*, and *where* consumers are interacting with your brand (Solis, 2010). The challenge for advertising scholars would be to clearly define and devise ways in which social media engagement can be measured so we can better understand how it influences persuasion.

There are several ways in which engagement can be measured on social media. Solis (2010) suggests using conversations with brand representatives, time spent viewing or taking action, using the size and shape of the social network tied to the brand, as well as browsing and interacting with online content related to a brand. Additionally, some industry experts have called for a new pricing model based on engagement. For instance, David Berkowitz (2009) suggests using a cost per social action (CPSA) model wherein companies pay specifically for something social and relationship oriented. Several marketers are already testing the new engagement model. One of the world's largest advertisers, P&G, recently launched a results-based online ad model that rewards publishers for consumer engagement (Bearne, 2009). Industry researchers are also looking at creating an engagement index using both a brand's extent (breadth) of engagement across social media and the level of engagement (depth) (Solis, 2010). Using this index, ENGAGEMENTdb report lists Starbucks (127), Dell (123), eBay (115), Google (105), and Microsoft (103) as the top five engaging brands in 2009 along with the scores they received on this index (ENGAGEMENTdb report, 2009).

Another new metric that social media introduces is Razorfish's (2009) Social Influence Marketing Score (SIM score). Solis (2010) explains it as "the representation of online conversations related to a brand and then further categorized by brand and comparative industry sentiment. It is designed to capture the state of brand health" (p. 342). Industry leaders have also mentioned other metrics for measuring social media effects such as social media leads, bounce rates, activity ratios, conversions, virality, and brand interactions (Dash, 2010). Some of these metrics are similar to traditional metrics while others are only relevant to social media environment. For instance, virality relates to the degree to which something could be or might be shared on social media in a short amount of time. Virality leverages the power of existing social networks online and this is something not usually observed or used as a metric in a traditional context.

Research Agenda

The proliferation of social media presents numerous opportunities for research for advertising scholars. First, advertising scholars can begin by asking questions about the *Who* and *What* from Figure 1.1, and how the changing nature of these two components changes our understanding of advertising effects. For instance, Daugherty, Eastin, and Bright (2008) examined the motivations for user-generated content and Gangadharbatla (2008) investigated the factors that influence consumers' attitudes toward content on social media. Cheong and Morrison (2008) and Bae and Lee (2010) looked at consumers' perceptions and reliance on recommendations via user-generated content. However, an area that is somewhat lacking in research is an understanding of the outcomes or consequences of user-generated content creation and consumption. More precisely, what effect does user-generated content have on attitudes, intentions, and purchase behavior of consumers? Other related issues include investigating the impact of user-generated content on branding, the shift in power from advertisers to consumers, and the co-creation of brands with consumers and its impact on persuasion.

Second, communication researchers are yet to fully examine how information travels on social media. Several questions remain unanswered about the propagation of information on social media, all of which are ripe areas for research for advertising scholars. Do social media eliminate the barriers to entry and produce a truly democratic medium for individuals to create and share content? Do opinion leaders exist on social media? If so, how are they different or similar to opinion leaders in traditional media? How does information propagate on social media and what factors influence it? What role do users (or actors) play in determining the speed and nature of information propagation on social media? Finally, how does message propagation on social media influence persuasion (and processing of advertising messages)?

Third, the interconnectedness of "receivers" of social media presents numerous research opportunities for theory revision and construction in advertising. For instance, does increased connectivity translate to increased effectiveness of messages? The concept of user interconnectedness also has implications for advertising costs and effectiveness measures such as reach and cost per thousand (CPM), as the value of consumers in a connected environment should be a function of their networks. Not all consumers are created equal. In other words, the more individuals a single consumer is connected to (and can potentially influence), the greater should be the cost to reach him or her with advertising messages. This pilots the idea of a dynamic model for advertising costs based on an individual's rank, power, and influence within a network (similar to Razorfish's (2009) SIM score). Other areas for future research include an examination of its strengths and the influence on persuasion, attitudes, and affinity toward the group or community one belongs to and its effect on persuasion, and, finally, the consequences of increased connectivity of audiences on persuasion. As an example, consider the theory of reasoned action, which states that behavior is determined by beliefs about attributes, evaluation of those attributes, normative beliefs about others, and the motivations to comply with those beliefs (Fishbein & Ajzen, 1975). In a social media environment—with increased connectedness or a perception of increased connectedness—both normative beliefs and individuals' motivations to comply with those beliefs can be amplified. For instance, the pressure to contribute to a charity—a normative belief—may be amplified if you notice 90% of your friends on Facebook have already donated to the cause and will know that you have not. Either way, it should be interesting to examine the role of increased connectedness of "receivers" in the advertising model and its effect on persuasion.

And fourth, as social media become more prevalent, newer and more effective metrics for measuring the success of advertising on social media should emerge. Creating such new metrics, and then relating/comparing them to traditional measures of ad effectiveness, will be another ripe area for future research. The first step to measuring any "message effects" in social media should begin with "listening in." As denoted earlier in the chapter, social media users are creating and sharing incredible amounts of what is essentially "data" online. Most of this data is publicly available for advertisers to aggregate and mine to effectively target their consumers with relevant brand messages. The astronomical amount of data consumers generate on social media is the distinguishing feature of advertising on social media compared to traditional media. The quality, richness, and quantity of this data—in terms of millions of Facebook and MySpace profiles, billions of tweets, thousands of blogs, opinions, and reviews, and millions of check-ins—have the capacity to fundamentally change how advertising effects are measured in future. Companies now have the technological capabilities to conduct "buzz monitoring" and trend watching on social media and anticipate and respond to problems even before they occur. Buzz monitoring and trend watching relate to keeping track of consumer responses to products and services online.

Social media metrics is a ripe area of research for advertising scholars. Particularly, a network analysis approach to understanding social media and effectiveness of advertising on social media will be one of the hottest areas of research for advertising scholars. Network analysis and data mining will identify key influencers or opinion leaders on social media, links between various actors, shared connections, or commonalities among these actors. This is a necessary step to understanding how advertising on social media works.

Conclusion

Social media are being increasingly used in advertising and marketing. According to eMarketer, 80% of companies with 100 or more employees plan to use social media in their marketing campaigns next year (Williamson, 2010). Many brands are already on social media and have been experiencing varying levels of success. For instance, Dell computers used Twitter to generate $6.5 million in direct sales last year (Ostrow, 2009b), Ford generated awareness for its 2011 Ford Explorer using social media and now has over half a million followers across Twitter and Facebook, and JetBlue has over 1.6 million followers on Twitter, which it uses extensively as a two-way communication/conversation tool (Elliott, 2010). Therefore, it is important that advertising scholars devote more attention to understanding how this medium works. The current chapter enumerated some ways in which social media can and are impacting advertising theory.

No other recent phenomenon perhaps impacts advertising theory as much as the advent of social media. First, social media empower consumers to create and share content more easily than traditional media leading to the addition of a new set of individuals to the types of sources that could be classified as "message sources." Second, the notion of "messages" is itself evolving to include both implicit and explicit notifications in the form of recommendations, check-ins, and purchase behavior to everyone on social media. Third, information propagation on social media appears to be different from that of traditional media leading to a re-evaluation of the role of "channels" in social media. Fourth, "receivers" of messages on social media appear to be different from traditional receivers in that they are more interconnected in ways that are not limited by time and space. And, finally, social media present numerous opportunities for redefining advertising effects to include new measures like engagement and SIM score.

Social media, as a whole, are moving the field of advertising toward the direction of "connected experiences." Connected experiences is a manifestation of a broader symptom of technological changes on the Internet that are commonly referred to as Web 2.0 technologies. Social networking sites, social shopping, and social gaming are a direct result of Web 2.0 way of life on the Internet. There is an increasing tendency to involve others in every aspect of our daily lives be it work, shopping, leisure, and entertainment, or information consumption. More and more individuals are sharing their work, shopping, and purchase behaviors, media consumption habits, and even their personal lives on social media.

This phenomenon has led to the creation of numerous technology start-ups such as Groupon that address the idea of "connected experiences." Groupon is a community-based local deal-of-the-day search website that allows consumers to sign up for various offers and if a certain number of consumers sign up for it, then the deal is made available to everyone. Other indicators of the rise of a "connected experiences" movement on the Internet include the proliferation of services, websites, and apps that stress a community-based approach to (a) shopping (Grooster, SocialShopper, LivingSocial, BuyWithMe, Kaboodle, Yelp, ShopSocially, Blippy, Swipely, LooptStar, SCVNGR, and Shopkick), (b) gaming (Farmville, Fishville, Mafiawars, Cityville, and MMORPG games like SecondLife and World of Warcraft), and (c) entertainment including music, TV shows, movies, and print media (GetGlue, Philo, Tunerfish, and Miso).

Ultimately, it appears that the future of advertising theory when it comes to social media lies in this idea of connected experiences. While social media impact individual components of the advertising framework, as detailed in this chapter, the overarching influence of social media on the field of advertising would be to connect all the components of advertising theory in a more robust way that is a reflection of the "connected experiences" that the Web as a whole is moving toward.

References

Andreas, K., & Haenlein, M. (2010). Users of the world, unite! The challenges and opportunities of social media. *Business Horizons, 53* (1), 59–68.

Bae, S., & Lee, T. (2010). Gender differences in consumers' perception of online consumer reviews. *Electronic Commerce Research, 11* (2), 201–214.

Bearne, S. (2009, September 16). P&G to pay publishers based on online engagement. *MarketingWeek*. Retrieved December 15, 2010, from www.marketingweek.co.uk/news/pg-to-pay-publishers-based-on-online-engagement/3004476.article.

Berkowitz, D. (2009, August 4). CPSA: The new pricing model for social media? *Social Media Insider*. Retrieved December 15, 2010, from www.mediapost.com/publications/?fa=Articles.showArticle&art_aid=111081.

Bowman, J. (2010). Location-aware services: Are they worth the effort? *CBC News*. Retrieved December 10, 2010, from www.cbc.ca/technology/story/2010/11/08/f-smallbiz-foursquare-small-business-facebook-places.html.

boyd, d. m., & Ellison, N. B. (2007). Social network sites: Definition, history, and scholarship. *Journal of Computer-Mediated Communication, 13* (1), 210–230.

Cheong, H. J., & Morrison, M. A. (2008). Consumers' reliance on product information and recommendations found in UGC. *Journal of Interactive Advertising, 8* (2), 1–29.

comScore. (2011). The comScore 2010 U.S. digital year in review. Retrieved February 9, 2011, from www.comscore.com/Press_Events/Presentations_Whitepapers/2011/2010_US_Digital_Year_in_Review.

Dash, A. (2010, February 24). The 10 social media metrics your company should monitor. *Social Times*. Retrieved December 15, 2010, from www.socialtimes.com/2010/02/social-media-metrics/.

Daugherty, T., Eastin, M. S., & Bright, L. (2008). Exploring consumer motivations for creating user-generated content. *Journal of Interactive Advertising, 8* (2), 1–24.

Dunbar, R. I. (1993). Co-evolution of neocortex size, group size and language in humans. *Behavioral and Brain Sciences, 16* (4), 681–735.

Eckler, P., & Rodgers, S. (2010). *Viral marketing on the internet*. Wiley International Encyclopedia of Marketing. Retrieved February 7, 2011, from http://onlinelibrary.wiley.com/doi/10.1002/9781444316568.wiem04009/full.

Elliott, A. (2010). Social media success: 5 lessons from in-house corporate teams. *Mashable*. Retrieved December 12, 2010, from http://mashable.com/2010/12/07/social-media-business-success/.

ENGAGEMENTdb Report. (2009). Social media brand engagement report. Retrieved December 15, 2010, from www.engagementdb.com/Report.

Facebook (2010). Facebook statistics. Retrieved December 10, 2010, from www.facebook.com/press/info.php?statistics.

Fishbein, M., & Ajzen, I. (1975). *Belief, attitude, intention, and behavior: An introduction to theory and research*. Reading, MA: Addison-Wesley.

Fredrix, E. (2010, December 10). Gap gets rid of new logo. *Huffington Post*. Retrieved February 8, 2011, from www.huffingtonpost.com/2010/10/12/gap-gets-rid-of-new-logo_n_759131.html.

Gangadharbatla, H. (2008). Facebook me: Collective self-esteem, need to belong, and Internet self-efficacy as predictors of the iGeneration's attitudes toward social networking sites. *Journal of Interactive Advertising, 8* (2), 1–28.

Gaudin, S. (2010, December 9). Study: 8 percent of Americans use Twitter. *PC World*. Retrieved December 10, 2010, from www.pcworld.com/article/213135/study_8_percent_of_americans_use_twitter.html.

Giegerich, C. (2011, January 3). The art of the checkin: From location to content to brand. *Mashable*. Retrieved February 7, 2011, from http://mashable.com/2011/01/03/art-of-checkin/.

Gillin, P. (2007). *The new influencers: A marketer's guide to the new social media*. Sanger, CA: Quill Driver Books.

Katz, E., & Lazarsfeld, P. (1955). *Personal influence*. New York: The Free Press.

Lasswell, H. (1948). The structure and function of communication in society. In L. Bryson (Ed.), *The communication of ideas* (pp. 37–51). New York: Harper and Brothers.

Mayfield, A. (2008). What is social media. *Networks, V1.4 UPDAT*, 36. iCrossing. Retrieved December 15, 2010, from www.icrossing.co.uk/fileadmin/uploads/eBooks/What_is_Social_Media_iCrossing_ebook.pdf.

McCombs, M. E., & Shaw, D. L. (1972). The agenda-setting function of mass media. *Public Opinion Quarterly, 36* (2), 176.

McGuire, W. J. (1969). An information-processing model of advertising effectiveness. In H. L. Davis & A. J. Silk (Eds.), *Behavioral and management science in marketing*. New York: Ronald Press, 156–180.

Mooney, K., & Rollins, N. (2009). *The open brand: When push comes to pull in a web-made world*. Berkeley, CA: New Riders.

Neilsen (2010a, August 2). What Americans do online: Social media and games dominate activity. Retrieved August 4, 2010, from http://blog.nielsen.com/nielsenwire/online_mobile/what-americans-do-online-social-media-and-games-dominate-activity/on.

Nielsen (2010b). Changing models: A global perspective on paying for content online. Retrieved December 10, 2010, from http://blog.nielsen.com/nielsenwire/reports/paid-online-content.pdf.

Ostrow, A. (2009a). Social media marketing spend to hit $3.1 billion by 2014. *Mashable*. Retrieved December 10, 2010, from http://mashable.com/2009/07/08/social-media-marketing-growth/.

Ostrow, A. (2009b). Dell rides Twitter to $6.5 million in sales. *Mashable*. Retrieved December 12, 2010, from http://mashable.com/2009/12/08/dell-twitter-sales/.

Qualman, E. (2009). *Socialnomics: How social media transforms the way we live and do business*. Hoboken, NJ: John Wiley & Sons.

Razorfish (2009). Fluent: The Razorfish social influence marketing report. Retrieved December 15, 2010, from http://fluent.razorfish.com/publication/?m=6540&l=1.

SAS Institute (2010). Social media metrics: Listening, understanding and predicting the impacts of social media on your business. Retrieved December 12, 2010, from www.sas.com/resources/whitepaper/wp_19861.pdf.

Shaw, E. F. (1979). Agenda setting and mass communication theory. *Gazette, 25* (2), 101.

Shirky, C. (2008). *Here comes everybody: The power of organizing without organizations*. New York: Penguin.

Shirky, C. (2010) *Cognitive surplus: Creativity and generosity in a connected age*. New York: Penguin Press.

Solis, B. (2010). *Engage! The complete guide for brands and businesses to build, cultivate, and measure in the new web*. Hoboken, NJ: John Wiley & Sons.

Tapscott, D. (2009). *Grown up digital: How the net generation is changing your world*. New York: McGraw-Hill.

Thomaselli, R. (2010, May 17). If consumer is your agency, it's time for a review. *Advertising Age*. Retrieved December 12, 2010, from http://adage.com/article?article_id=143896.

Williamson, D. A. (2010, December 8). How much money will you spend on social-media marketing next year? *Advertising Age*. Retrieved December 12, 2010, from http://adage.com/digitalnext/post?article_id=147544.

YouTube (2010). YouTube fact sheet. Retrieved December 10, 2010, from www.youtube.com/t/fact_sheet.

Additional Readings

Gillin, P. (2007). *The new influencers: A marketer's guide to the new social media*. Sanger, CA: Quill Driver Books.

Li, C., & Bernoff, J. (2008). *Groundswell: Winning in a world transformed by social technologies*. Boston, MA: Harvard Business Press.

Qualman, E. (2011). *Socialnomics: How social media transforms the way we live and do business* (Rev. ed.). Hoboken, NJ: John Wiley & Sons.

Shirky, C. (2008). *Here comes everybody: The power of organizing without organizations*. New York: Penguin.

Solis, B., & Kutcher, A. (2010). *Engage! The complete guide for brands and businesses to build, cultivate, and measure success in the new web*. Hoboken, NJ: John Wiley & Sons.

Tapscott, D., & Williams, A. D. (2008). *Wikinomics: How mass collaboration changes everything*. New York: Portfolio Trade.

Part VI

Organizations

Chapter 27

Toward a Social Ecology of Advertising

Christine Wright-Isak

An Institution and a Profession?

When we consider theories of advertising we tend to think first about explaining how ads work. In contrast, this chapter views advertising as a human enterprise centered on a particular field of work. In order to consider advertising in this holistic way we need a different kind of theoretical framework. I begin by calling advertising a profession—but only as a hypothesis with which to step outside the field and view it as a whole.

This approach allows us to take a sociological view of advertising as an institution along three dimensions: knowledge, organizations, and individuals. In any profession there is a *body of scientific knowledge* that is its differentiating characteristic, *organizations* in which *individuals* (scholars) add to that body of knowledge via scientific research, and other *organizations* in which *individuals* (practitioners) apply the special knowledge to specific problems. Unifying them into a single profession that can defend its work processes, enhance the perceived value of what its professionals do, or appreciate the positive solutions it may offer to solve important problems of society is a challenge that calls for a sociological perspective.

In the case of advertising, the solutions to these problems can directly foster social good and enhance the commercial realm of society; both are important to the national culture. Thinking about advertising as a societal institution fills the gap between understanding what the boundaries of our scientific knowledge are, and what the central issues of our academic research are on one hand, and the experiences of practitioners as they apply that knowledge on the other.

Thinking of advertising as a societal institution also encourages us to think about ourselves as a community united by a work specialty and to focus on how non-advertisers influence the sources and valuation of our work. This may lead us to think differently about why practitioners and scholars have so few regular interactions, why practitioners do not read academic journals, and how to create richer connections than just trying to place students in ad agencies after they graduate.

Clarifying what the institution of advertising consists of, drawing sharper boundaries around its unique area of knowledge, and developing confidence in the importance of its work are all topics that have been discussed throughout the field, especially recently. All three are also central to problems of any profession. For the most part, theory in advertising focuses on making proper additions to our collective body of knowledge. However, in this chapter we step back and view advertising from a society-wide perspective, delving inside it only to better understand how the entire enterprise functions in its cultural environment.

Figure 27.1 represents advertising as a profession. The entities included are not comprehensive; they are intended to be pertinent examples of what comprises the knowledge, organization, and individual levels of the social system referred to throughout the chapter.

In searching for a definition of advertising itself Jef Richards and Catharine Curran (2002) recognize the importance of the social system context in which the research and applied work of advertising is conducted, i.e., the definition we use also has practical implications. It can determine what is taught in advertising courses, what is covered in advertising trade publications, and the domain

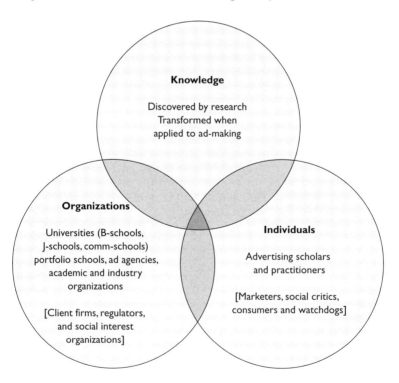

Figure 27.1 Analytical Levels for Studying Advertising as an Institution.

of the field's professional organizations (Richards & Curran, 2002). When a court or a regulator assesses whether an activity is "advertising," the definition applied can have far-reaching impact (p. 64).

In their investigation, Richards and Curran canvassed multiple sources in both the academic and practitioner sectors of advertising and were unable to come up with a single definition. That is an important finding itself for an understanding of advertising as a field (see related discussion in Chapter 1 of this text). Their purpose was to open a discussion on what is a complex issue. This chapter builds on that discussion, attempting to provide a theoretical framework for explaining the complexity with examining a social ecology of advertising. We begin with a discussion of advertising as a profession.

Examining Advertising as a Profession

Scholars already investigate questions involving all three institutional levels of advertising, but placing their findings into a broader theoretical perspective has not yet been accomplished. Much of advertising research today is rooted in psychology and involves the ways consumers comprehend and process communications. These variables and theories tend to focus on advertising in terms of individuals and ads, not on an institutional level of analysis.

Work on creativity and ad making has recently suggested that a useful way to understand previous work and carry theory forward is to focus on persons, places, and the actual processes involved in ad-making, thus investigating both individual and organizational levels of the field. A useful summary of this area is the lead article in the *Journal of Advertising* special issue on creativity. In it Sasser and Koslow (2008) open a lens beyond the individual level of analysis to examine work processes and work settings, drawing together the work of Kover, Goldberg, and James (1995), Johar, Holbrook, and Stern (2001) among others. However, they are necessarily focused on the practitioner portion of the field, not the field as a whole.

Numerous researchers have investigated aspects of client–agency relations, thus covering much of the organizational level of analysis from the practitioner side. Polonsky and Michael (2007), editing a special issue of the *Journal of Advertising* on responsibility, take a stakeholder approach to the organizational level of analysis, even drawing attention to the interactions of organizations that bridge the world of advertising and the larger societal environment. On the academic side, Ross and Richards (2008) provide a firm foundation for investigating organizational-level analysis in their 100-year history of education in this field. The challenge now is to provide an overarching framework that takes all these theories and research studies into account in a way that helps us talk about the field as a whole.

This chapter proposes that a social system framework will foster integration of findings from studies both of academic and of practitioner sectors so that their collective significance for understanding advertising as an institution is more evident. Using this approach, I combine the idea of construing our field as a profession with a dynamic human systems ecology dimension in order to explain how it interacts with other institutions and organizations in its cultural environment.

Formal Characteristics of Professions

Working from the perspective of the medical profession, Eliot Freidson (1988) offers this definition of "profession":

> In the most elementary sense, the profession is a group of people who perform a set of activities which provide them with the major source of their subsistence—activities which are called "work" rather than "leisure" and "vocation" rather than "avocation."

(p. 71)

The sociologist William Goode (1977) defined professions even more parsimoniously as having two fundamental attributes from which all others can be derived—specialized training in a body of abstract knowledge, and a collectivity

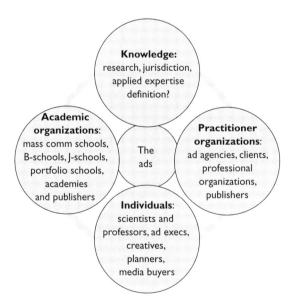

Figure 27.2 Characteristics of Advertising as a Profession.

or service orientation to their work. Drawing from Goode (1977), Freidson (1988) and other work (Merton, 1968; Ben-David, 1984; Abbott, 1988; Damon, Colby, Bronk, & Ehrlich, 2005; Gardner & Shulman, 2005), I suggest a set of characteristics of professions that can be used to examine the advertising profession.

A profession comprises:

- *A specialized body of knowledge* (jurisdiction) as its core differentiating element (Ben-David, 1984; Gardner & Shulman, 2005).
- *Academic organizations* that add to the body of professional knowledge:
  - *Schools of Mass Communication*, *Journalism Schools*, *Business Schools* that advance knowledge through scientific research and educating future practitioners (Abbott, 1988; Freidson, 1988);
  - *Portfolio schools* train practitioners in visual, aural, and technical skills (O'Guinn, Allen, & Semenik, 2008; Wells, Moriarty, & Burnett, 2006);
  - *publishers of scientific journals* (e.g., *Journal of Advertising*, *Journal of Advertising Research*) review and share additions to the scientific base of professional knowledge.

- Practitioner Organizations:
  - *ad agencies* employ those trained to create the ads, manage the creative and message delivery processes, or conduct research;
  - external to the profession, *clients—commercial firms or others—*value and pay for the work;
  - *professional organizations* promote work standards, encourage ethical behavior, and maintain a community of fellow professionals (e.g., Advertising Research Foundation, American Association of Advertising Agencies) (Wright-Isak & Faber, 1996).

- *People* train in the work of the profession, become members, and educate future professionals. They:
  - master and add to the body of knowledge/domain of practice (Gardner & Shulman, 2005);
  - perform work not able to be done without specific education and training (Ben-David, 1984; Gardner & Shulman, 2005);
  - are committed to serving clients but also society (Ben-David, 1984; Gardner & Shulman, 2005);
  - are guided by the ideals, responsibilities, and ethics of the profession (Ben-David, 1984; Gardner & Shulman, 2005).

A Human Ecology of Professions

Abbott (1988) offers a systems level framework with which to examine advertising. He describes this system not in terms of whether a given field is a profession or not, but *to what degree* a given field has the characteristics of a profession. In doing so he shifts the examination from taxonomic categorizations of work types—professional or not—to diagnostic examinations of any type of work in terms of how many characteristics of a profession each has, and what adaptive advantages the strength or weakness of its professionalization offers for its continuation.

Even more usefully, Abbott (1988) offers us a theoretical approach with which to understand the metabolism within a given field, asserting that:

> Each profession is bound to a set of tasks by ties of jurisdiction, the strengths and weaknesses of these ties being established in the processes of actual professional work. Since none of these links is absolute or permanent, the professions make up an interacting system, an ecology.
>
> (p. 33)

He points out that professions compete in a larger national culture for authority over specific types of problems and claim jurisdiction over the knowledge that is the basis for their solutions.

In examining *the degree to which* advertising is a profession we can analyze and diagnose (and perhaps devise solutions for) many of advertising's problems as a field. We can think about what aspects of advertising's structure and social function enhance or undermine its perceived value to the larger society. We can develop institutional explanations for why there is a divide between academic research and practitioner application of their knowledge. We can take new approaches to problems that arise when the field is judged unfairly or falls victim to inaccurate myths about its work. All of these are issues that frequently have been the topic of discussion among scholars and practitioners.

Assessing Advertising as a Professional Institution

Advertising in America today is comparable to that of the six blind men trying to understand the elephant, where the one standing by its tail thinks the animal is "like a rope" or the one standing by a leg thinks it is "like a tree." Each accurately identifies one or another characteristic but neither understands the size, daily behaviors, or vulnerability of the entire creature in its habitat. Within this book alone we see how different vantage points could lead to different characterizations of the field. Moreover, each species also thrives or fails in a larger environment of others competing for resources and survival. Advertising is such a creature and its "habitat" is the national system of social structures, cultural processes, and other professions that compete with advertising.

This characterization also encourages us to think about how the field as a whole must function in order to thrive. Abbott (1988) notes that: "From time to time, tasks are created, abolished or reshaped by external forces, with consequent jostling and readjustment within the system of professions" (p. 33). If each profession is constantly challenged by its societal environment then each must (1) grow in size and stature, (2) reproduce itself, and (3) establish its unique contributions to society, if it is to remain viable over the long run.

Fragmentation: The Main Problem of this Profession

Prompted by this human ecology approach, I suggest that the main problem facing the advertising field today is fragmentation at every level of institutional analysis. Advertising's knowledge jurisdiction has exceptionally permeable boundaries vulnerable to encroachment by numerous other fields. The problem of knowledge fragmentation is aggravated in the university by fragmentation at the organizational level, exemplified by the fact that advertising is taught and degrees are offered in three very different areas of the university: communication schools, journalism schools, and business schools. In each setting, the knowledge advertising research accumulates is more often tolerated than appreciated. One result for the field is that in the academy cutbacks cause departments of advertising to lose resources sooner than others and professors to lose positions to those who study or work in more "essential" fields. Portfolio schools provide yet another way in which the study of advertising is housed.

Within any advertising agency individuals have distinct and sometimes clashing types of expertise in management, creation of ads, consumer research, or media planning. In addition to ad agencies there are many other organizations (e.g., client firms, marketing, or branding firms) in which practitioners conduct their work.

Further fragmentation arises from the fact that in practitioner arenas, advertising knowledge and its professional application is judged from different points of view, often by contradictory criteria driven by diverse interests of the organizations in which advertising is a function. Critics insist advertising's influence on consumers is powerful and pernicious. Businesses complain it is not nearly effective enough in persuading people to consume. Organizations that use advertising to promote social good, trust it will persuade people to admirable attitudes and behaviors. The cumulative effect on the profession is that of being "nibbled to death by ducks." The fact that in some situations exceptional individuals have personally overcome negative perceptions on behalf of our field is not reassuring. Any field whose stature rests on the reputations of particular individuals is institutionally endangered.

In looking through the social system lens, we can ask whether we have been attempting to investigate or even solve the institutional problems of negative perception from the wrong direction—by focusing on individuals who are committed to the profession acting singly or in small groups. In bridge situations, such as when practitioners are invited to address scholarly groups, the two sides often find their interests seem unrelated or appreciation results that barely lasts the duration of the encounter. If such moments cannot be institutionalized, the effort to foster respect has to be repeated over and over. Respected advertising professionals in agencies take client goodwill toward advertising with them from one agency to another—and it disappears when either the client or the advertising professional retires from the field.

Some industry organizations have been explicitly formed to enhance the reputation of advertising. To the degree that their focus is on making ads to promote the value of making ads—an agenda that lacks credibility with the very audiences they wish to persuade—they may do more harm than good by reifying current perceptions of the field as superficial.

Future research is needed to understand each of these situations. The place to begin is by defining what the "special knowledge and expertise" of our field is, for without it, the fragmentation problem among organizations and individuals will persist despite our best efforts. From there we can proceed to understanding its relevant value to problem solving in the larger society and that can provide the basis for increased professional authority, respect, and jurisdiction over the knowledge of the profession and its application.

Studying Institutions Requires Unique Research Designs

Institutions are not phenomena that lend themselves to the experimental research tradition (Abbott, 2004). Rather, they require multiple investigations that triangulate various sources of data—investigations that extend beyond individuals as the case unit of analysis to organizations and institutions. This chapter has proposed a theoretical framework which can be used to accomplish this, a framework with scholarly as well as real world relevance. From this theoretical vantage point I suggest several areas of specific future research that foster direct study of advertising as an institution.

The Knowledge Level of Institutional Analysis

How do we investigate the question "What is the core knowledge of the profession of advertising?" Identifying what its legitimate jurisdictional boundaries are would help clarify its differentiated importance to the rest of society. The expert knowledge and jurisdiction of advertising is very difficult to describe because of the history of how it began and has evolved. Accompanying very diverse phenomena included in the work of advertising are very diverse work processes involved in applying advertising knowledge outside academia. Understanding this as the challenge may help clarify the field's proper domain by demonstrating why many scholars and practitioners are unable to articulate a single description of it.

Histories tell us advertising began as a business of brokering media opportunities to message senders in the middle of the nineteenth century (Fox, 1997; Marchand, 1985) and then early in the twentieth century added to its responsibilities the work of the creation of the art that conveys sponsors' messages and dramatizes their brands. Since that time, advertising as a field swings back and forth between declaring itself to be an industry or an art (Bogart, 1995; Fox, 1997; Lears, 1994). The problems it solves tend to be characterized as the need for mass messages designed to persuade specific audiences and delivered by mass media (O'Guinn et al., 2008; Wells et al., 2006).

The creation of art and the conduct of business have very different work processes and very different criteria for judging value of work outcomes (Becker, 1982). Management aims at achieving efficiency through routinization reassured by quantifiable metrics—typical of the media brokerage aspect of advertising work. The creative work of making the ads themselves requires nonlinear and intuitive work processes that are the antithesis of the rational calculative thinking habits that managers have been trained to use in making and justifying their decisions (O'Guinn et al., 2008).

Exacerbating the difference between the mind sets of rational-calculative managers and inspired spontaneous creative directors may be agency rhetoric itself and the clash of syntax between the two. In their efforts to legitimize the value of the work they do, agencies have claimed to offer "the big idea" or they call their strategic processes names like "the whole egg." These rhetorical images often strike client managers as being "light weight" when compared to their own calculative rhetoric. Yet, creative directors correctly assert that routine and predictability kill the very creativity needed to come up with these next "big ideas," many of which *do* prove to be effective in achieving the client's communications goals. The complexity of research language within academia and its journals is another area where language itself divides rather than unites the field. These situations make the work and the jurisdiction of the field very difficult to articulate.

However, there are possibilities for defining advertising's professional boundaries and research into the knowledge issues described above might illuminate them. For example, advertising academic and practitioner organizations might develop a definition of the "professional territory" of the field by legitimizing the *combination* of the business and art elements of how its work must be done and how it should be evaluated. Raising the level of discourse to this conceptual level might lead to identifying the profession as a bridge area of expertise that makes it *central* to bringing business and social messages to new generations of consumers who are more visually than verbally oriented in comparison to earlier generations.

Or advertising as a profession might incorporate its widely acknowledged expertise in "dramatizing brand meanings" into its definition by pointing out its capacity for creating new cultural symbols. Thus, looking outward from within the profession, research is needed about how perceptions of the institution of advertising both positive and negative arise and are perpetuated. Identifying what drives specific misconceptions may indicate how and when the larger society is likely to appreciate its work or attempt to restrict its function.

The Organizational Level of Institutional Analysis

Fragmentation of professional knowledge is amplified by fragmentation in the organization of the field in university and ad agency organizations. Within the academy, continuing research on curriculum history and the location of the field in different university structures is needed to understand the issues in this area. The work of Ross, Osborne, and Richards (2006) provides a critical beginning extended and amplified by Ross and Richards (2008) into the history of advertising in the academy. Their work immediately reveals the long history of organizational fragmentation of the field itself into its different academic locations, Schools of Communication, Journalism Schools, and Business Schools—and most recently Portfolio Schools. Future research must identify the conditions under which departments and schools of advertising lose autonomy to other disciplines within the university and the impact this has on professionalism within the field.

Histories of advertising have so far typically under-represented the development of advertising as an academic field in their narratives and have largely ignored the relationships between the two areas of the field over the past 100 years. Important organizational questions to investigate include how the academy can best accomplish the requirements of any profession: educating new members, transforming special knowledge into practice behaviors, and certifying or otherwise qualifying members.

While these artifacts of history may not be easily changed, and we may determine that unification of academic location may not be advantageous to the field in the long run, it is important to recognize now that the problems of strengthening the solidarity of members of the profession is more acute and more urgently in need of resolve as a result. Understanding the challenges or opportunities offered by diverse locations in the academy structure is critical to posing solutions.

Outside the academy, advertising work is no longer performed entirely within organizations labeled "ad agencies." Media buying and strategy companies that split off from parent agencies in the 1990s now pose threats to the creative function as new social media are perceived to "be the message." Media conglomerates who do the work of message delivery now pose threats to agency autonomy and perceived value as they innovate on program content that is increasingly "advertainment" (O'Guinn et al., 2008; Wells et al., 2006).

Research should extend current research on the creative process of ad making and processes of agency–client relations, building on the work of Henke (1995), Mitchell, Catequet and Hague (1992) or Mitchell and Saunders (1995) to examining the changing nature of the organizations that house creative processes. Whether "it is still advertising" to create advertainment messages for example is a question that affects how we define the boundaries of the field and the nature of professional knowledge within it.

The Individual Level of Institutional Analysis

When the knowledge and organizational fragmentation situations are reframed in this ecological perspective, the third problem, fragmentation of individuals' membership in the profession becomes more visible. Professions typically produce new generations of members not only by educating and training new scholars but also by socializing them into their identities as professionals and nurturing their continuing affiliation with their professional community. Beginning with the fragmentation of where new professionals are educated, these tasks are accomplished today through a patchwork quilt of organizations: universities, ad agencies, and professional consortiums like the American Advertising Federation (AAF) or the American Association of Advertising Agencies (4As). New research specifically regarding socialization of individuals into their professional identities and comparing advertising to other professions could help address the weak sense of membership and professional confidence that is the case today.

Once advertising majors leave the university, inadequate coordination of the many advertising organizations' efforts to nurture members and foster commitment to their professional community render the institution itself vulnerable to disregard. Losing touch with one's professional knowledge source in a situation of organizational fragmentation diminishes the confidence of individuals about their own work, and undermines their ability to command respect for that work. This may be the phenomenon underlying Schudson's 1984 observations about the uncertainties of individual practitioners regarding their work. It may also underlie more recent observations of continual pressure on agency individuals to reassert the value of the work to clients observed by numerous scholars of client–agency relations (Henke, 1995; Mitchell et al., 1992; Mitchell & Saunders, 1995).

Research on the practitioner sector of advertising demonstrates the vulnerability of professional autonomy in the absence of a professional consensus on the value of the work (Cook & Kover, 1997). This consensus is needed for credibility in educating the rest of society regarding the complexity of how advertising works in order to require greater accuracy from those who would credit its contributions or scapegoat it for society's problems, but such an effort is a strategic and long-term endeavor that few individuals can accomplish on their own. This underscores the importance of continuing research regarding how the actual work of making ads and managing production and media processes to enhance creative effectiveness gets done, building on existing research on copywriters' work process (Kover, 1995), creativity vs. effectiveness (Kover et al., 1995), and advertising design (Johar et al., 2001).

The conditions that foster the creativity of ad making need to be investigated in the future with the institutionally weak professional situation of advertising as its context. Key questions include how the work of ad making legitimately and usefully differs from the work of business management, how the performance of creative work should be properly assessed by academicians and practitioners, and under what management conditions the spontaneity of the process of message creation cannot only be respected but nurtured.

Accompanying this research direction is another very important area to investigate, i.e., the impact of different professional rhetorical styles and vocabularies on respect for professional boundaries. Talking about creative work in a rational calculative vocabulary may reassure clients but will operate at cross-purposes with those who create nonlinear and nonverbal message content. Such a capitulation to client language may open the door to clients suggesting specifics of how the creatives should do their work. Finally, we need to delineate social processes by which ads become cultural symbols, the circumstances under which they evolve, and why the larger culture overlooks the contribution of advertising to the lexicon of meanings in our national culture.

A Concluding Comment

In this chapter I have attempted to provide a picture of the social organization of advertising as an institution functioning in an environment of societal structures, processes, and cultural symbol systems. Using concepts common to sociological inquiry into institutions I hope to legitimize advertising research that examines the science of knowledge building and application of professional knowledge as it is carried out by advertising professionals, the interactions among organizations and individuals, and research into how external institutions affect the future operation of our field. This chapter has provided a theoretical basis for conducting this research as well as integrating some disparate bodies of existing research. If I have been persuasive, future investigators will find the human ecology approach to understanding professions valuable for posing questions and formulating and testing hypotheses in the future.

I hope that the theoretical perspective described in this chapter will support the other work in this book in provoking renewed interest in establishing an integrated, research-based understanding of advertising as an institution on all levels of social organization. The societal paradox of those who condemn advertising as damaging to society in contrast to others who doubt its effectiveness in influencing consumers begs for more complete clarification of what advertising can and cannot do before declarations are made about what it should or should not do.

This paradox underscores the importance of recognizing that advertising is not some foreign body in society, exerting benign or malignant influence on social processes. Instead it is made up of people and organizations that are *of the culture* and affected *by the culture*. The least obvious but most important implication of this insight is that any "cures" for such misunderstandings will necessarily be institution-wide rather than piecemeal if they are to have lasting success.

References

Abbott, A. (1988). *The system of professions.* Chicago: University of Chicago Press.

Abbott, A. (2004). *Methods of discovery, heuristics for the social sciences.* New York: W.W. Norton & Company.

Becker, H. (1982). *Art worlds.* Berkeley: University of California Press.

Ben-David, J. (1984). *The scientist's role in society.* Chicago: University of Chicago Press.

Bogart, M. H. (1995). *Artists, advertising, and the borders of art.* Chicago: University of Chicago Press.

Cook, W., & Kover, A. (1997). Research and the meaning of advertising effectiveness: Mutual misunderstandings. In W. D. Wells (Ed.), *Measuring advertising effectiveness* (pp. 13–20). Mahwah, NJ: Erlbaum Press.

Damon, W., Colby, A., Bronk, K., & Ehrlich, T. (2005). Passion and professionalism in balance. *Daedalus, 134* (3), 27–35.

Fox, S. (1997). *The mirror makers.* Urbana: University of Illinois Press.

Freidson, E. (1988). *The profession of medicine.* Chicago: University of Chicago Press.

Gardner, H., & Shulman, L. S. (2005). The professions in America today. *Daedalus, 134* (3), 13–26.

Goode, W. J. (1977). Encroachment, charlatanism, and the emerging profession. *American Sociological Review, XXV*, 902–914.

Henke, L. (1995). A longitudinal analysis of the ad agency–client relationship: Predictors of agency switch. *Journal of Advertising Research, 35* (2), 24–30.

Johar, G. V., Holbrook, M. B., & Stern, B. B. (2001). The role of myth in creative advertising design: Theory, process and outcome. *Journal of Advertising, 30* (2), 1–25.

Kover, A. J. (1995). Copywriters' implicit theories of communication: An exploration. *Journal of Consumer Research, 21* (4), 30–45.

Kover, A. J., Goldberg, S. M., & James, W. (1995). Creativity vs. effectiveness? An integrating classification for advertising. *Journal of Advertising Research, 35* (6), 30–45.

Lears, J. (1994). *Fables of abundance.* New York: Basic Books.

Marchand, R. (1985). *Advertising the American dream.* Berkeley: University of California Press.

Merton, R. (1968). *Social organization.* New York: Free Press.

Mitchell, P., & Saunders, N. (1995). Loyalty in agency–client relations: The impact of organizational context. *Journal of Advertising Research, 35* (2), 9–22.

Mitchell, P. C., Catequet, H., & Hague, S. (1992). Establishing the causes of disaffection in agency–client relations. *Journal of Advertising Research, 32*, 41–48.

O'Guinn, T. C., Allen, C. T., & Semenik, R. J. (2008). *Advertising and integrated brand promotion.* Mason, OH: Thomson Southwestern.

Polonsky, M. J., & Michael, H. (2007). A multiple stakeholder perspective on responsibility in advertising. *Journal of Advertising, 36* (2), 1–25.

Richards, J. I., & Curran, C. M. (2002). Oracles on "advertising": Searching for a definition. *Journal of Advertising, 31* (2), 63–77.

Ross, B. I., Osborne, A. C., & Richards, J. I. (2006). *Advertising education yesterday-today-tomorrow.* Lubbock, TX: Advertising Education Publications.

Ross, B. I., & Richards, J. I. (2008). *A century of advertising education.* Chicago: American Academy of Advertising.

Sasser, S. L., & Koslow, S. (2008). Desperately seeking advertising creativity. *Journal of Advertising, 37* (4), 1–25.

Schudson, M. (1984). *Advertising, the uneasy persuasion.* New York: Basic Books.

Wells, W. D., Moriarty, S., & Burnett, J. (2006). *Advertising principles and practice.* Saddle River, NJ: Prentice-Hall.

Wright-Isak, C., & Faber, R. J. (1996). Community: A hidden value in the advertising effectiveness awards. *Journal of Advertising Research, 36* (4), 64–74.

Additional Readings

Abbott, A. (1988). *The system of professions.* Chicago: University of Chicago Press.

Becker, H. (1982). *Art worlds.* Berkeley: University of California Press.

Ben-David, J. (1984). *The scientist's role in society.* Chicago: University of Chicago Press.

Bogart, M. H. (1995). *Artists, advertising, and the borders of art.* Chicago: University of Chicago Press.

Gardner, H., & Shulman, L. S. (2005). The professions in America today. *Daedalus, 134* (3), 13–26.

Chapter 28

Brand Concepts and Advertising

Dean M. Krugman and Jameson L. Hayes

Introduction

Brands are part of our everyday life. Take a look at your shirt, shoes, hat, or cell phone and chances are you will encounter a brand name or brand logo that is intended to communicate something about the item and likely something about you as well. Brands are what advertising is mostly about because they are the overt offerings of the marketer and convey ownership of the product or service. Marketing and advertising plans are centered around the brand. Brands are a focal point of the company or organization's efforts including how they market and communicate. Basically, a brand is a promise (Kotler, 2005; Landor Associates, 2010) and much of that promise is conveyed via advertising in traditional media, new media, social media, or any other vehicle used to disseminate the message.

Although the concept of branding is not at all new, the term "brand" has taken on added importance in our language and at times goes well beyond the identification and value of the offering. Most people intuitively understand what we mean by the concept of brand when it is associated with a marketer's products or services. However, the term has broadened and is now included in more parts of our conversations and descriptions than ever before. For example, our ears perked up a few years ago when at a university meeting one of our deans referred to her/his college as a brand; this was quickly followed by our university referring to itself as a brand.

The goal here is to demonstrate why branding serves as an integral part of advertising theory and to examine some of the key concepts that explain branding. The concept of brand intersects with almost all areas pointed out in Figure 1.1 "Components of the Advertising Process Circle" framework discussed in Chapter 1 of this text. While initially the province of the marketer that owns the brand, the brand operates in a social, political, and economic environment, and brand messages are communicated via traditional and nontraditional media. Brand consideration and use are negotiated processes where a reciprocal relationship is formed between the consumer, the social environment, and the organization.

We first discuss the importance of theory and how it relates to advertising and branding, the inseparable link between branding and advertising, and key concepts used to explain branding—ownership/market power, promise/trust, image/meaning, contact, negotiation/collaboration, and brand valuation. We also discuss challenges to the concept of brand and identify when the concept of brand loses its central meaning and tightness of explanation.

Theory and Explanation

In some professional areas, theory is often relegated to the land of the overly complex and obtuse. When someone says, "You are being too theoretical" they are generally not paying you a compliment! A more reasoned view is that theory serves as a guide and explanation. Good theory helps insure that practice can be accomplished successfully on a regular basis. Advertising is taught at our universities as an applied field where students are made ready for practice. As such, we need to embrace theory as a way to help explain how and why things work. Put simply, if you understand how practice works and why it works, you are more apt to be consistent in your solutions and applications.

We certainly understand and acknowledge that the creativity and alchemy of advertising is special and a good portion of the field defies formal or prescribed theory. However, many in practice rely on normative thinking and implicit models of how things operate (Nyilasy & Reid, 2009). It is important that we continually examine, understand, and explain how the field operates to advance both knowledge and practice.

When James W. Carey, among others (1979, p. 284), wrote, "nothing was as practical as good theory" he did so to expressively state that there was not, and should not, be a sharp division between theory and practice in communication-based fields. Theory does not reside in academic institutions far removed from what is happening in the world. Theory provides a template as to how things are organized, how things work, and what we can expect from social phenomena.

There is often a difference in research programs that are expressively developed for application to existing practical problems and research programs that are developed for broader knowledge; however, this division does not mean that the application-oriented research is less theoretical. More appropriately, the difference between research programs oriented toward practice rather than broader knowledge means that the former is specifically developed to be more applied than general and basic.

The division between applied and broader research must be observed with caution when noting their respective contributions to practice, especially in the field of communication where so many of the most important applications have come from broader research programs. To name a few—functionalism, diffusion, two-step flow, involvement, elaboration likelihood, cognitive dissonance, selective exposure and selective perception, attitude development and change, semiotics, spiral of silence—all have their roots in broader research programs and have greatly influenced the practice of communication. Although the distinction between applied and broader research can be made, it should not be associated with a distinction between theoretical and nontheoretical. Moreover, the distinction in no way implies broader research is void of application nor that applied research fails to sometimes advance broader research.

Theory spans the sciences, social sciences, and humanities. While the content and flow of these three major areas are very different, more often than not they all rely on theory to help define and explain concepts. Scholars in advertising generally reside in the social sciences and humanities. While it is beyond the scope of this chapter to discuss the tenets of theory in the sciences, social sciences, and humanities, it is generally agreed that theory must provide an explanation of the concept or phenomena at hand.

Denzin (1978) notes that the social sciences fall between the sciences and humanities in terms of the general approaches and language used to create knowledge and explanation. He argues that theory provides explanation, new images of reality, and a guide for future thought. Communication scholars Chafee and Berger (1987) use explanatory power as the first criterion in evaluating a theory. The discussion of theory and explanation sets the tone for looking at some of the key constructs used to describe and explain branding.

Advertising, Branding, and Explanation

Advertising and branding are inextricably linked because the concept of branding helps to explain advertising at its core. The brand can be any device such as a name, slogan, or symbol that is used to distinguish a product or service. Because brands are designed to create value, companies take legal brand protection steps to ensure that the benefits accrue to their enterprise.

Figure 28.1 points out some of the central concepts relating to and explaining branding. Ownership/market power, promise/trust, image/meaning, contact, negotiation/collaboration, and valuation are all key constructs of brands.

Ownership and Market Power

Branding conveys ownership. Early use of branding in the second century indicates that brand markings were proof of ownership, sign of quality, or other

Figure 28.1 Constructs of Brand (Six Major Areas Explaining Branding).

purposes (*Online Etymology Dictionary*). For example, in both the early and modern U.S. West, branding provided proof of ownership protection against rustlers. Ownership, art, and imagination are obvious in the brands (trademarks) registered with the Livestock Identification Bureau in Reno, Nevada (McPhee, 1993) (see Figure 28.2).

Beyond the concept of ownership is the creation of brand to gain power in the marketplace. Trademark protection allows the company to keep the brand name as a valuable economic resource and the brand becomes a key strategy to gain and maintain market power. Before the development of national advertising, manufacturers did little to distinguish themselves in the eyes of the consumer. As a result, the market power belonged to the retailers who were the key contact point for the consumer. Competing goods had little differentiation in the eyes of the consumer and were essentially viewed as commodities; hence, manufacturers of products received little recognition. Under this system the manufacturer primarily dealt with the retailer and competed only on price to have the retailer stock the product (Norris, 1980; Hovland &Wolburg, 2010). The development of national advertising allowed manufacturers to go directly to consumers to make arguments that their brand was better. Branding took on

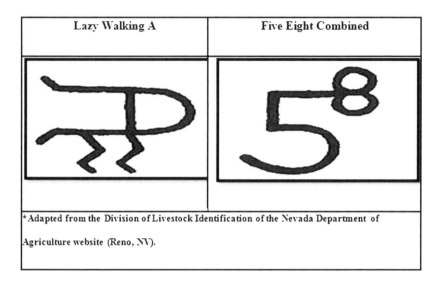

Lazy Walking A	Five Eight Combined

*Adapted from the Division of Livestock Identification of the Nevada Department of Agriculture website (Reno, NV).

Figure 28.2 Livestock Brands Indicating Ownership (Cattle Brands Artfully Used to Signify Ownership).

special importance because the "brand" now represented unique benefits and images. The producer's goal was, and still is, to gain power in the marketplace by having a brand that is meaningful and important to consumers, thus avoiding competition based solely on price. Consequently, advertising takes on great importance in the creation of brands and the development of differentiated goods.

The Uneeda Biscuits brand illustrates advertising's role in branding and differentiation. Booming in the late 1890s, the cracker industry was controlled by local retailers. Displayed in large wooden barrels and boxes, crackers were not differentiated by manufacturer and susceptible to quality variation and price competition (Twede, 1997). Uneeda's manufacturer, the National Biscuit Company, developed and patented a cost-effective method of packaging using paperboard cartons that provided crackers with moisture protection and physical protection from breakage (Peters, 1899) thus allowing for national distribution. Armed with this innovation, Uneeda launched what was at that time the largest advertising campaign in history communicating the unique benefits of Uneeda's package and urging consumers to ask stores to carry Uneeda Biscuits. As a result, Uneeda successfully built a relationship between consumers and the brand strong enough to shift power from retailers to the manufacturer (Twede, 1997).

So advertising and branding are bonded. The focus on brands changed the way products were bought and sold because a special relationship was forged between producer and the consumer. Brands take on special meaning and much of that meaning is developed and portrayed in advertising.

Promise and Trust

Brands make promises and seek to create trust between the producer and consumer. Both well-known scholars such as Philip Kotler, Distinguished Professor, Northwestern University, and acclaimed practitioners, such as Hayes Roth, President, Landor Associates, agree that a brand is a promise. Kotler (2005) states that the brand's promise determines how every facet of the company functions—product development, manufacturing, marketing, distribution—work to fulfill that promise. Roth notes that the brand's promise consists of everything that defines the offering and distinguishes it from competitors. The promise sets the stage for how a company will implement its offering and becomes the platform for planning and delivering the brand (Landor Associates, 2010).

The promise and trust built by the brand and conveyed via advertising, and all facets of marketing communication, serve as a cornerstone for success. Jennifer Aaker (1997) found that brands have distinctive personality traits such as sincerity, excitement, competence, sophistication, and ruggedness. The personality trait most often associated with successful brands is sincerity. The influence of sincerity as an important element of success is highly consistent with the notions of trust and promise as it is much easier to have trust in a brand that is viewed as sincere.

Image and Meaning

While promise and trust provide a cornerstone for a brand, image accounts for the way the brand promise is actualized. Brand image represents the total impression or net takeaway that a consumer has of the product or service and makes it easier on the consumer in terms of product selection and product use. The image serves as a mental shortcut that communicates quickly without requiring a great deal of thought on the part of the consumer. Brand image both reduces purchase complexity and at the same time adds meaning to the purchase and experience.

While serving as a mental shortcut to makes things easier, brand image remains a powerhouse of stored information and is the operational meaning of the brand (Sherry, 2005). Image development is dynamic and operates in a changing social and economic environment where organizations adapt, refine, and at times make major changes to the brand. While the company provides the signs, symbols, and other forms of information to construct the brand, it is the consumer who ultimately assigns the meaning.

A key goal is to provide an enduring image upon which the consumer can rely. The image often transforms the brand experience and serves to mentally "demonstrate" how the brand gets used and how to enjoy the brand. A visit to Ray Ban's website demonstrates that sunglasses are about "being cool" as much as they are about superior polarized eye protection. Some of the featured images are highly stylized and/or portray an "urban cool" look and feel. By comparison, Costa Del Mar's website also shows superior polarized eye protection but the image is directed to water sports, especially fishing. Using Costa Del Mar sunglasses enhances the angler's time on the water by serving as a prop and signaling he/she is a person who "knows how to fish" and "looks the part." In both situations, the image serves to transform the brand experience well beyond eye protection.

Master image maker and one of the most influential advertising professionals of modern times, David Ogilvy understood the importance of creating clear, consistent and non-contradictory messages when he stated that, "Every advertisement should be thought of as a contribution of the complex symbol which is the brand message" (Batra, Myers, & Aaker, 1996, p. 316).

However, the information environment is now much more complex making it difficult for the advertiser to deliver a clear and consistent message. People have much greater ability to seek out information and are also continually exposed to information that is negative or contradictory to the brand.

Contact

All brand messages are not the same and the level of brand contact can differ greatly. Schultz and Walters (1997) argue that brand contact consists of all messages, incentives, activities, or methods by which an individual comes in contact with the brand and leaves some trace of brand information and impact. Although some contact information includes positive information dispensed by the organization, other contact information from other sources may be negative (e.g., negative news reports or conversations with peers).

A useful distinction in understanding contact is seen in the concepts of *value* and *presence*. Company information that focuses on the benefits/attributes of price is seen as value based in terms of moving the customer toward purchase and use. Advertising is a key tool in providing value information.

Presence provides contact via activities that are not designed to communicate a great deal of meaning in terms of value, but rather to reinforce existing perceptions and reintegrate the consumer with the brand. Presence serves as a lubricant and motivates the customer by raising "salience" or moving the brand up in the consumer's agenda or thinking (Moran, 1990). Physical presence may come in such forms as shelf space or simply being exposed to the brand logo; mental presence may come in the form of very short ads or similar formats.

Of the two, value information is more robust because it offers more in both substance and tone. Although there is not always a clear-cut method for distinguishing between value and presence, it is important to note that level of contact can be very different.

Negotiation and Brand Collaboration

The information environment encourages people to negotiate with brands. Strategies devised by the company constitute only *one* part of the purchase process and marketers tend to overestimate their importance. People continually interact with social, economic, technical, and broader cultural factors that help shape their brand considerations. For example, the Apple iPad is part of a regiment of products geared to making information and entertainment portable, instantly accessible and "cool." The iPad did not create the culture of portability, accessibility, and "cool," but rather plays into it.

A basic premise is that the consumer determines and drives the value of the brand (Schultz & Schultz, 2005). We now have a model of collaboration where customers and prospective customers have the capacity to be much more interactive in their dealings with brands (Leadbeater, 2010). The reciprocity allows for communication from producer to customers/prospective customers, customers/prospective customers to producers, and customers/prospective customers to each other. Websites and social networks are no longer supplements but key agents in marketing and marketing communication. For example, "My Starbucks Idea" is social website with the stated goal of having customers take part in helping to co-create the company. Customers submit and review each product and service suggestion (Follows, 2010). Zappos Shoes goes to extraordinary lengths to interact with customers via online and telephone contact during the purchase process (Follows, 2010). The interaction makes consumers comfortable and helps to limit problems associated with not trying on the shoes.

Brand Valuation

In the last 20 years we have seen increased scrutiny for exploring and understanding the value of marketing, advertising, and branding for the company. Understanding the way brands are valued now plays a large role in explaining how well marketing and advertising work toward achieving overall company goals and justifying the marketing communications investment.

The brand is viewed as a dynamic entity that needs to be replenished and is open to both opportunity and threat. Because of its dynamic nature, it is critical that the role of brand value be continually assessed. We have learned that changes in the value added by the brand should be as routine a part of annual reviews and plans as changes in brand volume and sales (Crimmins, 1992).

David Aaker (1991), who is responsible for developing many of the constructs regarding brand value, argues that brand equity is a set of brand assets and liabilities linked to a brand that add to or subtract from the value to a firm and its customers.

While advertising and other forms of marketing communication are critical in conveying positive information about the brand, we also know that negative brand information can be instantly conveyed when problems occur. Consider the following Bloomberg *Businessweek* headline, "Toyota Sinks in Quality Survey After Recalls." Following its large recall of vehicles for brake issues, Toyota registered its record worst ranking in the annual J.D. Power & Associates new vehicle quality survey going from a perennial top brand to below the national average (Welch, 2010). Significant here is that high-scoring brands have the highest customer retention scores. Therefore, it is critical that any brand valuation method includes challenges to a brand's equity.

Interbrand, a management consulting group, provides an annual analysis of the best global brands. Revenue, earnings, and core brand strength (which include such factors as market, leadership, trends, diversification, support, and stability) are used to determine a brand's value. Table 28.1 shows the top 20 global brands as rated by Interbrand's method. Coke, IBM, Microsoft, GE, and Nokia remained stable and are in the top five brands over a 2-year period (Table 28.1 rankings are through 2009 and had not yet reflected the noted problems with Toyota). Figure 28.2 shows the top 10 best global brands using their logos or symbols. Can you note the difference in the understanding, look, and feel,

Table 28.1 Top 20 most valuable brands (revenue, earnings, and core brand strength used to determine brand value)

2009 rank	2008 rank	Brand	2009 rank	2008 rank	Brand
1	1	Coca-Cola	11	12	Hewlett Packard
2	2	IBM	12	11	Mercedes Benz
3	3	Microsoft	13	14	Gillette
4	4	General Electric	14	17	Cisco
5	5	Nokia	15	13	BMW
6	8	McDonald's	16	16	Louis Vuitton
7	10	Google	17	18	Marlboro
8	6	Toyota	18	20	Honda
9	7	Intel	19	21	Samsung
10	9	Disney	20	24	Apple

Source: adapted from http://www.interbrand.com/best_global_brands.aspx?year=2009 &type=desc&col=1&1angid=1000 (retrieved August 17, 2010).

between simply reading the standard text in Table 28.1 and viewing the symbols/logos in Figure 28.3? The difference is in branding.

James Crimmins (1992) presents the most straightforward way of measuring brand value by using the metric of cost. For example, if Brand A and Brand B are equally desirable and Brand A costs $110 versus Brand B $100, then Brand A is 10% more valuable ($110/100 - 1 = 10\%$). This method is straightforward and in some respects covers brand value but it does not explain why the value exists. Therefore, it is critical to understand what the consumer thinks because ultimately brand value lies in what consumers think and feel about the brand (Keller, 2001).

Schultz and Schultz (2005) provide an overview that shows three pathways for measuring brand value, (1) consumer-based metrics such as attitude data and tracking studies, (2) incremental-brand sales using market performance and marketing mix return on investment (ROI), and (3) branded business value using a valuation model. Pathway 1 uses information that relies on how consumers value various aspects of the product and then extrapolates value. Pathway 2 focuses on short-term value looking at sales, premium pricing, and end results attributed to brand activities. Pathway 3 combines financial data, research, and accounting methods to estimate brand value.

Figure 28.3 Symbols and Logos of Top Ten Most Valuable Brands (Note How Logos and Symbols Convey Brand Meaning).

Pathway 1 is generally the best understood and most used because of its inherent focus on consumers. David Aaker (1996) points out brand value measurements include brand loyalty, perceived quality, and leadership/popularity, associations such as perceived value, brand personality and organizational associations, brand awareness, and market share/distribution. Keller (2001) provides a similar consumer-based approach that focuses on the constructs of brand salience, performance, imagery, consumer judgments, feelings, and resonance.

Challenges to Branding

Widening the Concept of Brand

The above dimensions of—ownership/market power, promise/trust, image/meaning, contact, negotiation/collaboration, valuation—are common denominators in explaining the concept of brand as used by advertisers. We have good explanatory power and understanding and can apply the concepts to advertising and marketing communication. However, the concept and use of brand has taken on a broader meaning in popular culture. Specifically, the lexicon or language of brand has changed and the term is used in ways that transcend traditional explanation. Two recent examples illustrate the extension.

Vice President Joseph Biden remarked,

> "I told the president two things when he asked me to do the job," Biden said. "I said, 'Just two conditions, Mr. President. I'm not going to wear any funny hats, and I'm not changing my brand.' And I kept my promise."
>
> (Associated Press, 2010)

Isawa Elaigwu, who spoke on behalf of the members of Nigeria's rebranding committee, said that the program is a rebirth for the country.

> We are not happy with the Nigerian product we have now; hence we have decided to do something about it . . . All we hear in the past is that Nigeria is a fertile ground for credit fraud and all kinds of crime. We all can re-brand Nigeria. Once we continue to re-brand ourselves, then Nigeria can be re-branded.
>
> (*The Economist*, 2009)

We certainly mix things up a bit by extending the term and meaning beyond the conventional use. In Vice Presidents Biden's case, brand is used as an illustration of an individual's personality and behavior. In Nigeria's case, the use of brand is equated with helping to rebuild a country which inputs a power that is not likely possible.

Not all Contacts are Positive

We have noted several times that the nature of branding is dynamic and based upon a multitude of interactions. Branding is not an easy process and is made much more difficult in an environment where information is rapid and impact of mistakes spreads quickly.

The information environment is rich, competitive, and often filled with negative information that serves as a liability to the brand image. Figure 28.4 shows the photo attached to an Associated Press story titled, "Study: Kids' meals loaded with fat, salt and calories." The major brands in the picture are associated with areas that are detrimental to a child's health.

Immediacy of Communication

What now happens in one part of the world certainly does not stay in that part of the world. Frances Cairncross (1997) coined the term "The Death of Distance" in the mid 1990s to convey the fact that information rapidly transcends distance via the new communication technologies. Instant communication poses both an

Figure 28.4 News Story Headline and Picture Demonstrating Negative Brand Contact (Not All Brand Contacts are Positive).

opportunity to disseminate brand information and at the same time reveals brand problems as they arise throughout the world.

For example, one of the key reasons the Chinese government was reluctant to get heavy handed with striking workers at "big-brand" firms such as Honda is because such actions would attract instant global attention (*The Economist*, 2010). The global Honda brand draws instant attention.

Conclusion

Branding and advertising are inextricably linked. In many respects the brand is what advertising is all about. A key role of any theory is to provide explanation and we have seen how the concepts of ownership/market power, promise/trust, image/meaning, contact, negotiation/collaboration, and valuation help explain the meaning of brand.

There are challenges to the brand. In some instances the term brand has moved beyond the concepts noted and taken on a broader meaning in our language. Additionally, the fact that not all contacts are positive and the immediacy of communication have combined to make the management and control of the brand much more difficult.

References

Aaker, D. A. (1991). *Managing brand equity: Capitalizing on the value of a brand name*. New York: Free Press.

Aaker, D. A. (1996). Measuring brand equity across products and markets. *California Management Review, 38* (3), 102–120.

Aaker, D. A., & Myers, J. G. (1982). *Advertising management* (2nd ed.). Englewood Cliffs, NJ: Prentice Hall.

Aaker, J. L. (1997). Dimensions of brand personality. *Journal of Marketing Research, 34* (August), 347–356.

Associated Press (2010, July 10). Biden tells Leno US did fine in Russian spy swap.

Batra, R., Myers, J. G., & Aaker, D. A. (1996). *Advertising management* (5th ed.). Upper Saddle River, NJ: Prentice Hall.

Cairncross, F. (1997). *The death of distance: How the communications revolution is changing our lives*. Boston, MA: Harvard Business School Press.

Carey, J. W. (1979). Graduate education in mass communication. *Communication Education, 28*, 282–293.

Chaffee, S. H., & Berger, C. R. (1987). What communication scientists do. In C. R. Berger & S. H. Chaffee (Eds.), *Handbook of communication science* (pp. 99–122). Newbury Park, CA: Sage.

Crimmins, J. C. (1992). Better management and measurement of brand value. *Journal of Advertising Research, 32* (4), 11–19.

Denzin, N. K. (1978). *The research act: A theoretical introduction to sociological methods* (2nd ed.). New York: McGraw-Hill.

Follows, T. (2010, May). From adoption to adaption: Service brands in particular need to embrace the dawning of an era of "adaption" through collaboration with consumers, exemplified by brands such as Starbucks, Best Buy, Zappos and AT&T. *Admap*, 30–31.

Hovland, R., & Wolburg, J. M. (2010). *Advertising, society, and consumer culture*. Armonk, NY: M.E. Sharp.

Keller, K. L. (2001). *Building customer based brand equity: A blueprint for creating strong brands* (MSI Report 01–107). Cambridge, MA: Marketing Science Institute.

Kotler, P. (2005). Forward by Phillip Kotler. In A. M. Tybout & T. Calkins (Eds.), *Kellogg on branding* (pp. ix–x). Hoboken, NJ: John Wiley & Sons.

Landor Associates. (2010). Thinking: The essentials of branding. In *Landor*. Retrieved September 1, 2010, from http://landor.com/?do=thinking.article&storyid=788.

Leadbeater, C. (2010, May). Co-Creation: Think "with." *Admap*, 24–25.

McPhee, J. (1993, December 20). Irons in the fire. *New Yorker*, 94–113.

Moran, W. T. (1990). Brand presence and the perceptual frame. *Journal of Advertising Research, 30*, 9–16.

Norris, V. (1980). Advertising history: According to the textbooks. *Journal of Advertising, 9* (3), 3–11.

Nyilasy, G., & Reid, L. (2009). Agency practitioner theories of how advertising works. *Journal of Advertising, 38* (3), 81–96.

Online etymology dictionary. (n.d.). Brand. Retrieved August 4, 2010 from www.etymonline.com/index.php?term=brand.

Peters, F. M. (1899). *Method of and means for packing biscuit, crackers, or the like* (U.S. Patent No. 621,974). Washington, D.C.: U.S. Patent Office.

Schultz, D. E., & Schultz, H. F. (2005). Measuring brand value. In A. M. Tybout & T. Calkins (Eds.), *Kellogg on branding* (pp. 244–271). Hoboken, NJ: John Wiley & Sons.

Schultz, D. E., & Walters, J. S. (1997). *Measuring brand communication ROI*. New York: ANA.

Sherry, J. F. (2005). Brand meaning. In A. M. Tybout & T. Calkins (Eds.), *Kellogg on branding* (pp. 40–69). Hoboken, NJ: John Wiley & Sons.

The Economist. (2009, May 2). Rebranding Nigeria: Good people, impossible mission. *The Economist*, 50.

The Economist (2010, July 29). World economy: The rising power of the Chinese worker. *The Economist*, 9.

Twede, D. (1997). Uneeda Biscuit: The first consumer package? *Journal of Macromarketing, 17* (Fall), 82–87.

Welch, D. (2010, June 17). Toyota sinks in quality survey after recalls; Ford makes top 5. *Bloomberg Businessweek*. Retrieved July 28, 2010, from www.businessweek.com/news/2010–06–17/toyota-sinks-in-quality-survey-after-recalls-ford-makes-top-5.html.

Additional Readings

Baran, S. J., & Davis, D. K. (2008). *Mass communication theory: Foundations, ferment, and future* (5th ed.). Boston, MA: Wadsworth Cengage Learning.

Calder, B. J. (Ed.). (2008). *Kellogg on advertising & media*. Hoboken, NJ: John Wiley & Sons.

Gregory, J. R. (2004). *The best of branding: Best practices in corporate branding.* New York: McGraw-Hill.

Keller, K. L. (2008). *Strategic brand management: Building, measuring, and managing brand equity*. Upper Saddle River, NJ: Pearson/Prentice Hall.

Tybout, A. M., & Calkins, T. (Eds.). (2005). *Kellogg on branding*. Hoboken, NJ: John Wiley & Sons.

Chapter 29

I Know It When I See It

The Definability and Consequences of Perceived Fit in Corporate Social Responsibility Initiatives

Amanda B. Bower and Stacy Landreth Grau

I shall not today attempt to further define the kinds of material I understand to be embraced within that shorthand description; and perhaps I could never succeed in intelligibly doing so. But I know it when I see it.
(Justice Stewart on U.S. Supreme Court Jacobeliis v. Ohio, the case defining pornography, 1964)

In the early 1980s after a series of associations with local nonprofit causes (e.g., the Dallas Ballet, Mount Vernon), Jerry Walsh, the executive vice president of worldwide marketing and communications for American Express, was looking for a cause upon which to build a national campaign. Looking at the Statue of Liberty, which was being prepared for restoration, he realized that she was "arguably the most universally compelling cause to Americans" (Alden, 2009b). So, in 1983, American Express offered to donate 1 cent for each credit card transaction and $1 for each new credit card account opened toward the effort to restore the Statue of Liberty. Jeff Atlas, the lead creative director on the campaign, knew that the communication of this alliance needed to carefully balance the relationship between American Express and the Statue. To avoid cynical reactions on the part of the consumers, the emphasis in the advertising needed to be more on helping the statue's renovations and less on the use of or benefit to American Express cards (Alden, 2009a). The program raised $1.7 million of the $87 million restoration and the press coverage has been estimated at worth 10 times that amount. New card applications increased 45%, and in the first month alone card use increased 28% (Alden, 2009b). Jerry Walsh coined the term "cause-related marketing," defining it not as philanthropy, but "marketing through an artful association with a charitable cause" (Alden, 2009b).

Growth and Popularity of Corporate Social Responsibility Initiatives

The interest, excitement, press, and new business generated by American Express' relationship with the Statue of Liberty gave birth to a new strategic option in marketing: the corporate social responsibility initiative. Corporate social responsibility initiatives (CSRI) refer to social alliances of two or more parties (for profit and nonprofit) that develop a partnership with at least one noneconomic objective. Economic aspects of CSRI may include many types of resources including money, in kind product donations, time donations, professional expertise, volunteers, and communications support (see also Drumwright & Murphy, 2001; Lichtenstein, Drumwright, & Braig, 2004).

Each year, companies donate millions to charities. Spending on CSRI was $1.5 billion in 2009 (IEG Sponsorship, 2009) and is expected to increase more than 6% for 2010 (www.causemarketingforum.com, 2010). Perceptions of corporate America's "good deeds" are becoming more important to all stakeholders, especially consumers. To that end, corporations have increasingly embraced social alliances in order to showcase their impact within the community at large (see "organizations" in Figure 1.1 in Chapter 1). This rush to include CSRI into marketing strategy has led to an explosion of types of CSRIs that exist (e.g., methods of donations, levels of participation of consumers), as well as the types of pairings between causes and corporations. Home Depot and KaBOOM! teamed up for "1,000 Playgrounds in 1,000 days" which took employee volunteerism to a new level as Home Depot employees built places for kids to play within walking distance of their homes. The Lance Armstrong Foundation and Nike paired up to create and sell the ubiquitous "Live Strong" yellow bracelets, with proceeds going to cancer research. American Express allows their customers to determine where money should go and used social media to promote this effort. As a result, American Express has donated more than $4.5 million in 2 years to various causes (www.causemarketingforum.com, 2010).

One of the more popular causes is breast cancer, and one of the most effective nonprofits for this cause has been the Susan G. Komen for the Cure, with nearly 240 corporate relationships (Hutchison, 2010). One campaign that has become strongly associated with Komen's pink ribbon is Yoplait's Lids for Lives, which has run since 1999. Each fall, Yoplait asks customers to mail in the lids of their yogurt containers and Yoplait donates 10 cents for each lid redeemed to Komen for the Cure, raising more than $26 million in 12 years. The variety of Komen's corporate partnerships has also led to some criticism (e.g., Orenstein, 2003; Hutchison, 2010). One example is the 2010 Pink Bucket campaign with KFC. For every pink bucket sold, KFC would donate 50 cents to Komen. While the bucket did raise $2 million in the first week alone, the executive director of Breast Cancer Action, Barbara Brenner, strongly criticized the poor fit between the cause and the product, saying "They are raising money for women's health by selling a product that's bad for your health . . . it's hypocrisy" (Hutchison, 2010).

Thus, one of the greatest challenges associated with a CSRI is determining what constitutes the wise selection of partners in the cause/brand alliance, with a good fit between partners so as to heighten the "artfulness" (per Jerry Walsh) of the execution.

Importance of Fit in CSRI

One of the most researched CSRI variables by academics is that of fit. Or similarity. Or congruence. Or match up. Or one of the many other terms that have been used to describe this concept in the research. It has been explored in such a variety of different ways that there are an assortment of semantics, definitions, manifestations, and effects both in terms of the outcomes of fit but also the determinants of fit. The purpose of this chapter is to bring some coherence to the research on CSRI/fit issues. Within the McGuire (1969) model, we concern ourselves with both source and receiver issues; as per Cornwell (2008), a fit is determined both by the seemingly objective characteristics of the CSRI brand pairing and the knowledge and awareness of the receiver. Given the importance of these two issues, how the "fit" is presented within the messages is also a key consideration in determining what might be considered the effectiveness of fit.

Semantics and Explanation of "Fit"

While we are currently using the word "fit," researchers have used a variety of words, descriptors, and definitions to capture the idea of how two attitudinal objects are a suitable pairing, including congruence/congruity (Menon & Kahn, 2003; Pope, Voges, & Brown, 2004; Rifon, Choi, Trimble, & Li, 2004), complementarity (Strahilevitz & Myers, 1998), perceived fit/fit (Barone, Norman, & Miyazaki, 2007; Bloom, Hoeffler, Keller, & Meza, 2006; Lafferty, 2009, 2007; Pracejus & Olsen, 2004; Samu & Wymer, 2009), cause/brand fit (Nan & Heo, 2007), relatedness (Crimmins & Horn, 1996; Johar & Pham, 1999; Wakefield, Becker-Olsen, & Cornwell, 2007), match up (e.g., Gwinner & Eaton, 1999; Strahilevitz, 1999), and appropriateness (Menon & Kahn, 2003; Pope et al., 2004). Rifon et al. (2004) described it as "consumer perceptions of similarity but with variations," referring readers to Johar and Pham's (1999) description of fit as "relatedness and relevance" and Ruth and Simonin (2003) "compatibility." Bloom et al. (2006) describe an initiative as having a high level of fit if consumers can easily determine the logic behind the brand affiliation.

Why Do Consumers Perceive a Fit?

Menon and Kahn (2003) offer categories that would result in perceptions of fit. First, a partnership with a cause can align along product dimensions. For example, Marshall's Department Store may sponsor donations to an organization like Dress for Success to benefit lower income women looking for jobs. A second type is a partnership with a cause that is important to the target audience. Avon's campaign for breast cancer is a good example since women are the target audience. Third, the cause promotion can fit with the image of the brand. For example, Ben & Jerry's has been known for environmental advocacy. Last, cause promotions can be developed based on the involvement of a company's chief executive. For example, Ryka shoes support domestic violence causes due to the involvement of its founder. While these categories indicate what aspects of the nonprofit/for-profit pairing will result in fit, they do not quite capture why a consumer would perceive there to be a fit.

Cornwell (2008) argues that the key to understanding how consumers process communication information is based on associative networks (Anderson & Bower, 1973) and spreading activation (Collins & Loftus, 1975). The types of fit offered by Menon and Kahn (2003) indicate what aspects of the associative networks of each member of the CSRI might result in perceptions of fit. Essentially knowledge is stored in memory nodes, which are then activated by a stimulus; the activation of that stimulus then works to retrieve stored information. Therefore, the more that a consumer knows about a brand and cause, the greater the number of memory nodes that exist, and the stronger the resulting associative network (e.g., Keller, 1993). For example, a consumer can see a "fit" between computer software and education by the nature of the product and cause. But a consumer would have to know that Dave Thomas, founder of Wendy's, was adopted and supported adoption during his lifetime, in order to see a perceived fit between Wendy's and their cause of adoptions. Therefore, if a consumer has a stronger associative network, the idea of perceived fit is broadened and even nuanced to include a richer understanding of the partnership between the brand and the cause. In other words, perceptions of fit result when a profit and nonprofit either share memory nodes, or have nodes that are either connected or connectable.

Categories of Fit

The congruency of these conceptual traits may be categorized into the concepts of commonality (i.e., shared nodes) and complementarity (i.e., connected or connectable nodes) (Hoeffler & Keller, 2002). The first is "commonality" where the firm and the nonprofit share some sort of common associations, where the two objects "share much of the same meaning and elicit similar judgments and feelings" (p. 83). One might think of this as an overlap between the associations consumers might have of the firm (brand, product) and associations consumers might have of the nonprofit (cause type, reputation). For example, Gwinner and Eaton (1999) suggest that a firm would want to match the characteristics of the brand with the characteristics of the sponsorship. Similarly, Bower and Grau (2009) have as congruent categories one in which the nonprofit (a reading literacy group) would be one in which an overlap indicates an expertise regarding the company (e.g., Baby Einstein). Menon and Kahn (2003) also appear to put forth this type of congruence, where an herbal product fits with sponsoring a rain forest. This commonality conceptualization of fit would also be similar to Gwinner's (1997) "functional based similarity" where the sponsor's product is used during a sponsorship event. If Nike shoes are used during a sponsored charity basketball game, there is a clear overlap between the product/brand and sponsorship.

Hoeffler and Keller (2002) also suggest that a pairing can also be complementary. They indicate that a complementary pairing strategy is one where the nonprofit and the firm have few associations, and the firm may be attempting to add to the existing knowledge consumers might have of a brand. An example is Harley Davidson's sponsorship of the Muscular Dystrophy Association (MDA). Indeed, Hoeffler and Keller (2002) conceptualize a complementary strategy as being representative of low fit. However, we suggest shifting of our understanding of a complementary strategy not as being entirely lacking of appropriateness, but instead of a different kind of fit altogether. Instead of being an overlap, we conceive a complementary strategy as being two puzzle pieces fitting together without much redundancy, or, to return to the associate network conceptualization, two nodes that will easily be connected and thus, activated. Therefore, this type of fit could be a way to break through the clutter surrounding many of the most popular causes. According to Cornwell (2008), some pairings that might not have been considered by past research as being highly congruent could be conceived of as more relevant. Both the nonprofit and the firm have a network of associations with each having related multiple words, concepts, and visual images (e.g., Anderson & Bower, 1973; Nelson, Bennett, & Leibert, 1997; Nelson & McEvoy, 2002). A partnership between Harley Davidson and MDA might initially lack congruence because it is a pairing of a tough, burly biker image and ill children. But consumers might ultimately determine that Harley Davidson represents tough bikers with a heart of gold. This would represent a stronger and richer association between the cause and brand in the minds of consumers.

Strahilevitz (1999) and Strahilevitz and Myers (1998) examined "affect-based complementarity." Specifically, they found that a donation to charity would serve as more of a complement to hedonic (e.g., fancy chocolates) products relative to utilitarian (e.g., toilet paper) products. They argue that the feelings associated with consuming a more frivolous (even selfish) product would be complemented by the good feelings or even relief of guilt associated with a donation to charity such that the sum could be greater than the parts. So in other words, one might conceive of commonality and complementary strategies both as being strategies of fit, but referring to a greater or lesser overlap between the nonprofit and the firm.

Heightening Perceptions of Fit

With new CSRI (e.g., either a new brand partnering with a cause or a new cause partnering with a brand) partnerships, the ideas of memory recall and mediator concepts, words, or visuals become increasingly important (for more information on memory and recall in general see Nelson, McEvoy, & Pointer, 2003; Nelson, McKinney, Gee, & Jacurza, 1998; Nelson, Schreiber, & McEvoy, 1992). If a brand wants to heighten perceptions of fit between the brand and the nonprofit/cause, the communications may be structured to heighten those perceptions. Here, the brand manager may need to provide additional information to create a stronger network association. Cornwell (2008) argues that a concept might be emphasized to support the link, or that an associated pathway between the nonprofit and the marketer "that would otherwise not be activated" might make the connection between the firm and the nonprofit more logical.

For example, P&G was one of the sponsors of the 2010 Winter Olympics. While on the face of it there is little overlap between those two agents other than possibly the large scope of both, P&G created a campaign that emphasized the commonality reinforcing the fit. The "Moms" campaign reinforced the idea that moms sacrifice for their child athletes, and moms (and family) are the first to be embraced when a win (or disappointment) are had during the competition. And of course, mothers are a large part of the target market for many P&G products. In other words, even if the fit isn't readily obvious to the viewing market, advertisers can introduce that commonality themselves.

Consequences of Perceived Fit for CSRI

The various types of fit have been found to affect an assortment of corporate perceptions, including perceptions of corporate social responsibility (Bower & Grau, 2009; Menon & Kahn, 2003), corporate image or attitude (Lafferty, 2007, 2009; Nan & Heo, 2007; Pope et al., 2004; Rifon et al., 2004). Researchers have examined attitudes and intentions toward the brand (e.g., Barone, Miyazaki, & Taylor, 2000; Barone, Norman, & Miyazaki, 2007; Lafferty, 2007;

Nan & Heo, 2007; Samu & Wymer, 2009), attitudes toward the ad (e.g., Nan & Heo, 2007; Pope et al., 2004), and recall rates of sponsors (Wakefield et al., 2007). Although Jerry Welsh emphasizes the marketing aspect of CSRI-type actions, one dependent variable that has been explored on a limited basis is behavioral consequences. The effects of fit and CSRI on choice has been studied (e.g., Pracejus & Olsen, 2004; Strahilivitz, 1999; Strahilevitz & Myers, 1998). Of interest to nonprofits may be the fact that evidence suggests that fit may have consequences for the nonprofits as well, including attitude toward the cause (Samu & Wymer, 2009) or intentions towards the nonprofit (e.g., Barone et al., 2007; Samu & Wymer, 2009).

Given the various possible understandings of "fit" as well as the variety of dependent variables explored, it is not surprising that support for the effectiveness of "fitting" CSRIs has been mixed. Most of the research has found that a greater degree of fit is more effective at influencing positive consumer evaluations and reducing skepticism. This may result when the fit of the CSRI creates or reinforces something positive, whether affect (e.g., Strahilevitz, 1999; Strahilevitz & Myers, 1998), or product-relevant commonality (e.g., Bower & Grau, 2009). There are, however, exceptions. Therefore, those wishing to make decisions (whether managerial, conducting future research, etc.) based upon past research on fit must make sure that they are clear on how fit is defined and manifested (measured or manipulated) in the study, as well as how the effectiveness of fit is defined.

Of particular interest may be perceptions of the motivations of the brand/firm participating in the CSRI. If the consumers are suspicious of motives for participation whether resulting from higher or lower fit, this may result in deleterious effects (e.g., Menon & Kahn, 2003; Barone et al., 2007). For example, Ellen, Mohr, and Webb (2000) indicated that a higher degree of fit indicates to consumers how the marketer might benefit from CSRI sales, thus leading to some sort of consumer backlash. In their study, fit was manifested in the stimuli of donating food or cleaning supplies (congruent with grocery stores) or building supplies (congruent with building a supply store). However, the spreading activation model suggests that Ellen et al.'s (2000) findings were because the CSRI fit activated beliefs (such as schemer schema) regarding the suspicious motives for participating in the CSRI. Obviously, advertisers would want to activate different links, emphasizing more optimistic aspects of the association. With regard to the American Express/Statue of Liberty campaign that started CSRI (as well as this chapter), Jeff Atlas, the creative director for the American Express campaign puts it (Alden, 2009b):

> I wanted to be sure that we were not being perceived as trading on or cheapening the image of the Statue. If the headline had been, "The next

time you go shopping, buy one hat for you and one for her," people who take the Statue very seriously—and there are many who see it as a shrine to American values—would have been offended. They would have thought, American Express is trading on the reputation of the Statue of Liberty for their own profits.

Conclusion

While fit is an important consideration when selecting partners for CSRI as well as communicating that affiliation, an appreciation for the multidimensionality of fit may be as important for understanding and optimizing fit's consequences. Researchers need to take this into consideration before boldly and universally stating that fit is effective or ineffective in a particular situation. Advertisers and marketing strategists need a knowledge of consumer structure as well as a sense of how the two members of the CSRI alliance will be presented together in any messaging. These strategists will want to determine and reinforce how might the alliance reinforce or augment the brand rather than simply not appearing as a jarringly inconsistent pairing of brands. Given the varied dependent variables studied, advertisers will also want an awareness and definition of how that effectiveness will be determined. Is the goal of the campaign to heighten perceptions of corporate social responsibility, or is it to directly change behavior? Finally, given the possibility that fit functions differently across CSRI types (Bower & Grau, 2009), future consideration (both in research and strategy) will want to take into account how certain fits work differently in different CSRI types. For example (Ellen et al., 2000), consumers might see cause-related marketing as potentially self-serving under certain fit conditions; perhaps under those conditions, a simpler donation would better serve the marketer.

References

Alden, K. (2009a, February 14). Jeff Atlas remembers Amex's Statue of Liberty campaign. Retrieved September 2, 2010, from http://causerelatedmarketing.blogspot.com/2009/02/jeff-atlas-remembers-amexs-statue-of.html.

Alden, K. (2009b, February 17). An interview with cause-related marketing pioneer Jerry Walsh. Retrieved September 2, 2010, from http://causerelatedmarketing.blogspot.com/2009/02/interview-with-cause-related-marketing.html.

Anderson, J. R., & Bower, G. (1973). *Human associative memory: A brief edition*. Hillsdale, NJ: Lawrence Erlbaum.

Barone, M. J., Miyazaki, A., & Taylor, K. (2000). The influence of cause related marketing on consumer choice: Does one good turn deserve another? *Journal of the Academy of Marketing Science, 28* (2), 248–262.

Barone, M. J., Norman, A. T., & Miyazaki, A. (2007). Consumer response to retailer use of cause-related marketing: Is more fit better? *Journal of Retailing, 83* (4), 437–445.

Bloom, P. N., Hoeffler, S., Keller, K. L., & Meza, C. E. B. (2006). How social-cause marketing affects consumer perceptions. *MIT Sloan Management Review, 47* (2), 49–55.

Bower, A. B., & Grau, S. L. (2009). Implicit versus explicit third party endorsements: Do CSR initiatives imply a nonprofit organization endorsement? *Journal of Advertising, 58* (Fall), 113–126.

Cause Marketing Forum. (2010). Retrieved July 25, 2010 from www.causemarketing-forum.com.

Collins, A. M., & Loftus, E. F. (1975). A spreading activation theory of semantic processing. *Psychological Review, 82* (6), 407–428.

Cornwell, T. B. (2008). State of the art and science in sponsorship-linked marketing. *Journal of Advertising, 37* (3), 41–55.

Crimmins, J., & Horn, M. (1996). Sponsorship: From management ego trip to marketing success. *Journal of Advertising Research, 36* (4), 11–21.

Drumwright, M. E., & Murphy, P. (2001). Corporate societal marketing. In P. N. Bloom and G. T. Gundlach (Eds.), *Handbook for marketing and society* (pp. 162–183). Thousand Oaks, CA: Sage.

Ellen, P. S., Mohr, L. A., & Webb, D. J. (2000). Charitable programs and the retailer: Do they mix? *Journal of Retailing, 76* (3), 393–406.

Gwinner, K. P., & Eaton, J. (1999). Building brand image through event sponsorship: The role of image transfer. *Journal of Advertising, 28* (4), 47–57.

Hoeffler, S., & Keller, K. L. (2002). Building brand equity through corporate societal marketing. *Journal of Public Policy and Marketing, 21* (1), 78–89.

Hutchison, C. (2010, April 24). Fried chicken for the cure. Retrieved September 2, 2010, from http://abcnews.go.com/Health/Wellness/kfc-fights-breast-cancer-fried-chicken/story?id=10458830.

Johar, G. V., & Pham, M. T. (1999). Relatedness, prominence and constructive sponsor identification. *Journal of Marketing Research, 36* (3), 299–312.

Keller, K. L. (1993). Conceptualizing, measuring and managing customer-based brand equity. *Journal of Marketing, 57* (1), 1–22.

Lafferty, B. (2007). The relevance of fit in a cause–brand alliance when consumers evaluate corporate credibility. *Journal of Business Research, 60*, 447–453.

Lafferty, B. (2009). Selecting the right cause partners for the right reasons: The role of importance and fit in cause–brand alliances. *Psychology and Marketing, 26* (4), 359–382.

Lafferty, B., & Goldsmith, R. E. (2005). Cause–brand alliances: Does the cause help the brand or does the brand help the cause? *Journal of Business Research, 58* (4), 423–429.

Lichtenstein, D. R., Drumwright, M., & Braig, B. M. (2004). The effect of corporate social responsibility on customer donations to corporate-supported nonprofits. *Journal of Marketing, 68* (October), 16–32.

McGuire, W. J. (1969). An information-processing model of advertising effectiveness.

In H. L. Davis & A. J. Silk (Eds.), *Behavioral and management science in marketing* (pp. 156–180). New York: Ronald Press.

Menon, S., & Kahn, B. (2003). Corporate sponsorships of philanthropic activities: When do they impact perception of sponsor brand? *Journal of Consumer Psychology, 13* (3), 316–327.

Nan, X., & Heo, K. (2007). Consumer responses to corporate social responsibility initiatives: Examining the role of brand–cause fit in cause-related marketing. *Journal of Advertising, 36* (2), 63–74.

Nelson, D. L., Bennett, D. J., & Leibert, T. W. (1997). One step is not enough: Making better use of association norms to predict cued recall. *Memory and Cognition, 25* (6), 785–796.

Nelson, D. L., & McEvoy, C. L. (2002). How can the same type of prior knowledge both help and hinder recall? *Journal of Memory and Language, 46* (3), 652–663.

Nelson, D. L., McEvoy, C. L., & Pointer, L. (2003). Spreading activation or spooky action at a distance? *Journal of Experimental Psychology: Learning, Memory and Cognition, 29* (1), 42–52.

Nelson, D. L., McKinney, V. M., Gee, N. R., & Jacurza, G. A. (1998). Interpreting the influence of implicitly activated memories on recall and recognition. *Psychological Review, 105* (2), 299–324.

Nelson, D. L., Schreiber, T. A., & McEvoy, C. L. (1992). Processing implicit and explicit representations. *Psychological Review, 99* (2), 322–348.

Orenstein, S. (2003, February 1). The selling of breast cancer is corporate America's love affair with a disease that kills 40,000 women a year good marketing—or bad medicine? Retrieved September 2, 2010, from Business 2.0.

Pope, N. K., Voges, K. E., & Brown, M. R. (2004). The effect of provocation in the form of mild erotica on attitude to the ad and corporate image. *Journal of Advertising, 33* (1), 69–82.

Pracejus, J. W., & Olsen, G. D. (2004). The role of brand/cause fit in the effectiveness of cause-related marketing campaigns. *Journal of Business Research, 57*, 635–640.

Rifon, N. J., Choi, S. M., Trimble, C. S., & Li, H. (2004). Congruence effects in sponsorship: The mediating role of sponsor credibility and consumer attributions of sponsor motive. *Journal of Advertising, 33* (1), 29–42.

Ruth, J. A., & Simonin, B. L. (2003). Brought to you by Brand A and Brand B: Investigating multiple sponsors' influence on consumers' attitudes toward sponsored events. *Journal of Advertising, 32* (3), 19–30.

Samu, S., & Wymer, W. (2009). The effect of fit and dominance in cause marketing communications. *Journal of Business Research, 62*, 432–440.

Strahilevitz, M. (1999). The effect of product type and donation magnitude on willingness to pay more for a charity-linked brand. *Journal of Consumer Psychology, 8* (3), 215–241.

Strahilevitz, M., & Myers, J. G. (1998). Donations to charity as purchase incentives: How well they work may depend on what you are trying to sell. *Journal of Consumer Research, 24* (March), 434–446.

Vadarajan, P. R., & Menon, A. (1988). Cause-related marketing: A coalignment of marketing strategy and corporate philanthropy. *Journal of Marketing, 52* (July), 58–74.

Wakefield, K. L., Becker-Olsen, K., & Cornwell, T. B. (2007). I spy a sponsor: The effects of sponsorship level, prominence, relatedness, and cueing on recall accuracy. *Journal of Advertising, 36* (4), 61–74.

Additional Readings

Aaker, J., & Smith, A. (2010). *The dragonfly effect: Quick, effective, and powerful ways to use social media to drive social change.* San Francisco: Jossey-Bass.

Daw, J. (2004). *Cause marketing for nonprofits: Partners for purpose, passion and profits.* Hoboken, NJ: John Wiley & Sons.

Kotler, P., & Lee, N. (2004). *Corporate social responsibility: Doing the most good for your company and your cause.* New York: John Wiley & Sons.

Vadarajan, P. R., & Menon, A. (1988). Cause-related marketing: A coalignment of marketing strategy and corporate philanthropy. *Journal of Marketing, 52* (July), 58–74.

Part VII

Contexts of Advertising

Chapter 30

Ethics and Advertising Theory

Minette E. Drumwright

Advertising is not an easy context for ethics. Clients are demanding. Deadlines are never-ending. Short-term results are mandatory. Creative content must push the limits of what is familiar and acceptable to compete for attention. Media must interject itself into the crowded lives of message recipients, and ever-new devices provide recipients more and more opportunities to opt out of or otherwise control advertising messages. With the advent of new media, recipients, once passive, now create messages that can wreak havoc on corporate communication strategies. A common reaction is simply to avoid the topic of ethics. In such a context, having theory to guide practice and research is especially important, and yet there is little to none.

Citing from Nan and Faber (2004), Thorson and Rodgers assert in Chapter 1 of this text that advertising is a variable field in that it borrows theories from other fields and applies them to the unique context of advertising. Advertising ethics is no different. At times, some of the same theories from psychology and social psychology that are used to address other areas of advertising can be borrowed profitably to address advertising ethics (e.g., theories related to biases and heuristics in decision making). At other times, theories from areas that are not typically drawn on to study issues of advertising, such as philosophy and organizational studies, must be adopted to study issues of advertising ethics.

Because advertising ethics is a variable field, if we are going to borrow theory for it profitably, we must understand what advertising ethics is and what we know about it. If we look at theory and research in advertising generally—whether managerial or psychological[1]—such efforts focus primarily on questions of effectiveness. In contrast, ethics raises fundamentally different questions related not to what will be effective in advertising but to "what is right and good in the conduct of the advertising function. It is concerned with questions of what ought to be done, not just what legally must be done" (Cunningham, 1999, p. 500). Advertising ethics typically encompasses issues in two broad areas—(1) those related to "message ethics," the ethical issues involved in the creation and dissemination of the advertising message, and (2) those related to "business ethics," the ethics of the advertising business and the organizations that conduct or influence it (Drumwright & Murphy, 2009). As such, theory and research examining issues of advertising effectiveness often do not address issues of ethics directly.

To borrow theory profitably for advertising ethics, one must understand how ethics fits into Thorson and Rodgers' model presented in Figure 1.1 at the beginning of this text, and the role it plays in the advertising field more generally. Ethics is one of multiple broad contexts of the model, and, as such, it pervades every component of the model. In traditional media advertising, the onus of ethical decision making is primarily on three parties: (1) the creator of the advertising (e.g., the advertising practitioner), (2) the message sponsor or source (e.g., the client), and (3) the channel, the conveyor of the message (e.g., the mass media). The fact that the onus is on these three parties does not mean that ethical decision making necessarily occurs. For example, this trio has been referred to as the "unholy trinity" because of the tendency of ethics to sink to the lowest common denominator (Murphy, 1998), and some advertising practitioners have been characterized as having moral myopia, a distortion of moral vision that prevents ethical issues from coming clearly into focus (Drumwright & Murphy, 2004). As creators and disseminators of messages through new media, recipients are now subject to many of the same ethical issues related to messages as the traditional three parties. Individual decision makers are affected not only by their own character and values but also by the culture and climate of the organizations in which they work—the "advertising organizations" in the model. All parties are affected by the culture and trends of the larger society. For example, social norms regarding new media currently are relatively undeveloped as compared to traditional media, which has been described by advertising practitioners as a "Wild West" in which anything goes from an ethical perspective (Drumwright & Murphy, 2009).

The effects that advertising ethics is typically most concerned with are the ones that Thorson and Rodgers' Figure 1.1 refers to as the "unintended effects," i.e., the side effects of advertising that are potentially harmful, and these effects often are manifest at the societal level. As such, the ethical and social contexts of the model often overlap at the macro level when the unintended social consequences of advertising are examined through the lenses of ethical analysis. The ethical context also overlaps with the legal context of the model, and these two contexts must be differentiated. Laws are ultimately a reflection of ethical judgments, and we often make illegal what we consider most unethical (see also Chapter 31). A fundamental mistake, however, is to assume that because something is legal, it is ethical, or if something is unethical, it will be made illegal (Drumwright, 1993). Advertising law is a subset of the domain of advertising ethics. It does not and cannot encompass all of advertising ethics. Preston (1994) observed that for advertisers who believe that the law is sufficient, "ethics never really starts" (p. 128).

As the above discussion indicates, if one is to borrow theory profitably, advertising ethics must be examined at three different levels: (1) the micro level that focuses on the individual—individual consumers, individual advertising practitioners, individual ads or campaigns, and specific advertising practices, (2) the meso level of the organization or groups of organizations that conduct or influence the advertising business—whether agencies, clients, media, industry associations, or regulators, and (3) the macro level of advertising's effects on society or society's effects on advertising. We now turn to an examination of what we know about advertising ethics so that we can consider which theories have been or could be borrowed at each of the three levels—micro, meso, and macro. The theories discussed are not intended to be exhaustive but merely to highlight some possibilities for enriching advertising research and practice.

Micro-Level Theory

Examples of micro-level ethical issues. Should an advertising professional go online with various pseudonyms and post glowing testimonials that she has fabricated regarding her client's product? Should an advertising professional create a message with a claim that exaggerates the market research findings?

Because much of advertising research, in general, focuses on the micro level of the individual consumer, it is not surprising that there is more advertising ethics research at the micro level than at the other levels. Also not surprising is the fact that micro-level theory related to ethics draws heavily from psychology and social psychology as does advertising research in general. Two types of micro-level issues will be discussed: (1) individual characteristics, and (2) the decision-making process.

Individual Characteristics

Certainly, the personal characteristics of individual advertising practitioners will influence their ethical sensitivity and behavior. Two individual characteristics that appear to be particularly important are examined below—the individual's personal moral development and the individual's perception of the role of an advertising practitioner.

Personal Moral Development

The personal moral development of advertising practitioners no doubt will influence their ethical sensitivity, decision making, and behavior. Drawing theory from developmental psychology, Kohlberg's (1981, 1984) model of moral development can be helpful in assessing the maturity of advertising practitioners. Kohlberg asserted that individuals progress through three cognitive stages of moral development: (1) a pre-conventional stage in which individuals focus on their own needs and desires, (2) a conventional stage in which individuals focus on group-centered values and conforming to expectations, and (3) a principles stage in which individuals are concerned with upholding basic rights, values, and rules of society. These stages are likely to overlap, and, in reality, probably would be better represented as a continuum (Ferrell, 2005). A high degree of personal moral development is helpful in recognizing and analyzing an ethical issue, but many other factors also influence ethical behavior. For example, a high level of moral development may not be enough to prevent an individual from engaging in unethical behavior in an organizational context that encourages such behavior (Drumwright & Murphy, 2004, 2009). Findings regarding the moral development and level of ethical reasoning of advertising professionals are alarming. For example, advertising professionals demonstrated ethical reasoning at a lower stage of moral development than journalists (Cunningham, 2005; Wilkins & Coleman, 2005). Even more alarming, when advertising professionals were asked to consider ethical dilemmas in advertising, they demonstrated even lower levels of ethical reasoning than they had when responding to non-advertising dilemmas (Cunningham, 2005). Cunningham (2005) concluded that these findings may indicate that while advertising professionals are capable of reasoning at a higher stage of moral development, when asked to respond to an advertising issue, they suspend moral judgment to focus on the financial implications for them and their clients.

Perception of Role

Advertising practitioners who view ethical decision making as a part of their role as trusted business advisors are more likely to recognize relevant ethical issues and engage in ethical decision making (Drumwright & Murphy, 2004; Gentile, 2010). However, there is evidence that some advertising practitioners do not see ethical decision making as part of their professional roles (Drumwright & Murphy, 2004). Role theory from organizational studies can be helpful in understanding how individuals view their professional roles and responsibilities. A role has been defined as "shared normative expectations that prescribe and explain behaviors in a social system" (Biddle, 1986, p. 70) and as "the set of expected behaviors engaged in while performing job tasks" (Tubre & Collins, 2000, p. 156). Educators must also be cognizant of the influence that they have on advertising students' conceptions of their professional roles.

Ethical Decision-Making Process

Like other decision-making processes, ethical decision making often involves multiple steps that an individual must move through progressively. An advertising practitioner must, first, identify the ethical issue and then assess its moral intensity. If the moral intensity warrants proceeding to the analysis stage, the practitioner must evaluate the ethical issue and alternative responses. Finally, the ethical response must be implemented.

Identifying the Ethical Issue

Recognizing an ethical issue often is not an easy task for advertising practitioners, and they can succumb to rationalizations that prevent them from identifying or focusing on ethical issues (Drumwright & Murphy, 2004). From a theoretical perspective, these rationalizations are grounded in research in social psychology on biases and heuristics that can distort an individual's decision-making capability related to other areas of decision making in advertising (e.g., Kahneman & Tversky, 2000; Kahneman, Slovic, & Tversky, 1982; Nisbett & Ross, 1980). Observing that decision biases and heuristics had received scant attention in business and legal ethics, Prentice (2004) applied social psychology research to business ethics and identified a number of rationalizations that are potentially problematic with respect to business ethics—e.g., the self-interest bias, the social proof bias (everybody's doing it), the obedience to authority bias (the boss told me to do it). Gentile (2010) asserted that prompting business practitioners to identify these rationalizations is the first step in freeing them to put their values into action. In short, theory related to biases and heuristics, which has been applied to decision making with respect to advertising effectiveness, can also enrich an understanding of decision making related to advertising ethics.

Assessing the Moral Intensity of an Ethical Issue

After advertising practitioners recognize an ethical issue, they must determine its moral intensity to decide whether to proceed with the decision-making process. That is, the ethical issue itself must be assessed to determine its importance and urgency. If an ethical issue has a low level of moral intensity, advertising practitioners are likely to ignore it. Drawing on the arguments of moral philosophers, Jones (1991) introduced a model that specifies the characteristics that determine the moral intensity of an ethical issue: the magnitude of the consequences (i.e., the sum of the harms or benefits to various parties), the social consensus (i.e., the social agreement that the proposed action is good or evil), the probability of effect (i.e., the joint function of the probability that the proposed action will take place and that it will actually cause harm), the temporal effect (i.e., the length of time between the proposed action and the onset of its consequences), proximity (i.e., the feeling of nearness to the victims or beneficiaries), and the concentration of effect (i.e., an inverse function of the number of people affected by an act of a given magnitude). Understanding the moral intensity that advertising practitioners perceive helps one to predict which issues they are likely to be aware of or evaluate from a moral perspective.

Moral Evaluation of the Ethical Issue and Alternative Responses

If the moral intensity of an issue is sufficient, advertising practitioners or even message recipients engage in moral evaluation of the issue and their alternatives for responding to it. Some scholars have asserted that people need to develop moral imagination (Drumwright & Murphy, 2004; Werhane, 1999). Moral imagination involves thinking resourcefully—"outside the box"—and envisioning moral alternatives that others do not. Drumwright and Murphy (2004) found that advertising practitioners with moral imagination could reconceptualize a problem and find inventive solutions that enabled them to be both successful and ethical.

Once the issue and alternatives have been identified, theory from philosophy can be adopted to identify the rules or principles that individuals use to determine what is right and wrong. For example, models of ethical decision making in marketing have posited that message recipients use one of two approaches: (1) teleological approaches such as utilitarianism, in which right and wrong is determined based on an evaluation of consequences or outcomes, or (2) deontological approaches in which determining right and wrong is based on dimensions other than outcomes, such as intentions, duties, and the nature of the act itself (e.g., Hunt & Vitell, 1986, 2006). Of course, there is a difference in determining how individuals make moral evaluations and what is actually right and wrong. The latter issues are often left to moral philosophers and theologians. Research on how individuals make moral evaluations has been criticized for focusing too much on positive (i.e., descriptive) rather than normative (i.e., prescriptive) approaches (Laczniak & Murphy, 1993). That is, researchers focus on describing how people actually make ethical decisions (i.e., descriptive ethics) rather than engaging the tougher questions related to how people *should* make ethical decisions and what actually is right and wrong (i.e., normative ethics). While it is helpful to understand which philosophical approach individuals use, there is no universal agreement on the correct moral philosophy to use, and individuals tend to use different philosophical approaches in different situations (Ferrell, 2005). For example, Fraedrich and Ferrell (1992) found only 15% of their sample applied the same moral philosophy across both work and non-work situations. They speculated that the cognitive moral development issues that relate to home and family may not be the most significant factors in resolving ethical issues at work. For example, the values of an individual's work group or the pressure to meet economic goals may be a more important determinant of behavior than the individual's approach to ethical reasoning.

Implementing Ethical Decisions

Once advertising practitioners determine what the ethical alternative is in a given situation, they must implement it. Implementation is particularly important because even individuals who have reached a high stage of personal moral development and have identified the ethical response can make bad ethical decisions if they do not know how to act on their values. "Giving Voice to Values" (GVV) is a business ethics research and curriculum development initiative designed to enable individuals to develop the skills they need to put their values into action (Gentile, 2010). While it draws on multiple bodies of theory, it highlights the concept of scripts from social psychology theory (e.g., Ableson, 1981). Through GVV, individuals develop ethics-related scripts, which are cognitive structures that when activated help them organize and understand events related to ethics. In building these scripts, they practice articulating arguments and rehearsing action plans related to giving voice to their values and acting upon them (Gentile, 2010). People who have built scripts are those who are likely to have the courage to put their scripts into action in difficult circumstances (e.g., London, 1970).

Finally, one scholar has blended the ethical decision-making process with moral character. Rest's model (1984, p. 24) identifies the four components that determine moral behavior as the following: "1) moral sensitivity (interpreting the situation), 2) moral judgment (judging which actions are right and wrong), 3) moral motivation (prioritizing values relative to other values), and 4) moral character (having courage, persisting, overcoming distractions, implementing skills)." Drumwright and Murphy (2004) observed that the advertising professionals in their study who made responsible, ethical decisions appeared to have mastered all of the aspects of Rest's model. Of course, there are many other potential applications of theory to the micro level of individual decision making, but we turn now to illustrate how theory can enhance practice and research at the meso level.

Meso-Level Theory

Example of a meso-level ethical issue: Should an advertising agency encourage its media planners to pad their billable hours when the client is under budget?

Some leaders assume that if individuals (the micro level) have a high level of moral development and can make ethical decisions, then organizations (the meso level) will not have ethical problems, but this is far from the case (Ferrell, 2005). Organizations can impede ethical behavior through socialization processes, environmental influences, and hierarchical relationships (Smith & Carroll, 1984).

The difference in the focus on ethics at the micro and meso levels has been explained as the "bad apple vs. bad barrel" dichotomy (Edwards, Webb, Chappell, & Gentile, forthcoming). The "bad apple" approach puts emphasis on the ethical character of individuals and their personal decision making, while the "bad barrel" approach takes a structural view that emphasizes organizational environments and the characteristics that can contribute to unethical practices.

Advertising ethics research has been characterized having a "micro-macro" focus that largely neglects the meso level (Drumwright, 2007). Neglect of the meso level is particularly problematic not only because of the influence of organizations on the behavior of individual advertising practitioners (Drumwright & Murphy, 2004; Keith, Pettijohn, & Burnett, 2003), but also because solutions to some macro-level ethical problems to which advertising contributes require the collaborative efforts of organizations or groups of organizations (Brenkert, 1998; J. D. Bishop, 2000).

To borrow theory profitably for the meso level, factors that contribute to a "bad barrel" must be understood so that leaders can proactively work to create a "good barrel." Not surprisingly, the meso level draws theory from management, organizational studies, and sociology. Below, several organizational factors are discussed: organizational environments, the influence of co-workers and supervisors, and organizational myopia.

Organizational Environment

Philosophers have long observed that virtue is best lived out in community and that it is difficult to act virtuously if one is surrounded by vice (Aristotle, 1962; Woodruff, 2001). Woodruff (2001) defined virtue ethics as dealing with the strengths that people develop in community and specified that virtues have the greatest lasting power in close-knit communities. Two bodies of organizational theory that are particularly relevant to developing ethical environments in advertising organizations are organizational culture and ethical climate.

Organizational culture is the "shared set of values, beliefs, goals, norms and ways to solve problems" (Ferrell, 2005, p. 11). It establishes the formal and informal values, norms, and assumptions that guide behavior. An organization's ethical climate consists of "a combination of its members' perceptions of the ethical values and behaviors supported and practiced by organizational members" (Schwepker & Good, 2007, p. 329). It focuses on issues of right and wrong, and it has been described as the organization's character or conscience. It is influenced by codes of conduct, ethics policies, and top management's behavior related to ethics (Ferrell, Johnston, & Ferrell, 2007). A variety of other factors, such as incentive systems, leadership styles, and group dynamics, also contribute to organizational culture and ethical climate.

Influence of Supervisors and Coworkers

The supervisors, coworkers, and clients of advertising practitioners are likely to influence their ethical decision making and behavior. Indeed, research confirms that coworkers and supervisors have more impact on an employee's daily decisions than any other factor (Ferrell & Gresham, 1985). As such, their personal ethical values, their moral development, and their actions with respect to ethics are likely to have a profound influence. A number of theories of group influence are germane but of particular interest is social network theory, which emphasizes the relationships among individuals or collective groups (Seevers, Skinner, & Kelley, 2007). Social networks are defined by various types of interpersonal relationships such as friendship, communication, sentiment, advice giving, and influence (Bristor & Ryan, 1987). Understanding social networks and their influence on ethical behavior is of paramount importance.

Organizational Myopia

We move from issues related to "bad barrels" to issues related to the ethical and social impact of an advertising organization on those beyond its immediate constituencies. Advertising agencies and their clients, like people, can suffer from a myopia that makes it difficult for ethical issues to come clearly into focus. Smith et al. (2010) asserted that many companies have a new type of marketing myopia in which they focus on customers to the exclusion of other important stakeholders. They drew on a body of theory in management referred to as stakeholder management (Carroll, 2008; Freeman, 1984), which is based on the premise that companies have obligations to stakeholders who are affected by or can affect what a company does. Smith et al. (2010) urged greater attention to stakeholders so that companies can better recognize their ethical and social responsibilities. For a discussion of a stakeholder orientation in marketing and its relationship to distributive justice, see Ferrell and Ferrell (2008). The emphasis on stakeholders as a meso-level concern of advertising organizations introduces a discussion that can broaden to the macro level of advertising's impact on society.

Macro-Level Theory

Examples of a macro-level ethical issues. Does advertising junk food to young children contribute to childhood obesity? Does using ultra-thin models in fashion advertising contribute to unhealthy conceptions of beauty among young girls?

Macro-level criticisms of advertising focus on the aggregate effects of advertising. They are sometimes referred to as "advertising's unintended social consequences, the social by-products of the exhortations to 'buy products'" (Pollay, 1986, p. 19). They are a major part of the social and economic criticisms focused on the marketing system (Wilke & Moore, 1999).[2] Many of them fall into three categories: (1) encouraging excessive materialism, (2) creating, or at least reinforcing, problematic stereotypes, and (3) creating false values and the resulting problematic behavior (Drumwright, 2007). Although macro-level criticisms of advertising have a long history and cut across academic disciplines (e.g., F. P. Bishop, 1949; Galbraith, 1958, 1967; Leiser, 1979; Pontifical Council for Social Communication, 1997; Waide, 1987), there is little empirical work on macro-level concerns, let alone use of theory. Scholarship consists mostly of commentary and debate,[3] which typically raises a variety of far-reaching societal concerns rather than focusing on answering a single question. One reason there is little empirical research on macro-level criticisms of advertising is that they are difficult to research. As Pollay observed, "our research paradigms are at quite a loss in dealing with the fundamental questions in the macro market's evolution" (1986, p. 32). For example, since the alleged macro-level effects occur over time and are not typically directly observable, longitudinal effects must be captured, and appropriate measures are difficult and perplexing. But, beyond that, there is the daunting difficulty of researching environmental issues from within the environment in which all individuals are already "treated." Because of the difficulty of studying macro-level issues of advertising, Pollay (1986) called for greatly expanded research approaches that draw from other disciplines such as history, literary criticism, sociology, and anthropology. A few possibilities for borrowing macro-level theory from other disciplines are highlighted below.

Agenda Setting

Pollay (1986) typified writings by scholars from fields other than advertising and marketing as "a major indictment of advertising" (p. 31), which he characterized as "shocking" in its "veritable absence of perceived positive influence" of advertising (p. 19).[4] Despite these indictments, advertising practitioners have difficulty taking macro-level criticisms seriously. Drumwright and Murphy (2004) found that the advertising practitioners in their sample were least likely to recognize ethical issues at the macro level. Common defenses among practitioners and academics alike are that advertising does not create values—it merely reflects them—and that the real culprits are other parties—e.g., peers, parents, regulators, media (Lantos, 1987). When advertising practitioners do recognize macro-level issues of advertising (e.g., advertising's contribution to childhood obesity), the issues have become prominent on the public agenda. As such, agenda setting theory can provide guidance. Agenda setting theory deals primarily with the process by which issues get the attention of the public and the policy makers and how those issues proceed to make it onto the political decision agenda. Given the limitations of time, money, and other resources, getting onto the public agenda is a very difficult process, and many worthy issues never make it. In a seminal book on agenda setting, Kingdon (1984) provided a number of insights regarding how issues get on the political decision agenda. For example, when problems appear to have solutions, they are more likely to get on the agenda. To get on the agenda, coalition building is crucial, and it must often occur among unnatural allies. The media can play a powerful role by repeatedly drawing attention to a problem, and timing matters because windows of opportunity open and close. Since one of the major ways to get advertising practitioners to take responsibility for advertising's unintended effects is to get the issue on the political decision agenda, advertising scholars would profit from understanding agenda setting theory. Such an understanding will also be helpful to advertising practitioners promoting social causes such as anti-drinking and driving or healthy lifestyle behaviors.

Diffusion of Innovation

Advertising practitioners are also more likely to give attention to issues that are topics of widespread public concern even if they have not made it onto the political decision agenda. Here, theory related to diffusion of innovation is relevant. Diffusion of innovation theory wrestles with the manner in which a new idea spreads from its originator or source to its users or adopters (Rogers, 1962). It is, in essence, "the process of human interaction in which one person communicates a new idea to another person" (Rogers, 1962, p. 13). Diffusion theory demonstrates that targeting opinion leaders, prompting them to adopt early, and motivating them to influence others is central to diffusion. Identifying active rejecters of the innovation and attempting to neutralize their negative impact on others are important as well. Theory also suggests that certain key characteristics of a new idea influence its adoption in important ways: (1) its relative advantage over other competing ideas, (2) its compatibility with the existing culture and beliefs, (3) its complexity or the difficulty involved in understanding it, (4) its divisibility or the ability to try it on a limited basis, and (5) its communicability or how readily it can be observed and communicated. Irrespective of one's normative position, understanding how concern about an unintended effect of advertising diffuses through society can be informative because advertising practitioners are more likely to pay attention and take it seriously when there is widespread public concern.

Expanded Research Approaches

In keeping with Pollay's (1986) suggestions, some advertising scholars are drawing on a greatly expanded set of research approaches, such as history, literary criticism, feminist theory, visual studies, and philosophy. A few examples are provided by way of illustration. Ahuvia (1998, p. 143) advocated and demonstrated a "doubly integrated" approach to social criticism that combines literary analysis with the use of empirical data and also integrates the system by which ads are produced with the way they are comprehended. Schroeder and Borgerson (1998) used an interpretive method drawing from social psychology, feminist theory, and art history to analyze contemporary images of gender. Borgerson and Schroeder (2002) examined visual representations in ads from an interdisciplinary perspective that drew on ethics, visual studies, and critical race theory. Ferrell and Ferrell (2008) drew on the normative philosophy of distributive justice in creating a macromarketing ethics framework. They asserted that justice as it is applied to marketing ethics involves evaluations of fairness and a willingness to deal with the perceived injustices of others. The possibilities for expanding the theory base at the macro level are many.

Comprehensive Models of Marketing Ethics

We have examined theory and research related to advertising ethics at each of three levels—micro, meso, and macro. Several models of ethical decision making in marketing bring together all three levels in a single framework (e.g., Ferrell & Gresham, 1985; Hunt & Vitell, 1986; Ferrell, Gresham, & Fraedrich, 1989; Ferrell, 2005; Hunt & Vitell, 2006). These models are rich and detailed and move toward a comprehensive framework. Although they are from the marketing ethics literature, they are general enough to apply to any professional or managerial context, including advertising. It is encouraging that marketing ethics has advanced from descriptive studies of issues to positive decision-making models.

Conclusions

For those who work in the field of advertising ethics, the paucity of advertising theory is troubling. However, as this chapter demonstrates, theory can be borrowed profitably from a variety of sources—those fields from which advertising typically draws, such as psychology and social psychology, and those from which it does not routinely borrow from, such as organizational studies, political science, and philosophy. The burden for those who work in advertising is to modify and adapt the theories to the unique context of advertising. Such adaptation is particularly challenging in a field that is changing as rapidly and as radically as advertising.

Acknowledgment

The author thanks O. C. Ferrell and H. W. Perry, Jr. for their very helpful comments that helped shape this chapter.

Notes

1. Rodgers, Thorson, and Jin (2009) observed that since its beginnings in the late nineteenth century, advertising theory has taken two basic forms—managerial or psychological. Managerial theories provide managers with guidance regarding the stages that a consumer might go through between exposure to the ad and buying the product, while psychological theories focus on in-depth examinations of different kinds of memory.
2. Four of the eight classic social and economic debates concerning the marketing system that Wilke and Moore (1999, p. 215) identified were focused on advertising.
3. See the classic debate between Pollay (1986) and Holbrook (1987).
4. Pollay (1986) provides an excellent review of the criticisms of advertising by scholars outside marketing and advertising.

References

Abelson, R. P. (1981). Psychological status of the script concept. *American Psychologist*, *36* (7), 715–725.

Ahuvia, A. D. (1998). Social criticism of advertising: On the role of literary theory and the use of data. *Journal of Advertising*, *27* (1), 143–163.

Aristotle (1962). *Nicomachean ethics*. New York: Macmillan.

Biddle, B. J. (1986). Recent developments in role theory. *Annual Review of Sociology*, *12*, 67–92.

Bishop, F. P. (1949). *The ethics of advertising*. London: Robert Hale Limited.

Bishop, J. D. (2000). Is self identity image advertising ethical? *Business Ethics Quarterly*, *10* (2), 371–398.

Borgerson, J. L., & Schroeder, J. E. (2002). Ethical issues of global marketing: Avoiding bad faith in visual representation. *European Journal of Marketing*, *36* (5/6), 570–594.

Brenkert, G. G. (1998). Marketing to inner-city blacks: Powermaster and moral responsibility. *Business Ethics Quarterly, 8* (1), 1–18.

Bristor, J. H., & Ryan, M. J. (1987). The buying center is dead, long live the buying center. In M. Wallendorf & P. Anderson (Eds.), *Advances in consumer research* (pp. 255–258). Provo, UT: Association for Consumer Research.

Carroll, A. B. (2008). A history of corporate social responsibility: Concepts and practices. In A. Crane, A. McWilliams, D. Matten, J. Moon, & D. S. Siegel (Eds.), *The Oxford handbook of corporate social responsibility* (pp. 19–46). Oxford, UK: Oxford University Press.

Cunningham, P. H. (1999). Ethics of advertising. In J. P. Jones (Ed.), *The advertising business* (pp. 499–513). London: Sage.

Cunningham, A. (2005). Advertising practitioners respond: The news is not good. In L. Wilkins & R. Coleman (Eds.), *The moral media: How journalists reason about ethics* (pp. 114–124). Mahwah, NJ: Lawrence Erlbaum.

Drumwright, M. E. (1993). Ethical issues in advertising and sales promotion. In N. C. Smith & J. A. Quelch (Eds.), *Ethics in marketing* (pp. 607–625). Homewood, IL: Irwin.

Drumwright, M. E. (2007). Advertising ethics: A multi-level theory approach. In G. J. Tellis & T. Ambler (Eds.), *The handbook of advertising* (pp. 398–415). London: Sage.

Drumwright, M. E., & Murphy, P. E. (2004). How advertising practitioners view ethics: Moral muteness, moral myopia, and moral imagination. *Journal of Advertising, 33* (2), 7–24.

Drumwright, M. E., & Murphy, P. E. (2009). The current state of advertising ethics: Industry and academic perspectives. *Journal of Advertising, 38* (1), 83–107.

Edwards, M. G., Webb, D. A., Chappell, S., & Gentile, M. C. (forthcoming). Giving voice to values: A new perspective on ethics in globalized organizational environments. In C. Wankel & S. Malleck (Eds.), *Globalization and ethics.* Charlotte, NC: Information Age Publishing.

Ferrell, O. C. (2005). A framework for understanding organizational ethics. In R. A. Peterson & O. C. Ferrell (Eds.), *Business ethics: New challenges for business schools and corporate leaders* (pp. 3–17). Armonk, NY: M.E. Sharpe.

Ferrell, O. C., & Ferrell, L. (2008). A macromarketing ethics framework: Stakeholder orientation and distributive justice. *Journal of Macromarketing, 28* (1), 24–32.

Ferrell, O. C., & Gresham, L. G. (1985). A contingency framework for understanding ethical decision making in marketing. *Journal of Marketing, 49* (3), 87–96.

Ferrell, O. C., Gresham, L. G., & Fraedrich, J. (1989). A synthesis of ethical decision models for marketing. *Journal of Macromarketing, 9* (2), 55–64.

Ferrell, O. C., Johnston, M. W., & Ferrell, L. (2007). A framework for personal selling and sales management ethical decision making. *Journal of Personal Selling and Sales Management, 27* (4), 291–299.

Fraedrich, J. P., & Ferrell, O. C. (1992). Cognitive consistency of marketing managers in ethical situations. *Journal of the Academy of Marketing Science, 20* (3), 245–252.

Freeman, R. E. (1984). *Strategic management: A stakeholder approach.* Boston: Pitman.

Galbraith, J. K. (1958). *The affluent society*. Boston: Houghton Mifflin.

Galbraith, J. K. (1967). *The new industrial state*. Boston: Houghton Mifflin.

Gentile, M. C. (2010). *Giving voice to values: How to speak your mind when you know what's right*. New Haven, CT: Yale University Press.

Holbrook, M. B. (1987). Mirror, mirror on the wall, what's unfair in the reflections on advertising? *Journal of Marketing, 51* (3), 95–103.

Hunt, S. D., & Vitell, S. (1986). A general theory of marketing ethics. *Journal of Macromarketing, 6* (1), 5–16.

Hunt, S. D., & Vitell, S. J. (2006). The general theory of marketing ethics: A revision and three questions. *Journal of Macromarketing, 26* (2), 143–153.

Jones, T. M. (1991). Ethical decision making by individuals in organizations: An issue-contingent model. *Academy of Management Review, 16* (2), 366–395.

Kahneman, D., Slovic, P., & Tversky, A. (1982). *Judgment under uncertainty: Heuristics and biases*. Cambridge, UK: Cambridge University Press.

Kahneman, D., & Tversky, A. (2000). *Choices, values, and frames*. Cambridge, UK: Cambridge University Press.

Keith, N. K., Pettijohn, C. E., & Burnett, M. S. (2003). An empirical evaluation of the effect of peer and managerial ethical behaviors and the ethical predispositions of prospective advertising employees. *Journal of Business Ethics, 48* (3), 251–265.

Kingdon, J. W. (1984). *Agendas, alternatives, and public policies*. Boston: Little, Brown and Company.

Kohlberg, L. (1981). *The philosophy of moral development: Moral stages and the idea of justice*. Cambridge, MA: Harper & Row.

Kohlberg, L. (1984). *The psychology of moral development: The nature and validity of moral stages*. San Francisco: Harper & Row.

Laczniak, G. R., & Murphy, P. E. (1993). *Ethical marketing decisions: The higher road*. Needham Heights, MA: Allyn and Bacon.

Lantos, G. P. (1987). Advertising: Looking glass or molder of masses? *Journal of Public Policy and Marketing, 6* (1), 104–128.

Leiser, B. (1979). Beyond fraud and deception: The moral uses of advertising. In T. Donaldson & P. Werhane (Eds.), *Ethical issues in business* (pp. 59–66). Englewood Cliffs, NJ: Prentice-Hall.

London, P. (1970). The rescuers: Motivational hypotheses about Christians who saved Jews from the Nazis. In J. Macaulay & L. Berkowitz (Eds.), *Altruism and helping behavior: Social psychological studies of some antecedents and consequences* (pp. 241–268). New York: Academic Press.

Murphy, P. E. (1998). *Eighty exemplary ethics statements*. Notre Dame, IN: University of Notre Dame Press.

Nan, X., & Faber, R. J. (2004). Advertising theory: Reconceptualizing the building blocks. *Marketing Theory, 4* (1/2), 7–30.

Nisbett, R. E., & Ross, L. (1980). *Human inference: Strategies and shortcomings of social justice*. Englewood Cliffs, NY: Prentice-Hall.

Pollay, R. W. (1986). The distorted mirror: Reflections on the unintended consequences of advertising. *Journal of Marketing, 50* (2), 18–36.

Pontifical Council for Social Communications (1997). *Ethics in advertising*. Vatican City: Vatican Documents.

Prentice, R. (2004). Teaching ethics: Biases and heuristics. *Journal of Business Ethics Education, 1* (1), 57–74.

Preston, I. (1994). *The tangled web they weave*. Madison: University of Wisconsin Press.

Rest, J. R. (1984). The consequences of morality. In W. Kurtines & J. Gewirtz (Eds.), *Morality, moral behavior, and moral development* (pp. 24–38). New York: Wiley.

Rogers, E. M. (1962). *Diffusion of innovations*. New York: Free Press.

Rodgers, S., Thorson, E., & Jin, Y. (2009). Social science theories of traditional and internet advertising. In D. W. Stack & M. B. Salwen (Eds.), *An integrated approach to communication theory and research* (2nd ed., pp. 198–219). New York: Routledge.

Schroeder, J. E., & Borgerson, J. L. (1998). Marketing images of gender: A visual analysis. *Consumption, Markets, and Culture, 2* (2), 161–201.

Schwepker, C. H., Jr., & Good, D. J. (2007). Sales management's influence on employment and training in developing an ethical sales force. *Journal of Personal Selling and Sales Management, 27* (4), 326–341.

Seevers, M. T., Skinner, S. J., & Kelley, S. W. (2007). A social network perspective on sales force ethics. *Journal of Personal Selling and Sales Management, 27* (4), 343–355.

Smith, H. R., & Carroll, A. B. (1984). Organizational ethics: A stacked deck. *Journal of Business Ethics, 3*, 95–100.

Smith, N. C., Drumwright, M. E., & Gentile, M. C. (2010). The new marketing myopia. *Journal of Public Policy and Marketing, 29* (1), 4–11.

Tubre, T. C., & Collins, J. M. (2000). Jackson and Schuler (1985) revisited: A meta-analysis of the relationships between role ambiguity, role conflict, and job performance. *Journal of Management, 26* (1), 155–169.

Waide, J. (1987). The making of self and world in advertising. *Journal of Business Ethics, 6* (2), 73–79.

Werhane, P. L. (1999). *Moral imagination and management decision-making*. New York: Oxford University Press.

Wilke, W. L., & Moore, E. S. (1999). Marketing's contributions to society. *Journal of Marketing, 63* (4), 198–218.

Wilkins, L., & Coleman, R. (2005). *The moral media: How journalists reason about ethics*. Mahwah, NJ: Lawrence Erlbaum.

Woodruff, P. (2001). *Reverence: Renewing a forgotten virtue*. New York: Oxford University Press.

Additional Readings

Drumwright, M. E., & Murphy, P. E. (2004). How advertising practitioners view ethics: Moral muteness, moral myopia, and moral imagination. *Journal of Advertising, 33* (2), 7–24.

Ferrell, O. C., & Ferrell, L. (2008). A macromarketing ethics framework: Stakeholder orientation and distributive justice. *Journal of Macromarketing, 28* (1), 24–32.

Gentile, M. C. (2010). *Giving voice to values: How to speak your mind when you know what's right*. New Haven, CT: Yale University Press.

Hunt, S. D., & Vitell, S. J. (2006). The general theory of marketing ethics: A revision and three questions. *Journal of Macromarketing, 26* (2), 143–153.

Jones, T. M. (1991). Ethical decision making by individuals in organizations: An issue-contingent model. *Academy of Management Review, 16* (2), 366–395

Chapter 31

Theory and Law

Jef I. Richards

Advertising, like all industries, operates within a legal context. Thorson and Rodgers' Figure 1.1 in Chapter 1 notes the importance of this context, given the potential effects of advertising on society. Of course, no business is immune from at least some regulatory concerns, such as licenses, permits, hiring restrictions, and taxation. But in addition to the normal issues that affect virtually every other business, advertising is subject to its own unique set of issues, like deception, unfairness to children, promoting unhealthy products, etc.

In fact, each advertised product could carry its own unique regulatory concerns. Dog food, for example, is subject to restrictions by the Department of Agriculture, the Food and Drug Administration (FDA), as well as the Federal Trade Commission (FTC) at the federal level, in addition to several state agencies. It is subject to several specific laws like the Federal Food, Drug and Cosmetic Acts, the FTC Act, the Fair Packaging and Labeling Act, and many more. And, of course, media are subject to varied regulations as well so putting that dog food ad on television may be quite different from putting it on a billboard. Simply put, advertising is a heavily regulated industry. Indeed, it is the most regulated of all the communication industries.

Given that reality, any attempt at understanding advertising or how it works can be foolhardy if its legal environment is ignored. Imagine, for example, an advertising agency's researchers conducting a study for a client, resulting in a list of recommendations for that client, and those recommendations turn out to be illegal.

Researchers ignore the legal context at their own peril. As we consider the role of theory in advertising in this chapter, it is equally foolish to forget the law's role in theory.

Legal Theory

A few years ago I submitted a manuscript to a journal, and it was rejected. One reviewer clearly hated the paper, primarily because it "was not theory-driven."

Of course, every graduate student in marketing or communication quickly learns that research should be theory-driven. But the reviewer was wrong. The problem appeared to be that the reviewer didn't recognize this particular genus of theory: *legal* theory.

Too often researchers trained in one field or subfield learn a set of theories as part of their training, and too often they subsequently confine their understanding of what constitutes a theory to only that particular set and anything resembling that set. In advertising we often research consumer behavior, so we learn about bullet theory, limited effects theories, uses and gratifications theory, cultivation theory, spiral of silence theory, social learning theory, and so forth. In other words, most of our theories tend to be derived from psychology or social psychology. They are theories about how consumers' minds work, or how groups of consumers behave. But these are not the only "theory" concerns if we are to fully understand advertising. These are merely subcategories of a broader theory type we might call "consumer behavior" theories. Legal theory is a wholly different type, with its own subcategories.

Probably every field has its set of theories. Economists study advertising, principally trying to determine whether it is a worthwhile investment. Economics has its own type of theories, but its theories are about the behavior of money rather than the behavior of consumers' minds. Of course, there are many fields that generally have nothing to do with advertising, like physics and biology. They, too, have their theories. These are theories about the behavior of physical elements or the behavior of organic matter. Law is no different; but its theories concern, in effect, the behavior of judges, legislators, and more.

A good theory is predictive. The reason such a premium is put on theory-driven research is because theories can improve our ability to predict some effect or outcome. For advertising, consumer behavior theories hold the promise of predicting which advertisement will result in the most desirable consumer response; usually purchase behavior, i.e., sales. A theory might tell us, for instance, that changing a background color from blue to yellow should increase sales. And legal theory is no different, except that it generally is designed to predict the effect of a law. Figure 31.1 shows that legal theory is important in understanding *how law affects advertising*, just as behavioral and many other theories are needed to understand *how advertising affects the consumer*, the marketplace, and our society as a whole.

To appreciate the nature of legal theory, it is important to first recognize that in law—and here I confine myself to American jurisprudence, since there are variations from country to country—the courts tend to draw a sharp line between law and fact (Lawson, 1992). This is a convention that is used in allocating decision-making authority, helping to simplify an otherwise complicated judicial system.

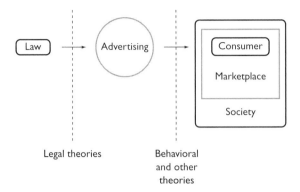

Figure 31.1 The Roles of Theories.

Lawson (1992) illustrates this distinction by the claim that "A has broken B's window," as compared to "A has broken B's law." The former is a question of fact while the latter is a question of law. Facts are proven by empirical evidence, such as finding A's shoe inside B's house with broken glass around it. Either a jury or judge can decide whether this constitutes sufficient "proof" of the allegation. The legal process still has rules regarding proof of facts, of course, assigning the responsibility for which party has the burden of proving a particular fact and instructing the judge or jury (the "fact finder") to meet some threshold standard like "beyond a reasonable doubt." Aside from those basic rules, though, the ultimate determination of what is or is not a fact remains totally up to the fact finder.

But "law" is more complex, arguably more important, and generally is assumed to take a higher level of expertise to assess; so while a jury can decide questions of fact, no jury of lay people is permitted to decide questions of law. As a consequence, appeals courts and even the Supreme Court will normally defer to the judgment of the original (trial) court on questions of fact. It is presumed that the jury or judge made the right decision as to facts. The original evidence, such as photographs of that broken glass, are not even shown to judges during appeals, because those judges confine themselves to deciding just questions of law. If the lower court says A broke the window, the appeals court will not question that finding. Whether breaking that window was a violation of the law, though, is fair game for the appeal.

Note that I asserted law is arguably more important than fact. This is because a set of facts (who hit whom, what time it happened, etc.) generally is confined to a single event or situation, while a law almost never is applicable only to one case. Therefore, when questions of law are decided those decisions must take into account not only the present fact situation but also any imaginable set of facts (Friedman, 1992).

A law that prohibits speeding, for example, is not intended just to prohibit driving 80 mph in a 55 mph speed zone, it also is designed to stop someone from driving 35 mph in a 30 mph zone. The facts vary, but the same law is used in both situations. It is easy to see that if a judge in the first situation declared the speeding law means you cannot drive 25 mph above the speed limit, this could give the driver in the second situation *carte blanche* to go fast. Determinations of law, then, must be made with more than the current set of facts in mind, which adds to the complexity.

A legal theory, then, is a proposition about how the law *should* be interpreted. It is a theory about how the law should work, taking into consideration other fact situations, what the law was designed to do, what other laws might conflict with it, and so forth. This is far from being a simple proposition, and much has been written about how a judge should decide which theory is the best (e.g., Friedman, 1992; Tamanaha, 1996). And while the system by which laws are interpreted has been systematized, and in some ways seemingly deified, an entire "legal positivism" movement and Critical Legal Studies have arisen that question the way decisions of law are made (Dworkin, 1986; Fuller, 1988; Gardner, 2001).

Every lawyer representing a client in adjudication really must develop a theory about how the law will apply in that particular situation. Some theories are simple and obvious, while others are more complex and/or creative.

Adjudication, in essence, is about competing theories: one theory for the plaintiff versus a completely different theory for the defendant. Lawyers advocate a theory that favors their client, and if that lawyer is able to convince the judge that his/her theory makes the most sense, that client will win the case.

The plaintiff's lawyer might theorize, for example, that the law is broken if A played any role at all in breaking the window, while the defendant's lawyer might theorize that A must "intend" to break the window for the law to be broken. It is up to the judge, then, to determine whether the law requires such intent.

Alternatively, the defendant's lawyer might theorize that the law prohibiting someone from breaking a window is somehow a violation of a superior law, like the U.S. Constitution, in which case the judge would need to decide whether the window-breaking law is valid.

Put another way, where behavioral advertising theories deal in probabilities of how *consumers* will behave, legal theories generally deal in probabilities of how *judges and courts* will behave. A "precedent" is a court decision about what a law means, and subsequent courts are supposed to follow applicable precedents. It is considered "settled law" that no longer is subject to competing theories. Therefore, the existence of a precedent that supports one particular theory increases the probability that a judge will adopt that particular theory just as the existence of a research study supporting a behavioral theory can be seen as increasing the probability that theory is correct.

While most legal theories are tied to a specific case and a specific set of facts, broader discussions about the law and how it should be interpreted also entail legal theories. These are topic-specific theories. An article arguing laws regulating tobacco advertising are inherently unconstitutional (e.g., Richards, 1996) would need to present a legal argument—a legal theory—to advance that proposition. In those situations the theory might be used to sway legislators or regulators instead of judges.

Even broader applications of legal theory can be found in the philosophy of law, delving into topics like the difference between law and justice and the relationship of law to morality (Dworkin, 1986). These debates extend back centuries.

In spite of the distinction I have drawn, fact and theory are not wholly unrelated. Different theories frequently require proof of entirely different facts, just as different behavioral theories may require different questions on a survey or different stimuli in an experiment. One legal theory could propose that the law is broken if A played any role in breaking the window. In that situation the only facts that need to be proved are (1) that the window was broken and (2) that A was involved. But a theory that the law is broken only if A is the person *most* responsible for breaking the window would require additional facts to be proved, showing (3) whether any other persons were involved and (4) whether A was more at fault than those other persons.

It is at this point legal theories and behavioral theories often cross paths, because legal theories about advertising can dictate what research is legally relevant. Hence, this can affect what behavioral theories are important in a legal setting. Too often researchers trained in the behavioral sciences engage in research intended to affect regulation or provide some legal evidence, but their research provides evidence of facts that are irrelevant to the legal process (Richards, 2009). That can be, and often is, a reflection of them not knowing or understanding the legal theories, and what those theories demand as proof.

Examples of legal theories can be found in most published court decisions. Perhaps the most seminal of advertising cases is the Supreme Court decision in Virginia State Board of Pharmacy v. Virginia Citizens Consumer Council (1976). In that decision the Court said this:

> Advertising, however tasteless and excessive it sometimes may seem, is nonetheless dissemination of information as to who is producing and selling what product, for what reason, and at what price. So long as we preserve a predominantly free enterprise economy, the allocation of our resources in large measure will be made through numerous private economic decisions.

It is a matter of public interest that those decisions, in the aggregate, be intelligent and well informed. To this end, the free flow of commercial information is indispensable.... And if it is indispensable to the proper allocation of resources in a free enterprise system, it is also indispensable to the formation of intelligent opinions as to how that system ought to be regulated or altered. Therefore, even if the First Amendment were thought to be primarily an instrument to enlighten public decision making in a democracy, we could not say that the free flow of information does not serve that goal.

The theory found here declares that because advertising delivers important information, indispensible to our economy, it is serving the purposes of the Constitution's First Amendment. The State of Virginia in that case had pushed the theory that its citizens needed to be protected from pharmacists' advertising because the pharmacists could take advantage of them, and that this was not speech worthy of protection because it was more about money than about pharmacists expressing important opinions. The Court rejected that theory, and the theory expressed in its decision is now the law of the land.

Over the years that theory has been extended and fine tuned by new theories. A few years later the Court declared that while advertising (a.k.a. "commercial speech") is protected under the First Amendment, it is not as protected as some other forms of speech (Central Hudson Gas & Electric Corp. v. Public Service Commission of New York, 1980). And several years after that the Court affirmed that hierarchy of speech by adopting a theory that commercial speech is less protected than other speech only because some regulation is necessary to ensure fair bargaining in the marketplace (*44 Liquormart, Inc. v. Rhode Island*, 1996).

Each of these opinions expresses adoption of a specific legal theory. And these theories, as adopted, draw the boundaries around what statements are permissible in advertisements, as well as the methods by which those ads are allowed to reach an audience. Those theories effectively define the way advertising is and can be practiced.

Legal theories affect advertising every day and in many ways. However, the relationship of law to theory is more complex than is manifest in the expression of legal theories.

Law Also Uses Behavioral and Other Theories

Figure 1.1 in this text depicted behavioral and other (i.e., "non-legal") theories as dealing with the impact of advertising on the consumer, marketplace, and society, but that is something of an over-simplification. Not only is legal theory important to non-legal theories, those non-legal theories can be important to legal theory, as they frequently are used in crafting the law and in developing legal theories. Of course, they also are used as proof of *facts* in legal proceedings.

Legal scholars, in developing their theories, frequently call upon behavioral theories and other theories to craft their arguments. The theory from the Virginia Pharmacy (1976) case, above, draws heavily on economic theory in its reference to the workings of the free enterprise system, for instance. The State of Virginia in that case actually pinned much of its own legal theory on economics, as reflected in another part of the Court's opinion:

> Price advertising, it is argued, will place in jeopardy the pharmacist's expertise and, with it, the customer's health. It is claimed that the aggressive price competition that will result from unlimited advertising will make it impossible for the pharmacist to supply professional services in the compounding, handling, and dispensing of prescription drugs. . . . It is also claimed that prices might not necessarily fall as a result of advertising. If one pharmacist advertises, others must, and the resulting expense will inflate the cost of drugs. . . . Finally, it is argued that damage will be done to the professional image of the pharmacist. . . . Price advertising, it is said, will reduce the pharmacist's status to that of a mere retailer.

The fact of what would happen if prescription drugs were advertised was unknown at that time, so Virginia used economic theory to predict an outcome and then used that prediction as a foundation of its legal theory.

Indeed, the legal system draws heavily upon economic theory when dealing with advertising. In Bates v. State Bar of Arizona (1977) the Court opined, "[W]here consumers have the benefit of price advertising, retail prices often are dramatically lower than they would be without advertising."

In another Supreme Court case, Zauderer v. Office of Disciplinary Counsel (1985), an attorney ran an advertisement that was declared a violation of a state law-regulating attorney advertising. The law at that time prohibited the use of illustrations in such ads. The Court adopted a theory that favored the lawyer, drawing from very basic communication theory, saying:

> The use of illustrations or pictures in advertisements serves important communicative functions: it attracts the attention of the audience to the advertiser's message, and it may also serve to impart information directly. Accordingly, commercial illustrations are entitled to the First Amendment protections afforded verbal commercial speech.

Of course, some court decisions make better and more sophisticated use of communication theory than others.

Behavioral and other relevant theories can be found throughout legal scholarship, including articles that talk about advertising (e.g., Preston & Richards, 1986; Solum, 1988; Richards, 1996; Calvert, 1998). Unfortunately, lawyers write most of that literature and, often, their understanding of these non-legal theories is limited, just as behavioral researchers too often miscomprehend legal theories (Preston & Richards, 1986; Richards, 2009).

For example, Armstrong and Russ (1975) made such an error in writing about how to detect deceptive advertising, stating, "For deception to occur it is not sufficient that the claims are false. They must also be believed." In reality, neither "falsity" nor "belief" is an element of deception in the United States. While those elements might seem to make sense from a behavioral sense, the law requires proof of slightly different elements. These authors may have thought they were publishing work with promise to influence law, but if the lawyers happened to see it these flaws probably made it useless to them. I see problems like these frequently in manuscripts I am asked to review.

As has been noted in the past, lawyers and scientists speak different languages (Pollay, 1969), which can lead to abuse and misuse of behavioral theories. It has been specifically suggested, in fact, that for law to work well in some venues, like product warnings, there needs to be a better integration of law and communication theory (Schwartz & Driver, 1983). However, in recent years the integration of law and the social sciences seems to have advanced markedly. Tamanaha (1996) even notes there is an emerging field of "sociolegal studies," which involves the application of social science to the study of law. At the same time, in the marketing field, the *Journal of Public Policy and Marketing* has grown to become one of the most highly respected journals in marketing. It and another well-regarded publication, the *Journal of Consumer Affairs*, now provide marketing researchers a choice of outlets for scholarship regarding the intersection of law and marketing.

Finally, of course, the use of expert witnesses from the social sciences is common in lawsuits dealing with advertising (e.g., Schwab v. Philip Morris USA, 2006). Those witnesses generally make use of theories to bolster their opinions. And because there is no general body of advertising-specific behavioral theories, it is common for them to draw upon psychology and other social sciences.

There continues to be a need for the integration of law with non-legal theories. Many of the biggest problems in the advertising industry today entail some legal dimensions in need of such theories in the quest for solutions. For example, in the area of Privacy alone, there is a need for theory regarding the value consumers place on their privacy (Lessig, 2002); whether consumers should be given the choice to opt-in or opt-out of email lists (Kracher & Corritore, 2004);

whether some products are more or less appropriate for radio frequency identification (RFID) enabled billboards (Peslak, 2005); and, more. In social marketing, we need behavioral theories that deal with consumer trust of product information provided on blogs, and economic theories regarding the monetary value of Facebook and Twitter, etc., as marketing tools (Maddox, 2009) in light of potential legal (and ethical) risks associated with these tools (McGeveran, 2009). These are just a few examples.

It is worth noting that not all issues related to advertising policy are consumer oriented. We also need to know about the advertising process, the advertisers, the advertising agencies, and the media companies. Theories about agency practices in monitoring the laws affecting their clients (e.g., Howard & Hulbert, 1973, pp. 36–38), for example, would be especially valuable. Theories about media vehicles' roles in monitoring the legality of advertising claims, too, would be helpful (e.g., Galloway, Rotfeld, & Richards, 2005). Obviously, there is plenty of room for theory development in the juncture between law and advertising.

Conclusion

The legal system is a regular user of theories related to advertising, and legal thinking provides its own theories affecting advertising. All of these can have profound implications for the practice of advertising. A researcher should never discount the value of a theory, no matter from what discipline it originates. The most important point, though, is that theories of all kinds are needed to make advertising regulation more effective and efficient. And, of course, we must never underestimate the power of a theory, be it a good theory or a bad one. In a sense, our laws are only as good as the theories behind them.

References

44 Liquormart, Inc. v. Rhode Island, 517 U.S. 484 (1996).

Armstrong, G. M., & Russ, F. A. (1975). Detecting deception in advertising. *MSU Business Topics, 23*, 21–32.

Bates v. State Bar of Arizona, 433 U.S. 350 (1977).

Calvert, C. (1998). Advertising: Excising media images to solve societal ills: Communication, media effects, social science, and the regulation of tobacco advertising. *Southwestern University Law Review, 27*, 401–471.

Central Hudson Gas & Electric Corp. v. Public Service Commission of New York, 447 U.S. 557 (1980).

Dworkin, R. (1986). *Law's empire*. Cambridge, MA: Harvard University Press.

Friedman, R. D. (1992). Legal theory: Standards of persuasion and the distinction between fact and law. *Northwestern University Law Review, 86*, 916–942.

Fuller, S. (1988). Playing without a full deck: Scientific realism and the cognitive limits of legal theory. *Yale Law Journal, 97*, 549–580.

Galloway, C. S., Rotfeld, H. J., & Richards, J. I. (2005). Holding media responsible for deceptive weight-loss advertising. *West Virginia Law Review, 107* (2), 353–384.

Gardner, J. (2001). Legal positivism: 5½ myths. *American Journal of Jurisprudence, 46*, 199–227.

Howard, J. A., & Hulbert, J. (1973). *Advertising and the public interest: A staff report to the Federal Trade Commission*. New York: Federal Trade Commission.

Kracher, B., & Corritore, C. L. (2004). Is there a special e-Commerce ethics? *Business Ethics Quarterly, 14* (1), 71–94.

Lawson, G. (1992). Legal theory: Proving the law. *Northwestern University Law Review, 86*, 859–904.

Lessig, L. (2002). Privacy as property. *Social Research, 69* (1), 247–269.

McGeveran, W. (2009). Disclosure, endorsement, and identity in social marketing. *University of Illinois Law Review, 2009*, 1105–1166.

Maddox, K. (2009). Some question payoff of social media efforts. *B to B, 94* (4), 1–28.

Peslak, A. R. (2005). An ethical exploration of privacy and radio frequency identification. *Journal of Business Ethics, 59* (4), 327–345.

Pollay, R. W. (1969). Deceptive advertising and consumer behavior: A case for legislative and judicial reform. *Kansas Law Review, 17*, 625–637.

Preston, I. L., & Richards, J. I. (1986). Consumer miscomprehension as a challenge to FTC prosecutions of deceptive advertising. *John Marshall Law Review, 19*, 605–635.

Richards, J. I. (1996). Politicizing cigarette advertising. *Catholic University Law Review, 45* (4), 1147–1212.

Richards, J. I. (2009). Common fallacies in law-related consumer research. *Journal of Consumer Affairs, 43* (1), 174–180.

Schwab v. Philip Morris USA, 449 F. Supp. 2d 992 (E.D. N.Y. 2006).

Schwartz, V. E., & Driver, R. W. (1983). Warnings in the workplace: The need for a synthesis of law and communication theory. *University of Cincinnati Law Review, 52*, 38–83.

Solum, L. B. (1988). Freedom of communicative action: A theory of the First Amendment Freedom of Speech. *Northwestern University Law Review, 83*, 54–135.

Tamanaha, B. Z. (1996). Pragmatism in U.S. legal theory: Its application to normative jurisprudence, sociolegal studies, and the fact-value distinction. *American Journal of Jurisprudence, 41*, 315–355.

Virginia State Board of Pharmacy v. Virginia Citizens Consumer Council, 425 U.S. 748 (1976).

Zauderer v. Office of Disciplinary Counsel, 471 U.S. 626 (1985).

Additional Readings

Fallon, R. H., Jr. (1999). How to choose a constitutional theory. *California Law Review, 87* (3), 535–579.

Golding, J. M., Warren, A. R., & Ross, D. E. (1997). On legal validity, internal validity, and ecological validity: Comment on Wasby and Brody. *Law and Human Behavior, 21* (6), 693–695.

Hastak, M., Mazis, M. B., & Morris, L. A. (2001). The role of consumer surveys in public policy decision making. *Journal of Public Policy and Marketing, 20* (2), 170–185.

LoPucki, L. M., & Weyrauch, W. O. (2000). A theory of legal strategy. *Duke Law Journal, 49* (6), 1405–1486.

Monahan, J., & Walker, L. (2006). *An introduction to social science in law.* Mineola, NY: Foundation Press.

Chapter 32

Four Theories of How IMC Works

Sandra Moriarty and Don Schultz

A set of foundational Integrated Marketing Communications (IMC) concepts has been with us in one form or another from IMC's earliest days, although as Kitchen and Schultz (2009) suggest, most of those concepts and constructs have changed as the field of IMC has matured. Thus, rather than a single concept, IMC represents a group of concepts. The challenge to scholars is to understand the interrelationships between and among them. Because these concepts work together, it is difficult to arrive at one single explanation, or even definition, of IMC. However, this chapter proposes four general theoretical frameworks that we believe are central to IMC. This chapter will also outline the underlying, supporting concepts that are basic to understanding how contemporary IMC works:

Interactive Communication Theory
Supporting Theories: Two-Way and Multi-Way Communication; Customer-Focused Communication; Contact Points.

Perceptual Integration Theory
Supporting Theories: Message Consistency; Synergy; Integration Theory.

Reciprocity Theory
Supporting Theories: Stakeholder and Relationship Theories; Reciprocity and Symmetry Theories.

IMC Process Theory
Supporting Theories: Outside-In Planning; Continuous Planning; X-functional Management.

Interactive Communication

Schultz, Tannenbaum, and Lauterborn (1993, p. 45) recognized the importance of the communication foundation of IMC: "If we think for a moment about traditional marketing, we begin to realize that almost all the marketing techniques and approaches that we have used over the years are essentially some form of communication." IMC focuses, however, on interactive communication, that is, from source to receiver and from receiver back to source.

The idea of ongoing dialogue between consumers and marketers is now a central marketing theme and one of the most important IMC paradigm shifts. That trend increases with the growing emphasis on word-of-mouth and social media. Duncan and Moriarty (1997) explored the notion that exchange is both a communication and a business process and that interactivity supports both by enhancing brand relationships.

Consumer Focus

In the past, traditional advertising and marketing communication practices focused on how best to target consumers and persuade them of a brand's superiority. Even with account planning, which introduced the voice of the consumer to strategic planning in the 1980s, the practice of targeting was still an instrumental tool designed to help marketers better persuade prospective customers.

The concept of "targeting" shifted in the early 1990s as the IMC program at Northwestern focused less on marketing organization and more on the customer and other stakeholders. Heralded as a change from inside-out to outside-in planning, the Northwestern approach launched a new data-driven, demand-based marketing system—recognizing that the communication objective was not only about persuasion and one-time exchanges, but also about ongoing engagement, negotiation, relationships, and discussions. The introduction of one-to-one strategies using direct-response tools also reinforced the idea of a database-driven IMC communication model. This early work (Schultz et al., 1993; Pepper & Rogers, 1993) was based on an important paradigm shift—the focus on identifiable consumer behaviors, not just on consumer attitudes.

Communication strategy takes an entirely new meaning when the goal is to engage customers in a conversation rather than target them with a persuasive message. In an interactive marketplace, where consumers often access and acquire as much external information as they receive from marketers, the basic concept of audience targeting is rapidly being made obsolete by shifts in communication technology. This paradigm shift involves seeing the customer as a participant, rather than just a target, in a dynamic ongoing communication network.

As the marketing communication model has shifted from one-way to two-way or multi-way communication, this new perspective also reflects the idea that consumers are not just the target of the promotional strategies, but may actually, at times, drive the communication process through customer-initiated messages (Duncan, 1995). Another change is found in the multiplicity of message encounters, both planned and unplanned.

Contact Points

IMC communication involves more than traditional outbound, marketer-controlled media systems, such as those used in advertising campaigns. Schultz et al. (1993) detailed the ways in which different aspects of the marketing mix say something about the brand and the person for whom the product was designed. Duncan (1995) described how "everything communicates" and that includes all aspects of the marketing mix, as well as every encounter by a consumer with something that sends a message about a brand.

Sometimes these contact points are traditional marketing communication messages, but often they are messages delivered by the marketing mix (what does the product design, price, or distribution say about the brand?), word-of-mouth interactions, and other brand experiences. The breadth of these message-delivering interactions is not new: Wayne DeLozier in his 1976 book on marketing communication treated all of the marketing mix elements as communication variables and proposed that each one must be considered in relation to all of the others in order to develop an integrated program. This idea of a system of contact points where stakeholders encounter brand messages reflects another paradigm shift as the traditional way of looking at media has been expanded to include a variety of brand contacts beyond traditional marketing communication.

Another dimension of the contact point concept is the idea of *touch points*. Sometimes contact points and touch points are used interchangeably, but Duncan and Moriarty (2006) argue that touch points are qualitatively different. A touch point means a consumer connects on an emotional level with the brand as a result of a brand experience. In other words, it's more than just coming in contact with a brand message. This is particularly important in service marketing, which is becoming more dominant than product marketing, as explained by Lusch and Vargo (2006).

Perceptual Integration Theory

What is it that integrated communication can accomplish in terms of consumer response? Keller (1996) explains that on a general level, "communication effects are what consumers saw, heard, learned, thought, felt, and so on while exposed to a communication" (pp. 106–197). More specifically, he said that, "the role of marketing communications is to contribute to brand equity by establishing the brand in memory and linking strong, favorable, and unique associations to it."

Keller explains that brand knowledge is not just facts, but also all the thoughts, feelings, perceptions, images, and experiences that create a set of associations to the brand in consumer memory. In addition to driving short-term effects of awareness, comprehension, and attitude-change, one test of IMC's effectiveness is its ability to form an integrated brand perception where all the consumer-received impressions come together in the consumer's mind as a coherent brand image. Keller (2009) also says IMC activities can contribute to brand equity and drive results in many ways, but ultimately these activities "must be integrated to deliver a consistent message and achieve the strategic positioning" (p. 146).

The idea of customer-focused planning calls for a deeper understanding of how customers actually integrate messages and experiences to create this integrated brand perception. It's important to recognize that corporate managers do not have a magic wand that enables them to move ideas from their strategy statements into the minds of consumers via well-conceived IMC strategies. Managers may have strategies for defining brand images and positions, but these images and positions actually exist in consumers' minds as subjective impressions—think of Swatch or Starbucks. Managers can only use communication to attempt to cue an intended favorable response (Franzen & Moriarty, 2009; Moriarty & Franzen, 2009).

A number of principles relate to this view of customer-driven meaning construction. One is that people automatically integrate messages whether the marketer provides the proper messages or tools to do so. Therefore the integration process occurs in spite of what is sometimes dysfunctional, silo-based planning (plans developed by different departments who don't talk to one another) that marketers often employ. Another insight is that a brand exists in the mind of the consumer only through the process of conceptual integration. The brand takes on meaning—perceptual integrity—to the degree that individual impressions and associations are connected, which contributes to Keller's (1996, 2009) notion of consumer-based brand equity.

Message Consistency

Consistency in message and graphics was the battle cry of the original "one sight–one sound" approach that launched IMC in the 1980s (see Thorson & Moore, 1996). Strategies were crafted to synchronize multi-channel communication to reach every market segment with a single, unified message. Initially

IMC was developed to help clients and agencies bring all their communication efforts together. This objective and the coordination efforts that supported it received extensive coverage in trade publications almost to the exclusion of the more strategic values that IMC could provide.

The idea that there are multiple sources for marketing communication (MC) messages and these messages need to be strategically coordinated drove the concern for consistency (Gronstedt & Thorson, 1993). Duncan (1995) developed a model of message consistency, identifying four message types (planned, intrinsic, maintenance, and unplanned) that needed to be managed and monitored for consistency. The value of consistency has been often discussed but it is difficult to test its value in the marketplace. Thus, IMC thinkers have leapt over the consistency issue and focused almost entirely on coordination of the various communication tools.

Synergy

Message consistency is presumed to lead to communication efficiency and effectiveness. Efficiency based on synergy (the idea that $2 + 2 = 5$) served as a starting point for the development of IMC practices in the late 1980s and early 1990s. The benefit of message consistency is synergy, which means that marketing communication can be more effective, efficient, and generate greater combined impact—meaning all of them connected together have more impact than single messages delivered on their own would have. In other words, the benefits of synergy (more impact) accumulate if messages from the various areas are coordinated around a common theme or delivered at a particular time (Kitchen, Brignell, Li, & Jones, 2004; Lee & Park, 2007; Stammerjohan, Wood, Chang, & Thorson, 2005). This synergistic effect of integration was explained by Interbrand's Carolyn Ray (2004) who said, "The Principle of Integration holds that all communications emanating from a single strategic platform will generate a significantly greater return on the communication investment than would be the case with traditional independent media executions" (p. 1).

The Interbrand work borrows from Information Integration Theory, which is a unified theory of judgment and decision making based in psychology and cognitive science (Anderson, 1971, 1981). The idea is that consumers cognitively integrate the barrage of messages they receive by "input interweaving," which is the process of integrating impressions from pieces and parts of previous exposures and experiences (Schumann, Dyer, & Petkus, 1996).

The basic tenets of psychological consistency theory, which is related to information integration, reside in Heider's (1946) balance theory, Osgood and Tannenbaum's (1955) congruity theory, and McGuire's (1976) analysis of cognitive consistency in consumer decision making. These early works suggest that there is a natural tendency for consumers to strive for simplicity and consistency and to integrate what and how they believe, experience, feel, and act. Inconsistency from different brand messages and experiences can create cognitive tension, which demands some kind of adjustment in their attitudes and knowledge base (Sheth & Parvatiyar, 1995).

The importance of synergy was highlighted in the 1992 DDB Needham "Synergy of Persuasive Voices" conference in Chicago. Presenters at this early IMC conference explored the definitions, theoretical foundations, management, and measurement of IMC. The DDB conference papers were edited by Thorson and Moore and appeared as a book in 1996. A concluding chapter in that book (Moriarty, 1996) looked at synergy in terms of memory impact based on the interaction of audience, the brand concept, and the communication channel. This chapter explored how multidimensional IMC programs deliver linkages and associations in a receiver's mind as a result of messages that connect—and this integration cues a coherent brand concept in the mind of the audience, all basic tenets of IMC.

Reciprocity Theory

A key element in the new view of IMC as interactive communication is reciprocity, the idea that all communication must sum to "win–win" situations for both the marketer and the customer, a very old concept that can be traced back to Greek philosopher Aristotle's *Nichomachean Ethics*. In most traditional exchange-theory marketing models (Bagozzi, 1975; Ennis, 1974; Kotler & Levy, 1969), the marketer builds value into the product, and this value can then be inventoried (the basis for all supply chain theory). Customers then extract that value at their leisure as they buy and use the product. In other words, if the value the consumer receives is as great or greater than the cost of acquiring that value, the customer would likely repurchase.

Today, IMC, based on communication relationships, complex communication networks, and interactivity, has evolved into a system where both the marketer and consumer receive value from the communication activity itself for it to be continued. Thus, in today's market, for brand relationships to be built and maintained through communication, the buyer and seller must both derive benefit. If the value is tilted too far on one side or the other, one of the parties will likely withdraw and the relationship will fail.

Grunig (1989) helped further explain the reciprocity concept in stakeholder relationships. What he called the *asymmetrical approach* (advertising targeting, for example) is manipulative because the communication impact benefits the organization rather than its publics. In contrast, the *two-way symmetrical approach* (for example, interactive communication) benefits both the organization and its publics. He explains that organizations using this approach "use bargaining, negotiating, and strategies of conflict resolution to bring about symbiotic changes in the ideas, attitudes, and behaviors of both the organization and its publics" (p. 29). Given the tremendous marketplace choice available to consumers today, reciprocity has and will become increasingly important in understanding customer–stakeholder–brand–marketer relationships. All these concepts are built around the concept of stakeholders and the connected relationship theories.

Stakeholders

The concept of *stakeholders*, i.e., anyone who has an interest in an organization or an activity, is well established. As a theory of organizational management, the notion of stakeholders first appeared in *Strategic Management: A Stakeholder Approach* by Freeman in 1984 but other writers have linked stakeholders to marketing as well (Gummesson, 1991; Donaldson & Preston, 1995; Jones, 1995; Mitchell, Agle, & Wood, 1997). Sheth and Parvatiyar stated the basic premise of relationships in consumer marketing in a 1995 article and a 2000 edited volume. Moriarty (1994) applied the concept to public relations, as did De Bussy and Ewing (1998). Additionally, a professional interpretation appeared as *The Stakeholder Corporation: A Blueprint for Maximizing Stakeholder Value* (1997) by Wheeler and Sillanpaa.

Gronstedt (1996) linked the objectives of marketing and public relations through his Stakeholder Relations Model. Building on Kotler's 1986 notion of "Megamarketing," Gronstedt's premise was that the concepts of "markets" and "publics" overlap. De Bussy, Ewing, and Pitt (2003) reviewed the development of the stakeholder concept within the IMC arena. A 1998 article by Duncan and Moriarty presented a communication-based model for managing brand relationships with multiple stakeholder groups on both the organization and consumer sides.

The stakeholder concept intersects with IMC theory in the notion of *strategic consistency* (Duncan, 1995), which is based on the idea that the multiple groups all have different message needs—both upstream (suppliers), internal (employees, investors), and downstream (distributors, retailers, and ultimately customers). Ruth and Simonin's model (1995) identified a system of horizontal and vertical integration that includes all the various IMC areas and tools, as well as corporate sources. In addition to these corporate sources, the communication environment includes community organizations and leaders, government officials and regulators, the media, the financial community, and special interest groups, such as activists—all of whom have something to say about the brand and the company. To further illustrate this point, McDonald, Christopher,

Knox, Payne, and Simms (2001) presented an integrated stakeholder model in *Creating a Company for Customers*.

We are beginning to recognize that we live in a networked communication system of overlapping interests. In addition to identifying a network of stakeholders, rather than just a single target group, an IMC principle is that people in these groups—and their roles—overlap. Any one individual may be an employee, a neighbor to the firm, a community leader, an activist—and a customer. Since stakeholders talk to one another about the brand, individual messages need to be differentiated depending upon the audience, although they may all be consistent in terms of some central brand message that anchors the communication strategy. That's the point of Duncan's theory of strategic consistency (Duncan & Moriarty, 1997).

Relationships

Related to the concept of stakeholders is the idea of brand relationships—relationships that drive brand loyalty and advocacy by customers on behalf of the brand. This emphasis on relationship marketing, rather than transactions and exchanges, is a paradigm shift that has evolved parallel to the development of IMC. Rather than targeting potential customers by a company for a brand-related message or even a campaign, IMC managers strive to develop long-term brand interactions that cement a positive relationship and deliver repeat business (brand loyalty), as well as positive comments within the stakeholder network.

The communication aspect of brand relationships specifically related to IMC was described by Grönroos and Lindberg-Repo in 1998, Duncan and Moriarty in 1999, and Finne and Grönroos in 2009. On the academic side, the Scandinavian school—Gummeson, Grönroos, and their colleagues—and the Cranfield Business School in Britain—Christopher, Payne, Ballantyne, among others—focused on relationship marketing and services, as well as brand communication throughout the stakeholder network. Sheth and Parvatiyar (2000) and Miller and Halinen (2000) were also important theorists linking stakeholders, relationships, marketing, and marketing communication. On the industry side, relationship marketing was introduced to professionals with the publication of McKenna's 1991 book, *Relationship Marketing*.

The brand relationship concept is also a shift in how IMC performance is measured. Traditional marketing communication is often driven by strategies that focus on short-term financial exchanges with measures of effectiveness—such as, awareness, trial, repeat purchase, and market share. IMC shifts some of the organization's focus to long-term impact, particularly as measured by various types of relationship metrics. Thus, in IMC, both long-term (brand relationships) and short-term measures (sales and share) are necessary indicators of marketplace success. There is increasing evidence in the social media literature that inter-market communication, that is references and referrals by existing customers, are linked to brand loyalty. Reichheld (1996) proposed this in his brand loyalty research in which he suggested that referrals are the best brand loyalty measure. Thus monitoring of and activation of comments by satisfied customers—i.e., positive word of mouth—is an important IMC outcome.

The reason brand relationships are important to IMC planners is that loyalty results from all types of brand messages and positive customer experiences. IMC provides a process to establish, monitor, and cement these relationships. Duncan and Moriarty (1998) pointed out that stakeholder communication via IMC was a complex set of relationships anchored by interactive communication.

As can be seen, changes in the conceptualization of IMC suggest the field is moving from a simple traditional source → receiver model that only emphasizes using a coordinated set of messages to reach the consumer, to complex systems of nodes, networks, and stimulus activation contact points. This demands a reconceptualization of the traditional linear S → R communication model by adding a third party, the social network, which engages stakeholders in a variety of word-of-mouth and increasingly electronically delivered digital social media. Thus, the system becomes a multi-modal, interconnected loop that includes the organization, all key stakeholders, the people they talk to, the people they hear from, all influenced by the voices of their various stakeholder communities.

These relationships are more than just conversations. Positive (or negative) relationships are important because ultimately they contribute to brand value (Duncan & Moriarty, 1997). Brand image, which drives brand value (the communication side of brand equity), can be seen as the aggregation of all these relationships—suppliers, vendors, distributors, financial, government, employees, and, yes, customers. The sum of the positive/negative relationships is an indication of brand strength—the intangible value that is so critical to the overall value of the brand and the impact that has on the marketing organization.

The three preceding theoretical frameworks all have academic and research potential and are supported by theories from related scholarly fields. The last area of IMC theory, however, is focused more on praxis (professional practice). Although still based on areas of management theory, its contribution lies in its support of several critical areas of IMC management and planning.

IMC Process Theory

So how is this complex communication system to be managed? Continuous planning, rather than start-and-stop campaigns and annual plans, is another management concept that has emerged as an answer to the problem of managing ongoing communication activities, such as brand-focused IMC programs (Duncan, 1995, 2009; Schultz & Schultz, 2004; Schultz, Barnes, Schultz, & Azzaro, 2009). Admittedly sales and market share are still a concern on one level, but IMC offers marketing managers a way to move communication planning from start-and-stop campaigns and short-term thinking to long-term relationships that lead to brand loyalty and a network of positive interactions and referrals.

Both the Schultz and Duncan models are circular and provide guidance to practitioners in similar ways. The circular process undergirds the notion of ongoing planning and monitoring. Once set in place, research leads to plans and implementation tactics that generate feedback which then lead to new plans. Duncan's model (2009), for example, includes (1) zero-based planning and objective setting, (2) message strategies, (3) contact point strategies, and (4) evaluation and measurement, leading back to (1). At the point of evaluation it spins off measures of sales, profits, and brand equity—the critical metrics that are continually monitored so the planning can be adjusted. The Schultz model (2004) includes (1) customer identification, (2) customer valuation, (3) creating and delivering messages and incentives, (4) estimating ROI, and (5) budget, evaluation and recycling. This is a similar continuous monitoring and enhancement approach that is somewhat different since it continuously focuses on the customer, not on the marketer.

Cross-Functional Management

In recognition of the notion that IMC is all about the organization and how it interacts with its customers and prospects, early academic papers investigated management structures—i.e., the challenge of functional silos—and then proposed new ways of organizing or at least aligning the marketing communication functions. Prensky and his colleagues (1996) explored the cause of silos identifying four models of structures that incorporated various types of corporate cultures and political structures. They concluded that traditionally "the firm's organizational structure, culture, and politics foster a distinct procedural framework that segregates them from practitioners of other communications forms, encouraging a myopic view of marketing communications that divides the content of integrated communications efforts" (p. 178).

One potential solution to silos is cross-functional management with representatives from all customer-facing units represented in management teams that monitor, as well as plan, brand communication (Duncan, 1995; Duncan &

Moriarty, 1997). However, as DeLozier suggested in 1976 and the Schultzes reiterated in 2004, it is not just customer-facing units but all units within the organization, including all message-producing sources, that need to be coordinated both inside and outside the organization.

Summary: Four Premises

The point of this review is that the concept of IMC has evolved over time as various sub-theories have emerged and connected in the practice of IMC. Initially the IMC concept meant outbound communication distributed by a marketing organization using various tools to generate returns for the firm. Today most of the activity in IMC scholarship, as well as practice, is focused on brands, relationships, and interactivity—i.e., customers and other stakeholders create as much of the conversation as the marketer. The notion of audience has broadened beyond just consumers to include a complex set of stakeholders who interact, not only with the brand, but with each other. The instrumental use of targeting as a way for marketers to manipulate consumers has given way to relationship-building programs. There's a new interest in shared values (reciprocity) between marketers, consumers, and other stakeholders. The concept of media and message delivery has expanded to include, not just traditional marketing communication, but a system focused on identifying and managing all contact points where a message is delivered or a brand impression created.

What has emerged through the 30 years of IMC development is recognition that communication is a complex system that involves new ways of thinking about messages, media, sources, receivers, targeting, and effectiveness measures that are all interrelated. Here are four premises that summarize the IMC theories that we have briefly discussed in this chapter.

Communication Premise: multi-way, interactive communication— from all ... to all ... everywhere—creates a system of total brand communication.

Perceptual Integration Premise: consistent brand messages create integrated perceptions that drive synergy.

Reciprocity Premise: reciprocal stakeholder relationships create brand value.

IMC Process Premise: X-functional, continuous, outside-in planning delivers brand communication effectiveness and organizational returns.

We began by suggesting that these theories are interrelated, so perhaps the next step by scholars might be to tie them together to determine if they can, in fact, be consolidated into one grand theory of IMC. Certainly another step would be to carve out a research program that would verify the theories and determine their validity in the world of professional practice. So what we propose here is the beginning, not the end, of the search for a validated IMC theory.

References

Anderson, N. H. (1971). Integration theory and attitude and change. *Psychological Review, 78* (3), 171–206.

Anderson, N. H. (1981). Integration theory applied to cognitive responses and attitudes. In R. E. Petty, T. M. Ostrom, & T. C. Brock (Eds.), *Cognitive responses in persuasion* (pp. 361–397). Hillsdale, NJ: Lawrence Erlbaum.

Bagozzi, R. (1975). Marketing as exchange. *Journal of Marketing, 39* (October), 32–39.

De Bussy, N. M., & Ewing, M. T. (1998). The stakeholder concept and public relations: Tracking the parallel evolution of two literatures. *Journal of Communication Management, 2* (3), 222–229.

De Bussy, N. M., Ewing, M. T., & Pitt, L. F. (2003). Stakeholder theory and internal marketing communications: A framework for analysing the influence of new media. *Journal of Marketing Communications, 9*, 146–161.

DeLozier, W. (1976). *The marketing communications process*. New York: McGraw-Hill.

Duncan, T. R. (1995, March 23–24). A macro model of integrated marketing communication. Paper presented at the American Academy of Advertising Conference, Norfolk, VA.

Duncan, T. R. (2009). The evolution of IMC. *International Journal of Integrated Marketing Communications, 1* (1), 17–23.

Duncan, T. R., & Moriarty, S. E. (1997). *Driving brand value: Using integrated marketing to manage profitable stakeholder relationships*. New York: McGraw-Hill.

Duncan, T. R., & Moriarty, S. E. (1998). A communication-based marketing model for managing relationships. *Journal of Marketing, 62* (2), 1–13.

Duncan, T. R., & Moriarty, S. E. (1999). Relationship-based marketing communication. *Australasian Marketing Journal, 7* (1), 118–120.

Duncan, T. R., & Moriarty, S. E. (2006). How integrated marketing communication's "touchpoints" can operationalize the service-dominant logic. In R. F. Lusch & S. L. Vargo (Eds.), *The service dominant logic of marketing* (Ch. 18). Armonk, NY: M.E. Sharpe.

Donaldson, T., & Preston, L. E. (1995). The stakeholder concept and public relations: Tracking the parallel evolution of two literatures. *Academy of Management Review, 20* (1), 71.

Ennis, B. (1974). *Marketing principles*. Pacific Palisades, CA: Goodyear Publishing.

Finne, Å., & Grönroos, C. (2009). Rethinking marketing communication: From integrated marketing communication to relationship communication. *Journal of Marketing Communications, 15* (2–3), 179–195.

Franzen, G., & Moriarty, S. E. (2009). *The science and art of branding*. Armonk, NY: M.E. Sharpe.

Freeman, R. (1984). *Strategic management: A stakeholder approach*. Boston: Pitman.

Grönroos, C., & Llindberg-Repo, K. (1998). Integrated marketing communications: The communication aspect of relationship marketing. *IMC Research Journal, 4* (1), 3-11.

Gronstedt, A. (1996). Integrating marketing communication and public relations: A stakeholder relations model. In E. Thorson & J. Moore (Eds.), *Integrated marketing communications: Synergy of persuasive voices* (pp. 287–304). Mahwah, NJ: Lawrence Erlbaum.

Gronstedt, A., & Thorson, E. (1993, August). In search of integrative communications excellence: Five organizational structures in advertising agencies. Paper presented at the Association for Education in Journalism and Mass Communication, Kansas City, MO.

Grunig, J. (1989). Symmetrical presuppositions as a framework for public relations theory. In C. Botan & V. Hazleton, Jr. (Eds.), *Public relations theory* (pp. 17–44). Hillsdale, NJ: Lawrence Erlbaum.

Gummesson, E. (1991). Marketing orientation revisited: The crucial role of the part-time marketer. *European Journal of Marketing, 24* (2), 60–75.

Heider, F. (1946). Attitudes and cognitive organization. *Journal of Psychology, 2* (January), 107–112.

Jones, T. M. (1995). Instrumental stakeholder theory: Synthesis of ethics and economics. *Academy of Management Review, 20* (20), 404–437.

Keller, K. L. (1996). Integrated marketing communications and brand equity. In E. Thorson & J. Moore (Eds.), *Integrated marketing communications: Synergy of persuasive voices* (pp. 103–132). Mahwah, NJ: Lawrence Erlbaum.

Keller, K. L. (2009). Building strong brands in a modern marketing communications environment. *Journal of Marketing Communications, 15* (2–3), 139–155.

Kitchen, P. J., Brignell, J., Li, T., & Jones, G. S. (2004). The emergence of IMC: A theoretical perspective. *Journal of Advertising Research, 44* (1), 19–30.

Kitchen, P. J., & Schultz, D. E. (2009). IMC: New horizon/false dawn for a marketplace in turmoil? *Journal of Marketing Communications, 15* (2–3), 197–204.

Kotler, P. (1986). Megamarketing. *Harvard Business Review*, March–April, 117–124.

Kotler, P., & Levy, S. (1969). Broadening the concept of marketing. *Journal of Marketing, 33* (January), 10–15.

Lee, D. H., & Park, C. W. (2007). Conceptualization and measurement of multidimensionality of integrated marketing communications. *Journal of Advertising Research, 47* (3), 222–236.

Lusch, R. F., & Vargo, S. L. (Eds.). (2006). *The service dominant logic of marketing*. Armonk, NY: M.E. Sharpe.

McDonald, M., Christopher, M., Knox, S., Payne, A., & Simms, J. (2001). *Creating a company for customers*. London: Financial Times Prentice Hall.

McGuire, W. (1976). Some internal psychological factors influencing consumer choice. *Journal of Consumer Research, 2* (March), 302–319.

McKenna, R. (1991). *Relationship marketing*, Reading, MA; Addison-Wesley.

Miller, K., & Halinen, A. (2000). Relationship marketing theory: Its roots and direction. *Journal of Marketing Management, 16* (1–3), 29–54.

Mitchell, R. K., Agle, B. R., & Wood, D. J. (1997). Toward a theory of stakeholder identification and salience: Defining the principle of who and what really counts. *Academy of Management Review, 22* (4), 853–886.

Moriarty, S. E. (1994). PR and IMC: The benefits of integration. *Public Relations Quarterly* (Fall), 38–44.

Moriarty, S. E. (1996). The circle of synergy: Theoretical perspectives and an evolving IMC research agenda. In E. Thorson & J. Moore (Eds.), *Integrated communication: Synergy of persuasive voices* (pp. 51–64). Mahwah, NJ: Lawrence Erlbaum.

Moriarty, S. E., & Franzen, G. (2009). The I in IMC: How science and art are integrated in branding. *International Journal of Integrated Marketing Communications, 1* (1), 24–32.

Osgood, C., & Tannenbaum, P. (1955). The principle of congruity in the production of attitude change. *Psychological Review, 62*, 42–55.

Peppers, D., & Rogers, M. (1993). *The one to one future: Building relationships one customer at a time*. New York: Currency Doubleday.

Prensky, D., McCarty, J., & Lucas, J. (1996). Integrated marketing communication: An organizational perspective. In E. Thorson & J. Moore (Eds.), *Integrated communication: Synergy of persuasive voices* (pp. 167–184). Mahwah, NJ: Lawrence Erlbaum.

Ray, C. (2004). *Integrated brand communications: A powerful new paradigm*. Toronto, Canada: An Interbrand publication.

Reichheld, F. F. (1996). *The loyalty effect*. Boston: Harvard Business School Press.

Ruth, J., & Simonin, B. (1995, March 23–24). Reconceptualizing integrated marketing communications: the importance of vertical integration, corporate externalities and constituencies. Paper presented at the American Academy of Advertising, Norfolk, VA.

Schultz, D. E., Barnes, B. E., Schultz, H. F., & Azzaro, M. (2009). *Building customer–brand relationships*. Armonk, NY: M.E. Sharpe.

Schultz, D. E., & Schultz, H. F. (2004). *IMC: The next generation*. New York: McGraw-Hill.

Schultz, D. E., Tannenbaum, S., & Lauterborn, R. (1993). *Integrated marketing communications: Pulling it together and making it work*. Lincolnwood, IL: NTC Business Books.

Schumann, D., Dyer, B., & Petkus, E. (1996). The vulnerability of integrated marketing communication: The potential for boomerang effects. In E. Thorson & J. Moore (Eds.), *Integrated communication: Synergy of persuasive voices* (pp. 51–64). Mahwah, NJ: Lawrence Erlbaum.

Sheth, J., & Parvatiyar, A. (1995). Relationship marketing in consumer markets: Antecedents and consequences. *Journal of the Academy of Marketing Science, 23* (4), 255–271.

Sheth, J., & Parvatiyar, A. (Eds.). (2000). *Handbook of relationship marketing*. Thousand Oaks, CA: Sage.

Stammerjohan, C. A., Wood, C. M., Chang, Y., & Thorson, E. (2005). An empirical investigation of the interaction between publicity, advertising, and previous brand attitudes and knowledge. *Journal of Advertising, 34* (4), 55–67.

Thorson, E., & Moore, J. (Eds.). (1996). *Integrated communication: Synergy of persuasive voices*. Hillsdale, NJ: Lawrence Erlbaum.

Wheeler, D., & Sillanpaa, M. (1997). *The stakeholder corporation: A blueprint for maximizing stakeholder value*. London: Pitman Publishing.

Additional Readings

Duncan, T. R. (2009). The evolution of IMC. *International Journal of Integrated Marketing Communications, 1* (1), 17–23.

Duncan, T. R., & Moriarty, S. E. (1998). A communication-based marketing model for managing relationships. *Journal of Marketing, 62* (2), 1–13.

Franzen, G., & Moriarty, S. E. (2009). *The science and art of branding*. Armonk, NY: M.E. Sharpe.

Kitchen, P. J., & Schultz, D. E. (2009). IMC: New horizon/false dawn for a marketplace in turmoil? *Journal of Marketing Communications, 15* (2–3), 197–204.

Schultz, D. E., & Schultz, H. F. (2004). *IMC: The next generation*. New York: McGraw-Hill.

Chapter 33

Theories about Health and Advertising

Joyce M. Wolburg

Advertising is such a significant part of our culture that many scholars regard it as an *institution* in society—one that expresses American cultural ideology in a unique way and encourages people to pursue the American dream. Advertising has earned its place among institutions in society not only by regulating the distribution of wealth but by assisting corporations in their efforts to expand and become more powerful entities within the economic system. Furthermore, advertising orders relationships by teaching members of the culture to be consumers.

As we shift our thinking about advertising from a macro- to micro-level perspective, we focus on advertising's ability to promote products and services to consumers, help citizens to decide which political candidate to vote for, persuade them to take a particular stance on various causes (e.g., pro-life versus pro-choice), and provide information beneficial to their health and safety.

Advertising for health-related issues is the focus of this chapter, particularly the messages sent to receivers (see Figure 1.1 in Chapter 1). Essentially, this chapter examines advertising's role in three highly visible areas of health communication: modifying unhealthy behavior, solving health problems through products, and positioning a wide variety of products as means to a healthy lifestyle.

Modifying Unhealthy Behavior

One of the most challenging tasks for advertising is to motivate people to change their unhealthy ways—or to avoid making unhealthy choices in the first place. Consumers are exposed to a variety of messages for the sake of their health: quit smoking, drink in moderation, avoid driving under the influence, take precautions when engaging in sexual behavior, say no to drugs, use sunscreen, wear seatbelts, eat a balanced diet, get enough exercise, get regular medical screening tests, etc. These messages are part of social marketing campaigns and often come in the form of public service announcements (PSAs), which have traditionally been non-paid placements in the media that fill unpaid airtime or space. Consequently, they often appear at times when few audience members are present. Paid placements have a better chance of reaching the intended audience; however, few social marketing campaigns have the necessary budget. Even when the budget is not an issue, creating a compelling "anti-indulgence" message is far more difficult than creating a message that encourages consumption. It goes without saying that most advertising copywriters find it easier to create messages that resonate with consumers about the pleasures of consumption than the consequences.

Anti-consumption messages are challenging from a creative perspective for several reasons. At a minimum, messages must convince consumers that they are better off not engaging in unhealthy behavior, which usually means consumers are persuaded that making unhealthy choices puts them at risk for serious consequences. Furthermore, these messages must not be perceived as judgmental, preachy, or infringing upon personal freedom. Otherwise, they can have a boomerang effect that makes consumers more likely to engage in the unhealthy behavior (Ringold, 2002). Finally, messages must also take into consideration the ritual meaning of the unhealthy behavior consumers are asked to give up—the meaning derived from drinking, smoking, etc. Thus, we explore concepts of risk, reactance effects, and ritual behavior.

What We Know about Risk

Current risk theories tell us which points to consider when creating messages that ask for behavior modifications. Most messages that communicate risk do so by arousing a certain level of fear, and the Extended Parallel Process Model (EPPM) predicts that messages that include fear appeals generate two potential responses (Witte, 1994). Upon realizing they are at risk, consumers either control the danger by modifying their behavior (drink less, enter a smoking cessation program, use condoms, wear sunscreen, etc.), or they continue to engage in the risky behavior but, consequently, must control the fear they experience.

According to the theory, several factors must be in place for consumers to be motivated to change their behavior and, thereby, reduce the risk of serious consequences. For example, most consumers will only be willing to use condoms to avoid the risk of sexually transmitted diseases or pregnancy if four conditions are met: (1) if they feel that the threat is severe (e.g., not using condoms could result in pregnancy or exposure to serious STDs); (2) if they feel vulnerable to the threat (e.g., the consequences such as pregnancy or STDs can happen to them personally or their partner); (3) if they feel capable of changing their at-risk behavior (e.g., they believe they have the control and self-efficacy to take precautions by using condoms or asking their partner to do so); and (4) if they perceive the behavior change as effective in avoiding the threat (e.g., that condom use is an effective measure for eliminating the risk) (Witte, 1994; Reisen & Poppen, 1999). When all four conditions are met, consumers are likely to change their behavior to avoid the consequences; however, when only some conditions are met, the probability of behavior modification diminishes.

Even though most people believe that condoms are effective for avoiding pregnancy and STDs, not all individuals will take precautions. This is especially true for those who think their personal vulnerability is low, as in the case of an adult in a monogamous relationship, or for those who lack the self-confidence to ask a partner to use a condom for fear of risking rejection (Reisen & Poppen, 1999). Likewise, college students know that drinking in moderation is safer than binge drinking, but many feel "bulletproof." In situations when one or more risk factors are missing, the individual may disregard the consequences and continue engaging in the risky behavior (Wolburg, 2006).

The other behavior path predicted by the EPPM is motivated by fear. When consumers fail to heed the warnings from messages about health, they may experience a high level of fear, which can drive them to control the fear instead of the behavior. The person who feels at risk but lacks the self-efficacy to bring about change is a prime candidate for controlling the fear (e.g., the drinker who fears alcohol dependency and wants to cut back but can't help giving in to peer pressure). Fear can trigger denial, defiance, and even an escalation to riskier behavior. To illustrate the dark side of social marketing, the following quotes from college student smokers show the use of denial and defiance when confronted with anti-smoking messages. "Nothing bad will happen to me now so why bother [quitting]? Cigarettes serve a purpose by giving pleasure. No one wants to live forever" (Wolburg, 2006, p. 306). "I am going to have to die from something someday, and I like smoking, so why shouldn't this be my cause of death?" (Wolburg, 2006, p. 306).

According to the EPPM, the most effective way to avoid defensive responses when telling consumers that their behavior puts them at risk is to build their sense of self-efficacy so they believe they are capable of changing their behavior if they have the desire to do so.

What We Know about Reactance

In addition to effectively communicating risk, creators of social marketing campaigns must avoid heavy-handed messages, which have been known to elicit undesirable responses. Psychologists believe that many maladaptive responses such as denial and defiance can best be explained by "psychological reactance," which is a predictable reaction among people who believe their personal freedom is at stake (Brehm, 1966; Brehm & Brehm, 1981). When consumers encounter social marketing campaigns that tell them to change their behavior, they can potentially become argumentative, minimize the significance of the behavior, and assert their personal freedom (Miller & Rollnick, 1991). According to the theory, when people perceive a threat to personal freedom, they find the undesirable behavior all the more attractive and respond by "digging their heels in." Reactance accounts for various boomerang effects such as smokers celebrating their right to smoke during the national smoke-out event in November. The comments below in a study of college students' responses to anti-smoking messages illustrate how reactance affects smokers' thought processes. "All the 'truth' campaign does is convince me that I should go outside and light up another cigarette" (Wolburg, 2006, p. 294).

> Last summer on my way home from work, the "truth mobile" pulled right up next to me at a stoplight, and I couldn't believe it. I had smoked my last cigarette on my way to the car, and all I wanted to do was have a cigarette. I had no reasoning behind that but somewhere deep down maybe subconsciously, even though it is a bit childish, all I wanted to do was smoke.
>
> (Wolburg, 2006, p. 307)

A common response that bolsters reactance is the feeling of entitlement. For example,

> This is something I like doing. I don't do drugs. I don't drink excessively . . . Of all the vices, can't I have my one little cigarette? . . . All I'm doing is smoking. I'm not doing heavy drugs or robbing banks or murdering people. This is as bad as I get. Let me have my cigarette.
>
> (Wolburg, 2006, p. 309)

Social marketers who take reactance theory to heart create respectful messages that clearly allow consumers to believe they are in control. Any behavior change they make must be of their own free will, not one they are forced to make.

What We Know about Ritual

In addition to being mindful of risk theories and psychological reactance, creators of social marketing campaigns are well advised to understand the nature of rituals, especially when the unhealthy behavior has ritual meaning. Rook (1985) described ritual behavior as a symbolic activity that occurs in a fixed sequence that is repeated over time. He further identified the essential elements of rituals as an artifact, a script with rules and procedures, a performance, and an audience to observe the performance.

If we think of the drinking ritual, the performance and procedures include knowing how to drink as well as where and when to drink. The most important artifact is the alcohol itself whereas other drinkers become the audience.

Rituals also serve various functions. According to Driver (1991), they provide a sense of community, maintain order, and offer transformation. When focusing on alcohol consumption among college students, the ritual aspect of the behavior is apparent. Treise, Wolburg, and Otnes (1999, p. 26) observed that:

> When students drink with friends in a group, they establish a bond that fulfills the community function. When students observe the many rules associated with drinking, including how, when, and where to drink, they gain order and security in the social situation. Finally, when the alcohol releases inhibitions, alleviates stress, and offers a rite of passage, it transforms students from young adults who are anxious about social interactions to ones who are socially at ease.

A college student participant in an alcohol study (Wolburg, 2001) illustrates the community function further by addressing the transition from high school to college and the way alcohol eases the process by bringing new people together. For many, drinking is the one thing that they have in common with the strangers they encounter.

> Freshmen have just come from an environment [high school] where they know everything and have a very solid group of friends. They are thrust into a new city with all new people and a very difficult course load. Alcohol makes it easier to meet new people because it reduces your inhibitions.
>
> (Wolburg, 2001, p. 31)

Other comments address the ordering function—what days of the week and times of day are best for drinking, where drinking occurs for underage versus legal drinkers, how drinking games organize behavior, etc. One student explained that during a typical week, he would start drinking right after his last class, go to lunch and drink about six beers, go back home and drink some more until about 5 p.m. Friends would come over to drink until about 10 p.m., and then they would go to a bar or party to drink more. Drinking patterns varied from person to person, but all showed some degree of ordering related to the drinking ritual.

Alcohol consumption transforms drinkers in several ways because it is not only a rite of passage but an addictive substance. For some students, the appeal of alcohol is the ability to escape the pressures of college life and simply forget about the tension, feel comfortable, and be part of the social scene. A comment among college student drinkers illustrates the transformation that alcohol provides as social lubricant. "When I am sober, I often feel that there is a risk in speaking and talking with women. There is the risk of being rejected. However, when I am intoxicated, that risk seems to be null and void" (Wolburg, 2001, p. 32).

The significance of the drinking ritual is so great that when creators of social marketing campaigns ask students not to drink or to drink in moderation, they may not understand the magnitude of the behavior change they are requesting if they don't know the meaning of the ritual. Different strategies can be used, such as creating newer, less risky rituals to replace the harmful ones; however, the meaning of the ritual must be addressed one way or another for the effort to succeed.

Solving Health Problem with Products

The previous section addressed ways that advertisers and social marketers communicate with consumers when the goal is to solve health problems through behavior modification. This section addresses communication strategies when the solution to health problems comes from product use, particularly direct-to-consumer (DTC) prescription drugs, over-the-counter (OTC) drugs, and food supplements. Although the advertising of DTC prescription drugs carries specific legal requirements, the message strategy centers upon convincing consumers that the product provides a relatively easy and effective medical solution. Furthermore, the benefits of product use must seem worth any risks of side effects.

Prescription Drug Advertising

As we have seen in Chapter 18, the Food and Drug Administration (FDA) requires that all DTC prescription drugs must be approved before being advertised, and all printed promotional material must include a brief summary that names the drug and condition it treats, the scientific name, the side effects, contraindications, and effectiveness. Through the fair balance provision, the FDA requires television advertisers to identify both the risks and the benefits of all products.

Some current examples in magazines show how products deliver a compelling appeal to consumers. Turning now to Figure 33.1, a BOTOX® Cosmetic ad shows an attractive woman with the headline, "Once you get it, you really get it." Supporting statements reassure consumers that millions of women have experienced BOTOX® and that it is "proven year after year . . . with real, noticeable

Figure 33.1 Botox Ad.

results." Information on the back page addresses side effects, which include life-threatening problems with swallowing, speaking, or breathing due to weakening of associated muscles. However, the disclosure suggests that people with the highest risk have preexisting conditions, and that consumers can call their doctor or get medical help right away if they experience side effects.

Products that treat diseases use a similar formula. An ad for Pristiq® depicts a wind-up doll bent over with the headline, "Depression can make you feel like you have to wind yourself up to get through the day." Supporting statements define depression as a serious medical condition and reassure readers that Pristiq® is proven to treat depression. Ironically, noted side effects include suicidal thoughts or actions in children, teens, and young adults within the first few months of treatment.

Chapter 18 also points out that DTC prescription drug advertising is unique in directing consumers to a physician since they can't purchase it without a prescription. In this manner, the ads must not only arouse consumers' interest in the product but instruct then on ways to talk to physicians. The cosmetic ad instructs readers to "Ask your doctor if BOTOX® Cosmetic is right for you. There's only one BOTOX® Cosmetic," and the antidepressant ad tells readers that "Pristiq® may be a key in helping to treat your depression. So ask your doctor about Pristiq®."

Advertising of OTC Drugs and Dietary Supplements

In contrast to prescription drugs, consumers purchase dietary supplements and OTC drugs directly without the involvement of a third party. Thus, the advertising message only has to appeal to the consumer with a desirable solution to a problem that appears to carry minimal risks.

Although the advertising for OTC drugs and food supplements has fewer restrictions upon the messages that can be directed to consumers, the Federal Trade Commission's Bureau of Consumer Protection examines advertising practices directed toward those product categories in addition to alcohol, tobacco, and high-tech products (FTC, 2010). The FTC works in cooperation with the FDA to ensure that: (1) advertising is truthful and not misleading, and that (2) advertisers must have adequate substantiation for all objective product claims (FTC, 2001). Advertisers must consider expressed and implied claims as well as explicit claims and, thus, are cautioned that they must consider the total impression conveyed by all elements of the ad, not just the written text but also the product name and depictions. For example,

> An ad for a vitamin supplement claims that 90% of cardiologists regularly take the product. In addition to the literal claim about the percentage of cardiologists who use the product, the ad likely conveys an implied claim that the product offers some benefit for the heart. Therefore, the advertiser must have adequate support for both representations.
>
> (FTC, 2001)

Ads can sometimes be considered deceptive for what they fail to say. For example, an advertiser claims that its herbal product is a natural pain reliever "without the side effects of over-the-counter pain relievers." However, there is substantial evidence that the product can cause nausea in some consumers when taken regularly. Because of the reference to the side effects of other pain relievers, consumers would likely understand this ad to mean that the herbal product posed no significant adverse effects. Therefore, the advertiser should disclose information about the adverse effects of the herbal product.

Current guidelines also require advertisers to make clear and prominent disclosures to avoid deception. Disclosures at the bottom of a print ad or buried in a body of text or a brief video superscript in a television ad are inadequate. Consider the following example. A marketer promotes a supplement as a weight loss aid. There is adequate substantiation to indicate that the product can contribute to weight loss when used in conjunction with a diet and exercise regimen. The banner headline claims "LOSE 5 POUNDS IN 10 DAYS," the ad copy discusses how easy it is to lose weight by simply taking the product three times a day, and the ad includes dramatic before-and-after pictures. A fine print disclosure at the bottom of the ad, "Restricted calorie diet and regular exercise required," would not be sufficiently prominent to qualify the banner headline and the overall impression that the product alone will cause weight loss. The ad should be revised to remove any implication that the weight loss can be achieved by use of the product alone. This revision, combined with a prominent indication of the need for diet and exercise, may be sufficient to qualify the claim. However, if the research does not show that the product contributes anything to the weight loss effect caused by diet and exercise, it would be deceptive, even with a disclosure, to promote the product for weight loss.

Historically, some marketers have made unrealistic claims, and consumers seeking remedies that are "too good to be true" (e.g., take off the weight without diet and exercise) are particularly vulnerable to biased thinking. Persuasion theories, such as the Elaboration Likelihood Model discussed in Chapter 4, propose that consumers with a high level of involvement will process information centrally, and will carefully weigh the pros and cons rather than simply respond to peripheral cues such as the attractiveness of the product endorser. However, for consumers who are desperate to lose weight or solve acute health problems, high involvement can overwhelm rational thinking. When the result is wishful thinking rather than rational processing, consumers who should know better often don't.

Embracing a Healthy Lifestyle

Thus far we've explored ways that advertising presents solutions to health problems through behavior modification and product use. However, advertising also promotes a healthy lifestyle across multiple product categories including health and beauty aids, food items, beverages, and OTC drugs. Health claims not only promise such things as greater energy and stronger bones through nutritious food products but also improved appearance from products that repair damaged skin, hair, etc. Health messages of this type utilize a wide range of strategic options.

Transmission Strategies

One theoretical model that helps us understand the wide variety of strategic messages for persuasive purposes is the Six-Segment Advertising Strategy Wheel (Taylor, 1999). Taylor divided message strategies into two categories—transmission and ritual—each with three segments. Transmission messages impart information from a sender to receiver and are well suited for conveying data about the product, price, and benefits—a process that is depicted in Figure 1.1 of Chapter 1. On the other hand, ritual messages go beyond transmitting information and depict consumers using products to create a sense of identity, not only to others but also to oneself. The complexity and meaning of ritual communication will require the development of additional models. At a minimum, these models must address how consumers interpret visual communication, which relies on images rather than text and provides insights into the way that consumers identify with those depicted in ads.

Transmission strategies include the routine, acute need, and ration segments. According to Taylor (1999), purchase decisions for the *routine* segment are based on rational motives but are usually driven by habit because consumers do not invest large amounts of time deliberating. Communication for the routine segment has two functions: first, by providing a cue that a brand can satisfy needs and, second, by reminding consumers to continue buying the brand so they don't lose the habit. Appeals to convenience and product efficacy are common, and when combined with health claims are likely to promote the product's effectiveness among other healthy options, even if the comparison is only implied rather than explicit. Abundant examples exist: Aveeno Nourish + Moisturize Shampoo® invites consumers to "discover a transformation in hair care" with a product that is "clinically shown to repair damage, nourishing hair back to life in just 3 washes"; Wish-Bone Salad Dressing® "doesn't just add great flavor"—it helps "absorb more of the vitamins in your salad." These products are consumed in a relatively short time period and need to be repurchased frequently (see Figure 33.2).

Establishing a desirable position for routinely purchased products helps generate repeat purchases. For instance, positioning Wish-Bone Salad Dressing® as a healthier option than other salad dressings will increase the chances that nutritious-minded consumers will purchase Wish-Bone Salad Dressing® again instead of

Figure 33.2 Wish-Bone Salad Dressing® Ad.

buying a competing brand. Decisions in the *acute need* segment are typically made by consumers under pressure who are trying to make the best decision among readily available options in order to satisfy a critical need (Taylor, 1999). These consumers desire information, but their search is limited by the amount of time it takes to gather information as well as the time to deliberate. Building familiarity before the acute need arises is a common strategy among advertisers so that once in need, consumers already know and trust the brand. Healthcare providers, emergency clinics, hospitals, and law firms that specialize in accident cases are among those who find this strategy effective. For example, Figure 33.3 shows that the MD Anderson Cancer Center at the University of Texas claims that "when cancer strikes, we strike back." Personal injury attorney David Gruber tells television viewers that his firm represents people who have been injured in a car, truck,

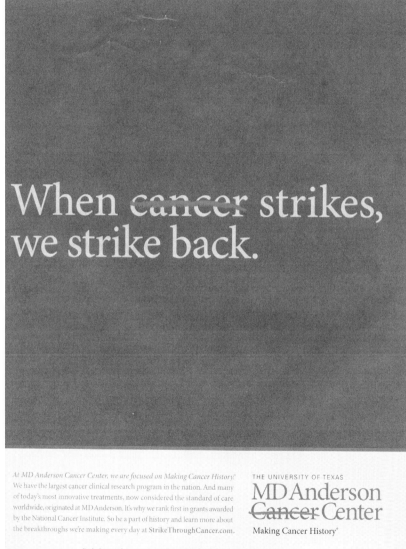

Figure 33.3 MD Anderson Cancer Center Ad.

or motorcycle accident with "experienced, talented and caring personal injury attorneys and staff who are dedicated to helping our clients get what they deserve." Until the need arises, these ads may have little relevance, but when "in need" consumers know whom to turn to.

Consumers who have a higher level of involvement and are willing to invest more time and effort in their deliberations typically represent the decisions in the *ration* segment (Taylor, 1999). Because consumers in high involvement situations are believed to be calculating, conscious, and rational in their thinking, the advertising goal is to use product information to inform and persuade them. Communication includes positioning strategies, use of a unique selling proposition, and preemptive claims, among others. A common example of product that combines a ration strategy with a health claim is the organic food category, which often uses a message with copious information to position the product as highly nutritious in comparison to its non-organic counterpart or as part of the slow food movement rather than a fast-food option. For example, an ad for Horizon® Organic Reduced Fat Milk promoted its nutrition content of DHA Omega-3 as "a nutrient which supports healthy brain development." The body copy further enhances the health claim by explaining that Horizon® brand organic milk contains "all the goodness of organic, plus an extra nutritional boost for growing minds and bodies."

Ritual Strategies

In contrast to the transmission messages, ritual messages in the Strategy Wheel are more often about drama than information. Based on the work of James Carey, ritual communication constructs and maintains "an ordered, meaningful cultural world that serves as a control and container for human action" (Taylor, 1999, p. 8). In this view of communication, news is not just information; it is drama between various forces played out in an arena. To make the concept more accessible, Taylor cites Rothenberg (1994), who observed that when a consumer purchases a pair of Nikes after viewing a Nike campaign that features athletes, the purchase serves the consumer like the communion ritual. A man or woman is "literally consuming part of a hero and taking on elements of his (or later her) character" (Taylor, 1999, p. 8).

Those who support a ritual view of communication do not deny the existence of the transmission view, especially for delivering product information; they merely believe that communication fulfills a ritual as well as a transmission function (e.g., Carey, 1975).

Within the Advertising Strategy Wheel, the three ritual strategies are ego, social, and sensory. Messages that utilize an *ego* strategy are image based and relate to emotional needs that can be fulfilled by products. Purchase decisions are emotionally important and "allow the consumer to make a statement to him/herself about who he/she is" (Taylor, 1999, p. 12). Consumers require little information and instead seek cues that show how the product fits within their definition of who they are. Appeals to vanity and self-actualization help define the individual, and health messages that use an ego strategy are abundant.

For example, Figure 33.4 shows a recent ad in *Real Simple* magazine showing the image of an aggressive, attractive, well-toned woman doing kickboxing with the headline, "be-HOT, be a better you." In the ad, the body copy promises that

Figure 33.4 GNC's be-HOT® Ad.

GNC's be-HOT® Exercise Enhancing Turbopak program will take workouts to the next level, increase metabolism, boost energy, and support lean muscle tone, but the visual communicates an ego-driven message about being "hot."

Ego messages appeal to both men and women, and an ad for Skechers® Shape-ups athletic shoes offers men a way to "get back in the game." The ad in Figure 33.5 depicts Joe Montana holding the shoe like a football and promises that wearing the shoes will burn more calories, tone muscles, and reduce stress on

Figure 33.5 Skechers® Ad.

back and legs. Much like the Nike example, wearing the product allows men to consume part of a hero and take on certain elements of Joe Montana's character.

The *social* segment delivers messages about products that are used to make a statement to others, unlike products in the ego segment which make a statement to one's self. Conspicuous consumption is an important part of this segment because products that are visible to others often meet emotional needs. Ads that depict the user in social situations are appropriate strategies in this category because consumers can imagine themselves as the user of the product as well as the impression that they will make on others.

An example can be seen in Figure 33.6 for the ever-popular "got milk?" campaign. In a recent *Redbook* ad, readers see a close up of chef Tyler Florence drinking a glass of milk with the message: "Milk the Moment. At dinnertime, my family and I always raise a glass—of milk. It's naturally nutrient rich like no other beverage . . . It brings everyone together no matter what life dishes up." The ad ends with the famous line, "got milk?" and evokes an emotion of togetherness as a family while advertising the nutritional value of milk.

While some products in the social segment are used publicly, others are consumed privately but for public results. For example, a Norateen® Hollywood Body ad for a muscle-building supplement in *Men's Health* shows an attractive, bare-chested man with a woman lusting after him, hugging him from behind while fingering the muscles in his chest. The only body copy is the headline, "Be admired."

Other brands of muscle-building products offer similar benefits for being noticed or standing out from the crowd. As shown in Figure 33.7, Hydroxycut Advanced Thermogenic promises men that they can "Own the Summer" whether they want to "hit the beach hard, explode off the lines, show some extra hustle on the field, or just show up your friends on the court." Ironically, some ads in the social segment promise to bring people together whereas others promise to separate them by providing a competitive edge.

Finally, the *sensory* segment works for healthy lifestyle products that offer a "moment of pleasure," whether it is based on taste, sight, hearing, touch, or smell. The role of advertising is to explicitly show how the product can produce sensory pleasure. For example, Figure 33.8 shows a recent Metromint® ad for spearmint water that uses a bright shade of green on a silver bottle with multiple bright colors to represent other flavors. The body copy reinforces the sensual appeal by saying,

> Your mouth is in for a treat. Metromint is pure water infused with real mint that cools and refreshes with every sip. The rest of your body will like it, too. Metromint is all natural . . . So you can refresh to your heart's content, 100% guilt-free.

Figure 33.6 "Got Milk?" Ad.

Figure 33.7 Hydroxycut Advanced Thermogenic Ad.

Figure 33.8 Metromint® Ad.

Conclusion

This chapter has addressed three theoretical perspectives to gain insights into the ways that advertisers and marketers communicate about health. First, it examined approaches when asking consumers to modify unhealthy behaviors, such as not smoking, not drinking in excess, not engaging in unprotected sex. In order to be successful, messages should effectively address risk (Witte, 1994), avoid eliciting psychological reactance (Brehm, 1966; Brehm & Brehm, 1981), and respect the meaning of rituals (Rook, 1985; Driver, 1991).

The second way that advertisers and marketers communicate about health is through the promotion of products that solve health problems, such as DTC prescription drugs, OTC remedies, and dietary supplements. These products offer relatively easy solutions for consumers, compared to the difficulty of modifying behavior; however, the risks of side effects and other undesirable outcomes have created a greater need for consumer protection in the form of advertising regulation.

The third way that advertisers and marketers communicate about health is through the promotion of a healthy lifestyle. At first glance, the use of health claims might appear to limit the creative strategy of the advertised brand; however, the Six-Segment Message Strategy Model (Taylor, 1999) shows a wide variety of approaches that advertisers can use, whether the product is routinely purchased, acutely needed, or one that requires great deliberation. Advertisers can also show consumers how to use products to make a statement to themselves or to others, or to enjoy the sensual pleasures that healthy products offer.

Attaining a healthy lifestyle is valued in American society, for it allows consumers to look and feel their best and stand out from others—a hallmark of an individualistic society.

References

Brehm, J. W. (1966). *A theory of psychological reactance*. New York: Academic Press.

Brehm, S. S., & Brehm, J. W. (1981). *Psychological reactance: A theory of freedom and control*. New York: Academic Press.

Carey, J. W. (1975). A cultural approach to communication. *Communication, 2* (December): 1–22.

Driver, T. (1991). *The magic of ritual*. New York: HarperCollins.

Federal Trade Commission (2001). Dietary supplements: An advertising guide for industry, facts for business. Retrieved August 1, 2010, from www.ftc.gov/bcp/edu/pubs/business/adv/bus09.shtm.

Federal Trade Commission (2010). Bureau of Consumer Protection. What we do. Retrieved August 1, 2010, from www.ftc.gov/bcp/edu/microsites/recruit/what-wedo.html.

Miller, W. R., & Rollnick, S. (1991). *Motivational interviewing: Preparing people to change addictive behavior*. New York: Guilford.

Reisen, C. A., & Poppen, P. J. (1999). Partner-specific risk perception: A new conceptualization of perceived vulnerability to STDs. *Journal of Applied Social Psychology, 29* (4), 667–684.

Ringold, D. J. (2002). Boomerang effects in response to public health interventions: Some unintended consequences in the alcoholic beverage market. *Journal of Consumer Policy, 25* (1), 27–63.

Rook, D. (1985). The ritual dimension of consumer behavior. *Journal of Consumer Research, 12* (December), 252–264.

Rothenberg, R. (1994). *Where the suckers moon*. New York: Vintage Books.

Taylor, R. E. (1999). A six-segment message strategy wheel. *Journal of Advertising Research, 39* (6), 7–17.

Treise, D., Wolburg, J. M., & Otnes, C. (1999). Understanding the "social gifts" of college drinking rituals: An alternative framework for PSA developers. *Journal of Advertising, 28* (2), 35–49.

Witte, K. (1994). Fear control and danger control: A test of the extended parallel process model (EPPM). *Communication Monographs, 61* (2), 113–134.

Wolburg, J. M. (2001). The "risky business" of binge drinking among college students: Using risk models for PSAs and anti-drinking campaigns. *Journal of Advertising, 30* (4), 24–39.

Wolburg, J. M. (2006). College students' responses to anti-smoking messages: Denial, defiance, and other boomerang effects. *Journal of Consumer Affairs, 40* (2), 293–323.

Additional Readings

Cialdini, R. B. (2009). *Influence: Science and practice* (5th ed.). Boston: Pearson Education.

Golan, G., & Zaidner, L. (2008). Creative strategies in viral advertising: An application of Taylor's six-segment message strategy wheel. *Journal of Computer-Mediated Communication, 13*, 959–972.

Huh, J., & Langteau, R. (2007). Presumed influence of direct-to-consumer (DTC) prescription drug advertising on patients: The physicians' perspective. *Journal of Advertising, 36* (3), 151–172.

Otnes, C. C., & Lowrey, T. M. (2004). *Contemporary consumption rituals: A research anthology*. Mahway, NJ: Lawrence Erlbaum.

Ringold, D. J. (2002). Boomerang effects in response to public health interventions: Some unintended consequences in the alcoholic beverage market. *Journal of Consumer Policy, 25* (1), 27–63.

Part VIII

The Future of Advertising Theories

Chapter 34

Human Barriers to Using Theory and Research on Responses to Advertising Messages

Ivan L. Preston

ME: Here's a newspaper headline that says: "Police Find Man With Cleaver in Temple."

YOU: Oh, I hope he didn't disrupt the religious service.

ME: No way! It means the cleaver was in the side of his head.

YOU: No way yourself!

The headline is from the "Lower Case" column in *Columbia Journalism Review* (2010), which in each issue features a group of such items taken from newspapers. *The Tonight Show*'s Jay Leno uses similar content in a feature called "Headlines." The items indicate failure by writers and editors to see a potential for ambiguity, resulting in double meanings that readers find entertaining. Readers also see an implication that the writer's goal may not have been achieved, which is humorous too, but also serious.

Creators and audiences of all sorts of messages typically have goals to pursue, often via transmission and reception of accurate information. Ambiguity or other errors may thwart their purpose, especially when senders are left unaware of whether their intended messages were actually transmitted and whether recipients had accurate or inaccurate understandings of them.

School teachers promote awareness of such problems with a brief game called "Telephone" in which students line up in a row. The teacher whispers a sentence containing some facts into the first one's ear, then each passes the secret to the next. The last student in line states out loud what came through, which is almost always a seriously different message. The mix-up is so predictable that the game is played little by anyone beyond the teaching mode. Most communications in the real world, however, are transmitted outside teachers' scrutiny and are free to create havoc that may remain undiscovered at critical moments.

In the advertising world, research on messages has long been available and provides the best means for ad people to identify responses to advertisements and/or ad messages. A major type of response, as illustrated above, involves what recipients understand the message to be telling them. While that response will be stressed here, the discussion applies also to other message effects, such as attitudes toward the advertised item, intention to buy, and buying brand loyalty. Such steps have been best described in work on Hierarchies of Effects, which although not emphasized in recent times, has been discussed at length in the past (Preston & Thorson, 1984; Preston, 1982).

There are various other topics of advertising research, such as values, lifestyle, brand share, and media audiences. This chapter, however, addresses only research on responses to the ad message. The main point to address is that some ad people may obstructively reject or ignore research findings because of the unpleasant implications of the revealed responses. They then may impose substitute conclusions that, by being strictly personal viewpoints, are invalid, unreliable, and biased, failing to reach the standard of being scientific while also blocking the use of established methods. The principal goal of this chapter is to describe such preemption and examine how to minimize the havoc it can create.

To begin, ad people have varying attitudes toward reports of how people respond to their creations. Some appreciate that messages can reasonably mean different things to different people and so are willing to accept research findings no matter how unpleasant they find such uncertainty. We may call these people the Flexibles. Other people refuse to accept uncertainty and prefer to conclude that only a single perceived message should possibly exist, applying to all of a message's recipients to the exclusion of any other choices. While the Flexibles may be applauded for being open to having their hopes contradicted by research data, these other people see nothing to correct. They persist in the face of contrary findings, even if from research. They can appropriately be called the Inflexibles. As with Potter Stewart, their logic requires that anyone who disagrees with them cannot be right.

Stewart was the Supreme Court justice who said he had no definition for pornography but then declared that "I know it when I see it" (Jacobellis v. Ohio, 1964). He did not consider that others applying the same term to the same challenged media content might disagree on whether it was pornography. He seemed not to realize that the same conclusion could be reached only if all observers applied the same standard, i.e., the same set of facts, to the concept. Without such a shared basis, the social science weatherman could easily predict potential havoc just around the corner and, in fact, Stewart acknowledged later that he had drawn many questioning and negative comments about his statement.

An old saying is that while we are entitled to our own opinions, we are not entitled to our own facts. What messages tell us are facts as we see them, and the Flexibles either acknowledge or at least do not reject the idea that perceptions of message content may vary from one person to another. They may wish it weren't so, but they appreciate that that's how things work.

The Inflexibles, by contrast, reject the idea of different people seeing different messages. Some of them do it with a quick and decisive reaction; they are the Knee-Jerk Inflexibles. They may, for example, use a secondary source such as a dictionary definition and say, well, that's the meaning right there, for me and for everybody else. They are "reasoning" in their way, and they may be unacquainted with arguments that refute their method. They may be sincere in believing that when there is one message there should be but one response.

Another group may be called the Agenda Inflexibles. They decide that people understand a message as they do because it supports a predetermined agenda they have. They would prefer not to acknowledge or discuss the agenda because of not wanting to expose the arbitrariness. So they copy the Knee-Jerk Inflexibles in claiming that their preferred understanding is the only one that can possibly exist. They may not be very sincere in doing so. This category of persons could be the biggest source of havoc concerning questions of what is communicated.

In combination, the Flexibles see the possibility of uncertainty, the Knee-Jerk Inflexibles do not, and the Agenda Inflexibles do but pretend they do not. Any person may be any of the three types for any given message, and, by going from instance to instance, individuals can be any two or even all three types over time.

The pertinence of these types of people to advertising theory and research is that Inflexibles reject not only other people's contrary understandings but necessarily also any research findings that counteract their rejection. Yes, the business has copy testing (also called other names such as pre-testing or copy point playback). But the point here is not whether ad people have research but whether they respect it and use it. To reject it makes a big difference because research findings almost invariably support the Flexibles by finding a variety of understandings of messages.

It would seem from this that we could use research as the antidote for the Inflexibles' behavior. Their only evidence of what consumers perceive is in their own heads, while theory and research operate in the more pertinent location of consumers' heads. Paralleling that strength, however, is the problem that the Inflexibles are poison for research.

I propose the latter as a topic for study. The idea, coming from anecdotal observations over the years, of course, is speculative. It comes to mind because I have sensed for a long time that research on message response has no great acceptance from what I take to be substantial numbers of the people who actually make the ads—people such as copywriters and art directors—as contrasted to others such as account supervisors or top executives.

My point is a narrow one—creatives seem generally appreciative of research prior to doing their creating while seeming less favorable to studies done after the fact. As to the latter, I have heard creative people say they rely instead on expectations derived from their own experience. I have heard that response research is one of the first things to go when budgets must be cut.

Consequently, this chapter proposes an effort to promote thinking and acting on these issues. In continuing, I examine (1) how research got into advertising education and practice, (2) why advertising creative people may often be Inflexibles, and, finally, (3) how researchers might break down the Inflexible barrier and play a greater role in producing knowledge of communication in the best way possible.

Research and Advertising Education and Practice

To begin, let's see how theory and research on advertising and other mass media messages arrived and eventually thrived in the curricula of our mass media and marketing programs. Academic advertising programs began about a century ago, mostly as single courses in journalism programs, reflecting the presence of ad departments in newspaper and magazine offices. Eventually, they became departments that offered majors, or sequences, specializations, etc., in those schools, many of which took names such as media or mass communications.

Research was absent from the earliest programs, but became a staple item starting after World War II. A strong force for the change was a body of social psychology surveys and experiments done during the war by social psychologists for the U.S. Army on the effects of propaganda (Simpson, 1994). Those efforts were highly regarded for their findings and methods, and so prompted academic programs in communications and marketing to take up such topics. The universities also wanted these units to modify the "trade school" image by emulating others on campuses in hiring PhDs and publishing research.

Thus, communication and marketing departments, in reflection of psychology's stimulus-response (S-R) model, switched from their original emphasis solely on the message stimuli to examining responses to those messages as well. The transition was not entirely smooth, since students and faculty, the latter typically with backgrounds of professional activity, were very happy with courses on writing, design, editing, production, and transmission of news stories and advertisements. When such orientation then was diluted, the old newspaper hands and the new social psychologists found themselves in uncomfortable proximity. The former had the "old time religion" on their side, but the latter more easily integrated themselves into the university community. Even worse was the concern of professional faculty that they might be required to take up publishing in order to avoid perishing.

Despite some vestiges still remaining of the transition period, integration of the two areas has now been essentially complete for a long time and cooperation is the norm. Students, and eventually the organizations they join, now benefit from learning not just how to create messages but how to evaluate them. That is the fundamental difference between studying advertising/marketing/journalism, and studying communications.

I first encountered this difference in my graduate study at Michigan State's communication college in a department newly created to specialize in theory and research. In my first class in 1959, we were told that many academics and others place the meaning of a message *in the message*. Thus, we were constantly given the catch phrase that "Meanings are in people, not in messages"—not in words, pictures, or sounds—nowhere in messages. It was like a mantra. We didn't actually chant it, but we certainly said it often.

Our mission for our coming careers as professors was to establish this more correct viewpoint in the many programs where it was not yet accepted. Today the missionary zeal has subsided in light of the level of success accomplished.

One interesting example that became evident over the years is that dictionaries were tending less toward being authoritative in their orientation. Instead of labeling their content as an inviolable set of rules about what words mean, they became reporters of whatever usage was occurring. They were going with the flow of society by changing from prescriptive to descriptive.

That amounts to a recognition that changes in meaning were becoming quite normal and acceptable. A good example is the word "media," which the Macintosh computer's dictionary, the *New Oxford American*, now interprets as acceptably singular in some usages rather than always being plural.

Still, the claim of success we can make about giving communication a research orientation mostly involves academic programs. In the wider society, we do not see the same level of accomplishment.

Why Advertising Creative People May Often be Inflexibles

Turning now, let's discuss the effects of message research beyond academia and return to the problem of the Inflexibles. As a beginning point, it is not without common sense to think that if a message or any stimulus is the same for all, then what people perceive it to be must also be the same.

Yet all those who gather data on such responses know that message recipients typically vary in what they perceive. Accordingly, communications faculties interpret responses to mass media as being made individually in our separate minds. Despite that, other types of people stick to the older and more traditional message orientation.

To say that the automatic response of the Knee-Jerk Inflexibles is simply an aspect of human nature is a fair point. But, given that they fool themselves in doing so, there is no choice but to criticize the habit. It lets egos get in the way of seeing that there may be different responses for different people. There also seems to be another common knee-jerk belief, however false, that advertising, including both subliminal and supraliminal content, has a power to control minds so strongly that everyone takes it literally. That, too, leads to the conclusion that everyone sees it the same way (Broyles, 2006).

Over the 50 years that I have been contemplating the "meanings are in people" paradigm, I believe that the proportion of people who understand and accept the idea has not increased very much. There are more of us academics who follow the principle than before, and the number of students who learn about it is surely growing all the time. But the point has not really been instilled into the public consciousness.

What about the Agenda Inflexibles? While the Knee-Jerks have their thinking driven by their understanding, correct or incorrect, of how communication works, these people may be driven by the agendas they are pursuing.

For example, two consumer economists presented a content analysis of cigarette ads at a Public Policy and Marketing Conference prior to publication (Ringold & Calfee, 1989). They reported what claims the ads explicitly stated and also what messages consumers took those claims to be telling them. They reported those two things as being exactly the same in all cases. A consumer psychologist objected to the perceptions being inferred only from the messages, and one hell of an argument broke out.

The psychologist later wrote that the study "found only what was said and not what was communicated" (Cohen, 1989). The responses conceivably *could* be the same as the stimuli; but communication researchers know that such a result is infrequent and, in any event, the research in question produced no evidence that addressed the question.

The economists had two agendas, one being that their traditional economics training assumes rational behavior, which would best be borne out if all message recipients see the same message. The other was that they opposed strong regulation of cigarettes, and the literal content of the ads suggested that strong regulation was not needed to protect smokers. That, too, would best be supported if the literal content of the ads were what smokers perceived the ads to be saying.

Yet, in concluding that the perceived messages were what they wanted them to be, the economists were identifying the response only by examining the stimulus. And they could not understand the consequences of that. They thought everything is evident from what is said. As reviewers of manuscripts submitted for publication are well aware, this is a problem that often occurs with interpretation of content analyses. That many researchers make such assumptions was supported recently by a marketing researcher who is a former editor of the *Journal of Advertising* (Carlson, 2008). The problem is also noted by Petty (2008).

Herb Rotfeld, editor of *Journal of Consumer Affairs*, reports frequently about having to eliminate errors on the same point in his letters to prospective authors (Rotfeld, 2008). And Rotfeld, along with Ray Taylor, while editing a special issue of the *Journal of Advertising*, reported seeing a number of articles assuming that what is communicated is identified sufficiently by what is said (H. Rotfeld, personal communication, 2009).

Elsewhere, the Federal Trade Commission for some time has been using consumer economists as substitutes for consumer psychologists. The switch does not work when economists rely on assumptions about response while psychologists make actual observations. Some economists have abandoned such habits, but not enough to eliminate the problem of what amounts to suitable evidence.

Much of my own experience pertinent to this topic has been with government regulators. I first became interested when I saw that they identify deceptive claims based on their findings of what is communicated—a perfect fit with what I had studied. But in 1971 when the Commission asked me to be an expert witness on what was communicated, I disagreed with their proposed method, which was simply to have me state my presumably expert opinion.

Instead, I proposed a consumer survey; but they said they had no money for it. I countered that I could use student subjects and do it almost for free, and ultimately they agreed. It worked and was the first of many surveys they have commissioned over all these years (Sun Oil Co., 1974). I feel it is the most significant thing I have done professionally.

I also found, however, that with claims of opinion or valuation, called puffery, the regulators do not make observations—they just make the assumption that consumers take "puffs" to mean nothing that would influence their buying decision. Regarding the accuracy of that, they unfortunately have no idea, having never looked to see. Like the economists cited, they identify the response by examining the stimulus. They decide merely by their legal authority, which for puffery is typically by citing precedents, with the earliest coming about 250 years before psychology even became a discipline (Preston, 1996).

That is the essential foundation of what I have written about puffery (Preston, 1996). Many see it as a consumer protection issue, which, of course it is, but to me it is predominantly about people not knowing because of not looking. Such procedure is, among other things, incredibly disrespectful of research. They often display the pattern of using us when they think our findings will suit their purpose, but not using our research when they don't think it fits their purpose.

My viewpoint is buttressed by other academics that worked at the FTC, including Keith Hunt of the University of Utah in 1973–1974. Recently, he wrote this by email to Herb Rotfeld:

> It was a fantastic experience, an immersion in the problems you and Ivan and Jef [Richards] and others have addressed. We are sure we have "truth" that is valuable to the lawyers, when, in fact, all our "truth" does is make their world more difficult. Of course, they don't want behavioral science in their world of precise words and logic structures. So it goes on and on and on. I appreciate your continuing exhortations that the behavioral scientists share some of the blame because we don't adequately understand the law. However, in the end, the law is its own universe with no need for alien "truths" to enhance it. Indeed, anything external to the law itself only muddies things and keeps legal truth from emerging.
>
> (K. Hunt, personal communication, June 23, 2009)

These comments about economists and lawyers point toward identifying them as Inflexibles. Some may not be, of course, but we may assume at a high level of probability that they follow the belief that if there is only one stimulus then there must be only one response. The response need not be observed independently because examining the stimulus can identify it a priori. Refusal to use research to check their conclusions puts them in the Knee-Jerk category and also reveals the effect of their prior agendas. Economists want to maintain their long-running assumption that people are rational. Lawyers want to maintain their long-running belief that precedents from the past should continue to prevail in the present.

What, though, can we say about the degree of flexibility of advertising people? Do they have particular traits, or are they in particular situations, that push them one way or the other? I suggest that many of the creatives, meaning those who are most hands-on in choosing, devising, and arranging the content of ads, are Agenda Inflexibles to a considerable degree simply because that trait can readily be built in to what a creative *is*.

What does it mean, after all, to be a copywriter, an artist, or art director, even a media buyer? Creative people working in various other areas can be entirely free and independent of working for anyone other than themselves, but you cannot be so when you have advertisers as clients. And as the creator of your clients' messages you are even more importantly the creators of the resulting effects, and you are supposed to know in advance what those effects will be regarding your own agendas of, first, selling ads and, then, selling the products and services depicted in those ads.

But while that orientation prompts creatives to want predetermined results regarding what is actually communicated, data on message effects can spoil the fun. The researcher may step in and show that the result was not what the creatives expected, either by being another message, or, as usually happens, by being a variety of different messages.

Although such research may be done after the fact, it also may be done beforehand, i.e., pre-testing. My concern, however, includes the possibility that even if the research is available, the creatives' agenda may lead to twisting the findings or just ignoring them.

The question of which is the better communication expert, the creator/seller or the researcher, is something that involved parties cannot find easy to be impartial about. The question is also complicated because people become identified as experts in different ways. A student upon graduation may be designated an engineer or lawyer and therefore, however tentatively, an expert. Being a success is something different, however. Success presumably requires a more definite display of expertise, and therefore will take a while longer.

Professors function in that way. They must show evidence of expertise in order to be considered for publication. If they then get published and their work is heralded, then they can claim success. Such achievement, thus, comes only after the establishing of their expertise.

The process works differently in advertising. The designation of "expert" tends to come *after* the achievement of success. Like professors, creatives must gain approval for publication, but the process does not include presenting a degree, as with a professor or lawyer. There is no degree they can get that paints the word "expert" across their foreheads before they are hired. Those to whom creatives submit their work necessarily make their judgments in a more speculative way, and more permanent judgments are made only later. Approval is followed by production and publication, and only after that can success be shown. Creatives found to have been successful, via evidence such as findings of high or higher levels of consumer awareness, comprehension, or purchasing, etc., will then be saluted as experts.

On a personal note, when I once was an assistant to an account executive, I inquired about the possibility of becoming a copywriter. I already knew that there were no assistants in that department. I then learned further that they only hire a person for that job who already is a copywriter. So you had to be one to get a job, but you needed a job in order to be one.

The agency, Ketchum MacLeod and Grove, now departed, was about twentieth in billings nationally, and I believe its size made that policy possible. If I went to a small shop I could have gotten experience via on-the-job training, which I might have done had I not eventually chosen graduate school instead.

Of course, creatives can improve their lot by having a success, and on the next round, those who did have success would *begin* as experts. Even then, though, the process will remain tentative. If there is failure at a later time, the designation "expert" can be removed as fast as it was given. Like a baseball player, you're only as good as your last at bat. "What have you done for me lately?" is a prevailing attitude.

The point of this discussion is that the slender link that creatives may have with expertise and success is thinned even further by message research that comes along and belittles their accomplishment. To embrace it looks too much like conceding that you're not an expert. An expert doesn't need research. That's a big blow for a strong ego to take.

Of course, such research objectively may be entirely appropriate from the standpoint of the companies involved. It's just that people with agendas aren't dedicated to objectivity, and they will decide such things whenever permitted to.

Breaking Down the Inflexible Barrier and Playing a Greater Role in Producing Knowledge of Communication

From this, my conclusion is that advertising theorists/researchers, particularly those outside the industry, i.e., academics, need not just produce research but also must sell it.

The easiest and most obvious place to sell it is in teaching. Michigan State in my time, 1959–1964, had a beginning course called "The Process of Communication." My experience as a graduate assistant and discussion group leader made clear that its emphasis was on social psychological matters, the human process, rather than on the nature of the media.

Had student reaction been examined, I would not have been surprised to find that those taking that course gained insights not acquired by others. From that experience I feel such teaching should be emphasized in all programs involving mass media. It could teach about the potential for research to contribute to their success, and also explain the agendas and egotistical urges that prompt people to ignore research.

Another thing that might usefully be taught to students of research, and used by research professionals, involves the way research is presented to advertising people or anyone else not trained in it. Presentations might usefully vary in style from that used by researchers when speaking to each other. For example, what looks like a wonderfully conceived spread of data across a page or a screen might be taken by a lay audience as an incomprehensible bunch of meaningless numbers. As to speaking, points made orally might be presented more slowly and with more redundancy than researchers would use when presenting to each other.

Another item to teach is that researchers might usefully avoid stating or implying that science is always valid, always superior, cannot be disagreed with, and other such things that may reveal them to be—horrors!—Inflexibles themselves. Talking down to people or claiming too much are definitely things to avoid. Be prepared to admit, when pressed, or even voluntarily, that research is less than perfect. Restraining the ego is always a good idea.

Just as ad people study consumers to find out what they want, researchers might well acquire some knowledge of their clients' needs and how research can contribute to their goals. It is essential to show deference to the perspectives of those to whom you are presenting. Such an orientation not only helps clients but also helps researchers themselves who might usefully remember that they are in their own competitive environment in which other researchers may be competing with them for business.

While suggestions for topics in the classroom are easy to make, what can researchers do in their own world? In general, things out there seem to be more difficult. We could try to create publications, programs, or talks that could reach the general public. What we really need are people who can get their comments into the press in the manner that is so often accomplished these days by economists, political scientists, sociologists, psychiatrists, and any other experts on newsworthy matters. We could offer ourselves as experts in the same way. That's all easier said than done, of course, but we should keep the idea before us as a goal.

It could include trying to reach advertising creatives, although, candidly, I can't imagine much luck in trying to rewire people who've been in the business for a long time. Probably our best hopes would be to make our students as much aware as possible about these issues and hope that the next generation of creative people has their egos better under control.

I have always found dealing with the effects of all sorts of messages to be a fascinating area, for its complexities and intricacies and also for its contribution toward keeping society functioning and growing. We should regard it proudly as being a satisfying area in which to be working and providing a valuable resource for businesspeople and citizens alike.

Acknowledgment

Earlier versions of parts of this discussion were used in the commentary "Understanding Communication Research Findings," *Journal of Consumer Affairs, 43* (Spring 2009), 170–173.

References

Broyles, S. J. (2006). Subliminal advertising and the perpetual popularity of playing to people's paranoia. *Journal of Consumer Affairs, 40* (Winter), 392–406.

Carlson, L. (2008). Use, misuse, and abuse of content analysis for research on the consumer interest. *Journal of Consumer Affairs, 42* (Spring), 100–105.

Cohen, J. B. (1989). Counting advertising assertions to assess regulatory policy: When it doesn't add up. *Journal of Public Policy and Marketing, 8*, 24–29.

Lower Case. (2010, July/August). The lower case headlines that editors probably wish they could take back. *Columbia Journalism Review*, July–August, inside back cover.

Jacobellis v. Ohio, 378 U.S. 184 (1964).

Petty, R. D. (2008). Pet peeves: Trademark law and the consumer enjoyment of brand pet parodies. *Journal of Consumer Affairs, 42* (Fall), 461–470.

Preston, I. L. (1982). The association model of the advertising communication process. *Journal of Advertising, 11* (2), 3–15. See also: Errata. *Journal of Advertising, 11* (3), 24.

Preston, I. L., (1996). *The great American blow-up: Puffery in advertising and selling* (Rev. ed.). Madison: University of Wisconsin Press.

Preston, I. L., & Thorson, E. (1984). The expanded association model: Keeping the hierarchy concept alive. *Journal of Advertising Research, 24* (1), 59–65.

Ringold, D. J., & Calfee, J. E. (1989). The informational content of cigarette advertising: 1926–1986. *Journal of Public Policy and Marketing, 8*, 1–23.

Rotfeld, H. J. (2008). Can you really say that? *Journal of Consumer Affairs, 42*, 484–487.

Simpson, C. (1994). "Worldview warfare" and World War II. Retrieved March 17, 2011, from www.icdc.com/~paulwolf/oss/worldview.htm.

Sun Oil Co. (1974). *Federal Trade Commission Decisions, 84*, 247–261.

Chapter 35

Toward Theories of Advertising
Where Do We Go From Here?

Marla B. Royne

Theory is an integral part of almost all academic disciplines because it is a critical tool for understanding why things happen; as a result, it helps to establish disciplinary knowledge. According to Webster, there are seven current definitions of a theory (dictionary.com, 2010):

1. a coherent group of general propositions used as principles of explanation for a class of phenomena;
2. a proposed explanation whose status is still conjectural, in contrast to well-established propositions that are regarded as reporting matters of actual fact;
3. in mathematics, a body of principles, theorems, or the like, belonging to one subject (e.g., number theory);
4. the branch of a science or art that deals with its principles or methods, as distinguished from its practice (e.g., economic theory);
5. a particular conception or view of something to be done or of the method of doing it; a system of rules or principles;
6. contemplation or speculation; and
7. a guess or conjecture.

Clearly, the basic concept of theory has more than one interpretation. And while theory is important to establishing an academic discipline, the nature of theory in the academic world is still debated. In classic marketing theory, Hunt (1991, p. 148), notes that

> Although theory would have to rank high among the most abused terms in marketing, there is probably more unanimity among philosophers of science as to what constitutes a theory than there is agreement among them concerning the nature of laws and explanations. This is not to say that there is a universal consensus concerning the nature of theoretical constructions. Rather, different uses of the term "theory" in philosophy of science are more apparent than real, more superficial than substantive.

Whether the different terminology is superficial or substantive, there is obviously a difference across researchers' perspectives. In the advertising arena, theory is generally used to provide an explanation of why people respond to advertising in a particular manner or why certain advertisements are more effective. That is, academic advertising researchers—social scientists—use theory just as the physical scientists do.

Reviewers of top academic advertising journals, such as the *Journal of Advertising*, continue to argue that for research to make a contribution to advertising and warrant publication in the *Journal*, it must contribute to advertising theory. However, the *Journal*'s purpose— as stated in the editorial guidelines— is for articles to contribute to advertising theory *and its relationship to practice*. The questions raised, then, are: what really constitutes advertising theory, and how does theory contribute to advertising practice as a whole, including academics and practitioners? Only by answering these questions can we then identify what theoretical directions the discipline needs. Yet, even before these questions can be answered, a more fundamental question demanding an immediate response with today's rapidly changing society is "what is advertising?"

For many years, a definition of advertising found in many textbooks included such characteristics as paid, mass-mediated, and persuasive (e.g., O'Guinn, Allen, & Seminik, 2009). And while some textbooks today still cling to this antiquated definition, despite the current positioning of the particular textbook in which it appears, the definition of advertising has not evolved so much over the years inasmuch as definitions have blurred, as noted in Chapter 1 of this volume. This is evidenced by Quesenberry's (2010) discussion of the current winners of the prestigious Cannes award, where public relations, integrated communications, and Internet campaigns earned top honors. As he notes, some of the "most respected leaders in the industry are now rewarding campaigns that fuse public relations, advertising and digital media" (Quesenberry, 2010, p. 7). Quesenberry (2010) also notes that this recognition is what clients have been demanding and what has been working in the marketplace. The bestowing of such accolades on these newer "fused" approaches is clearly a reflection of the well-accepted changes in the advertising field.

With this recognition clearly filtering through the industry, it is essential to determine if these changes are being reflected in the development of advertising theory. This can only be assessed by examining what has been submitted to and published in the leading theoretically-based journals in the advertising discipline. Even more important is to determine if this theoretically-grounded research is applicable to the practice of advertising.

An analysis both of submissions to and of publications in the *Journal of Advertising* suggests that, indeed, the scope and definition of advertising are changing and expanding. Submitted and published articles run the gamut to include the Internet, mobile advertising, product placement, advergames, and the integration of advertising and publicity, among others. This supports the notion of moving away from classic definitions of advertising, and developing a more relevant set of characteristics that more accurately reflect what is going on in the current marketplace. Perhaps the word "integrated" is not quite appropriate, but the term convergence—where two or more things come together—is more applicable because the concept of blended campaigns includes the use of two or more types of media.

Even with a clearer definition of advertising, the next task may prove more difficult than the first. As a definition, advertising probably fits best into the fourth theoretical definition presented above: the branch of a science or art that deals with its principles or methods, as distinguished from its practice—in this case—advertising theory. It can also be argued that advertising theory is a particular conception or view of something to be done or of the method of doing it (definition 4) or even a system of rules or principles (definition 5).

But an examination of the other definitions of theory reinforces that as a discipline, advertising has few theories of its own because it borrows regularly from other disciplines such as psychology, sociology, anthropology, economics, marketing, and others. So the coherent group of general propositions that are used as principles of explanation for a class of phenomena—advertisements (definition 1), a proposed explanation whose status is still conjectural, in contrast to well-established propositions that are regarded as reporting matters of actual fact (definition 2) are not truly advertising theories. Thus, it is the theories from other fields that help advertising researchers explain their findings. While this is not necessarily a "bad" thing, it is one that must be clearly acknowledged, because the advertising discipline cannot claim such theories as its own. This is not unusual, however, as other disciplines (e.g., marketing) face the same challenge. Consequently, a question remains about what theory can, and should, be developed within the advertising discipline.

Next, it is important to determine whether theory is being applied to the practice of advertising. With campaign winners outside the traditional scope of advertising capturing top honors at the prestigious industry awards, there is a strong indication that the knowledge of practitioners is far beyond the academic world. This is hardly surprising because academic theory in business-related disciplines often lags behind practice. And Madison Avenue is no exception with top agencies on the cutting edge of creativity. These top agencies are well regarded and well known for engaging in consumer research to ensure accurate information and consumer understanding to assist in the development of effective advertising campaigns. Potential results or the changing of consumer behaviors drives advertising campaigns. There is no indication that these agencies use theory to guide their research or campaign planning. Hence, we might then ask, why do we need theory at all?

A noted scholar once said, "there is nothing as practical as a good theory" (Lewin, 1951). But if theoretical explanations have no place in the "real" advertising world, then, indeed, why should we develop theory at all? In short, for advertising as an industry to move forward, advertising theory must inform practice and provide implications. In doing so, it must focus on predicting, explaining, and understanding advertising phenomenon for practitioners. It must also go beyond traditional definitions of advertising because they no longer hold. Rather, advertising must be viewed in holistic terms and must include all aspects of communication to audiences. As noted earlier, understanding convergence of media and consumer reactions to these media have the promise of moving both the academic and practitioner worlds forward.

But many advertising-related constructs, such as Integrated Marketing Communications, are practitioner based. Does academia have a role, a responsibility, or even an obligation to better understand the theoretical meanings behind these constructs? While the tools of advertising may change, human behavior generally does not. Does that mean that existing theories can be used to understand the current tools? And, if so, are these theories considered advertising theory? As noted, the advertising discipline borrows theories from other disciplines to establish its own discipline, and these theories do not always inform advertising practice.

So where do we go from here? How can researchers in the academic advertising arena best contribute to the advertising discipline as a whole? Abandoning theory is hardly an option, because at the very least, theory is what sets the foundation for the development of new ideas and defines the legitimacy of a particular area. And without theory, we are left with outcome research that is simply situation based, not a better understanding of how and why things work. That said, academic advertising researchers need to develop a body of theoretical understanding that separates advertising from other disciplines in the social sciences. With the seeming demise of the "grand theory" across different disciplines, we must accumulate the important data collected and used by practitioners in an effort to come up with a better understanding of our field. While data-driven research is hardly the approach advanced and taught by scientists, it appears that much of "science" may be going that way, and, hence, this may be the best way for advertising academicians to contribute to the discipline. Partnering with practitioners *and* their data may help practitioners understand the consumer by using theory to explain marketplace happenings in a more systematic way. Helping the industry understand these occurrences through the use of theory to explain consumers and their behaviors has the potential for advertising academicians to advance the advertising discipline as a whole.

References

dictionary.com (2010, December). Retrieved December 1, 2010, from http://diction-ary.reference.com/browse/theory.

Hunt, S. D. (1991). *Modern marketing theory: Critical issues in the philosophy of marketing science.* Cincinnati, OH: Southwestern Publishing.

Lewin, K. (1951). *Field theory in social science.* London: Harper & Brothers.

O'Guinn, T. C., Allen, C., & Semenik, R. J. (2009). *Advertising and integrated brand promotion* (5th ed.). Mason, OH: Thomson-Southwestern.

Quesenberry, K. A. (2010). The ad age is over: A call for interdisciplinary instruction. *AAA Newsletter*, 7–9.

Chapter 36

Advancing Advertising Theories and Scholarship

Hairong Li

Advertising is a profession of ideas—creative ideas that can foster the market growth of businesses and the economic and social welfare of a nation and, thus, a better life for everyone. The charge to advertising scholars is to contribute to the profession by cultivating advertising students and professionals with domain-specific knowledge. Advertising scholars create useful knowledge through rigorous academic research and disseminate it to students and professionals. For the knowledge to be useful, it must be new, either theoretically or managerially, and ideally both. As a founding editor of the *Journal of Interactive Advertising*, an editorial board member of several journals in the US, Europe, and Asia, and an ad hoc reviewer of many journals over the past decade, I often ponder how innovative advertising research and scholarship really are. I would like to share some of my thoughts here.

Research Innovativeness and Theories About Advertising

I tend to see a study in terms of its degree of innovativeness. Studies of one type are those that use new phenomena of our field to substantiate an existing theory. We are fortunate to be in a field that has experienced many advances. Using online advertising forms as an example, we have seen the development of display ads, sponsorship, search ads, viral ads, and, more recently, blogs and microblogs, social ads, user-generated content, widgets, and mobile apps. On the other hand, popular theories have been developed over the years, including attribution theory, social identity theory, social learning theory, the elaboration likelihood model, theory of reasoned action and theory of planned behavior, uses and gratifications, the technology acceptance model, and many more. If a study studies a new phenomenon such as the adoption of mobile advertising, participation in social media, or response to viral ads to support any theory, I usually see it as less innovative because such a study adds little to our understanding of the new phenomenon under study. I would rather see a study that fails to support an existing theory with a new advertising form or under a new context, though studies of this type are usually difficult to get published. Thus, my attitude is that if a theory has been tested numerous times and consistently supported, further studies to substantiate it are unnecessary.

A more innovative approach is to revise an existing theory or model to better describe a new development. Popular theories of advertising were most often established years ago under conditions that now no longer exist. It is reasonable to assume that the explanatory power of an existing theory should be increased if it finds support when tested under a new condition. This approach is actually quite common. For example, a ScienceWatch analysis (2009) of recent research on the Technology Acceptance Model found 28 highly cited studies between 2003 and 2009 whereby most studies revised the original model. A doctoral student in our program recently used the Technology Acceptance Model to explain the intention to adopt mobile websites in an educational setting. The study added "perceived enjoyment" to the perceived ease of use and perceived usefulness to the model, and the expanded model accounted for a greater amount of the variance (Sung, 2010).

Revisions also can be made to conceptual models. For example, Harvey (1997) expanded the Advertising Research Foundation's 1961 model that specified a six-level advertising process. Increasingly used measures such as recall, click-through, and lead generation as well as profits, loyal customers, and return on investment enabled the expansion of this popular model. Integrating ideas of industry experts, Harvey presented a new model to include two renamed levels of the previous model and four new levels, increasing the model to 10 levels. The model could be customized for measuring both traditional and interactive advertising effectiveness.

In another example, Dentsu, the largest advertising agency in Japan, developed the AISAS model (Kobayashi, 2008). The model consists of five stages—awareness, interest, search, action, and share. The model does not assume linear relationships among these stages. That is, consumers in the search stage may jump to the share stage and consumers in the interest stage may share with other consumers as well. This model is a revision of the model of hierarchical advertising effects, which posits linear stages from awareness to interest, desire, memory, and action. I would argue the AISAS model is more innovative and useful as a planning framework today because it calls for search and sharing mechanisms in marketing communications planning. When the hierarchy model was developed, there were no search engines and social media!

The most innovative approach is normally found in those who establish new theories and models, which are "new paradigms" to use Kuhn's (1962) term. These theories and models, largely induced from keen observations and empirical tests regarding new phenomena, offer unique perspectives. Let me give a few examples. In one of the first conceptualizations of marketing on the Internet, Hoffman and Novak (1996) stated that the many-to-many communication model turned traditional principles of mass media advertising based on the one-to-many model inside out, making obsolete marketing and advertising approaches that assumed a passive, captive consumer. They proposed a model of network navigation in computer-mediated environments, and many of the concepts and relationships in the model have guided future studies of the Web and interactive advertising. Rodgers and Thorson (2000) developed a structural model that portrayed how users perceive and process online ads. The model started with user motives for Internet use, including shopping, research, communication, and socializing; these motives might be goal-directed or just playful. Next was the layer of information processes, involving attention, memory, and attitude. In the middle of the model came advertiser-controlled factors, including ad types, ad formats, and ad features. And, finally, the model ended with a set of user responses, consisting of attention to ads, clicks on ads, and purchases made online. The layers and elements of the model were detailed and served as a useful conceptual map of interactive advertising.

More recently, Rappaport (2007) claimed a paradigm shift in advertising from the interruption model to models centered on relevance—a change attributed to new technologies and associated changes in consumer behavior, resulting in three new advertising models. The On-Demand Model sees consumers as content aggregators, filterers, schedulers, exposers, and disposers; and the media and advertisers as providers of necessary platforms and tools for consumers to generate their own content and customize product information to their interests, needs, and tastes. The Engagement Model emphasizes the high relevance of brands to consumers and the development of an emotional connection between consumers and brands. This model is highly visible in many successful campaigns these days. Finally, the Advertising As Service Model takes for granted the role of advertising in providing consumers with information and capabilities that can smooth transactions or enhance brand engagement. It is evident that each of the models stresses certain aspects of advertising, and in combination these models are very relevant for advertising in today's marketplace.

Methodological Sophistication

Innovative research can be carried out with any method. Experiments and surveys have probably been the most common methods in advertising research for decades. The trendy methods in advertising studies seem to have become diversified, and I see three levels of intriguing exploration. On the micro level, neuroscience knowledge and methods such as functional magnetic resonance imaging, electroencephalography, facial coding, eye tracking, skin conductance, and body posture are increasing in use in advertising, communication, and marketing research (Duffy & Foster, 2007; Page & Raymond, 2006; Bolls, Wise, & Bradley, this volume). More recently, the *Journal of Consumer Psychology* published a call for papers for a special issue on brand insights from psychological and neurophysiological perspectives (Yoon, 2010).

On the macro level, data mining is gaining increasing popularity. Massive data are cumulated as a by-product of normal consumption of interactive media and advertising. Online panels are widely used in the US and markets overseas. With privacy issues appropriately addressed, user data can be a goldmine for advertising researchers. For example, marketing researchers in China recently used tracked data in model development. Li, Pan, and Wang (2010) proposed a Poisson regression model that links advertising effectiveness to keyword characteristics. Through empirical tests with a real data set obtained from the website of a service company, they found that analyzing features of keywords affects advertising effectiveness, which could help advertisers create and select new keywords for paid search advertising campaigns. Wang, Zhang, Li, and Zhu (2010) explored how media publicity and word of mouth (WOM) about a to-be-released new movie drive movie-going behavior in China. Using the Bass new product diffusion model and empirical data from the industry, the authors found that pre-release media publicity and online WOM influence movie-going decision making differently. That is, media publicity determines movie goers' innovation probability whereas WOM determines both innovation and imitation probability.

Managerially, data mining methods play an essential role in computational advertising, "a new scientific sub-discipline, at the intersection of information retrieval, machine learning, optimization, and microeconomics. Its central challenge is to find the best ad to present to a user engaged in a given context" (Broder & Josifovski, 2009). The potential of computational advertising resides in converting advertising waste and annoyance to opportunity by employing computational technologies to process user-specific information drawn from previously collected data, context, and real-time user responses. This enables the targeted delivery of ads to individual members of media audiences based on their specific consumption needs and preferences. Computational advertising likely represents the future direction of the advertising business.

On the aggregate level, a promising method called "perspective meta-analysis" is catching some advertising scholars' attention. In the field of interactive advertising, numerous studies have been published. However, they are difficult to subject to a meta-analysis for universal effects because they are not directly comparable. Even on a same subject, say the effect of display ads, studies might be conducted with different participants, using various stimulus materials, and measuring different variables. Medical researchers who are eager to find real solutions from trials propose the adoption of perspective meta-analysis. Reade et al. (2009, p. 16) wrote,

> By planning a meta-analysis before trials commence, many of the listed barriers can be overcome. Hypotheses and intended analytical techniques for subgroup analyses can be specified in advance, and randomization may even be stratified by subgroups relevant to the meta-analysis but of less interest to one or more of the constituent trials. Advantages of a perspective design include consistent entry criteria, study protocols and outcome measures, consistent data collections, and the avoidance of criticism on "data dredging."

For advertising scholars who are in constant search of effective solutions, such perspective meta-analysis is certainly useful in generating more robust findings.

Practical Relevance

As we talk about the future of advertising scholarship, the practical relevance of academic research may need our renewed attention. The issue of bridging the gap in advertising research between academia and the industry was discussed in a panel session at the 2006 American Academy of Advertising conference in Reno, Nevada (Li, 2006). Panelists from both sectors explored the causes of the gap as well as possible solutions. Little progress seems to have been made in this regard since then. It is still the reality that "advertising academics know little about the findings of applied research, and advertising practitioners could care less about the results of academic research" (Li, 2006, p. 75). Thus, I share some of the solutions proposed by a panelist: work in teams of academic and practitioner researchers to do research that translates basic research into research that is useful to the practice of advertising; build databases and index them so that they are convenient to use by practitioners; make the relevance of academic research a priority within the academy; identify the most timely and relevant issues for younger academic researchers to pursue; do more programmatic research and fewer one-shot studies; and publish in forms practitioners do read, e.g., books. A consensus of that panel was that academic researchers should "translate" the findings of their studies into something understandable and useful to practitioners. This is indeed something worth pursuing in the near future. Nyilasy and Reid's chapter in this book offers great insights on the relationships between practitioner and academic theories of advertising, and their research encourages more exploration of this important issue of practical relevance of academic studies.

Summary

As marketing researcher Deighton (1996, p. 151) states,

> The profession of marketing, its theories, its practices, and even the basic sciences it draws on are determined by the tools at its disposal at any moment. When the tools change, the discipline adjusts, sometimes quite profoundly and usually quite belatedly.

The Internet has fundamentally changed the way companies do business and consumers shop and buy goods and services, resulting in significant paradigm shifts in marketing communications from a predominantly push approach to a mixed push and, largely, a pull approach. Advertising scholars have carried out numerous studies in addressing emerging issues by developing new concepts and theories to intellectually prepare for the profession to meet a new reality (for a review, see Cho & Khang, 2006; Ford & Merchant, 2008; Ha, 2008; Kim & McMillan, 2008).

The profession of advertising always needs better knowledge from academic research that is most innovative in conceptualization, conducted more sophisticatedly, and is more relevant to real issues. This will be the future of academic scholarship and, thus, the goal of the next generation of advertising scholars.

References

Broder, A., & Josifovski, V. (2009). *Introduction to computational advertising*. Retrieved January 5, 2010, from course at Management Sciences and Engineering Department, Stanford University website: www.stanford.edu/class/msande239/.

Cho, C., & Khang, H. K. (2006). The state of Internet-related research in communication, marketing, and advertising: 1994–2003. *Journal of Advertising, 35* (3), 142–163.

Deighton, J. (1996). The future of interactive marketing. *Harvard Business Review*, November–December, 51.

Duffy, M., & Foster, A. (2007). Neuroscience and the power of newspaper advertising. *Admap, 486* (September), 43–46.

Ford, J. B., & Merchant, A. (2008). A ten-year retrospective of advertising research productivity, 1997–2006. *Journal of Advertising, 37* (3), 69–94.

Ha, L. (2008). Online advertising research in advertising journals: A review. *Journal of Current Issues and Research in Advertising, 30* (1), 31–48.

Harvey, B. (1997). The expanded ARF model: Bridge to the accountable advertising future. *Journal of Advertising Research, 37* (March/April), 11–20.

Hoffman, D. L., & Novak, T. P. (1996). Marketing in hypermedia computer-mediated environments: Conceptual foundations. *Journal of Marketing, 60* (3), 50–68.

Kim, J., & McMillan, S. J. (2008). Evaluation of Internet advertising research: A bibliometric analysis of citations from key sources. *Journal of Advertising, 37* (1), 99.

Kobayashi, Y. (2008). The concept of engagement: State of the art and developments in Japan. *Communicative Business, 1*, 110–129.

Kuhn, T. S. (1962). *The structure of scientific revolution*. Chicago: University of Chicago Press.

Li, H. (2006). Bridging the gap in advertising research between the academia and the practice: Challenges and solutions. In J. Richards (Ed.), *Proceedings of the 2006 American Academy of Advertising conference* (pp. 75–79). Reno, NV: American Academy of Advertising.

Li, J., Pan, R., & Wang, H. (2010). Selection of best keywords: A Poisson regression model. *Journal of Interactive Advertising, 11* (1), 27–35.

Page, G., & Raymond, J. E. (2006, September). *Cognitive neuroscience, marketing and research: Separating fact from fiction*. ESOMAR, Annual Congress, London.

Rappaport, S. D. (2007). Lessons from online practice: New advertising models. *Journal of Advertising Research, 47* (2), 135–141.

Reade, M. C., Delaney, A., Bailey, M. J., Harrison, D. A., Yealy, D. M., Jones, P. G., et al. (2009). Prospective meta-analysis using individual patient data in intensive care medicine. *Intensive Care Medicine, 36*, 11–21.

Rodgers, S., & Thorson, E. (2000). The interactive advertising model: How users perceive and process online ads. *Journal of Interactive Advertising, 1* (1), 42–61.

ScienceWatch (2009, August). *Technology acceptance model: Research front map*. Retrieved December 12, 2010, from http://sciencewatch.com/dr/tt/2009/09-augtt-ECO/.

Sung, J. (2010). Interactivity effects on the usefulness, ease of use, and enjoyment of university mobile websites. Unpublished manuscript, Michigan State University.

Wang, F., Zhang, Y., Li, X., & Zhu, H. (2010). Why do moviegoers go to the theater? The role of prerelease media publicity and online word of mouth in driving moviegoing behavior. *Journal of Interactive Advertising, 11* (1), 50–62.

Yoon, C. (2010, December 1). CFP reminder: JCP special issue on brand insights from psychological and neurophysiological perspectives. Retrieved December 1, 2010, from http://mail.sjdm.org/pipermail/jdm-society/2010-December.txt.

Chapter 37

Adventures in Misplaced Theories

Herbert Jack Rotfeld

Virtually every introductory textbook for university programs in advertising, public relations, or marketing describes a model of innate human needs that first appeared in a 1943 psychology journal article titled, "A Theory of Human Motivation," often reproducing a pyramid-shaped chart illustrating each need as occupying a distinct level. Yet, despite many instructors' unquestioning acceptance of this theory as something important enough to place on exams, the ubiquitous content contains inescapable self-contradictions that should be readily evident to anyone more perspicacious than a member of the Flat Earth Society. Within the space of a single page of the textbook I now use for a course devoted to the marketing and advertising theories of the field known as "consumer behavior," it asserts (as do books by many other authors):

1. "The [model] appears to be closely bound to contemporary American culture," with citations from management journal articles from the 1970s, or, at latest, a quarter of a century ago (e.g., Hofstede, 1984, who also called the model "ethnocentric").
2. "It cannot be tested empirically."
3. "There is no way to measure precisely how satisfied one level of need must be before the next higher need becomes operative," so research can't discern who possesses which of the various needs described.
4. "Despite these concerns, the theory is still useful as a framework for developing advertising appeals. It enables marketers to focus their advertising appeals on a need level that is likely to be shared by a large segment of the target audience."

To not realize that the fourth statement contradicts the first three requires suspension of all critical thinking to the point of perceiving "Star Wars" movies as historical documentaries.

If the model is culture bound, it can't claim to describe innate human needs or drives, not to mention that the "contemporary" American culture of 1943, or even 1984, cannot provide a useful description of advertising audiences in the first decades of the twenty-first century. At a more basic level, if it cannot be tested, it is not a theory. An alleged scientific theory that cannot be tested by observation or experiment cannot be considered either scientific or a theory. The primary pragmatic utility of a theory for advertising decisions would be the ability to make predictions, which both the second and third statements say it cannot provide. If research is unable to tell which people are at each level of the model, then the model cannot identify audience segments, nor can it tell if a segment is large enough to be a target.

Despite these self-contradictions, this intuitive descriptive metaphor, composed from one researcher's ethnocentric perceptions of North American culture in the middle of the last century, remains a collection of textbook statements students must memorize to pass tests in business classes. And these same textbooks, in turn, are cited in papers submitted to journals as authoritative statements of advertising theory.

So the question remains why theories such as this one still appear in popular textbooks. This is not to criticize textbooks, because the more important question is whether students and their instructors discuss advertising theories with a critical review of the background, history, applications, and assessments of how businesses can, or can't, actually use those perspectives for making decisions. The pragmatic use of a theory, any theory, would be its ability to predict what would happen in a given situation where a decision is to be made and new data might not be immediately available. Unfortunately, this appears to be something few students are ever told. To judge by papers submitted to journals, many researchers are equally oblivious.

In a book on advertising theory such as this, authors make varied efforts to provide a definition of a theory: quoting from dictionaries; citing what other advertising scholars say about theories; or merely saying that a theory is exemplified by what they are describing as one. Their difficulty is not unexpected because it is a task rarely encountered. It is presumed everyone "knows." After years of their own research, it envelops their thinking. As the noted adman of the mid-twentieth century Howard Luck Gossage is frequently noted as having said, "We don't know who discovered water, but we know it wasn't a fish."

However, my experiences after a decade as editor of an international interdisciplinary journal indicate that many advertising researchers don't understand the meaning of scientific theories. I would be surprised if they are able to rattle off the three basic requirements that a theory must (1) explain existing data, (2) based on that explanation make predictions of future events, and (3) by virtue of those predictions, is falsifiable, meaning that is open to being demonstrated to be false.

Theories That Never Die

Compounding the problem of misunderstanding the basic definitions of theories, there is the extended near-immortal life of theories that actually have been falsified. In the world of advertising research articles submitted to journals, theories are never really shown to be false, but at some point become described as having "mixed support." New papers continue to cite old theories such that, over time, the background collection of theories grows, with each past author on the topic characterized as having "argued" a particular perspective, while the understanding of the phenomenon never progresses.

Over the years, I have endured too many research manuscript submissions in which the citations are more aptly described as an eclectic list than a review, an ill-conceived effort to reference all articles that might be written on the topic. The paper would list other data findings, maybe even mention a theory, but never pay attention to how the data are explained by the theories. Relevant literature would be listed but not integrated, then ignored in planning the research or interpreting the results. Sometimes, after a journal's double-blind editorial reviewers note additional relevant theory or research that could influence the context or interpretation of the data, these authors would merely add gratuitous citations to their list in a fashion that indicates they failed to read the article they now cite.

In that bygone era when a physical copy of a journal was needed to read the articles it contains, I tracked down a French article from a limited distribution French-titled psychology journal that appeared in many reference lists on my research topic. To my surprise, all of those citations to the paper were actually taking a sentence or two from an English language abstract printed in the front of the journal, an abstract that was not a translation of any sentences from the published article itself. This could only mean that the English-speaking authors citing this article apparently never read it beyond the abstract, or it is equally likely that many of the authors just copied the descriptive sentences and citation from someone else. (For more on this tale, see Rotfeld, 2010.)

This is an extreme example of when a literature review is used only to list articles instead of providing a basis for a study. Yet, too many research articles submitted to the journals, too often, exhibit too little ability to understand the pragmatic need to connect theory and research.

But then, maybe the problem is more basic than that.

This discussion started with an example from textbooks, but part of the problem might be found in the textbooks. Conventional wisdom holds that advertising textbooks are based on established concepts, with an assumption that their contents reliably summarize research findings. In what is assumed to be a virtuous reciprocal relationship, knowledge is generated in research, published in journal articles, and then collected and summarized in our textbooks. At least, that is how textbook authors claim it works. At the same time, many academic journal articles often cite textbooks for authority. In a process I called the "textbook effect" (Rotfeld, 2000), it is easy to document the embedding of old, defunct, unsubstantiated theories in our textbooks, with an undesirable impact on pragmatic understanding of advertising theory that gets repeated in the research submitted for publication in academic journals.

This is not just a problem for advertising research.

Scholars in any field can lock in old thinking to the detriment of future research. As Nobel Prize-winning economist George Stigler (1985) observed, "Once an idea is widely accepted, it is guaranteed a measure of immortality" (p. 112). Gould (1985, p. 384) has repeatedly pointed out how

> Facts achieve an almost immortal status once they pass from primary documentation into secondary sources, . . . errors are copied from generation to generation and seem to gain support by sheer repetition. No one goes back to discover the fragility of original arguments.

For example, almost all basic sociology textbooks state that Margaret Mead found that the Tchambuli of New Guinea reversed sex roles, despite the fact that from when she published her work on the Tchambuli in 1935 until her death, she repeatedly asserted that she never made such a claim (Goldberg, 1996). In studies of persuasive communications, an off-hand comment in two studies over five decades ago resulted in most textbooks and many research articles today still listing an "optimal level of fear for persuasion" as a theory explaining consumer responses to public health and safety messages, even though it has never been supported in the literature. The original authors dropped all discussion of the comment from their later research on the topic. A 1970 effort in a prestigious marketing journal to explain the "mixed" support for the original comment—a comment that had long since been elevated to the status of a theory in advertising research—actually made the statement incapable of falsification (Rotfeld, 1988, 2000). Yet, to this day, it still appears as one established theory in many academic journals and textbooks.

The dogmatic retention of unsupported and outdated theories in textbooks is inexorably linked to the implicit endorsement and propagation of them in journal articles. As a result, many researchers also lock in and defend theories that have failed to establish any explanatory utility. And, as a partial result of that, researchers also lock into efforts to tortuously explain or support perspectives that have been repeatedly discredited.

To make the confusion worse, textbooks misuse past advertising materials when discussing consumer theories. Almost every textbook discussion of theory—right, wrong, never supported, or weird—is accompanied with an illustration of advertising as an example of the theory's application. However, what the textbooks never reveal, and what few instructors ever explain, is that each illustration is chosen because it looks like it might be an application of the theory. Was that advertisement written because the copywriters had that theory in mind? Did the predicted consumer response ever materialize? The textbook authors probably do not know. The questions are never asked. Instead, the assessment is merely whether the illustration looks good, if the theory might fit in a face validity sort of way, and whether the copyright holder gave permission to reprint it.

The problem for research, or, rather, the problem for researchers who learned from the textbooks, is their pervasive inability to critically assess existing literature, or to propose new concepts or perspectives. They become focused on the experiment or the test, with a search for statistical significance while missing the pragmatic significance. In the end, they have a problem understanding just what is meant by a theory.

Data without Theories

A further problem is the unfortunate number of academic writers who consider theory irrelevant for their work, or something to be added to data gathered for some other purpose, possibly because the data were collected only because subjects were available to use in experiments.

When using research to make a business decision, the simple research question could turn on which test commercial is more persuasive. A government agency might want to test nutritional information formats to see which one is most likely to be used with certain types of people or which warning label has the strongest impact on a sample of young people (e.g., Sabbane, Lowrey, & Chebat, 2009). However, academic research tries to provide broader guidance than the narrow choice of a message tactic with a specific target audience (e.g., Tangari, Burton, Howlett, Cho, & Thyroff, 2010).

A manuscript that had been revised and resubmitted for a second round of reviews at the *Journal of Consumer Affairs* provides an extreme example. The authors were directed to provide a stronger theoretical context for their study, but they asserted that they considered it unnecessary, explaining they were not concerned with theory because "we are behaviorists."

At the most basic level, they misunderstood that the original term for the perspective-originating psychologists referenced a direction for social science research that, by ignoring all human thought, would allow control and measurement of all experimental variables. Instead of speculating as to what might transpire in people's minds, research participants, whether they were humans, cats, dogs, or rats, would all be "response organisms." Only behaviors would be measured in relation to test stimuli, with resulting experiments providing stronger scientific tests of theoretical predictions. In other words, behaviorism was a route to claims of social science being more like the so-called "hard" sciences such as chemistry. This more directly measurable focus, in turn, allowed for greater use of controlled experiments using scientific methods for testing theories.

However, ignorant of this background, these self-designated behaviorist manuscript authors became atheoretical data pile generators, providing no context, understanding, or reason why anyone should care about any of their analysis. They might be the rare example where authors actually revealed the basis for their research myopia, but they are not unique.

This is a particularly notable problem for research on advertising topics related to consumer protection and public policy. Not unlike the plethora of television police procedural programs, academic advertising articles often have extensive pedantic introductory paragraphs ripped from today's headlines (e.g., see discussion in: Rotfeld & Taylor, 2009). Instead of a research question driven by the application of a theory, the multi-page introductions to these papers could be summarized with one or two simple sentences of a news media "controversy" or public fear of advertising, such as:

- *People are fat and we can cite people who say so, with proposed solutions involving restrictions on the marketing of soft drinks, fast food, and candy.*
- *High school students purchase cigarettes, so advertising restrictions are proposed to "not cause" sales.*
- *Identity theft is on the rise, with misleading online advertising the implied culprit.*
- *Buzz agents, product placements, and other covert marketing tools entice unwary consumers into excessive purchase situations.*
- *Pharmaceutical companies spend millions of dollars on direct to consumer advertising of prescription drugs, and since these companies (presumably) won't waste money, they must be doing it because they know they can bypass doctors and improperly influence malleable patients* (see discussion in Royne & Myers, 2008).

If the problem with this approach to research is not intuitively obvious, take one enduring controversy built on ignorance of theory-based research, the public paranoia of subliminal advertising's alleged ability to influence consumer sales responses. Although consumers might believe that they are manipulated by advertising mind control, the basic established theories of human perception and mass communications explain how such fears are not based in reality (e.g., see Broyles, 2006). But if one ignores theory, then researchers could merely design a copy test of possible advertising messages with supposed hidden messages. By the variation of human samples, as well as the uncertain variables that are unavoidable in the data collection of social science research, someone could "discover," by accident and research artifact, that people seemed to be influenced by the subliminal messages (e.g., see discussion in Rotfeld, 2008). However, the preliminary research question is not if a business critic can "see" a hidden message, or whether a test message with hidden content seems to persuade people at a better than chance rate. The required first research question is whether existing established theory of perception provides a testable prediction of when, or if, a hidden message can influence anyone.

Research articles need more than the presentation of a new data set. Without a theoretical context, the data become idiosyncratic meaningless artifacts. Although few would dare to explicitly say they consider theory irrelevant, that appears to be the implicit case with many manuscripts submitted to research journals. And, unfortunately, some of these papers do get published.

Too often, for too much research, the existence of numbers to analyze becomes more important than a theoretical context. A colleague at another university sarcastically describes these too-common research projects as adherents of the bad research model of "find data, analyze it using big hairy [quantitative] models." The late naturalist Stephen Jay Gould said that, "Numbers suggest, constrain, and refute; they do not, by themselves, specify the content of scientific theories" (1981, p. 106). As the numbers or methods gain greater attention, some might forget—or maybe they just ignore—the need for a conceptual foundation that must precede the analysis. In other writing, Gould repeatedly explained that

> We often think, naively, that missing data are the primary impediments to intellectual progress—just find the right facts and all problems will dissipate. But barriers are often deeper and more abstract in thought. We must have access to the right metaphor, not only the requisite information. Revolutionary thinkers are not, primarily, gatherers of facts, but weavers of new intellectual structures.
>
> (1985, p. 151).

I have expressed my own long time concerns about an overwhelming focus on data analysis to the exclusion of thinking (Rotfeld, 2007), or times where the research method seems selected to serve the presence of available convenience samples, usually students (Rotfeld, 2003). Past editorials and commentary in *Journal of Consumer Affairs*, as a collective, provide a research guide for consumer scholars on both methods and related theoretical applications (see Additional Readings).

The important realization is that while data collection can be expensive and time consuming, it really is the easy part of research. As the late Muzafer Sherif was frequently credited by his former students as having said, if the existing theory is properly assessed, "By the time you get around to gathering data, the game has largely been played."

In Theory, This Should Work

At professional meetings or in articles written by practitioners, it is easy to summarize their most common complaints about academic advertising research: "show me one product that is moved off the shelves by an academic study," "they endlessly discuss useless theories that no one understands," or "this does not help me set a budget, write an ad, or purchase a mass media vehicle at a good price." Of course, if they see everything in terms of short run immediate decisions with related fast outcomes, theory can be irrelevant.

And yet, the advertising teachers—and the writers of the articles—only have themselves to blame for these critics, many of whom have read our academic literature or read the textbooks where that research is supposedly compiled and reported. They might have taken our classes. But the reason they do not understand the value of a theory-based research journal is that they do not know the meaning of a theory or its pragmatic applications in practice. No one ever told them. We never told them.

From my personal interests of public policy concerns, it is not that difficult to find important theory-based research questions for the consumers' interest (Rotfeld & Royne Stafford, 2007). Public policy and consumer protection activities of government are driven by some assumptions or expectations of consumers in the marketplace (e.g., France & Bone, 2005). Efforts to change consumers' unsafe habits need an understanding of how the targeted audiences respond to public health messages, knowing that it might be in ways not generally expected or understood (e.g., Haley, Avery, & McMillan, 2011; Rotfeld, 2009; Rotfeld, 2011; Smith & Stutts, 2006; Mandal, 2010; Tangari et al., 2010; Wolburg, 2006).

Theories predict. What they predict, how well they predict, or under what conditions the predictions might be wrong should provide the basis for research in advertising journals.

In advertising practice, no decision maker can research everything. Maybe, sometimes, in some cases, intuition, experience, and gut feelings can make a successful prediction. But for all the money spent on mass communications, some of the more insightful practitioners see the value in the knowledge of a theoretical perspective that indicates whether something would work as expected or whether that money might be wasted.

References

Broyles, S. J. (2006). Subliminal advertising and the perpetual popularity of playing to people's paranoia. *Journal of Consumer Affairs, 40* (Winter), 392–406.

France, K. R., & Bone, P. F. (2005). Policy makers' paradigms and evidence from consumer interpretation of dietary supplement labels. *Journal of Consumer Affairs, 39* (Summer), 27–51.

Goldberg, S. (1996). The erosion of the social sciences. In K. Washburn & J. F. Thornton (Eds.), *Dumbing down: Essays in the strip mining of American culture* (pp. 97–114). New York: W.W. Norton and Company.

Gould, S. J. (1981). *The mismeasure of man*. New York: W.W. Norton and Company.

Gould, S. J. (1985). *The flamingo's smile: Reflections in natural history*. New York: W.W. Norton and Company.

Haley, E., Avery, E. J., & McMillan, S. J. (2011). Developing breast health messages for women in rural populations. *Journal of Consumer Affairs, 45* (Spring), 33–51.

Hofstede, G. (1984). The cultural relativity of the quality of life concept. *Academy of Management Review, 9* (3), 389–398.

Mandal, B. (2010). Use of food labels as a weight loss behavior. *Journal of Consumer Affairs, 44* (Fall), 516–527.

Rotfeld, H. J. (1988). Fear appeals and persuasion: Assumptions and errors in advertising research. *Current Issues and Research in Advertising, 11* (1), 21–40.

Rotfeld, H. J. (2000). The textbook effect: Conventional wisdom, myth, and error in marketing. *Journal of Marketing, 64* (April), 122–126.

Rotfeld, H. J. (2003). Convenient abusive research. *Journal of Consumer Affairs, 37* (Summer), 191–194.

Rotfeld, H. J. (2007). Mistaking precision for reality. *Journal of Consumer Affairs, 41* (Summer), 187–191.

Rotfeld, H. J. (2008). The stealth influence of covert marketing and much ado about what may be nothing. *Journal of Public Policy and Marketing, 27* (Spring), 63–68.

Rotfeld, H. J. (2009). Health information consumers can't or don't want to use. *Journal of Consumer Affairs, 43* (Summer), 373–377.

Rotfeld, H. J. (2010). Editors talking. *Journal of Consumer Affairs, 44* (Fall), 615–619.

Rotfeld, H. J. (2011). The public as the problem of public health. *Journal of Consumer Affairs, 45* (Spring), 165–168.

Rotfeld, H. J., & Royne Stafford, M. (2007). Toward a pragmatic understanding of the advertising and public policy literature. *Journal of Current Issues and Research in Advertising, 29* (Spring), 67–80.

Rotfeld, H. J., & Taylor, C. R. (2009). The advertising regulation and self-regulation issues ripped from the headlines with (sometimes missed) opportunities for disciplined multidisciplinary research. *Journal of Advertising, 38* (Winter), 5–14.

Royne, M. B., & Myers, S. D. (2008). Recognizing the consumer issues in DTC pharmaceutical advertising. *Journal of Consumer Affairs, 42* (Spring), 60–80.

Sabbane, L. I., Lowrey, T. M., & Chebat, J. (2009). The effectiveness of cigarette warning label threats on non-smoking adolescents. *Journal of Consumer Affairs, 43* (Summer), 332–345.

Smith, K. H., & Stutts, M. A. (2006). The influence of individual factors on the effectiveness of message content in antismoking advertisements aimed at adolescents. *Journal of Consumer Affairs, 40* (Winter), 261–293.

Stigler, G. J. (1985). *Memoirs of an unregulated economist.* New York: Basic Books.

Tangari, A., Burton, H. S., Howlett, E., Cho, Y., & Thyroff, A. (2010). Weighing in on fast food consumption: The effects of meal and calorie disclosures on consumer fast food evaluation. *Journal of Consumer Affairs, 44* (Fall), 431–462.

Wolburg, J. M. (2006). College students' responses to antismoking messages: Denial, defiance and other boomerang effects. *Journal of Consumer Affairs, 40* (Winter), 294–323.

Additional Readings

Carlson, L. (2008). Use, misuse, and abuse of content analysis for research on the consumer interest. *Journal of Consumer Affairs, 42* (Spring), 100–105.

Preston, I. L. (2009). Understanding communication research findings. *Journal of Consumer Affairs, 43* (Spring), 170–173.

Rotfeld, H. J. (2003). Convenient abusive research. *Journal of Consumer Affairs, 37* (Summer), 191–194.

Rotfeld, H. J. (2005). Aliterates' scholarship. *Journal of Consumer Affairs, 39* (Summer), 229–232.

Rotfeld, H. J. (2007). Mistaking precision for reality. *Journal of Consumer Affairs, 41* (Summer), 187–191.

Rotfeld, H. J. (2008). How do you know that? *Journal of Consumer Affairs, 42* (Spring), 123–126.

Rotfeld, H. J. (2008). Can you really say that? *Journal of Consumer Affairs, 42* (Fall), 484–487.

Rotfeld, H. J. (2009). Disciplined conduct of interdisciplinary research. *Journal of Consumer Affairs, 43* (Spring), 181–183.

Royne, M. B. (2008). Cautions and concerns in experimental research on the consumer interest. *Journal of Consumer Affairs, 42* (Fall), 478–482.

Chapter 38

IMC, Advertising Research, and the Advertising Discipline

Patricia B. Rose

Having spent 20-plus years in various marketing positions with medium-sized companies and agencies prior to joining academe, I have been involved with IMC during my entire career—well before it was even termed IMC. Academic theory provided me with perspectives and paradigms for what I had done in industry. My academic positions and ultimately my membership on the accrediting council of the Accrediting Council on Education in Journalism and Mass Communications (ACEJMC) has afforded me the opportunity to look at various advertising programs and review IMC's role within them. And, as editor of the *Journal of Advertising Education* (*JAE*), devoted to research and commentary on instruction, curriculum, and leadership in advertising education, I was able to monitor the pedagogical research being done in the field. Started in the mid-1990s, the *Journal* emerged within the IMC world.

Note, however, that the IMC world, to a major extent, is still in its infancy: it is still developing and, consequently, changing. What started as "one sight, one sound" has advanced to strategic consistency. While IMC was first seen as a marketer interacting with a customer, the concept has broadened to all of management interacting with all stakeholders. The original turf war between public relations and advertising has morphed into a bigger issue of communications vs. management. Indeed, scholars are still searching for a universally accepted definition of IMC. As Chapter 32 by Moriarty and Schultz aptly states, "Communication is a complex system that involves new ways of thinking about messages, media, sources, receivers, targeting, and effectiveness measures that are all interrelated."

Advertising educators realize this, and, while a number of the articles in *JAE* encompass IMC, or integrated marketing communications, the impact of IMC theory tends to be more subtle than overt. True, there has been some, repeat *some*, good research done in the field; unfortunately, it has been done by a limited number of people. While a number of tactical articles have been written, few have centered on theory.

That said, however, if one analyzes the content of current advertising research, one finds that IMC has forged important, even if subtle, influences on the overall discipline. For instance, early advertising focused on the product. Discussions and research on IMC forced researchers and educators to start focusing on the customer, which meant there was less emphasis on persuasion per se, and far more prominence given to consumer insights and engagement. From a tactical and educational standpoint, it validated account planning and allowed it to be accepted as a valid discipline by educators. Today, even the traditional portfolio schools have integrated account planning into their initial creative-only curriculum. Indeed, the Miami Ad School offers a special "Boot Camp for Account Planners."

As a corollary to the above, marketing communications shifted from one-way to two-way, and ultimately to multi-way, interactions. The shift from product to consumer focus and behavior changed the way marketers looked at the communication process and opened the way for social media to be perceived as a communication tool.

Part of the shift in IMC's original "one sight, one sound" philosophy was the realization that there were multiple stakeholders in the success or failure of a brand, that these stakeholders tended to morph in and out of various roles, and that depending on which role they found themselves, they had different messaging needs. Thus, the concept of "one look, one voice" shifted to one of strategic consistency. Strategy became a substitute for integration. And, out of strategy and multiple stakeholders grew the realization that relationships needed to be built and maintained. Relationship marketing became a buzzword; and researchers looked at "how" this relationship could best be achieved so that loyalty—and referrals—developed.

And, as the definition of IMC slowly moved away from sameness, researchers were at a loss to agree on a single definition. True, many use words that included terms like interactive, manages and monitors communication, multiple media, and integrated brand perception; but no one definition is used universally. And, while researchers are still searching for a common, acceptable definition of IMC, they are also stymied by a changing perception and definition of advertising. As Chapter 1 notes, it has become more and more difficult to define advertising as "a paid form of non-personal presentation for the promotion of ideas, goods, or services by an identified sponsor." Messaging has become much more!

Indeed, IMC has made message delivery, and consequently media choice, far more important in the messaging process. In essence, acknowledging the consumer as the point of focus opened the way for publicity, promotions, word-of-mouth, direct and interactive marketing, and personal experiences to be deemed part of messaging. The medium has, indeed, become the message rather than solely the creative message. The best examples of this are the American Advertising Federation's National Student Advertising Competition, which dictates an IMC campaign; the Direct Marketing Education Foundation's Echo competition, which is used in many advertising classes; and, indeed, *JAE*'s production of two special issues of the *Journal* in conjunction with the Direct Marketing Education Foundation.

Accordingly, communication and its evaluation are now seen in a far more holistic way. Indeed, marketers are no longer satisfied with short-term measures of success (reach and frequency, awareness, trial, etc.) but look for longer-term measurements of brand success and value. The brand has become the focal point and all communications should be geared to enhance its value. Thus, all elements of a "long term communication plan become equally important in forming an integrated brand perception." While much of the above has faded into "general advertising theory," it is safe to say that the impetus for much of the current holistic view of advertising emanated from the discussions and research into IMC.

IMC and Advertising Education

The long-term impact of IMC's influence on advertising education is yet to be determined. IMC, in some form or another, has been taught—in a variety of ways—for multiple years, even preceding the 1980s. Marketing texts have always talked about advertising as part of promotions (including public relations' marketing tools as part of the process). Advertising texts have always had chapters on promotions, direct marketing, etc. Thus, the fact that some author(s) now used IMC as part of the title cannot be considered a breakthrough.

Of note, the "talk" of IMC made a notable difference in advertising programs. However, most of this was perceptual. Discussions regarding IMC and the wisdom of including public relations' marketing tools forged the growth of combined Ad/PR programs. Ross, Osborne, and Richards (2006), in "*Advertising Education: Yesterday–Today–Tomorrow*" reports that combined programs showed consistent growth starting in the early 1990s through at least the mid-2000s. However, the vast majority of these programs were, and remain, solely focused on advertising and public relations; even database marketing, key to the original concept of IMC, is rarely taught in most programs.

There have been some other changes. While almost all schools now include an account planning class, stressing a consumer focus, this is not necessarily "integrated" into the curriculum. Far too many schools continue to have minimal "core" courses and a plethora of electives which may—or may not—give the student a more integrated view of communications. Without a basic integration of all IMC concepts and a refocusing of the curriculum, with the exception of a campaigns course, IMC "components" are normally taught as stand-alone topics.

In short, the complexity of the field has not really altered the teaching of advertising to any major extent. However, the reality of social and interactive media might do so. Social media epitomizes two-way and multi-way communication as well as relationship theory. More importantly, since social media is new to academia, there are no turf wars. Indeed, in order to catch up with our students, academicians are forced to learn about and think about its influence on communications—especially with their day-to-day constituency. Equally important, accrediting bodies, such as ACEJMC, are insisting that "new media" be taught and incorporated into the curriculum. Accordingly, a plethora of courses are being developed—and a great deal of research produced. What influence this will have on IMC in general is yet to be determined, but the interest and pedagogic similarities are cause for hope. So far, the jury is out.

Reference

Ross, B. I., Osborne, A. C., & Richards, J. I. (2006). *Advertising education: Yesterday–Today–Tomorrow*. Lubbock, TX: Billy I. Ross Advertising Education Publications.

Glossary

Ability A component of message response involvement theory referring to the capacity for a message recipient to process marketing communications due to insufficient product knowledge/experience, limited intelligence, or complex message design.

Academician–practitioner gap in advertising The differences in attitudes, knowledge content, and presuppositions about how advertising works between advertising workers and university researchers.

Accessibility of motives The ability to recognize a motive from another person; for example, recognition of a persuasion agent's motive. More information about the person usually leads to increased accessibility.

Account planner An advertising professional who creates advertising strategy from research to guide the creation of advertising communication.

Adjudication A judge makes a decision about the application of a law; decides between conflicting claims.

Advergame A free online game primarily developed for promoting advertisers' brands or branded products. In a typical advergame, one brand is featured and the embedded brand or product is a central part of the game.

Advertising A paid communication from an identified sponsor for using mass media to persuade an audience.

Advertising agency Independent business composed of both business and creative people who are strategic partners with clients in the planning, development, placement, and evaluation of advertising.

Advertising channel A technological platform delivering unique, motivated sensory experience in the process of delivering a brand message.

Advertising exposure Often used loosely to represent a person who is exposed to the media vehicle in which an ad is placed.

Advertising response curve A curve representing the estimated probability of response (y-axis) to different numbers of advertising exposures (x-axis). The curve is generally assumed to be concave in nature (exhibiting continually diminishing returns on added numbers of exposures) or S-shaped (exhibiting a threshold, beyond which it exhibits increasing returns, followed by diminishing returns).

Advertising skepticism   General tendency toward disbelief of advertising claims.

Affect Transfer Theory   Positive feelings induced by game play are likely to be transferred to gamers' attitude toward the brand.

Affective feelings   Discrete emotions such as happiness, anger, fear, and disgust. This term is generally used by scholars subscribing to a dimensional theory of emotion that defines emotion as a response occurring along the dimensions of arousal (intensity) and valence (positive/negative).

Affordance or Affordances   The capacity possessed by the medium to initiate or facilitate a certain action, as inferred by the user, upon visual inspection of the medium's interface. Technologies may determine the presentation of information as well as consumers' states of mind when using it.

Agency affordance   Agency affordance refers to the ability of the interface to serve as source of content. Individuals cannot only realize self-agency but also encounter other users as sources of information.

Agency philosophy   A theory or attitude that acts as a guiding principle for the behavior of an advertising agency.

Agency portfolio   The range of clients held by an advertising agency.

Agent knowledge   The target's beliefs (whether true or false) about characteristics of the persuasion agent such as their goals, effectiveness, and ethics.

Ambient advertising   A category of non-traditional advertising that is seen in unusual and unexpected places often with unconventional executions and generally being the first or only ad execution to do so.

Amygdala   Part of the limbic system, and generally understood to be the central hub for emotional memory and response.

Analogy   A creative thinking technique first used in Synetics. An analogy is saying that one thing is like another, so in creative thinking it allows for solving problems in novel ways. When finding an original solution, using analogy might suggest an alternative solution. Metaphor is a similar term.

Analytical processing   Involves close examinations of product attribute information, as encouraged by advertisements that present products' features and attributes in a list.

Appetitive system   Drives approach-related responses to environmental stimuli and is generally activated by information perceived as pleasant.

Appropriateness   Something that is useful or relevant to a task. Creativity is usually defined as originality plus "something else." This "something else" may often be appropriateness. Some consumers might think that creative advertising is original and relevant to the product category, but relevance may not actually be persuasive. Advertisers use appropriateness for on-strategy hoping it will persuade the targeted segment.

Associative hierarchies   The ability to bring otherwise mutually remote ideas into contiguity to facilitate a creative solution—creatives are more able to make original associations and, thus, have more creative ideas.

Associative network   Knowledge is stored in memory nodes, which are then activated by a stimulus; the activation of that stimulus then works to retrieve stored information.

Attitude   General valenced evaluations of objects, issues, or persons; object-evaluation associations.

Attitude strength   Stronger (vs. weaker) attitudes have a greater influence on coloring perceptions, lasting over time, resisting change, or guiding behavior. The nature of attitude structure, attitude accessibility, attitude certainty, and degree of elaboration in formation or change, are things associated with attitude strength.

Attitude toward advertising   Evaluations of advertising that have both valence and intensity.

Authority constraints   The social and legal norms that encompass a limited space occupation in terms of rules, laws, economic barriers, and power relations, which determine who does or does not have specific access to specific domains at specific times in specific spaces.

Aversive system   Drives defensive avoidance of threatening stimuli and is generally activated by unpleasant information.

Backlash effects   The unintended consequences of negative political ads, due to voter disapproval of negative advertising, which might result in more negative feelings toward the sponsor (Jasperson & Fan, 2002).

Behaviorism   An epistemological paradigm that dominated psychology from the late nineteenth century until halfway through the twentieth century. This school of thought maintained that behavior is the only proper focus of scientific research in psychology and discounted as unscientific any effort to index the occurrence of mental processes and events.

Billings   The amount of business conducted in a given time by a client through an agency.

Bottom-up processing   Direct response to primary sensory input without conscious involvement.

Brainstorming   A group creativity technique that generates a listing of creative ideas. There is no evaluation of whether these ideas are good or bad, the main focus is just to think of and list items. From four to eight people participate and build onto the listing rather than discussing particular ideas. It is widely misconstrued as an individual listing of ideas.

Brand   A symbol representing a specific manufacturer's product that distinguishes it from other products and conveys ownership of a product or service. As a symbol, a brand embodies all the meanings that a consumer has for that product.

Brand collaboration   Customers and prospective customers have the capacity to be much more interactive in their dealings with brands.

Brand loyalty   Consistent purchase of a brand over time by consumers. Brand-loyal consumers often do not consider purchasing competitive brands.

Brand narratives   Stories that marketers tell about their brands, which usually resonate with consumers' desires, identities, or lifestyles; when consumers choose to own a brand, they possess the narrative associated with it too.

Brand prominence   A placement strategy in relation to the brand location in games is referred.

Brand valuation   Different ways to measure how much a brand is worth.

Capability constraints   The user's resources and ability to overcome spatial separation at a specific moment. They circumscribe the amounts of effort needed.

Capacity Theory of Attention   An advertising theory stating that audiences have limited amount of cognitive resources at any given time and that these resources may be allocated across multiple tasks, such as talking and viewing an ad, with the amount of cognitive resource dedicated to any one task being a function of the demands imposed by the task and the individual's personal drive. For example, the more someone engages in a deep conversation, the fewer resources are made available to view an ad.

Captive audience   Message recipients that are stationary with respect to non-traditional advertising such as sitting in a movie theater or waiting for a bus.

Causal proposition   An assertion that a specific cause-and-effect sequence will occur whenever the necessary conditions are present.

Cause-related marketing   Marketing through an artful association with a charitable cause.

Central and peripheral nervous systems   The broadest division of the human nervous system. The central branch of the nervous system consists of the brain and spine. The peripheral branch of the nervous system consists of all the other organs, glands, and muscles.

Central processing   Occurs when motivation, opportunity, and ability to process the message are sufficient.

Central route to persuasion   Attitude change achieved via active and involved processing of information.

Clutter The busy environment in which advertising is located embedded in editorial content, close to the advertising for other products, and even other brands of the same product.

Co-creation Where joint creation evolves between creatives, clients, and possibly customers in a collaborative process based upon willingness to explore, an open interactive relationship dialogue and co-construction of experiences and/or something of value as in an integrated advertising campaign.

Cognition The mental process of acquiring knowledge and understanding.

Cognitive capacity Enough "brain power" or available resources to process and respond to incoming information (whether from a media source or persuasion agent or other stimulus).

Cognitive congruency An end state in advertising design such that the amount of cognitive resources required to process a message is commensurate with those available to the consumer. Cognitive congruency is based upon the principles of the resource-matching hypothesis.

Cognitive Consistency Theories A set of theories from psychology that suggest people prefer mental status or balance over dissonance or imbalance. As such, people act to preserve or restore mental balance.

Cognitive defenses Resources internal to receivers used to interpret and/or counter persuasion attempts in advertising messages.

Cognitive psychological stimuli Influencers on internal mental process.

Cognitive resources In cognitive psychology and the information processing literature, a term used to describe the limited amount of attention a person has available to allocate to memory processes involved in encoding, storing, and retrieving information.

Cognitive revolution A paradigm shift occurring in psychology about halfway through the twentieth century. This revolution ushered in a new school of thought in psychology focused on developing research techniques for measuring the actual operation of the human mind/brain and drawing inferences about meaningful mental processes as the foundation for behavior.

Commonality of fit Two attitudinal objects are a suitable pairing in corporate social responsibility ads because of an attribute(s) they hold in common ("shared nodes"), e.g., Marshall's department stores and a "dress for success" campaign.

Complementarity of fit Two attitudinal objects are a suitable pairing in corporate social responsibility ads because they have complementary features—that is, they are like two separate pieces of a puzzle fitting together.

Confluence The synthesizing of several factors simultaneously. Creativity often results when several factors coincide with one another. The resulting interactions make it more challenging to isolate factors predicting creativity because it is not based upon solely linear effects.

Connected experiences Refers to the increasing tendency of Internet users to share and involve others in every aspect of their daily lives including, but not limited to, work, shopping, traveling, leisure, and entertainment, and information gathering.

Consumer behavior Behaviors exhibited by people in relation to the acquisition, use, and disposal of products and services.

Consumer Culture Theory A family of theoretical perspectives, which address the dynamic relationships between consumer actions, the marketplace, and cultural meanings.

Consumer socialization The process by which individuals learn how to become consumers; includes many different elements such as age, family communication structure, co-shopping, and advertisements/mass media. Consumer socialization also influences the development of brand preferences, as well as materialistic tendencies.

Contraindication A condition or factor that speaks against a certain measure. It is mostly used in medicine, with regard to factors that increase the risks involved in using a particular drug, carrying out a medical procedure, or engaging in a particular activity.

Convergent thinking A thought process or strategy that focuses or collapses together existing ideas in a coherent way, like a funnel. Characterized by a set of rational thinking steps that lead to one "correct" solution.

Coping behavior A target's responses to the agent's persuasion attempts based on his/her own knowledge and goals in the persuasion episode, presented by various thoughts and behaviors.

Core capabilities A business process or set of processes that a firm excels at and that serves as the firm's basis for competitive advantage.

Corporate social responsibility initiative Efforts to connect a firm with a non-profit activity, like fundraising for Susan B. Komen Breast Cancer Fund, to the mutual benefit of both the firm and the non-profit.

Cost and targeting indices Indices used in conventional media planning to adjust the cost per rating point used when allocating media exposures across an advertising schedule to reflect differences in the average cost and targeting efficiency of different media classes.

Cost-per-thousand effective target market exposures (CPM$_{ETM}$) A quantitative criterion for evaluating alternative media vehicles, considering the cost, the strategic audience quality and receptiveness, and the quality of the advertising exposure likely to occur in the media vehicle environment.

Coupling constraints A set of instrumental, physiological, and cognitive limitations that requires the user's presence at a specific time and place.

Creatives   A person whose job is to create advertising ideas and tactics.

Creativity   Relating to or involving the use of imagination or original ideas to create something.

Credibility   The quality of an information source, which leads communication recipients to believe the information. In the mass communication research tradition, credibility is used as an umbrella concept that embraces trustworthiness, believability, and other related terms.

Cross-media effects   The interaction effects that make ad exposures in different media different from comparably placed exposures in the same media.

Cue   Any salient aspect of the mediated presentation that might allow for quick evaluation of the underlying product information, possibly by triggering heuristics.

Culture   Conceptualized following Hofstede's (1997) view of culture as "the collective mental programming of the mind, which distinguishes the members of one group or category of people from another" (p. 5). It is a system of shared meanings (Geertz, 1973).

Cultural dimensions   Variables that help to categorize and verbalize groups on a number of different characteristics.

Cumulation   Repetition of advertising messages.

Cutaneous   Sensory nerves in the skin behind the ear, side, and front of the neck.

Declarative memory   Memories that can be consciously retrieved and understood in terms of verbal repetition or visual images.

Defocused attention   The number of elements that an individual is able to keep in mind at one time.

Deontological approaches to ethical theory   Assert that actions are best judged as good or ethical in and of themselves without regard to consequences. These approaches are based on the premise that certain actions are "right" because they stem from certain fundamental obligations. Assessments of duties, intentions, and motivations often are used to determine whether an act is ethical or unethical.

Descriptive ethics   Provides an empirical or neutral description of the values or ethical behavior of individuals and groups. For example, to say that advertising professionals in a given agency approve of disguising their identities and assuming pseudonyms to create positive word of mouth for their clients is a descriptive statement. Descriptive ethics is typically classified as a social science rather than as a philosophical activity.

Dietary supplements   Products that are intended to supplement the diet, contain one or more dietary ingredients (including vitamins, minerals, herbs or other botanicals, amino acids, and other substances) or their constituents, and are labeled on the front panel as being a dietary supplement.

Digital advertising   A category of non-traditional advertising that is created and/or displayed using computer technology such as the Internet, email, or text messaging.

Direct motivations   External incentives to stimulate behavior change.

Direct-to-consumer (DTC) prescription drug advertising or DTC advertising   Any promotional effort by a pharmaceutical company to present prescription drug information to the general public and the lay media rather than healthcare professionals.

Direct-to-consumer (DTC) websites   Consumer-targeted websites specifically created by pharmaceutical companies to promote prescription drug brands.

Dispositional trust or disposition to trust   The extent to which one displays a consistent tendency to be willing to depend on others, in general, across a broad spectrum of situations and persons.

Distinctiveness Theory   This suggests that people tend to define themselves on traits that are numerically rare in their local environment, such as ethnicity (Appiah, 2004).

Distributive justice   The normative ethical philosophy that is concerned with fairness of the goals, processes, and outcomes. The benefits derived and equity of rewards are key concerns.

Divergent thinking   A thought process or thinking strategy that expands or explodes different ideas outward like a blast. The term divergent or divergence typically describes the thinking process itself rather than the resulting concepts and ideas that are exponential variations or solutions.

Drama advertisements   A subtype of narrative advertisements, which encompass all advertisements featuring plots acted out by advertising characters but that also may be interpreted by narrators.

Dual broadcasting system   The system in which private broadcasters operate alongside public broadcasting corporations.

Dual Process Models   A class of theories that posit two modes for information processing: systematic processing and heuristic processing. That is, we do not always process the central arguments of an advertising message actively and effortfully (systematic processing). Oftentimes, "peripheral cues" embedded in the context of advertising lead us to apply judgmental rules to make quick decisions or "heuristics."

Effective exposure   This refers to a person who is actually exposed to an ad in the manner specified by a campaign objective.

Effective reach and frequency   A media planning approach that assumes advertising must achieve a certain number of exposures (effective frequency) in order for the advertising to be effective. Planning then seeks to develop a media schedule that will expose a desired proportion of the target market at the effective frequency level (i.e., achieve effective reach).

Elaboration continuum The amount and type of thinking operating along a continuum, ranging from low to high elaboration as characterized by the ELM. Anchored by the peripheral route at one end and the central route at the other. The processes by which variables influence persuasion differ depending on the point on the elaboration continuum.

Elaboration Likelihood Model (ELM) A leading theory of persuasion, which asserts that there are two ways that consumers process a message: (1) central, and (2) peripheral.

Embodied Motivated Cognition Theory A general theoretical framework through which the human mind can be understood in a manner that allows for more precise explication of psychological concepts (e.g., attention, attitudes) advertisements are believed to impact.

Embodiment Perceiving someone else's emotion, experiencing that same emotion as a result, and using that emotional knowledge.

Engagement In a social media context, this roughly translates to some evidence that the individual, i.e., audience member, an advertiser is trying to reach is responding in some way to the message, e.g., by clicking the "like" button or commenting on your wall on Facebook.

Epistemology A philosophy used to define a particular scope of knowledge and valid methods for producing knowledge related to a specific general phenomenon.

Ethnic cultural groups Groups with cultures of origin different from the one in the society in which they currently reside.

Explicit memory Involves retrieval of previously encoded information through conscious recollection.

Exposure frequency distribution An estimated distribution showing the proportion of a target audience exposed at each of several different levels (0, 1, 2, 3, 4, and so forth).

Exposure interval effects The effect of intervals between advertising exposures on the cumulative effect of multiple exposures (frequency) during an advertising campaign.

External validity The extent to which results of a study can be legitimately generalized to populations and situations.

Extrinsic motivation The desire to engage in a behavior for outside reasons or because of a reward or recognition. For example, incentives are often given to encourage creative ideas or innovations.

Family communication patterns Four distinct parent–child communication interactions that are defined by two communication dimensions, one in which parent–child communications are designed to develop pleasant home environments, while in the other, parent–child communications are oriented toward aiding the growth of children's autonomy. The resulting four communication patterns are Laissez-faire, Protective, Pluralistic, and Consensual.

Fixed advertising   Non-traditional advertising vehicles that are stationary with respect to the audience viewing the ad such as billboards, bus shelters, or airport terminal displays.

Flow   Involves experiencing an enjoyable sense of control and total concentration in an activity, which requires an adequate level of skill and challenge (Csikszentmihalyi, 1990).

Foreign consumer culture positioning   Strategy in which brand mystique is built around a specific foreign culture.

Frequency   Average number of advertising exposures received by a group of people who have been exposed to advertising in a specified period of time.

Frequency value planning   An alternative to effective reach and frequency planning in which response probabilities for different levels of advertising exposure from an estimated advertising response curve are weighted by the proportion of a target population in order to evaluate the effectiveness of a particular advertising schedule.

Generalization   Asserting that a causal sequence found in a particular data set will occur in any other similar environment.

Genius   A person who is both highly creative and highly intelligent, as these two traits are closely linked in such people.

Global consumer culture positioning   Strategy by which the brand is identified as a symbol of a given global culture by the advertiser.

Global Marketing Strategy Theory   A broad theory that integrates the standardization, configuration–coordination, and integration perspectives of global marketing strategy. IT suggests that a global strategy comprises eight first-order dimensions.

GLOBE'S nine cultural dimensions:

1. **Power distance**. The degree to which members of an organization (should) accept distinctions between members on the basis of organizational position. Includes such things as perquisites, status, and decision-making power.

2. **Uncertainty avoidance**. The degree to which members of an organization (should) actively attempt to reduce ambiguity in organizational life by relying on norms, rules, and policies.

3. **Humane orientation**. The degree to which members of an organization (should) encourage and reward individuals for being fair and kind to other organization members.

4. **Assertiveness**. The degree to which members of an organization are (should be) assertive, dominant, and demanding in their interactions with other organization members.

5. **Gender egalitarianism**. The degree to which men and women are (should be) treated equally in the organization in terms of tasks assigned and opportunities for training and advancement.

6. **Future orientation**. The degree to which an organization (should) encourages and rewards long-term versus short-term planning and projects.

7. **Performance orientation**. The degree to which an organization (should) focuses on and rewards high performance and efforts to improve quality.

8. **Individualism collectivism**. The degree to which an organization (should) focuses on individual accomplishment versus group accomplishment.

9. **Organizational collectivism**. The degree to which organizational members (should) take pride in being associated with the organization.

Gross rating points (GRPs)   The number of potential advertising exposures delivered, expressed as a percentage of the overall population. Thus, 400 GRPs is four times as many advertising exposures as there are in the overall population (See also Target Rating Points).

Grotesque   Bizarre, weird imagery, generally negative in character, and perceived as a violation of the normal or customary.

Hard money advertisements   Advertisements "which call for electing or defeating a particular candidate" (Shen & Wu, 2002).

Heuristic processing   Less thorough processing mode relying on peripheral cues embedded in the context of a message to make a quick judgment by applying judgmental rules. The mental shortcut used as a judgment rule (often based on generalizations of knowledge and experience) for making quick evaluations. At times, these short cuts can introduce bias and distortion into the decision-making process.

Hierarchy of Effects   The presumed order of steps that must be accomplished in order to move a consumer toward an action.

Hofstede's five cultural dimensions:

1. **Power distance**. The extent to which power is distributed equally within a society and the degree that society accepts this distribution. A high power distance culture prefers hierarchical bureaucracies, strong leaders, and a high regard for authority. A low power distance culture tends to favor personal responsibility and autonomy.

2. **Uncertainty avoidance**. The degree to which individuals require set boundaries and clear structures: a high uncertainty culture allows individuals to cope better with risk and innovation; a low uncertainty culture emphasizes a higher level of standardization and greater job security.

3. **Individualism versus collectivism**. The degree to which individuals base their actions on self-interest versus the interests of the group. In an individual culture, free will is highly valued. In a collective culture, personal needs are less important than the group's needs. This dimension influences the role government is expected to play in markets.

4. **Masculinity versus femininity**. A measure of a society's goal orientation: a masculine culture emphasizes status derived from wages and position; a feminine culture emphasizes human relations and quality of life.

5. **Time orientation**. The degree to which a society does or does not value long-term commitments and respect for tradition. Long-term traditions and commitments hamper institutional change.

Identification Theory   Refers to the manner in which people make similarity judgments by assessing their level of similarity with a source during an interaction (Kelman, 1961).

Implicit memory   Typically measured by how accessible information is when people are given an ambiguous stimulus.

Inference of manipulative intent   Target consumers' beliefs that the persuasion agent may be trying to persuade using unfair methods.

Informational advertising   Advertising that provides consumers with credible, factual, and relevant information, thus giving consumers greater confidence in their ability to logically assess the nature of a product or brand.

In-game advertising   Refers to the placement of advertisers' brands in a commercial game to promote their products or services to the target demographic.

Institutional trust   Beliefs that favorable conditions are in place that are conducive to situational success in an endeavor or aspect of one's life. In the Internet context, it translates to beliefs that the Internet has legal or regulatory protections for consumers.

Integrated marketing communications   The notion that everything a company does must be considered part of its marketing communications program, and that it must all be carefully coordinated to service the company's strategic marketing objectives.

Interactivity   The medium is responsive to users' needs and, therefore, takes into account variations in users' input during the interaction.

Interactivity affordance Interactivity affordance refers to the ability of medium to provide choices and be responsive to users' inputs.

Internal validity In an experimental context, the degree to which one is confident that the treatment administered was the cause of the outcomes observed.

Intrinsic motivation The desire to engage in a behavior purely for passion, love, inherent fulfillment, or true belief of the importance of the act of creation. Driven to creative thinking for pure joy rather than finding it to be a chore.

Key influencers Individuals or groups of individuals who yield a great amount of influence when it comes to perception, attitudes, beliefs, and purchasing behavior of other consumers or the public at large.

Lawlike generalizations Phenomena/occurrences within a discipline that have achieved empirical support over time thereby implying validation of the phenomenon. For example, the Product Life Cycle may qualify as a lawlike generalization.

Learning Theories A broad set of theories from psychology that address how people learn.

Legal Theory A proposition about how the law *should* be interpreted, how the law should work, what the law was designed to do, and what other laws might conflict with it.

Level fields Disciplines that develop around an interest in a specific level of analysis. Anthropology (societal or cultural level), sociology (group level), and psychology (individual level) are examples.

Limbic system An area in the forebrain, home to the amygdala and hippocampus, and considered critical for emotion and other innate responses required for survival.

Local consumer culture positioning Strategy in which the advertiser emphasizes cultural meaning that is shared by the local culture.

Location-based services Information or entertainment services that use the geographical position of a mobile device to inform other users of the service and individual's whereabouts.

MAIN model Classifies technology affordances into four broad categories: Modality (M), Agency (A), Interactivity (I), and Navigability (N).

Media audience The people reached through a particular advertising medium or media program.

Media class decisions The first level of traditional media planning in which the advertising budget is allocated among general classes of media, such as television, radio, magazines, out-of-home, and so forth.

Media-market matching The process of evaluating media according to the relative proportion of target market members (generally represented by product users) in their audiences. Direct media market matching does this by using single-source data to evaluate the proportion of product users who are in each media audience, while indirect media-market matching looks for demographic categories that contain relatively high concentrations of product users, then using the demographic categories to represent product users.

Media planner   An advertising professional who plans in what media advertising should be placed in order to optimally reach a specified target market within a specified budget.

Media scheduling   Decisions regarding the timing of ad placements to create a pattern of advertising exposures.

Media usage plans   The specific series of intentions that govern audience members' behavior as they dedicate attention to a particular medium.

Media vehicle decisions   Decisions regarding specific programs, stations, publications, and so forth to carry the actual advertising messages.

Mediator variables   "In general, a given variable may be said to function as a mediator to the extent that it accounts for the relation between the predictor and the criterion. . . . Whereas moderator variables specify when certain effects will hold, mediators speak to how or why such effects occur" (Baron & Kenny, 1986, p. 1176).

Mental model   An explanation of someone's view of the world.

Mental simulation   Participants who are directly invited to imagine themselves in consumption situations, as opposed to those who are not, are more likely to engage in narrative processing.

Message argument   Typically verbal, but any element in a message that when scrutinized carefully, leads to elaborative thoughts on the topic at hand. Argument quality manipulations are used as tools to examine the extent of elaboration in a given context.

Message coordination   Advertising is presented as extended, coordinated campaigns rather than single messages.

Message Response Involvement Theory   An advertising theory used to explain how message recipients respond to advertising for reasons of motivation, opportunity, and ability. The more motivated a message recipient is, the greater is the opportunity to process the message and/or the greater is the consumer's ability to comprehend a message, the deeper is the level of cognitive elaboration and subsequent processing of the marketing communication. Deeper processing can lead to more favorable outcomes such as attitudes toward the ad and brand, purchase intent, and persistence of ad and brand elements in memory.

Message strategy   "What to say" in advertising in order to achieve the advertising goal.

Message task allocation matrix   A planning framework in which media are classified according to the degree to which they tend to draw audiences with a high versus a low need for information and a high versus a low capacity for processing information. This helps media planners to match media to the creative demands of particular types of advertising messages.

Metacognition   The art of thinking about thinking, usually in the sense of thinking about when and how to use certain thinking strategies.

Mindscribe   When engaging in creative thinking, making mental notes to oneself. Considerable mindscribing is frequently the mark of a skilled creative.

MOA   An abbreviation for motivation, opportunity, and ability.

Mobile advertising   Non-traditional advertising vehicles that are moving with respect to the audience viewing the ad such as taxi or bus ads or airplane banners.

Mobile audience   Message recipients that are moving with respect to non-traditional advertising such as walking, driving, or riding on a bus or train.

Modality affordance   Modality is the ability of the interface to offer variety in the modes of content presentation and the modes with which users can interact with it.

Modeling   The process of demonstrating a behavior or cognitive concept.

Moderator variables   "In general terms, a moderator is a qualitative (e.g., sex, race, class) or quantitative (e.g., level of reward) variable that affects the direction and/or strength of the relation between an independent or predictor variable and a dependent or criterion variable" (Baron & Kenny, 1986, p. 1174).

Motivated mental processes   Mental processes that are involved in the execution of basic approach and avoid motivational responses to stimuli encountered in the environment. Such responses can include variation in attention, memory, feelings, attitudes, and behavior.

Motivated sensory experience   A term used to highlight the fact that sensory experience is first and foremost organized and interpreted according to the degree to which it results in patterns of appetitive and aversive motivational activation.

Motivation   A component of Message Response Involvement Theory referring to the desire to process marketing communications based upon individual need or interest.

Narrative   In an advertising context, an ad that tells a story, or invites the audience to construct a story using the raw materials provided by an ad.

Navigability   An interface's ability to facilitate user navigation or movement through the device, site, or even a multi-layered advertisement.

Navigability affordance   Navigability affordance refers to the medium's ability to facilitate user navigation or movement through the device, site, or even a multi-layered advertisement.

Need for affect   A stronger dispositional tendency to approach emotions.

Need for cognition (NFC)   An individual difference that indexes how motivated people are for information.

Negative political advertising   Advertisements that attacks the opponent or opposing idea, rather than discussing the positive attributes of the sponsoring candidate, party, or issue (Kaid, 2008).

Neuromarketing   A branch of marketing research grounded in neuroscience that primarily utilizes techniques for indexing central nervous system activity directly occurring in the human brain (e.g., Functional Magnetic Resonance Imaging and EEG) when consumers interact with marketing stimuli like advertisements.

Neuropsychology   A subdiscipline of psychology dedicated to understanding human nature as it is embodied in the central and peripheral nervous system of the human body.

Nondeclarative emotional memory   Unconscious emotional associations that inform conscious processing.

Normative ethics   Seeks to develop and defend judgments of right and wrong, good and bad, virtue and vice. For example, to say that it is wrong for advertising professionals to disguise their identities and assume pseudonyms to create positive word of mouth for their clients is a normative statement.

Opportunity   A component of message response involvement theory referring to factors that may either impede or aid in message processing such as message length or available time to process.

Opportunity-to-see (OTS)   Often used loosely to represent a person who is exposed to the media vehicle in which an ad is placed.

Organic   An evolution of a natural system, usually neither planned nor intended. An organic thought process or organic creativity does not use an obvious metacognitive strategy, but appears to naturally lead to a creative solution.

Organizational culture   The social behavior, ideas, and customs of a particular organization.

Originality   Something that is genuinely different, novel, unusual, unique, new, or statistically rare. Most informed observers can usually agree when something is original, especially something as public as advertising.

Outdoor advertising   A subcategory of out-of-home advertising referring specifically to billboards, street furniture (e.g., bus benches, bus shelters, newsstands, kiosks), transit (e.g., airport, rail, bus), and alternative (i.e., ambient) advertising.

Out-of-home advertising   A category of non-traditional advertising that reaches a message recipient while he or she is outside the home such as billboards, bus and taxi advertising, and cinema advertising.

Over-the-counter (OTC) or nonprescription drugs   Drugs that are used to self-treat mild transitory symptoms, conditions, and illnesses and do not require physician approval and supervision.

PAD   One of the most widely accepted models of emotional response that uses pleasure, arousal, and dominance (PAD) as the three necessary and sufficient dimensions of emotion.

Paradox   A seemingly contradictory proposition that, upon investigation, may be well founded.

Parental styles   Four distinct types of parental orientations toward children as defined by two dimensions of how children are socialized by parents, i.e., warmth versus hostility and restrictiveness versus permissiveness. The resulting four "parental styles" are Authoritative, Authoritarian, Indulgent, and Neglecting.

Passion   A very intense type of intrinsic motivation that drives artists and creatives that is associated with intimacy, commitment, and even love.

Perceived brand globalness   The degree to which the brand is measured as a function of the interaction of the brand's positioning and consumer perceptions of the brand.

Perceived fit   How consumers view the linkage between a firm and a non-profit effort that are paired in a corporate social responsibility campaign.

Peripheral processing   Occurs when little attention is paid to the message and heuristic cues are used to form impressions and make decisions.

Peripheral cue   A message or context factor that can serve as the basis of positive or negative feelings toward an attitude object, typically under low elaboration conditions.

Persistence   The extent to which an attitude changes in extremity over time; less change = greater persistence.

Personal extensibility   The ability of a person (or group) to overcome the friction of distance through transportation or communication.

Persuasion agent   The person(s) responsible for designing and constructing a persuasion attempt, such as advertising agency professionals.

Persuasion attempt   The target consumers' perceptions of the agent's persuasion behavior, including tactics such as advertisements or product placements, but also thoughts about the agent's motives, intentions, and consequences of the attempt.

Persuasion episode   The actual persuasion tactic—and features or characteristics of the tactic. It is the tangible persuasion event, i.e., what the agent creates, such as publicity, commercials.

Persuasion knowledge   All knowledge related to persuasion. Usually refers to the target consumer's beliefs and understanding about a persuasion agent's (e.g., marketer) persuasion tactics.

Persuasion target   The consumer or audience for whom a persuasion attempt is intended.

Phatic   An expression of emotion that does not make any claims about the world.

Political advertising   Any controlled message communicated through any channel that promotes the political interest of individuals, parties, groups, government, or other organizations (Holtz-Bacha & Kaid, 2006).

Political electoral broadcasts   Free broadcasting time on public channels offered to political parties, on an equal or proportional basis (Brants, 2006; Holtz-Bacha & Kaid, 2006).

Positioning   Giving the consumer a unique way to think about your product or service in relation to your competition.

Practitioner knowledge autonomy   The relative independence of advertising practitioners' cognitive structures about the workings of advertising from academic advertising theories and research.

Practitioner meta-theories   Advertising practitioners' presuppositions about the epistemological and ontological standing of advertising knowledge.

Practitioner theories   Advertising practitioners' beliefs about how advertising works and what works best in advertising.

Precedent   A court decision about what a law means, and subsequent courts are supposed to follow applicable precedents.

Prescription drugs   Drugs available only with a written prescription from a doctor.

Primacy hypothesis   Asserts that positive and negative affective reactions can be evoked with minimal stimulus input and virtually no cognitive processing.

Primary demand   The total sales of all brands in a given product or service category.

Primary process cognition   The ability to switch between primary and secondary cognitive modes, primary being the mode of dreaming, reverie, psychosis, and hypnosis and secondary process cognition is the abstract, logical, reality-oriented waking consciousness side.

Priming   An advance exposure to an idea or concept, like a preview or stimulus, that later influences thinking without necessarily being cognizant of the earlier exposure. In problem solving, priming effects normally dampen original solutions. Most creative thinking techniques work by attempting to use priming to move users to different places from typical patterns.

Prior learning effects The impact of previous advertising exposure and/or brand experience on the effectiveness of additional advertising exposures.

Privacy policy A statement about what information is being collected, how the information being collected is being used, how an individual can access his/her own data collected, how the individual can opt out, and what security measures are being taken by the parties collecting the data.

Production processes Cognitive processes that transfer information into guides for behavior.

Profession An occupation with a special prestige and standing in society differentiated by an "esoteric" (unique and complex) theoretical knowledge base.

Professional paradox of advertising The perceived impossibility to establish a knowledge base in advertising that is both theoretically sound and esoterically complex for the purposes of professionalization.

Professionalization The process by which an occupation strives to achieve the status of a profession.

Proportional representation Refers to an ethnic group's representation expressed through its numeric proportion in the society.

Proprioceptive The unconscious sense of the relative position of one body part to another.

Pseudo-media New forms of communication growing out of the concept of integrated marketing communications, where everything a company does is seen as a potential means of communicating with consumers.

Pseudo-professionalization tactics Knowledge-based social practices among advertising agency practitioners attempting to alleviate the consequences of the professional paradox of advertising.

Psychophysiological research A form of research emerging from the intersection of psychology, physiology, and anatomy that attaches psychological significance to patterns of nervous system activity in the organs, glands, and muscles of the body.

Psychophysiology The scientific study of social, psychological, and behavioral phenomena as related to and revealed through physiological principles and events in functional organisms.

Pull mobile advertising Any content sent to, or displaced by, a wireless subscriber upon request or voluntary exposure. Any wireless platform with the capacity to browse content may be used for pull advertising. The WAP and HTML-type platforms are the most widely used.

Push mobile advertising Any content sent by or on behalf of advertisers and marketers to a wireless mobile device at a time other than when the subscriber requests it. Push mobile advertising includes audio, short message service, email, multimedia messaging service, picture, surveys, and any other pushed content.

QR code   A two-dimensional bar code containing encoded information that can be read by mobile phones, cameras, and scanners. Information usually consists of text, URL, or other data.

Reach   The number or percentage of a population group being reached at least once by an advertising campaign.

Reaction triad   The most generally acknowledged understanding of emotion, defining it in terms of physiological arousal, motor expression, and subjective feeling.

Recall   A measure of advertising effectiveness, which tests if consumers can remember and report something specific after seeing an advertisement, such as the brand name or advertising message.

Reception environment   The context in which a message is encountered or received by the audience.

Recognition   A measure of advertising effectiveness that tests if consumers can identify something specific after seeing an advertisement.

Repetition   The presentation of the same ad message repeatedly.

Resistance   The extent to which an attitude is maintained in the face of contrary factors; less change = greater resistance. Sometimes considered a process rather than an outcome.

Resource Advantage Theory   Theory that argues that competitive advantage is dependent on effective deployment of the bundle of resources available to the firm.

Resource-matching hypothesis   An advertising principle where the effectiveness of advertising is believed to be maximized when the amount of cognitive resources required to process an ad matches the amount of cognitive resources available to the message recipient.

Rhetoric   The body of knowledge concerned with the "how to" of persuasion.

Rhetorical Theory of Advertisement   A set of causal sentences about a set of ad forms and outcomes within a specified reception environment.

Risk   A situation where there is uncertainty to the outcome.

Risk management   The process of dealing with uncertainty of outcomes.

Risk taking   A decision where there is uncertainty to the outcome.

SAM   A nonverbal, visual, manikin-based approach to measuring emotion along the three dimensions of pleasure, arousal, and dominance.

Secondary or selective demand   The sales of a specific brand within a product category.

Selective exposure   The idea that people either avoided persuasive media content designed to change their opinions, or seek out media that reinforces their beliefs (Lazarsfeld, Berelson, & Gaudet, 1944).

Self-efficacy   The feeling of self-worth and competence to intrinsically motivate an individual.

Self-produced motivators   Self-gratifying activities that provide positive associations with the past.

Semantic differential   Measures people's reactions to a stimulus in terms of ratings on bipolar scales defined with contrasting adjectives at each end (e.g., lively/dull, interesting/boring).

Single-source data   Data that contain measures of target market membership (generally product usage) and media-audience membership in the same database, thus, facilitating direct media-market matching. This contrasts with double-source data where target market membership and media audience membership come from different studies, thus, requiring indirect media-market matching.

Skepticism   Psychological reactance, leading to questioning the motives of and claims made by the persuaders.

Skunkworks   A team of experts across various areas who come together on a temporary basis like a task force to solve a seemingly intractable problem. Typically, they are physically separated from the rest of their organizations and work autonomously. An advertising agency could be thought of as a variant in that it is an institutionalized skunkworks or thinktank for ideas.

Social categorization   Refers to the way individuals organize people according to certain salient characteristics to facilitate their social interactions (Fiske and Taylor, 1991).

Social interaction   An association between two or more people that may range from fleeting to enduring.

Social media   The shift from a one-to-many/broadcast system to a many-to-many model where individuals act both as content creators and receivers during the communication process.

Socialization agent   People or groups who influence self-concept emotions, attitudes, and behaviors of a person.

Sociolegal studies   Involve the application of social science to the study of law.

Soft money advertisements   Advertisements that "focus on issues or candidates' positions on certain issues" instead of calling "for electing or defeating a particular candidate" (Shen & Wu, 2002, pp. 395–396).

Source credibility   An aspect of a message or individual presenter that conveys expertise or trustworthiness.

Sponsorships   The linkage that firms create between themselves and, usually, non-profit efforts.

Spreading activation   The activity that occurs in associative network representations of the human brain such that connections between nodes in the network allow retrieval of memory information.

Standardization   The degree to which the firm uses uniform marketing (or advertising) strategies in the markets in which it operates.

Strategy   Specific objectives and goals of the campaign targeted to the specified consumer audience through integrated marketing communications and the media.

Systematic processing   More thorough and effortful processing mode focusing on the central argument(s) of a message.

Target   A prospect point to where an organization is directing its efforts and decisions about messaging mix, developed to persuade the target of the desired action.

Target audience   The practical translation of the target market membership into specific characteristics by which media audiences are measured and targeted.

Target market   The people being targeted by a particular communications program.

Target Rating Points (TRPs)   The number of target market exposures, expressed as a percentage of the target market (see also Gross rating points).

Technology Acceptance Model (TAM)   An information systems theory that explains perceived usefulness and usage intentions in terms of social influence and cognitive instrumental processes (Davis, 1989). In TAM, perceived usefulness and ease of use are identified as fundamental determinants of user acceptance of a technology.

Teleological approaches to ethical theory   These are sometimes called consequences-oriented approaches because a decision or action is judged as ethical or unethical depending on the consequences or outcomes. These approaches typically focus on creating the greatest balance of benefits over harms and generally give equal weight to everyone affected.

Telepresence   Individuals' immersion or transportation ("you are there") in an experience, like a game.

Templates   A thinking technique for developing creative ideas that mimics the patterns seen in award-winning advertising campaigns. For example, one template, subtraction, takes a critical element away from an advertising idea, e.g., title, copy, or image deleted. Another, extreme consequences, might elaborate on the exaggerated results of using the product.

Theoretical knowledge base   In Professionalization Theory, the unique and complex foundation and legitimatizing for a professionalizing occupation's practices, supplied by academic scholarship.

Theory   A supposition or set of ideas intended to explain something based upon general principles.

Theory of Reasoned Action   A behavioral model that posits that individual behavior is driven by behavioral intentions, where behavioral intentions are a function of an individual's attitude toward the behavior and subjective norms surrounding the performance of the behavior.

Time-geography   An approach to spatial human activities as a scientific discipline, as the Swedish geographer Torsten Hägerstrand proposed.

Tokenism   Refers to members of the ethnic minority group being treated as tokens of their respective cultural group category.

Top-down processing   The use of conscious information and knowledge to interpret primary sensory information.

Topic knowledge   A target's (or agent's) beliefs about the topic of the persuasion message (usually content related to the product, brand, or company).

Top-of-mind awareness (TOMA)   TOMA has traditionally been defined as "the percent of respondents who, without prompting, name a specific brand or product first when asked to list all the advertisements they recall seeing in a general product category over the past 30 days." Another way to explain TOMA is to ask, "Whom do you think of first when you think of [product/service]?" The answer to that question is the company that has achieved Top of Mind Awareness with you. TOMA varies from consumer to consumer (Wikipedia.org).

Transformational advertising   Advertising that transforms the nature of a brand by associating it with psychological characteristics that make the usage experience unique in the product category.

Transportation   The degree to which a reader becomes immersed or absorbed in stories and undergoes a mental process that entails imagery, affect, and attentional focus.

Transportation-Imagery Model   Suggests that there are more routes to persuasion than just the central and peripheral routes of the Elaboration Likelihood Model.

Ubiquitous computing   A post-desktop model of human–computer interaction in which computers and software are carefully integrated and tuned to offer users unobtrusive assistance in their navigation and personal lives.

User-generated content (UGC)   Video, audio, or written content created by end-users of a website that is largely public and available for others to consume, comment on, or modify.

Uses and Gratifications Theory   An axiomatic theory that suggests that media users play an active role in choosing and using the media, and are goal oriented in their media use.

Utilitarianism   Perhaps the most commonly applied teleological or consequences-oriented approach to ethical theory. There are many variations of utilitarianism, but the basic idea is that a decision is ethical only if it creates the greatest good for the greatest number of individuals. "Good" typically refers to the net benefits that accrue to all the parties affected by the decision. As such, utilitarians determine the ethical choice by calculating the net benefits for each of the available alternatives.

Values　Enduring beliefs that motivate people to prefer one set of outcomes over another (de Mooij, 2010). According to de Mooij (2010), values are at the core of culture and are the standards that drive people's beliefs, attitudes, and behavior.

Variable fields　When a significant number of researchers become interested in a specific phenomenon. Political science, archeology, linguistics, education, marketing, journalism, and advertising are examples of variable fields.

Vicarious motivators　Behaviors and reactions can be learned by observing models and experiencing consequences of the behaviors.

Wear-in　Involves learning, which fosters familiarity with advertising stimuli and, thus, enhances brand memory and attitudes.

Wear-out　Repetition leads to boredom, irritation, or psychological reactance toward the ad stimuli, which diminishes positive attitudinal effects while failing to augment brand memory.

Web 2.0　A collective term for Internet-based technologies and web-based services that stem from an ideology of sharing and collaboration.

Website trust　Willingness of a consumer to be vulnerable to the actions of an Internet merchant based on the expectation that the Internet merchant will behave in certain agreeable ways.

Zipping　Fast-forwarding through commercials.

Zapping　Jumping between programs during commercial breaks.

References

Appiah, O. (2004). Effects of ethnic identification on web browsers' attitudes toward and navigational patterns on race-targeted sites. *Communication Research, 31* (3), 312–337.

Baron, R. M., & Kenny, D. A. (1986). The moderator–mediator variable distinction in social psychological research: Conceptual, strategic and statistical considerations. *Journal of Personality and Social Psychology, 51,* 1173–1182.

Brants, K. (2006). Sure to come, but temporarily delayed: The Netherlands in search of the political ad. In L. L. Kaid & C. Holtz-Bacha (Eds.), *The Sage handbook of political advertising* (pp. 227–239). Thousand Oaks, CA: Sage.

Csikszentmihalyi, M. (1990). *Flow: The psychology of optimal experience.* New York: Harper and Row.

Davis, F. D. (1989). Perceived usefulness, perceived ease of use, and user acceptance of information technology. *MIS Quarterly, 13* (3), 319–340.

De Mooij, M. (2010). *Global marketing and advertising: Understanding cultural paradoxes* (3rd ed.). Thousand Oaks, CA: Sage.

Fiske, S. T., & Taylor, S. E. (1991). *Social cognition* (2nd ed.). New York: McGraw-Hill.

Geertz, C. (1973). *The interpretation of culture*. New York: Basic Books.

Hofstede, G. (1997). *Cultures and organizations: Software of the mind*. New York: McGraw-Hill International.

Holtz-Bacha, C., & Kaid, L. L. (2006). Political advertising in international comparison. In L. L. Kaid & C. Holtz-Bacha (Eds.), *The Sage handbook of political advertising* (pp. 3–13). Thousand Oaks, CA: Sage.

Jasperson, A. E., & Fan, D. P. (2002). An aggregate examination of the backlash effect in political advertising: The case of the 1996 U.S. Senate race in Minnesota. *Journal of Advertising, 31* (1), 1–12.

Kaid, L. L. (2008). Political advertising. In W. Donsbach (Ed.), *The international encyclopedia of communication* (pp. 3664–3667). Oxford, UK: Wiley-Blackwell.

Kelman, H. C. (1961). Processes of opinion change. *Public Opinion Quarterly, 25*, 57–78.

Lazarsfeld, P. F., Berelson, B., & Gaudet, H. (1944). *The people's choice: How the voter makes up his mind in a presidential campaign*. New York: Duell, Sloan and Pearce.

Shen, F., & Wu, H. D. (2002). Effects of soft-money issue advertisements on candidate evaluation and voting preference: An exploration. *Mass Communication and Society, 5* (4), 395–410.

Index

Page numbers in *italics* denote tables, those in **bold** denote figures.

A relations 33–4
Aaker, D. A. 87, 442, 444
Aaker, J. L. 167, 439
Abbott, A. 424, 425
Abernethy, A. 330
ability 341, 342, 567; and persuasion
　process 53, 59, 60
Abruzzo, J. 76
absorption propensity 264
academic organizations 419, 423, 428–9
academician-practitioner gap 33, 36–7,
　42, 44, 550, 567
accessibility of motives 181–2, 567
accommodation 168
account planners 129–30, 567
actual advertising exposure 327
acute need strategy 515, 516–18
Adams, P. C. 384
Adaval, R. 242, 245, 246
adolescents 144, 185, 275
AdSam (attitude self-assessment manikin)
　91, 92, 96
Advances in Consumer Research 51
advergames 110, 181, 183–4, 388–99, 567
advertainment 429
advertising 567; as a profession 421–6; as
　a scientific field 12–14; scope and
　definition of 542–4; as societal
　institution 419–21, 424–5, 426–30
advertising agencies 423, 425, 429,
　543–4, 567; client-agency relations
　421; client diversification 221–2;
　philosophy 120, 202–3, 221, 568

advertising channels 5, *8*, 9, 58, 106,
　108, 109, 110, 164, 567; social media
　407, 413
advertising education 423, 425, 428–9,
　532–3, 564
advertising exposure *see* exposure
advertising organizations 5, *8*, 419, 421,
　423, 425, 428–9; *see also* advertising
　agencies
Advertising Process Circle **3**, 5, 8–10,
　69, 121
Advertising Research Foundation 255,
　547
advertising response curve 328–30, 331,
　332, 567
advertising skepticism 568; children's
　140, 144; consumer 20, 179, 180,
　183; epistemological 40, 41;
　ontological 40, 41
advocacy, brand 125, 498
advocacy advertising 180, 304
affect 69, 85, 108, 272; need for 263,
　582; negative 22; positive 250;
　transfer 391, 393, 395, 397, 568; *see
　also* emotion(s)
affordances 357–66, 568; agency 357,
　361–3, 367; interactivity 357–8,
　363–5, 367; modality 357, 358,
　359–61, 367; navigability 357, 358,
　365–6, 367, 582
agencies *see* advertising agencies
agency affordances 357, 361–3, 367, 568
Agenda Inflexibles 531, 534

agenda setting 472–3
agent knowledge 176, 179, 568
Ahluwalia, R. 179
Ahn, H.-Y. 51–68
Ahuvia, A. D. 474
AIDA model 121
AISAS model 547
Ajzen, I. 11, 86, 378
alcohol consumption 510–11
Alden, D. L. 152, 153, 154, 155
Allen, D. 247
Allen, M. 303–4
Allport, G. W. 85
Altaras, S. 151, 153
Amabile, T. M. 191–2, 195, 197, 198, 203
ambient advertising 342, 353, 568
ambiguity 529
Ambler, T. 38, 39
American Academy of Advertising
    conference (2006) 550
American Advertising Federation (AAF)
    429; Student Advertising Competition
    564–5
American Association of Advertising
    Agencies (4As) 429
American Express 449, 450, 455–6
Amine, L. 154
amydala 70–2, 74, 79, 81, 82, 568
analogy 198, 201, 214, 568
analytical processing 241, 242–3, 245, 568
Anand, P. 233, 243
Anderson, J. R. 392
Andreas, K. 402
Andrews, J. C. 12
Ang, S. H. 195, 201
Angelini, J. R. 116
animatics 88
animation ads 360–1
Ansolabehere, S. 303
Appel, M. 259, 262, 263
appetitive system 107, 568
Appiah, O. 360
Apple 27, 442
applied research 13, 435–6, 550
approach avoidance 73, 82
appropriateness 194–5, 195, 202, 213,
    568
Archpru, M. A. 152, 155

Arens, W. F. 6
arguments 52–3, 54, 55–6, 57, 60, 61,
    128, 256–7, 580; qualitative 349;
    quality of 58, 61; quantitative 347;
    strong v. weak 61, 233–5
Argyris, C. 34
Aristoff, M. 196
Armstrong, G. 7, 140, 487
Arnold, M. 154
Arnould, E. J. 150–1
Aronoff, J. 80
arousal 89, 90, 91, 98–9
artfulness 39
Ashley, C. 196
assertiveness 157, 158, 577
associations, brand 20–1, 29, 494
associative hierarchies 213, 214, 569
Associative Learning Theory 21
associative models of creativity 198, 214
associative networks 452, 569
asymmetrical approach 496
Atlas, J. 449, 455–6
attention 22, 24, 25–6, 38, 112, 120;
    capacity theory of 337, 341–2, 390,
    392, 394, 396, 397, 570; cognitive
    258, 262; defocused 214; lack of 25;
    unconscious 75
attitude formation 38, 52, 62, 86, 87,
    108; emotional 38; and purchase
    behavior 121
attitude toward advertising 389, 569
attitude(s) 11, 38, 47, 54, 85, 242, 341,
    342, 378, 569; and behavior 86; brand
    141–2, 393, 394, 395, 397, 398, 399;
    change 23–4, 25, 29, 51, 52, 86, 129;
    conative 92; to DTC websites 288,
    289–90, 291, 292; persistence/
    resistance 54–5, 583; rational 38;
    reinforcement 24, 29, 52; strength 53,
    62, 569
attributes: brand 11, 20; product 242, 243
audience(s) 8, 9, 314; captive 338, 342,
    343–4, 344, 345, 570; characteristics
    314–15; media 314, 315, 316, 326,
    327, 530, 549, 579; mobile 338, 342,
    343, 345; social media 407–8; target
    314, 315, 326, 327, 338, 492, 501,
    588; see also receivers

audio advertising 111–12
augmented reality 339
authority constraints 382, 383, 569
aversive system 107, 569
avoidance behavior 73
awareness 29; brand 24, 26, 38
awareness, interest, and desire (AIDA)
    model 121
axiomatic theories 135

B relations 33–4
Baack, D. W. *196, 201*
Babin, L. A. 245
backlash effects 303–4, 305, 569
Badzinski, D. 141
Baker, G. F. 88
balance theory 495
Bandura, A. 273, 274
banner advertisements 363–4, 366
Barban, A. M. 6
Barnes, S. J. 374, 375
Barron, F. 194
Bartholomew, A. 185
Barwise, P. 374
basic research 13
Bates v. State Bar of Arizona (1977) 486
Batra, R. 87, 152, 154
Baumgartner, H. 248–9
Baumrind, D. 142, 143
BBH agency 204
Bearden, W. O. 6
beauty 93–5
behavior: change/modification 5, 24, 86,
    99, 274, 277, 278, 506–11; imitative
    274
behavioral intention 11, 86, 87, 91, 92,
    108, 288–9, 291–2, 361, 366, 378,
    379
behavioral theory 106, 485–7, 488
behaviorism 106, 569
Belch, G. E. and Belch, M. A. 7
beliefs 11, 22, 54–5, 91, 121, 128–9,
    140, 164, 165, 176, 242, 300, 378,
    411; change in 231, 235, 255, 257,
    258, 259, 265, 266; creative 221
Belk, R. 154
Benoit, W. L. 300, 301
Berger, C. R. 436

Berkowitz, D. 409
Berntson, G. G. 107
Berthon, P. *205*
biases, decision 467
Biden, J. 444
billboards 337, 347; digital 340
billings 221, 569
Binet, A. 193
Bitner, M. J. 61
BMW 339, *442*
Bobo doll experiments 273
Bolen, W. H. 6
Bolls, P. D. 105–19
Borgerson, J. L. 474
Borghini, S. *201*
Borrell Associates Inc. 298
borrowed theories 12–13
Boster, F. J. 61, 62
BOTOX 511–12, **512**
bottom-up processing 70, 110–11, 569
Boush, D. M. 140, 185
Bovée, C. L. *6*
Bower, A. B. 449–59
boyd, d. m. 402–3
BP 128
Bradley, M. M. 88
Bradley, S. D. 105–19, 116
Bradt, G. 218
brain: emotion and 70–2, 77–8, 79–80,
    81, 82, 89, 93, 112; motivation and
    105–17
brainstorming 193, 199, 200, 569
brand(s) 434–48, 570; advocacy 125,
    498; associations 20–1, 29, 494;
    attitudes 141–2, 393, 394, 395, 397,
    398, 399; attributes 11, 20; awareness
    24, 26, 38; building 5; co-creation of
    410; collaboration 441, 570;
    commitment 121–1; communities
    125, 129; contact 440–1, 445;
    enduring involvement with 125;
    equity 442, 494, 499, 500; exposure
    27, 28; familiarity 179; global 151,
    153, 154–5; image 439–40; and
    instant communication 445–6; loyalty
    24, 91, 92, 125, 444, 498, 499, 564,
    570; meaning 439–40; memory 22–3,
    390, 391, 392–3, 394, 396, 397, 399,

494; narratives 243, 570; negative contact 445; negotiation with 441; placements 388, 390–9; positioning 152, 153, 154, 155; preferences 20; presence 440–1; prominence 391, 570; as a promise 439; recall 391, 393, 395, 398; recognition 22, 27–8, 122, 391, 393, 398; relationships 498–9; selection 24; valuation 441–4, 570; value 440–1, 499; widening concept of 444
break through and engage theory 38, 42
Brenner, B. 451
Bright, L. 410
Bristol, T. 144
Britton, J. E. 246
Brock, T. C. 250, 258, 264, 265
Brommel, B. 142
Brown, D. 27
Brucks, M. 140
Brumbaugh, A. M. 167
Burke, M. C. 87
Burke, R. R. 205
Burnkrant, R. E. 179
Burns, A. C. 245
Burrell, N. 304
bus advertising 340, 343
Bush, G. W. 298
business ethics 464, 467
buzz monitoring 412
Bylund, C. 142

Cacioppo, J. 51, 52, 53, 58, 86, 107, 141
Cairncross, F. 445
Calvert, S. L. 389, 396
campaign objectives 40
Campbell, M. C. 181
Camras, L. A. 79
Cannon, H. M. 194, 313–36
capability constraints 382, 383, 570
Capacity Theory of Attention 337, 341–2, 390, 392, 394, 396, 397, 570
captive audiences 338, 342, 343–4, 344, 345, 570
Carey, J. W. 435, 518
caring theory 204
Carlson, L. 135–48

Carpenter, K. M. 249
Categorization Theory 153
Cateora, P. 164
Cauberghe, V. 389, 391, 392, 394–5
causal process theories 135, 231, 235, 237
cause-related marketing 179, 180, 570; see also corporate social responsibility (CSR) initiatives
Cavusgil, S. T. 156
celebrity endorsement 54
Central Hudson Gas & Electric Corp. v. Public Service Commission of New York (1980) 485
central nervous system 113, 570
central processing 141–2, 570
central route to persuasion 52, 53, 60, 86, 570
Chafee, S. H. 436
Chaney, I. M. 389, 390, 393
Chang, C. 241–54, 262, 263
Chao, M. C. H. 154
charities 179; see also corporate social responsibility (CSR) initiatives
Charles, R. E. 202
Chattopadhay, S. 300
Chen, Q. 364
Chervany, N. L. 286
children: advergames play 395–6, 397–8; brand attitudes 141–2; cognitive defenses 140, 145; development 136–7; disclaimer content, understanding of 140–1, 145–6; information processing abilities 141–2; metaphors, understanding of 141; moderators of the influence of advertising on (parents/family 141–4, 146; peers 144–5, 146); persuasion knowledge 140–1, 144, 183–4, 185; persuasive intent, understanding of 139–40, 183; skepticism 140, 144; socialization 142–5, 146
children's advertising 5, 135–48
Cho, S. 288
Chong, M. 201
Christopher, M. 498
Churchill, G. 142, 144
Cialdini, R. B. 249

cinema advertising 343–4
Cisco *442*
citizenship, creative 194
Clemons, D. S. 54
client-agency relations 421
client diversification 221–2
Clore, G. L. 73
clutter 22–3, 343, 571; competitive
    22–3; non-competitive 22
co-creation 410, 571
Co-Creation Index (CCI) model 192,
    197
coactive activity 107
Coca-Cola 20–1, 27–8, 442
cognition 86, 91, 92, 93, 272, 571; need
    for 53, 54–5, 57, 236, 264, 582;
    primary process 213–14, 584
cognitive attention 258, 262, 393, 397,
    571
cognitive capacity, and persuasion
    knowledge 181–2, 397
cognitive congruency 346–50, 353, 571
Cognitive Consistency Theories 128,
    495, 496, 571
cognitive defenses 140, 145, 571
cognitive elaborators 58, 92, 93
cognitive misers 58, 59, 92–3
cognitive processing 52, 93, 248–50
cognitive resources 341, 344, 346, 347,
    353, 357, 571
cognitive revolution 106, 571
Cohen, D. 6
collectivism 578; in-group 157;
    institutional/organizational 157, 577
Columbia Journalism Review 529
commitment: high 121–2; low 122;
    product or brand 121–2
commonality of fit 452–3, 454, 571
communication process models 19, 164,
    169
Compeau, L. 285
competition 230
competitive advantage 155–6, 215
complementarity of fit 452, 453–4, 571
complexity of messages 53, 55–6,
    347–50
comprehension/miscomprehension 25
computational advertising 549

conation 272, 361
conative attitude 92
confidence 58
confluence model of individual creativity
    192, 571–2
congruence, and product/brand
    placements 392, 397
Congruity Theory 165, 495
connected experiences 413, 572
conscious memory 112
conscious processing 70, 75
consistency: cognitive 128, 495, 496; in
    message 494–5; strategic 497–8, 564
Constantin, C. D. *389*, 391
consumer culture 10, 150–1, 572; global
    150, 151–3; glocal 153; local 153
Consumer Culture Theory (CCT) 150–1
consumer identity 150
consumer ratings 362
consumer referrals 499, 564
consumer response theories 227
consumer skepticism 20, 140, 144, 179,
    180, 183
Consumer Socialization Theory 275–7,
    278, 572
consumption, socio-historic patterning of
    151
consumption visions 248–9
contact points 492
Contemporary Marketing Practices
    group 37
context 9–10, 14, 158
contraindications 270, 271, 511
convergence, media 543, 544
convergent thinking 198, 202, 572
Cook, E. W. 90
coordination of marketing activities 156
coping behavior 177, 182, 184, 572
core capabilities 155–6, 572
core competences 155
Cornwell, T. B. *389*, 390, 391, 393,
    452, 453, 454
corporate advertising 5, 126
corporate social responsibility (CSR)
    initiatives 180, 572; growth and
    popularity of 450–1; motives for
    455–6; perceived fit in 451–9
cost of ads 325–6

cost indices 323–4, 572
cost-per-thousand effective target market exposures (*CPM_ETM*) 328, 332, 572
coupling constraints 382, 383, 572
Courneya, K. S. 56
coworkers 471
Craig, R. T. 34, 37 creative beliefs 221
creative concept 43, 44
creative tactics 75
creativity 39–40, 41, 42, 191–211, 421, 427, 573; appropriateness dimension of 194–5, 202, 213; associative models of 198, 214; brainstorming 193, 199, 200; confluence model of 192, 571–2; convergent and divergent thinking 198, 202; cross-cultural/ global studies of 195; culture and 193–4; definitions 212–13; defocused attention model of 214; environment place-based theories of 202–4, *205*; ethnicity and 193–4; flow 197–8; implicit communication models 198; individually-oriented theories of 191–5, *196*; innate 193; intelligence and 193; intuitive thinking and 193; learned 199–200, 202; mathematical model of 198; motivation theories 199, 200; organizational effects on 194; passion theories of 199, 200; primary process cognition model of 213–14; priming theories 199, 200; process theories 195, 197–202; and risk 203, 212, 214–22; sociological theories of 193–4; templates method of 198, 199, 588; think tanks 193; two-step process of 200
credibility 375, 573; source 56, 58, 60, 128, 284, 287, 587
Crewe, B. 193
Crigler, A. 300
Crimmins, J. 443
cross-functional management 500–1
cross-market segmentation 151–2, 156
cross-media effects 331, 332–3, 573
cues 358, 359, 573; heuristic 356–7, 358–66; peripheral 56, 57, 58, 60, 356–7, 366, 514, 583
Culp, J. *389*

cultural dimensions 157–8, 165, 573
cultural diversity 165–9
cultural globalization 151
cultural symbols 151
culture 149, 151, 162–73, 276, 573; and creativity 193–4; and emotions 88, 91; marketplace 150; and narrative prototypes 246; organizational 218, 220, 470–1, 500, 582; political 299; *see also* consumer culture
cumulation, message 230, 573
Cunningham, A. 466
Cunningham, P. H. 463
Curran, C. M. 4, 7, 19, 420–1
Czinkota, M. R. 7

Dahlén, M. *196*, *205*, 243
Damasio, A. 93
Darke, P. R. 183
data: collection 559–60; mining 411–12, 549; without theories 557–60
Daugherty, T. 410
Davis, F. D. 379
Davis, J. H. 285
Day, E. 125–6
De Bussy, N. M. 497
de Mooij M. K. 164
De Pelsmacker, P. *389*, 391, 392, 394–5
deception 487, 513–14
decision biases 467
decision heuristics 467
decision making 249; ethical 467–9
declarative memory *see* explicit memory
definitions of advertising 3–4, 6–7
defocused attention 214, 573
Deighton, J. 250, 256, 551
delayed retention 25
Dell 410, 412
DeLorme, D. E. 284
DeLozier, W. 493, 501
demand: primary 24, 584; secondary or selective 24, 586
Dentsu 547
Denzin, N. K. 436
deontological approaches to ethical theory 468, 573
descriptive ethics 468, 573
Deshpande, R. 167

developmental psychology 136–7, 466
devices *8*, 9
Devinney, T. *196*
Dewitte, S. *196*
Dholakia, U. M. 378
dietary supplements 511, 513–14, 525, 573–4
diffusion of innovation theory 473–4
digital advertising 9, 337, 339, 340, 342, 353, 355, 542; *see also* Internet; Multimedia Message Service (MMS) advertising; Short Message Service (SMS) advertising
direct to consumer (DTC) advertising 95; motivators 274–5; of prescription drugs 269–78, 281–93, 511–13, 525
Direct Marketing Education Foundation 565
direct media-market matching 315, 326
direct motivators 274, 275, 574
direct-to-consumer (DTC) websites 286–93
disclaimer content 140–1, 145–6
disclosures 514
discounts 325–6
dismissal 229–30
Disney 125, 128–9, *442*
dispositional trust 286, 287, 288, 289, 290, 574
distance 230, 237
Distinctivenes Theory 167–8, 574
distinctiveness 231–5
distraction 53, 60, 262, 361
distractor evaluation 28
distributive justice 474, 574
divergent thinking 198, 202, 574
doctors, and DTC advertising 271, 272, 277–8
dominance 89, 90, 91, 98–9
Doner agency 204
Dotson, M. J. 57
Dou, W. 203
Dou, X. 355–72
Drake, M. *205*
drama advertising 244, 246, 247, 574
drive reduction and induction 73
Driver, T. 510
driving purchase 5

drugs: over-the-counter (OTC) 511, 513–14, 525; prescription 269–78, 281–2, 283–5, 287–93, 511–13, 525
Drumwright, M. E. 13, 463–79
Du Plessis, E. 106
dual broadcasting system 299, 574
dual process model 356–7, 574
Duchenne smile 80–1
Duff, B. R. L. 18–32
Dulan, R. J. 70
Duncan, T. R. 492, 493, 495, 497, 498, 499
Dunn, S. W. 6
Dutta, R. 380
Dutton, J. M. 34

Eagly, A. 62
Eastin, M. S. 410
Eaton, J. 453
eBay 410
economic theory 486, 488
Edell, J. A. 87
education, advertising 423, 425, 428–9, 532–3, 564
EEG 115
effective exposure 327, 333, 574
effective frequency 329, 330, 331, 574–5
effective reach 329, 330, 574–4
effects 5, 10, 38–9, 41, 69, 465; duration of 301; hierarchy-free theories of 39; hierarchy of 19, 38, 121, 272, 530, 547, 577; intended 9; mutation of 38, 39, 40, 42, 178; negative/positive 182–4; political advertising 300–5; social media 409–10, 411; unintended 5, 9, 464, 474; wear-in 20, 394–5, 590; wear-out 20, 394–5, 590
ego strategy 518–21
Ehrenberg, A. S. C. 24
Eisenhower, D. D. 297
Ekman, P. 81
El-Murad, J. *196*, *201*
elaboration likelihood continuum 52, 54, 59, 60, 575
Elaboration Likelihood Model (ELM) 13, 51–63, 86, 92, 128, 233–4, 255, 267,

366, 514; future research 62–3;
issues, misunderstandings and
challenges 58–62; review of theory
and tenets 52–3; variables involved in
research 54–8
Elaigwu, I. 444
Ellen, P. S. 455
Ellison, N. B. 402–3
Embodied Motivated Cognition (EMC)
Theory 105–17, 575
embodiment, emotional 77–8, 80, 81,
575
emotional appeal 57
emotional embodiment 77–8, 80, 81,
575
emotional intelligence 193
emotional involvement 12, 122–3, 124,
258, 259, 263, 265
emotional memory 70–2, 74–5, 81–2
emotional profiles 87
emotion(s) 69–84, 85; authentic 78, 81;
and behavioral intention 86, 87, 91,
92; brain and 70–2, 77–8, 79–80, 81,
82, 89, 93, 112; categorical models of
88; and culture 88, 91; and gender 88;
measurement of 88–9, 98–9
(nonverbal measures 89–92, 99);
mirroring of 78; and motivation 70,
73–4, 82; narrative processing and
250–1; and persuasion 86–99, 250,
251; pleasure, arousal, dominance
(PAD) model 89–91, 98–9; primary
69, 77; secondary or social 69; three-
dimensional models of 88–93, 98–9
empathy 156, 251, 256, 257–8, 264
empirical generalizations (EGs) 135–6
encoding/decoding 164
endorsers 56; celebrity 54; status 57
engagement, social media 409–10, 413,
575
Engagement Model 548
entertainment 375, 378
epistemological skepticism 40, 41
epistemology 113, 575
Escalas, J. E. 244, 246, 249, 250, 251
ethics 10, 463–79; business 464, 467;
deontological approach to 468, 573;
descriptive 468, 573; message 463;

moral intensity 467–8; normative 468,
582; organizational 470–2;
practitioners 465–9; scripts 469;
teleological approach to 468, 588;
virtue 470
ethnic identity 168
ethnicity 165–9; and creativity 193–4
Eureka Ranch 193
Ewing, M. T. 196, 497
exchange-theory 496
excitatory stimuli 74
expectancy-value models 242
expert witnesses 487
expertise 192, 200–1, 537–8
explicit memory 26, 27, 70, 74, 392,
575
exposure 567; actual 327; brand 27, 28,
394–5; effective 327, 333, 574;
effectiveness 327–8; frequency of
328–31; impact 327, 332–3; interval
effects 331, 332, 575; mode of 394,
397; repeated 14, 20–1, 22, 26, 53,
54, 55, 62, 86, 394–5; selective 215,
300, 436; value 330–1
exposure frequency distribution 329, 575
Extended Parallel Process Model 507
eye blink startle response 116
eye gaze 81

Faber, R. 259
Faber, R. J. 12, 18–32, 389, 392, 393
Faber, T. 259
Facebook 197, 402, 405, 406, 412, 488
facial EMG 115
facial expression 72, 77, 78, 79–81, 82,
89
facial feedback hypothesis 79
family, as moderators of advertising
influences 142–4, 146
family communication patterns (FCPs)
143, 575
Fan, D. P. 302, 305
Farn, C. 57
FCB (Foote, Cone, and Belding) grid
122–4, 319
fear 73
Federal Trade Commission (FTC) 480,
513, 535

femininity/masculinity 157, 578
feminist theory 474
Ferrell, L. 471, 474
Ferrell, O. C. 469, 471, 474
field of advertising 12–14
Fishbein, M. 11, 86, 378
Fisher, E. 179
Fiske, S. T. 166, 249
fixed advertising 338–40, 342, 344, 345, 576
Flexibles 530–1
flow 576; creativity 197–8; game players experience of 390–1
food advergames 395–6, 397–8
Food and Drug Administration (FDA) 269, 270–1, 277, 480, 511, 513
Foote, Cone, and Belding (FCB) grid 122–4, 319
Ford, C. 194
Ford company 217–18, **219**, 412
Ford, J. 205
forms 229, 231, 232, 235–7, 239
44 Liquormart, Inc. v. Rhode Island (1996) 485
Fraedrich, J. P. 469
fragmentation: knowledge 425, 427–8; organizational 425–6, 428–9
framing 55, 56
Franke, N. 361
Franz, M. M. 298, 301
Freeman, R. 497
Freidson, E. 422
frequency 576; of advertising exposure 328–31; distribution 329; effective 329, 330, 331, 574–5
frequency value planning 328–31, 332, 576
Friestad, M. 39, 140, 174, 175, 176, 181, 185
Frijda, N. H. 73
functional magnetic resonance imaging (fMRI) 79, 89, 116, 548–9
fusiform gyrus 72
future orientation 157, 577

Galvin, K. 142
gaming see advergames; in-game advertising

Gangadharbatla, H. 402–16
GAP 407
Garramone, G. M. 303
gaze 81
GE 442
Gelb, B. 165
gender: egalitarianism 157, 577; and emotion 88; and political advertising 301
General Motors 325–6
generalization 19, 40, 41, 135–6, 231, 233, 234, 239–40, 359, 576
genius theory 193
Gentile, M. C. 467
Gilbert, D. T. 259
Gillette 442
"Giving Voice to Values" (GVV) initiative 469
global advertising see international advertising
global brands 151, 153, 154–5
Global Consumer Culture Positioning (GCCP) theory 152, 153, 155, 576
Global Consumer Culture Theory (GCCT) 150, 151–3
global consumer cultures (GCC) 152–3
Global Information Technology Report, The 380
global market participation 156
Global Marketing Strategy (GMS) Theory 156, 576
globalization 150, 151, 152, 163
GLOBE study 157–8, 165, 576–7
glocal consumer cultures (GLCC) 153
glocalization 153
GNC **519**, 519–20
Goldberg, M. E. 138, 140, 198, 205, 421
Goldenburg, J. 196, 199
Goode, W. 422–3
Google 410, 442; "Parisian Love" 245
Gordon, W. J. J. 199
Gorn, G. J. 138
Gossage, H. L. 554
"Got Milk" campaign 24, 521, **522**
Gould, S. J. 556, 559
Graham, J. 164
Grau, S. L. 449–59

Green, M. C. 250, 255, 258–9, 264, 265
Greenbaum, P. E. 90
Gregory, W. L. 249
Grier, S. A. 167
Griffin, W. G. *196*, 199, 200
Griffith, D. A. 155, 364
Grigorovici, D. M. *389*, 391
Griver, A. 85
Grönroos, C. 498
Gronstedt, A. 497
Gross, I. 198, 199, *201*
Gross, M. L. 392, 398
gross rating point (GRP) 323, 577
grotesque images 238–9, **239**, 577
Groupon 413
Grunig, J. 496
Gudykunst, W. B. 163, 164, 165
Guilford, J. P. 193, 198, 202
guilt 179
Gummeson, E. 498
Gwinner, K. P. 453

habit 24, 122, 125, 515
Hackley, C. *196*
Haenlein, M. 402
Hägerstrand, T. 381
Haley, E. 120–31
Halinen, A. 498
Hall, E. T. 158, 165
Ham, C. D. 174–87
Hamel, G. 155
Hamilton, M. 61–2
Hammond, L. J. 73–4
Handbook of Psychophysiology 113
happiness 73, 80–1
hard money advertisements 304, 577
Harley Davidson 125, 215, 243, 453
Harrington, D. M. 194
Harvey, B. 547
Haugtvedt, C. P. 51–68
Havlena, W. J. 88
Haxby, J. V. 81
Hayes, J. L. 434–48
He, Y. 153
health advertising 5, 55, 56, 92, 95–7, 506–26, 560; dietary supplements 511, 513–14, 525; direct-to-consumer

(DTC) prescription drugs 269–78, 281–2, 283–5, 287–93, 511–13, 525; to modify unhealthy behavior 506–11, 560; over-the-counter (OTC) drugs 511, 513–14, 525; to promote healthy lifestyle 514–24, 525
heart rate 115
Heath, R. G. *196*
Heider, F. 495
Heiser, R. S. *196*
Heo, N. 360, 366
Herington, C. 245
Herrman, D. J. 89
heuristic processing 356–7, 358–66, 577
Heuristic-Systematic Model 51
heuristics, decision-making 467
Hewlett Packard *442*
hierarchical linear analysis 29
hierarchy-free theories 39
hierarchy of effects models 19, 38, 121, 272–3, 530, 547, 577
Higgins, E. T. 181
Hill, R. *205*
Hill, S. J. 301
hippocampus 71, 74
Hirschman, E. C. *205*
Hoeffler, S. 453
Hoffman, D. L. 381, 548
Hofstede, G. 157, 158, 163–4, 165, 577–8
Holbrook, M. B. 86, 87, 88, 198, 421
Holland, E. A. 79
Holtz-Bacha, C. 298
Home Depot 450
Honda *442*, 446
House, R. J. 157, 158
Houston, M. J. 124
Hovland, C. 51, 52
Hovland, R. 10
Huber, J. 249
Huddleson, S. 140
Huh, J. 277, 281–96
humane orientation 157, 576
Hunnicutt, G. 140–1
Hunt, K. 536
Hunt, S. 34, 136
Hunter, J. 62
Hyatt, E. M. 57

Hydroxycut Advanced Thermogenic 521, **523**
hypersexuality 95

IBM 27, 442
idea mapping 198
Identification Theory 166, 167, 578
identity: consumer 150; ethnic 168; heuristic 362
imagery, mental 258–9, 262–3, 265
"imagine yourself ..." advertisements 244–5
implicit learning 75
implicit (nondeclarative) memory 26, 27–8, 70, 71, 74, 75, 78, 392, 398, 578
indirect media-market matching 315, 326
individual differences 53, 165, 194, 236, 242, 246–7, 251
individualism 157, 578
Inflexibles 531, 533–4, 536
information, need for 319, 320, 325
Information Integration Theory 495
information processing 69–??? 85, 106, 107–8, 313–17
information processing: bottom-up 70, 110–11, 569; capacity 316, 319, 320, 325; by children 141–2; conscious 70; strength of involvement and 128–9; top-down 70, 110–11, 589; unconscious 70
information processing memory-based model of 301
informational advertising 55, 57, 87, 124, 319, 578
informativeness 375, 378
infotainment 375, 378
in-game advertising 388–95, 578
in-group collectivism 157
inhibitory stimuli 74
innate creativity 193
innovation, diffusion of 473–4
innovativeness 41; research 546–8
institution of advertising 419–21, 424–5, 426–30
institutional collectivism 157, 577
institutional trust 286, 578

Integrated Marketing Communications (IMC) 22, 202–3, 313, 315, 317–20, 491–505, 563–6, 578; and conventional media planning 318–20; and interactive communication theory 491, 492–3, 501; and perceptual integration theory 491, 493–6, 501; process theory 500–1; and reciprocity theory 496–9, 501
Intel *442*
intellectual involvement 12
intelligence: and creativity 193, 194; emotional 193
intention, behavioral 11, 86, 87, 91, 92, 108, 288–9, 291–2, 361, 366, 378, 379
interactive advertising 109, 281–2, 287–8, 292, 316, 549
interactive communication theory 491, 492–3, 501
interactivity 390–1, 578
interactivity affordances 357–8, 363–5, 367, 579
Interbrand 442, 495
international advertising 149–61, 162, 164–5
International Affective Picture System (IAPS) 90–1
Internet 4, 58, 197, 355–68, 548, 551; agency affordances 357, 361–3; banner ads 363–4, 366; click-through-rate (CTR) 183; credibility as information source 284, 287; direct-to-consumer advertising 271–2, 273, 281–93 (website trust 286–93, 590); interactivity affordances 357–8, 363–5; mobile 380–1; modality affordances 357, 358, 359–61; navigability affordances 357, 358, 365–6; pop-ups 360, 361; *see also* social media
interpersonal communication 276–7
Interpersonal Reactivity Index 264
intrinsic motivation 192, 199, 204, 390
intrusiveness 361
intuitive thinking, and creativity 193
involvement 57, 120–31, 247; emotional 12, 122–3, 124, 258, 259, 263; enduring 124, 125; high 54, 122, 123,

124, 128, 129; intellectual/rational
12, 122–3, 124; and learning 121–3;
low 54, 121, 122, 123, 124, 128; with
the medium 126–7; and message
strategy 123–4; negative v. positive
127–8; product 12, 57, 58, 514;
relationships among types of 125–6;
relevance and 129; situational 124
IPG agency 203–4
irritation 375, 378
issue advertising 5
Iyengar, S. 303

James, W. 421
Janelle, D. 383
Jasperson, A. E. 302, 305
Jayant, R. K. *205*
Jerry, J. 298
JetBlue 412
Johar, G. V. 198, *201*, 421
John, D. R. 139
Johnson, B. 62
Johnson, L. W. *205*
Jones, E. E. 168
Jones, J. P. *196*
Jones, L. W. 56
Jones, T. M. 467–8
Journal of Advertising 137, 421, 542
Journal of Advertising Education (JAE) 563,
565
Journal of Advertising Research 376, 388
Journal of Consumer Affairs 487
Journal of Consumer Psychology 549
Journal of Consumer Research (JCR) 137
*Journal of Current Issues in Research and
Advertising (JCIRA)* 137
*Journal of Public Policy and Marketing
(JPP&M)* 137, 487
Jupiter Research 255
Just, M. 300
justice 474
JWT agency 221

Kahn, B. 452, 453
Kahneman, D. 216
Kaid, L. L. 298, 300, 301, 302
Kalyanaraman, S. 360
Kanter, R. M. 166

Kardes, F. R. 57
Kasof, J. 194
Kassarjian, H. H. 123
Katz, H. 7
Kaufman, L. 6
Keller, K. L. 444, 453, 493–4
Keller, P. A. 243
Kelman, H. C. 166
Kent, R. J. 22
Keum, H. *389*, 393
key influencers 412, 579
KFC 450–1
Khan, B. E. 180
Kilduff, M. 35
Kilgour, M. 195, *196*, 200, 202
Kim, B. H. *205*
Kim, J. 364
Kim, J. Y. 91, 92
Kim, N. Y. 362
Kim, S. 126
King, G. 181
King, K. W. 287
Kingdon, J. W. 473
Kirmani, A. 181
Kleijnen, M. 381
Knee-Jerk Inflexibles 531, 534
knowledge 419, 427–8; creation 43, 44;
fragmentation 425, 427–8; prior 264;
reflexive 70
Koh, Y. J. 363, 364
Kohlberg, L. 466
Komen for the Cure 450
Koslow, S. 191–211, 421
Kotler, N. 297
Kotler, P. 7, 297, 439, 497
Kotowski, M. R. 51–68
Kover, A. J. 37, 76, 178, *196*, 198, *201*,
205, 421
Krugman, D. M. 434–48
Krugman, H. 121, 126
Kunkel, B. A. *205*

La Ferle, C. 162–73
Laczniak, R. N. 12, 135–48
Lamb, C. W. 7
Lance Armstrong Foundation 450
Lang, P. J. 90, 91
Langteau, R. 277

language 90, 112
Lasswell, H. 19, 404
Lau, R. R. 302, 303, 304
Lauterborn, R. 492
Lavidge, R. J. 272
law 464–5, 480–90
lead generation 5
learning 276; implicit 75; involvement
    and 122–3; unconscious 75
learning theory 121–2, 579
Leckenby, J. D. 7, 330
LeDoux, J. E. 93
Lee, B. 276
Lee, M. 388–401
Lee, M. K. O. 285
Lee, S. 116
Lee, W.-N. 162–73
Lee, Y. H. 195
legal theory 480–5
Lenntorp, B. 381
Leno, J. 529
Leong, S. M. 195
Leshner, G. M. 300
level fields 12, 19, 579
Lewin, K. 34
Li, H. 7, 203, *205*, 546–52
Liang, T. 375
limbic system 77–8, 82, 579
limited capacity model of attention 390,
    392, 394, 396, 397
limited capacity model of motivated
    mediated message processing
    (LC4MP) 110–11
Lin, C. A. 377
Lindberg-Repo, K. 498
Linville, P. W. 168
literary criticism 474
livestock branding 437
Local Consumer Culture (LCC) theory 153
local consumer culture positioning
    (LCCP) 153, 579
location-based services 406, 579
long-term advertising response 332
Louis Vuitton *442*
Lowrey, T. M. 55–6
loyalty, brand 24, 91, 92, 125, 498, 499,
    564, 570
Lubart, T. I. 192

Lundqvist, D. 80
Lutz, R. J. 87, 141

Maarek, P. J. 301
McCain, J. 298
McCarthy, E. J. 7
McDonald, M. 497–8
McDonald's 175, 176, 177, *442*
McGill, A. L. 243
McGuire, W. 18, 19, 33, 52, 164, 169,
    495
McKenna, R. 498
Macklin, M. C. 137, 139
McKnight, D. H. 286
MacLachlan, J. 198
McLuhan, M. 355
McQuarrie, E. F. 14, 227–40
magazines 121, 126, 127, 235–9
Main, K. J. 179
MAIN model 357–68, 579
Mallalieu, L. 139
Mallinckrodt, V. 183, *389*, 396
management, cross-functional 500–1
Mangleburg, T. 144
manipulation 179
Mao, E. 379
March, J. G. 218
market power 436–9
marketing mix 4, 169, 493
marketplace culture 150
markets, target 314–15, 588
Marlboro *442*
Martin, M. C. 139
masculinity/femininity 157, 578
mass media 4, 151, 276
materialism 10
Mattila, A. S. 242, 247
May, W. H. 89
Mayer, R. C. 285
Mazursky, D. *196*, 198
meaning 439–40; change of 182–4
meaning systems, consumer 129–30
media audience 314, 315, 316, 326,
    327, 530, 549, 579
media availability 316
media brokerage 427
media class allocations and scheduling
    321–5

media class decisions 318–20, 321, 325, 579

media convergence 543, 544

media data services 315

media-market matching 314, 315, 579–80; direct 315, 326; indirect 315, 326

media options 325

media planners 127, 266, 314, 315, 317, 320, 321, 326, 327, 329, 331, 470, 580

media schedule evaluation 328–31

media usage plans 316–17, 327, 580

media vehicle decisions 321–2, 325–8, 580

medial prefrontal cortex 72

Mednick, S. A. 214

Mehabrian, A. 89, 90, 98

Mehra, A. 35

Melamed, B. G. 90

memory 108, 111; accessibility 26, 29; brand 22–3, 390, 391, 392–3, 394, 396, 397, 399, 494; conscious 112; emotional 70–2, 74–5, 78, 81–2; explicit or declarative 26, 27, 70, 74, 392, 575; implicit

or nondeclarative 26, 27–8, 70, 74, 75, 78, 392, 398, 578; information processing and 301; interference 22–3; working 71, 74–5, 342

Menon, S. 180, 452, 453

mental imagery 258–9, 262–3, 265

mental models 36, 39, 213, 580

mental simulation 248–9, 257, 580

Mercedes Benz 442

Merz, M. 153, 197

message learning perspective 51

Message Response Involvement Theory 337, 341–2, 580

message task allocation matrix 317–20, 581

message(s) 5, 106, 108–9, 110, 164, 241–2; ambiguity 529; arguments see arguments; complexity of 53, 55–6, 265, 347–50; consistency 494–5; coordination of 20, 22, 580; cumulation 230; distant 230, 237; effects see effects; ethics 463; forms

229, 231, 232, 235–7, 239; framing of 55, 56; incongruity 347; marketing mix 493; modality of 265–6; purpose 227, 229, 231, 232, 235, 239; quality of 58, 61, 265; reception environment 229–31, 232, 234, 239; repetition see repetition; responses to 529–40; rhetorical theory 227–40; ritual 515, 518–21; and social media 405–6, 407, 411, 412; sources 8, 54, 56–7, 69, 404–5; strategy 580; and involvement 123–4; time compression and processing of 58; transmission 515–18

meta-cognition 55, 581

meta-theories, practitioner 40–2, 44–5, 584

metaphors 141

metrics, social media 410, 411–12

Metromint 521, **524**

Metzler, A. E. 56

Michael, H. 421

Michell, P. C. 205

Mick, D. G. 237

Microsoft 410, 442

Miller, B. 180

Miller, K. 498

mind-scribing 199, 581

Mira, I. 380

Miron, M. S. 89

Mitchell, N. 141

Mizerski, D. 183, 389, 396

MOA see motivation; opportunity; ability

mobile advertising 340, 342–3, 345, 373–87, 581; pull 373, 375, 378, 551, 585; push 373, 374–5, 378, 551, 585; spending on 373

mobile audiences 338, 342, 343, 345

mobile phones 315, 337, 339–40, 344

Modality-Agency-Interactivity-Navigability (MAIN) model 13

modality affordances 357, 358, 359–61, 367

moderator variables 53, 581

Mohr, L. A. 455

mood 58, 69, 87

Moore, D. L. 58

Moore, E. S. 141, 389, 395

Moore, M. C. 246

Moorman, M. 297–309
moral character 469
moral development 465–6
moral evaluation 468–9
moral imagination 468
moral intensity 467–8 Moriarty, S. 491–505
Morris, J. D. 85–104, 116
Morrison, D. 200
Moschis, G. 142, 144
motivated sensory experience 109, 581
motivation 234, 341, 342, 581; creativity and 199, 200; emotion and 70, 73–4, 82; homeostatic concept of 74; intrinsic 192, 199, 204, 390; moral 469; negative 75–6; persuasion agents 181–2; positive 75–6; sponsor 180; see also Embodied Motivated Cognition (EMC)
motivational variables, and persuasion process 53, 58, 59–60
motivators: direct 274, 275, 574; self-produced 274, 275, 587; vicarious 274, 275, 590
Mowrer, O. H. 73
Muehling, D. D. 12
Mueller, B. 149–61, 154
Muk, A. 378
multiattribute theories 11
multiculturalism 166
Multimedia Message Service (MMS) advertising 373
Murphy, P. E. 468, 473
mutation of effects theory 38, 39, 40, 42, 178
Myers, J. G. 453

Nan, X. 12, 18–32, 259
narrative advertising 243–51; persuasion and 250, 251, 255–67
narrative(s): brand 243, 570, 581; outcome-focused 265; pre-reading instructions 265; process-focused 265; processing 241–51, 256–7, 266; prototypes 246, 251; realism of 266; understanding 247–8
National Biscuit Company 438

navigability 581
navigability affordances 357, 358, 365–6, 367, 582
Nayakankuppam, D. 55
need 553; acute 515, 516–18
need for affect 263, 582
need arousal 316, 317, 319
need for cognition (NFC) 53, 54–5, 57, 236, 264, 582
need for information 319, 320, 325
Neely, S. 138–9
negative affect 22
negative political advertising 302–5, 582; backlash or boomerang effects 303–4, 305
Neijens, P. 297–309
Nelson, M. R. 174–87, 388, 389, 391, 393, 394
neuromarketing 105, 582
neuropsychology 105, 107
newspapers, advertising revenues 10
NFO Healthcare Influencer study 95–6
Nicholson, C. 285
Niedenthal, P. M. 78
Nielsen surveys 404
Nijman, J. 151
Nike 215, 450, 453, 518
Nixon, S. 193
Nokia 442
non-traditional advertising message processing (NAMP) framework 13, 337–53
nondeclarative memory see implicit memory
Norateen 521
normative ethics 468, 582
Novak, T. P. 548
Nyilasy, G. 33–47, 178, 196

Obama, B. 298
Obermiller, C. 61
objectification, of women 95
occipital cortex 72
O'Connor, G. C. 198, 201
O'Donohue, S. 185
Ogilvy, D. 440
Ogilvy & Mather 221
O'Guinn, T. C. 7

Öhman, A. 80, 91
Okazaki, S. 149–61, 154, 156, 373–87
Oliver, J. D. *196*
Olson, J. C. 248–9
Omnicom 203
On-Demand Model 548
online advertising *see* Internet
ontological skepticism 40
opinion leaders 407, 411
opportunity, to process advertisements 341, 342–3, 582
opportunity to see (OTS) 327, 582
orbital frontal cortex 72
Organic digital agency 203
organizational collectivism 157, 577
organizational culture 218, 220, 470–1, 500, 582
organizational fragmentation 425–6, 428–9
organizational myopia 471–2
organizational politics 500
organizational structure 500
organizations, advertising 5, *8*, 419, 421, 423, 425, 428–9; *see also* advertising agencies
originality 194, 195, 202, 213, 222, 582
Ortony, A. 73
Osborne, A. C. 428, 565
Osgood, C. 89, 165, 495
Otnes, C. 510
out-of-home advertising 342, 583
outdoor advertising *196*, 315, 339, 340, 342, 353, 582
over-the-counter (OTC) drugs 511, 513–14, 525, 583
ownership 436–9
Özsomer, A. 151, 153, 154

PAD (pleasure, arousal, dominance) measures 89–91, 583
Padgett, D. 247
Paek, H. 276
Palan, K. M. 139
parents, as moderators of advertising influences 141–4, 146
Parvatiyar, A. 497, 498
passion 192, 199, 200, 583
Patterson, M. J. 79

Pavlou, P. A. 288
Pawlowski, D. 141
Payne, A. 498
Pechman, C. 182
peers 144, 146, 275
Pempek, T. A. *389*, 396
PEPS framework for creativity 192
Perceived Brand Globalness (PBG) 154–5, 583
perceived fit, in corporate social responsibility (CSR) initiatives 451–9, 583
perception, selective 120
perceptual integration theory 491, 493–6, 501
Percy, L. 69–84, 319
performance orientation 157, 158, 577
peripheral cues 56, 57, 58, 60, 356–7, 366, 514, 583
peripheral nervous system 115, 570
peripheral processing 52, 53, 56, 57, 58, 60, 86, 141, 142
persistence of attitudes 54–5, 583
Perrault, W. D. 7
personal extensibility theory 383–4, 583
personal relevance 53, 129
personal selling 4–5
personalization 362, 374
perspective meta-analysis 549–50
persuasion 19, 23–6, 85, 163, 234; ability variables and 53, 59, 60; appropriateness of 179; central route to 52, 53, 60, 86, 570; channel variables and 54, 58; children's understanding of 139–40; emotion and 86–99, 250, 251; mental simulation and 249; message arguments and 52–3, 54, 55–6, 57, 60, 61; motivational variables and 53, 58, 59–60; narrative advertising and 250, 251, 255–67; online 355–68; outcomes 176, 179, 180, 181–4; peripheral route to 52, 53, 56, 57, 58, 60, 86, 141, 142; receiver variables 54, 57–8; social media and 411; source variables 54, 56–7, 58; *see also* Elaboration Likelihood Model

persuasion agents 175–6, 177–8, 583; motives 181–2; persuasion knowledge 174, 175, 177–8; target knowledge 176; topic knowledge 176

persuasion attempts 176–7, 583

persuasion cognitive response model of 51

persuasion episodes 177, 583

persuasion knowledge 584; and accessibility of agent motives 181; agents 174, 175, 177–8; children's 140–1, 144, 183–4, 185, 397; cognitive capacity and 181–2; developmental and longitudinal understanding of 185; targets 174, 175, 176–7, 178–9, 180, 181–5

Persuasion Knowledge Model (PKM) 39, 174; application of 177–80; commentary and critique 184–5; overview 175–7; processing and outcomes 181–4

persuasion targets 176, 584; agent knowledge 176, 179; coping mechanisms 177, 182, 184, 472; persuasion knowledge 174, 175, 176–7, 178–9, 180, 181–5; skepticism 179, 180, 183; topic knowledge 176, 180

persuasion/communication model 18, 164

Petty, R. 51–2, 53, 54, 56, 57, 58, 86, 141

PEW Research Center 402

Pfau, M. 304

Pfeiffer, M. 333

pharmaceutical industry 270–1, 283

Phelps, J. E. 255–68

Phillips, B. J. 14, 227–40

Phillips, D. M. 245, 248–9

philosophy of science 36, 135–6, 541

Phinney, J. S. 168

Piaget, J. 136–7

Pieters, F. G. M. 201

Piller, F. 361

Pitt, L. F. 497

Planned Behavior, theory of 11, 366

pleasure 89, 90, 91, 93, 98–9

Poels, K. *196*

Polarized Appraisal Theory 168

political advertising 5, 10, 91, 116, 127–8, 229, 232, 297–309, 584; and electoral system 299; image content 301, 302; by independent groups 302; issue content 301, 302; and media system 299; negative 302–5, 582 (backlash or boomerang effects 303–4, 305, 569); effects of 300–5; and political culture 299; third-party 304–5

political electoral broadcasts 299, 584

Pollay, R. W. 471–2

Polonsky, M. J. 421

Pomper, G. M. 304

pop-ups 360, 361

portfolio schools 423, 425, 428, 568

positioning 152, 153, 154, 155, 584

power distance 157, 576, 577

practitioner-academician gap 33, 36–7, 42, 44, 550

Practitioner Knowledge Autonomy model 37, 38, 44, 45, 584

practitioner meta-theories 40–2, 44–5, 584

practitioner theories 14, 33, 37, 38–40, 44, 584

practitioners 419, 423, 429–30, 536–7; coworkers 471; ethics 465–9; perception of role 466; supervisors 471

Prahalad, C. K. 155

preferences, brand 20

Prensky, D. 500

Prentice, R. 467

prescription drugs 269–78, 281–2, 283–5, 287–93, 511–13, 525, 584

presence, brand 440–1

Preston, I. 464–5, 529–40

Presumed Influence Model 277–8

price advertising 486

Priester, J. R. 55, 56

primary demand 24, 584

primary emotions 69, 77

primary process cognition 213–14, 584

priming 192, 584

priming creativity theories 198–202

prior knowledge 264

prior learning effects 331–2, 585

privacy 487, 585
problem-orientated research 34
Proctor and Gamble (P&G) 409, 454
product attitudes 242
product attributes 242, 243
product categories 40; involvement with 126
product commitment 120–1
product involvement 12, 57, 58, 126, 514
product placements 318, 320, 388, 390–9; congruence/incongruence 392, 397; prominent (or focal) 391, 394, 396; subtle (or peripheral) 391–2, 394
product usage 326–7
production processes 274, 585
products, routinely purchased 515–16
professional organizations 423
professional paradox of advertising 42, 44, 585
professionalization 35, 36, 585; pseudo- 42–3, 45, 585
profession(s) 585; advertising as a 421–6; formal characteristics of 422–3; human ecology of 424
promotion 4–5
Proportional Representation theory 167, 168, 585
prospect theory 216–17
pseudo-media 315, 320, 585
pseudo-professionalization 42–3, 45, 585
psychological consistency theory 495
psychological reactance 508–9, 525
Psychology and Marketing 376
psychophysiology 105, 112–17, 585
public relations 4, 565
public service announcements 92, 251, 506–7, 560
Publicis 203
pull mobile advertising 373, 375, 378, 551, 585
pulvinar 79
purchase behavior, and attitude formation 121
purpose, message 227, 229, 231, 232, 235, 239
push mobile advertising 373, 374–5, 378, 551, 585

Puto, C. P. 124

QR coding 350, 586
qualitative arguments 349
Qualman, E. 407
quantitative arguments 347
Quesenberry, K. A. 542

radio 109
Randazzo, S. 243
Rappaport, S. D. 548
rate cards 325
ration strategy 515, 518
Ray, C. 495
Raybeck, D. 89
Rayne, M. B. 541–5
Razorfish 410, 411
reach 328, 329, 330, 586; effective 329, 330, 574–5
reactance 20, 508–9, 525
reaction triad 69, 586
Reade, M. C. 550
realism 266
reasoned action, theory of 11, 378–9, 411, 588
recall 26–7, 122, 128, 586; brand 391, 393, 395, 398
receiver(s) 8, 9, 69, 106–8, 164, 242; social media 413; variables 54, 57–8; see also audience(s)
reception environment 229–31, 232, 234, 239, 586
reciprocity theory 491, 496–9, 501
recognition 26–7, 586; brand 22, 27–8, 122, 391, 393, 398
Red Bull 340
referrals, customer 499, 564
reflective practitioner 37
reflexive knowledge 70
Reid, L. N. 33–47, 178, 196, 198, 201, 205, 287
reinforcement, attitude 24, 29, 52
relationship management 43, 44
relationship marketing 498–9, 564
relevance 53, 129, 213, 222
repetition 14, 20–1, 22, 26, 53, 54, 55, 62, 86, 230, 237, 394–5; variation strategies 248

research 532–3, 538–9, 544; applied 13,
    435–6, 550; basic 13; innovativeness
    546–8; validity of 42
resistance 39, 54, 178, 586
Resnik, A. 138
Resource Advantage Theory 155–6, 586
resource-matching hypothesis 337, 345,
    346, 586
Rest, J. R. 469
retention, delayed 25
Reynolds, P. 135, 136
rhetorical tactics 43–4
rhetorical theory 227–40, 586
Richards, J. I. 4, 7, 19, 420–1, 428,
    480–90, 565
Richter, T. 259, 262, 263
Rideout, V. *389*, 395
Ridout, T. N. 298, 301
Riordan, E. A. 195, 200
risk 507–8, 525, 586; creative 203, 212,
    214–22
risk management 216–18, 586
Ritchie, R. J. B. 183
ritual 509–11
ritual messages 515, 518–21
roadside advertising 343
Roberts, M. S. 88
Robertson, T. S. 121, 122, 139
Rodgers, S. 3–17, 180, 548
Roedder, D. L. 141
Roethlisberger, F. J. 33, 34, 37
Rogers, E. M. 194, 473
role theory 466
Roner, L. 255
Rook, D. 509
Rosch, E. 153
Rose, G. M. 140, 185
Rose, P. B. 563–6
Ross, B. I. 421, 428, 565
Ross, D. 273
Ross, S. 273
Rossiter, J. R. 73, 74, 76, 81, 139, *201*,
    319
Rotfeld, H. J. 198, *201*, 535, 553–62
Roth, H. 439
Rothenerg, R. 518
Rothschild, M. J. 124
Rousseau, J.-J. 136

routinely purchased products 515–16
Runco, M. A. 202
Russ, F. A. 487
Russell, J. A. 89, 90, 98
Ruth, J. 497

Saatchi 203
sales promotion 4
Salmon, C. 276
SAM (self-assessment manikin) scale
    90–1, 586
Samsung *442*
Sanbonmatsu, D. M. 57
Sandelands, L. E. 34
Sasser, S. L. 191–211, 421
Schneider, L. *389*, 390, 391, 393
Schneider, S. K. 248, 249
Schon, D. A. 37
Schoorman, F. D. 285
Schorin, G. A. 198
Schroeder, J. E. 474
Schudson, M. 430
Schultz, D. E. 440, 491–505
Schumann, D. W. 51–68, 138–9, 141
Schwartz, S. H. 165
ScienceWatch 547
scientific field, advertising as 12–14
scripts, ethics-related 469
secondary emotions 69
secondary or selective demand 24, 586
segmentation, cross-market 151–2, 156
segments 9; global consumer 152
selective exposure 215, 300, 436
selective perception 120
self-assessment manikin (SAM) scale
    90–1, 586
self-awareness 264
self-consciousness 264
self-efficacy 273, 274, 508, 586
self-produced motivators 274, 275, 587
self schema 57
semantic differential scales 89, 90, 587
sensory appeal 521
sensuality 94–5
Seris, M. 559–60
Service Model 548
set-of-laws theories 135–6
Sethi, R. 285

Severin, W. J. 18
sexiness 94–5
sexualization 95
Shapira, Z. 218
Shavitt, S. 169
Shaw, D. R. 301
Sheean, K. Bartel 269–80
Shen, F. 304, 364
Sheth, J. 497, 498
Shimp, T. A. 87
Shin, W. 281–96
Shiv, B. 249
Short Message Service (SMS) advertising 373, 374–5, 378, 379
short-term advertising response 332
silos, functional 500
SIM score 410, 411, 413
Simonin, B. 497
simulation, mental 248–9, 257
sincerity 439
Sinclair, J. 180
Sinclaire, R. C. 56
Singh, A. J. 93
single-source data bases 315, 587
Six-Segment Advertising Strategy Wheel 515–21, 525
Skechers **520**, 520–1
skepticism *see* advertising skepticism
smiling 78, 80–1
Smith, B. L. *196*
Smith, N. C. 471
Smith, R. E. 195, *201*
smoking 508, 509
Social Categorization theory 166–7, 587
Social Cognitive Theory 273–5, 278
social ecology 419–31
social emotions 69
Social Influence Marketing Score (SIM score) 410, 411, 413
social interaction 78, 167, 176, 273, 384, 510, 587
social media 197, 361, 402–16, 499, 564, 566, 587; advertising effects 409–10, 411; and agency autonomy 429; audiences 407–8; brand-based sharing 406; channels 407, 413; content-based sharing 406; data mining 411–12; engagement 409–10,
413, 575; location-based services 406; messages 405–6, 407, 411, 412; metrics 410, 411–12; virality 410
social network theory 471
social networks 499; *see also* social media
social norms 11
socialization: agents 142–5, 146, 275–6, 587; of children 142–5, 146; consumer 275–7, 278
society 10
sociolegal studies 487, 587
soft money advertisements 304, 305, 587
Soh, H. 287
Solis, B. 403, 409
Soloman, S. 198
Solution People 193
somatusensory cortex 72
Sony 182–3
sources 241, 361; credibility of 56, 58, 60, 128, 284, 287, 587; message *8*, 54, 56–7, 69, 404–5; trustworthiness 56
space-time perspective 381–3
Sparks, B. 245
sponsors 183, 587; motivations 180
spreading activation theory 392, 393, 587
Spyridakis, J. H. 365–6
Stafford, M. R. 125–6
stakeholder management theory 471–2
Stakeholder Relations Model 497
stakeholders 497–8, 499, 501, 564
standardization 152, 153, 156, 587
Starbuck, W. H. 34
Starbucks 410
Starch *Adnorms* 327
Stayman, D. M. 87, 167
Steenkamp, J. B. 152, 154–5
Steiner, G. A. 272
stereotyping 10, 166, 167
Stern, B. B. 138, 198, 251, 421
Sternberg, R. J. 192
Sternberg model of commitment, intimacy, passion, and trust 204
Sternthal, B. 233
Stewart, D. W. 85, 288
Stewart, P. 530

Stiff, J. B. 61
Stigler, G. 556
Stone, G. *201*
storyboards 88
Strahilevitz, M. 453
strategic consistency 497–8, 564
strategy 43, 44, 195, 202, 588
street branding 340
Strong, C. 374
Stuhlfaut, M. W. 193, *196*
Stutts, M. 140, 140–1
Subaru 243
subcortical pathways 79, 80
Sundar, S. S. 355–72
superior coliculus 79
supervisors 471
Sutherland, J. *205*
Swait, J. 91
symbols, cultural 151
sympathy 251
synergy 495–6
synetics training 199
Systematic Inventive Thinking (SIT) 193, 198
systemic processing 356, 588

tacit skill 41, 42
Tamanaha, B. Z. 487
Tankard, J. Jr. 18
Tannenbaum, P. H. 165
Tannenbaum, S. 492, 495
target audience 314, 315, 326, 327, 338, 492, 501, 588
target market 314–15, 588
target rating point (TRP) 323, 324, 588; cost per 328
targeting indices 323–4, 572
targets, persuasion *see* persuasion targets
Taylor, C. R. 149–61, 150, 154, 156
Taylor, R. E. 124, 194, *205*, 515, 535
Taylor, S. E. 166, 248, 249
Technology Acceptance Model (TAM) 379, 547, 588; ease of use (EOU) 379; perceived usefulness (PU) 379
technology affordances 357–68
teleological approaches to ethical theory 468, 588
telepresence 391, 397, 588

television 109, 121, 126, 127; direct-to-consumer advertising 271, 274; political advertising 297–8
Tellegen, A. 264
templates, creativity 198, 199, 588
Terlutter, R. 181
textbooks 555–7
Thamodaran, K. 58
theoretical knowledge base 35, 36, 43, 588
theory 541–5, 546–52, 588; axiomatic 135; borrowed 12–13; causal process 135, 231, 235, 237; definitions of 541, 555; falsification of 555; ignoring 557–60; misplaced 553–62; set-of-laws 135–6
theory-practice relations 33–5; in advertising 36–7
Theory of Reasoned Action 11, 378–9, 411, 588
Thill, J. V. 6
Thomas, K. W. 34
Thompson, C. J. 150–1
Thorson, E. 3–17, 548
Till, B. D. *201*, 337–54
time-geography 381–2, 384, 589
time orientation, long-term v. short-term 157, 578
time-space convergence 383
time-space perspective 381–3, 384
Tinkham, S. F. 300–1
Tippins, M. J. *205*
tokenism 166, 589
top-down processing 70, 110–11, 589
top-of-mind (T-O-M) awareness 26, 589
topic knowledge 176, 180, 589
Tormala, Z. L. 56
total exposure value 330–1
touch points 493
Toyota 442
trademarks 437
traditional media 315, 403–4
transformational advertising 87, 124, 319, 589
transmission messages 515–18
transportation 250, 391, 589; cognitive attention antecedent of 258, 262; emotional involvement antecedent of

258, 259, 263, 265; individual
    moderators of 263–4; mental imagery
    antecedent of 258–9, 262–3, 265;
    message moderators of 264–6
Transportation-Imagery Model 13,
    255–6, 258–67
Treise, D. 510
trend watching 412
trust 163, 281, 285–6, 356, 379, 439,
    488; and behavioral intention 291–2;
    dispositional 286, 287, 288, 289, 290,
    574; in DTC advertising websites
    286–93; institutional 286, 578;
    interpersonal 286
trustworthiness 56
Tsang, M. 375, 378
Turban, E. 285
Turner, C. 90
Tversky, A. 216
Twitter 402, 412, 488
two-way symmetrical approach 496–7
Tymon, W. G. Jr. 34

ubiquitous computing 380, 589
ubiquity 380–1, 382, 384
Umphrey, L. R. 55
uncertainty 212, 221
uncertainty avoidance 157, 167, 576,
    578
unconscious attention 75
unconscious learning 75
unconscious processing 70
uncoupled activation 107
Uneeda Biscuits 438
unintended effects 5, 9, 464, 474
unique theories 12, 13
user-generated advertising 4
user-generated content 402, 405, 406,
    410, 589
uses and gratifications 317, 375, 377–8,
    589
utilitarianism 468, 589
utilities of advertising messages 5

Vaitl, D. 91
Vakratas, D. 38, 39, 332
validity of research 42
value, brand 440–1, 499

values 164, 165, 590
Van Meurs, L. *196*
Vance, D. 140
Vanden Bergh, B. G. 7, 198, *201*, *205*
variable fields 12, 19–20, 590
Vaughn, R. 123
verbal details 245
Verbeke, W. *205*
vicarious motivators 274, 275, 590
viral marketing 406
virality 410
Virginia State Board of Pharmacy v.
    Virginia Citizens Consumer Council
    (1976) 484–5, 486
virtue ethics 470
visual cortex 79, 80
visual stimulus 56–7
Volz, Y. Z. 156–7

Waiguny, M. 181
Waine, C. A. 90
Wallach, L. 300
Walsh, A. 143
Walters, G. 245
Walters, J. S. 440
Wang, E. T. G. 57
Wang, F. 549
Wang, G. 203
Wang, K. 57
Wang, L. 182
Waters, M. 151
Watson, R. T. 381
wear-in effects 20, 394–5, 590
wear-out effects 20, 394–5, 590
Web 2.0 technologies 402, 413, 590
Webb, D. J. 455
webisodes 339
website trust 286–93, 590
Wei, L. P. 88
Wei, M. 179
Weick, K. E. 33, 34, 35, 37
Weiser, Marc 380
Wells, W. D. 7, 124, 247, 256–7,
    319
Welsh, J. 449, 455
Wertley, C. 144
West, D. C. 196, 201, 205, 212–26
White, A. 196

Willemain, T. R. 198
Williams, J. D. 169
Wilson, R. T. 337–54
Winston, J. S. 70
Wise, K. 105–19, *389*, 391, 393
Wish-Bone Salad Dressing 515, 516
Wohlburg, J. 10
Wolberg, J. M. 506–26
women: and beauty 93–5; objectification of 95
Woo, C. 93
Wood, M. L. M. 184
Woodruff, P. 470
word of mouth (WOM) 376, 549
working memory 71, 74–5, 342
Wright-Iask, C.419–33
Wright, P. 39, 174, 175, 176, 181
Wu, H. D. 304
Wyer, R. S. Jr. 242, 245, 246

Xerox Palo Alto Research center (PARC) 380
Xu, Q. 355–72

Yalcinkaya, G. 155
Yang, M. *389*
Yang, X. *201*
Yaprak, A. 194
Yaros, R. A. *389*, 393
Yoo, C. Y. 183
Youn, S. 388–401
Young, C. E. *196*
YouTube 197, 402, 405

Zajonc, R. B. 86
Zaltman, G. 37
zapping 315, 590
Zauderer v. Office of Disciplinary Counsel (1985) 486
Zhang, J. 165, 379
Zheng, L. 255–68
Zhou, N. 154, 203
Zikmund, W. G. 7
Zinkhan, G. M. *201*
Zinnbauer, M. 333
zipping 315, 590
Zou, S. 156, 156–7